Christianity beyond the Crossroads

The Son and the Father

BY THE SAME AUTHOR

Islam at the Crossroads
A Companion to the Study of *Epistle to the Son of the Wolf*

Christianity beyond the Crossroads

The Son and the Father

Lameh Fananapazir

OXFORD
GEORGE RONALD

George Ronald, Publisher
Oxford
www.grbooks.com

©Lameh Fananapazir 2022
All Rights Reserved

A catalogue record for this book
is available from the British Library

ISBN 978-0-85398-643-0

Cover design: Steiner Graphics

CONTENTS

Preface, by Hooper C. Dunbar   vii
Acknowledgements   viii
Foreword, by JoAnn Borovicka   ix
Introduction   1

PART I. WHAT DEFINES A CHRISTIAN?

1. Taking stock: The darkening spiritual horizons   11

2. Revisiting Christian virtues and relearning to walk in Christ's footsteps   27

3. Discarding obsolete teachings, outworn shibboleths and injurious superstitions   58

PART II. PROMISES OF NEW DIVINE INTERVENTIONS

4. The times of rebirth and renewal of faith   107

5. The advent of the world redeemer in the Hebrew Bible (Old Testament)   116

6. The 'good news' of the Gospels and the signs of the times in the New Testament   133

PART III. DIFFICULTIES AND OBSTACLES

7. Objections to Jesus as the Messiah — 175

8. Stumbling blocks at the Second Coming — 206

9. Further impediments — 244

PART IV. CHURCH DOGMA AND REALIZED ESCHATOLOGY

10. Review of some Christian themes — 279

11. Resurrection — 305

12. The Trinity — 338

13. Sacraments and ordinances — 351

14. Biblical criteria to validate truth — 364

15. Biblical promises fulfilled — 384

PART V. RENEWAL AND RESURRECTION

16. Bahá'u'lláh's proclamation — 413

17. Continuity of divine purpose: Multiple religions but one common faith — 428

18. Reaffirmation of earlier moral and ethical teachings — 462

19. New social paradigms for a global society — 490

Bibliography — 515
Notes and References — 535
Index — 573

PREFACE

Dr Lameh Fananapazir's new volume, *Christianity Beyond the Crossroads*, conveys its convincing arguments through the same general expository methods he employed so effectively in his previous work on Islam and the challenges presently facing the Islamic world. In that volume, his approach was a persuasive one, gently placing his keen insights and observations before us, informed and reinforced with relevant passages from authentic Muslim scriptures, both from the Qur'án and its traditions.

The result was a clear demonstration of the continuity of divine revelation with respect to Islam and its connection with the Holy Writings of the Twin Founders of the Bahá'í Faith, Bahá'u'lláh and the Báb. This was all done in such a manner as to draw the attention of the reader to his earlier and possibly erroneous assumptions, and persuade him to reconsider certain fundamental points.

Here, Dr Fananapazir has taken up the same task, but this time with the vast scriptures and traditions of Judaism and Christianity. Considering the diversity of views currently weighing on Jewish and Christian communities around the globe, the content of this volume holds the promise of new vision and understanding. It is addressed to the sincere followers of these Faiths and to other fair-minded people seeking a united way forward – a way which corresponds with the urgent worldwide need for unity and wholeness. One that enables souls to resolve the perplexities of our broken past. Before us, then, lies the prospect of promoting a worldwide fraternity based on God-given scriptures, the common heritage of us all. The keys are at hand.

Amidst the darkness besetting us, the words and teachings of Bahá'u'lláh shine out as a beacon of hope, illumining the path ahead – they constitute, as demonstrated here, the consummate gift of God to our distracted age.

Hooper C. Dunbar

ACKNOWLEDGEMENTS

I wish to express my profound gratitude to May Hofman for her editorial expertise, dedicated work and patience. Without her guidance, persistence and encouragement this work would not have been completed. My heartfelt thanks also to Erica Leith for the complex job of typographical design and typesetting. I am also grateful to my wife Karen for her able assistance and support.

FOREWORD

It is statistically evident that the Christian churches are undergoing an upheaval of some sort. Over the past generation large numbers of church closings have been regularly reported in the United States and Europe.[1] It is estimated that 'somewhere between four thousand and seven thousand churches close their doors every year' in the United States with only about one thousand new churches being built annually.[2] Christians represent a significantly smaller percentage of the general population than they did a generation ago and the numbers continue to fall.[3] This is not isolated to a particular Christian denomination. In the words of Rachel Held Evans, a popular Christian writer, 'Just about every denomination in the American church – including many evangelical denominations – is seeing a decline in numbers, so if it's competition, then we're all losing, just at different rates.'

This loss is a multi-generational phenomenon. A certain percentage of adults are abandoning church, and young people born into Christian families are, more and more, opting to identify themselves as 'spiritual but not religious'. When surveyed as to their religious affiliation they often respond by checking 'None'.[4] Currently the 'Nones' comprise about 20 per cent of all Americans, and about a third of Americans under thirty years of age.[5] This dramatic trend has moved Dr Steve McSwain, a Christian speaker and advisor to congregations, to bemoan, 'God's marvelous Church has become culturally irrelevant.'[6]

Reasons offered to explain this mass exodus include the politicization of Christianity, a greater number of interfaith marriages, globalization, economic factors, problems with church leadership, troubled relationships within the church, and disagreements with church doctrine and policies.[7] It is noteworthy, however, that a reason that does not seem to be offered in these many and varied explanations is disagreement with the foundational teachings of Jesus Christ Himself. For example, one does not hear of Christians abandoning a church because they disagreed with the Sermon on the Mount or had problems with the Parable of the Good Samaritan. People may disagree with scriptural interpretations, church doctrines, people, or the doings of an institution, but disagreement with the foundational teachings of Christ is not generally offered as a reason why people leave the church. This calls for reflection. And it is at precisely this point where insights gleaned from the Bahá'í Writings may encourage the hearts of the followers of Christ.

The Bahá'í Faith, the newest of the world's revealed religions, views the phenomenon of religion from a unique perspective. In the Bahá'í Writings religion is not seen as a 'multiplicity of sectarian organizations'.[8] Rather, the concept of religion is described as 'the principal force impelling the development of consciousness'.[9] This divine force, the Bahá'í Writings describe, manifests itself in stages throughout human history. All of these stages of divine Revelation work toward a common, unchangeable, and fundamental purpose – the establishment of 'affinity between the hearts of the world of humanity' in an 'ever-advancing civilization'.[10] From this perspective each of the world's religions, including the religion of Christ, are seen as having two distinct realities. The first reality is the divine teachings that are the spiritual foundation of the religion. These foundational teachings are in agreement with and constitute the spiritual 'collective centre' of all of the sacred religions.[11] The second reality consists of the social laws and organizational structures unique to a particular historical Dispensation. These social laws and systems will naturally differ between religions due to cultural differences, stages of development, accidents of history, and varying requirements of the times in which the religions were revealed.

As explained in the Bahá'í Writings, the foundational spiritual teachings of the revealed religions are always relevant, true, and in agreement. Describing this spiritual aspect or big picture of religion Bahá'u'lláh states, 'This is the changeless Faith of God, eternal in the past, eternal in the future.'[12] However, the social laws and organizational structures that are either dispensed by the divine Messenger or that develop through human means and become associated with a particular Revelation do eventually become obsolete. This is due to a number of factors including the evolving needs of an ever-changing society and various human influences that, with time, distort the original laws and teachings.[13]

With the above in mind, let us return to the concern of falling church membership. Might it be possible that the reason why many feel disinclined to establish or maintain affiliation with a church is because of the 2,000-year distance that church doctrines and institutions have travelled since Jesus Christ appeared? For centuries institutionalized Christianity has largely presented itself as a timeless system of belief and organization that was divinely mandated and delivered, fully formed, in the past. 'Yet Christianity's actual history is a story of change and adaptation', involving many human decisions regarding church organizations, interpretations of scripture, dogmas, rituals, social policies, and affiliations.[14] That various Christian systems of belief and organization have not always remained consistent with the foundational teachings of Christ is evident in the history of the church. The Christian Testament proclaims a radical unity and equity: 'There is neither Jew nor Greek, there is neither slave nor free, there is neither male nor female: for ye are all one in Christ Jesus' (Gal. 3:28).

Yet history shows that the Christian Testament has been used to promote and defend violent inequity and crippling disunity in the form of anti-Semitism, slavery, racism, subjugation of women, colonial imperialism, and demonization of the 'other'.[15] For many churches, rhetoric and actions inconsistent with the spiritual teachings of Christ continue. These are unintended tragic outcomes. They are also predictable outcomes from the point of view of the Bahá'í understanding of religion as characterized, first, by eternal spiritual verities common to all Faiths and, second, by social laws and systems with divine expiration dates and inevitable accumulated human failings.

From a Bahá'í perspective, the fundamental teachings of Christ – identical to the fundamental teachings of the Bahá'í Faith and every revealed religion – are sufficient proof of His eternal Majesty. The Spirit of Christ is unscathed by the changes and chances of history. That Christians are falling away from the church does not, to a Bahá'í, lessen the importance and divinity of Christ. And yet, organization and communion around the Word of God is a responsibility and bounty of the believers, and so the decline of the churches is concerning.

The title of this book, *Christianity Beyond the Crossroads*, suggests that we live in a time that requires critical decision-making of both institutional and individual followers of Moses and Christ. To the degree that loss in church membership and the popularity of the claim among former churchgoers to be 'spiritual but not religious' indicates a longing to return to the foundational teachings of Christ, then perhaps this trend is a healthy wake-up call. In response, individuals as well as churches might ask themselves, 'To what degree am I crucifying myself by hanging onto outdated institutions and manmade dogmas at odds with the fundamental teachings of Christ? How can I align myself with the Spirit of Christ as both my means and my end?' and 'How can I join with others in this endeavour?' While considering these questions, churches, Christians, and 'Nones' may do well to ponder the following guidance from 'Abdu'l-Bahá, the Centre of the Covenant of the Bahá'í Faith. Addressing all believers in His *Tablets of the Divine Plan* 'Abdu'l-Bahá states:

> Hence the intention must be purified, the effort ennobled and exalted, so that you may establish affinity between the hearts of the world of humanity. This glorious aim will not become realized save through the promotion of divine teachings which are the foundations of the holy religions.[16]

JoAnn Borovicka

INTRODUCTION

Faith and the many challenges facing humanity

It is a truism to say that global society is becoming increasingly interdependent, and that the welfare of any section of humanity on our planet ultimately affects us all. Yet most of us tend to ignore the plight of the rest of the world as we pursue our own personal and local interests. In this context, Bahá'u'lláh, the Founder of the Bahá'í Faith, admonishes us: 'Let your vision be world-embracing, rather than confined to your own self.'[1]

And when we do direct our attention to the state of the world we readily appreciate that mankind faces incalculable challenges. These include climate change; environmental pollution and destruction; rapid deterioration in the health of the global ecosystem and vanishing biodiversity; hunger and malnutrition in impoverished countries and, in contrast, health problems associated with overindulgence and obesity in affluent countries; uneven economic growth; inharmonious international trade and investment; diminishing planetary resources; rapid and ultimately unsustainable population growth; an increasing gap between the rich and the poor; functional and cultural illiteracy; gender rights violations; human trafficking and slavery; political polarization of societies; international conflicts and terrorism with attendant refugee and migrant problems; drug addiction and related gang violence; and the scourge of emerging and reemerging infectious diseases. In the latter context, Covid-19 has highlighted the vital need for cohesive action and cooperation at both national and international levels if humanity is to stem the tide of this dire plague. Sadly, everywhere, but more specifically in the United States, the fires of prejudice and racism are being stoked. The following statement in the Bahá'í Writings, written just before World War II but still relevant today, presaged a dismal situation:

> Who knows but that these few remaining, fast-fleeting years, may not be pregnant with events of unimaginable magnitude, with ordeals more severe than any that humanity has as yet experienced, with conflicts more devastating than any which have preceded them. Dangers, however sinister, must, at no time, dim the radiance of their new-born faith. Strife and confusion, however bewildering, must never befog their vision. Tribulations, however afflictive, must never shatter their resolve. Denunciations, however clamorous, must never sap their loyalty . . .[2]

To this disconcerting list may be added the decidedly negative part played by what passes as religion in many recent conflicts. Arguably, this is not the only cause of the hostilities but there is no denying the part played by religion either actively or through its inability to mediate peace and foster harmony. Bahá'u'lláh predicted 150 years ago: 'Religious fanaticism and hatred are a world-devouring fire, whose violence none can quench. The Hand of Divine power can, alone, deliver mankind from this desolating affliction.'[3]

The relevance of faith in a world increasingly oblivious of its Creator

As is fairly evident, we may wish to retreat from the world, but the global concerns will ultimately have their impact on all of us. The fact that many of the problems have a scientific and sociological basis, and hence are potentially remediable, begs the question as to why we have been impotent to eradicate the issues despite the expenditure of significant resources and the sincere efforts of many organizations. For example, using scientific methods, we should theoretically be able to eradicate many of the infectious diseases, and eliminate hunger and malnutrition, and yet we have failed to do so. This is because the issues cannot be solved by a materialistic approach only, as the underlying problem has to do with how we view and treat one another. The question that is vital to our survival and that of our fragile planet is whether we continue to regard each other as strangers with alien beliefs and customs, or recognize one another as members of one human race. Will we pursue only our own selfish interests, clinging to unreasonable theories such as excessive nationalism, or, whilst espousing a sane patriotism, consider mankind as co-inhabitants of one land? Will we continue to merely imitate ancestral beliefs, or instead study the reality of all religions and determine whether, as currently practised, they accord with reason and advance the best interests of humanity? We may well conclude that to bring about the cultural changes that will effectively rescue the planet demands a spiritual transformation and renewal of faith. Exulting in our own Christian Faith, and reaffirming time-expired beliefs, dogma and rituals, referred to by some Christians a century and a half ago as 'Churchianity',[4] will not be enough to turn the downward spiral.

This presentation relies largely on the scriptures and is one attempt to help us understand the specific issues that confront Christianity. It discusses their possible solutions, particularly in the light of Bahá'u'lláh's revelation.

The Bahá'í Faith

In the year 1844 and at the time when there was great world-wide excitement about the fulfilment of biblical prophecies, a young man named the Báb declared that God would soon manifest the One promised in all of the sacred scriptures. He and many thousands of His followers were cruelly martyred. Nine years later, Bahá'u'lláh (in English 'Glory of God') announced that He was the One foretold by the Báb and all earlier divine mediators. In His turn, He suffered untold hardships, mainly at the hands of Shí'ih and Sunni monarchs and religious leaders. Despite this, His Faith has now spread to all corners of the world.

Relation of the Bahá'í Faith to Judeo-Christianity

In the following pages we will explore the mission of Christ and its relationship to the Bahá'í Faith. This also requires us to examine briefly the deteriorating state of Christianity. However, it must be stated at the outset that Bahá'ís love Christ and have an absolute and abiding conviction in the validity, efficacy and goodness of the Christian revelation. Their genuine love and appreciation for Christianity is grounded in the Bahá'í Writings which emphasize the indispensability of the Christian Faith and emphatically eulogize Christ, as exemplified by the following passage:

CHRISTIANITY BEYOND THE CROSSROADS

> Jesus Christ gave His life upon the cross for the unity of mankind. Those who believed in Him likewise sacrificed life, honour, possessions, family, everything, that this human world might be released from the hell of discord, enmity and strife. His foundation was the oneness of humanity. Only a few were attracted to Him. They were not the kings and rulers of His time. They were not rich and important people. Some of them were catchers of fish. Most of them were ignorant men, not trained in the knowledge of this world . . . All of them were men of the least consequence in the eyes of the world. But their hearts were pure and attracted by the fires of the Divine Spirit manifested in Christ. With this small army Christ conquered the world of the East and the West. Kings and nations rose against Him. Philosophers and the greatest men of learning assailed and blasphemed His Cause. All were defeated and overcome, their tongues silenced, their lamps extinguished, their hatred quenched; no trace of them now remains. They have become as nonexistent, while His Kingdom is triumphant and eternal.
>
> . . . His name, beloved and adored by a few disciples, now commands the reverence of kings and nations of the world. His power is eternal; His sovereignty will continue forever, while those who opposed Him are sleeping in the dust, their very names unknown, forgotten. The little army of disciples has become a mighty cohort of millions. The Heavenly Host, the Supreme Concourse are His legions; the Word of God is His sword; the power of God is His victory.[5]

Moreover, although the Bahá'í revelation claims to be the fulfilment of the promise of all ages, 'it does not attempt, under any circumstances, to invalidate those first and everlasting principles that animate and underlie the religions that have preceded it':

> The God-given authority, vested in each one of them, it admits and establishes as its firmest and ultimate basis. It regards them in no other light except as different stages in the eternal history and constant evolution of one religion, Divine and indivisible, of which it itself forms but an integral part. It neither seeks to obscure their Divine origin, nor to dwarf the admitted magnitude of their colossal achievements. It can countenance no attempt that seeks to distort

> their features or to stultify the truths which they instil. Its teachings do not deviate a hairbreadth from the verities they enshrine, nor does the weight of its message detract one jot or one tittle from the influence they exert or the loyalty they inspire. Far from aiming at the overthrow of the spiritual foundation of the world's religious systems, its avowed, its unalterable purpose is to widen their basis, to restate their fundamentals, to reconcile their aims, to reinvigorate their life, to demonstrate their oneness, to restore the pristine purity of their teachings, to coordinate their functions and to assist in the realization of their highest aspirations.[6]

Hence, the Bahá'í Faith has no intention to belittle Christ, to whittle down any of His teachings, to obscure, however slightly, the radiance of His revelation, to oust Jesus from the hearts of His followers, or to abrogate the fundamentals of His teachings.[7] This presentation attempts to adhere assiduously to the above principles.

The Bahá'í Writings underline the fact that faith 'has been the basis of all civilization and progress in the history of mankind'.[8] It is a matter of historical record that the three Abrahamic revelations, Judaism, Christianity and Islam, created, unaided and persecuted at their origins, great civilizations based on fundamentally similar moral and ethical principles, demonstrating the power of faith to enable humanity to discard the effete and to propel it to a new stage of endeavour and spiritual and social achievement.

However, when the Bahá'í Faith speaks of religion it is not referring to 'the dogmas and blind imitations which have gradually encrusted it',[9] the denominationalism and sectarianism. It is these that have caused the spiritual health of mankind to be in the trough of a major decline today.

Bahá'u'lláh warned of the impending decline in faith, but emphasized that, as in the past, the power of the divine Word has the capacity to remedy it:

> The vitality of men's belief in God is dying out in every land; nothing short of His wholesome medicine can ever restore it. The corrosion of ungodliness is eating into the vitals of human society; what else but the Elixir of His potent Revelation can cleanse and revive it? Is it within human power . . . to effect in the constituent elements of

any of the minute and indivisible particles of matter so complete a transformation as to transmute it into purest gold? Perplexing and difficult as this may appear, the still greater task of converting satanic strength into heavenly power is one that We have been empowered to accomplish . . . The Word of God, alone, can claim the distinction of being endowed with the capacity required for so great and far-reaching a change.[10]

The importance of true faith in upraising moral standards, reducing acts of violence, and ensuring the peace of mankind is emphasized:

There can be no doubt that the decline of religion as a social force, of which the deterioration of religious institutions is but an external phenomenon, is chiefly responsible for so grave, so conspicuous an evil. 'Religion', writes Bahá'u'lláh, 'is the greatest of all means for the establishment of order in the world and for the peaceful contentment of all that dwell therein. The weakening of the pillars of religion hath strengthened the hands of the ignorant and made them bold and arrogant. Verily I say, whatsoever hath lowered the lofty station of religion hath increased the waywardness of the wicked, and the result cannot be but anarchy.' 'Religion . . . is a radiant light and an impregnable stronghold for the protection and welfare of the peoples of the world, for the fear of God impelleth man to hold fast to that which is good, and shun all evil. Should the lamp of religion be obscured, chaos and confusion will ensue, and the lights of fairness, of justice, of tranquillity and peace cease to shine.'[11]

In the revelation of Bahá'u'lláh we find that the fundamental realities of Christianity, that is, the essential teachings, have been restated, amplified and thereby reinvigorated. Promoting a world-embracing vision, it prescribes the moral, ethical and social principles that must govern a global society today.

The Bahá'í Writings inculcate belief in the oneness of faith and declare the validity of all revealed religions. They seek to reconcile and unify the major religions of mankind.

Investigation of the Bahá'í Faith without prejudice, ascertaining that its 'fruits', namely, the love and unity that it creates in the hearts of its followers from diverse religions and denominations, are good, and therefore, that it emanates from the same God that inspired earlier dispensations, is an urgent responsibility of every true follower of Moses and Christ. In this process, the trappings, the dogma and rituals must needs be discarded and replaced by an understanding that faith is one and eternal. Truth and salvation have not been revealed solely and exclusively in any single religion. Today, God's Faith addresses the whole of mankind, and amongst other admonitions, declares the oneness of humanity that includes equal gender rights and the complementary nature of science and religion.

Christ has declared that both in His day and on the day of His return those that heard and responded to the divine message will be spiritually resuscitated, and live:

> Verily, verily, I say unto you, The hour is coming, and now is, when the dead shall hear the voice of the Son of God: and they that hear shall live. (John 5:25)

In the same vein, Bahá'u'lláh exhorts:

> Arise, and lift up your voices, that haply they that are fast asleep may be awakened . . . Whoso hath been reborn in this Day, shall never die; whoso remaineth dead, shall never live.[12]

In spite of the gloomy and depressing events currently affecting Christian institutions, Bahá'ís are optimistic of the final outcomes:

> Such institutions as have strayed far from the spirit and teachings of Jesus Christ must of necessity, as the embryonic World Order of Bahá'u'lláh takes shape and unfolds, recede into the background, and make way for the progress of the divinely-ordained institutions that stand inextricably interwoven with His teachings. The indwelling Spirit of God which, in the Apostolic Age of the Church, animated its members, the pristine purity of its teachings, the primitive brilliancy of its light, will, no doubt, be reborn and revived as the inevitable consequence of this redefinition of its fundamental verities, and the clarification of its original purpose.[13]

And yet while the shadows are continually deepening, might we not claim that gleams of hope, flashing intermittently on the international horizon, appear at times to relieve the darkness that encircles humanity?[14]

Although the thoughts expressed in this book are inspired by the Bahá'í teachings, the arrangements and conclusions are those of the author and are not a doctrine of the Bahá'í Faith except where there are direct quotations from the Bahá'í Writings.[15]

My earnest hope is that this book will open eyes and ears, and empower individuals to investigate the truth for themselves, unfettered by preconceived ideas, and to endeavour to study the Bible and to judge the tree of God's latest revelation by its fruits.

Lameh Fananapazir

PART I

WHAT DEFINES A CHRISTIAN?

I

TAKING STOCK: THE DARKENING SPIRITUAL HORIZONS

The phenomenal initial growth of Christianity may in part be attributed to the fact that it represented a transforming experience in the life of not only the individual but also the community, based on a belief in the centrality of Jesus Christ as the agent of God's saving grace. In the words of the Apostle Paul:

> . . . for we walk by faith, not by sight . . . Therefore, if anyone is in Christ,[1] he is a new creation.[2] The old has passed away; behold, the new has come.[3] (II Cor. 5:7, 17)

Compelled by Christ's love and sacrifice for them, Paul wrote that they had become reconciled to God (II Cor. 5:18–20). His own life testified to this transformation. Previously he had been a zealous persecutor of the Christians, but he was now ready to give his life to promote the cause of Christ, his Lord. He urged his fellow believers not 'to be conformed to this world', that is, not to embrace its values, customs, traditions and rituals, but to 'be transformed by the renewal of your mind, that by testing you may discern what is the will of God, what is good and acceptable and perfect' (Rom. 12:2). Similarly, Simon and his brother Andrew had been quite content with catching fish in the Sea of Galilee, but were called to become the 'fishers of men' (Matt. 4:19). Simon, whom Jesus renamed as Peter, died as a martyr in Rome.

So it was that, faithful to the Divine Word, the outlook of the early Christians became changed, making them effective witnesses to Christ and His teachings, and examples of the 'good fruits' of His revelation. As stated by the Apostle Paul:

> for at one time you were darkness, but now you are light in the

Lord. Walk as children of light [for the fruit of light is found in all that is good and right and true], and try to discern what is pleasing to the Lord. (Eph. 5:8–10)

The Book of Acts states that 'all the believers met together in one place and shared everything they had' (New Living Translation: Acts 2:44), and again, 'the full number of those who believed were of one heart and soul, and no one said that any of the things that belonged to him was his own, but they had everything in common' (Acts 4:32). The Apostles' Creed, a document of the fourth-century church, refers to the infant Christian community as the 'communion of saints'.[4] William Barclay, Professor of Divinity and Biblical Criticism at Glasgow University, explained:

> The word *saints* is used . . . in its New Testament sense and not in its modern sense. The saints are not those who have the word 'Saint' prefixed to their names; they are not the famous examples of holiness and piety who have been canonized into saints in the ecclesiastical sense of the term . . .
>
> The first and simplest interpretation of the phrase *the communion of saints* takes it to be a description of *the way in which Christian people in mutual care and love share everything with each other*. This caring and sharing has always been the mark of the church when it was truly Christian . . .
>
> The Christians were like the members of a body. Each member had care for every other member. The need of one was the need of all and the suffering of one was the suffering of all (I Cor. 12:25–26).[5]

The Epistle to Diognetus, written in the late second century in defence of the much-maligned early Christian community, describes eloquently the distinguishing features of this group of individuals:

> For Christians are not distinguished from the rest of humanity by country, or by speech, or by customs. For they do not dwell in cities of their own, or use a different language, or practise a peculiar life. This knowledge of theirs has not been discovered by the thought and the effort of inquisitive men, they are not champions of a human doctrine, as some men are. But while they dwell in Greek or barbarian cities, according as each man's lot was cast, and follow the customs of the

land in clothing and food and other matters of daily life, yet the conditions of citizenship which they exhibit is wonderful, and admittedly beyond all expectation. They live in their countries of their own, but only as sojourners; they share the life of citizens, they endure the lot of foreigners; every foreign land is to them a fatherland and every fatherland is to them a foreign land. They marry like the rest of the world, they beget children, but they do not cast their children adrift. They have a common table but not a common bed. They exist in the flesh, but live not after the flesh. They spend their existence upon earth, but their citizenship is in heaven. They obey the established laws, but in their own lives they surpass the laws. They love all men, and are persecuted by all. They are unknown, and yet they are condemned; they are put to death, yet they give proof of new life. They are poor, yet they make many rich; they lack everything, yet in everything they abound. They are dishonoured, yet their dishonour becomes their glory; they are reviled, and yet are vindicated. They are insulted, and repay insult with honour. They do good, and are punished as evildoers; and in their punishment they rejoice as finding new life therein. The Jews were against them as aliens; the Greeks persecute them, and yet they that hate them can state no ground for their enmity.

In a word, what the soul is to the body, Christians are to the world . . .

. . . (Dost thou not see them) flung to the wild beasts, to make them deny their Lord, and yet unconquered. Dost thou not see that the more of them are punished the more their numbers increase? These things look not like the achievements of man; they are the power of God; they are proof of His presence.[6]

The Christian community continued to grow steadily over the centuries and across the world. In 2005, Christianity, in all of its various denominations (Catholic, Protestant, Anglican, Eastern Orthodox, Syrian, Anabaptist, Restorationist, etc.), represented the largest religion on the planet comprising a third of the world's population.

Increasing issues facing the church

While Christianity as a whole continues to be the world's dominant religion, recent statistics show its institutions in the West experiencing an unprecedented and disturbing downward spiral in their fortunes. The church hierarchy faces a bewildering array of serious challenges on a truly global scale. Christian institutions, unable to offer coherent solutions to the new issues facing humanity, have also had to contend with a number of tragic and disturbing moral lapses.

Far from wishing to criticize or engage in fault-finding, the purpose here is to briefly examine the current state of Christian institutions and demonstrate the need for spiritual revival and fundamental change.

Waning commitment to institutional religion – flagging church membership and attendance

Recent surveys demonstrate that the Christian experience in the West has undergone a steep decline during the past 60 years, gauged by such factors as church membership and worship service attendance.[7]

In the United Kingdom, the population describing itself as Anglican has dropped from 30% in 2000 to 15% today, and it is projected that if these trends continue, Anglicanism will become insignificant in Britain by 2033.[8] In Scotland, church attendance has fallen by more than half over the past 30 years.[9] Indeed, many people across Europe have no religious affiliation: France (28%), Germany (25%), Italy (12%) and the Netherlands (42%).[10] Consequently, Europe's churches have had to close at an alarming rate, reflecting 'the rapid weakening of the [Christian] faith in Europe, a phenomenon that is painful to both worshipers and others who see religion as a unifying factor in a disparate society',[11] a trend described as the 'philosophical, spiritual floundering of Europe'.[12]

Although the United States is still an overwhelmingly Christian country, a recent survey found that it is following the same trend as Europe. The percentage of adult Americans who described themselves as Christian fell from about 86% in 1990 to 76% in 2008[13] and to 71% in 2014.[14]

Recent articles note that in a dozen countries most young people do not follow a religion.[15]

Reasons for the precipitous decline

Several reasons have been cited for these trends. Reflecting perhaps the spirit of this age, the Barna research group recently reported that the reasons why young people aged 13 to 18 years do not see a need to go to church include a conviction that they can find God elsewhere; that church rituals are empty; and that the church is out of date.[16]

Lack of familiarity with the Scriptures and lack of reliance on God's Word

Most Christians ignore their personal responsibility to investigate diligently the profound truths of Christ's Message. As reported by one Christian organization, Christians are fond of the Bible but rarely study it; most Christians in the United States have apparently read little or nothing of the Bible.[17] Less than half can name the first book of the Bible and only a third know who delivered the Sermon on the Mount – this despite the fact that millions of copies of the Bible are sold or distributed every year.[18]

Discouragement of religious and scientific enquiry

The relationship between the Catholic Church and science has a chequered history. A prime example is the persecution of Galileo Galilei (1564–1642) considered the father of modern science. His advocacy of a heliocentric universe earned him enemies among the Catholic Church leaders. He was forced to recant and was placed under house arrest for the rest of his life. On several other issues, scientific truths have been clearly subordinate to faith, as defined by the Catholic Church:

> ***By faith,*** man completely submits his intellect and his will to God. With his whole being man gives his assent to God the revealer. Sacred Scripture calls this human response to God, the author of revelation, 'the obedience of faith'.[19]
>
> ***Faith and science:*** 'Though faith is above reason, there can never be any real discrepancy between faith and reason. Since the same God who reveals mysteries and infuses faith has bestowed the light of reason on the human mind, God cannot deny himself, nor can truth ever contradict truth.' 'Consequently, methodical research in all branches of knowledge, provided it is carried out in a truly scientific manner and does not override moral laws, can never conflict

with faith, because the things of the world and the things of faith derive from the same God. The humble and persevering investigator of the secrets of nature is being led, as it were, by the hand of God in spite of himself, for it is God, the conserver of all things, who made them what they are.'[20]

Although it is reasonable to assume that true faith and true science must be complementary and not contradictory, it is incorrect to assume that there has never been any real discrepancy between faith as defined by the church and scientific reasoning; 'Since 1633, when Galileo Galilei faced the Roman Inquisition to account for his discovery that the earth revolves around the sun, there has been an often uneasy relationship between church and science.'[21] There is continued argument over teaching evolution versus creationism, with some Christian institutions wishing to control education and the scientific narratives. The Catholic Church has also recently reaffirmed its opposition to embryonic stem cell research.[22]

A new study reports 'that most Americans (59%) say, in general, that science often is in conflict with religion, and only a minority of adults (38%) consider science and religion to be mostly compatible'.[23] In this context, the success and dominance of science naturally erodes faith in traditional and fundamentalist religious belief. Some Christians continue to feel frustrated that legitimate doubt is prohibited and reasonable questions get dismissed with pat and often trite answers.[24]

Deteriorating sexual morality in the clergy and institutional failures in dealing with the problem

Christianity was founded on purity of character and motive. The Apostle Paul had warned:

> But sexual immorality and all impurity or covetousness must not even be named among you, as is proper among saints. Let there be no filthiness nor foolish talk nor crude joking, which are out of place, but instead let there be thanksgiving. For you may be sure of this, that everyone who is sexually immoral or impure, or who is covetous (that is, an idolater), has no inheritance in the kingdom of Christ and God. (Eph. 5:3–5)

It is therefore a deepening concern amongst people of faith that morality has declined not only in the United States and Europe, but throughout the world.[25] Even as early as the late medieval period, Thomas à Kempis, a Christian theologian and German–Dutch canon, felt impelled to remind his fellow believers in *The Imitation of Christ* of what it means to be Christian.

Assertion of the exclusivity and finality of a particular brand of Christianity

Christ emphasized the temporary nature of the outward trappings of religion (Luke 5:33–39). The relative insignificance of religious affiliation is also illustrated by the following Gospel account of miraculous power over evil being independently exercised in Jesus's name, which the disciples found quite disturbing:

> John answered, 'Master, we saw someone casting out demons in your name, and we tried to stop him, because he does not follow with us.' But Jesus said to him, 'Do not stop him, for the one who is not against you is for you.' (Luke 9:49–50)

Nevertheless, several Christian denominations assert that they alone represent the one true church. This belief, similar to that held by the followers of Moses at the time of Christ, is an important but not fully recognized contributor to the continuing decline of the Christian faith since it imbues individuals and institutions with an unmerited and overwhelming sense of superiority. It puts them at odds with other religions, and impedes their ability to question traditional beliefs, to investigate new realities and to understand what God has willed for today. It sidesteps biblical teachings that God is 'the Lord, the God of all mankind' (New International Version: Jer. 32:27, also, Ps. 103:13; Is. 63:16), a merciful heavenly Father, and through Abraham, 'the father of us all', and 'the father of many nations' (Matt. 6:9–10; Rom. 4:16–17; II Cor. 11:3).

Denominationalism

The Apostle Paul recommended that the worship of God in churches should not be disorderly: 'Because God is not chaotic, but peaceful, as in all the assemblies of The Holy Ones' (Aramaic Bible in Plain English: I Cor. 14:33). The American Presbyterian clergyman and theologian Rev. Albert Barnes (1798–1870), provided the following explanation in his extensive biblical commentary:

> ***God is not the author of confusion.*** His religion cannot tend to produce disorder. He is the God of peace; and his religion will tend to promote order. It is calm, peaceful, thoughtful. It is not boisterous and disorderly . . . wherever the true religion was spread, that it tended to produce peace and order. This is as true now as it was then. And we may learn, therefore:
> (1) That where there is disorder, there is little religion. Religion does not produce it; and the tendency of tumult and confusion is to drive religion away.
> (2) True religion will not lead to tumult, to outcries, or to irregularity . . .[26]

Christ desired that His followers be known by the love that they had for their fellow human beings (John 13:35) and warned that 'if a kingdom is divided against itself, that kingdom cannot stand. And if a house be divided against itself, that house will not be able to stand' (Mark 3:25). The Apostle Paul defined 'the fruit of the Spirit' as 'love, joy, peace, patience, kindness, goodness, faithfulness', (Gal. 5:22). But the church has allowed itself to be fragmented into many competing denominations based on disagreements over dogma, tradition and rituals, while still maintaining that it is the only way to God. Indeed, the initial impulse of Christians is often not to call themselves the followers of Christ's teaching but instead to identify themselves as Baptist, Catholic, Orthodox, Lutheran, Adventist, or one of the numerous other sects within the Christian Faith. Sadly, even being 'non-denominational' and accepting members of other denominations has itself become a sect and part of the fragmentation. The number of Christian sects was estimated at about 43,000 in 2012 and is projected to rise astonishingly to 55,000 by 2025.[27] In addition, the Protestant churches in the United States are segregated according to race: 87% of the Christian churches are completely made up of only white or only African–American parishioners.[28] This background of endless division and animosity ensures that the decline in belief will gain momentum.

It is clear from ecclesiastical history that the root cause of denominationalism is church dogma. Throughout the centuries, layer upon layer of doctrine and spurious practices have been added to the Faith of Christ, to the extent that it has become virtually unrecognizable and alienated from its origins. For example, the Catholic doctrine of the Immaculate Conception of Mary, a reference to the sinless state of Mary proclaimed by Pope Pius IX on 8 December 1854, has been the cause of many dissensions and lacks biblical support. Similarly, the doctrine of the Assumption of Mary, proclaimed by Pope Pius XII in November 1950, which states that the 'immaculate Virgin' was assumed body and soul into heaven after the completion of her earthly life, the belief of the Perpetual Virginity of Mary, and Mary as Co-Redemptrix, have no basis in the New Testament.[29]

Thus, from the cradle to the grave, Christians are trapped by man-made traditions and rituals which make it virtually impossible for them to make independent decisions about their faith without incurring feelings of guilt or official censure. A bewildering number of churches exist which testify to the disunity of the Christian Faith, representing monuments devoted to sectarian interests rather than dedicated to the promotion of unity, indiscriminating love and fellowship.[30]

Interdenominational and interreligious disputes, rivalries and animosities

The twentieth century witnessed several devastating nationalistic and ethnic conflicts between Europe's 550 million Christians. These have included two world wars that resulted in the deaths of many millions of members of European Catholic, Protestant, Orthodox, Anglican and Lutheran denominations at the hands of their fellow Christians. The bitter church feuds and fractionation show no sign of abating and are not always based on theological differences but may occasionally have their origins in geopolitical tensions, as demonstrated in the Rwanda conflict[31] or by the recent split of the Ukrainian Orthodox Church from its Russian counterpart.[32]

Increasing departure from the pristine purity of Christ's teachings

There is a stark dichotomy between Christ's teachings and what has been and is being perpetrated in His blessed name:

> Through His death and teachings we have entered into His Kingdom. His essential teaching was the unity of mankind and the attainment of supreme human virtues through love. He came to establish the Kingdom of peace and everlasting life. Can you find in His words any justification for discord and enmity? The purpose of His life and the glory of His death were to set mankind free from the sins of strife, war and bloodshed. The great nations of the world boast that their laws and civilization are based upon the religion of Christ. Why then do they make war upon each other? The Kingdom of Christ cannot be upheld by destroying and disobeying it. The banners of His armies cannot lead the forces of Satan . . . Therefore, these wars and cruelties, this bloodshed and sorrow are Antichrist, not Christ. These are the forces of death and Satan, not the hosts of the Supreme Concourse of heaven.
>
> No less bitter is the conflict between sects and denominations. Christ was a divine Center of unity and love. Whenever discord prevails instead of unity, wherever hatred and antagonism take the place of love and spiritual fellowship, Antichrist reigns instead of Christ. Who is right in these controversies and hatreds between the sects? Did Christ command them to love or to hate each other? He loved even His enemies and prayed in the hour of His crucifixion for those who killed Him. Therefore, to be a Christian is not merely to bear the name of Christ . . . To be a real Christian is to be a servant in His Cause and Kingdom, to go forth under His banner of peace and love toward all mankind, to be self-sacrificing and obedient, to become quickened by the breaths of the Holy Spirit, to be mirrors reflecting the radiance of the divinity of Christ, to be fruitful trees in the garden of His planting, to refresh the world by the water of life of His teachings – in all things to be like Him and filled with the spirit of His love.[33]

Taking Stock: The Darkening Spiritual Horizons

Scriptural warnings of a difficult period ahead

Christ emphasized the importance of distinguishing a good tree by its spiritual fruits (Matt. 7:16–20) rather than by its foliage, bark or flowers. He then followed this teaching with the startling warning that in 'that Day' His followers would exult in the fact that they had preached and performed miracles in His name, but that His response would be: 'I never knew you: depart from me, ye that work iniquity' (King James Version: Matt. 7:22–23). In his commentary, the biblical scholar Joseph Benson (1749–1821), a leader in the Methodist movement, provides the following explanation for this disturbing prediction:

> ***Then will I profess unto them, I never knew you*** – Though I called you to be my servants, and you professed yourselves such, I never knew you to be such, nor approved of you. So that even the working of the greatest miracles, and the uttering the most undoubted prophecies, is not a sufficient proof that a man possesses saving faith, nor will any thing of that kind avail to prove that we are now accepted of God, or are in the way to meet with acceptance of him at the day of final accounts, without the faith productive of true and universal holiness.[34]

Rev. Albert Barnes provides the following analysis:

> ***I never knew you*** – That is, I never approved of your conduct; never loved you; never regarded you as my friends. This proves that, with all their pretensions, they had never been true followers of Christ. Jesus will not then say to false prophets and false professors of religion that he had once known them and then rejected them; that they had been once Christians and then had fallen away; that they had been pardoned and then had apostatized but that he had never known them – they had never been true Christians. Whatever might have been their pretended joys, their raptures, their hopes, their self-confidence, their visions, their zeal, they had never been regarded by the Saviour as his true friends. I do not know of a more decided proof that Christians do not fall from grace than this text. It settles the question; and proves that whatever else such people had, they never had any true religion.[35]

The Hebrew Bible warns that 'the time of the end' will be a period when 'the wicked shall act wickedly. And none of the wicked shall understand, but those who are wise[36] shall understand' (Daniel 12:10) This state of affairs has reminded some Christians[37] also of the New Testament predictions of the spiritual deterioration and weakening of the foundations of faith at the time when Christ is expected to return. Metaphorically:

> Immediately after the tribulation of those days the sun will be darkened, and the moon will not give its light, and the stars will fall from heaven, and the powers of the heavens will be shaken. (Matt. 24:29)

Specifically:

> And then many will fall away and betray one another and hate one another. And many false prophets will arise and lead many astray. And because lawlessness[38] will be increased, the love of many will grow cold. (Matt. 24:10–12)

> But watch yourselves lest your hearts be weighed down with dissipation and drunkenness and cares of this life, and that day come upon you suddenly like a trap. For it will come upon all who dwell on the face of the whole earth. But stay awake at all times, praying that you may have strength to escape all these things that are going to take place, and to stand before the Son of Man. (Luke 21:34–36)

> . . . for that day will not come, unless the rebellion comes first[39] (II Thess. 2:3)

> Now the Spirit expressly says that in later times some will depart from the faith by devoting themselves to deceitful spirits and teachings of demons, through the insincerity of liars whose consciences are seared . . . (I Tim. 4:1–2)

Christianity at the crossroads and beyond: The fateful hour of decision

Quo vadis? – Given the current situation, Christians may do well to consider where Christianity is headed and what Christ would do today.

TAKING STOCK: THE DARKENING SPIRITUAL HORIZONS

We are reminded of an ancient legend that describes the Apostle Peter retracing his steps and recalibrating his priorities on encountering Christ:

> His friends, so runs the story, had entreated the Apostle to save his life by leaving the city. Peter at last consented, but on condition that he should go away alone. But when he wished to pass the gate of the city, he saw Christ meeting him. Falling down in adoration he says to Him 'Lord, whither goest Thou?' [Latin, *quo vadis?*] And Christ replied to him 'I am coming to Rome to be again crucified.' And Peter says to Him 'Lord, wilt Thou again be crucified?' And the Lord said to him 'Even so, I will again be crucified.' Peter said to Him 'Lord, I will return and will follow Thee.' And with these words the Lord ascended into Heaven . . . And Peter, afterwards corning to himself, understood that it was of his own passion that it had been spoken, because that in it the Lord would suffer. The Apostle then returned with joy to meet the death which the Lord had signified that he should die.[40]

By accepting Christ as his Lord, the Apostle Peter had not lost his faith in Moses or his conviction in the revelation that had descended from Mount Sinai. Whilst he and his fellow disciples remained faithful to the fundamental verities of Judaism, true to the teachings of Christ, they were not impressed by the glitter and tinsel of the Jewish institutions or enticed by their trappings (Mark 13:1–2). Christ had admonished them: 'Do not judge by appearances, but judge with right judgment' (John 7:24). They were able to attribute the failure of the Jewish leaders to recognize Jesus as their Messiah to their lack of understanding of their own scriptures which had been read daily for several centuries in their synagogues (John 5:45–47).

It is a sobering lesson for us that despite a lifetime of transcribing and studying the Torah and the Talmud, and having observed every detail of the minutest laws of Moses, in the end the Scribes and Pharisees rejected Christ – they thus failed to appreciate the intent of their scriptures. In his commentary on John 5:45–47, the German Lutheran scholar Heinrich August Wilhelm Meyer (1899–1873) wrote:

> In concluding, Jesus sweeps away from under their feet the entire ground and foundation upon which they based their hope, by

representing Moses, their supposed saviour, as really their *accuser*, seeing that their unbelief implied unbelief in Moses, and this latter unbelief made it impossible for them to believe in Jesus.[41]

The lesson for the followers of Christ today is evident: their response to the Second Coming will indicate how diligently they have followed the admonishments of the Gospels.

We may again ask ourselves what Jesus expects of His followers today. What does it mean to walk in Jesus's footsteps and to be truly Christian? What set of virtues, degree of righteousness, and receptivity must a Christian cultivate and evince to ensure that he will be prepared for the promised return of Christ in the glory of the Father? And is the necessary spiritual transformation and rebirth feasible by remaining faithful members of obsolete religious institutions? As with the First Coming, could it be that the resurrection of the Christians will come about once again through the creative power of the divine Word (*Logos*)?

If Christianity is to redeem itself and be reborn, it cannot afford to ignore the 'good news' of the advent of the Kingdom of God, the central theme of the Gospels and the salvation of Christianity

Finally, as will hopefully be clear later, the church has not recognized the promised new revelation and the return of Christ in the glory of the Father at the Second Coming. This failure has disconnected it from the saving grace of the Holy Spirit, and eliminated the opportunity of renewal and rebirth. The church is now two thousand years old. During this period Christians have preached the 'good news' of the coming of the Kingdom and prayed for the Second Coming of Christ in the glory of the Father, and yet at the same time they have stubbornly failed to genuinely consider how this would happen, enacting a similar failure of the followers of Moses to read aright their predictions concerning the advent of the Messiah at the First Coming. In spite of the New Testament warning that Christians must 'be watchful, and stand firm in the faith' (I Cor. 16:13), this central Christian expectation itself has changed significantly, as attested by the late Professor William Barclay:[42]

> ... we must think of the Christian teaching concerning the Second Coming of our Lord, and we will see that in modern times it has undergone a curious experience. For some people it is a belief which has simply vanished from the forefront of their minds, taking its place on the circumference, and even among the eccentricities of Christian doctrine. They seldom preach on it, and simply lay it aside. For other people it is the very centre of Christian belief. It dominates their whole thought and their whole thinking, and it is not far from being the culmination of every sermon which they preach ...
>
> What if it be true that the key to the correct understanding of the Second Coming is indeed to be found in John's Gospel in the words which tell how Father and Son will come and make their dwelling in the loving and the obedient heart? (John 14:25)[43]

The Prophet Jeremiah advised that when an individual faces a crossroads of faith he should pause and consider the past, as the 'ancient paths' may provide clues to the current issues and their solutions. He must then take the time to ascertain 'where the good way is; and walk in it' (Jer. 6:16).

Most members of the various religions, including Judaism and Christianity, have tackled the challenge that they face in one of three ways.

Some have discarded institutionalized faith altogether and become atheist or agnostic, endeavoring to lead moral lives while not following any particular religion. They ignore the fact that the moral life of one person is considered sinful by others, accounting for some of the many divisions in Western society.

Others have joined 'reformed' congregations which are considered by fundamentalists to have adulterated the original intent of the Scripture by adding changes to make it more compatible with modernity. They lack credibility, for the God Who revealed their Faith originally must surely be cognizant of the fact that their religion stands in dire need of being reformed, renewed and re-voiced to mankind. If individuals themselves can reform the religion, what is the relevance of the God Who revealed their Faith initially and promised that in due course He would address the need for new teachings?

Yet others have retreated into deep-rooted orthodoxy and conservatism, maintaining that as their religion was from God and was originally a force for good, they should return to the past fundamentals of their Faith. This viewpoint, however, does not consider that some of their teachings no longer serve the best interests of society. Their intolerant and dogmatic attitudes rely on extreme literal interpretations of the scriptures that are patently unreasonable, unscientific and untenable, and risk alienating other Christians and members of other Faiths.

An alternative path, one that is open to everyone, is to make choices that go beyond entrenched beliefs that are maintained through an accident of birth. Preliminary steps are to recommit to a virtuous life, one that is dedicated to validating without prejudice the awesome claim that the promised 'good news' of the Gospels has been fulfilled. Christians who have been true to Christ's call for vigilance in spite of all adversities have been made special mention of in the Bible:

> But stay awake at all times, praying that you may have strength to escape all these things that are going to take place, and to stand before the Son of Man. (Luke 21:36)

> The one who conquers will have this heritage, and I will be his God and he will be my son.[44] (Rev. 21:7)

2

REVISITING CHRISTIAN VIRTUES AND RELEARNING TO WALK IN CHRIST'S FOOTSTEPS

Arguably, the tragedies that have beset Christian institutions are in part the result of individuals and society ignoring the spiritual teachings of Christ and failing to follow His way. It will therefore be helpful to examine, according to the Bible, what it means to be a Christian.

The word 'Christian' occurs only three times in the New Testament. The disciples were first called Christians in Antioch (Acts 11:26). The Greek word is *Christianos* (Χριστιανός), meaning the follower of *Christos* (the Anointed). Initially a derogatory term given by outsiders, the name was adopted with pride by those to whom this label was given.[1] They endeavoured to follow the example set for them by their Lord, to make Him known, and to preach the advent of the Kingdom throughout the world.

The Apostle Peter counselled his fellow believers that they should emulate the example of Christ and follow in his steps (I Peter 2:21). Christ's injunction 'follow me!' (John 21:22) may have prompted the following statement:

> Whoever says he abides in him [Jesus] ought to walk in the same way in which he walked. (I John 2:6)

Obeying Christ's commandments

Christians often assert that they love Jesus, but the Gospels make it clear that no one can claim to love and praise Christ and at the same time ignore His basic teachings. He did not seek anyone's adulation but instead wished His followers to obey His teachings:

> Why do you call me 'Lord, Lord,' and not do what I tell you? (Luke 6:46)
>
> I do not receive glory from people. (John 5:41)

This obedience represented a firm and lasting foundation of faith (Luke 6:47–49). God loves the obedient individual and Christ would manifest Himself to him:

> If you love me, you will keep my commandments . . . Whoever has my commandments and keeps them, he it is who loves me. And he who loves me will be loved by my Father, and I will love him and manifest myself to him . . . if you love me, you will keep my commandments.[2] Whoever does not love me does not keep my words. And the word that you hear is not mine but the Father's who sent me. (John 14:15, 24)

The spiritual teachings of Jesus form the heart of the Gospels. They define the very essence of what it means to be a follower of Christ, and constitute the most endearing and enduring aspects of the Faith of Jesus. The virtues have a value that unlike theology is independent of dogma and tradition; they are lasting and derive their inspiration directly from God's Word. Notably, the divine principles are part of the scriptures of most religions, and are vital not only to the spiritual well-being of individuals, but also moderate and elevate the conversation and conduct of all members of the global human family.

The Judeo-Christian experience – continuity of the divine purpose

The shared Jewish and Christian spiritual values and aims allowed Jesus to reassure the followers of Moses of His time that He had no intention of abolishing 'the Law' or destroying their faith in Moses and the Prophets of Israel (Matt. 5:17–19).

He designated as the most important teaching of His Dispensation the Jewish *Shema* ('Hear') prayer (Deut. 6:4–5), which declares unequivocally the oneness of God:

> And one of the scribes came up and heard them disputing with one another, and seeing that he answered them well, asked him, 'Which commandment is the most important of all?' Jesus answered, 'The most important is, 'Hear, O Israel: The Lord our God, the Lord is one. And you shall love the Lord your God with all your heart and with all your soul and with all your mind and with all your strength.' (Mark 12:28–30).

In this connection, the Apostle Paul stated at his trial before the Roman procurator of Judea Province, Marcus Antonius Felix:

> I worship the God of our fathers, believing everything laid down by the Law and written in the Prophets, having a hope in God, which these men themselves accept, that there will be a resurrection of both the just and the unjust. (Acts 24:14–15)

The impermanent social teachings and outward structures of religion

In contrast to the core moral and ethical laws, the social teachings and practices of a religion serve the needs of a particular people for a pre-ordained period of time. They represent the outward form of faith and are referred to in the Hebrew Bible as fountains and cisterns that hold the water of life but which may break and become dry (Prov. 5:15; Jer. 2:13). In the New Testament they are referred to as 'waterless springs and mists driven by a storm' (II Peter 2:17), an 'old garment', and 'old wineskins' that if made to hold the new spiritual wine would burst (Matt. 9:16–17; see also Chapter 3).

Fundamentals of the Christian Faith

The essential or lasting teachings of the Christian Faith are its moral and ethical imperatives.

Love God

This love must be unfeigned: 'let love be genuine. Abhor what is evil; hold fast to what is good' (Rom. 12:9) – a 'love that issues from a pure heart and a good conscience and a sincere faith' (I Tim. 1:5). In turn, God loves His creatures:

> So we have come to know and to believe the love that God has for us. God is love, and whoever abides in love abides in God, and God abides in him. (I John 4:16)

This love must translate into obeying the divine teachings:

> For this is the love of God, that we keep his commandments . . . (I John 5:3; also, II John 1:6)

It must be evident through actions rather than words:

> But be doers of the word, and not hearers only, deceiving yourselves. If anyone thinks he is religious and does not bridle his tongue but deceives his heart, this person's religion is worthless. Religion that is pure and undefiled before God the Father is this: to visit orphans and widows in their affliction, and to keep oneself unstained from the world. (James 1:22, 26–27)

Put your trust in God and not in your own understanding

> Trust in the Lord with all your heart, and do not lean on your own understanding. (Prov. 3:5)

We must have the certitude that God will hear us as long as our wishes are in conformity with His will and purpose:

> And this is the confidence that we have toward him, that if we ask anything according to his will he hears us. (I John 5:14)

Love of God must be manifested by love for fellow Christians

This love would define the followers of Christ:

> A new commandment I give to you, that you love one another: just as I have loved you, you also are to love one another. By this all

people will know that you are my disciples, if you have love for one another. (John 13:34–35; also, Matt. 5:44–48)

Benson writes in his commentary:

> ***By this shall all men know that you are my disciples*** – Your loving one another sincerely and fervently, and in the manner and degree I now enjoin, will be the most acceptable and the most ornamental token of your relation to me, and the noblest badge of your profession. The reader will not need to be told how remarkably this new precept of our Lord was exemplified in the spirit and conduct of the first Christians, when he recollects their historian has attested, (Acts 4:32) that though they were a great multitude, consisting of many thousands, they were all of one heart and of one soul; insomuch that not any of them accounted any of the things which he possessed as his own, but they had all things in common. And the ancient apologists for Christianity inform us, that the persecuting heathen themselves could not help exclaiming in rapture, on observing the prevalence of this grace among them, See how these Christians love one another![3]

The Apostles reiterated this vital principle:

> And above all these [virtues] put on love, which binds everything together in perfect harmony.[4] (Col. 3:14)

> Now concerning brotherly love you have no need for anyone to write to you, for you yourselves have been taught by God to love one another… (I Thess. 4:9; also, I Pet. 1:22, I John 4:7–8, and I John 5:1–2)

The Apostle Paul underlined the importance of faith being fortified by love:

> If I speak in the tongues of men and of angels, but have not love, I am a noisy gong or a clanging cymbal. And if I have prophetic powers, and understand all mysteries and all knowledge, and if I have all faith, so as to remove mountains, but have not love, I am nothing. If I give away all I have, and if I deliver up my body to be burned, but have not love, I gain nothing. Love is patient and

kind; love does not envy or boast; it is not arrogant or rude. It does not insist on its own way; it is not irritable or resentful; it does not rejoice at wrongdoing, but rejoices with the truth. Love bears all things, believes all things, hopes all things, endures all things. Love never ends . . . So now faith, hope, and love abide, these three; but the greatest of these is love. (I Cor. 13:1–8, 13)

This love must also translate to love for all humanity

Christ stated that after the love of God the second greatest commandment was: 'You shall love your neighbour as yourself. On these two commandments depend all the Law and the Prophets' (Matt. 22:39–40; also, Mark 12:28–33). This love therefore also fulfilled the purpose of the Law of Moses:

> For the whole law is fulfilled in one word: 'You shall love your neighbor as yourself.' (Gal. 5:14; also, Rom. 13:8)

Individuals who accepted Christ were from diverse backgrounds. They therefore had to abandon their ancient prejudices, foster an abiding love and respect for all mankind, and strive for the unity and harmony of all humanity. Christ's eulogy of a believing Roman centurion (Matt. 8:10–12), and a Good Samaritan (Luke 10:25–37) paved the way. This love was on a par with devotion to the welfare of individuals from their own ethnic background. The Apostle Paul elaborated:

> The God who made the world and everything in it, being Lord of heaven and earth...
> he himself gives to all mankind life and breath and everything. And he made from one man every nation of mankind to live on all the face of the earth . . . he is actually not far from each one of us . . . (Acts 17:24–26, 27)

According to the Book of Revelation, Jesus gave His life on the cross for people from all races and all backgrounds:

> . . . for you were slain, and by your blood you ransomed people for God from every tribe and language and people and nation . . . (Rev. 5:9)

That this love 'supposes a general love to mankind' was emphasized by the Welsh non-conformist minister and prodigious biblical commentator, Matthew Henry (1662–1714).[5] Indeed, the litmus test for true transformation and spiritual resurrection on the part of the followers of Jesus is whether they love others:

> We know that we have passed out of death into life, because we love the brothers. Whoever does not love abides in death. Everyone who hates his brother is a murderer, and you know that no murderer has eternal life abiding in him. (I John 3:14–15)

Furthermore, the Gospel of John[6] declares that Christ was the Light of Truth which illuminates every person who comes into the world. Therefore a Christian, whose soul reflects that universal divine Light, will not be at ease with belief systems that directly or indirectly segregate humanity, by insisting that they are the only way to God, righteousness and heaven. This love necessarily calls for eschewing all denominational differences and animosities, a course of action that is fortified by the scriptural warning that no one who is illuminated by the light of Christ can afford to alienate himself from his fellow men:

> . . . the darkness is passing away and the true light is already shining. Whoever says he is in the light and hates his brother is still in darkness. Whoever loves his brother abides in the light, and in him there is no cause for stumbling. But whoever hates his brother is in the darkness and walks in the darkness, and does not know where he is going, because the darkness has blinded his eyes. (I John 2:8–11)

Fear of God

> And from the throne [of God] came a voice saying, 'Praise our God, all you his servants, you who fear him, small and great.' (Rev. 19:5)

Being mindful of the Divine Presence impels us to be righteous:

> . . . bringing holiness to completion in the fear of God. (II Cor. 7:1)

The Apostle Peter stated that irrespective of state affiliation anyone who fears God and is righteous is acceptable to God:

> So Peter opened his mouth and said: 'Truly I understand that God shows no partiality, but in every nation anyone who fears him and does what is right is acceptable to him.' (Acts 10:34–35)

The Apostle Paul explained that the chief sin is to have 'no fear of God' (Rom. 3:18). The well-known Protestant reformer John Calvin observed that 'without the fear of God, men do not even observe justice and charity among themselves'.[7]

Be devoted and dedicated to the divine message

> Therefore, my beloved brothers, be steadfast, immovable, always abounding in the work of the Lord, knowing that in the Lord your labour is not in vain. (I Cor. 15:58; also, see Rom. 12:12, I Cor. 16:13–14, Heb. 10:23)

The supreme function of faith is to transform the character of individuals

The acceptance of Christ entailed a profound spiritual change:

> But to all who did receive him, who believed in his name, he gave the right to become children of God, who were born, not of blood nor of the will of the flesh nor of the will of man, but of God. (John 1:12–13)

The Apostle Paul further exhorted Christians to 'be renewed in the spirit of your minds, and to put on the new self, created after the likeness of God in true righteousness and holiness' (Eph. 4:23–24), that is, to be reborn and renewed, and abandon the old self. They should not be concerned with what is considered acceptable by society, but instead, continually seek what is pleasing to God:

> Do not be conformed to this world, but be transformed by the renewal of your mind, that by testing you may discern what is the

will of God, what is good and acceptable and perfect. (Rom. 12:2)

Christians must be true to the divine ordinances and cleanse themselves from the obscuring dust of earlier misapprehensions so that they may be worthy of gaining eternal life and entering the kingdom of heaven:

> Blessed are those who wash their robes, so that they may have the right to the tree of life and that they may enter the city by the gates. (Rev. 22:14)

As explained by the Apostle Paul, the First Coming entailed a renewal of faith and a transformation of one's outlook:

> Therefore, if anyone is in Christ, he is a new creation. The old has passed away; behold, the new has come. All this is from God . . . (II Cor. 5:17–18)

> . . . to put off your old self, which belongs to your former manner of life and is corrupt through deceitful desires, and to be renewed in the spirit of your minds, and to put on the new self, created after the likeness of God in true righteousness and holiness. (Eph. 4:22–24)

Avoid any semblance of being superior to others in any way

> Judge not, that you be not judged. For with the judgment you pronounce you will be judged, and with the measure you use it will be measured to you. Why do you see the speck that is in your brother's eye, but do not notice the log that is in your own eye? Or how can you say to your brother, 'Let me take the speck out of your eye,' when there is the log in your own eye? You hypocrite, first take the log out of your own eye, and then you will see clearly to take the speck out of your brother's eye. (Matt. 7:1–5; also Gal. 6:3–4)

Love humanity – have an abiding concern for the welfare of the stranger

It was very normal in Jewish times for a servant of the house to wash the feet of guests who came to visit. Jesus washed the feet of His disciples and by this lowly act exhorted them to be humble in their service to others, to manifest the same spirit that He did, and to emulate His actions:

> When he had washed their feet and put on his outer garments and resumed his place, he said to them, 'Do you understand what I have done to you? You call me Teacher and Lord, and you are right, for so I am. If I then, your Lord and Teacher, have washed your feet, you also ought to wash one another's feet. For I have given you an example, that you also should do just as I have done to you. Truly, truly, I say to you, a servant is not greater than his master, nor is a messenger greater than the one who sent him. If you know these things, blessed are you if you do them. (John 13:12–17)

Those who show concern for the needy, the stranger, and the oppressed will be rewarded:

> When the Son of Man comes in his glory, and all the angels with him, then he will sit on his glorious throne ... Then the King will say to those on his right, 'Come, you who are blessed by my Father, inherit the kingdom prepared for you from the foundation of the world. For I was hungry and you gave me food, I was thirsty and you gave me drink, I was a stranger and you welcomed me, I was naked and you clothed me, I was sick and you visited me, I was in prison and you came to me.' Then the righteous will answer him, saying, 'Lord, when did we see you hungry and feed you, or thirsty and give you drink? And when did we see you a stranger and welcome you, or naked and clothe you? And when did we see you sick or in prison and visit you?' And the King will answer them, 'Truly, I say to you, as you did it to one of the least of these my brothers, you did it to me.' (Matt. 25:31, 34–40)

Be courteous and inclusive of others

A true follower of Christ avoids alienating others – instead, he must strive to promote love, unity and harmony:

> Do nothing from selfish ambition or conceit, but in humility count others more significant than yourselves. Let each of you look not

only to his own interests, but also to the interests of others. (Philip 2:3–4)

Love one another with brotherly affection. Outdo one another in showing honour. (Rom. 12:10)

Care for strangers and show them hospitality

Contribute to the needs of the saints[8] [fellow Christians] and seek to show hospitality.[9] (Rom. 12:13)

Let brotherly love continue. Do not neglect to show hospitality to strangers for thereby some have entertained angels unawares. Remember those who are in prison, as though in prison with them, and those who are mistreated, since you also are in the body. (Heb. 13:1–3)

Be humble, kind, and gentle

In the Beatitudes, Jesus states that the seeker who is humble and admits his spiritual poverty is truly fortunate (Matt. 5:3,5). Indeed, the Apostles Peter and James regarded humility as the key to spiritual success:

Humble yourselves, therefore, under the mighty hand of God so that at the proper time he may exalt you ... (I Pet. 5:6; also, James 4:10)

Christ added that His followers should appreciate the truth with the simplicity and unpretentiousness of children – they should not approach God's truth arrogantly and oppose it with sophisticated theological arguments:

Truly, I say to you, unless you turn[10] and become like children, you will never enter the kingdom of heaven. Whoever humbles himself like this child is the greatest in the kingdom of heaven. (Matt. 18:3–4)

The Bible commentator Rev. Joseph Benson (1749–1821), explains this admonishment:

Observe well, reader, the first step toward entering into the kingdom of grace is to become as little children: lowly in heart, knowing ourselves utterly ignorant and helpless, and hanging wholly on our Father who is in heaven, for a supply of all our wants.[11]

Adopt the golden rule which is also the sum ethical teaching of Judaism[12]

So whatever you wish that others would do to you, do also to them, for this is the Law[13] and the Prophets. (Matt. 7:12)

Do not overestimate the approval of others; counter the evil of hatred with love; and be kind to those who wish you harm

Woe to you, when all people speak well of you, for so their fathers did to the false prophets. But I say to you who hear, Love your enemies, do good to those who hate you, bless those who curse you, pray for those who abuse you. To one who strikes you on the cheek, offer the other also, and from one who takes away your cloak do not withhold your tunic either. (Luke 6:26–29)

Do not be overcome by evil, but overcome evil with good. (Rom. 12:21; also, I Peter 3:8–9)

Shun division and sectarianism

There must be unity. Avoid creating feelings of alienation:

If a kingdom is divided against itself, that kingdom cannot stand. And if a house is divided against itself, that house will not be able to stand. (Mark 3:24–25)

Finally, all of you be like-minded [united in spirit], sympathetic, brotherly, kindhearted [courteous and compassionate towards each other as members of one household] and humble in spirit. (Amplified Bible: I Peter 3:8)

I appeal to you, brothers, by the name of our Lord Jesus Christ, that

> all of you agree, and that there be no divisions among you, but that you be united in the same mind and the same judgment. (I Cor. 1:10)

> As for a person who stirs up division, after warning him once and then twice, have nothing more to do with him (Titus 3:10)

Be a peacemaker and avoid strife

> Blessed are the peacemakers, for they shall be called sons of God. (Beatitude no. 7: Matt. 5:9)

> ... let him keep his tongue from evil and his lips from speaking deceit; let him turn away from evil and do good; let him seek peace and pursue it ... (I Peter 3:10–11)

Reminding his fellow Christians of the injunctions of the Torah, the Apostle Paul explained that justice belongs ultimately to God – humanity is in the grasp of His hand and it is He Who shows mercy and delivers justice. Individuals should learn to forgive and not seek revenge: 'Repay no one evil for evil ...'; to the contrary, 'if your enemy is hungry, feed him; if he is thirsty, give him something to drink ... (Rom. 12:17, 20)

Encourage one another

> And let us consider how to stir up one another to love and good works, not neglecting to meet together, as is the habit of some, but encouraging one another, and all the more as you see the Day drawing near. (Heb. 10:24–25)

Endeavour to be of service to one another

Help others through their difficulties and sufferings:

> Brothers, if anyone is caught in any sin, you who are spiritual [that is, you who are responsive to the guidance of the Spirit] are to restore such a person in a spirit of gentleness [not with a sense of superiority or self-righteousness], keeping a watchful eye on yourself, so that

you are not tempted as well. Carry one another's burdens and in this way you will fulfill the requirements of the law of Christ [that is, the law of Christian love]. (Amplified Bible: Gal. 6:1–2)

Attend to the welfare of the destitute

Religion that is pure and undefiled before God the Father is this: to visit orphans and widows in their affliction, and to keep oneself unstained from the world. (James 1:27)

Exercise self-denial and be self-sacrificing: consecrate and dedicate your lives to God

I appeal to you therefore, brothers, by the mercies of God, to present your bodies as a living sacrifice, holy and acceptable to God, which is your spiritual worship. (Rom. 12:1)

Set your minds on things that are above, not on things that are on earth . . . Put to death [mortify] therefore what is earthly in you: sexual immorality, impurity, passion, evil desire, and covetousness, which is idolatry. (Col. 3:2, 5)

Christ was well aware that proclaiming the good news of the Gospel would entail hardships, sacrificial efforts and, not infrequently, martyrdom in remote lands for His apostles:

Blessed are those who are persecuted for righteousness' sake, for theirs is the kingdom of heaven. (Beatitude no. 8: Matt. 5:10)

Greater love has no one than this, that someone lay down his life for his friends. (John 15:13; also, I John 3:16)

Using a farming analogy, Christ clarified the need for sacrificial efforts. He taught that a seed only realizes its full potential when it sacrifices itself and becomes a plant, which in turn yields fruit. The individual should by the same token not consider his or her limited capacity, but remember that a small mustard seed grows into a mighty tree (Matt. 17:20; Luke 13:19):

> Truly, truly, I say to you, unless a grain of wheat falls into the earth and dies, it remains alone; but if it dies, it bears much fruit. Whoever loves his life loses it, and whoever hates his life in this world will keep it for eternal life. If anyone serves me, he must follow me . . . (John 12:24–26; also, Luke 9:23–25)

In another statement along the same lines, and one that must have come as a great surprise to the people of His time who dreamed of celebrating Messianic triumphs, Jesus explained that anyone who was not prepared to sacrifice himself could not be described as His follower:

> Whoever loves father or mother more than me is not worthy of me, and whoever loves son or daughter more than me is not worthy of me. And whoever does not take his cross and follow me is not worthy of me. Whoever finds his life will lose it, and whoever loses his life for my sake will find it. (Matt. 10:37–39; also Luke 14:27)

The Apostles Peter and James emphasized the need to endure suffering:

> . . . if when you do good and suffer for it you endure, this is a gracious thing in the sight of God . . . Christ also suffered for you . . . leaving you an example, so that you might follow in his steps. He committed no sin, neither was deceit found in his mouth. When he was reviled, he did not revile in return; when he suffered, he did not threaten, but continued entrusting himself to him who judges justly. (I Peter 2:20–23)

> Count it all joy, my brothers, when you meet trials of various kinds, for you know that the testing of your faith produces steadfastness. And let steadfastness have its full effect, that you may be perfect and complete, lacking in nothing. (James 1:2–4)

The Apostle Paul exhorted Christians to live a sacrificial life and reject worldly standards of conduct:

> I appeal to you therefore, brothers, by the mercies of God, to present your bodies as a living sacrifice, holy and acceptable to God, which is your spiritual worship. Do not be conformed to this world, but be

transformed by the renewal of your mind, that by testing you may discern what is the will of God, what is good and acceptable and perfect. (Rom. 12:1–2)

Reject materialism

Excessive and ostentatious materialism does not sit well with many of the Gospel teachings, since seeking the kingdom of heaven requires a Christian to maintain a proper perspective concerning this earthly life. To be effective, Christians were to be in the world but remain uncontaminated by it:

> Sell your possessions, and give to the needy. Provide yourselves with moneybags that do not grow old, with a treasure in the heavens that does not fail, where no thief approaches and no moth destroys. For where your treasure is, there will your heart be also. (Luke 12:33–34)

> They are not of the world, just as I am not of the world. Sanctify them in the truth [set them apart for Your purposes, make them holy]; Your word is truth. Just as You commissioned and sent Me into the world, I also have commissioned and sent them (believers) into the world. For their sake I sanctify Myself [to do Your will], so that they also may be sanctified [set apart, dedicated, made holy] in [Your] truth. (Amplified Bible: John 17:16–19)

The Epistle of James gives the following stern warning to the rich:

> Come now, you rich, weep and howl for the miseries that are coming upon you. Your riches have rotted and your garments are moth-eaten. Your gold and silver have corroded, and their corrosion will be evidence against you . . . (James 5:1–3)

Christ exhorted His followers not to pray for material things, 'for your Father knows what you need before you ask him' (Matt. 6:8). His response to a rich ruler underlines the dangers of a materialistic existence and, in contrast, the importance of seeking what pertains to the kingdom of heaven:

> And a ruler asked him, 'Good Teacher, what must I do to inherit eternal life?' And Jesus said to him, . . . 'You know the commandments: "Do not commit adultery, Do not murder, Do not steal, Do not bear false witness, Honour your father and mother."' And he said, 'All these I have kept from my youth.' When Jesus heard this, he said to him, 'One thing you still lack. Sell all that you have and distribute to the poor, and you will have treasure in heaven; and come, follow me.' But when he heard these things, he became very sad, for he was extremely rich. Jesus, seeing that he had become sad, said, 'How difficult it is for those who have wealth to enter the kingdom of God! For it is easier for a camel to go through the eye of a needle than for a rich person to enter the kingdom of God.'[14] Those who heard it said, 'Then who can be saved?' But he said, 'What is impossible with man is possible with God.' (Luke 18:18–27; also Matt. 19:23–24)

As soldiers in God's army, Christians must avoid mundane distractions:

> Share in suffering as a good soldier of Christ Jesus. No soldier gets entangled in civilian pursuits, since his aim is to please the one who enlisted him. (II Tim. 2:3–4)

Individuals are also warned about desiring excessive wealth and material possessions:

> Keep your life free from love of money, and be content with what you have, for he has said, 'I will never leave you nor forsake you.' (Heb. 13:5)

In particular, the clergy were warned not to covet riches or desire worldly pleasures:

> . . . an overseer[15] must be above reproach, the husband of one wife, sober-minded, self-controlled, respectable, hospitable, able to teach, not a drunkard, not violent but gentle, not quarrelsome, not a lover of money. He must manage his own household well, with all dignity keeping his children submissive, for if someone does not know how to manage his own household, how will he care for God's church? . . .

Deacons likewise must be dignified, not double-tongued [devious in speech], not addicted to much wine, not greedy for dishonest gain. (I Tim. 3:2–5, 8; also Titus 1:7–9, and I Peter 5:1–3)

Responsibility to work and earn one's keep

... aspire to live quietly, and to mind your own affairs, and to work with your hands, as we instructed you, so that you may walk properly before outsiders and be dependent on no one. (I Thess. 4:11–12)

If anyone is not willing to work, let him not eat. For we hear that some among you walk in idleness, not busy at work, but busybodies. Now such persons we command and encourage in the Lord Jesus Christ to do their work quietly and to earn their own living. (II Thess. 3:10–12)

Be patient in the face of hardship, rejection and persecution

Count it all joy, my brothers, when you meet trials of various kinds, for you know that the testing of your faith produces steadfastness. And let steadfastness have its full effect, that you may be perfect and complete, lacking in nothing ... Blessed is the man who remains steadfast under trial, for when he has stood the test he will receive the crown of life, which God has promised to those who love him. (James 1:2–4, 12)

As an example of suffering and patience, brothers, take the prophets who spoke in the name of the Lord. Behold, we consider those blessed who remained steadfast. You have heard of the steadfastness of Job, and you have seen the purpose of the Lord, how the Lord is compassionate and merciful. (James 5:10–11)

Be truthful: shun gossip and slander

The Apostle Peter advised:

So put away all malice and all deceit and hypocrisy and envy and all slander. (I Pet. 2:1)

> ... let him keep his tongue from evil and his lips from speaking deceit ... (I Pet. 3:10)

The New Testament further admonishes:

> Therefore, having put away falsehood, let each one of you speak the truth with his neighbour, for we are members one of another ... do not let the sun go down on your anger... (Eph. 4:25–26)

> ... to speak evil of no one, to avoid quarreling, to be gentle, and to show perfect courtesy toward all people. (Titus 3:2)

See also Christ's warning in Luke 6:41–42.

God overlooks your faults – therefore, forgive the shortcomings of others

> And forgive us our debts, as we forgive our debtors ... For if you forgive others their trespasses, your heavenly Father will also forgive you, but if you do not forgive others their trespasses, neither will your Father forgive your trespasses. (Matt. 6:12, 14–15)

> Then Peter came up and said to him, 'Lord, how often will my brother sin against me, and I forgive him? As many as seven times?' Jesus said to him, 'I do not say to you seven times, but seventy-seven times.' (Matt. 18:21–22; also, Col. 3:13)

> Judge not, that you be not judged. For with the judgment you pronounce you will be judged, and with the measure you use it will be measured to you. Why do you see the speck that is in your brother's eye, but do not notice the log that is in your own eye? (Matt. 7:1–5)

Pray, and be joyful and grateful

For a Christian, true and proper worship is a life devoted to doing what is 'holy and acceptable to God' (Rom. 12:1). He supplicates God unceasingly, and persistently:

Rejoice always, pray without ceasing, give thanks in all circumstances; for this is the will of God in Christ Jesus for you. (I Thess. 5:16–18; also, Rom. 12:12)

Be sincere – avoid ostentatious and hypocritical worship

He also told this parable to some who trusted in themselves that they were righteous, and treated others with contempt: Two men went up into the temple to pray, one a Pharisee and the other a tax collector. The Pharisee, standing by himself, prayed thus: 'God, I thank you that I am not like other men, extortioners, unjust, adulterers, or even like this tax collector. I fast twice a week; I give tithes of all that I get.' But the tax collector, standing far off, would not even lift up his eyes to heaven, but beat his breast, saying, 'God, be merciful to me, a sinner!' I tell you, this man went down to his house justified, rather than the other. For everyone who exalts himself will be humbled, but the one who humbles himself will be exalted. (Luke 18:9–14)

And when you pray, you must not be like the hypocrites. For they love to stand and pray in the synagogues and at the street corners, that they may be seen by others. Truly, I say to you, they have received their reward. But when you pray, go into your room and shut the door and pray to your Father who is in secret. And your Father who sees in secret will reward you. And when you pray, do not heap up empty phrases as the Gentiles do, for they think that they will be heard for their many words. (Matt. 6:5–7)

Be charitable

A Christian's charity is not for the purpose of being noticed and admired by his fellow-believers:

Beware of practising your righteousness before other people in order to be seen by them, for then you will have no reward from your Father who is in heaven. Thus, when you give to the needy, sound no trumpet before you, as the hypocrites do in the synagogues and in the streets, that they may be praised by others. Truly, I say to you, they have received their reward. But when you give to the needy, do not let your left hand know what your right hand is doing, so that your giving may be in secret. And your Father who sees in secret will reward you. (Matt. 6:1–4)

The amount donated is less important than the quality and sincerity of the intent:

And he sat down opposite the treasury and watched the people putting money into the offering box. Many rich people put in large sums. And a poor widow came and put in two small copper coins, which make a penny. And he called his disciples to him and said to them, 'Truly, I say to you, this poor widow has put in more than all those who are contributing to the offering box. For they all contributed out of their abundance, but she out of her poverty has put in everything she had, all she had to live on.' (Mark 12:41–44)

Be compassionate

Put on then, as God's chosen ones, holy and beloved, compassionate hearts, kindness, humility, meekness, and patience, bearing with one another and, if one has a complaint against another, forgiving each other; as the Lord has forgiven you, so you also must forgive. And above all these put on love, which binds everything together in perfect harmony. (Col. 3:12–14)

A follower of Christ shares his good fortune with others

Bear fruits in keeping with repentance . . .
'. . . Every tree therefore that does not bear good fruit is cut down and thrown into the fire.' And the crowds asked him, 'What then shall we do?' And he answered them, 'Whoever has two tunics is to share with him who has none, and whoever has food is to do likewise.' (Luke 3:8–11)

Be merciful

Blessed are the merciful, for they shall receive mercy. (Matt. 5:7)

Seek truth sincerely and desire righteousness

Jesus also selected for praise those individuals who had an intense yearning for righteousness, which was akin to the thirst and hunger that one experienced living in the desert:

> Blessed are those who hunger and thirst for righteousness, for they shall be satisfied. (Matt. 5:6)

> So Jesus said to the Jews who had believed him, 'If you abide in my word, you are truly my disciples, and you will know the truth, and the truth will set you free. ' (John 8:31–32)

Christ prayed that the truth would set His disciples apart for holy service to God:

> Sanctify them in the truth; your [God's] word is truth. (John 17:17)

Occasionally, an individual attains this truth by accident and without much personal effort, searching or investigation. This was the case with some of the disciples of Jesus:

> For truly, I say to you, many prophets and righteous people longed to see what you see, and did not see it, and to hear what you hear, and did not hear it. (Matt. 13:17; also, Luke 10:24)

However, this inestimable bounty is uncommon, and for most it is imperative that Christians cultivate an abiding desire for truth and a genuine quest for faith. They are warned not to become spiritually 'sluggish' (Heb. 6:12), or complacent about their faith. They are asked to: 'Examine yourselves, to see whether you are in the faith. Test yourselves' (II Cor. 13:5), while the Apostle Peter advised:

> Like newborn infants, long for the pure spiritual milk, that by it you may grow up into salvation . . . (I Peter 2:2)

Divine reciprocity

To seek divine mercies and guidance is a clear and specific commandment of the Gospels. A believer should take the first step through his own efforts, assured that God will assist him with the next.

In the preceding dispensation, the Psalms lamented the failure of the children of Israel to submit to the divine will – God would have fed them if they would only open their mouths:

> Open your mouth wide, and I will fill it. But my people did not listen to my voice; Israel would not submit to me. So I gave them over to their stubborn hearts, to follow their own counsels. (Ps. 81:10–12)

Similarly, God declares in the Hebrew Bible:

> Call to me and I will answer you, and will tell you great and hidden things that you have not known. (Jer. 33:3)

Christ also taught:

> Ask, and it will be given to you; seek, and you will find; knock, and it will be opened to you. For everyone who asks receives, and the one who seeks finds, and to the one who knocks it will be opened. Or which one of you, if his son asks him for bread, will give him a stone? Or if he asks for a fish, will give him a serpent? If you then, who are evil, know how to give good gifts to your children, how much more will your Father who is in heaven give good things to those who ask him! (Matt. 7:7–11)

The opportunity to address the heavenly Father is not meant to be taken up by requests for personal material gain: 'for your Father knoweth what things ye have need of, before ye ask him' (Matt. 6:8). The supplication for divine mercies instead includes a desire for God's revelation and for His truth:

> And the tempter came and said to him, 'If you are the Son of God, command these stones to become loaves of bread.' But he answered,

'It is written, Man shall not live by bread alone, but by every word that comes from the mouth of God.' (Matt. 4:3–4)

The quest of the Christian should be for spiritual enlightenment and not for material gain, for Christ also stated:

Therefore I tell you, do not be anxious about your life, what you will eat or what you will drink, nor about your body, what you will put on. Is not life more than food, and the body more than clothing? (Matt. 6:25)

Notably, one of the final warnings in the New Testament reiterates that at the Second Coming only those who desire truth will receive enlightenment (Rev. 21:6; see Matt. 5:6).

Adopt a childlike receptivity to and acceptance of the truth

A true Christian is humble and is without pretension, and is blessed because he is 'poor in spirit' (Matt. 5:3) and recognizes that, as with the First Coming, the Second Coming will bring new understanding (Is. 52:15; John 16:13–15; Ephes. 1:18; I Cor. 13:12), and, therefore, should not be judged by former comprehensions. Hence, by acknowledging that his cup is empty he allows himself to be filled with the new wine of God's Spirit.

Christ counselled that individuals with an infant-like temperament and attitude to the truth that is, 'teachable, mild, humble, and free from prejudice and obstinacy,'[16] were more likely to accept the kingdom of God than the worldly-wise who judged according to their limited understanding:

Then children were brought to him that he might lay his hands on them and pray. The disciples rebuked the people, but Jesus said, 'Let the little children come to me and do not hinder them, for to such belongs the kingdom of heaven.' (Matt. 19:13–14)

It was this child-like wonderment and purity of heart that allowed Simon Peter, Andrew, James the Elder, and John, son of Zebedee, who were simple fishermen, and Matthew, who was a tax collector (tax collectors were considered bullies and were reviled by the Jews and their leaders because they worked for Rome), to recognize Jesus as their Messiah – they saw with their own eyes and heard with their own ears and not through the prejudiced eyes and ears of the theologically wise. In contrast, the High Priest, Joseph Caiaphas, and other chief priests of the Sanhedrin, conceited with pride and blinded by their theological wisdom, denied Christ. For this reason, Christ gloried in His disciples' pure-hearted acceptance of His revelation:

> In that same hour he rejoiced in the Holy Spirit and said, 'I thank you, Father, Lord of heaven and earth, that you have hidden these things from the wise and understanding and revealed them to little children; yes, Father, for such was your gracious will . . .' (Luke 10:21)

Avoid engaging in contentious and idle arguments about faith and truth

Instead of trying to win arguments through the strategic use of biblical verses, a follower of Jesus lovingly and humbly shares Christ's words, always eager to receive and increase his understanding:

> . . . charge them before God not to quarrel about words, which does no good, but only ruins the hearers . . . Have nothing to do with foolish, ignorant controversies; you know that they breed quarrels. And the Lord's servant must not be quarrelsome but kind to everyone, able to teach, patiently enduring evil, correcting his opponents with gentleness. God may perhaps grant them repentance leading to a knowledge of the truth, and they may come to their senses and escape from the snare of the devil, after being captured by him to do his will. (II Tim. 2:14, 23–26)

> Do not grumble against one another, brothers, so that you may not be judged; behold, the Judge is standing at the door. As an example of suffering and patience, brothers, take the prophets who spoke in the name of the Lord. Behold, we consider those blessed who remained steadfast. (James 5:9–11)

Possess a pure heart, sanctified from the obscuring dust of human conjecture – only then can one see and understand

Addressing an audience immersed in Hebrew tradition, Jesus in the Sermon on the Mount announced:

> Blessed are the pure in heart, for they shall see God. (Matt. 5:8)

God is not a physical entity that can be seen or perceived by mortal eyes. Indeed, God Himself states in the Torah that 'you cannot see my face, for man shall not see me and live' (Ex. 33:20), and the Gospel of John (1:18) explains that 'no man has ever seen God'. It is therefore likely that the above Beatitude is referring to those individuals who had purified themselves from traditional understandings, and hence were able to appreciate God's revelation.

In an effort to investigate the truth and the Second Coming, a Christian shuns biased opinion. Truth does not require embellishments – too many ornate lampshades prevent the divine light from shining through.

Ascertain the truth

The Apostle Paul urged his fellow Christians not to reject 'prophecies' out of hand but to ascertain their validity with an unprejudiced mind:

> Rejoice always, pray without ceasing, give thanks in all circumstances; for this is the will of God in Christ Jesus for you. Do not quench the Spirit. Do not despise prophecies, but test everything;[17] hold fast what is good. Abstain from every form of evil. (I Thess. 5:16–22)

Avoid blindly following others

The Prophet Ezekiel was instructed:

> Son of man, look with your eyes and hear with your ears and set your heart and mind on all that I will show you. (Ezek. 40:4)

Christ unambiguously warned that one's faith should not depend on others, but on God alone:

> How can you believe, when you receive glory from one another and do not seek the glory that comes from the only God? (John 5:44)

Faith is too important to be an accident of birth; as with science, it should be the product of sincere searching and endeavour. A Christian is reminded that most of the followers of Moses rejected Christ out of hand because they defined themselves more by the traditions and practices they had inherited, such as what food was kosher and what food was not pure, rather than by demonstrating in their speech and, more importantly, actions, the true meaning of their scripture:

> . . . it is not what goes into the mouth that defiles a person, but what comes out of the mouth; this defiles a person. Then the disciples came and said to him, 'Do you know that the Pharisees were offended when they heard this saying?' He answered, 'Every plant that my heavenly Father has not planted will be rooted up . . . Let them alone; they are blind guides. And if the blind lead the blind, both will fall into a pit.' (Matt. 15:11–12, 14)

Hence, the Bible's injunction is that Christians emulate only that which is acceptable to God:

> Beloved, do not imitate evil but imitate good. Whoever does good is from God; whoever does evil has not seen God. (III John 1:11)

The worth of an individual's faith is judged by his response to the fulfilment of the 'good news'

The most important and frequently mentioned glad-tidings of the New Testament is the establishment of the kingdom of God on earth, when the Will of the Father 'will be done on earth as it is in heaven' (Matt. 6:10), and when Christ will return in the Glory of the Father (Matt. 16:27; Mark 13:26; Luke 21:27). Christ in the Gospel of Matthew refers to the event as the 'gospel of the kingdom'[18] (Matt. 24:14). Christ repeatedly commanded His followers to 'watch' for the event (Matt. 24:42–44; 25:13) as it would happen unexpectedly.

> Behold, I am coming like a thief! Blessed is the one who stays awake,

keeping his garments on, that he may not go about naked and be seen exposed! (Rev. 16:15; also, Luke 12:35–40; Luke 21:34–35; Rev. 3:3).

Christ wished the rest of humanity to also hear the good news of the coming of a universal Redeemer. Hence, His last instruction to His disciples was that they should disperse far and wide and proclaim this Gospel:

And he said to them, 'Go into all the world and proclaim the gospel to the whole creation'.[19] (Mark 16:15)

To follow in Christ's footsteps requires a Christian to announce and to prepare for this significant event:

Now after John [the Baptist] was arrested and taken into custody, Jesus went to Galilee, preaching the good news of [the kingdom of] God, and saying, 'The [appointed period of] time is fulfilled, and the kingdom of God is at hand; repent [change your inner self – your old way of thinking, regret past sins, live your life in a way that proves repentance; seek God's purpose for your life] and believe [with a deep, abiding trust] in the good news [regarding salvation].' (Amplified Bible: Mark 1:14–15)

Soon afterward he went on through cities and villages, proclaiming and bringing the good news of the kingdom of God. And the twelve were with him . . . (Luke 8:1)

. . . and he [Jesus] sent them out to proclaim the kingdom of God and to heal. And they departed and went through the villages, preaching the gospel and healing everywhere. (Luke 9:2, 6)

The Apostle Paul thus described the blessed status of the disciples:

. . . in every way you were enriched in him in all speech and all knowledge – even as the testimony about Christ was confirmed among you – so that you are not lacking in any gift, as you wait for the revealing of our Lord Jesus Christ, who will sustain you to the end . . . (I Cor. 1:5–8)

The singular priority at the First Coming was the message of Christ's return at the Second Coming:

> But seek first the kingdom of God and his righteousness, and all these things will be added to you. (Matt. 6:33)

> Therefore stay awake – for you do not know when the master of the house will come, in the evening, or at midnight, or when the rooster crows, or in the morning . . . lest he come suddenly and find you asleep. And what I say to you I say to all: Stay awake. (Mark 13:35–36)

Do not be discouraged by the fact that not all Christians will be 'awake' or 'watching'

> Stay dressed for action[20] and keep your lamps burning, and be like men who are waiting for their master to come home from the wedding feast, so that they may open the door to him at once when he comes and knocks. Blessed are those servants whom the master finds awake when he comes. (Luke 12:35–37)

The Apostle Paul wrote that Christians should become worthy of the Kingdom:

> . . . we exhorted each one of you and encouraged you and charged you to walk in a manner worthy of God, who calls you into his own kingdom and glory. (I Thess. 2:12)

The New Testament describes the transformation that must precede the Second Coming:

> For the grace of God has appeared, bringing salvation for all people, training us to renounce ungodliness and worldly passions, and to live self-controlled, upright, and godly lives in the present age, waiting for our blessed hope, the appearing of the glory of our great God and Savior Jesus Christ . . . (Titus 2:11–13)

The Apostle Peter asked that his fellow Christians consider what type of individuals they should be, given that everything was likely to be different at the Second Coming, and advising them that they should prepare themselves for the event by living spiritually transformed lives (II Pet. 3:11–13).

Be as farmers and spread the good news

Christ asked His followers to act as farmers by sowing the seed of faith and truth and cultivating the promise of a future rebirth. As farmers, they would be aware that there are various reasons for lack of success in planting seeds. Only the seed that germinates in a good or receptive soil will bear spiritual fruits:

> [Jesus] said in a parable, 'A sower went out to sow his seed. And as he sowed, some fell along the path and was trampled underfoot, and the birds of the air devoured it. And some fell on the rock, and as it grew up, it withered away, because it had no moisture. And some fell among thorns, and the thorns grew up with it and choked it. And some fell into good soil and grew and yielded a hundredfold.' As he said these things, he called out, 'He who has ears to hear, let him hear.' (Luke 8:4–8)

Truth will in the end triumph through the services of spiritually transformed individuals:

> [Jesus] answered, The one who sows the good seed is the Son of Man. The field is the world, and the good seed is the sons of the kingdom. The weeds are the sons of the evil one, and the enemy who sowed them is the devil. The harvest is the end of the age, and the reapers are angels. (Matt. 13:37–39)

In the interim period, Christians were to follow the example of Christ and continue to plant the seeds in collaboration with others, proclaim the good news, trusting that God would provide the rain and bless them with a rich harvest:

> What then is Apollos [a Jewish–Christian who was well versed in scriptures]? What is Paul? Servants through whom you believed, as the Lord assigned to each. I planted, Apollos watered, but God gave

the growth. So neither he who plants nor he who waters is anything, but only God who gives the growth. He who plants and he who waters are one, and each will receive his wages according to his labour. For we are God's fellow workers. (I Cor. 3:5–9)

3

DISCARDING OBSOLETE TEACHINGS, OUTWORN SHIBBOLETHS AND INJURIOUS SUPERSTITIONS

Impermanent teachings

In their current form, earlier religions no longer serve the best interests of humanity. The world desperately needs an alternative to 'the workings of the moribund and obsolescent institutions to which a perverse generation is desperately clinging'.[1] The time has certainly come to discard the 'hollow and outworn institutions, the obsolescent doctrines and beliefs, the effete and discredited traditions',[2] and embrace spiritual rebirth and a new social order:

> Those who care for the future of the human race may well ponder this advice. 'If long-cherished ideals and time-honoured institutions, if certain social assumptions and religious formulae have ceased to promote the welfare of the generality of mankind, if they no longer minister to the needs of a continually evolving humanity, let them be swept away and relegated to the limbo of obsolescent and forgotten doctrines. Why should these, in a world subject to the immutable law of change and decay, be exempt from the deterioration that must needs overtake every human institution? . . .'[3]

In contrast to the core moral and ethical laws discussed earlier, the social teachings and practices of each religion serve the needs of a particular people for a preordained period of time. They represent the outward forms of faith and, as previously mentioned, are referred to metaphorically in the Hebrew Bible as fountains and cisterns that hold the water of life but which may break and become dry (Jer. 2:13); and in the

Gospels as the 'skins' that hold the spiritual wine, which if aged, may burst; and also as the external 'garment' that clothes faith but which ages and may become torn (Matt. 9:16–17).

In this context, a major factor likely to have contributed to the decline of Christianity is the diminished relevance of the social agenda of the church. Several teachings of the Bible are outdated or are no longer of benefit to humanity, and are in most instances ignored by even the most ardent Jews and Christians. Renewal of faith demands jettisoning these outdated concepts, and becoming liberated from this 'prison' of a 'waterless pit' (Zech. 9:11) described as 'The dry and barren depth of human misery, where are no streams of righteousness, but the mire of iniquity':[4]

> Thus says God, the Lord . . . who gives breath to the people on it (the earth) . . . and spirit to those who walk in it: 'I am the Lord; I have called you in righteousness; I will take you by the hand and keep you; I will give you as a covenant for the people, a light for the nations, to open the eyes that are blind, to bring out the prisoners from the dungeon, from the prison those who sit in darkness. I am the Lord; that is my name; my glory I give to no other, nor my praise to carved idols. Behold, the former things have come to pass, and new things I now declare. (Is. 42:5–9)

Using similar metaphors, the English Baptist pastor and scholar John Gill (1697–1771) noted in his commentary:

> ***To open the blind eyes*** . . . Of the idolatrous Gentiles, who were spiritually blind, and knew not the wretchedness of their case; the exceeding sinfulness of sin; their need of a Saviour, and who he was; as they did, when their eyes were opened by means of the Gospel sent among them, through the energy of the divine Spirit; for this is a work of almighty power and efficacious grace:
> ***to bring out the prisoners from the prison***; who were concluded in sin, shut up in unbelief, and under the law, the captives of Satan, and held fast prisoners by him and their own lusts, under the dominion of which they were:
> ***and them that sit in darkness out of the prison house***: of sin, Satan, and the law; being under which, they were in a state of darkness

and ignorance as to things divine and spiritual. The allusion is to prisons, which are commonly dark places.[5]

The English theologian Charles Ellicott (1819–1905) similarly wrote:

> The 'prison' is that of the selfishness and sin which hinder men from being truly free. In the 'prisoners of hope' of Zechariah 9:12, and the 'spirits in prison' of I Peter 3:18, we have different aspects of the same thought.[6]

The disciples maintained that they were now freed from the shackles of the Law:

> For sin will have no dominion over you, since you are not under law but under grace. (Rom. 6:14)

> Likewise, my brothers, you also have died to the law . . . (Rom. 7:4)

In other words, the Law, given to Moses by God, had lost its value. Writing to the Christians in Galatia (modern-day Turkey), the Apostle Paul explained that Christ through His sacrifice had freed His followers from this limitation so that the divine blessings might reach a greater section of humanity:

> so that in Christ Jesus the blessing of Abraham might come to the Gentiles, so that we might receive the promised Spirit through faith. (Gal. 3:14)

Colossians and Hebrews further explain that the Law was not immutable, but only a prelude to a higher calling:

> Therefore let no one pass judgment on you in questions of food and drink, or with regard to a festival or a new moon or a Sabbath. These are a shadow of the things to come, but the substance belongs to Christ. (Col. 2:16–17; see also Heb. 10:1)

He exhorted his fellow Christians to cherish the freedom they had gained through Christ and not to be enslaved again by effete ideas and practices:

> For freedom Christ has set us free; stand firm therefore, and do not submit again to a yoke of slavery. (Gal. 5:1)

Albert Barnes explains:

> ***Stand fast, therefore*** – Be firm and unwavering... The sense is, that they were to be firm and unyielding in maintaining the great principles of Christian liberty. They had been freed from the bondage of rites and ceremonies; and they should by no means, and in no form, yield to them again.[7]

It readily follows that Christians must, at the Second Coming, similarly abandon earlier understandings, traditions and rituals if they are to be empowered to perceive and embrace new realities and bring God's redeeming mercies to all nations.

The transition from outworn garments, old wine and wineskins

Some Christians have found the term 'dispensation' a valuable concept to explain distinct ages such as that of Noah, Abraham, Moses, and Christ, as incremental steps in the evolution of one divine purpose and plan for the spiritual education of humanity.[8] The term may also be applied to other major religions of mankind that have appeared in different parts of the world such as Zoroastrianism, Hinduism, Buddhism, Islam and the Bahá'í Faith.

In this connection, every dispensation has an outer form and an inner reality. A time comes when the outward forms of a dispensation, that is, its traditions, rituals, dogma and social laws, no longer serve the best interests of humanity (Luke 5:36–38). Today, it may be argued, the same applies to many of the outworn creeds, ceremonies and man-made institutions of the church.

Precedence for changes in the divine Law

The seven Noahide Laws given to Adam and Noah were replaced by the Ten Commandments in the revelation received by Moses on Mount Sinai about three thousand years ago.

Rabbi Maimonides compiled a list of 613 commandments that are binding on the followers of Moses; 248 are 'positive commandments' consisting of injunctions to perform an act, and 365 are 'negative commandments' to abstain from certain acts. It is estimated that even in the State of Israel, the followers of Moses can comply with only 369 of the laws, and of these, 99 of the laws, while still applicable, may not ever be enacted, since one may never encounter in one's lifetime a situation where that law applies.[9]

The Christian thus has examples of the abrogation/modification of the Law of Noah and some of the laws of Moses, and their replacement with new commandments by Christ. It is to be expected that the Second Coming will also entail similar changes.

A complicating factor that was not entirely resolved at the First Coming was whether the teachings of the Torah that were not abrogated by Jesus were binding on Christians. This ambiguity has intruded into the teachings and practices of the church. Christ had early on strongly affirmed the Law:

> Do not think that I have come to abolish the Law or the Prophets; I have not come to abolish them but to fulfil them. For truly, I say to you, until heaven and earth pass away, not an iota [an infinitesimal amount; the smallest letter of the Hebrew alphabet 'yod' or 'i'], not a dot, will pass from the Law until all is accomplished. Therefore whoever relaxes one of the least of these commandments and teaches others to do the same will be called least in the kingdom of heaven, but whoever does them and teaches them will be called great in the kingdom of heaven. For I tell you, unless your righteousness exceeds that of the scribes and Pharisees, you will never enter the kingdom of heaven. (Matt. 5:17–20)

His frequent references to the Torah indicate clearly that Jesus considered His revelation to be continuous with that of Moses. In general, He ratified the Law but modified some of its harsher provisions. He explained the wider and spiritual implications of the teachings of the preceding dispensation, and the need for its followers to become transformed spiritually in preparation for the coming of the Kingdom of the Father.

It is worth noting in this context that the tensions between Christ and the Jewish religious leaders, evident throughout His approximately three-year ministry, emanated not so much because of disagreements concerning the written Torah but were largely due to different interpretations of the oral tradition. Christ did not approve the additions and redactions, describing these doctrines as 'the commandments of men'[10] (Matt. 15:9) and not ordained by God. He maintained that the Pharisees and rabbis had deviated from the original divine intent of the Law: their duty was to accept that He had also been sent by, and spoke in place of, God and it was His teachings that now ensured their salvation.

Even the Apostle Paul, not an avid proponent of the Law of Moses, saw merit in a legal system which, if utilized properly, was necessary to deal with a variety of societal misdemeanors (I Tim. 1:8–11). However, he too warned about the false presentations of the Jewish Faith:

> ... Therefore rebuke them sharply, that they may be sound in the faith, not devoting themselves to Jewish myths[11] and the commands of people who turn away from the truth. (Titus 1:13–14)

Capital punishment and observance of Sabbath: examples of unsettled issues concerning the laws of Moses

The Torah prescribed capital punishment for any transgression of the Ten Commandments; for example, death by stoning for working during the Sabbath (Friday evening to Saturday evening, later changed to Sunday by the Roman Emperor Constantine). Christ did not entirely abrogate the Sabbath but indicated that the restrictions of the Holy Day observance must not be followed blindly. He remarked:

> The Sabbath was made for man, not man for the Sabbath. So the Son of Man is lord even of the Sabbath. (Mark 2:27–28)

He did not make any specific changes to its observance. There remained therefore confusion as to what extent and in what manner one should follow the Law and observe the Sabbath. In some Christian communities the Sabbath was observed strictly and enforced with as much zeal as in the time of Moses, as Alice Earle describes:

> 'No one shall travel, cook victuals, make beds, sweep house, cut hair, or shave on the Sabbath Day.'

'No Woman shall kiss her child on the Sabbath or fasting day.'

'No one shall ride on the Sabbath Day, or walk in his garden, or elsewhere except reverently to and from meeting' . . .

Thus in New London [Connecticut] we find in the latter part of the seventeenth century a wicked fisherman presented before the Court and fined for catching eels on Sunday; another 'fined twenty shillings for sailing a boat on the Lord's Day;' while in 1670 two lovers, John Lewis and Sarah Chapman, were accused of and tried for 'sitting together on the Lords Day under an apple tree in Goodman Chapman's Orchard,' – so harmless and so natural an act. In Plymouth a man was 'sharply whipped' for shooting fowl on Sunday; another was fined for carrying a grist of corn home on the Lord's Day, and the miller who allowed him to take it was also fined. Elizabeth Eddy of the same town was fined, in 1652, 'ten shillings for wringing and hanging out clothes'. A Plymouth man, for attending to his tar-pits on the Sabbath, was set in the stocks. James Watt, in 1658, was publicly reproved 'for writing a note about common business on the Lord's Day, at least in the evening somewhat too soon'. A Plymouth man who drove a yoke of oxen was 'presented' before the Court, as was also another offender, who drove some cows a short distance 'without need' on the Sabbath . . .

In Wareham, in 1772, William Estes acknowledged himself 'Gilty of Racking Hay on the Lord's Day' and was fined ten shillings; and in 1774 another Wareham citizen, 'for a breach of the Sabbath in puling apples,' was fined five shillings. A Dunstable soldier, for 'wetting a piece of an old hat to put in his shoe' to protect his foot – for doing this piece of heavy work on the Lord's Day, was fined, and paid forty shillings.[12]

The Sabbatarians, most notably the Seventh Day Adventist Church, are Christians who believe that the Hebrew Sabbath should continue to be observed today.

The lack of clarity as to which laws of Moses were binding resulted in the first rupture within the Christian community. It was precipitated by the conversion of the first Gentiles. The question arose as to which Hebrew laws they should follow. Dietary laws and circumcision were emblematic of the issue at hand. An argument broke out, known as the 'incident at Antioch' between the Apostle Paul and the Apostles Peter and James, the brother of Peter and the first head of the church in Jerusalem, as to whether the Gentile converts should undergo circumcision and follow the dietary laws of the Torah. Notably, when St Paul, who regarded himself as the apostle to the Gentiles (Rom. 11:13), introduced his convert Timothy, whose father was Greek, to the Hebrew Christians, he thought it prudent to first circumcise him (Acts 16:3). This question was dealt with at the Council of Jerusalem about twenty years after Christ's crucifixion. A compromise was reached whereby the Gentile Christians were not required to be circumcised or to follow the dietary laws, but the Law was made binding on the Hebrew-Christians. The Apostle Paul later expressed his antipathy to the proceedings and to this compromise (Gal. 2:7, 9, 11–14; 6:15).

• • • • •

The following sections examine some of the social teachings of the New Testament which no longer serve the interests of humanity, demonstrating the need for a fresh revelation.

Slavery

The subject of slavery continues to this day to be a source of great concern. There are currently about 40 million slaves in the world 'living as forced laborers, forced prostitutes, child soldiers, child brides in forced marriages and, in all ways that matter, are treated as pieces of property, chattel in the servitude of absolute ownership.'[13]

Slavery is condoned in the Torah (Lev. 25:39–46). The story of the Patriarch Noah provides the scriptural justification for this practice. Noah had three sons: Shem, Ham and Japheth. Medieval Christianity believed that following the flood they were the founders of the populations of Europe, Africa and Asia, respectively.[14] We are told that Ham discovered his father naked and in a deep sleep after drinking wine, and told his two brothers what he had seen. On waking, Noah cursed Ham and his son Canaan:

> When Noah awoke from his wine and knew what his youngest son had done to him, he said, 'Cursed be Canaan; a servant of servants[15] shall he be to his brothers.' (Gen. 9:24–25)

Ham was believed to have been the ancestor of Africans who were therefore presumed to be all black, although this entire conviction has no merit. Nevertheless, the curse of Noah in the Bible has been used in racist arguments to justify the slavery of Blacks. Even if the story is taken at its face value, the curse of Noah applied only to Ham's son Canaan, whose descendants occupied the Eastern Mediterranean. It was Ham's other sons who allegedly populated Africa. Furthermore, the Torah specifies that a curse is effective for only three to four generations (Ex. 20:5). Slaves were not to be mistreated and escaped slaves were not to be returned to cruel masters (Deut. 23:15–16).

Slavery was hence a fact of life at the time of Christ and for centuries before His advent. It was culturally acceptable everywhere, and was an integral part of the society and economy. Although Christ did not abrogate slavery and was generally silent on the prevailing custom, the compassion and the unconditional and universal love with which He imbued His followers were essential to the eventual emancipation of slaves. He did not address the subject of literal slavery but recast the subject, emphasizing the spiritual freedom that came through the divine Word:

> So Jesus said to the Jews who had believed him, 'If you abide in my word, you are truly my disciples, and you will know the truth, and the truth will set you free.' They answered him, 'We are offspring of Abraham and have never been enslaved to anyone. How is it that you say, "You will become free?"' Jesus answered them, 'Truly, truly, I say to you, everyone who practises sin is a slave to sin . . . So if the Son sets you free, you will be free indeed . . .' (John 8:31–34, 36)

Elaborating on this theme, the disciples taught that the followers of Christ were to be free of passions and illicit pleasures (Titus 3:3), and to become 'slaves of God' (Rom. 6:22) instead of 'slaves of corruption' (II Peter 2:19).

It is fair to state that although the New Testament teachings did not empower slaves with any greater civil rights and freedoms than the Torah or Talmud, they encouraged a more just and fair treatment of slaves – both master and slave were the subjects of one compassionate Heavenly Father. Also, in considering the harsh statements of the New Testament regarding slavery, one has to be aware that some scholars dispute whether the Pauline writings are not in fact his, but represent interpolations (pseudepigraphy) – misrepresentations of his teachings following his death, designed to maintain the status quo.[16] In particular, it is believed that the Apostle Paul did not write the Pastoral letters (I and II Timothy and Titus), Ephesians, or Colossians.[17]

Despite these uncertainties, the following troubling verses about slavery remain part of the New Testament:

> Bondservants [Greek 'douloi': slaves], obey your earthly masters with fear and trembling, with a sincere heart, as you would Christ, not by the way of eye-service, as people-pleasers, but as bondservants of Christ, doing the will of God from the heart, rendering service with a good will as to the Lord and not to man, knowing that whatever good anyone does, this he will receive back from the Lord, whether he is a bondservant or is free. Masters, do the same to them, and stop your threatening, knowing that he who is both their Master and yours is in heaven, and that there is no partiality with him. (Eph. 6:5–9)

Again:

> Bondservants, obey in everything those who are your earthly masters . . . Whatever you do, work heartily, as for the Lord and not for men, knowing that from the Lord you will receive the inheritance as your reward. You are serving the Lord Christ. (Col. 3:22–24)

Christian slaves were not to take advantage of the fact that their master was also a Christian; such a master had to be served with even more fidelity:

> Let all who are under a yoke as bondservants regard their own masters as worthy of all honor, so that the name of God and the teaching may not be reviled. Those who have believing masters must not be disrespectful on the ground that they are brothers; rather they must serve all the better since those who benefit by their good service are believers and beloved. Teach and urge these things. (I Tim. 6:1–2)

Being enslaved is portrayed as mattering less than the imperative that the followers of Christ should uphold the tenets of the Christian Faith:

> Bondservants are to be submissive to their own masters in everything; they are to be well-pleasing, not argumentative, not pilfering, but showing all good faith, so that in everything they may adorn the doctrine of God our Saviour. (Titus 2:9–10)

Despite questions of authorship, there is agreement that two passages concerning Christian slaves are attributable to the Apostle Paul:

> Each one should remain in the condition in which he was called. Were you a bondservant when called? Do not be concerned about it. (But if you can gain your freedom, avail yourself of the opportunity.) For he who was called in the Lord as a bondservant is a freedman of the Lord. Likewise he who was free when called is a bondservant of Christ. (I Cor. 7:20–22)

The approach to slavery is further illustrated by the story of the slave Onesimus who had worked for a Christian master, Philemon. When accused of theft he ran away but was caught and thrown into the same prison as the Apostle Paul (most probably in Rome or Caesarea) where he accepted Christ. Notably, Paul did not advise him that as a Christian and working for a Christian, he should consider himself a free man. Instead he wrote to Philemon, begging him to forgive Onesimus and take him back as a slave (Philem. 1:1, 10–18).

The biblical teachings concerning slavery shaped Christian thought and actions for many centuries. They cannot be attributed solely to the Apostle Paul, since an epistle of the Apostle Peter recommends that cruel and unjust treatment of the household staff, slave or free, should be borne by them with resignation:

> Servants, be subject to your masters with all respect, not only to the good and gentle but also to the unjust. For this is a gracious thing, when, mindful of God, one endures sorrows while suffering unjustly. For what credit is it if, when you sin and are beaten for it, you endure? But if when you do good and suffer for it you endure, this is a gracious thing in the sight of God. (I Pet. 2:18–20)

Tragically, the Bible was quoted frequently to justify slavery of Blacks.[18] The arguments were compounded by the belief that the white and black belonged to separate species. J. H. Van Evrie, the publisher of a widely disseminated pamphlet entitled *The Negro's Place in Nature*, wrote in 1866:

> The Human Family is composed of a certain number of species or races, just as all other forms of being which are generally alike but specifically unlike. The White or Caucasian, is the most elevated, and the Negro the most subordinate of all the Races in their organic structure, and therefore in their faculties. This is *fact*, unchanging, immovable, everlasting fact, fixed by the hand of the Almighty, but whether so at the beginning of all thing, or by subsequent decree of the Eternal, mortals are not permitted to know. We know the *fact*, and God holds us responsible for our mode of dealing with it, and when we willfully shut our eyes, disregard and ignore it altogether, and impiously strive to degrade our race *down*, or force the Negro *up*, to 'impartial freedom,' or a forbidden level, we are blindly striving to reverse the natural order, and to reform the work of the Almighty ...[19]

Ellicott's commentary describes slavery as perhaps the most difficult issue Christianity has had to deal with. It acknowledges that the New Testament did not abrogate the practice directly, but indicates that Christ's teachings began the gradual transformation that heralded realization of the oneness of mankind:

> It was perhaps the most perplexing of all the questions Christianity had to face – this one of slavery. It entered into all grades and ranks. It was common to all peoples and nations. The very fabric of society seemed knit and bound together by this miserable institution. War and commerce were equally responsible for slavery in the Old World. To attempt to uproot it – to preach against it – to represent it in public teaching as hateful to God, shameful to man – would have been to preach and to teach rebellion and revolution in its darkest and most violent form. It was indeed the curse of the world; but the Master and His chosen servants took their own course and their own time to clear it away. Jesus Christ and His disciples, such

as St. Paul and St. John, left society as they found it, uprooting no ancient landmarks, alarming no ancient prejudices, content to live in the world as it was, and to do its work as they found it – trusting, by a new and lovely example, slowly and surely to raise men to a higher level, knowing well that at last, by force of unselfishness, loving self-denial, brave patience, the old curses – such as slavery – would be driven from the world. Surely the result, so far, has not disappointed the hopes of the first teachers of Christianity.[20]

At the same time the Bible promises the advent of a more universal revelation when the Father would address the spiritual needs of all nations and which would allow the spiritual principles of justice and equality to evolve further. The Gospel of Luke, quoting Is. 40:5, states that in that Day 'all flesh'[21] shall see the salvation of God' (Luke 3:6).

Restrictions on social interactions

One can discern an evolution from strict segregation towards social and spiritual harmonization of the diverse sections of humanity in the Bible.

The Torah forbade associating with seven Canaanite nations and marrying non-Jews (Gentiles or *goyim*) (Gen. 24:2–4; 28:1; Deut. 7:3–4; Joshua 23:11–13; Ezra 9:11–12; Neh. 13:24–27) through fear that the offspring would be lost to Israel and that the foreign wives would induce their husbands to follow other gods and pagan religions, causing Israel to become once again tainted by idolatry. However, the natural law of attraction did not permit this ruling to be observed strictly. Moses's wife was from another country and Aaron and Miriam were punished for criticizing the interracial marriage (Num. 12:1–15); Ruth, a Moabite, was a virtuous great-grandmother of King David; King Solomon loved many foreign women (I Kings 11:1–2); and Rahab, a Canaanite harlot, who protected the spies of Joshua, is included in the lineage of Christ (Matt. 1:5; Joshua 2:9–13).

Furthermore, the Talmud, written at a later time in Jewish history, declares that a righteous Gentile, that is, one that follows the seven laws of Noah, also has a share in the 'world to come'.[22]

To the extent feasible in His time, Christ attempted to remove the barriers between Jews and non-Jews:

But I say to you, Love your enemies and pray for those who persecute you, so that you may be sons of your Father who is in heaven. For he makes his sun rise on the evil and on the good, and sends rain on the just and on the unjust. For if you love those who love you, what reward do you have? Do not even the tax collectors do the same? And if you greet only your brothers, what more are you doing than others? Do not even the Gentiles do the same? (Matt. 5:44–47)

An effective method that Jesus used was to recast the Law in ways designed to overcome Jewish insularity. For example, when an expert in the Law asked Him, 'And who is my neighbour?' Jesus responded with a story that restored the intent of the Law and at the same time illustrated that even despised strangers and non-orthodox Jews could fit the definition of a neighbour:

Jesus replied, 'A man was going down from Jerusalem to Jericho, and he fell among robbers, who stripped him and beat him and departed, leaving him half dead. Now by chance a priest was going down that road, and when he saw him he passed by on the other side. So likewise a Levite, when he came to the place and saw him, passed by on the other side. But a Samaritan, as he journeyed, came to where he was, and when he saw him, he had compassion. He went to him and bound up his wounds, pouring on oil and wine. Then he set him on his own animal and brought him to an inn and took care of him. And the next day he took out two denarii and gave them to the innkeeper, saying, "Take care of him, and whatever more you spend, I will repay you when I come back." Which of these three, do you think, proved to be a neighbor to the man who fell among the robbers?' He said, 'The one who showed him mercy.' And Jesus said to him, 'You go, and do likewise.' (Luke 10:30–37)

In yet another remarkable example, Christ made a surprising announcement that an idolatrous Roman centurion, part of the despised foreign force that occupied the Holy Land, possessed a faith that was greater than any Jew in the whole of Israel. Additionally, He warned that foreigners such as the Romans would gain admittance to the Kingdom of God, while those for whom the kingdom was primarily intended might find themselves deprived of that bounty:

> When he had entered Capernaum, a centurion came forward to him, appealing to him, 'Lord, my servant is lying paralyzed at home, suffering terribly.' And he said to him, 'I will come and heal him.' But the centurion replied, 'Lord, I am not worthy to have you come under my roof, but only say the word, and my servant will be healed. For I too am a man under authority, with soldiers under me. And I say to one, "Go," and he goes, and to another, "Come," and he comes, and to my servant, "Do this," and he does it.'
>
> When Jesus heard this, he marveled and said to those who followed him, 'Truly, I tell you, with no one in Israel have I found such faith. I tell you, many will come from east and west and recline at table with Abraham, Isaac, and Jacob in the kingdom of heaven, while the sons[23] of the kingdom will be thrown into the outer darkness. In that place there will be weeping and gnashing of teeth.' (Matt. 8:5–12)

Notably, the three distinguished foreigners or 'Magi' whom the Gospels celebrate as having come from the East to visit the infant Christ belonged to a non-Jewish religion. The word *magi* is derived from Old Persian *maguš*, a title given to priests of the ancient Persian religion of Zoroastrianism, a monotheistic faith that promulgates righteous thoughts, righteous deeds, and righteous speech, and differentiates between the divine light of true understanding and the evil darkness of ignorance.[24] It would be incongruous to accept the adoration of the Magi but to deny the truth of the inspiration/revelation that prompted them to make the long and arduous journey to Bethlehem.

The Apostle Peter directly addressed the issue of religious and racial prejudice in a large mixed group that included Cornelius, a devout Roman centurion and the first foreign convert to the cause of Christ:

> And as he talked with him, he went in and found many persons gathered. And he said to them, 'You yourselves know how unlawful it is for a Jew to associate with or to visit anyone of another nation, but God has shown me that I should not call any person common or unclean. So when I was sent for, I came without objection . . .' (Acts 10:27–29)

At one stage, he admonished them that they were all one in Christ irrespective of their backgrounds:

> ... in Christ Jesus you are all sons of God, through faith. For as many of you as were baptised into Christ have put on Christ. There is neither Jew nor Greek, there is neither slave nor free, there is no male and female, for you are all one in Christ Jesus. (Gal. 3:25–28)

However, the issue of racial and religious bias is not as clear-cut in the New Testament as one might expect. Sentiments are included that sadly became a barrier to unity and indiscriminate fellowship. There are suggestions that faith and hope are intended only for the deserving and not for others who behave like animals:

> These twelve Jesus sent out, instructing them, 'Go nowhere among the Gentiles and enter no town of the Samaritans, but go rather to the lost sheep of the house of Israel. And proclaim as you go, saying, "The kingdom of heaven is at hand."' (Matt. 10:5–7)

> Do not give dogs what is holy, and do not throw your pearls before pigs, lest they trample them underfoot and turn to attack you. (Matt. 7:6)

When a Gentile woman from Canaan, who is also described as a Greek and a Syro-Phoenician by birth, pleaded with Jesus to heal her daughter, He initially refused but later agreed to her request in view of her faith. In this way He not only placated Jewish sentiment about healing a Gentile but also showed that it was possible to be compassionate to a foreigner:

> He answered, 'I was sent only to the lost sheep of the house of Israel.' But she came and knelt before him, saying, 'Lord, help me.' And he answered, 'It is not right to take the children's bread and throw it to the dogs.' She said, 'Yes, Lord, yet even the dogs eat the crumbs that fall from their masters' table.' Then Jesus answered her, 'O woman, great is your faith! Be it done for you as you desire.' And her daughter was healed instantly. (Matt. 15:24–28)

Even the Apostle Paul, self-styled as a skilled master builder (I Cor. 3:10) and with a personal mission to evangelize the Gentiles (Rom. 11:13; Ephes. 3:8), acknowledged that the Gospels had a special relevance for the Jews and they were to be given priority in this respect:

> So I am eager to preach the gospel to you also who are in Rome. For I am not ashamed of the gospel of Christ: for it is the power of God unto salvation to every one that believeth; to the Jew first, and also to the Greek. (Rom. 1:15–16)

Ellicott's *Commentary* explains:

> 'Greek' is intended to cover all who are not 'Jews'. Before the Apostle was making, what may be called, the secular classification of men, here he makes the religious classification. From his exceptional privileges the Jew was literally placed in a class alone.
>
> It is not quite certain that the word 'first' ought not to be omitted. In any case the sense is the same. St. Paul certainly assigns a prerogative position to the Jews. They have an 'advantage' (Romans 3:1–2). To them belong the special privileges of the first dispensation (Romans 9:4–5). They are the original stock of the olive tree, in comparison with which the Gentiles are only as wild branches grafted in (Romans 11:17 *et seq.*). It was only right that the salvation promised to their forefathers should be offered first to them, as it is also said expressly in the Fourth Gospel, that 'salvation is of the Jews' (John 4:22).[25]

Paul was perhaps concerned that taking the Gospel message to the Gentiles and pioneering to foreign lands entailed the risk that the Christian faith would become contaminated and adulterated by alien customs, practices, forms of worship and philosophies. This may be the reason for the often quoted statement attributed to him that the followers of Christ should avoid consorting with unbelievers:

> Do not be unequally yoked with unbelievers. For what partnership has righteousness with lawlessness? Or what fellowship has light with darkness? What accord has Christ with Belial? ['the King of Evil', responsible for causing man's wickedness] Or what portion does a believer share with an unbeliever? What agreement has the temple of God with idols? For we are the temple of the living God ... (II Cor. 6:14–16)

Matthew Henry's commentary justifies this passage as follows:

> We should not yoke ourselves in friendship and acquaintance with wicked men and unbelievers. Though we cannot wholly avoid seeing, and hearing, and being with such, yet we should never choose them for our bosom-friends.
>
> Much less should we join in religious communion with them; we must not join with them in their idolatrous services, nor concur with them in their false worship, nor any abominations; we must not confound together the table of the Lord and the table of devils . . . What an absurdity is it to think of joining righteousness and unrighteousness, or mingling light and darkness, fire and water, together! Believers are, and should be, righteous; but unbelievers are unrighteous. Believers are made light in the Lord, but unbelievers are in darkness; and what comfortable communion can these have together? Christ and Belial are contrary one to the other; they have opposite interests and designs, so that it is impossible there should be any concord or agreement between them . . . There is a great deal of danger in communicating with unbelievers and idolators, danger of being defiled and of being rejected; therefore the exhortation is (v. 17) to come out from among them, and keep at a due distance, to be separate, as one would avoid the society of those who have the leprosy or the plague, for fear of taking infection, and not to touch the unclean thing, lest we be defiled.[26]

Rev. Albert Barnes admits that the ban raises many uncomfortable and not entirely resolved questions for Christians:

> It is implied in the use of the word that there is a dissimilarity between believers and unbelievers so great that it is as improper for them to mingle together as it is to yoke animals of different kinds and species. The ground of the injunction is that there is a difference between Christians and those who are not, so great as to render such unions improper and injurious. The direction here refers doubtless to all kinds of improper connections with those who were unbelievers. It has been usually supposed by commentators to refer particularly to marriage. But there is no reason for confining it to marriage. It doubtless includes that, but it may as well refer to any other intimate connection, or to intimate friendships, or to participation in their amusements and employments, as to marriage. The

radical idea is, that they were to abstain from all connections with unbelievers – with infidels, and pagans, and those who were not Christians, which would identify them with them; or they were to have no connection with them in anything as unbelievers, pagans, or infidels; they were to partake with them in nothing that was special to them as such.

They were to have no part with them in their paganism unbelief, and idolatry, and infidelity; they were not to be united with them in any way or sense where it would necessarily be understood that they were partakers with them in those things. This is evidently the principle here laid down, and this principle is as applicable now as it was then . . . There is no principle of Christianity that is more important than that which is here stated by the apostle; and none in which Christians are more in danger of erring, or in which they have more difficulty in determining the exact rule which they are to follow. The questions which arise are very important. Are we to have no contact with the people of the world? Are we cut loose from all our friends who are not Christians? Are we to become monks, and live a recluse and unsocial life? Are we never to mingle with the people of the world in business, in innocent recreation, or in the duties of citizens, and as neighbors and friends? It is important, therefore, in the highest degree, to endeavor to ascertain what are the principles on which the New Testament requires us to act in this matter.[27]

Gender rights

The social status of women, as defined by the oral law (Talmud and Mishna), and taught by rabbis and Pharisees in Jesus's day, was anything but favourable or liberating by today's standards. A few examples are presented here for illustration.

According to the Tosefta ('addition'), a book of Jewish oral law, a man is obligated to say three blessings (Berachot) during morning prayers:

Blessed are You Hashem, our God, King of the world, for not making me a gentile (non-Jew).
   Blessed are You Hashem, our God, King of the world, for not making me a woman,

> Blessed are You Hashem, our God, King of the world, for not making me a boor (who is not afraid of sin) . . .²⁸

The Gemara, a component of the Talmud, also records:

> The Sages taught: Three objects should not be allowed to pass between two people [men] walking along a road, and people should not walk between two of them: A dog, a palm tree and a woman. And some say: also a pig. And some say: Also a snake.²⁹

Interaction with a Samaritan woman

Although hailed as a rabbi, Jesus on one occasion broke convention and spoke privately to someone who was not only to a woman but also from Samaria – Samaritans lived and worshipped separately from the Jews. They were also referred to as *Kutim* as they had migrated to Israel from a city in Southern Iraq called Kutha (c. 701–681 BCE). They converted to Judaism but kept some of their old practices. A small community of Samaritans still exists. They believe in the Torah but do not accept the Prophets of the Hebrew Bible or their writings. There was mutual hostility between this Jewish minority and other Jews. An orthodox Jew would not use utensils of Samaritans because they considered them unclean.

Christ's encounter with a Samaritan woman was the more remarkable as it occurred during a period when there was opposition to the religious education of women: 'Anyone who teaches his daughter Torah teaches her *tiflut* (promiscuity).'³⁰

He explained patiently and politely the spiritual nature of His teachings:

> A woman from Samaria came to draw water. Jesus said to her, 'Give me a drink.' (For his disciples had gone away into the city to buy food.) The Samaritan woman said to him, 'How is it that you, a Jew, ask for a drink from me, a woman of Samaria?' (For Jews have no dealings with Samaritans.) Jesus answered her, 'If you knew the gift of God, and who it is that is saying to you, "Give me a drink," you would have asked him, and he would have given you living water.' The woman said to him, 'Sir, you have nothing to draw water with,

and the well is deep. Where do you get that living water? Are you greater than our father Jacob? He gave us the well and drank from it himself, as did his sons and his livestock.' Jesus said to her, 'Everyone who drinks of this water will be thirsty again, but whoever drinks of the water that I will give him will never be thirsty again. The water that I will give him will become in him a spring of water welling up to eternal life.'

... Just then his disciples came back. They marveled that he was talking with a woman, but no one said, 'What do you seek?' or, 'Why are you talking with her?' So the woman left her water jar and went away into town and said to the people, 'Come, see a man who told me all that I ever did. Can this be the Christ?' (John 4:7–14, 27–29)

On another occasion, Jesus praised the great faith of a woman:

And there was a woman who had had a discharge of blood for twelve years, and who had suffered much under many physicians, and had spent all that she had, and was no better but rather grew worse. She had heard the reports about Jesus and came up behind him in the crowd and touched his garment. For she said, 'If I touch even his garments, I will be made well.' And immediately the flow of blood dried up, and she felt in her body that she was healed of her disease. And Jesus, perceiving in himself that power had gone out from him, immediately turned about in the crowd and said, 'Who touched my garments?' And his disciples said to him, 'You see the crowd pressing around you, and yet you say, "Who touched me?"' And he looked around to see who had done it. But the woman, knowing what had happened to her, came in fear and trembling and fell down before him and told him the whole truth. And he said to her, 'Daughter, your faith has made you well; go in peace, and be healed of your disease.' (Mark 5:25–34)

Imposition of a number of restrictions on the role of women in the Christian community

The New Testament teachings on how women should be treated remained fundamentally the same as the Hebrew Bible. The Apostle

Peter explicitly expected a Christian wife to be deferential to her husband. She was to submit herself to her husband and address him as master:

> Likewise, wives, be subject to your own husbands, so that even if some do not obey the word, they may be won without a word by the conduct of their wives, when they see your respectful and pure conduct. Do not let your adorning be external – the braiding of hair and the putting on of gold jewelry, or the clothing you wear – but let your adorning be the hidden person of the heart with the imperishable beauty of a gentle and quiet spirit, which in God's sight is very precious. For this is how the holy women who hoped in God used to adorn themselves, by submitting to their own husbands, as Sarah obeyed Abraham, calling him lord . . .
>
> Likewise, husbands, live with your wives in an understanding way, showing honor to the woman as the weaker vessel, since they are heirs with you of the grace of life, so that your prayers may not be hindered. (I Pet. 3:1–7)

The word *Kyrion* or Lord used here is a Greek title also used to refer to God (Matt. 4:10), to Christ (John 11:2), and the Lord and master of a slave (Matt. 10:24). Sarah addressed her husband Abraham by the Hebrew equivalent *adonai* (Orthodox Jewish Bible: I Peter 3:6). This subservience was considered so important that it was recommended that the tradition should be observed even if the husband was not a Christian, so that he might be persuaded thereby to accept Christ. (I Peter 3:1)

Judaism had considered it sinful for women to rule over men or influence rulers (Is. 3:12). The letter to the Ephesians also considers man to be the head of the woman, and the difference in status between woman and man, according to the letter to the Corinthians to be of the same magnitude as the disparity between man and Christ, and Christ and God:

> Wives, submit to your own husbands, as to the Lord. For the husband is the head of the wife even as Christ is the head of the church, his body, and is himself its Savior. Now as the church submits to Christ, so also wives should submit in everything to their husbands.

> Husbands, love your wives, as Christ loved the church and gave himself up for her . . . his mystery is profound, and I am saying that it refers to Christ and the church. However, let each one of you love his wife as himself, and let the wife see that she respects her husband. (Eph. 5:22–25, 32–33)

Again:

> Wives, submit to your husbands, as is fitting in the Lord. Husbands, love your wives, and do not be harsh with them. (Col. 3:18–19)But I want you to understand that the head of every man is Christ, the head of a wife is her husband, and the head of Christ is God. (I Cor. 11:3)

Rev. Albert Barnes commented:

> ***That the head*** . . . The word 'head,' in the Scriptures, is designed often to denote 'master, ruler, chief'. . .
> ***And the head of the woman is the man*** – The sense is, she is subordinate to him, and in all circumstances – in her demeanor, her dress, her conversation, in public and in the family circle – should recognize her subordination to him. The particular thing here referred to is, that if the woman is inspired, and speaks or prays in public, she should by no means lay aside the usual and proper symbols of her subordination.[31]

Women were required not to preach

The ability of women to become rabbis has been intensely debated in some Jewish communities. There is some agreement that there is no direct halakhic objection to the acts of training and ordaining a woman to be a rabbi, preacher or teacher. Hence, in the last few decades, there have been an increasing number of women graduating from rabbinical schools. Most women rabbis today have been ordained from Conservative, Reform and Reconstructionist seminaries, but a few Orthodox women have also become rabbis, and an effort is under way to incorporate more women into the Orthodox rabbinate; its success is at present uncertain.[32]

As in the Jewish tradition, the New Testament states women must not speak in a congregation.

> . . . the women should keep silent in the churches.³³ For they are not permitted to speak, but should be in submission, as the Law also says. If there is anything they desire to learn, let them ask their husbands at home. For it is shameful³⁴ [Greek: αἰσχρὸν, aischron, disgraceful] for a woman to speak in church. (I Cor. 14:34–35)

A literal interpretation of Genesis is relied on to justify this stance:

> Let a woman learn quietly with all submissiveness. I do not permit a woman³⁵ to teach or to exercise authority over a man; rather, she is to remain quiet. For Adam was formed first, then Eve; and Adam was not deceived, but the woman was deceived and became a transgressor.³⁶ Yet she will be saved through childbearing – if they continue in faith and love and holiness, with self-control. (I Tim. 2:11–15)

Rev. Albert Barnes explained:

> ***Let your women keep silence*** – This rule is positive, explicit, and universal. There is no ambiguity in the expressions; and there can be no difference of opinion, one would suppose, in regard to their meaning. The sense evidently is, that in all those things which he had specified, the women were to keep silence; they were to take no part . . .
> ***And if they will learn anything*** – If anything has been spoken which they do not understand; or if on any particular subject they desire more full information, let them inquire of their husbands in their own dwelling. They may there converse freely; and their inquiries will not be attended with the irregularity and disorder which would occur should they interrupt the order and solemnity of public worship.
> ***For it is a shame*** – It is disreputable and shameful; it is a breach of propriety. Their station in life demands modesty, humility, and they should be free from the ostentation of appearing so much in public as to take part in the public services of teaching and praying. It does not become their rank in life; it is not fulfilling the object which God

evidently intended them to fill. He has appointed people to rule; to hold offices; to instruct and govern the church; and it is improper that women should assume that office upon themselves . . .[37]

However, one also notes certain remarkable exceptions and contradictions. The Apostle Paul mentions Phoebe, also known as Priscilla, whom he entrusted to deliver his letter to the Romans, in glowing terms:

> I commend to you our sister Phoebe, a servant [or deaconess] of the church at Cenchreae,[38] that you may welcome her in the Lord in a way worthy of the saints, and help her in whatever she may need from you, for she has been a patron of many and of myself as well. Greet Prisca and Aquila, my fellow workers in Christ Jesus, who risked their necks for my life, to whom not only I give thanks but all the churches of the Gentiles give thanks as well. (Rom. 16:1–4)

Also, in early Christianity women did participate in the leadership of small communities. This came to an end when Pope Gelasius decreed in 494 CE that women could no longer be ordained to the priesthood. In recent years, an increasing number of women are being ordained in Protestant denominations, but the practice remains forbidden in the Catholic Church.[39]

Restrictions on women's attire: Christ did not specify what His followers should wear. However, as in Judaism, wives are required in the New Testament to be modest, not to show off their beauty, jewellery or finery, and to cover their heads when praying.

> Every man who prays or prophesies with his head covered dishonours his head, but every wife who prays or prophesies with her head uncovered dishonours her head, since it is the same as if her head were shaven. For if a wife will not cover her head, then she should cut her hair short. But since it is disgraceful for a wife to cut off her hair or shave her head, let her cover her head. For a man ought not to cover his head, since he is the image and glory of God, but woman is the glory of man. For man was not made from woman, but woman from man. Neither was man created for woman, but woman for man. (I Cor. 11:4–9)

The above passage is followed by words of caution, and a change in the teaching, lest the previous declaration of the subordination of woman to man might be exaggerated or perverted:

> Nevertheless neither is the man without the woman, neither the woman without the man, in the Lord. For as the woman is of the man, even so is the man also by the woman; but all things of God. Judge in yourselves: is it comely that a woman pray unto God uncovered? Doth not even nature itself teach you, that, if a man have long hair, it is a shame unto him? But if a woman have long hair, it is a glory to her: for her hair is given her for a covering. But if any man seem to be contentious, we have no such custom, neither the churches of God. (I Cor. 11:11–16)

Again:

> ... likewise also that women should adorn themselves in respectable apparel, with modesty and self-control, not with braided hair and gold or pearls or costly attire, but with what is proper for women who profess godliness – with good works. (I Tim. 2:9–10)

Matthew Henry, in the 19th century, provided the following explanation:

> Here is a charge, that women who profess the Christian religion should be modest, sober, silent, and submissive, as becomes their place. 1. They must be very modest in their apparel, not affecting gaudiness, gaiety, or costliness (you may read the vanity of a person's mind in the gaiety and gaudiness of his habit), because they have better ornaments with which they should adorn themselves, with good works. Note, Good works are the best ornament; these are, in the sight of God, of great price. Those that profess godliness should, in their dress, as well as other things, act as becomes their profession; instead of laying out their money on fine clothes, they must lay it out in works of piety and charity, which are properly called good works. 2. Women must learn the principles of their religion, learn Christ, learn the scriptures; they must not think that their sex excuses them from that learning which is necessary to salvation. 3. They must be silent, submissive, and subject, and not usurp

authority. The reason given is because Adam was first formed, then Eve out of him, to denote her subordination to him and dependence upon him; and that she was made for him, to be a help-meet for him. And as she was last in the creation, which is one reason for her subjection, so she was first in the transgression, and that is another reason. Adam was not deceived, that is, not first; the serpent did not immediately set upon him, but the woman was first in the transgression (2 Co. 11:3), and it was part of the sentence, Thy desire shall be to thy husband, and he shall rule over thee, Gen. 3:16. But it is a word of comfort (v. 15) that those who continue in sobriety shall be saved in child-bearing, or with child-bearing – the Messiah, who was born of a woman, should break the serpent's head (Gen. 3:15); or the sentence which they are under for sin shall be no bar to their acceptance with Christ, if they continue in faith, and charity, and holiness, with sobriety.[40]

The Apostle Peter imposed similar restrictions on women (I Pet. 3:3–5). Churches that have images of the Virgin Mary depict her as wearing a veil. Veiling was mandated in the Catholic Church and women were required to cover their heads during Mass well into the 20th century:

> It is desirable that, consistent with ancient discipline, women be separated from men in church. Men, in a church or outside a church, while they are assisting at sacred rites, shall be bare-headed, unless the approved mores of the people or peculiar circumstances of things determine otherwise; women, however, shall have a covered head and be modestly dressed, especially when they approach the table of the Lord.[41]

This ruling was abrogated by not being reissued in the 1983 Code of Canon Law. Today, the practice of veiling in church continues in many Eastern Christian communities, especially those in the Orthodox tradition, where rules for women covering their hair (and men removing their hats) upon entering a church are enforced.

The attitude of many churches today towards women has progressed as they have focused on reading the scripture in light of the spiritual message of Christ.

Marriage

Christ was silent on the subject of marriage except to state, when asked about levirate marriage (Deut. 25:5–6) – the marriage between a widow and her deceased husband's brother – that 'they neither marry nor are given in marriage' in the kingdom of heaven (Matt. 22:30). However, the New Testament does stress that both women and men have marital rights (I Cor. 7:3).

Polygamy

There are several instances of polygamy in the Hebrew Bible. Polygamy was also practised by some Jewish-Christians when the early church was established. There was no unambiguous statement in the New Testament that all Christians should be monogamous. Several passages state that the church leaders should be the 'husband of one wife' (I Tim. 3:2, 12; Titus 1:6). Some Christian denominations interpreted this as a prohibition of polygamy. Others argued that polygamy was allowed, but not for church leaders. Still others argued that the passage recommends that the church leaders should not divorce their first wives.

Martin Luther, the founder of the 16th-century Reformation, was a counsellor to Landgrave Philip of Hesse, a Protestant convert and one of the German champions of the Reformation. When the latter wished to take a second wife he sought Luther's guidance. Luther noted that in the Old Testament polygamy had evidently been practised without divine disapproval, and counselled Philip into a second, albeit secret, marriage.[42] He wrote:

> I confess that I cannot forbid a person to marry several wives, for it does not contradict the Scripture. If a man wishes to marry more than one wife he should be asked whether he is satisfied in his conscience that he may do so in accordance with the word of God. In such a case the civil authority has nothing to do in the matter.[43]

As a previous monk, Martin Luther's own marriage to Katharina von Bora, a former nun who had fled from a convent, was opposed by many of his friends who saw in it the downfall of the Reformation. Others saw it as permission for Protestant clergymen to marry.

Jan Van Leyden, also known as John of Leiden (1509–1536), a Dutch Anabaptist leader and reformist who had many wives, also proclaimed that polygamy was according to God's will.[44]

Divorce

According to the Talmudic understanding of Torah law (Deut. 24:1–4), there was a unilateral (and apparently unrestricted) right to divorce by the husband, with no right to divorce by the wife except in rare circumstances. The Prophet Malachi however cautions:

> So guard yourselves in your spirit, and let none of you be faithless to the wife of your youth. For the man who does not love his wife but divorces her, says the Lord, the God of Israel, covers his garment with violence, says the Lord of hosts. So guard yourselves in your spirit, and do not be faithless. (Mal. 2:15–16)

Christ forbade divorce except in cases of infidelity, and regarded marriage to a divorcee as adultery:

> It was also said, 'Whoever divorces his wife, let him give her a certificate of divorce.' But I say to you that everyone who divorces his wife, except on the ground of sexual immorality, makes her commit adultery, and whoever marries a divorced woman commits adultery. (Matt. 5:31–32)

The Apostle Paul reminded Christians that they must not divorce, regardless of whether or not the spouse believed in Christ. However, a non-Christian spouse was free to divorce the Christian partner:

> To the married I give this charge (not I, but the Lord): the wife should not separate from her husband (but if she does, she should remain unmarried or else be reconciled to her husband), and the husband should not divorce his wife.
>
> To the rest I say (I, not the Lord) that if any brother has a wife who is an unbeliever, and she consents to live with him, he should not divorce her. If any woman has a husband who is an unbeliever, and he consents to live with her, she should not divorce him.

> For the unbelieving husband is made holy because of his wife, and the unbelieving wife is made holy because of her husband. Otherwise your children would be unclean, but as it is, they are holy. But if the unbelieving partner separates, let it be so . . . (I Cor. 7:10–15)

Only the death of her husband freed a Christian woman to marry again, but even then the Apostle Paul did not recommend that she should remarry:

> A wife is bound to her husband as long as he lives. But if her husband dies, she is free to be married to whom she wishes, only in the Lord. Yet in my judgment she is happier if she remains as she is . . . (I Cor. 7:39–40)

In the 18th and early 19th centuries, divorce in England was only possible by an Act of Parliament but became legal in 1857. Divorce has become legal in most European Catholic countries only relatively recently: Italy in 1974; Spain in 1981; Argentina in 1987; the Republic of Ireland in 1997; Chile in 2005; and Malta in 2011. Divorce amongst Catholics remains illegal in the Philippines and Vatican City. After more than 20 years of debate the Church of England finally gave its blessing to the remarriage of divorced people in 2002.[45]

Celibacy

Ancient Judaism was strongly opposed to celibacy. In Jesus's time, the priests of the Essenes (c. 200 BC to 200 CE), a strict ascetic Jewish sect, practised celibacy. The Romans viewed celibacy as an aberration and legislated fiscal penalties against it, with a sole exception granted to the Vestal Virgins, the priestesses of Vesta, goddess of the hearth, the sacred eternal flame in Ancient Rome.

Jesus never decreed celibacy. However, the Apostle Paul was celibate and recommended it to his fellow Christians as an ideal state:

> Now concerning the matters about which you wrote: 'It is good for a man not to have sexual relations with a woman.' But because of the temptation to sexual immorality, each man should have his own

> wife and each woman her own husband . . . To the unmarried and the widows I say that it is good for them to remain single, as I am. But if they cannot exercise self-control, they should marry. For it is better to marry than to burn with passion. (I Cor. 7:1–2, 8–9)

But even the Apostle Paul confessed that his judgements were not based on any explicit teaching of Christ. His recommendation that if at all possible Christians should not marry was not based on any antipathy towards the institution of marriage but was based on the belief that the time available for individuals to proclaim the Kingdom was too short for them to be preoccupied with marriage and worldly affairs:

> Now concerning the betrothed, I have no command from the Lord . . . it is good for a person to remain as he is. Are you bound to a wife? Do not seek to be free. Are you free from a wife? Do not seek a wife. But if you do marry, you have not sinned, and if a betrothed woman marries, she has not sinned. Yet those who marry will have worldly troubles, and I would spare you that. This is what I mean, brothers: the appointed time has grown very short. From now on, let those who have wives live as though they had none . . . I want you to be free from anxieties. The unmarried man is anxious about the things of the Lord, how to please the Lord. But the married man is anxious about worldly things, how to please his wife, and his interests are divided. And the unmarried or betrothed woman is anxious about the things of the Lord, how to be holy in body and spirit. But the married woman is anxious about worldly things, how to please her husband. I say this for your own benefit, not to lay any restraint upon you, but to promote good order and to secure your undivided devotion to the Lord. (I Cor. 7:25–29, 32–35)

It is clear from the New Testament accounts that the Apostle Peter was married (Matt. 8:14–15). It is safe to assume that, based on Jewish law and custom, all the Apostles, except for John, were married and had families.[46]

In the early 3rd century the Canons of the Apostolic Constitutions decreed that clerics of lower rank might still marry after their ordination, but marriage of bishops, priests and deacons was forbidden.[47] Thus, without any direct mandate from Christ, Christians in the

Middle Ages and, in particular, the Catholic Church, came to insist on celibacy as a prerequisite for holding religious office. The Eastern Orthodox Church never adopted it and most other churches rejected the discipline. Despite the church decrees, for the first millennium of the church's existence priests, bishops and 39 popes were married.[48] Pope Urban II (1042–1099) tried to enforce celibacy rigorously. He ordered that married priests who ignored the celibacy laws be imprisoned for the good of their souls. He had the wives and children of those married priests sold into slavery, and the money went to the church coffers.[49]

The status of women worsened with pronouncements of the church fathers on the matter. In 401 CE, Augustine, one of the early fathers of the church, wrote that 'nothing is so powerful in drawing the spirit of a man downwards as the caresses of a woman'.[50]

Condoning violence

In self-defence

The sixth commandment of the Law of Moses states 'You shall not murder' (Ex. 20:13). However, the right to self-defence is well established within Jewish law. The Torah states: 'you shall not stand up against the life of your neighbor [Orthodox Jewish Bible: neither shalt thou stand aside while thy neighbor's blood is shed]' (Lev. 19:16). Notably, the law of *rodef* (the pursuer) dictates that someone who is chasing after another person to kill him, can be killed by anyone:

> And these are the ones who are saved from transgressing even at the cost of their lives; that is to say, these people may be killed so that they do not perform a transgression: One who pursues another to kill him, or pursues a male to sodomize him, or pursues a betrothed young woman to rape her. But with regard to one who pursues an animal to sodomize it, or one who seeks to desecrate Shabbat, or one who is going to engage in idol worship, they are not saved at the cost of their lives. Rather, they are forewarned not to transgress, and if they proceed to transgress after having been forewarned, they are brought to trial, and if they are found guilty, they are executed.[51]

Forgiveness vs. justice

The story of Joseph in Genesis may be said to set the standard of forgiveness. When Joseph was sold by his brothers into slavery and was eventually reunited with them, his brothers feared his revenge, assuming they would now be punished for their transgression. Joseph explained that through divine wisdom the evil they had committed had become the means of salvation (Gen. 50:19–21).

Several verses of the Torah also encourage love and forgiveness and forbid revenge and bearing grudges:

> You shall not hate your brother in your heart, but you shall reason frankly with your neighbor, lest you incur sin because of him. You shall not take vengeance or bear a grudge against the sons of your own people, but you shall love your neighbor as yourself: I am the Lord. (Lev. 19:17–18)

However, the injunctions of the Torah were revealed for a harsh desert environment. Hence, forgiveness had to be balanced and reinforced with justice. Thus we find that, similar to the earlier Babylonian Code of Hammurabi (1754 BCE),[52] the Torah permits equitable retaliation which extends even to livestock:

> Whoever takes a human life shall surely be put to death. Whoever takes an animal's life shall make it good, life for life. If anyone injures his neighbor, as he has done it shall be done to him, fracture for fracture, eye for eye, tooth for tooth; whatever injury he has given a person shall be given to him. Whoever kills an animal shall make it good. And whoever kills a person shall be put to death. You shall have the same rule for the sojourner and for the native, for I am the Lord your God. (Lev. 24:17–22)

The law of forgiveness was repeated and amplified by Christ. He was less concerned that His followers seek personal justice in this evanescent world, and more interested that they undergo a spiritual transformation.

> You have heard that it was said, 'An eye for an eye and a tooth for a tooth.' But I say to you, do not resist the one who is evil. But if anyone

slaps you on the right cheek, turn to him the other also. And if anyone would sue you and take your tunic [a long garment worn under the cloak next to the skin], let him have your cloak as well. And if anyone forces you to go one mile, go with him two miles. (Matt. 5:38–41)

This teaching did not preclude society seeking redress for the wrongs done to individuals. However, Christ gave no guidance in this respect.

Justifiable war and holy war

This is of particular interest given the recent escalation of terrorism in the name of religion. Christians were called to be 'peacemakers' (Matt. 5:9). Sadly, despite the emphasis in the Gospels on love, forgiveness and unity, the concept of fighting for God, perhaps borrowed from the Hebrew Bible, entered into the teachings and practices of the church soon after it assumed temporal power.

There are two instances when Christ appears to condone violence. The first states:

Do not think that I have come to bring peace to the earth. I have not come to bring peace, but a sword. For I have come to set a man against his father, and a daughter against her mother, and a daughter-in-law against her mother-in-law. And a person's enemies will be those of his own household. (Matt. 10:34–36)

However, the passage simply reflects that God's revelation always incites opposition to it.

The second instance has been more problematic for Christian commentators: Christ, without preamble and inexplicably, orders His disciples to sell their earthly possessions and buy weapons:

He said to them, 'But now let the one who has a moneybag take it, and likewise a knapsack. And let the one who has no sword sell his cloak and buy one. For I tell you that this Scripture must be fulfilled in me: "And he was numbered with the transgressors." For what is written about me has its fulfillment.' And they said, 'Look, Lord, here are two swords.' And he said to them, 'It is enough.' (Luke 22:36–38)

According to the explanation by Rev. Albert Barnes:

> ***And he that hath no sword*** *–* There has been much difficulty in understanding why Jesus directed his disciples to arm themselves, as if it was his purpose to make a defense. It is certain that the spirit of his religion is against the use of the sword, and that it was not his purpose to defend himself against Judas. But it should be remembered that these directions about the purse, the scrip, and the sword were not made with reference to his 'being taken' in the garden, but with reference 'to their future life'. . . . It amounts, then, to a 'prediction' that they would soon leave the places which they had been accustomed to, and go into scenes of poverty, want, and danger, where they would feel the necessity of money, provisions, and the means of defense. All, therefore, that the passage justifies is:
>
> 1. That it is proper for people to provide beforehand for their wants, and for ministers and missionaries as well as any others.
> 2. That self-defense is lawful.
>
> Men encompassed with danger may lawfully 'defend' their lives. It does not prove that it is lawful to make 'offensive' war on a nation or an individual.[53]

It should also be noted that Christ Himself neither had a sword nor used a sword, even when He and His followers were threatened physically. Only once did one of His disciples, the Apostle Peter, briefly use a sword that he had been instructed to buy, when he saw His master being arrested in the dead of night. Even then Christ did not sanction his action but observed that violence begets more violence and expressed His wish to abide by what God had willed for Him (John 18:10–11; Matt. 26:52). The reason, he explained to the Roman governor, Pontius Pilate, that His followers did not fight was because it was not His mission to establish an earthly kingdom but to proclaim the good news of the heavenly Kingdom of the Father (John 18:36).

The Christian church and holy war

When Emperor Constantine adopted the Christian Faith in, or about, 312 CE, Christianity became transformed from a persecuted religion into one that was able and eager to persecute other religions and 'heresies'.[54] The church leaders suddenly found themselves in charge of an empire that they had to help defend against the barbarian forces that were prone to attack Rome. As a result, the Gospel message was interpreted in ways that allowed them to justify the use of force. The influential father of the church Augustine of Hippo claimed in the 5th century CE that, while individuals should not resort to violence, God had given the sword to governing authorities for good reason (Rom. 13:3–4). He argued that Christians, as part of a government, need not be ashamed of protecting peace and punishing wickedness when forced to do so by a government.[55] He developed the concept of 'just war' in his work *The City of God* (Book XIX, ch. 7). Thomas Aquinas, 800 years later, using the authority of St Augustine, defined the conditions under which a war could be justified:

> the war must be conducted by a legitimate authority, for a just cause, and with an upright intention.[56]

In 1095, at the Council of Clermont, Pope Urban II declared that some wars were not only a *bellum justum* or 'just war', but could, in certain cases, rise to the level of a *bellum sacrum* or 'holy war'. Jill Claster, Dean of New York University College of Arts and Science, characterizes this as a remarkable transformation in the ideology of war, shifting the justification of war from being not only just but also spiritually beneficial.[57] Richard L. Crocker asks in *The Holy War*, a book which examines the Christian concept of holy war, 'how a culture formally dedicated to fulfilling the injunction to "love thy neighbour as thyself" could move to a point where it sanctioned the use of violence against the alien both outside and inside society'.[58] He further writes: 'Certainly the holy war, as the term is now generally understood, appears to have been the invention of the West.'[59] Referring to a paper in the same book by Montgomery Watt (1909–2006), Professor of Arabic and Islamic Studies in Edinburgh, Scotland, he further states that it is clear that the usual image of a horde of rabid Muslims sweeping all civilizations before them in war without quarter, a horde crying 'Convert or die,' is, like so many other faces of the enemy, a caricature.[60]

The sanctioning of holy war was a turning point in Christian attitudes towards violence, as Thomas Patrick Murphy points out: 'Pope Gregory VII (c. 1015–1085) made the Holy War possible by drastically altering the attitude of the church towards war ... Hitherto a knight could obtain remission of sins only by giving up arms, but Pope Urban II (1042–1099) invited him to gain forgiveness 'in and through the exercise of his martial skills.' A holy war was defined by the Roman Catholic Church as 'war that is not only just, but justifying; that is, a war that confers positive spiritual merit on those who fight in it'.[61]

With little or no scriptural justification the church unleashed unspeakable violence on all perceived enemies. The list of violence in the name of Christ includes: the Inquisition; the Crusades; the devastating wars between Catholics, Orthodox and Protestants; and anti-Semitism.[62] To this list, J. Denny Weaver (Professor of Religion at Bluffton College in Ohio) adds, 'warrior popes, support for capital punishment, corporal punishment under the guise of "spare the rod and spoil the child", justification of slavery, worldwide colonialism in the name of propagating Christianity, the systemic violence of women subjected to men'.[63] A well-known controversial hymn written in 1864, nowadays generally understood as spiritual battle but with national and militaristic overtones,[64] is a reminder of a violent tradition:

> Onward, Christian soldiers, marching as to war,
> With the cross of Jesus going on before.
> Christ, the royal Master, leads against the foe;
> Forward into battle see His banners go! ....[65]

Sectarian violence

Following the Protestant Reformation in 1517, the two main denominations of western Christianity waged a series of internecine wars in Europe between 1522 and 1713 resulting in devastation, with more than six million dead. The conflict intensified after the Catholic Church mounted the Counter-Reformation in 1545 against the growth of Protestantism, culminating in the Thirty Years War which devastated Germany, killing a third of its population, a mortality twice that of World War I.[66]

The gruesome inquisitions, institutions within the judicial system of the Catholic Church whose aim was to combat heresy, often Protestantism, and the sacking of Constantinople, the capital of the Orthodox Byzantine Empire, by the Catholic Crusader army in 1204, are further examples of Christian violence.

The Hebrew scriptures were often employed to justify these hostilities. The exploits of Joshua in the name of Yahweh continued to have profound repercussions centuries later as Christians sought scriptural reasons to attack fellow Christians. Thus, in the view of a Bishop of the Anglican Church, in 1845 the Catholics represented Babylon of the Book of Revelation:

> 'Thus Jericho' a great and fortified city and chief defense of the Canaanites, 'was the type of Rome in its pagan and papal state, as the great enemy which prevents the Church of God from taking possession of the promised inheritance of the whole earth, according to the word, Ask of me, and I will give thee the heathen for thine inheritance, and the uttermost parts of the earth for thy procession. This great enemy, the Babylon described in the Book of Revelation, has ever been so strong in its walls and bulwarks, that the power of the Church, in itself, and by its own means only, is utterly unequal to gain the conquest. But we have a Captain of our salvation, the same who appeared to Joshua (v. 13-15) and through him our complete and full victory is sure.'[67]

The blatantly sectarian 'troubles' in Northern Ireland resulted in many thousands of deaths of both Catholics and Protestants. Both sides considered their part in the conflict to be justified and holy. Thus, the atrocities committed against the Catholics by the Protestants were portrayed as the continuation and completion of God's work against the Canaanites. To the Catholics it was just as clear that they were reliving the suffering of the Israelites under a tyrannical Pharaoh:

> To the Catholic Gaelic Irish of the same period – and later it seemed equally obvious to compare their sufferings with those of 'the children of Israel in Egypt under the oppression of the enemies of God'. . .[68]

This led Conor Cruise O'Brien (1917–2008), an Irish intellectual and politician, to comment at the height of the troubles in the 1970s that Ireland was really inhabited not by Catholics and Protestants but by two Christian denominations that considered their plight to be similar to that of the children of Israel:

[In the minds of] Irish patriots, the sufferings of Christ and those of the Irish (Catholic) people were in a particular sense one: the sacrifice of Irish patriots was analogous to the sacrifice of Christ; and the resurgence of the national spirit that such a sacrifice could set in motion was analogous to the resurrection of Christ. The timing of the Rising for Easter was no coincidence . . .

The Bible is the story of a Chosen People, and the various sets of people who have laid claim to it have habitually regarded themselves as chosen . . . The Gaels were the children of Israel and of course 'the enemies of God' were the Protestants, who were themselves the children of Israel in their own eyes.

One could say that Ireland was inhabited, not really by Protestants and Catholics but by two sets of imaginary Jews.

In theory Irish Catholics and Ulster Protestants shared a religion of love. But they shared also a belief in a God of love, who is ready to torture throughout eternity anyone who seriously offends Him. In these conditions 'love' becomes something of a technical term. You were supposed to love your neighbour, even of the opposite religion, but as his beliefs and behaviour were obviously so offensive as to mark him out for hell-fire it did not matter if you knocked him about a bit, if only to prepare him for what was coming to him in the next. It didn't mean you didn't 'love' him, as God 'loved' the sinner to whom he handed out eternal torment.

Crude perversions of Christian belief no doubt, yet they, and generations of Christian clergy propounding something very like them have helped to shape the present scene . . .[69]

Christian aggression towards other religions

Anti-Semitism

The Apostle Paul had never met Jesus or heard Him preach. As Saul, he had spearheaded Jewish persecutions of the Nazarenes. Following his conversion, and now as 'an apostle of Christ by the will of God' (Eph. 1:1), he had clashed, as noted earlier, with the first Apostle Peter, James, John and the early church in Jerusalem. Until the end of his life, he saw it as his mission to mold Christian communities around the Mediterranean to his understanding of Christ's mission. Several scholars have commented on the tensions between Petrine or Jewish Christianity and Pauline Christianity.[70]

As the number of Gentile converts began to overwhelm the Hebrew converts, the rift between the two Christian factions widened. The letter to Diognetus, possibly written by Justin Martyr in the second century, contains derogatory remarks concerning Jewish practices, and conveniently ignores the fact that the laws were ordained in the same Bible that Christians also hold sacred:

> With regards, however, to their scruples about meats, and their superstitious observance of the Sabbath, and their pride in circumcision, and the affectation of their keeping of fast and new moon – things ridiculous and undeserving of consideration – I think thou hast not any need to learn of me. For to accept some of the things created by God for the use of man as rightly created, and to reject others as useless and necessary, is not this plainly wrong? To misrepresent God as forbidding a man to do a good deed on the Sabbath day, is not this irreverent? To boast of the mutilation of the flesh (fasting) as a testimony of their election (i.e. chosen people of God) though they were especially beloved by God on that account, is not this ridiculous? . . . I think therefore that thou hast now learned sufficiently that Christians are right in holding aloof from the vanity and delusion of the pagan world and the punctiliousness and pride of the Jews . . .[71]

The Gentile-dominated church continued to issue statements designed to divorce Christianity from all that was Jewish, and had no inclination to have anything to do with the commandments of the Torah, festivals, the Sabbath, or circumcision, denying in the process the special relationship of Israel and Jews to God. It considered all of these as things of the past. In the Epistle of Ignatius, Bishop of Antioch, to the Magnesians in 115 CE, Christians were warned of the error of looking to Judaism:

> To profess Jesus Christ while continuing to follow Jewish customs is an absurdity. The Christian faith does not look to Judaism, but Judaism looks to Christianity . . .[72]

Many of the early church fathers and saints began uttering strong anti-Jewish sentiments, including St John Chrysostom (349–407 CE), St Augustine of Hippo (354–430 CE), St Ambrose of Milan (340–397 CE), St Jerome (347–420 CE), and Ephraim the Syrian (306–373 CE). It was not long after its denunciations of the Jews that the church took action against them. The second council of the Synod of Macon in 583 CE imposed a curfew against Jews, banning them from the streets at all times between Maundy Thursday, the day before Easter, and Easter Sunday. It also prohibited the Jews from talking to nuns.[73]

The early church in Rome never explained satisfactorily its stance against Judaism, the background of the Christian Faith, and why it accepted Hebrew scripture as the Word of God but discarded its provisions so easily. Their final rendering of Christianity had little in common with what Jesus had said about the Law, or what He and His twelve disciples, witnesses to Jesus's teachings, practised. Indeed, most of the evolution in church thinking was based on Pauline elaborations rather than the actual statements of Christ.

There are several explanations as to why the church, and predominantly the Catholic Church, persecuted the Jews so vehemently for almost two millennia. A primary reason appears to have been the inability of Christians and the church to convince the Jews that Jesus had fulfilled the biblical prophecies and was indeed their Messiah. It was therefore more convenient for the church to blame the Jews for being stubborn, evil and an enemy of Christ and Christians.

The term 'scapegoat' refers to a goat that was sent ('escaped') into the wilderness after the sins of the people had been heaped upon it (Lev. 16:20–22). Christians with the complicity of the church have scapegoated Jews for two thousand years.

For example, unexplained deaths or disappearance of children were blamed on the Jews. The accusation is that they kidnapped and killed Christian babies and used their blood as part of their religious rituals during Jewish holidays, and for the baking of matzos for Passover, a 'blood libel' 'that had first appeared in Oxford at the time of the Second Crusade in the twelfth century'.[74] The accusation is particularly unjust and tragic, since the Jews are forbidden to consume blood and commanded not to kill.

According to the Gospel of Matthew the Jewish contemporaries of Jesus claimed responsibility for His death (Matt. 27:22–25). This provided perhaps the most damaging example of scapegoating – the accusation of deicide,[75] namely, the crucifixion of Jesus Who according to church dogma was God incarnate. The accusation of deicide appeared first in a sermon in 167 CE by Melito of Sardis entitled *Per Pascha* (On the Passover). This text squarely blamed the Jews for allowing King Herod and Caiaphas to execute their Messiah and in so doing were guilty of killing God Himself. It only mentions that Pontius Pilate washed his hands of the guilt. Its purpose may have been therefore to appeal to Rome to spare the Christians.[76] St John Chrysostom (c. 347 CE) made the charge of deicide the cornerstone of his theology. He was perhaps the first to use the term 'deicide'[77] and the first Christian preacher to apply it to the Jewish nation. He held that for this putative 'deicide' there was no expiation, pardon or indulgence possible. Again, early on, another Catholic saint, Peter Chrysologus (c. 380–450 CE) endorsed the use of the word (*deicida*) in his Latin sermon (number 172). He wrote: *Iudaeos [invidia] . . . fecit esse deicidas*, i.e., '[envy] made the Jews deicides'.[78] The church's labelling of the Jews as 'Christ-killers' and 'God-killers' justified for centuries the many atrocities perpetrated against Jews.

Attacks on Islam

As early as 14 years after the death of the Prophet, an orthodox saint, John of Damascus, wrote in 746 CE a malicious account of Muhammad:

> From that time to the present a false prophet named Mohammed has appeared in their midst. This man, after having chanced upon the Old and New Testaments and likewise, it seems, having conversed with an Arian monk, devised his own heresy. Then, having insinuated himself into the good graces of the people by a show of seeming piety, he gave out that a certain book had been sent down to him from heaven. He had set down some ridiculous compositions in this book of his and he gave it to them as an object of veneration . . . There are many other extraordinary and quite ridiculous things in this book which he boasts was sent down to him from God. But when we ask: 'And who is there to testify that God gave him the book? And which of the prophets foretold that such a prophet would rise up?' – they are at a loss.[79]

The Byzantine monastic chronicler, Theophanes the Confessor (c. 752/760–818 CE) wrote disparagingly:

> In this year [actually, in 632] died Muhammad, the Saracens' ruler leader and false prophet. He had previously chosen his relative Abu Bakr as his successor. As soon as rumor of him arrived, everyone became afraid.
>
> When he first appeared, the Hebrews were misled and thought he was the Anointed One [Messiah or Christ] they expected, so that some of their leaders came to him, accepted his religion, and gave up of that of Moses, who had looked on God. Those who did this were ten in number, and they stayed with Muhammad until his death. But when they saw him eating of a camel they knew he was not the man they had thought. They were at a loss as to what to do; as they were afraid to give up his religion, they stayed at his side and taught him the lawless behavior towards us Christians.[80]

Since then, and up to the present day,[81] Christian scholars have not been able to rein in their pens to resist the temptation of unfairly disparaging the Prophet of Islam. Christian–Muslim animosity has fuelled many crusades and bloody wars. Currently, there are a number of ongoing conflicts between the two religions worldwide, and both sides share some of the blame.

Forced conversion of Hindus

Religious oppression in the Indian state of Goa was carried out by the Portuguese from the 16th to 17th centuries. With the complicity of zealous Franciscan and Jesuit missionaries, the natives, mostly Hindus, were brutally persecuted and forcibly converted to Catholicism.[82] In north Goa, many temples and mosques were destroyed, Hindu rituals and use of Hindu sacred scripture were banned, and all inhabitants older than 15 years were forced to listen to Christian teachings, compelled to abandon their local language and to speak Portuguese.[83]

Other examples of Gospel teachings which are incompatible with the practices of most modern-day societies

Underlining the need for a fresh revelation are several New Testament instructions which were intended to teach Christ's disciples compassion and to make them more spiritual and less grounded in material existence. However, if applied at societal level, they may be considered subversive. Hence, none of the government institutions in western Christian democracies adhere to these social teachings of the Gospels.

Recommendation to come quickly to terms with a plaintiff or aggressor

The Hebrew Bible admonishes:

> Go not forth hastily to strive, lest thou know not what to do in the end thereof, when thy neighbour hath put thee to shame.

Christ confirms this teaching:

> Settle matters quickly with your adversary who is taking you to court. Do it while you are still together on the way, or your adversary may hand you over to the judge, and the judge may hand you over to the officer, and you may be thrown into prison . . . And if anyone wants to sue you and take your shirt, hand over your coat as well. (New International Version: Matt. 5:25, 40; also Luke 12:58)

Do not take oaths

> Do not take an oath at all, either by heaven, for it is the throne of God, or by the earth, for it is his footstool, or by Jerusalem, for it is the city of the great King. And do not take an oath by your head, for you cannot make one hair white or black. Let what you say be simply 'Yes' or 'No'; anything more than this comes from evil. (Matt. 5:34–37; also James 5:12)

Ellicott comments: 'Not a few interpreters, and even whole Christian communities, as e.g. the Society of Friends, see in these words and in James 5:12, a formal prohibition of all oaths, either promissory or evidential, and look on the general practice of Christians, and the formal teaching of the Church of England in her Articles (*Art.* xxxix.), as simply an acquiescence in evil.'[84] Others believe that 'the prohibition must be understood of rash and careless oaths in conversation, not of solemn asseveration in Courts of Justice.'[85]

Go the extra mile and concede to apparently unreasonable demands and avoid contentions

> And if anyone forces you to go one mile, go with him two miles. (Matt. 5:41)

Matthew Henry comments:

> The plain instruction is, Suffer any injury that can be borne, for the sake of peace, committing your concerns to the Lord's keeping. And the sum of all is, that Christians must avoid disputing and striving. If any say, Flesh and blood cannot pass by such an affront, let them remember, that flesh and blood shall not inherit the kingdom of God; and those who act upon right principles will have most peace and comfort.[86]

Love your enemies (Matt. 5:43–46)

Christian authorities have for two thousand years fought their enemies, often with the blessing of the church.

Lending with interest and borrowing

This practice is frowned upon in the New Testament but is essential to the workings of all current financial institutions. It is the basis of the modern-day banking system, as well as church financing:

> And if you lend to those from whom you expect to receive, what credit is that to you? Even sinners lend to sinners, to get back the same amount. But love your enemies, and do good, and lend, expecting nothing in return, and your reward will be great, and you will

be sons of the Most High, for he is kind to the ungrateful and the evil. Be merciful, even as your Father is merciful. (Luke 6:34–36; also, Matt. 5:42)

Obeying civil authorities

Here there is a fundamental difference between Judaism and Christianity. The former believes Israel to be a nation established by God and endowed by Him with kings and rulers. It therefore resisted being subjugated by foreign nations. Jewish kings were to be obeyed and cursing a Jewish king carried the death sentence (I Kings 21:13).

In contrast, the New Testament teaches that the abode of Christ's followers was in heaven. They therefore should not love their earthly life and had no reason to go against earthly powers:

> Remind them to be submissive to rulers and authorities, to be obedient, to be ready for every good work. (Titus 3:1)

> Be subject for the Lord's sake to every human institution, whether it be to the emperor as supreme, or to governors as sent by him to punish those who do evil and to praise those who do good. For this is the will of God . . . (I Peter 2:13–15)

Christ had earlier instructed that the imperial tax should be paid to Caesar. However, here again the emphasis is that Christians concern themselves with spiritual rather than material matters:

> And they sent to him some of the Pharisees and some of the Herodians, to trap him in his talk. And they came and said to him, 'Teacher, we know that you are true and do not care about anyone's opinion. For you are not swayed by appearances, but truly teach the way of God. Is it lawful to pay taxes to Caesar, or not? Should we pay them, or should we not?' But, knowing their hypocrisy, he said to them, 'Why put me to the test? Bring me a denarius and let me look at it.' And they brought one. And he said to them, 'Whose likeness and inscription is this?' They said to him, 'Caesar's.' Jesus said to them, 'Render to Caesar the things that are Caesar's, and to God the things that are God's.' And they marvelled at him. (Mark 12:13–17)

PART II

PROMISES OF NEW DIVINE INTERVENTIONS

4

THE TIMES OF REBIRTH AND RENEWAL OF FAITH

In common with the Holy Writings of other religions, the Bible anticipates new divine revelations. These will renew, reform and revitalize the fundamental realities of faith – that is, the essential moral virtues and ethical values – and revoice them to mankind. At the same time, God will abrogate or alter some of the obsolete past social teachings, and introduce new laws that must govern human society.

The Apostle Paul explained that a rebirth had occurred through Christ: 'according to his own mercy by the washing of regeneration and renewal of the Holy Spirit' (Titus 3:5). There is a dire need for a similar resurrection and regeneration today – not through renovation and man-made devices but, as in the past, through a fresh outpouring of the Holy Spirit and the creative and transformative power of the Divine Word:

> Having purified your souls by your obedience to the truth for a sincere brotherly love, love one another earnestly from a pure heart, since you have been born again, not of perishable seed but of imperishable, through the living and abiding word of God. (I Peter 1:22–23).

The Hebrew Bible prepares the Children of Israel for restoration and new teachings

The Bible introduces the topic of new revelations in a variety of ways. The Prophet Isaiah warned that in that Day the Children of Israel must not allow the past to prevent them from recognizing the day of their redemption.

> Remember not the former things, nor consider the things of old. Behold, I am doing a new thing; now it springs forth, do you not perceive it? I will make a way in the wilderness and rivers in the desert. (Is. 43:18–19)

> For behold, I will create new heavens and a new earth. The former things will not be remembered, nor will they come to mind. (Is. 65:17)

Again:

> ... behold, I will again do wonderful things with this people, with wonder upon wonder; and the wisdom of their wise men shall perish, and the discernment of their discerning men shall be hidden. (Is. 29:14)

As the commentator Ellicott writes: 'All the wonders of the great historic past of Israel were to be as nothing compared with the new manifestation of the power of Jehovah.'[1]

The Hebrew Bible announces that God will also establish a 'new covenant':

> Behold, the days are coming, declares the Lord, when I will make a new covenant with the house of Israel and the house of Judah, not like the covenant that I made with their fathers on the day when I took them by the hand to bring them out of the land of Egypt, my covenant that they broke, though I was their husband, declares the Lord. For this is the covenant that I will make with the house of Israel after those days, declares the Lord: I will put my law within them, and I will write it on their hearts. And I will be their God, and they shall be my people ... (Jer. 31:31–33)

This will be necessary, as earlier covenants that God had established with the Children of Israel and humanity would have been violated:

> The earth lies defiled under its inhabitants; for they have transgressed the laws, violated the statutes, broken the everlasting covenant. (Is. 24:5)

THE TIMES OF REBIRTH AND RENEWAL OF FAITH

> Come, everyone who thirsts, come to the waters; Incline your ear, and come to me; hear, that your soul may live; and I will make with you an everlasting covenant . . . (Is. 55:1, 3)

The new everlasting covenant will coincide with the establishment of the Jews in the land of Israel:

> I will make with them an everlasting covenant, that I will not turn away from doing good to them. And I will put the fear of me in their hearts, that they may not turn from me. I will rejoice in doing them good, and I will plant them in this land in faithfulness, with all my heart and all my soul. (Jer. 32:40–41)

> They shall ask the way to Zion, with faces turned toward it, saying, 'Come, let us join ourselves to the Lord in an everlasting covenant that will never be forgotten.' (Jer. 50:5)

> They shall dwell in the land that I gave to my servant Jacob, where your fathers lived. They and their children and their children's children shall dwell there forever, and David my servant shall be their prince forever. I will make a covenant of peace with them. It shall be an everlasting covenant with them. And I will set them in their land and multiply them, and will set my sanctuary in their midst forevermore. My dwelling place shall be with them, and I will be their God, and they shall be my people. Then the nations will know that I am the Lord who sanctifies Israel, when my sanctuary is in their midst forevermore. (Ezek. 37:25–28)

God will create 'new heavens and a new earth':

> For as the new heavens and the new earth that I make shall remain before me, says the Lord, so shall your offspring and your name remain. From new moon to new moon, and from Sabbath to Sabbath, all flesh shall come to worship before me, declares the Lord. (Is. 66:22–23)

God will cleanse His people with a sprinkling of the water of life, and endow them with 'a new heart' and 'a new spirit'. He will multiply the spiritual fruits of His divine tree, and transform the faithful into a more united, perceptive and compassionate section of humanity:

> I will give them a heart to know that I am the Lord, and they shall be my people and I will be their God, for they shall return to me with their whole heart. (Jer. 24:7)

> I will take you from the nations and gather you from all the countries and bring you into your own land. I will sprinkle clean water on you, and you shall be clean from all your uncleannesses, and from all your idols I will cleanse you. And I will give you a new heart, and a new spirit I will put within you. And I will remove the heart of stone from your flesh and give you a heart of flesh. And I will put my Spirit within you, and cause you to walk in my statutes and be careful to obey my rules . . . I will make the fruit of the tree and the increase of the field abundant, that you may never again suffer the disgrace of famine among the nations. (Ezek. 36:24–27, 30)

God will open the eyes of the spiritually blind and bring a new light to all. He will cure humanity of its heedlessness and free it from the prison of self and passion, imitation and vain imagination:

> I will give you as a covenant for the people, a light for the nations, to open the eyes that are blind, to bring out the prisoners from the dungeon, from the prison those who sit in darkness. I am the Lord; that is my name; my glory I give to no other, nor my praise to carved idols. (Is. 42:6–8)

The invitation is extended to all mankind:

> Bring out the people who are blind, yet have eyes, who are deaf, yet have ears!
>   All the nations gather together, and the peoples assemble. (Is. 43:6–9)

He will introduce a 'sweet wine', abundant milk, and a new fountain of the water of life; in other words, He will reveal new truths.

> So you shall know that I am the Lord your God, who dwells in Zion, my holy mountain... And in that day the mountains shall drip sweet wine, and the hills shall flow with milk, and all the streambeds of Judah shall flow with water; and a fountain shall come forth from the house of the Lord... (Joel 3:17–18)

God will remove spiritual difficulties and guide the children of Israel and humanity back to the light:

> And I will lead the blind in a way that they do not know, in paths that they have not known I will guide them. I will turn the darkness before them into light, the rough places into level ground. These are the things I do, and I do not forsake them. (Is. 42:16)

God will introduce a 'new name', a 'better name', 'an everlasting name', and 'another name':

> I will give in my house and within my walls a monument and a name better than sons and daughters; I will give them an everlasting name that shall not be cut off. (Is. 56:5)

> The nations shall see your righteousness, and all the kings your glory, and you shall be called by a new name that the mouth of the Lord will give. (Is. 62:2)

> ... his servants he will call by another name... (Is. 65:15)

The people are enjoined to sing 'a new song':

> Sing to the Lord a new song, his praise from the end of the earth ... let the habitants of Sela sing for joy, let them shout from the top of the mountains. Let them give glory to the Lord... (Is. 42:10–12)

The advent of 'the Lord's chosen Servant' (Is. 42:1) will be an occasion for rejoicing and singing (Is. 65:13–14). Rev. Albert Barnes comments:

> **Sing unto the Lord a new song** – ... Here the prophet calls upon all people to celebrate the divine mercy in a song of praise in view of

his goodness in providing a Redeemer. The sentiment is, that God's goodness in providing a Saviour demands the thanksgiving of all the world.

A new song – A song hitherto unsung; one that shall be expressive of the goodness of God in this new manifestation of his mercy. None of the hymns of praise that had been employed to express his former acts of goodness would appropriately express this. The mercy was so great that it demanded a song expressly made for the occasion.

And his praise from the end of the earth – From all parts of the earth. Let the most distant nations who are to be interested in this great and glorious plan, join in this celebration.[2]

God will reveal the meaning of divine mysteries:

> He uncovers the deeps out of darkness and brings deep darkness to light.[3] (Job 12:22)

> Blessed be the name of God forever and ever, to whom belong wisdom and might. He changes times and seasons; he removes kings and sets up kings; he gives wisdom to the wise and knowledge to those who have understanding; he reveals deep and hidden things; he knows what is in the darkness and the light dwells with him (Dan. 2:20–22)

> Call to me and I will answer you, and will tell you great and hidden things that you have not known. (Jer. 33:3)

Kings, rulers and nations will receive new teachings; a sprinkling of the water of life will purify them and endow them with new perceptions and considerations:

> Behold, my servant shall act wisely; he shall be high and lifted up, and shall be exalted . . . so shall he sprinkle many nations. Kings shall shut their mouths because of him,[4] for that which has not been told them they see, and that which they have not heard they understand. (Is. 52:13, 15)

The New Testament also promises the advent of new revelations

The Second Coming will be another opportunity for rebirth and renewal. Christians should be prepared to forgo their former way of life and 'be born again' (John 3:3). The demise of the old is predicted, and there will be an advent of the times of refreshing and restitution (restoration) of all things. The old heaven and the old earth will pass away and will be replaced by a new heaven, a new earth and a New Jerusalem (Rev. 21:1–2).

Given that all earlier precepts will be questioned and discarded, the Apostle Peter also anticipated that there will be both a spiritual renewal and revitalization of faith (a new heaven), new perceptions and understandings, and new social order (a new earth):

> Repent therefore, and turn back,[5] that your sins may be blotted out, that times of refreshing may come from the presence of the Lord, and that he may send the Christ appointed for you, Jesus, whom heaven must receive until the time for restoring all the things about which God spoke by the mouth of his holy prophets long ago. (Acts 3:19–21)

> Since all these things are thus to be dissolved, what sort of people ought you to be in lives of holiness and godliness, waiting for and hastening the coming of the day of God, because of which the heavens will be set on fire and dissolved, and the heavenly bodies will melt as they burn! But according to his promise we are waiting for new heavens and a new earth in which righteousness dwells. (II Pet. 3:11–13)

Christians will be able to avoid the spiritual suffering and death complicating the First Coming precisely because 'the former things have passed away' (Rev. 21:4) – a time when God will renew all things (Rev. 21:5). It is to be hoped that they will successfully transition to the Second Coming and embrace the 'new'. True (sincere) seekers will be introduced to a (new) source of the water of life:

> I will give unto him that is athirst of the fountain of the water of life freely. (Rev. 21:6)

Both the First and Second Coming require individuals to abandon their 'old self', to become a new creation, and to not look back:

> Jesus said to him, 'No one who puts his hand to the plow and looks back is fit for the kingdom of God.' (Luke 9:62)

> Therefore, if anyone is in Christ, he is a new creation. The old has passed away; behold, the new has come. (II Cor. 5:17)

> ... to put off your old self, which belongs to your former manner of life and is corrupt through deceitful desires, and to be renewed in the spirit of your minds, and to put on the new self, created after the likeness of God in true righteousness and holiness. (Eph. 4:22–24)

> But one thing I do [focus on]: forgetting what lies behind [the past] and straining [looking] forward to what lies ahead ... (Philip. 3:13)

Like the Hebrew Bible, the New Testament announces that God will introduce a new name, new teachings and manifest what had hitherto been concealed:

> For nothing is hidden except to be made manifest; nor is anything secret except to come to light.[6] (Mark 4:22)

The bestowal of a new name implies that the anticipated revelation will entail both a profound external and spiritual transformation:

> He who has an ear, let him hear what the Spirit says to the churches. To the one who conquers I will give some of the hidden manna and I will give him a white stone, with a new name written on the stone that no one knows except the one who receives it. (Rev. 2:17)

Bible commentators have written:

> ***Will I give to eat of the hidden manna*** – The true spiritual food; the food that nourishes the soul. The idea is, that the souls of those who 'overcame', or who gained the victory in their conflict with sin, and in the persecutions and trials of the world, would be permitted

to partake of that spiritual food which is laid up for the people of God, and by which they will be nourished forever.

A new name – The giving of new names is not uncommon in the Bible: for example, Abraham, Israel, Boanerges [name given to John and James], Peter. The new name expressed the step which had been taken into a higher, truer life, and the change of heart and the elevation of character consequent upon it.[7]

'New' implies something altogether renewed and heavenly.[8]

5

THE ADVENT OF THE WORLD REDEEMER IN THE HEBREW BIBLE (OLD TESTAMENT)

The Hebrew Bible is replete with prophecies about the coming of an Anointed King or Messiah, and a universal Redeemer. Many of these signs were fulfilled by Jesus at what is referred to by Christians as the First Coming. However, some of the expectations of the Messiah relate to the 'end time', the 'last days' and the 'latter days', and thus, to a more distant future. These are equivalent to the promises concerning the Second Coming in Christianity.

What is the role of prophecy?

We may begin by examining the role and importance of prophecies. We note that while the faith of some early Christians in Jesus as the Saviour may have been strengthened by the Hebrew biblical promises, most Jews were hindered from recognizing the truth. Similarly, while today some Christians have recognized the fulfilment of the biblical prophecies, most are unconvinced. The question therefore is, what function do these prophecies serve?

The following allegory may help. In a country known for its bleak weather, it is customary for the weatherman to predict more wintry weather. Now if the weatherman predicts that the next day the sun will shine brightly, it is likely that his declaration will be received with incredulity and jeers, and that he will be pronounced delusional. However, if against all expectations, on the following day there is glorious sunlight, what will people say then? Some may treat the prediction as a hoax, unworthy of further investigation. Others will miss the bright day entirely as they remain in their darkened houses with the curtains drawn. But no one witnessing the sunshine will conclude that the sun is shining because the weatherman predicted its appearance. The sun will be evident by its light and heat. What just might happen is that at least some individuals will be led to consider the prophetic insights of the weatherman, and listen to whatever else he has to say. Similarly, although there are ample forecasts of gloom in the Bible, there are also, like the predictions of the weatherman, anouncements by the Prophets that the wintry nights will be followed by an epecially glorious bright day (Is. 4:2; 30:26). The fulfilment of their prophecies gives credance to all that they have said, and interlinks all of the days of God.

Similarly, Christ and Bahá'u'lláh do not depend on the prophecies of the Bible for validation of their missions. The light and truth of their revelations are manifest by the fruit and transformative power of their Words. The fulfilment of the prophecies demonstrates the interdependence of the dispensations, and the continuity of divine purpose.

Prophecies also provide an opportunity to gain new spiritual insights

The new revelation explains the true and hidden meaning of some of the prophecies, which are often expressed metaphorically. For instance, we come to appreciate that John the Baptist was the return of the power and spirit of Elijah (Luke 1:17); that is, the return of the reality, not the body, of Elijah. Again, the explanations of terms such as heaven and earth, coming in clouds, the darkening of the sun and the moon, the fall of stars, and earthquakes, are part of the 'all truth' promised by Christ to his disciples (John 16:13).

For the prophecies to be of value requires that the scripture not be interpreted too literally (II Cor. 3:6). It should not be asserted dogmatically that a particular prophecy applies exclusively to one historical event. We must also be mindful that the prophecies were not revealed by man, but by Messengers sent by God (II Peter 1:20–21), and that it is they who provide us with the most reliable interpretations of earlier scriptures.

The advent of the Manifestation of God: Some references from the Hebrew Bible

The coming of God the Lord

Among the many references to the coming of the Lord are the following:

> The Mighty One, God the Lord, speaks and summons the earth from the rising of the sun to its setting. Out of Zion, the perfection of beauty, God shines forth. Our God comes; he does not keep silence (Ps. 50:1–2)

Also: 'My God will hear me'; 'He will bring me out to the light'; 'He will tend his flock like a shepherd' (Is. 40:10–11); He will humble 'the haughtiness of man' and bring low 'the lofty pride of men', and 'the Lord alone will be exalted in that day. And the idols shall utterly pass away.' (Is. 2:17–18).

> ... on this mountain He will destroy the covering that is (cast) over all peoples, And the veil (of death) that is woven and spread over all the nations. He will swallow up death (and abolish it) for all time. And the Lord God will wipe away tears from all faces, And He will take away the disgrace of His people from all the earth; for the Lord has spoken. It will be said in that day, 'Indeed, this is our God for whom we have waited that He would save us. This is the Lord for whom we have waited; Let us shout for joy and rejoice in His salvation.' (Amplified Bible: Is. 25:7–9)

'A Redeemer will come to Zion'; 'the Holy One of Israel'; 'the God of my salvation'; and 'The God of the whole earth'

A prayer expressed in Psalms is 'Restore us again,[1] O God of our salvation, and put away your indignation toward us!' (Ps. 85:4)

> And a Redeemer will come to Zion, to those in Jacob who turn from transgression, declares the Lord. (Is. 59:20)

God is sanctified above any coming and going – the anticipated

Redeemer is thus a Manifestation of the Lord:

> Our Redeemer – the Lord of hosts is his name – is the Holy One of Israel. (Is. 47:4)

> ... the Lord of hosts is his name; and thy Redeemer the Holy One of Israel; The God of the whole earth shall he be called. (King James Version: Is. 54:5)

> Therefore I will look unto the Lord; I will wait for the God of my salvation: my God will hear me ... I will bear the indignation of the Lord, because I have sinned against him, until he plead my cause, and execute judgment for me: he will bring me forth to the light, and I shall behold his righteousness. (King James Version: Micah 7:7, 9)

'The King of Glory' and 'the Lord of Hosts'

> Lift up your heads, O gates! And be lifted up, O ancient doors, that the King of glory may come in. Who is this King of glory? The Lord, strong and mighty, the Lord, mighty in battle! Lift up your heads, O gates! And lift them up, O ancient doors, that the King of glory may come in. Who is this King of glory? The Lord of hosts, he is the King of glory! (Ps. 24:7–10).

There are several other references to 'the Glory of God' (Ps. 19:1; 72:19; Hab. 2:14); 'the God of Glory' (Ps. 29:3); 'the Glory of the Lord' (Is. 40:5; 60:1; Ezek. 43:4); and 'the Glory of the God of Israel' ('the Kavod Elohei Yisroel'; Ezek. 43:2). 'Glory' describes the manifestation of God's presence, fame, majesty, greatness, might, and beauty as perceived by humanity. This glory had been revealed earlier at the time of Moses (Ex. 24:16–17; Num. 20:6; Deut. 5:24) but is anticipated to be revealed again (Is. 60:2). Notably, the Prophet Haggai states:

> I [God] will fill this house with glory ... The latter glory of this house shall be greater than the former, says the Lord of hosts. And in this place I will give peace, declares the Lord of hosts. (Hag. 2:7, 9)

'The Judge'

The One Who will decide between right and wrong, 'the Lord, for he comes to judge the earth':

> He comes to judge the earth.
> He will judge the world with righteousness
> and the peoples with equity. (Ps. 98:9)

> He will crush kings in the day of His wrath. He will judge the nations, heaping up the dead; He will crush the leaders far and wide. (Ps. 110:5–6; also, Is. 2:4)

> 'The Sun of Righteousness . . .will arise with healing in its wings' (Mal. 4:2)

'The Ancient of days' (Dan 7:9, 22), that is, the One Who speaks in all the Days (dispensations) of God.

'A son of man'

> . . . behold, with the clouds of heaven there came one like a son of man, and he came to the Ancient of Days and was presented before him. And to him was given dominion and glory and a kingdom, that all peoples, nations, and languages should serve him; his dominion is an everlasting dominion, which shall not pass away, and his kingdom one that shall not be destroyed (Dan. 7:13–14).

Some of these titles and expectations may be taken to refer to the Messiah or Christ, and thus to the First Coming, but others appear to apply more specifically to one who is expected to appear in the end of days:

> For to us a child is born, to us a son is given; and the government shall be upon his shoulder, and his name shall be called Wonderful Counselor, Mighty God, Everlasting Father, Prince of Peace. Of the increase of his government and of peace there will be no end, on the throne of David and over his kingdom, to establish it and to uphold

it with justice and with righteousness from this time forth and forevermore. The zeal of the Lord of hosts will do this. (Is. 9:6–7)

Jesus stated clearly that the kingdom of the Heavenly Father would be established on earth in the future, and referred to Himself as 'the Son' and not 'the Father'. Christ's relation to God was that of the 'Son' to the 'Father'. His primary mission was the salvation of the individual and to proclaim the advent of the kingdom of God. He denied any intention of establishing an earthly sovereignty, as is evident from His response to the question as to which authority the Jews should pay their taxes:

'Is it lawful for us to give tribute to Caesar, or not?' But he perceived their craftiness, and said to them, 'Show me a denarius. Whose likeness and inscription does it have?' They said, 'Caesar's.' He said to them, 'Then render to Caesar the things that are Caesar's, and to God the things that are God's.' (Luke 20:22–25)

As for the title 'Prince of Peace', Jesus stated: 'Do not think that I have come to bring peace to the earth. I have not come to bring peace, but a sword' (Matt. 10:34).

Other such examples include: 'The Desire of all nations' (King James Version: Hag. 2:7): Jesus stated: 'I was sent only to the lost sheep of the house of Israel' (Matt. 15:24); 'I will set over them one shepherd' (Ezek. 34:23): Christ explained that there were sheep that were not of His fold, which God intended to gather so that there would be one flock and one shepherd (John 10:16); and the Lord's 'Servant' who will proclaim justice to the nations (Matt. 12: 18 quoting Is. 42:1–4).

A king and a descendant of King David; 'the righteous Branch'

Behold, the days are coming, declares the Lord, when I will raise up for David a righteous Branch, and he shall reign as king and deal wisely, and shall execute justice and righteousness in the land. In his days Judah will be saved, and Israel will dwell securely. And this is the name by which he will be called: The Lord is our righteousness. (Jer. 23:5–6)

Behold, the days are coming, declares the Lord, when I will fulfill the promise I made to the house of Israel and the house of Judah. In those days and at that time I will cause a righteous Branch to spring up for David, and he shall execute justice and righteousness in the land. (Jer. 33:14–15)

Isaiah refers to 'a shoot from the stump of Jesse,[2] and that 'a Branch from his roots shall bear fruit' (Is. 11:1–5). The image here is of a tree that has been so destroyed that only a stump remains. The expected person would be from the Davidic line (Jesse was the father of King David). He will usher in peace but also, like the conquering David, be a ruler who will render just and righteous decisions.

The Messiah

The word 'Messiah' is derived from the Hebrew *mashah* (to anoint) and, in the Bible, refers to anyone who has been anointed and has a divine commission, such as a king or priest. There are several individuals who were thus anointed in the Bible, including Aaron the High Priest, King Saul and King David. The Persian King Cyrus was also considered to be an anointed shepherd because he acted as God's instrument by allowing the Israelites to return from their exile in Babylonia (Is. 44:23–24; 45:1). 'The Anointed' also refers to God's Prophets (Is. 61:1). Christ, which is a Greek name meaning 'the Anointed One' or Messiah, represented the return of the righteous King David. Thus Messiah is rightly a title of Jesus, but also of the universal Redeemer expected at the end of time.

A man of sorrows

He was despised and rejected by men, a man of sorrows and acquainted with grief; and as one from whom men hide their faces he was despised, and we esteemed him not. Surely he has borne our griefs and carried our sorrows; yet we esteemed him stricken, smitten by God, and afflicted. But he was pierced for our transgressions; he was crushed for our iniquities; upon him was the chastisement that brought us peace, and with his wounds we are healed . . . and the Lord has laid on him the iniquity of us all. He was oppressed, and he was afflicted, yet he opened not his mouth; like a lamb that is led to the slaughter, and like a sheep that before its shearers is silent, so he opened not his mouth. By oppression and judgment he was taken away; and as for his generation, who considered that he was cut off out of the land of the living, stricken for the transgression of my people? (Is. 53:3–8)

Some signs of that day

Peace will extend even to ferocious wild animals (savage aggressive nations)

Through the transformative influence of His universal revelation, warring nations will learn to coexist in the Messianic Age. Intolerance, animosity and war will cease (Micah 4:2–3). Hostile nations will learn to forgo their predatory instincts:

> The wolf shall dwell with the lamb, and the leopard shall lie down with the young goat, and the calf and the lion and the fattened calf together; and a little child shall lead them. The cow and the bear shall graze; their young shall lie down together; and the lion shall eat straw like the ox. The nursing child shall play over the hole of the cobra, and the weaned child shall put his hand on the adder's den. They shall not hurt or destroy in all my holy mountain; for the earth shall be full of the knowledge of the Lord as the waters cover the sea. (Is. 11:6–9) [3]

The Messiah will exemplify humility, and triumph through teaching peace

The Prophet Zechariah states that, instead of mounting a horse, the Messiah will ride a lowly animal such as an ass or a colt; riding a horse would have signified earthly pomp and majesty. By so doing, He portrays humility and peaceful intentions:

> Rejoice greatly . . . Behold, your king is coming to you; righteous and having salvation is he, humble and mounted on a donkey, on a colt, the foal of a donkey . . . and he shall speak peace to the nations . . . (Zech. 9:9–10)

Mark 11:1–10, Luke 19:28–35, and John 12:14–15 describe the disciples obtaining a colt or a young donkey for Jesus's triumphal journey to Jerusalem (a distance of about 19 miles) during His final week. Matthew, perhaps misunderstanding the double Jewish symbolism of the humility of the Messiah, has Jesus riding on both an ass and a colt to Jerusalem (Matt. 21:1–11), presumably not at the same time![4]

The Messiah will at the same time rule with a rod of iron

> The Lord said to me, 'You are my Son; today I have begotten you. Ask of me and I will make the nations your heritage, and the ends of the earth your possession. You shall break them with a rod of iron and dash them in pieces like a potter's vessel.' Now therefore, O kings, be wise; be warned, O rulers of the earth. Serve the Lord with fear, and rejoice with trembling. (Ps. 2:7–11)

This prophecy was not fulfilled literally in Jesus's time. The Book of Revelation defers it to 'the end' or the Second Coming:

> ... hold fast what you have until I come. The one who conquers and who keeps my works until the end, to him I will give authority over the nations, and he [Greek, 'shepherd'] will rule them with a rod of iron, as when earthen pots are broken in pieces, even as I myself have received authority from my Father. (Rev. 2:25–27)

The words 'rod' and 'staff' are largely interchangeable. A staff is used by shepherds to guide the sheep. It was therefore figurative of divine care, guidance and correction.[5] It is with reference to this spiritual guidance that David, previously a shepherd by profession, states: 'your rod and your staff, they comfort me' (Ps. 23:4). Rev. Albert Barnes comments:

> ***And he shall rule them with a rod of iron.*** ... To rule with a scepter of iron, is not to rule with a harsh and tyrannical sway, but with power that is firm and invincible. It denotes a government of strength, or one that cannot be successfully opposed; one in which the subjects are effectually subdued.
> ***As the vessels of a potter shall they be broken to shivers –*** ...
> The image here is that of the vessel of a potter – a fragile vessel of

THE ADVENT OF THE WORLD REDEEMER IN THE HEBREW BIBLE

clay – struck with a rod of iron and broken into fragments. That is, as applied to the nations, there would be no power to oppose His rule; the enemies of his government would be destroyed. Instead of remaining firm and compacted together, they would be broken like the clay vessel of a potter when struck with a rod of iron. The speaker does not intimate when this would be; but all that is said here would be applicable to that time when the Son of God will come to judge the world, and when His saints will be associated with him in his triumphs.[6]

An immortal Messiah whose reign will be forever

This belief was probably based on the biblical statements that the Redeemer will be 'a priest forever' (Ps. 110:4), and that 'the God of heaven will set up a kingdom that shall never be destroyed' (Dan. 2:44). It may explain the question that a crowd asked Jesus about the immortality of the Messiah when He alluded to His death:

> '. . . And I, when I am lifted up from the earth, will draw all people to myself.' He said this to show by what kind of death he was going to die. So the crowd answered him, 'We have heard from the Law that the Christ remains forever. How can you say that the Son of Man must be lifted up? Who is this Son of Man?' (John 12:32–34)

Christ's immortality clearly did not refer to His body but to His everlasting Spirit and the permanence of His spiritual teachings.

Designations and signs of 'that Day', the 'latter days', and the 'end time' in the Hebrew Bible

'That Day' is variously referred to as the 'day of the Lord' (Jer. 46:10; Zech. 12:8; Ezek. 303) or 'the great and awesome day of the Lord' (Mal. 4:5). The Prophet Jeremiah announced: 'Alas! That day is so great there is none like it . . .' (Jer. 30:7)

The day of divine visitation, and a day of distress and anguish, gloom, and darkness

And what will ye do in the day of visitation, and in the desolation which shall come from far? To whom will ye flee for help? And where will ye leave your glory? (King James Version: Is. 10:3)

Wail, for the day of the Lord is near; as destruction from the Almighty it will come! . . . Behold, the day of the Lord comes, cruel, with wrath and fierce anger, to make the land a desolation and to destroy its sinners from it. Behold, the day of the Lord comes, cruel, with wrath and fierce anger, to make the land a desolation and to destroy its sinners from it. For the stars of the heavens and their constellations will not give their light; the sun will be dark at its rising, and the moon will not shed its light. (Is. 13:6, 9–10; see also Zeph. 1:7, 14–15, 17).

The day of justice but also of divine mercy

Therefore the Lord waits to be gracious to you, and therefore he exalts himself to show mercy to you. For the Lord is a God of justice; blessed are all those who wait for him. (Is. 30:18)

The day when the high and mighty will be punished and humbled; the day when the idols of men will be destroyed

Enter into the rock and hide in the dust from before the terror of the Lord, and from the splendour of his majesty. The haughty looks of man shall be brought low, and the lofty pride of men shall be humbled, and the Lord alone will be exalted in that day. For the Lord of hosts has a day against all that is proud and lofty, against all that is lifted up – and it shall be brought low; And the haughtiness of man shall be humbled, and the lofty pride of men shall be brought low . . . the Lord alone will be exalted in that day. And the idols shall utterly pass away. (Is. 2:10–12, 17–18)

I will punish the world for its evil, and the wicked for their iniquity; I will put an end to the pomp of the arrogant, and lay low the pompous pride of the ruthless. (Is. 13:11)

> In the wilderness prepare the way of the Lord; make straight in the desert a highway for our God. Every valley shall be lifted up, and every mountain and hill be made low; the uneven ground shall become level,[7] and the rough places a plain. (Is. 40:3–4)

There will be social and spiritual reversals and upheavals: prominent individuals, institutions, and seemingly unassailable cherished beliefs and rituals (mountains and hills) will be laid low (disgraced) but lowly and humble individuals (valleys) will be lifted up (exalted).

The dispersion of the Jews (at the First Coming), and their ingathering and return from many countries to the Holy Land (at the Second Coming)[8]

Several Prophets of the Hebrew Bible had anticipated that at a future time the Messiah would bring about the political and spiritual redemption of Israel by returning the Jews to their homeland:

> In that day the remnant of Israel and the survivors of the house of Jacob will no more lean on him who struck them, but will lean on the Lord, the Holy One of Israel, in truth. A remnant will return, the remnant of Jacob, to the mighty God. For though your people Israel be as the sand of the sea, only a remnant of them will return. Destruction is decreed, overflowing with righteousness. (Is. 10:20–22)

> In that day the Lord will extend his hand yet a second time to recover the remnant that remains of his people, from Assyria, from Egypt, from Pathros, from Cush, from Elam, from Shinar, from Hamath, and from the coastlands of the sea. He will raise a signal for the nations and will assemble the banished of Israel, and gather the dispersed of Judah from the four corners of the earth. (Is. 11:11–12)

> . . . bring my sons from afar and my daughters from the end of the earth, everyone who is called by my name, whom I created for my glory, whom I formed and made. (Is. 43:6–7)

This latter return to the Holy Land was considered by some prominent

Zionist Christians in the 1840s to be in accordance with biblical prophecy and a prerequisite for the Second Coming of Christ.[9]

It is now a fact of history that these two most remarkable events, namely, the dispersion of the Jews before and after the crucifixion of Christ, and their return to the Holy Land after about 1,800 years of living as wanderers and exiles in many countries, have come to pass.

The relevance of this return to the advent of the Messiah is underlined by the opposition by some Orthodox Jews (Haredim) to the formation of the State of Israel. They argue that only the coming of the Messiah would legitimize the process.[10] Most Haredim still do not celebrate Israel's national Independence Day, but many now support the State.

Divine teachings will proceed out of Zion and God will address all mankind from His holy mountain

> It shall come to pass in the latter days that the mountain of the house of the Lord shall be established as the highest of the mountains, and shall be lifted up above the hills; and all the nations shall flow to it, and many peoples shall come, and say: 'Come, let us go up to the mountain of the Lord, to the house of the God of Jacob, that he may teach us his ways and that we may walk in his paths.' For out of Zion shall go forth the law, and the word of the Lord from Jerusalem. (Is. 2:2–3; repeated in Micah 4:1–2)

> The wilderness and the dry land shall be glad; the desert shall rejoice and blossom like the crocus; it shall blossom abundantly and rejoice with joy and singing. The glory of Lebanon shall be given to it, the majesty of Carmel and Sharon. They shall see the glory of the Lord, the majesty of our God. (Is. 35:1–2)

> How beautiful upon the mountains are the feet of him who brings good news, who publishes peace, who brings good news of happiness, who publishes salvation, who says to Zion, 'Your God reigns.' (Is. 52:7)

THE ADVENT OF THE WORLD REDEEMER IN THE HEBREW BIBLE

The Day when God will reveal His glory to all nations (His revelation will have universal appeal)

The coming of the Messiah will not be an exclusively Jewish affair; according to the Bible it will also concern the rest of humanity. The Hebrew Bible speaks of a day and a revelation when the Lord will teach many nations, both Jews and Gentiles (Micah 4:1–3). People from diverse ethnic backgrounds, and, presumably, followers of all religions, will be united in belief in one God and one common faith:

> And the Lord will be king over all the earth. On that day the Lord will be one and his name one. (Zech. 14:9)

> ... all the earth shall be filled with the glory of the Lord ... (Num. 14:21)

> And the glory of the Lord shall be revealed, and all flesh shall see it together, for the mouth of the Lord has spoken. (Is. 40:5)

> ... so shall he sprinkle many nations. Kings shall shut their mouths because of him, for that which has not been told them they see, and that which they have not heard they understand. (Is. 52:15)

> Arise, shine, for your light has come, and the glory of the Lord has risen upon you. For behold, darkness shall cover the earth, and thick darkness the peoples; but the Lord will arise upon you, and his glory will be seen upon you. And nations shall come to your light, and kings to the brightness of your rising. (Is. 60:1–3)

> The nations shall see your righteousness, and all the kings your glory ... (Is. 62:2–4)

> Sing and rejoice, O daughter of Zion, for behold, I come and I will dwell in your midst, declares the Lord. And many nations shall join themselves to the Lord in that day, and shall be my people. And I will dwell in your midst, and you shall know that the Lord of hosts has sent me to you ... Be silent, all flesh, before the Lord, for he has roused himself from his holy dwelling. (Zech. 2:10–11, 13)

> ... for the earth will be filled with the knowledge of the glory of the Lord as the waters cover the sea (Is. 11:9, also Hab. 2:14)

The age will be characterized by increased knowledge and mobility:

> But you, Daniel, shut up the words and seal the book, until the time of the end. Many shall run to and fro, and knowledge shall increase. (Dan. 12:4)

'To and fro' denotes 'from one place to another' and the prophecy may be considered a prediction of the phenomenal rise in global travel. The increase in knowledge may be a reference not only to the sudden staggering advances in human knowledge and travel but also an allusion to the removal of physical and spiritual barriers that exist between the diverse sections of humanity.

A time when the divine light will be unclear

Humanity in that day will be besieged by perplexing problems for which it will not have solutions:

> On that day there shall be no light, cold, or frost. And there shall be a unique day, which is known to the Lord, neither day nor night, but at evening time there shall be light. (Zech. 14:6–7)

It is described as a 'day of wrath' (Is. 13:9), of spiritual darkness, when only the enlightened will understand the significance of the dire world events and the timeliness of the promised divine interventions (Dan. 12:10):

> ... for the day of the Lord is coming; it is near, a day of darkness and gloom, a day of clouds and thick darkness! Like blackness there is spread upon the mountains ... their like has never been before, nor will be again after them through the years of all generations ... For the day of the Lord is great and very awesome; who can endure it? (Joel 2:1–2, 11)

The sun, the moon and the stars shall darken

> For the stars of the heavens and their constellations will not give their light; the sun will be dark at its rising, and the moon will not shed its light. (Is. 13:10)

Paradoxically, the Day of the Lord will simultaneously be especially brilliant (Is. 30:26). The darkening of the stars is in part due to the fact that they are undetectable when the sun is shining brilliantly: 'before the sun and the light and the moon and the stars are darkened' (Eccles 12:2).

The stars shall fall

> All the stars in the sky will be dissolved and the heavens rolled up like a scroll; all the starry host will fall like withered leaves from the vine, like shriveled figs from the fig tree. (New International Version: Is. 34:4)

The earth will be shaken and the heavens shall tremble and vanish

> Therefore I will make the heavens tremble, and the earth will be shaken out of its place . . . (Is. 13:13)

> Lift up your eyes to the heavens, and look at the earth beneath; for the heavens vanish like smoke, the earth will wear out like a garment, and they who dwell in it will die in like manner; but my salvation will be forever, and my righteousness will never be dismayed. (Is. 51:6)

A time for spiritual resurrection and reawakening

The Hebrew Bible promises a spiritual resurrection:

> Thus says the Lord God: Behold, I will open your graves and raise you from your graves, O my people. And I will bring you into the land of Israel. And you shall know that I am the Lord, when I open

your graves, and raise you from your graves, O my people. And I will put my Spirit within you, and you shall live, and I will place you in your own land. Then you shall know that I am the Lord (Ezek. 37:12–14)

And many of those who sleep in the dust of the earth shall awake, some to everlasting life, and some to shame and everlasting contempt. (Dan. 12:2)

Some Jewish scholars have considered sleep as a state akin to death, when the soul leaves the body but returns refreshed. Similarly, it is the destiny of the Jews to regain their souls after a period of spiritual death:

When one lends new things to a person of flesh and blood, he [the borrower] returns them worn and torn; but the Holy One, blessed be He, is given them worn and torn and returns them new. Know that the laborer works all day, and his soul is tired and worn, and when he sleeps he returns his soul to the Holy One, blessed be He, and it is deposited with Him, and in the morning it returns to his body as a new creation, as it is written: New every morning, abundant is your faith (Lam 3:23). We believe and acknowledge that You return our souls at the [time of the] resurrection of the dead.[11]

However, as predicted, many will resist being roused up from their death-like slumber:

But a man dies and is laid low; he breathes his last and is no more . . . so he lies down and does not rise; till the heavens are no more, people will not awake or be roused from their sleep. (Job 14:10, 12)

6

THE 'GOOD NEWS' OF THE GOSPELS AND THE SIGNS OF THE TIMES IN THE NEW TESTAMENT

A central theme of the New Testament is the glad tidings of the advent of the Kingdom of God – a day of divine visitation which 'will come upon all who dwell on the face of the whole earth' (Luke 21:35).

An urgent and immediate day

Although some professing Christians, perhaps subconsciously, have pushed the message of Christ's coming to a distant future, the New Testament strongly emphasizes the urgent nature of the event. In this regard, it is notable that the early Christians often greeted each other or ended their conversations with reference to the Coming of the Lord. Instead of the Jewish greeting *shalom* or 'peace', they would refer to the blessed event by saying *Maranatha* which is Aramaic or Syriac for 'our Lord cometh' or 'O Lord come!' (I Cor. 16:22):

> Yet a little while, and the coming one[1] will come and will not delay . . . (Heb. 10:37)

> I am coming soon. Hold fast what you have, so that no one may seize your crown. (Rev. 3:11)

> And behold, I am coming soon. Blessed is the one who keeps the words of the prophecy of this book . . . Behold, I am coming soon, bringing my recompense with me, to repay each one for what he has done . . .' He who testifies to these things says, 'Surely I am coming soon.' Amen. Come, Lord Jesus! (Rev. 22:7, 12, 20)

Christians must accordingly sanctify and prepare themselves for the momentous event:

> Now may the God of peace himself sanctify you completely, and may your whole spirit and soul and body be kept blameless at the coming of our Lord Jesus Christ. (I Thess. 5:23)

The critical need for spiritual receptivity is underlined by the fact that although Christ provided many signs associated with His return He also warned that His revelation did not contain the precise knowledge of the manner in which it would unfold:

> But concerning that day or that hour, no one knows, not even the angels in heaven, nor the Son, but only the Father. Be on guard, keep awake. For you do not know when the time will come. It is like a man going on a journey, when he leaves home and puts his servants in charge, each with his work, and commands the doorkeeper to stay awake. Therefore stay awake – for you do not know when the master of the house will come, in the evening, or at midnight, or when the rooster crows, or in the morning – lest he come suddenly and find you asleep. And what I say to you I say to all: Stay awake. (Mark 13:32–37; also, Matt. 24:36; Dan. 12:8–10)

The meaning of the prophecies will become apparent only after the event has already taken place[2] – when the thief has come and departed.

The destruction of the heavens and earth

Some of the concepts and social principles of earlier religions are predicted to vanish, an event that would escape the attention of most individuals:

> But the day of the Lord will come like a thief, and then the heavens will pass away with a roar, and the heavenly bodies will be burned up and dissolved, and the earth and the works that are done on it will be exposed. Since all these things are thus to be dissolved, what sort of people ought you to be in lives of holiness and godliness, waiting for and hastening the coming of the day of God, because of

which the heavens will be set on fire and dissolved, and the heavenly bodies will melt as they burn! But according to his promise we are waiting for new heavens and a new earth in which righteousness dwells. (II Pet. 3:10–13)

The advent of God the Father

Christ drew a sharp distinction between His own Dispensation, the Dispensation of the 'Son', and the anticipated greater event associated with the Heavenly Father, 'the master of the house' (Mark 13:32). The Lord's Prayer, which Christians have read every Sunday for almost two thousand years, supplicates the Heavenly Father to hasten that Day:

> May your Kingdom come soon. May your will be done on earth, as it is in heaven. (New Living Translation: Matt. 6:10).

God will make His home among men

> And I heard a loud voice from the throne saying, 'Behold, the dwelling place[3] of God is with man. He will dwell with them, and they will be his people, and God himself will be with them as their God.' (Rev. 21:3)

The Lord, the righteous judge

> Henceforth there is laid up for me the crown of righteousness, which the Lord, the righteous judge, will award to me on that day, and not only to me but also to all who have loved his appearing. (II Tim. 4:8)

The Alpha and Omega, the First and the Last, and the Beginning and the End

God's new revelation will be continuous with past dispensations. It will thus encompass the pre-Christian revelations, the First Coming (*the Alpha*, the first letter of the Greek alphabet), and the Second Coming (*the Omega*, the last letter of the Greek alphabet). The Lord will satisfy the sincere yearnings of every seeker:

> 'I am the Alpha and the Omega,' says the Lord God, 'who is and who was and who is to come, the Almighty. (Rev. 1:8)

> I am the Alpha and the Omega, the beginning and the end. To the thirsty I will give from the spring of the water of life without payment . . . (Rev. 21:6; also 22:12–13)

The Chief Shepherd who will bestow an incorruptible and imperishable crown of glory

> And when the chief Shepherd appears, you will receive the unfading crown of glory.[4] (I Peter 5:4)

The Glory of God

The New Testament announces that the 'God of glory' who appeared to Abraham (Acts 7:2), and was re-manifested by Christ (John 1:14), would reappear (Rev. 15:8). The earlier sun would become eclipsed or darkened by such factors as disunity over dogma, rituals and tradition and struggles over the leadership of the Christian community. This in fact happened quite early on, as described in the New Testament (Gal. 2:11–14): a bruising dispute broke out in Antioch between the Apostle Paul and the Apostles Peter and James known as the 'incident' or 'conflict'. The controversies only grew thereafter, as the process of fragmentation accelerated.

However, the New Testament gives the glad-tidings that in the promised Day of God the eternal light of unity will illuminate the world. The source of this spiritual illumination will be the Glory of God:[5]

> And the city has no need of sun or moon to shine on it, for the glory of God gives it light . . . By its light will the nations walk, and the kings of the earth will bring their glory into it, and its gates will never be shut by day – and there will be no night there. They will bring into it the glory and the honour of the nations. But nothing unclean will ever enter it, nor anyone who does what is detestable or false . . . (Rev. 21:23–27)

THE 'GOOD NEWS' OF THE GOSPELS AND THE SIGNS OF THE TIMES

The Lord of the vineyard

In the parable of the 'wicked tenants' (Luke 20:9–16), God sends a series of His servants (Prophets) to Israel/the world (His vineyard). They are all mistreated or killed by those in charge. The Lord of the Vineyard then sends His Son (Jesus) who is killed by the husbandmen. Thereafter, He will come Himself 'and destroy those tenants and give the vineyard to others'.

The Lord of the harvest

> Then he said to his disciples, 'The harvest is plentiful, but the labourers are few; therefore pray earnestly to the Lord of the harvest to send out labourers into his harvest.' (Matt. 9:37–38)

The Parable of the Sower

Christ likened 'the word of the kingdom' to the good seed planted by the 'Sower'. Due to one of several adverse factors, some of the seeds failed to grow and to manifest their full potential. (Matt. 13:3–9. 19–30)

The Son of Man coming in clouds

> When the Son of Man comes in his glory, and all the angels with him, then he will sit on his glorious throne. Before him will be gathered all the nations ... (Matt. 25:31–32; also Matt. 26:24; Mark 14:21; Luke 7:34, 22:22)

> And then they will see the Son of Man coming in clouds with great power and glory. And then he will send out the angels and gather his elect from the four winds, from the ends of the earth to the ends of heaven. (Mark 13:26–27; also Matt. 16:27; Luke 21:27–28)

Return of the Lord and Christ

You heard me say to you, 'I am going away, and I will come to you.' If you loved me, you would have rejoiced ... (John 14:28)

... and that he may send the Christ who hath been appointed for you, even Jesus ... (Acts 3:20)

... so that you are not lacking in any gift, as you wait for the revealing of our Lord Jesus Christ. (I Cor. 1:7)

When Christ who is your life appears, then you also will appear with him in glory. (Col. 3:4)

... when the Lord Jesus is revealed from heaven with his mighty angels ... (II Thess. 1:7)

... so Christ ... will appear a second time, not to deal with sin but to save those who are eagerly waiting for him. (Heb. 9:28)

A Saviour from heaven

But our citizenship is in heaven, and from it we await a Saviour, the Lord Jesus Christ ... (Philip. 3:21)

A Prophet similar in stature to Moses[6]

Moses said, 'The Lord God will raise up for you a prophet like me from your brothers. You shall listen to him in whatever he tells you. And it shall be that every soul who does not listen to that prophet shall be destroyed from the people.' (Acts 3:22–23 quoting Deut. 18:15, 18)

The Prince

The word 'prince' denotes a leader or ruler. The term is thus applied to God Who has authority over the temporal and spiritual affairs of humanity. The expected Messiah is also referred to as the 'Prince of Peace' (Is. 9:6). Notably, Christ is also referred to as the 'Prince of life' (King James Version: Acts 3:15),[7] and 'the Prince of the kings of the earth' (King James Version: Rev. 1:5).[8]

Prophecies of the 16th Chapter of the Gospel of John

Christ warned His disciples of future persecutions and opposition from the Jewish institutions:

> I have said all these things to you to keep you from falling away. They will put you out of the synagogues. Indeed, the hour is coming when whoever kills you will think he is offering service to God. And they will do these things because they have not known the Father, nor me. But I have said these things to you, that when their hour comes you may remember that I told them to you. (John 16:1–3)

The advent of the Helper[9]

At a time when Jesus's followers were saddened by His intimation of His imminent departure, He reassured them that they would not be left alone: He promised that He would send a Helper. Evidently He did not wish for His own person to become a distraction:

> But because I have said these things to you, sorrow has filled your heart. Nevertheless, I tell you the truth: it is to your advantage that I go away, for if I do not go away, the Helper[10] will not come to you. But if I go, I will send him to you. (John 16:6–7)

Also, described as another Helper, the Holy Spirit:

> And I will ask the Father, and he will give you another Helper [*allon Paraklēton*] to be with you forever, even the Spirit of truth, whom the world cannot receive, because it neither sees him nor knows him. You know him, for he dwells with you and will be in you . . . These things I have spoken to you while I am still with you. But the Helper, the Holy Spirit, whom the Father will send in my name, he will teach you all things and bring to your remembrance all that I have said to you. (John 14:16–17; 25–26)

This reference to another Helper cannot be explained simply by the disciples' spiritual experiences of the Holy Spirit following the crucifixion when they realized that the spirit of Christ was alive and was present with them.

The Spirit of truth who will glorify Christ and reveal all truth

Addressing His disciples, Jesus stated that He had been able to reveal only part of the truth – He had much more to say but they, His followers, did not have the capacity to comprehend the greater revelation. However, Jesus reassured them that in due time the Spirit of truth would divulge 'all truth', and provide a fuller understanding:

> I still have many things to say to you, but you cannot bear them now. When the Spirit of truth comes, he will guide you into all the truth, for he will not speak on his own authority, but whatever he hears he will speak, and he will declare to you the things that are to come. He will glorify me, for he will take what is mine and declare it to you . . . therefore I said that he will take what is mine and declare it to you. (John 16:12–15)

The word 'All' is a prefix usually reserved for God: for instance, He is the 'Almighty' (Job 33:4; Rev. 16:7), Who knows 'all hearts' (New Living Translation: Rom. 8:27); and the 'all in all' (I Cor. 15:28; and Eph. 4:6). The phrase used for the Spirit of truth in the original Greek is τὸ Πνεῦμα τῆς ἀληθείας, *to Pneuma tēs alētheias*. 'Pneuma' translates as 'air' or 'breath' and has no gender. However, the 'One who is coming' is specified as a male and is referred to multiple times as He or Him (John 16:13). Moreover, this person will convict (reprove) the world of sin' (John 16:8); he will be 'sent' (John 16:7); he hears and speaks (John 16:13) – again, making it abundantly clear that it will be a physical reality, and distinct from the Holy Ghost that appeared to the disciples at Pentecost and inspired them but did not reveal any additional truth.

In revealing 'all truth' and reminding Christians of Christ's teachings (John 14:26), the Spirit of truth would take what Jesus had revealed and adapt it to the exigencies of the Second Coming. He would correct in the process all accumulated falsities.

Given their belief that Christ's revelation was the final and complete Word of God, certain commentators have had difficulty explaining the above verses. Some have tried to interpret them purely in the context of the First Coming, implying that the same followers who had been told by Jesus that what the Spirit of truth would bring in the future was beyond their understanding, would shortly be able to grasp everything:

> ***But ye cannot bear them now*** – But the weakness of your understanding, your desire and expectation of my erecting a temporal kingdom, your prejudices in favour of your own nation and law, and your aversion to the Gentiles, are so great, that you cannot yet bear the discovery. For which reason I judge it more prudent to be silent for the present. The things which our Lord had in view probably concerned his passion, death, resurrection, and the consequences of it; the abrogation of the ceremonial law, the abolition of the whole Jewish economy, the doctrine of justification by faith without the deeds of the law, the rejection of the Jews, and the reception of believing Gentiles, without subjecting them to the law of Moses.[11]
>
> ***I have yet many things to say*** – There were many things pertaining to the work of the Spirit and the establishment of religion which might be said. Jesus had given them the outline; he had presented to them the great doctrines of the system, but he had not gone into details. These were things which they could not then bear. They were still full of Jewish prejudices, and were not prepared for a full development of his plans. He probably refers here to the great change which were to take place in the Jewish system – the abolition of sacrifices and the priesthood, the change of the Sabbath, the rejection of the Jewish nation, etc. For these doctrines they were not prepared, but they would in due time be taught them by the Holy Spirit.[12]

One may additionally wonder, if 'all truth' was revealed to the disciples soon after the crucifixion of Christ, why so many differences of opinion have arisen on almost every aspect of Christ's teachings. The Bahá'í teachings explain that the Spirit of truth is a direct reference to the revelation of a universal faith which will address the unresolved issues of Christianity and the rest of humanity.[13] In this context, the Bahá'í Writings contain numerous truths that were not part of Judaism or Christianity (see Chapter 14). Bahá'u'lláh has elucidated those allegorical and abstruse passages of the scriptures which have bred these age-long misunderstandings, doubts and animosities.[14]

In addition, John (16:13) prophesies that the Spirit of truth would 'declare things that are to come'. For some of the predictions made by Bahá'u'lláh that have since been realized, see Chapter 12. The Spirit of truth would also declare the intent of what Christ had revealed (John 16:14). Many of the Bahá'í Writings[15] explore and explain themes from the New Testament.

He will glorify me (John 16:14)

As noted earlier, the Bahá'í Writings frequently eulogize Christ. For example:

> Jesus Christ . . . was content to suffer. His abasement was His glorification; His crown of thorns, a heavenly diadem. When they pressed it upon His blessed head and spat in His beautiful face, they laid the foundation of His everlasting Kingdom. He still reigns, while they and their names have become lost and unknown. He is eternal and glorious; they are nonexistent. They sought to destroy Him, but they destroyed themselves and increased the intensity of His flame by the winds of their opposition.
>
> Through His death and teachings we have entered into His Kingdom . . .[16]

Bahá'u'lláh pays the following glowing tribute to the sacrifice of Christ and the spiritual power released by His crucifixion:

> We testify that when He came into the world, He shed the splendour of His glory upon all created things. Through Him the leper recovered from the leprosy of perversity and ignorance. Through Him, the unchaste and wayward were healed. Through His power, born of Almighty God, the eyes of the blind were opened, and the soul of the sinner sanctified.
>
> Leprosy may be interpreted as any veil that interveneth between man and the recognition of the Lord, his God. Whoso alloweth himself to be shut out from Him is indeed a leper, who shall not be remembered in the Kingdom of God, the Mighty, the All-Praised. We bear witness that through the power of the Word of God every leper was cleansed, every sickness was healed, every human infirmity

was banished. He it is Who purified the world. Blessed is the man who, with a face beaming with light, hath turned towards Him.[17]

Signs of the Second Coming according to the 24th Chapter of the Gospel of Matthew

At one stage during Christ's ministry, Jesus, attempting to wean the disciples from the trappings of Judaism, explained that the external symbols of Jewish institutional power and glory were not destined to last but to be destroyed (Matt. 24:2).

Later, on the Mount of Olives, this prompted the disciples to ask: 'Tell us, when will these things be, and what will be the sign of your coming and of the end of the age?' (Matt. 24:3). The fact that they asked this question underlines the fact that they anticipated an event that would happen long into the future.

False Christs who will come in the name of Jesus

Early on in the chapter Jesus gave a warning about false Christs:

> For many will come in my name, saying, 'I am the Christ', and they will lead many astray (Matt. 24:5).

There were several Jewish Messiah claimants during the First Coming, including Simon Bar Kokhba ('the Star'), Moses of Crete, and Yudghan ('Al-Ra'i or the Shepherd of the flock of his people). Indeed, some Jews regard Jesus as the most influential and, consequently, the most damaging of the 'false Messiahs'. Many charismatic Christian leaders have claimed to speak in the name of Jesus or to represent His return.[18] Jesus warned Christians to be alert and not be deceived by those among them who claim to be inspired by God's Word and who perform 'miracles':

> And many false prophets will arise and lead many astray . . . Then if anyone says to you, 'Look, here is the Christ!' or 'There he is!' do not believe it. For false christs and false prophets will arise and perform great signs and wonders, so as to lead astray, if possible, even the elect. (Matt. 24:11, 22–24)

Matthew Henry explained that deceivers from within the church posed the greatest danger in this respect, betraying both the trust of their followers and the Gospel message:

> Some think, the seducers here pointed to were such as had been settled teachers in the church, and had gained reputation as such, but afterward betrayed the truth they had taught, and revolted to error; and from such the danger is the greater, because least suspected. One false traitor in the garrison may do more mischief than a thousand avowed enemies without . . . The devil and his instruments may prevail far in deceiving poor souls; few find the strait gate, but many are drawn to the broad way; many will be imposed upon by their signs and wonders, and many drawn in by the hopes of deliverance from their oppressions. Note, Neither miracles nor multitudes are certain signs of a true church . . .[19]

A world beset by wars, famines, earthquakes, and epidemics

> And you will hear of wars and rumours of wars: see that you are not alarmed, for this must take place, but the end is not yet. For nation will rise against nation, and kingdom against kingdom, and there will be famines[20] and earthquakes in various places. (Matt. 24:6–7; see also Luke 21:9–10)

One hears today incessantly about 'wars and rumours of wars' (Matt. 24:6) and repetitively that 'nations have arisen against nation, and kingdom against kingdom' (Matt. 24:7). In the past two centuries, there has been a proliferation of tribal, national, and international conflicts. Humanity has witnessed an unparalleled number of conflicts, including two world wars, multiple genocides, and acts of terrorism. Religion itself has played a significant role in about a dozen international conflicts. We have had some of the worst famines and plagues, precipitated by sectarian, national and tribal animosities.[21] In addition to these calamities, Amos 8:11–12 explained that in the latter days there would also be a 'famine of hearing the words of the Lord', a prominent feature of this day.

Earthquakes may refer literally to the shaking of the earth, but they may also be taken figuratively as referring to the many upheavals resulting in the destruction of the old, and the implementation of new ideas and principles. Faith plays a part in this process. For example, the Apostle Paul stated that Jesus's 'voice shook the earth', alluding to the upheavals caused by the divine Word. He added that God will 'yet once more . . . shake not only the earth, but also the heavens' (Heb. 12:26). The Apostle Peter warned that the old heavens would be destroyed in the commotion and perish, to be replaced by 'new heavens and a new earth' (II Pet. 3:12–13; also, Rev. 21:1) when all things would be renewed, restored and refreshed (Acts 3:21; Rev. 21:4).

Birth pangs of a new era

Matt. 24:8 states: 'all these are but the beginning of the birth pains'. The Hebrew oral traditions also speak of the coming of the Messiah as a period characterized by birth pangs (*chevlei MaShi'ihch*) of a new era, ushering in a new social and spiritual civilization. The New Testament also warns of the tribulations that will precede or accompany the Second Coming (Matt. 24:10, 12; Luke 21:34–36; II Thess. 2:3; II Tim. 3:1–5) as 'the beginning of the birth pains' (Matt. 24:8). The Gospel of John (16:21) uses a similar metaphor for the solemn event but explains that the birth pains will be followed by a blissful period.

Spread of lawlessness, loss of faith and diminished genuine love

> And then many will fall away[22] and betray one another and hate one another . . . And because lawlessness will be increased,[23] the love of many will grow cold. But the one who endures to the end will be saved. (Matt. 24:10, 12)

Matthew Henry explained:

> *The abounding of iniquity*; though the world always lies in wickedness, yet there are some times in which may be said, that iniquity doth in a special manner abound; as when it is more extensive than ordinary . . .
> *The abating of love* . . . it may be understood more particularly of brotherly love. When iniquity abounds . . . this grace commonly

waxes cold. Christians begin to be shy and suspicious one of another, affections are alienated, distances are created, parties made, and so love comes to nothing . . .[24]

Another biblical scholar, Rev. Joseph Benson, stated:

> **Then shall many be offended** – That is, shall stumble and fall, or shall be turned out of the right way . . . Some will openly desert the faith, as verse 10; others corrupt it, as verse 11; and others grow indifferent about it, as verse 12.[25]

Christ rhetorically asked:

> Nevertheless, when the Son of Man comes, will he find faith on earth? (Luke 18:8)

This is a remarkable statement given all the signs that are predicted to accompany the event and that there are more than two billion Christians in the world today. It is a clear indication of the pervasiveness of the issues that will beset the Christian community, and to what extent it is expected to distance itself from the original teachings of Jesus and thus fail to recognize His return. The commentaries of Rev. Albert Barnes, and Jamieson, Fausset and Brown explain this passage similarly:

> Nevertheless . . . Though this is true that God will avenge his elect, yet will he find his elect 'faithful?' The danger is not that 'God' will be unfaithful – he will surely be true to his promises; but the danger is that his elect – his afflicted people – will be discouraged; will not persevere in prayer; will not continue to have confidence in him; and will, under heavy trials, sink into despondency. The sole meaning of this phrase, therefore, is, that 'there is more danger that his people would grow weary, than that God would be found unfaithful and fail to avenge his elect.'[26]

> Yet ere the Son of man comes to redress the wrongs of His Church, so low will the hope of relief sink, through the length of the delay, that one will be fain to ask, Will He find any faith of a coming avenger left on the earth? From this we learn: (1) That the primary and historical

reference of this parable is to the Church in its widowed, desolate, oppressed, defenseless condition during the present absence of her Lord in the heavens; (2) That in these circumstances importunate, persevering prayer for deliverance is the Church's fitting exercise; (3) That notwithstanding every encouragement to this, so long will the answer be delayed, while the need of relief continues the same, and all hope of deliverance will have nearly died out, and 'faith' of Christ's coming scarcely to be found.[27]

The Antichrist

Correcting false news circulating in Thessalonica that he had said that the Second Coming had already happened, the Apostle Paul explained that the event would take place only after the general falling away, that is, a defection or mass apostasy, a return to past evil ways, and the appearance of the 'man of sin', 'the son of perdition' or the 'lawless one' (that is, not bound by spiritual laws), identified as the Antichrist (II Thess. 2:3–4, 7–10).

Christian scholars have proposed a number of events that they believe fulfilled the foretold apostasy associated with the advent of the Antichrist, such as the persecutions by Emperor Nero; the break of the Orthodox churches from Rome; or the fall of Constantinople, the capital of Byzantium, to Muslim forces. Protestants such as Martin Luther, John Calvin, Thomas Cranmer and John Knox labelled the Popes whose lives negated Christian ideals as Antichrists – while in their turn some Catholics have interpreted the Reformation as the predicted apostasy.

> Of the Papists, a part affirm that the apostasy is the falling away from Rome in the time of the Reformation, but the greater portion suppose that the allusion is to Antichrist, who, they say, will appear in the world before the great day of judgment, to combat religion and the saints.[28]

> Of the popes, Platina (a Roman Catholic) says: 'The chair of Saint Peter was usurped, rather than possessed, by monsters of wickedness, ambition, and bribery. They left no wickedness unpracticed' ... To no succession of men who have ever lived could the appellative, the man of sin, be applied with so much propriety as to this

succession. Yet they claim to have been the true successors of the apostles, and there are Protestants who deem it of essential importance to be able to show that they have derived the true 'succession' through such men.[29]

The Antichrist refers to the evil forces which oppose the blessed teachings of Christ. For example, Christ taught His followers to be united, and to love not only each other, their friends and neighbours, but also the stranger and their enemy (Matt. 5:43–47). Sectarian animosity and hostility offend the Christ spirit and may be regarded as the manifestation of the spirit of the Antichrist.[30]

Spread of false teachings and the appearance of individuals who will blatantly ridicule faith

> But you must remember, beloved, the predictions of the apostles of our Lord Jesus Christ. They said to you, 'In the last time there will be scoffers, following their own ungodly passions.' It is these who cause divisions, worldly people, devoid of the Spirit. (Jude 1:18–19)

Apparent holiness, false asceticism, superstitions and fads will proliferate. They will hinder recognition of God's Faith, and obscure and replace true spirituality and obedience to His Will:

> Now the Spirit expressly says that in later times some will depart from the faith by devoting themselves to deceitful spirits and teachings of demons, through the insincerity of liars whose consciences are seared, who forbid marriage and require abstinence from foods that God created to be received with thanksgiving by those who believe and know the truth. For everything created by God is good, and nothing is to be rejected if it is received with thanksgiving, for it is made holy by the word of God and prayer. (I Tim. 4:1–5)

The resurrection of the spiritually alive, as well as the spiritually dead

The Second Coming of Christ is predicted to be associated with the judgement of the spiritually dead as well as those Christians who despite adversities and obstacles placed in their path had remained spiritually alive (the quick). The Gospel of Matthew (24:13) reports Jesus as saying: 'But he that shall endure unto the end, the same shall be saved.' Everyone will be accountable for his or her own response to the new revelation:

> I tell you, on the day of judgment people will give account for every careless word they speak, for by your words you will be justified, and by your words you will be condemned. (Matt. 12:36–37)

> I charge you in the presence of God and of Christ Jesus, who is to judge the living and the dead, and by his appearing and his kingdom ... (II Tim. 4:1)

> ... but they will give account to him who is ready to judge the living and the dead. (I Pet. 4:5)

The Gospel 'will be proclaimed throughout the whole world'

> This good news of the kingdom [the gospel] will be preached throughout the whole world as a testimony to all the nations, and then the end [of the age] will come. (Amplified Bible, Matt. 24:14)

The Preterits, that is, those who interpret the prophecies of Matthew as having come to pass by 70 CE, explain that 'then shall the end come' refers to the destruction of Jerusalem by the Romans. Their explanations centre on the fact that the Greek word for 'all the world', *oikoumene*, may be interpreted as 'all inhabited earth' and, at a stretch, applies solely to the confines of the Roman Empire. Rev. Joseph Benson stated that the Gospels had been widely disseminated as early as 70 CE:

> Not universally; this is not yet done; but in general, through the several parts of the world, and not only in Judea. And this was done by St. Paul and the other apostles, before Jerusalem was destroyed... The Acts of the Apostles, it must be remembered, contain only a small part of the history of the history of a small number of the apostles, and yet even in that history we see the gospel was widely disseminated, and had taken root in the most considerable parts of

the Roman Empire . . . It appears from the writers of the history of the church, that before the destruction of Jerusalem the gospel was not only preached in the Lesser Asia, Greece, and Italy, the great theatres of action then in the world; but likewise propagated as far north as Scythia; as far south as Ethiopia; as far east as Parthia and India; as far west as Spain and Britain.[31]

Rev. Albert Barnes also explained:

The evidence that this was done is to be chiefly derived from the New Testament, and there it is clear. Thus Paul declares that it was preached to every creature under heaven (Col. 1:6, 1:23); that the faith of the Romans was spoken of throughout the whole world (Rom. 1:8); that he preached in Arabia (Gal. 1:17), and at Jerusalem, and round about unto Illyricum (Rom. 15:19). We know also that He traveled through Asia Minor, Greece, and Crete; that he was in Italy, and probably in Spain and Gaul, (Rom. 15:24–28). At the same time, the other apostles were not idle; and there is full proof that within thirty years after this prophecy was spoken, churches were established in all these regions.

For a witness unto all nations. This preaching the gospel indiscriminately to 'all' the Gentiles shall be a proof to them, or a witness, that the division between the Jews and Gentiles was about to be broken down.[32]

And Charles J. Ellicott wrote:

The words must not be strained beyond the meaning which they would have for those who heard them, and they were certain to see in 'all the world' (literally, *the inhabited earth,* as in Luke 2:1; Acts 11:28) neither more nor less than the Roman empire; and it was true, as a matter of fact, that there was hardly a province of the empire in which the faith of Christ had not been preached before the destruction of Jerusalem . . .[33]

Some may still argue that not every individual or tribe has heard the 'good news'. However, following the heroic efforts to spread the Gospel in the eighteenth and nineteenth centuries, several Christian groups such as the Adventists concluded in the 1840s that this prophecy had been fulfilled:

> This appearing is again intimately connected with the preaching of the Gospel to all nations ... We have ourselves in the last half century witnessed an unparalleled wide diffusion of the Gospels among all nations, and the uttermost parts of the earth have received the Law of Christ.[34]

Since then, there has been an even greater effort by the various churches to bring the Gospel to the attention of all humanity. Evangelists have been sent to every country and there is no ethnic group that has not been approached. Although it is generally agreed that preaching the Gospel can be verbal, an estimated five to six billion copies of the Bible have been sold and it remains the most widely distributed book in the world. Again, the prophecy does not require that the New Testament be published in every language, but the Bible has been translated into many languages – for example, by 2008 the Catholic Bible had been translated into 2,454 languages.[35] A Protestant group has also declared that 'as of October 2017 the full Bible has been translated into 670 languages, the New Testament alone into 1,521 languages and Bible portions or stories into 1,121 other languages. At least some portion of the Bible has been translated into 3,312 languages.'[36] Also, multiple English translations and translations in other languages are available on the internet.

The ending of the 'abomination of desolation'

> So when you see the abomination of desolation spoken of by the prophet Daniel, standing in the holy place (let the reader understand) ... (Matt. 24:15)

Christ thus referred the reader to the Book of Daniel which describes an important sign of the Second Coming, namely, 'the abomination of desolation' signifying the end of foreign occupation of the Holy Land. From the prophecies of Daniel, the Gospel of Matthew, and the Book of Revelation, many Christian scholars worked out the date of the

Second Coming as 1843/1844 CE, which coincides with the year that the Báb, the Forerunner of Bahá'u'lláh, declared His Mission.

'Abdu'l-Bahá[37] has explained the relevance of the Islamic calendar year of 1260 AH (1844 CE) which ended the period that Jerusalem was trodden under foot:

> This is a prophecy concerning the duration of the Dispensation of Islam, when Jerusalem was trodden underfoot, meaning that it was dishonoured, while the Holy of Holies remained preserved, guarded, and honoured. This state of affairs continued until the year 1260. This 1,260 years is a prophecy concerning the advent of the Báb, the 'Gate' leading to Bahá'u'lláh, which took place in the year A.H. 1260. As the period of 1,260 years has been completed, the Holy City of Jerusalem is now beginning to prosper and flourish again. Anyone who saw Jerusalem sixty years ago, and who sees it again today, will recognize how it has come to prosper and flourish and how it has regained its honour.[38]

A light from the East illuminating the West

> For as the lightning comes from the east and shines as far as the west, so will be the coming of the Son of Man (Matt. 24:27)

The 'Son of Man' will come in an unexpected and precipitous manner, as 'lightning'. There is also an allusion to his coming from the East and his light shining in the West. It is noteworthy that two thousand years earlier, three Magi, Zoroastrian priests known as *majús*, travelled from Persia westward to Bethlehem because they had seen the sign of Christ, represented by a star, in the East (Matt. 2:1–2).

The light of the Báb and Bahá'u'lláh arose in Persia, which is to the East of where Jesus was. With lightning speed it has illuminated the West and spread to virtually all parts of the world. In this connection Bahá'u'lláh writes:

> Say: In the East the light of His Revelation hath broken; in the West have appeared the signs of His dominion. Ponder this in your hearts, O people, and be not of those who have turned a deaf ear to the admonitions of Him Who is the Almighty, the All-Praised. Let

the Breeze of God awaken you. Verily, it hath wafted over the world. Well is it with him that hath discovered the fragrance thereof and been accounted among the well-assured.[39]

Again,

> We called unto her[40] from behind the Tabernacle of Majesty and Grandeur: 'O Bethlehem! This Light hath risen in the orient, and travelled towards the occident, until it reached thee in the evening of its life. Tell Me then: Do the sons recognize the Father, and acknowledge Him, or do they deny Him, even as the people aforetime denied Him [Jesus]?'[41]

The challenge facing Christians is whether they will heed God's summons, or will Bahá'u'lláh's origins become an issue for them, as was the coming of Jesus from Nazareth and Galilee for the Jews at the First Coming?

Anticipated spiritual death

> Wherever the corpse is, there the vultures will gather. (Matt. 24:28)

Most English translations of the Bible render the Hebrew word *nesher* and its Greek equivalent ἀετός as 'vultures' but some, including, the King James Version, translate it as 'eagles'. One commentary explains:

> **Wheresoever the carcase is.** – Two interpretations of this verse may, without much risk of error, be at once rejected: – (1) That which sees in the 'eagles' the well-known symbols of the strength of the Roman legions, and in the 'carcass' the decayed and corrupted Judaism which those legions came to destroy. This, true as far as it goes, is too narrow and localised in its range for so wide and far-reaching a comparison. (2) The strange fantastic imagination of many of the Fathers that the 'carcass' is Christ Himself, as crucified and slain, and that the eagles are His true saints and servants who hasten to meet Him in His coming. Those who picture to themselves with what purpose and with what results the vultures of the East swoop down on the carrion which they scent far off upon the breeze, will surely find such

an explanation at once revolting and irrational. What the enigmatic proverb (if indeed it be enigmatic) means, is that wherever life is gone, wherever a church or nation is decaying and putrescent, there to the end of time will God's ministers of vengeance, the vultures that do their work of destruction, and so leave room for new forms of life by sweeping off that which was 'ready to vanish away'. . .[42]

Another commentator writes:

There is not a need to be too concerned about a clear-cut distinction in the use of the word in Scripture. The word ἀετός is simply a reference in some passages to birds that are gathering to feast on dead bodies, of which both vultures and (at least some) eagles are characterized to do. The fact that the Bible indicates such is occurring in those passages means that even if they fall under the classification of modern day 'eagle', they are of the type that *does* eat carrion as well, like vultures.

Probably the leaning toward 'vulture' today in translations is because in our modern classifications, that type of bird better pictures one that gathers to eat dead things, whereas many people think of a 'bird of prey' (a hunter) when they hear 'eagle'.[43]

Tribulation and signs in the heavens: the darkening of the sun and the moon and fall of stars

Immediately after the tribulation of those days the sun will be darkened, and the moon will not give its light, and the stars shall fall from heaven, and the powers of the heavens will be shaken . . . (Matt. 24:29)

With specific reference to this passage Bahá'u'lláh remarks that one of the greatest oppressions (the word 'tribulation' is translated as 'oppression' in the New Heart English Bible) is the inability of souls to investigate the truth at the dawn of every dispensation because of the actions and control of the clergy:

As to the words –'Immediately after the oppression of those days' – they refer to the time when men shall become oppressed and afflicted, the time when the lingering traces of the Sun of Truth and the fruit of the Tree of knowledge and wisdom will have vanished from the midst of men, when the reins of mankind will have fallen into the grasp of the foolish and ignorant, when the portals of divine unity and understanding – the essential and highest purpose in creation – will have been closed, when certain knowledge will have given way to idle fancy, and corruption will have usurped the station of righteousness. Such a condition as this is witnessed in this day when the reins of every community have fallen into the grasp of foolish leaders, who lead after their own whims and desire. On their tongue the mention of God hath become an empty name; in their midst His holy Word a dead letter. Such is the sway of their desires, that the lamp of conscience and reason hath been quenched in their hearts, and this although the fingers of divine power have unlocked the portals of the knowledge of God, and the light of divine knowledge and heavenly grace hath illumined and inspired the essence of all created things . . .

. . . What 'oppression' is more grievous than that a soul seeking the truth, and wishing to attain unto the knowledge of God, should know not where to go for it and from whom to seek it? For opinions have sorely differed, and the ways unto the attainment of God have multiplied. This 'oppression' is the essential feature of every Revelation. Unless it cometh to pass, the Sun of Truth will not be made manifest. For the break of the morn of divine guidance must needs follow the darkness of the night of error. . . namely that iniquity shall cover the surface of the earth and darkness shall envelop mankind.[44]

A similar prophecy in the Hebrew Bible (Joel 2:28–32), quoted by the Apostle Peter in Acts as having been fulfilled at the time of Christ, helps us to understand what is expected to occur at the Second Coming. The passage begins with a reassurance that the disciples were not intoxicated. What they were witnessing was the realization of the biblical predictions:

> But others mocking said, 'They are filled with new wine.' But Peter, standing with the eleven, lifted up his voice and addressed them: 'Men of Judea and all who dwell in Jerusalem, let this be known to

you, and give ear to my words. For these people are not drunk, as you suppose, since it is only the third hour of the day. But this is what was uttered through the prophet Joel: "And in the last days it shall be, God declares, that I will pour out my Spirit on all flesh, and your sons and your daughters shall prophesy, and your young men shall see visions, and your old men shall dream dreams; even on my male servants and female servants in those days I will pour out my Spirit, and they shall prophesy. And I will show wonders in the heavens above and signs on the earth below, blood, and fire, and vapour of smoke; the sun shall be turned to darkness and the moon to blood, before the day of the Lord comes, the great and magnificent day.'" (Acts 2:13–20)

Clearly, the disciples did not view these prophecies and their fulfilment literally.

Bahá'u'lláh explains that one of the meanings of the 'sun' is the light of the Manifestations of God such as Moses and Christ:

> . . . by the 'sun' in one sense is meant those Suns of Truth Who rise from the dayspring of ancient glory, and fill the world with a liberal effusion of grace from on high . . . Thus it is that through the rise of these Luminaries of God the world is made new, the waters of everlasting life stream forth, the billows of loving-kindness surge, the clouds of grace are gathered, and the breeze of bounty bloweth upon all created things. It is the warmth that these Luminaries of God generate, and the undying fires they kindle, which cause the light of the love of God to burn fiercely in the heart of humanity. It is through the abundant grace of these Symbols of Detachment that the Spirit of life everlasting is breathed into the bodies of the dead . . .[45]

Christ, as mentioned earlier in the chapter (Matt. 24:10, 12) warned that there would be a spiritual dimming of the horizons of faith at the Second Coming. The light of both the sun and the moon, that is, the spiritual values and the social principles which derive their light and inspiration from the moral and ethical teachings, was predicted to fail and the Christian 'moon' would be converted to 'blood'[46] (Joel 2:31 and Acts 2:20).

Elsewhere, speaking on the same theme, the Apostle Peter predicts the destruction of the heavens and earth – the efficacy of the spiritual

THE 'GOOD NEWS' OF THE GOSPELS AND THE SIGNS OF THE TIMES

and social teachings will vanish, an event that will escape the attention of most of the faithful:

> For they deliberately overlook this fact, that the heavens existed long ago, and the earth was formed out of water and through water by the word of God, and that by means of these the world that then existed was deluged with water and perished. But by the same word the heavens and earth that now exist are stored up for fire, being kept until the day of judgment and destruction of the ungodly . . . But the day of the Lord will come like a thief, and then the heavens will pass away with a roar, and the heavenly bodies will be burned up and dissolved, and the earth and the works that are done on it will be exposed. Since all these things are thus to be dissolved, what sort of people ought you to be in lives of holiness and godliness, waiting for and hastening the coming of the day of God, because of which the heavens will be set on fire and dissolved, and the heavenly bodies will melt as they burn! But according to his promise we are waiting for new heavens and a new earth in which righteousness dwells. (II Pet. 3:5–7, 10–13)

Concerning the prophecy that 'the stars shall fall from heaven' (Matt. 24: 29), a dramatic meteor shower convinced some Adventists that this sign had been fulfilled literally:

> The great star shower took place on the night of November 13, 1833. It was so bright that a newspaper could be read on the street. One writer says, 'For nearly four hours the sky was literally ablaze.' It is most fascinating, and a sign of Christ's coming.
> 'No language, indeed, can come up to the splendor of that magnificent display . . . no one who did not witness it can form an adequate conception of its glory. It seemed as if the whole starry heavens had congregated at one point near the zenith, and were simultaneously shooting forth, with the velocity of lightning, to every part of the horizon; and yet they were not exhausted – thousands swiftly followed in the tracks of thousands, as if created for the occasion.'[47]

However, the fall of the stars also has a figurative explanation. The Book of Daniel describes those who are wise as stars that guide the caravans during the night through arid deserts (Dan. 12:3). Hence, the 'stars' of the firmament of faith may refer to religious leaders who will fail to direct their followers during the period of spiritual nighttime.

Notably, Bahá'u'lláh likens the Christian ecclesiastical orders to 'fallen stars': satiated with dogmas, traditions and rituals, they prevent their followers from investigating the truth and drinking from the fountain of life. He castigates them as 'clouds' for shunning and ignoring God's revelation, and for having 'interposed themselves between their flock and Christ returned in the glory of the Father:'[48]

> These 'fallen stars' of the firmament of Christendom, these 'thick clouds' that have obscured the radiance of the true Faith of God, these princes of the Church that have failed to acknowledge the sovereignty of the 'King of kings', these deluded ministers of the Son who have shunned and ignored the promised Kingdom which the 'Everlasting Father' has brought down from heaven, and is now establishing upon earth – these are experiencing, in this 'Day of Reckoning', a crisis which is . . . widespread and significant.[49]

Another explanation is that the passage refers to the dimming of the light of the religious leaders when in the presence of the brilliant sun of the new revelation:

> It is evident and manifest unto every discerning observer that even as the light of the star fadeth before the effulgent splendour of the sun, so doth the luminary of earthly knowledge, of wisdom, and understanding vanish into nothingness when brought face to face with the resplendent glories of the Sun of Truth, the Day-star of divine enlightenment . . .[50]

Consistent with the above explanations, Rev. John Lightfoot made the following sober observation about 400 years ago:

> The sun is the religion of the Church; the moon is the government of the state; and the stars are the judges and doctors of both.[51]

In addition, John Gill (1697–1771), an English Baptist writer and theologian, wrote in his commentary of this passage:

> Shall the sun be darkened: not in a literal but in a figurative sense . . . and the stars shall fall from heaven; which phrase, as it elsewhere intends the doctors of the church, and preachers falling off from purity of doctrine and conversation; so here it designs the Jewish Rabbins and doctors, who departed from the word of God, and set up their traditions above it, fell into vain and senseless interpretations of it, and into debates about things contained in their Talmud; the foundation of which began to be laid immediately upon their dispersion into other countries and the powers of the heavens shall be shaken; meaning all the ordinances of the legal dispensation; which shaking, and even removing of them . . . Gospel ordinances . . . shall not be shaken, so as to be removed, but remain till the second coming of Christ.[52]

Rev. Albert Barnes also observed:

> The images used here are not to be taken literally. They are often employed by the sacred writers to denote 'any great calamities'. As the darkening of the sun and moon, and the falling of the stars, would be an inexpressible calamity, so any great catastrophe – any overturning of kingdoms or cities, or dethroning of kings and princes is represented by the darkening of the sun and moon, and by some terrible convulsion in the elements . . . To the description in Matthew, Luke has added, (21:25) there should be 'distress of nations, with perplexity; the sea and the waves roaring; men's hearts failing them for fear, and for looking after those things which are coming upon the earth'. All these are figures of great and terrible calamity. The roaring of the waves of the sea denotes great tumult and affliction among the people, Perplexity means doubt, anxiety; not knowing what to do to escape. Men's hearts failing them for fear, or by reason of fear. Their fears would be so great as to take away their courage and strength.[53]

The Pulpit Commentary similarly explains:

> More generally the luminaries are explained in a good sense. The sun is Christ or his truth, which shall be obscured in the last days; the moon is the Church, darkened by heresy and unbelief, and

borrowing no light from its sun; the stars are they who once were foremost in the faith, but now shall fall from their steadfastness, or be unable to diffuse light, owing to the gross darkness and mistiness of those evil days.[54]

Matthew Henry links the changes to the demise of the old and the need to restore all things:

> Now concerning Christ's second coming . . . *the sun shall be darkened, and the moon will not give her light.* The moon shines with a borrowed light, and therefore if the sun, from whom she borrows her light, is turned into darkness, she must fail of course, and become bankrupt. *The stars shall fall;* they will lose their light, and disappear, and be as if they were fallen; and the powers of heaven shall be shaken. This intimates . . . That there shall be a great change, in order to the making of all things new (Rev. 21:5). Then shall be the *restitution of all things* when the heavens . . . *shall pass away with a great noise,* that there may be *new heavens* (II Pet. 3, 10, 13).[55]

Mourning on earth, the Son of Man coming in the clouds of heaven

> Then will appear in heaven the sign of the Son of Man, and then all the tribes of the earth will mourn, and they will see the Son of Man coming on the clouds of heaven with power and great glory. (Matt. 24:30)

Matthew Henry writes:

> **He will come with power and glory:** his first coming was in weakness and great meanness [humility]; (II Cor. 13:4) but his second coming will be with power and great glory, agreeable both to the dignity of his person and to the purposes of his coming.[56]

Bahá'u'lláh elucidates:

> These words signify that in those days men will lament the loss of the Sun of the divine beauty, of the Moon of knowledge, and of

the Stars of divine wisdom. Thereupon, they will behold the countenance of the promised One, the adored Beauty, descending from heaven and riding upon the clouds. By this is meant that the divine Beauty will be made manifest from the heaven of the will of God, and will appear in the form of the human temple. The term 'heaven' denoteth loftiness and exaltation, inasmuch as it is the seat of the revelation of those Manifestations of Holiness, the Day-springs of ancient glory. These ancient Beings, though delivered from the womb of their mother, have in reality descended from the heaven of the will of God. Though they be dwelling on this earth, yet their true habitations are the retreats of glory in the realms above. Whilst walking amongst mortals, they soar in the heaven of the divine presence. Without feet they tread the path of the spirit, and without wings they rise unto the exalted heights of divine unity. With every fleeting breath they cover the immensity of space, and at every moment traverse the kingdoms of the visible and the invisible . . .[57]

Clouds of heaven: One explanation of clouds is that they provide rain – namely, the water of life. The Pentateuch describes divine instructions as rain which provides spiritual life and revivifies the earth:

> May my teaching drop as the rain, my speech distill as the dew, like gentle rain upon the tender grass, and like showers upon the herb. (Deut. 32:2)

Jeremiah lamented the fact that the children of Israel had rejected true faith and adhered to the empty shell of religious institutions:

> . . . my people have committed two evils: they have forsaken me, the fountain of living waters, and hewed out cisterns for themselves, broken cisterns that can hold no water. (Jer. 2:12–13)

Clouds also prevent the light of the sun from shining through, and in this connection refer to the false teachings, dogmas, traditions and superstitions that conceal the divine light. Hence, the Prophet Zephaniah predicts:

> The great day of the Lord is near, near and hastening fast; the sound

of the day of the Lord is bitter; the mighty man cries aloud there. A day of wrath is that day, a day of distress and anguish, a day of ruin and devastation, a day of darkness and gloom, a day of clouds and thick darkness, a day of trumpet blast and battle cry against the fortified cities and against the lofty battlements. I will bring distress on mankind, so that they shall walk like the blind . . . (Zeph. 1:14–15)

Sadly, many religious leaders have used their combined energies and resources to obscure the light of truth and to prevent their followers from seeing God's promised Kingdom.

Dispatch of angels and God's deafening trumpet blast

And he will send out his angels with a loud trumpet call, and they will gather his elect from the four winds, from one end of heaven to the other. (Matt. 24:31)

Rev. Albert Barnes explains:

Angels signify, literally, messengers, Lu. vii 24; ix. 52. The word is applied to . . . anything that God employs to rescue his people from danger (Ps. civ. 4), but it most commonly refers to the race of intelligent beings more exalted than man, who are employed often in the work of man's rescue from ruin, and aiding his salvation . . .[58]

As promised, 'the Lord himself' has descended today from heaven 'with a cry of command, with the voice of an archangel, and with the sound of the trumpet of God' (I Thess. 4:16). His revelation has sounded the trumpet – a blast of divine spirit that has breathed a new life into humanity, awoken many that slumbered, raised the spiritually dead, and transformed and gathered the elect from the heaven of every dispensation:

Once more hath the eternal Spirit breathed into the mystic trumpet, and caused the dead to speed out of their sepulchers of heedlessness and error unto the realm of guidance and grace. And yet, that expectant community still crieth out: When shall these things be? When shall the promised One, the object of our expectation, be made manifest . . .?[59]

The Gospel of Matthew indicates that, in spite of all of the signs enumerated in the chapter, exactly how or when the Second Coming will take place is known only to God:

> But concerning that day and hour no one knows, not even the angels of heaven, nor the Son, but the Father only. For as were the days of Noah, so will be the coming of the Son of Man. For as in those days before the flood they were eating and drinking, marrying and giving in marriage, until the day when Noah entered the ark, and they were unaware until the flood came and swept them all away, so will be the coming of the Son of Man. (Matt. 24:36–39; see also Luke 17:26–28, 30)

Some individuals will be unaware that the Second Coming has occurred – history would thus repeat itself. Jesus gives this admonition:

> Therefore, stay awake, for you do not know on what day your Lord is coming. But know this, that if the master of the house had known in what part of the night the thief was coming, he would have stayed awake and would not have let his house be broken into. Therefore you also must be ready, for the Son of Man is coming at an hour you do not expect. (Matt. 24: 42–44)

Insights regarding the Second Coming from the Book of Revelation

A 'new heaven' and a 'new earth', and the descent of 'a new Jerusalem'

The penultimate chapter of the Book of Revelation specifies that spiritual death and anguish will be avoided because of the demise of the 'first heaven and the first earth' and their replacement by a 'new heaven and a new earth':

> Then I saw a new heaven and a new earth, for the first heaven and the first earth had passed away, and the sea was no more. And I saw the holy city, new Jerusalem, coming down out of heaven from God, prepared as a bride adorned for her husband. And I heard a

loud voice from the throne saying, 'Behold, the dwelling place of God is with man. He will dwell with them, and they will be his people, and God himself will be with them as their God. He will wipe away every tear from their eyes, and death shall be no more, neither shall there be mourning, nor crying, nor pain anymore, for the former things have passed away.' (Rev. 21:1–4)

The Bahá'í Writings explain:

> Consider how unmistakably 'the first heaven' and 'the first earth' refer to the outward aspects of the former religion . . . That is, the earth is the arena of the last judgement, and in this arena there will be no more sea, meaning that the law and teachings of God will have spread throughout the earth, all mankind will have embraced His Cause, and the earth will have been entirely peopled by the faithful. Thus there will be no more sea, for man dwells upon solid land and not in the sea – that is, in that Dispensation the sphere of influence of that religion will encompass every land that man has trodden, and it will be established upon solid ground whereon the feet do not falter.
>
> Likewise, the religion of God is described as the Holy City or the New Jerusalem. Clearly, the New Jerusalem which descends from heaven is not a city of stone and lime, of brick and mortar, but is rather the religion of God. For it is obvious that the Jerusalem which is built of stone and mortar does not descend from heaven and is not renewed, but that what is renewed is the religion of God.
>
> Furthermore, the religion of God is likened to an adorned bride who appears with the utmost grace . . .[60]

The promised City will not depend on the light of the sun and moon of earlier dispensations (their spiritual and social principles respectively) for the Glory of God [Bahá'u'lláh] will be its light. Due to the nature of its covenant which shields against divisions His revelation will not be followed by night (Rev. 21:23–27).

> Entrance to the City is promised to those who have not been heedless and have undergone the necessary transformation:
> Blessed are those who wash their robes, so that they may have the

right to the tree of life and that they may enter the city by the gates. that they may have right to the tree of life, and may enter in through the gates into the city. (Rev. 22:14)

Bahá'u'lláh explains that the Holy City refers to God's revelation and divine certitude:

> When the channel of the human soul is cleansed of all worldly and impeding attachments, it will unfailingly perceive the breath of the Beloved across immeasurable distances, and will, led by its perfume, attain and enter the City of Certitude . . . How unspeakably glorious are the signs, the tokens, the revelations, and splendours which He Who is the King of Names and Attributes hath destined for that City! The attainment unto this City quencheth thirst without water, and kindleth the love of God without fire . . . It bestoweth wealth without gold, and conferreth immortality without death . . . Once in about a thousand years shall this City be renewed and re-adorned. . . . That City is none other than the Word of God revealed in every age and dispensation.[61]

The followers of all religions, both high and low, will be judged by the content of their own Scripture:

> And I saw the dead, great and small, standing before the throne, and books were opened. Then another book was opened, which is the book of life. And the dead were judged by what was written in the books, according to what they had done. (Rev. 20:12)

A new name and renewal of 'all things'

> I am coming soon. Hold fast what you have, so that no one may seize your crown. The one who conquers, I will make him a pillar in the temple of my God. Never shall he go out of it, and I will write on him the name of my God, and the name of the city of my God, the new Jerusalem, which comes down from my God out of heaven, and my own new name. He who has an ear, let him hear what the Spirit says to the churches.' (Rev. 3:11–13)

And he who sat on the throne said, 'Behold, I am making all things new.'[62] (Rev. 21:5)

God will provide hitherto 'hidden' (spiritual) food (Rev. 2:17); God will bestow 'a new name' (Rev. 2:17; 3:12; see also Is. 62:2); humanity will sing a 'new song' or a new divine melody (Rev. 14:3). Charles J. Ellicott explained the repeated use of the phrase 'new':

> The characteristic word which runs throughout the description is the word '*new*'. All things are to be made *new*: the heavens and earth are *new*; the Jerusalem is *new*. There are two words which are translated *new* in our English version: one of these (*neos*) relates to time; the other (*kainos*) relates to quality. The one would be applied to what had recently come into existence; the other to what showed fresh features . . . the wine-skins (called 'bottles' in our English version) required for the new wine were not necessarily wine-skins only just prepared for service, but they were skins which had not grown withered, but retained their freshness and elasticity . . . the second word (*kainos*) is employed to describe them . . . The newness which is pictured is the newness of freshness: the old, decaying, enfeebling, and corrupting elements are swept away. The aspects and features which will surround the inhabitants of that new earth will be full of novelty to satisfy the progressive instincts of our nature; but the imagery no less conveys the assurance that the conservative instinct, which clings to what is old, and finds sanctity in the past, will not be disregarded. All things may be new, full of fresh and fair beauty; but all things will not be *strange*; there must be some correspondency between the old and the new, when the new things are called new *heavens*, new *earth*, new *Jerusalem*. The description is figurative, but the spirit of it implies that in the restitution age the sweetness of things loved and familiar will blend with the charm of all that is fresh and new.[63]

Timing of the advent of the Messiah and of the Second Coming

Biblical measures of time

As a preliminary to assessing prophecies, we note that a 'time' in biblical language denotes a year (Dan. 4:32). In the story of the flood, five months is equated with 150 days (Gen. 7:24 and 8:3–4); thus, a biblical year of 12 months equals 360 days. A 'day' is also equal to one year (Num. 14:34; Ezek. 4:6).

Prophecy of the Patriarch Jacob

This remarkable prophecy is perhaps the earliest biblical prediction of two events: the loss of authority to administer the Law of Moses when Shiloh (the name of the Messiah according to Sanhedrin 98B; 'He that is sent', 'the peaceable and prosperous one', or 'the seed of the tribe of Judah' – an idiomatic reference to the Messiah[64]) comes and is rejected; and the regaining of sovereignty by the Israelites and the gathering of the dispersed of Judah at 'the end of days', again associated with Shiloh:

> Then Jacob called his sons and said, 'Gather yourselves together, that I may tell you what shall happen to you in days to come. Assemble and listen, O sons of Jacob, listen to Israel your father. The sceptre[65] shall not depart from Judah, nor the ruler's staff from between his feet, until tribute comes to him; and to him shall be the obedience of the peoples'.[66] (Gen. 49:1–2, 10)

In Ellicott's commentary we read:

> The passage has always been regarded as Messianic, not merely by Christians, but by the Jews, all whose ancient writers, including the Talmud, explain the name Shiloh, or Sheloh, of the Messiah . . .
> **Until Shiloh come . . .** the translation into Aramaic treats the word as a proper name, and renders, 'Until Sheloh come.' Onkelos [Aramaic translation of the Torah] boldly paraphrases, 'Until Messiah come, whose is the kingdom;' and, finally, the Syriac has, 'Until he come, whose it is.'
> . . . Not Israel only, 'the people', but all nations are to obey Him 'whose is the kingdom'.[67]

First event: Loss of temporal authority and the dispersion of the Jews

According to Hosea (c. 750 BCE) the loss of sovereignty will last a long time, and endure until the coming of King David (Messiah, the descendant of King David) in the 'latter days' or last days':

> For the children of Israel shall dwell many days without king or prince, without sacrifice or pillar, without ephod or household gods. Afterward the children of Israel shall return and seek the Lord their God, and David their king, and they shall come in fear to the Lord and to his goodness in the latter days. (Hos. 3:4–5)

The Bible provides the following account of the vision of Daniel concerning the destruction of Jerusalem:

> Forces from him shall appear and profane the temple and fortress, and shall take away the regular burnt offering. And they shall set up the abomination that makes desolate . . . but the people who know their God shall stand firm and take action. And the wise among the people shall make many understand (Dan. 11:31–32).

Rev. Joseph Benson in his commentary on Daniel 11:31 wrote:

> ***And arms shall stand on his part*** – His arms shall so prevail as to make an entire conquest of the Jews, to profane the temple, and cause the daily service performed there to cease . . . The temple is here called *the sanctuary of strength,* either because it was fortified after the manner of a castle, or else because it was a token of the divine protection, as being the place God had chosen to be worshipped in. We are informed by Josephus, by the author of the Maccabees, and others, that Antiochus's soldiers entered the temple and plundered it, and that afterward he ordered that the Jews should not be suffered to offer up the daily sacrifices, which, according to the law, they were accustomed to offer; that he compelled them also to omit their worship of the true God, and to pay divine honours to them whom he regarded as gods, and to make shrines in every city and village, and to build altars, and daily to sacrifice swine upon them: see Joseph . . .

THE 'GOOD NEWS' OF THE GOSPELS AND THE SIGNS OF THE TIMES

> ***And they shall place the abomination that maketh desolate***
> – In the Scriptures, idols are commonly called abominations. This was a prediction of the great profanation Antiochus should cause to the temple, in placing an idol upon the altar of burnt-offerings . . . It is probable, that the idol was Jupiter, because we find that they dedicated the temple anew to Jupiter Olympius. It is here called, the abomination that maketh desolate, because it banished the true worship of God, and his worshippers from the place.[68]

As mentioned earlier in this chapter, Jesus, referring to this prophecy, warned of the imminent destruction of Jerusalem by another manifestation of this 'abomination that maketh desolate':

> So when you see the abomination of desolation spoken of by the prophet Daniel, standing in the holy place (let the reader understand), then let those who are in Judea flee to the mountains. Let the one who is on the housetop not go down to take what is in his house, and let the one who is in the field not turn back to take his cloak. And alas for women who are pregnant and for those who are nursing infants in those days! Pray that your flight may not be in winter or on a Sabbath. For then there will be great tribulation, such as has not been from the beginning of the world until now, no, and never will be. (Matt. 24:15–21)

'The abomination of desolation' is a Hebrew expression meaning the desolation or hateful destroyer of the Jewish faith and culture. The Gentiles were all held in abomination by the Jews, as is implied in the Book of Acts (10:28) and the abomination of desolation referred particularly to any alien occupying army. Israel's experience of the abomination began with the Babylonian king Nebuchadnezzar, but the tragedy was to be repeated and to continue until the time of the end.[69] In Jesus's time it referred to the occupying Roman army (Luke 21:20). Its symbol was the eagle (*aquila*), part of the Roman standard, the bird of the god Jupiter and a symbol of Rome:

> To the ancients the eagle [was] divine, owing first to its closeness to the heavens as well as to the domineering and lordly manner with which Aristotle describes it looking over the earth. It is easily seen

then why the bird is heavily associated with the king sky god Zeus/Jupiter, as well as the sky itself . . .[70]

The Roman soldiers sacrificed to the eagle within the sacred precincts of the Temple in Jerusalem:

> The ensigns were more than military flags or standards signifying Rome and its many legions, the ensigns were idols in the most literal sense of the word as they were regularly worshipped by the soldiers of the Roman army. In fact, the Roman army worshipped and offered sacrifices to the ensigns on the eastern gate of the Temple in A.D. 70 . . .[71]

Some Christian scholars also refer to the actual Roman occupation of Jerusalem as the desolating abomination.

The Messiah 'shall be cut off'

The timing of the return of Christ has been estimated based on a prophecy in the Book of Daniel concerning when the Messiah would be killed:

> . . . for you [Daniel] are greatly loved. Therefore consider the word and understand the vision. Seventy weeks [490 days or 490 years] are decreed about your people and your holy city, to finish the transgression, to put an end to sin, and to atone for iniquity, to bring in everlasting righteousness, to seal both vision and prophet, and to anoint a most holy place. Know therefore and understand that from the going out of the word to restore and build Jerusalem to the coming of an anointed one, a prince, there shall be seven weeks. Then for sixty-two weeks it shall be built again . . . [King James Version: seven weeks, and threescore and two weeks]. And after the sixty-two weeks, an anointed one shall be cut off and shall have nothing. (Dan. 9:23–26)

Four decrees pertaining to the rebuilding of Jerusalem and the Temple were issued by Persian kings in favour of the Jews. The first was the decree of Cyrus issued in 536/537 BCE (Ezra 1:1 and 6:3). The second was given by Darius in 519/520 BCE (Hag. 1:1). The third, the decree of Artaxerxes, was given in 457/458 BCE in the seventh year of his reign (Ezra 7:11–13). The fourth, a second decree from Artaxerxes, was given in 444/445 BCE. The favourable decrees of Artaxerxes are believed to have been a result of the influence of his Jewish wife, Queen Esther. Ancient sources date Artaxerxes' reign as beginning in 465 BCE, and the book of Nehemiah states that the command was given in the 20th year of Artaxerxes' reign. This would suggest a date of 445 BCE for the timing of Artaxerxes' second decree to rebuild Jerusalem.

Daniel predicted that an anointed one would be cut off some time after 62 weeks. He also provided 70 weeks or 490 years for this event to occur:

> Seventy weeks are decreed about your people and your holy city, to finish the transgression, to put an end to sin, and to atone for iniquity, to bring in everlasting righteousness, to seal both vision and prophet, and to anoint a most holy place. Know and understand this: From the issuance of the decree to restore and rebuild Jerusalem, until the Messiah, the Prince, there will be seven weeks and sixty-two weeks (Dan. 9:24–25).

The Adventists found that the most appropriate edict was the one dated 457/458 BCE. Although the date of Christ's crucifixion and His age when He died are uncertain, 457 BCE appeared to generally fit the expectations. Armed with this knowledge, they could now use it to decipher the second date that appears in Daniel.

Second event: The regathering of the Jews

This process would be accelerated when Israel regained its sovereignty, an event again associated with the coming of Shiloh.

> Then I heard one saint speaking, and another saint said unto that certain saint which spake, How long shall be the vision concerning the daily sacrifice, and the transgression of desolation, to give both the sanctuary and the host to be trodden under foot? And he said unto me, Unto two thousand and three hundred days; then shall the sanctuary be cleansed. (Dan. 8:13–14)

As we have seen, Christ refers to this prophecy of Daniel:

> And they shall fall by the edge of the sword, and shall be led away captive into all nations: and Jerusalem shall be trodden down of the Gentiles, until the times of the Gentiles be fulfilled. (Luke 21:24)

Using the 457 BCE prophecy of Daniel that corresponds with the timing of the crucifixion of Christ, Christians were able to decode that the cleansing of the sanctuary would occur in (2,300 minus 457) years or 1843/1844 CE.

PART III

DIFFICULTIES AND OBSTACLES

7

OBJECTIONS TO JESUS AS THE MESSIAH

For several hundred years the followers of Moses supplicated fervently for the advent of their Messiah but yet failed to recognize Jesus. The Hebrew Bible had warned them of the difficulties that they would face in this regard.[1] The Prophet Isaiah stated that the appearance of the Lord of Hosts would provide a safe haven from the evils afflicting mankind, but cautioned that it would also act as an obstacle to belief and understanding, particularly for the religious leaders:

> But the Lord of hosts, him you shall honour as holy. Let him be your fear, and let him be your dread. And he will become a sanctuary and a stone of offence and a rock of stumbling[2] to both houses of Israel, a trap ('gin') and a snare to the inhabitants of Jerusalem. And many shall stumble on it.[3] They shall fall and be broken; they shall be snared and taken. (Is. 8:13–15)

Rev. Albert Barnes commented:

> ***A stone of stumbling*** – A stone against which one should impinge, or over which he should fall. The idea is, that none could run against a hard, rough, fixed stone, or rock, without injuring himself. So the Jews would oppose the counsels of God; instead of making him their refuge and strength, they would resist his claims and appeals, and the consequence would be their destruction. It is also to be remembered, that God is often represented in the Scriptures as a rock, a firm defense, or place of safety, to those who trust in him. But instead of their thus taking refuge in him, they would oppose themselves to this firm rock, and ruin themselves . . . Many of the ancient Jewish commentators applied this to the Messiah . . . It is

also applied to Christ in the New Testament, I Peter 2:8.
A rock of offence – A rock over which they should fall. The English word offence, had that meaning formerly, and retains it in our translation of the Bible . . .
To both the houses of Israel – To the two kingdoms of Judah and Israel; that is, to the wicked portion of them, not to those who were truly pious.
For a gin – A net, or snare, to take birds. The idea is the same as in the former part of the verse. By rejecting the counsel of God; by despising his protection, and by resisting his laws, they would be unexpectedly involved in difficulties, as birds which are caught in a snare.[4]

Unwittingly, the reverend scholar Rabbi Maimonides confirmed this prophecy by maintaining in his extensive writings that the real obstacles to true Judaism were Jesus and Christianity:

Can there be a greater stumbling block than [Christianity]? All the prophets spoke of Moshiach as the redeemer of Israel and their savior, who would gather their dispersed ones and strengthen their [observance of] the mitzvos. In contrast [the founder of Christianity] caused the Jews to be slain by the sword, their remnants to be scattered and humiliated, the Torah to be altered, and the majority of the world to err and serve a god other than the Lord.[5]

An English writer and devout Catholic, John Heywood (1497–1589), wrote: 'there are none so blind as those who will not see. The most deluded people are those who choose to ignore what they already know.'[6]
'Abdu'l-Bahá observed:

They were expecting His coming; by day and night they mourned and lamented, saying, 'O God! Hasten Thou the day of the advent of Christ,' expressing most intense longing for the Messiah; but when Christ appeared, they denied and rejected Him . . . Why did this happen? Because they were blindly following imitations . . . tenaciously holding to it and refusing to investigate the reality of Christ. Therefore, they were deprived of the bounties of Christ, whereas if they had forsaken imitations and investigated the reality of the Messiah, they would have surely been guided to believing in Him. Instead of this they said, 'We have heard from our fathers and have read in the Old Testament that Christ must come from an unknown place; now we find that this one has come from Nazareth' [John 1:46]. Steeped in the literal interpretation and imitating the beliefs of fathers and ancestors, they failed to understand the fact that although the body of Jesus came from Nazareth, the reality of the Christ came from the unknown place of the divine Kingdom. They also said that the sceptre of Christ would be of iron – that is to say, He should wield a sword [Ps. 2:9]. When Christ appeared, He did possess a sword; but it was the sword of His tongue with which He separated the false from the true. But the Jews were blind to the spiritual significance and symbolism of the prophetic words. They also expected that the Messiah would sit upon the throne of David [Is. 9:7], whereas Christ had neither throne nor semblance of sovereignty; nay, rather, He was a poor man, apparently abject and vanquished; therefore, how could He be the veritable Christ? This was one of their most insistent objections based upon ancestral interpretation and teaching. In reality, Christ was glorified with an eternal sovereignty and everlasting dominion – spiritual and not temporal. His throne and Kingdom were established in human hearts, where He reigns with power and authority without end. Notwithstanding the fulfilment of all the prophetic signs in Christ, the Jews denied Him and entered the period of their deprivation because of their allegiance to imitations and ancestral forms.

Among other objections they said, 'We are promised through the tongue of the prophets that Christ at the time of His coming would proclaim the law of the Torah, whereas now we see this person abrogating the commands of the Pentateuch, disturbing our blessed Sabbath [Matt. 12:1–8; Mark 2:27] and abolishing the law of divorce [Matt. 5:31–32]. He has left nothing of the ancient law of Moses; therefore, he is the enemy of Moses.' In reality, Christ proclaimed and completed the law of Moses. He was the very helper and assister of Moses. He spread the Book of Moses throughout the world and established anew the fundamentals of the law revealed by Him. He abolished certain unimportant laws and forms which were no longer compatible with the exigencies of the time, such as divorce and plurality of wives [Matt. 19:9] . . .

> They, likewise, said, 'Through the tongues of the prophets it was announced that during the time of Christ's appearance the justice of God would prevail throughout the world, tyranny and oppression would be unknown, justice would even extend to the animal kingdom, ferocious beasts would associate in gentleness and peace, the wolf and the lamb would drink from the same spring, the lion and the deer meet in the same meadow, the eagle and quail dwell together in the same nest; [Is. 11:6] but instead of this, we see that during the time of this supposed Christ the Romans have conquered Palestine and are ruling it with extreme tyranny, justice is nowhere apparent, and signs of peace in the animal kingdom are conspicuously absent.' These statements and attitudes of the Jews were inherited from their fathers – blind allegiance to literal expectations which did not come to pass during the time of Jesus Christ. The real purport of these prophetic statements was that various peoples, symbolized by the wolf and lamb, between whom love and fellowship were impossible would come together during the Messiah's reign, drink from the same fountain of life in His teachings and become His devoted followers.[7]

Thus, the remedy in part is not to interpret the scriptures literally, but to examine their underlying spiritual message and reality.

The children of Israel were not told in the Torah to follow their religious teachers blindly but were instructed to ascertain the truth of a matter, to 'inquire and make search and ask diligently'(Deut. 13:14). The Prophet Jeremiah had also advised them that when they encountered a crossroads in their lives they should take the time to recall the past way, and in the light of this earlier experience enquire what was a good road ahead, and then confidently tread that path (Jer. 16:6).

When we consider the past we find that the transition from one dispensation to another has never been easy. Christ faced constant opposition to His teachings from the Jewish religious leaders. The Apostle Paul pleaded with his fellow Christians: 'let us not pass judgement on one another any longer, but rather decide never to put a stumbling block or hindrance in the way of a brother' (Rom. 14:13). We will examine here some of the objections to Jesus and His disciples at the First Coming, as many of these same objections are being repeated today.

Should you acquaint yourself with the indignities heaped upon the Prophets of God, and apprehend the true causes of the objections voiced by their oppressors, you will surely appreciate the significance of their position. Moreover, the more closely you observe the denials of those who have opposed the Manifestations of the divine attributes, the firmer will be your faith in the Cause of God.[8]

1. Jesus did not fulfil the scriptural expectations concerning the Messiah

Jewish writers have maintained that the Christians have been too zealous in their attempts to prove that Jesus was literally the one referred to in their scriptures. They contend that the Gospel accounts of the birth and life of Jesus were made to fit the prophecies in the Hebrew Scriptures. They have accused Christians of cherry-picking the Bible and quoting scriptural references entirely out of their historical context. The arguments are articulated comprehensively in the writings of Maimonides, which are considered to be foundational to Jewish thought and study.

Born in Cordova, Spain, Maimonides and his family faced exile after refusing to convert to Islam, and eventually settled in Fez, Morocco. For Maimonides, the Messiah would be born of human parents, and would not be a god or demi-god that possessed supernatural qualities. His objections were penned after the First Coming (Christ), and therefore he uses an admixture of prophecies relating to the First and Second Coming to refute Christ. He pointedly explains that the Messiah is not expected to perform signs or wonders, but instead is expected to be a descendant of David. The Messiah was to restore the throne of David, rebuild the Temple, re-establish its worship, gather together the Jewish exiles and return them to the Holy Land. He reasoned that none of these events had happened with Jesus.

In response, the church has argued that the Jews were and are simply too blind, stiff-necked and unreasonable to recognize Jesus as their Messiah.

Jewish scholars have in turn denounced church dogmas and the literal explanations of incarnation, trinity and bodily resurrection as being for the most part inconsistent with the teachings of the Torah, and therefore blasphemous. For example, Maimonides asserted that since God is incorporeal, this means that God assumes no physical form. Therefore, God is eternal, above time, infinite, and beyond space – He cannot be born, and He cannot die.

The Hebrew Bible also predicted the darkening of the sun, the conversion of moon into blood, the fall of the stars, and other miraculous physical events, none of which came to pass literally at the time of Christ.

The literal interpretation of the Scriptures explains the difficulties that the Synagogue experienced at the First Coming and that many Christians face today concerning the Second Coming. Christians would have been more convincing had they emphasized that religious truth should be free of ancestral beliefs and institutional prejudices, and that the Jewish prophecies were fulfilled for the most part allegorically and spiritually, but not, as expected, literally. The Christians could then have applied a similar method to their own prophecies concerning the Second Coming, supported by the following statements of Christ:

> It is the Spirit who gives life; the flesh is no help at all. The words that I have spoken to you are spirit and life. (John 6:63)

> So he said to them again, 'I am going away, and you will seek me, and you will die in your sin. Where I am going, you cannot come.' So the Jews said, 'Will he kill himself, since he says, "Where I am going, you cannot come"?' He said to them, 'You are from below; I am from above. You are of this world; I am not of this world.' (John 8:21–23)

Jesus came from Nazareth but the Messiah was expected to come suddenly from an unknown place and appear in the temple

> Behold, I send my messenger, and he will prepare the way before me. And the Lord whom you seek will suddenly come to his temple; and the messenger of the covenant in whom you delight, behold, he is coming, says the Lord of hosts. But who can endure the day of his coming, and who can stand when he appears? For he is like a refiner's fire and like fullers' soap.[9] (Mal. 3:1–2)

This idea was familiar amongst the Jews at the time of John, and may also be gleaned from the following question of Nathaniel in the Gospel of John:

> Some of the people of Jerusalem therefore said, 'Is not this the man whom they seek to kill? And here he is, speaking openly, and they say nothing to him! Can it be that the authorities really know that this is the Christ? But we know where this man comes from, and when the Christ appears, no one will know where he comes from.' (John 7:25–27)

He was surprised when he found out that Jesus had come from Nazareth in Galilee. This was particularly objectionable, as Nazareth and Galilee, though fertile regions, did not have a wholesome reputation:

> Philip found Nathanael and said to him, 'We have found him of whom Moses in the Law and also the prophets wrote, Jesus of Nazareth, the son of Joseph.' Nathanael said to him, 'Can anything good come out of Nazareth?' Philip said to him, 'Come and see.' (John 1:45–46)

The Gospel of Matthew (2:1) states that 'Jesus was born in Bethlehem in Judea'. There are however, supposedly two Bethlehems (*Bet Leḥem; 'House of Bread'* in Hebrew'); one, 'Bethlehem of Judea', about five to six miles southwest of Jerusalem (the traditional birthplace of Christ and King David, and the site of the Church of the Nativity), and a second Bethlehem in the north 'Bethlehem of the Galilee' (Bethlehem of the North or *Bet Leḥem HaGlalit* in Hebrew), near Kiryat Tivon about six miles from Nazareth.[10]

The Gospel of Matthew adds that Jesus later 'lived in a city called Nazareth, so that what was spoken by the prophets might be fulfilled, that he would be called a Nazarene' (Matt. 2:23). Notably, 'Nazareth' and 'Nazarene' do not appear in the Hebrew Bible – perhaps because Nazareth was an insignificant town in Galilee, itself a region distant from Jerusalem and the centres of religious scholarship. The family allegedly then returned to Nazareth after having fled to Egypt to escape Herod. Jesus's connection to Bethlehem and to Nazareth through the lineage of Joseph was tenuous, and was dismissed by the Pharisees (John 7:41–42, 50–52): 'Search and see that no prophet arises from Galilee' (John 7:52).[11]

Jesus is the specific name or title of the Messiah in the Hebrew Bible

Two names are used to refer to Jesus in the New Testament:

'Emmanuel' ('God is with us') occurs only once in the New Testament (Matt. 1:23 taken from Is. 7:14).

Jesus: in Luke 1:31 Mary is told to call her child Jesus, and in Matt. 1:21 Joseph is told to name the child Jesus. Some researchers hold that this is a transliteration made by the New Testament authors of the name 'Yeshua' (a saviour, deliverer), which translates in English as Joshua, is related to and is a shortened form of the biblical Hebrew form *Yehoshua* (יְהוֹשֻׁעַ). Yeshua and Joshua were the names of several individuals in the Hebrew Bible,[12] and were common names at the time of Christ, occurring several times in the Hebrew Bible. They are not understood to be the specific name or title of the expected Messiah.[13]

2. Why did Jesus refuse to perform miracles?

Moses and Elijah had performed extraordinary miracles. Why then did Jesus refuse to do so as a proof that He was indeed the Messiah? This is discussed later, in Chapter 9.

3. Jesus and His disciples were guilty of heresy and blasphemy

> And when Jesus saw their faith, he said to the paralytic, 'Son, your sins are forgiven.' Now some of the scribes were sitting there, questioning in their hearts, 'Why does this man speak like that? He is blaspheming! Who can forgive sins but God alone?' (Mark 2:5–7)

> Jesus answered them . . . 'I and the Father are one.' The Jews picked up stones again to stone him. Jesus answered them, 'I have shown you many good works from the Father; for which of them are you going to stone me?' The Jews answered him, 'It is not for a good work that we are going to stone you but for blasphemy, because you, being a man, make yourself God.' (John 10:25, 30–33)

> Jesus answered, 'If I glorify myself, my glory is nothing. It is my Father who glorifies me, of whom you say, "He is our God." . . . Your father

Abraham rejoiced that he would see my day. He saw it and was glad.' So the Jews said to him, 'You are not yet fifty years old, and have you seen Abraham?' Jesus said to them, 'Truly, truly, I say to you, before Abraham was, I am.' So they picked up stones to throw at him, but Jesus hid himself and went out of the temple. (John 8:54, 56–59)

The disciples were accused similarly:

For we have found this man (Apostle Paul) a plague, one who stirs up riots[14] among all the Jews throughout the world and is a ringleader of the sect[15] of the Nazarenes.[16] (Acts 24:5)

4. Those most familiar with Jesus did not endorse His teachings and actions

Even the inhabitants of His hometown of Nazareth considered His teachings blasphemous and worthy of death. Perhaps, due to their familiarity with the details of His earthly life, they did not appreciate His divine reality:

> ... and coming to his hometown he taught them in their synagogue, so that they were astonished, and said, 'Where did this man get this wisdom and these mighty works? Is not this the carpenter's son? Is not his mother called Mary? And are not his brothers James and Joseph and Simon and Judas? And are not all his sisters with us? Where then did this man get all these things?' And they took offense at him. But Jesus said to them, 'A prophet is not without honor except in his hometown and in his own household.' And he did not do many mighty works there, because of their unbelief. (Matt. 13:54–58)

Jesus's own siblings opposed Him and wished Him to go elsewhere:

> So his brothers said to him, 'Leave here and go to Judea, that your disciples also may see the works you are doing . . . For not even his brothers believed in him. (John 7:3, 5)

Indeed, His family was of the opinion that He had lost His mind, and that He needed to be saved from Himself:

> Then he went home, and the crowd gathered again . . . And when his family heard it, they went out to seize him, for they were saying, 'He is out of his mind' . . . And his mother and his brothers came, and standing outside they sent to him and called him. And a crowd was sitting around him, and they said to him, 'Your mother and your brothers are outside, seeking you.' And he answered them, 'Who are my mother and my brothers?' And looking about at those who sat around him, he said, 'Here are my mother and my brothers! For whoever does the will of God, he is my brother and sister and mother.' (Mark 3:20–21, 31–34)

5. Why did those in authority who were in a position to know – scholars and religious leaders – not believe in Jesus?

> And there was much muttering about him among the people. While some said, 'He is a good man,' others said, 'No, he is leading the people astray.' Yet for fear of the Jews no one spoke openly of him . . . The officers then came to the chief priests and Pharisees, who said to them, 'Why did you not bring him?' The [arresting] officers answered, 'No one ever spoke like this man!' The Pharisees answered them, 'Have you also been deceived? Have any of the authorities or the Pharisees believed in him? But this crowd that does not know the law is accursed.' (John 7:12–13, 45–49)

Instead, the religious leaders plotted to ruin Him, and accused Him of being an imposter (Matt. 27:63):

> But the Pharisees went out and conspired against him, how to destroy him. (Matt. 12:14; Mark 3:6; and Luke 6:11)

They objected that they did not know what commission Jesus had received, or who had sent Him:

> . . . we are disciples of Moses. We know that God has spoken to Moses, but as for this man, we do not know where he comes from. (John 9:28–29)

6. Jesus must have been possessed by demons

His ability to cast out evil spirits (diseases) was thought to be through the demonic assistance and power.

> And the scribes who came down from Jerusalem were saying, 'He is possessed by Beelzebul,'[17] and 'by the prince of demons he casts out the demons'. (Mark 3:22)

7. Jesus and His disciples led sinful lives that were inconsistent with the teachings of the Torah and the Talmud

His disciples were not sufficiently righteous, illustrated by the fact that they did not fast:

> Now John's disciples and the Pharisees were fasting. And people came and said to him, 'Why do John's disciples and the disciples of the Pharisees fast, but your disciples do not fast?' (Mark 2:18)

They appeared to disregard the laws of ritual cleanliness:

> Then Pharisees and scribes came to Jesus from Jerusalem and said, 'Why do your disciples break the tradition of the elders? For they do not wash their hands when they eat.' (Matt. 15:1–2; also, Mark 7:5 and Luke 11:37–38)

Notably, they broke the Sabbath by picking their food on that day:

> One Sabbath he was going through the grainfields, and as they made their way, his disciples began to pluck heads of grain. And the Pharisees were saying to him, 'Look, why are they doing what is not lawful on the Sabbath?'. . . And he said to them, 'The Sabbath was made for man, not man for the Sabbath. So the Son of Man is lord even of the Sabbath.' (Mark 2:23–24, 27–28; see also Luke 6:1–2)

Jesus also broke the Law by healing on the Sabbath:

> Again he entered the synagogue, and a man was there with a

withered hand. And they watched Jesus, to see whether he would heal him on the Sabbath, so that they might accuse him . . . And he said to them, 'Is it lawful on the Sabbath to do good or to do harm, to save life or to kill?' But they were silent. And he looked around at them with anger, grieved at their hardness of heart, and said to the man, 'Stretch out your hand.' He stretched it out, and his hand was restored. (Mark 3:1–2, 4–5)

He did not live a consecrated life:

For John came neither eating nor drinking, and they say, 'He has a demon.' The Son of Man came eating and drinking, and they say, 'Look at him! A glutton and a drunkard, a friend of tax collectors and sinners!' (Matt. 11:18–19)

He associated with people of ill repute:

And as Jesus reclined at table in the house, behold, many tax collectors and sinners came and were reclining with Jesus and his disciples. And when the Pharisees saw this, they said to his disciples, 'Why does your teacher eat with tax collectors and sinners?' But when he heard it, he said, 'Those who are well have no need of a physician, but those who are sick. Go and learn what this means: "I desire mercy, and not sacrifice." For I came not to call the righteous, but sinners.' (Matt. 9:10–13; also: Luke 5:29–32)

He recognized a chief tax collector at Jericho, Zacchaeus,[18] stating that he was a son of Abraham, and invited Himself to his house:

And behold, there was a man named Zacchaeus. He was a chief tax collector and was rich. And he was seeking to see who Jesus was, but on account of the crowd he could not, because he was small in stature. So he ran on ahead and climbed up into a sycamore tree to see him, for he was about to pass that way. And when Jesus came to the place, he looked up and said to him, 'Zacchaeus, hurry and come down, for I must stay at your house today.' So he hurried and came down and received him joyfully. And when they saw it, they all grumbled, 'He has gone in to be the guest of a man who is a sinner.'

And Zacchaeus stood and said to the Lord, 'Behold, Lord, the half of my goods I give to the poor. And if I have defrauded anyone of anything, I restore it fourfold.' And Jesus said to him,' Today salvation has come to this house, since he also is a son of Abraham. For the Son of Man came to seek and to save the lost.' (Luke 19:2–10)

He associated with, and accepted a gift from, a sinful woman:

> One of the Pharisees asked him to eat with him, and he went into the Pharisee's house and reclined at table. And behold, a woman of the city, who was a sinner, when she learned that he was reclining at table in the Pharisee's house, brought an alabaster flask of ointment, and standing behind him at his feet, weeping, she began to wet his feet with her tears and wiped them with the hair of her head and kissed his feet and anointed them with the ointment. Now when the Pharisee who had invited him saw this, he said to himself, 'If this man were a prophet, he would have known who and what sort of woman this is who is touching him, for she is a sinner'. . . And he said to her, 'Your sins are forgiven.' Then those who were at table with him began to say among themselves, 'Who is this, who even forgives sins?' And he said to the woman, 'Your faith has saved you; go in peace.' (Luke 7:37–39, 48–50)

8. If Jesus was the Messiah, why did the Prophet Elijah not descend from heaven beforehand as promised in the Bible?

According to the Hebrew Bible, Elijah,[19] one of the greatest Prophets, did not suffer death. While talking to his disciple and successor, Elisha, Elijah was suddenly transported to heaven on a chariot of fire (II Kings 2:11). In the closing verses of the Hebrew Bible the Prophet Malachi promises that Elijah, 'the messenger of the covenant', will return from heaven, before the coming of the Messiah, 'the great and dreadful day of the Lord' (Mal. 3:1–2; 4:5–6). The Jewish leaders therefore questioned why Elijah had not come prior to Christ (John 1:21).

9. The Gospel explanations concerning Jesus's birth and early life misrepresented the scriptures

Creative but conflicting genealogies of Jesus that attempt to link Him to King David

The Jews at the time of Christ expected two Messiahs: one would come from the family of Joseph followed by one from the family of David. The Gospel of Luke states:

> He will be great and will be called the Son of the Most High. And the Lord God will give to him the throne of his father David, and he will reign over the house of Jacob forever, and of his kingdom there will be no end. (Luke 1:32–33)

Jesus did not literally reign over the Jews. Nevertheless, two genealogies, Matt. 1:1–17 and Luke 3:23–38, attempt to demonstrate that Jesus was the descendant of King David. Surprisingly, both family trees trace Jesus's ancestry not through His mother Mary, as might be expected because of the Christian belief in the Virgin Birth, but through Joseph, who is described in the genealogy of Matthew as 'the husband of Mary'. In the genealogy of Luke, Jesus is described as being the son (as was supposed) of Joseph (Luke 3:23). Neither genealogy traces Jesus's ancestry to Joseph, the son of Jacob. Instead, Jesus's genealogy is traced to the fourth son of Jacob, Judah, born to Leah. Side-by-side comparison shows that the two genealogies differ irreconcilably as to how Jesus was related to King David.

Virgin birth

According to the Gospel of Luke, the angel Gabriel announced to Mary, a virgin 'espoused to Joseph', that she would give birth to a son. Mary and Joseph lived 'in a city of Galilee, named Nazareth' where Jesus was conceived. In the same town of Nazareth, 'an angel of the Lord' also appeared to Joseph in a dream saying, 'Joseph, thou son of David, fear not to take unto thee Mary thy wife: for that which is conceived in her is of the Holy Ghost. And she shall bring forth a son, and thou shalt call his name Jesus: for he shall save his people from their sins' (Matt. 1:20–21).

The Gospel of Matthew explains that this all happened to fulfil a prophecy of Isaiah:

> Now the birth of Jesus Christ took place in this way. When his mother Mary had been betrothed to Joseph, before they came together she was found to be with child from the Holy Spirit. And her husband Joseph, being a just man and unwilling to put her to shame, resolved to divorce her quietly ... All this took place to fulfil what the Lord had spoken by the prophet: 'Behold, the virgin[20] shall conceive and bear a son, and they shall call his name Immanuel (which means, God with us). (Matt. 1:18, 22–23; see Is. 7:14)

Scholars contend that Matthew misunderstood Isaiah's prophecy and argue that it does not apply to Jesus. Most Jewish sources translate 'the young woman is with child' as referring to a young woman of marriageable age (*'almâh*) and not to a virgin (*bĕthûlâh*). Moreover, there is no indication that the child would be the Messiah. Six months before Mary was visited by the angel Gabriel, Zechariah, a priest and the husband of Mary's cousin Elizabeth, who lived in Nazareth, was also visited by the same angel who announced the birth of a son whom they would call John. He later became known as John the Baptist.

Birth in Bethlehem, 'the city of David'

Mary, heavily pregnant with Jesus, and Joseph had to travel from Nazareth to Bethlehem in Judea, a perilous journey of about 80 miles through Samaria which normally took about four days to complete. According to Luke, Bethlehem, the city of King David, was the ancestral city of Joseph who was 'of the house and lineage of David'. The reason for the unusual journey was apparently to comply with a Roman census (Quirinus) decreed for tax purposes. In this way, Jesus's birth would satisfy a prophecy associating the Messiah with Bethlehem (Micah 5:2) even although Joseph was not the father of Jesus, and Mary was not native to Bethlehem.

Emigration to Egypt

The Gospel of Matthew records that, having heard the Magis' announcement of the birth of a new king of the Jews, Herod the Great ordered that all male infant children be killed. This caused Mary, Joseph and the infant Jesus to flee to Egypt, where they remained 'until the death of Herod', after which they returned to Nazareth via Judea. This journey is not mentioned anywhere else in the New Testament. Their recall from Egypt, the Gospel of Matthew states, fulfils another prophecy recorded in the Hebrew Bible:

> And he [Joseph] rose and took the child and his mother by night and departed to Egypt and remained there until the death of Herod. This was to fulfill what the Lord had spoken by the prophet, 'Out of Egypt I called my son.' (Matt. 2:14–15)

Jewish scholars object that the prophecy referred to in the above verse does not apply to Jesus but instead clearly applies to the Children of Israel who escaped bondage in Egypt:

> When Israel was a child, I loved him, and out of Egypt I called my son. (Hosea 11:1)

Notably, Luke has a divergent account. According to this Gospel Jesus was brought to the Temple in Jerusalem eight days after his birth and afterwards the family returned to Nazareth (Luke 2:21–39). Jesus hence spent the greater part of his life in Nazareth and occasionally visited Jerusalem with his family. According to the Gospel of Matthew He left Nazareth and dwelt in Capernaum so that another prophecy of Isaiah might be fulfilled:

> Now when he heard that John had been arrested, he withdrew into Galilee. And leaving Nazareth he went and lived in Capernaum by the sea, in the territory of Zebulun and Naphtali, so that what was spoken by the prophet Isaiah might be fulfilled: 'The land of Zebulun and the land of Naphtali, the way of the sea, beyond the Jordan, Galilee of the Gentiles – the people dwelling in darkness have seen a great light, and for those dwelling in the region and

shadow of death, on them a light has dawned.' (Matt. 4:12–16)

Matthew possibly had the following promise of Isaiah in mind – a prophecy that refers more directly to the Second Coming as it predicts the advent of the Father and the Prince of Peace:

> The people who walked in darkness have seen a great light; those who dwelt in a land of deep darkness, on them has light shone. You have multiplied the nation; you have increased its joy; they rejoice before you as with joy at the harvest, as they are glad when they divide the spoil. For the yoke of his burden, and the staff for his shoulder, the rod of his oppressor, you have broken as on the day of Midian. For every boot of the tramping warrior in battle tumult and every garment rolled in blood will be burned as fuel for the fire. For to us a child is born, to us a son is given; and the government shall be upon his shoulder, and his name shall be called Wonderful Counsellor, Mighty God, Everlasting Father, Prince of Peace. Of the increase of his government and of peace there will be no end, on the throne of David and over his kingdom, to establish it and to uphold it with justice and with righteousness from this time forth and forevermore. The zeal of the Lord of hosts will do this. (Is. 9:2–7)

10. Moses has ascendancy over all other Prophets, and the Torah is the immutable Word of God

As with the followers of other religions, the followers of Moses insist that their dispensation is the exclusive, complete and final expression of God's Will. The Jewish leaders were angered by Christ daring to author a new revelation, although the Hebrew Bible maintained that nothing is too hard for God (Jer. 32:27). Their excessive devotion to the Patriarchs, Moses, and the Torah blinded them and led them to ask Him somewhat presumptuous and inappropriate questions that spoke volumes about their lack of understanding:

> Are you greater than our father Jacob? He gave us the well and drank from it himself, as did his sons and his livestock. (John 4:12)

The Jews said to him, 'Now we know that you have a demon! Abraham died, as did the prophets, yet you say, "If anyone keeps my word, he will never taste death." Are you greater than our father Abraham, who died? And the prophets died! Who do you make yourself out to be?' (John 8:52–53)

The assertion that Moses is in place of God

Yahweh (God) sent Moses as God to Pharaoh, accompanied by Aaron, with the command that the ruler of Egypt release the Children of Israel from bondage:

> And the Lord said to Moses, 'See, I have made you like God to Pharaoh, and your brother Aaron shall be your prophet. You shall speak all that I command you, and your brother Aaron shall tell Pharaoh to let the people of Israel go out of his land.' (Ex. 7:1–2)

The assertion that God spoke to Moses directly but indirectly to other Prophets

Moses tended to stammer and God chose His brother Aaron, who understood Moses, to speak for Him. When Moses married a non-Israelite woman from Cush (Ethiopia), Aaron and his sister Miriam questioned His leadership, which led to a rebellion in the ranks of the children of Israel. For questioning Moses, they were admonished severely:

> Miriam and Aaron spoke against Moses because of the Cushite woman whom he had married, for he had married a Cushite woman. And they said, 'Has the Lord indeed spoken only through Moses? Has he not spoken through us also?' And the Lord heard it. Now the man Moses was very meek, more than all people who were on the face of the earth. And suddenly the Lord said to Moses and to Aaron and Miriam, 'Come out, you three, to the tent of meeting.' And the three of them came out. And he said, 'Hear my words: If there is a prophet among you, I the Lord make myself known to him in a vision; I speak with him in a dream. Not so with my servant Moses. He is faithful in all my house. With him I speak mouth to mouth,

clearly, and not in riddles, and he beholds the form of the Lord. Why then were you not afraid to speak against my servant Moses?' (Num. 12:1–4, 6–8)

Moses is thus known as the Prophet who spoke directly to God, and was His interlocutor. One reasonable conclusion would have been that since Moses received His revelation directly from God, the many inputs from numerous Jewish scholars were not required. However, the deduction of the renowned Rabbi Maimonides was that Moses was peerless amongst the Prophets. The seventh of his *Thirteen Principles of the Faith* expresses a dogmatic belief in the primacy of Moses:

> . . . that Moses was the father of all the prophets – of those who came before him and of those who came after him; all were beneath him in rank, and that he was the chosen of God from among the entire species of humanity and that he comprehended more of God, may He be exalted, than any man ever existed or will exist, ever comprehended or will comprehend and that he, peace be upon him, reached a state of exaltedness beyond humanity such that he perceived the level of sovereignty and became included in the level of the angels. There remained no veil which he did not pierce, no material hindrance burdened him. The imaginative and sensible faculties in his perceptions were stripped from him, his considerate faculty was still, and he remained pure intellect only. For this reason, they remarked of him that he discoursed with God without the intermediacy of an angel . . .
>
> Every other prophet received inspiration only when in a state of sleep . . . every other prophet receives inspiration only in a vision and by means of an angel . . . every other prophet did not receive inspiration by his own choice but by the will of God . . . But Moses our Teacher, was able to say whenever he wished . . .[21]

In his zeal to prove the superiority of Moses, Maimonides ignores the fact that although some Prophets, such as Isaiah and Daniel, received their divine inspiration indirectly through visions and dreams,[22] God spoke to others, such as Noah and Abraham, directly and without intermediaries.[23]

The assertion that the teachings and Dispensation of Moses are perfect

> The law of the Lord is perfect, reviving the soul; the testimony of the Lord is sure, making wise the simple; the precepts of the Lord are right, rejoicing the heart; the commandment of the Lord is pure, enlightening the eyes; the fear of the Lord is clean, enduring forever; the rules [or just decrees] of the Lord are true . . . (Ps. 19:7–9)

The assertion that no new revelation is needed since the Torah is complete

In particular, the Pentateuch repeatedly instructs that nothing should be added or subtracted from the Word of God. The Torah instructs the Jews several times not to add to or subtract from this Law:

> And now, O Israel, listen to the statutes and the rules that I am teaching you, and do them, that you may live, and go in and take possession of the land that the Lord, the God of your fathers, is giving you. You shall not add to the word that I command you, nor take from it, that you may keep the commandments of the Lord your God that I command you. (Deut. 4:1–2; also, Prov. 30:6)

> Take care lest you forget the Lord your God by not keeping his commandments and his rules and his statutes, which I command you today . . . (Deut. 8:11)

> These are the statutes and rules that you shall be careful to do in the land that the Lord, the God of your fathers, has given you to possess, all the days that you live on the earth. Be careful to obey all these words that I command you, that it may go well with you and with your children after you forever, when you do what is good and right in the sight of the Lord your God. (Deut. 12:1, 28)

The Torah reminds the Children of Israel that the Holy Land belongs to God, and they are 'foreigners and sojourners with Him' (Lev. 25:23). Moreover, their continued possession of the land was contingent on their submission and obedience to the Lord (Lev. 26:33 and Deut. 8:1).

The Hebrew Bible adds:

> If one turns away his ear from hearing the law, even his prayer is an abomination. (Prov. 28:9)

The final injunction of the Hebrew Bible is a reminder of the importance of the Law of Moses:

> Remember the law of my servant Moses, the statutes and rules that I commanded him at Horeb for all Israel. (Mal 4:4)

In his *Principles* Maimonides declares:

> The Eighth Principle is that the Torah is from heaven; to wit, it [must] be believed that the whole of this Torah which is in our hands today is the Torah that was brought down to Moses, our Teacher; that all of is from G-d.
>
> The Ninth Principle is the [denial of the] abrogation [of the Torah] to wit, that this Torah of Moses; our Teacher, shall not be abrogated or transmuted; nor shall any other law come from G-d. It may not be added to, nor subtracted from – not from its texts nor from its explanation . . .[24]

The Jews are additionally reminded that their Redeemer is unique and eternal ('the first' and 'the last') (Is. 44:6; 48:11–12). Furthermore, the statutes of the Torah must be observed by Israel in perpetuity.[25] Jewish leaders such as Maimonides thus concluded that all of the provisions of the Torah were immutable forever.

Therefore, at first glance it would appear that the Torah precludes the appearance of any future divine revelation. It requires understanding and a degree of humility to appreciate that the commandment to obey the laws of a particular dispensation is not incompatible with God revealing new laws in the future which will also have to be followed. In this connection it may be asked legitimately whether Moses did not in fact set precedence by changing the divine laws of Noah, known as the Noahide Laws.

Jewish scholars such as Maimonides ignored the fact that no one has fully understood the mind of God:

For he is manifold in understanding... 'Can you find out the deep things of God? Can you find out the limit of the Almighty? It is higher than heaven – what can you do? Deeper than Sheol – what can you know? (Job 11:6–8)

One concludes from Maimonides' observations that God's hands are shackled by the Torah, and that the omnipotent Lord, for whom nothing is too hard or difficult (Gen. 18:14; Job 42:2; Jer. 32:27), will be unable to teach any further truths. This understanding undermines Isaiah's statement that God's hand 'is stretched out over all nations' (Is. 14:27);[26] that is, He is not fettered. Isaiah further warns that there is no limit to God's ability to redeem His creatures:

Behold, the Lord's hand is not shortened, that it cannot save; neither his ear heavy, that it cannot hear (Is. 59:1)

The concept of finality is also incompatible with the appreciation of a God who is almighty, infinite and everlasting – whose understanding has no limit and whose divine mercies never fail, and who is not to be questioned of His doings:

Great is our Lord, and abundant in power; his understanding is beyond measure. (Ps. 147:5)

Have you not known? Have you not heard? The Lord is the everlasting God, the Creator of the ends of the earth. He does not faint or grow weary; his understanding is unsearchable. (Is. 40:28)

I prayed to the Lord, saying: 'Ah, Lord God! It is you who have made the heavens and the earth by your great power and by your outstretched arm! Nothing is too hard for you.' (Jer. 32:16–17)

The steadfast love of the Lord never ceases; his mercies never come to an end... The Lord is good to those who wait for him, to the soul who seeks him. It is good that one should wait quietly for the salvation of the Lord. (Lam. 3:22, 25–26)

Hence, the warnings not to add or subtract from the Torah were meant for the Jewish religious leaders such as Maimonides, but not the divine Messengers such as Christ, who by contrast did not say anything of their own, and whose words and deeds were according to what God had decreed to them (Deut. 18:18; John 5:19). The Hebrew Bible adds that whenever circumstances demand it, God, and not human wisdom, will guide His creation:

> Trust in the Lord with all your heart; and do not lean on your own understanding. In all thy ways acknowledge him, and he will make straight your paths. Be not wise in your eyes; fear the Lord . . . (Prov. 3:5–7)

Instead of forgetting the former things, as advised in Isaiah 43:18, they added layer upon layer of interpretation to God's Word, adulterating its spiritual intent. A prime example of this is the Talmud, which was compiled many centuries after the Torah, and comprises the pronouncements and debates of several prominent Rabbis.

The assertions that 'Moses is our Saviour' and that salvation comes to the Jewish people through the teachings of the Torah

Salvation, appearing in Hebrew as '*yasa*' (to save, help in peril, rescue, deliver, set free), is also an important theme of the Tanakh and is spoken of more often than in the New Testament. There are several examples of divine salvation in the Hebrew Bible.

Noah's dispensation, His ark of salvation, saved his family and 'animals' from the depravity of the world (Gen. 6:11–19) and from God's wrath. Again, on meeting his brothers who had sold him into slavery in Egypt, Joseph reassured them that the unfortunate episode was a means whereby God had demonstrated His power to save:

> So Joseph said to his brothers, 'Come near to me, please.' And they came near. And he said, 'I am your brother, Joseph, whom you sold into Egypt. And now do not be distressed or angry with yourselves because you sold me here, for God sent me before you to preserve life . . . And God sent me before you to preserve for you a remnant on earth, and to keep alive for you many survivors. So it was not you who sent me here, but God.' (Gen. 45: 4–5, 7–8).

The Psalmist declares that His salvation comes from God:

> For God alone, O my soul, wait in silence, for my hope is from him. He only is my rock and my salvation, my fortress; I shall not be shaken. On God rests my salvation and my glory; my mighty rock, my refuge is God. Trust in him at all times, O people; pour out your heart before him; God is a refuge for us. (Ps. 62:5–8)

The Prophet Hosea predicts that the Lord, their God, will have mercy on the house of Judah and will save them (Hosea 1:7). The Prophet Isaiah defines salvation as being liberated from the prison (of self and passion) by the Sovereign Lord, and being rescued and delivered from evil and harm by Him (Is. 61:1). The Prophet Jeremiah prays that God, 'the salvation of Israel' may deliver the Jews from their sins and heedlessness (Jer. 3:21–23, 25). The Prophet Ezekiel also stresses the need for salvation from sin or transgressions, uncleanness, iniquity and idolatry. Here salvation involves the gift of a new heart and a new spirit, which will finally empower his people to keep the commandments. He urged Israel to seek this life-bestowing transformation and confirmation:

> Repent and turn from all your transgressions, lest iniquity be your ruin. Cast away from you all the transgressions that you have committed, and make yourselves a new heart and a new spirit! Why will you die, O house of Israel? For I have no pleasure in the death of anyone, declares the Lord God; so turn, and live. (Ezek. 18:30–32)

The assertion that 'we have already received salvation from sin through the Lord Yahweh – why do we need to be saved through Jesus?'

The Jews also prayed for the compassionate God to 'wash' them 'thoroughly' from their 'inequities', sin and transgressions (Ps. 51:3–6). The Prophet Ezekiel announced that God will satisfy this wish:

> I will take you from the nations and gather you from all the countries and bring you into your own land. I will sprinkle clean water on you, and you shall be clean from all your uncleannesses, and

from all your idols I will cleanse you. And I will give you a new heart, and a new spirit I will put within you . . . (Ezek. 36:24–26)

The assertion that 'We already have Jehovah as our deliverer from death and Sheol'

The Psalmist declares:

> Like sheep they are appointed for Sheol; death shall be their shepherd. . . Their form shall be consumed in Sheol, with no place to dwell. But God will ransom my soul from the power of Sheol, for he will receive me. (Ps. 49:14–15)

> O God; I will render thank offerings to you. For you have delivered my soul from death, yes, my feet from falling,[27] that I may walk before God in the light of life. (Ps. 56:12–13) Blessed be the Lord, who daily bears us up; God is our salvation. Our God is a God of salvation, and to God, the Lord, belong deliverances from death. (Ps. 68:19–20)

• • • • •

Issue with the followers of John the Baptist

In His address to the adherents of His forerunner who were having difficulty accepting that the mission of their master had been so brief and was now superseded by the dispensation of Christ, Jesus blessed the few who were not deterred by such obstacles in their path:

> Go and tell John what you hear and see: the blind receive their sight and the lame walk, lepers are cleansed and the deaf hear, and the dead are raised up, and the poor have good news preached to them. And blessed is the one who is not offended by me. (Matt. 11:4–6)

The temporary desertion of Christ by His disciples immediately following the crucifixion

We also have a foretaste of lack of receptivity to the Second Coming in the reactions of Jesus's disciples when events at the end of Christ's ministry did not unfold as they had anticipated. Thus, despite all that they had witnessed, Christ's few followers became disheartened and began to doubt whether Jesus had indeed been the expected triumphant Messiah. Thus, at the first sign of persecution, His disciples deserted Him, fled, and were scattered (Matt. 26:56).

Christ spoke of the inevitable spiritual tests that His followers would experience, and denounced the individuals who would be responsible for such difficulties (Luke 17:1–2). He predicted that some of His followers would forsake Him once again:

> Behold, the hour is coming [Greek: ἔρχεται, erchetai), alluding to a future event],[28] indeed it has come [Greek: καὶ ἐλήλυθεν, kai elēlythen) alluding to the time of Christ], when you will be scattered, each to his own home, and will leave me alone. Yet I am not alone, for the Father is with me. (John 16:32)

'Many are called but few are chosen'

This warning of Christ means that few accept God's new revelation and attain salvation. Christ admonished His followers that they should enter God's Kingdom through the more arduous and less convenient path or gate, that is, painstakingly investigate personally the new revelation (Matt. 7:7–11) – tread the less familiar and solitary way, requiring diligence, rather than choose the easier option of trying to enter by 'the wider gate' of simply imitating the majority and following what is popular and mainstream:

> Enter by the narrow gate.[29] For the gate is wide and the way is easy that leads to destruction, and those who enter by it are many. For the gate is narrow and the way is hard that leads to life, and those who find it are few. (Matt. 7:13–14)

He further elaborated that if individuals did not make the difficult choices, they could find themselves left out, even if they considered themselves the natural heirs of the Kingdom:

> And someone said to him, 'Lord, will those who are saved be few?' And he said to them, 'Strive to enter through the narrow door. For

many, I tell you, will seek to enter and will not be able. When once the master of the house has risen and shut the door, and you begin to stand outside and to knock at the door, saying, "Lord, open to us," then he will answer you, "I do not know where you come from." Then you will begin to say, "We ate and drank in your presence, and you taught in our streets." But he will say, "I tell you, I do not know where you come from. Depart from me, all you workers of evil!" In that place there will be weeping and gnashing of teeth, when you see Abraham and Isaac and Jacob and all the prophets in the kingdom of God but you yourselves cast out. And people will come from east and west, and from north and south, and recline at table in the kingdom of God. And behold, some are last who will be first, and some are first who will be last.' (Luke 13:23–30)

Rev. Albert Barnes explained:

> ***Enter ye in at the strait gate*** – Christ here compares the way to life to an entrance through a gate. The words 'straight' and 'strait' have very different meanings. The former means 'not crooked', the latter, 'pent up, narrow, difficult to be entered'. This is the word used here, and it means that the way to heaven is 'pent up, narrow, close', and not obviously entered. The way to death is open, broad, and thronged. The Saviour here referred probably to ancient cities. They were surrounded with walls and entered through gates. Some of those, connected with the great avenues to the city, were broad and admitted a throng; others, for more private purposes, were narrow, and few would be seen entering them. So, says Christ, is the path to heaven. It is narrow. It is not 'the great highway' that people tread. Few go there. Here and there one may be seen – travelling in solitude and singularity. The way to death, on the other hand, is broad. Multitudes are in it. It is the great highway in which people go. They fall into it easily and without effort, and go without thought. If they wish to leave that and go by a narrow gate to the city, it would require effort and thought. So, says Christ, 'diligence' is needed to enter life ... None go of course. All must strive, to obtain it; and so narrow, unfrequented, and solitary is it, that few find it. His sentiment has been beautifully versified by Watts:[30]

> Broad is the road that leads to death,
> And thousands walk together there;
> But wisdom shows a narrower path,
> With here and there a traveller.[31]

In another parable, Jesus compared the failure to recognize the divine revelation to failure to response to a royal summons to a wedding:

> The kingdom of heaven may be compared to a king who gave a wedding feast for his son, and sent his servants to call those who were invited to the wedding feast, but they would not come. Again he sent other servants, saying, 'Tell those who are invited, "See, I have prepared my dinner, my oxen and my fat calves have been slaughtered, and everything is ready. Come to the wedding feast."' But they paid no attention and went off, one to his farm, another to his business, while the rest seized his servants, treated them shamefully, and killed them. The king was angry, and he sent his troops and destroyed those murderers and burned their city. Then he said to his servants, 'The wedding feast is ready, but those invited were not worthy. Go therefore to the main roads and invite to the wedding feast as many as you find.' And those servants went out into the roads and gathered all whom they found, both bad and good. So the wedding hall was filled with guests. But when the king came in to look at the guests, he saw there a man who had no wedding garment. And he said to him, 'Friend, how did you get in here without a wedding garment?' And he was speechless. Then the king said to the attendants, 'Bind him hand and foot and cast him into the outer darkness. In that place there will be weeping and gnashing of teeth.' For many are called, but few are chosen. (Matt. 22:2–14)

Christ in the Gospel of Matthew further states:

> ... many will come from east and west and recline at table with Abraham, Isaac, and Jacob in the kingdom of heaven, while the sons of the kingdom[32] will be thrown into the outer darkness. In that place there will be weeping and gnashing of teeth. (Matt. 8:12)

'The sons of the kingdom' refers to those to whom the kingdom properly and directly belonged. Hence, this term may well have applied to the Jews at the First Coming. However, it applies equally to Christians who, at the Second Coming, believe that the Kingdom of the Father is meant exclusively for them.

The Apostle Paul exhorted Christians to seek and live in the light of divine revelation, and to be spiritually sober and awake, and to possess discernment and perception. He predicted that many would miss the Second Coming because of their spiritual unpreparedness and preconceived notions:

> For you yourselves are fully aware that the day of the Lord will come like a thief in the night. But you are not in darkness, brothers, for that day to surprise you like a thief. For you are all children of light, children of the day. We are not of the night or of the darkness. So then let us not sleep, as others do, but let us keep awake and be sober. But since we belong to the day, let us be sober, having put on the breastplate of faith and love, and for a helmet the hope of salvation. (I Thess. 5:2, 4–6, 8)

Christians are therefore required to develop the spiritual capacity to discern the signs of the latter days and the advent of the Second Coming if they are to avoid repeating the mistakes of the First Coming. As Christians we ought to remind ourselves that, taken in their entirety, the biblical predictions of the Second Coming paint a most uncomfortable phase in human history and, in particular, for the Christian Faith. Christians should not therefore be too eager to reject out of hand God's new revelation because of misplaced feelings of loyalty and kinship to one denomination or another, or because they are unfamiliar with the external features of the new dispensation. Nor should they be too accepting of human interpretations of the scriptural prophecies, as their reality is destined to unfold only after the event actually takes place.

Both the Hebrew Bible and the New Testament urge the true seeker to possess eyes that see, ears that hear, and a heart that is attentive. Without the requisite receptivity the individual is likely to slip and falter. His efforts will be in vain, he will remain blinded to the truth, and he will reject the divine message even if all the signs of the new Day were to appear.

This heedlessness (neglect and inattention) has always been an issue (Ps. 119:70; Jer. 17:9; Zech. 7:11). Christ had to confront this same difficulty with the people of His time, as is evident from His quoting Isaiah 6:10 which described a similar situation:

> Indeed, in their case the prophecy of Isaiah is fulfilled that says: 'You will indeed hear but never understand, and you will indeed see but never perceive.' For this people's heart has grown dull, and with their ears they can barely hear, and their eyes they have closed, lest they should see with their eyes and hear with their ears and understand with their heart and turn, and I would heal them. But blessed are your eyes, for they see, and your ears, for they hear. For truly, I say to you, many prophets and righteous people longed to see what you see, and did not see it, and to hear what you hear, and did not hear it. (Matt. 13:14–17)

The New Testament often follows a certain teaching with the appeal: 'Who hath ears to hear, let him hear' (Matt. 11:15; 13:9; also Mark 4:9; 4:23; 7:16; 7:35; Luke 8:8; 14:35; also similar statements in Rev. 2:11, 17, 29; 3:6, 13, 22). The true sheep, He explained, are those who respond to the voice of the shepherd:

> So the Jews gathered around him and said to him, 'How long will you keep us in suspense? If you are the Christ, tell us plainly.' Jesus answered them, 'I told you, and you do not believe. The works that I do in my Father's name bear witness about me, but you do not believe because you are not among my sheep. My sheep hear my voice, and I know them, and they follow me . . .' (John 10:24–27)

Receptive souls such as His disciples had little difficulty in recognizing that Christ fulfilled Messianic expectations. The Jewish leaders, on the other hand, did not possess the necessary spiritual acuity to realize this:

> And the Pharisees and Sadducees came, and to test him they asked him to show them a sign from heaven. He answered them, 'When it is evening, you say, "It will be fair weather, for the sky is red." And in the morning, "It will be stormy today, for the sky is red and threatening." You know how to interpret the appearance of the sky, but you cannot interpret the signs of the times.' (Matt. 16:1–3)

Rev. Joseph Benson gave the following explanation in his commentary on the New Testament:

> As if he had said, It is evident you ask this out of a desire to cavil rather than to discern the divine will, for in other cases you take up with degrees of evidence far short of those which you here reject: as for instance, you know that a red sky in the evening is a presage of fair weather, and a red and lowering sky in the morning, of foul weather; thus ye can discern the face of the sky, and form from thence very probable conjectures concerning the weather; but can ye not discern the signs of the times – the signs which evidently show that this is the time of the Messiah?[33]

As with the hostile reception of Jesus by the Jewish leaders and the followers of John the Baptist at the First Coming, there is ample scriptural evidence that Christians will experience similar difficulty in recognizing the long-awaited return of Christ in the Glory of the Father. The reasons we have given in this chapter for the rejection of Christ by the Jews are summed up in this quotation from the Bahá'í teachings:

> Now inasmuch as the Jews were submerged in the sea of ancestral imitations, they could not comprehend the meaning of these prophecies. All the words of the prophets were fulfilled, but because the Jews held tenaciously to hereditary interpretations, they did not understand the inner meanings of the Holy Bible; therefore, they denied Jesus Christ, the Messiah. The purpose of the prophetic words was not the outward or literal meaning, but the inner symbolical significance. For example, it was announced that the Messiah was to come from an unknown place. This did not refer to the birthplace of the physical body of Jesus. It has reference to the reality of the Christ –that is to say, the Christ reality was to appear from the invisible realm – for the divine reality of Christ is holy and sanctified above place.[34]

8

STUMBLING BLOCKS AT THE SECOND COMING

We shall now examine some of the obstacles that may prevent Christians from recognizing God's promised revelation (see also Chapter 9).

1. Blind imitation instead of sincere investigation unfettered by prejudice

Faith is too important to be determined by an accident of birth. As with science, one must diligently investigate religious truth, and avoid being unduly influenced by others and choosing 'myth' above 'truth' and 'sound teaching' (II Tim. 4:3–4). A Christian's faith should not be defined by a particular church and clergy, the shape of a crucifix, type of clothing, birthplace, geographical location, family or social grouping, school or university, or even one's own personal name.

However, as noted earlier, few individuals follow Christ's commandment to ask, seek and knock (Matt. 7:7–8) or adhere to the Apostle Paul's injunctions to 'test every thing;[1] hold fast what is good' (I Thess. 5:21); and 'Do not be conformed to this world, but be transformed by the renewal of your mind, that by testing you may discern what is the will of God, what is good and acceptable and perfect' (Rom. 12:2). A minority assess their faith by the exhortation of John the Evangelist: 'Beloved, do not imitate evil but imitate good. Whoever does good is from God; whoever does evil has not seen God' (III John 1:11). Any such inquiry, rather than being greeted as the individual's right and duty as enshrined in the Gospels, is likely to be challenged by a religious leader as indicating the seeker's paucity of faith.

2. Pride when faced with the claim that the Father has, as promised, finally revealed His will and purpose to humanity

At the First Coming only Jesus had the divine authority to interpret the prophecies of the Hebrew Bible about His advent. Similarly, at the Second Coming, only One who manifests the will of the Father possesses the power to interpret the prophecies of earlier scriptures:

> . . . stay awake, for you do not know on what day your Lord is coming. But know this, that if the master of the house had known in what part of the night the thief was coming, he would have stayed awake and would not have let his house be broken into. Therefore you also must be ready, for the Son of Man is coming at an hour you do not expect. (Matt. 24:42–44)

Also,

> But concerning that day or that hour, no one knows, not even the angels in heaven, nor the Son, but only the Father. Be on guard, keep awake. For you do not know when the time will come. (Mark 13:32–33)

> For we know in part and we prophesy in part,[2] but when the perfect comes, the partial will pass away. When I was a child, I spoke like a child, I thought like a child, I reasoned like a child. When I became a man, I gave up childish ways. For now we see in a mirror dimly, but then face to face. Now I know in part; then I shall know fully, even as I have been fully known. (I Cor. 13:9–12)

There is therefore no excuse for disputing with God's promised revelation and basing our arguments on old theological arguments. In this connection, God in the Book of Isaiah admonishes:

> For my thoughts are not your thoughts, neither are your ways my ways, saith the Lord. For as the heavens are higher than the earth, so are my ways higher than your ways, and my thoughts than your thoughts. (Is. 55:8–9)

3. Reliance on literal interpretations of the scripture rather than perceiving their allegorical and spiritual significance

According to the Apostle Paul, a true follower of Moses was not one who relied on the praise of men but instead sought to please God, and was in tune with the spirit and not the letter of the Law:

> For no one is a Jew who is merely one outwardly, nor is circumcision outward and physical. But a Jew is one inwardly, and circumcision is a matter of the heart, by the Spirit, not by the letter. His praise is not from man but from God. (Rom. 2:28–29)

The expected Kingdom of God is a spiritual sovereignty, not a physical dominion

Questioned by the Pharisees as to when they would see the Kingdom of God, Christ warned:

> The kingdom of God is not coming in ways that can be observed, nor will they say, 'Look, here it is!' or 'here!' for behold, the kingdom of God is in the midst of you. (Luke 17:20–21)

Hence, the signs predicted in Matthew 24 of the Second Coming (See Chapter 6) have a spiritual dimension.

Literal interpretations of the scripture stifle the spirit, but spiritual explanations confer life

The Apostle Paul described a true Christian as a letter written by the Holy Spirit, and emphasized the importance of a spiritual understanding of scriptural teachings:

> You yourselves are our letter of recommendation, written on our hearts, to be known and read by all. And you show that you are a letter from Christ delivered by us, written not with ink but with the Spirit of the living God, not on tablets of stone but on tablets of human hearts. Such is the confidence that we have through Christ toward God. Not that we are sufficient in ourselves to claim anything

as coming from us, but our sufficiency is from God, who has made us sufficient to be ministers of a new covenant, not of the letter but of the Spirit. For the letter kills, but the Spirit gives life. (II Cor. 3:2–6)

Rev. Albert Barnes elaborates as follows on the last verse:

> **Not of the letter** – Not of the literal, or verbal meaning, in contradistinction from the Spirit . . . This is said, doubtless, in opposition to the Jews, and Jewish teachers. They insisted much on the letter of the Law, but entered little into its real meaning. They did not seek out the true spiritual sense of the Old Testament; and hence, they rested on the mere literal observance of the rites and ceremonies of religion without understanding their true nature and design. Their service, though in many respects conformed to the letter of the Law, yet became cold, formal, and hypocritical; abounding in mere ceremonies, and where the heart had little to do. Hence, there was little pure spiritual worship offered to God; and hence also they rejected the Messiah whom the old covenant prefigured, and was designed to set forth.
> **For the letter killeth** – The mere letter of the Law of Moses.
> . . . But the spirit giveth life – The spirit, in contradistinction from the mere literal interpretation of the Scriptures. . . the gospel, a spiritual system, is designed to impart life and comfort to the soul.[3]

More recently, John Crossan and Richard Watts have written:

> My point, once again, is not that those ancient people told literal stories and we are now smart enough to take them symbolically, but that they told them symbolically and we are now dumb enough to take them literally.[4]

Christ often spoke in parables to provide spiritual insights and explain divine mysteries to His deserving followers:

> Then the disciples came and said to him, 'Why do you speak to them in parables?' And he answered them, 'To you it has been given to know the secrets of the kingdom of heaven, but to them it has not been given . . .' (Matt. 13:10–11)

There are many instances where the language of the Bible may only be understood figuratively:

> Let the heavens be glad, and let the earth rejoice, and let them say among the nations, 'The Lord reigns!' Let the sea roar, and all that fills it; let the field exult, and everything in it! Then shall the trees of the forest sing for joy before the Lord, for he comes to judge the earth. (I Chr. 16:31–33)

> Let the sea roar . . .! Let the rivers clap their hands; let the hills sing for joy together before the Lord, for he comes to judge the earth. He will judge the world with righteousness, and the peoples with equity. (Ps. 98:7–9)

> For ye shall go out with joy, and be led forth with peace: the mountains and the hills shall break forth before you into singing, and all the trees of the field shall clap their hands. (Is. 55:12)

Several statements of Christ also indicate the spiritual nature of His teachings:

> For truly, I say to you, if you have faith like a grain of mustard seed, you will say to this mountain, 'Move from here to there,' and it will move, and nothing will be impossible for you. (Matt. 17:20)

Also:

> Behold, I have given you authority to tread on serpents and scorpions, and over all the power of the enemy, and nothing shall hurt you. (Luke 10:19)

Some evangelical Christian churches (Holiness, Pentecostal, Charismatic, and others) interpret this and related verses (Mark 16:17–18; Acts 28:3–6) literally. They include snake handling as part of their worship, with occasional lethal outcomes. However, others have emphasized the metaphorical nature of Christ's statement:

> ***To tread on serpents***, etc. – It is possible that by serpents and scorpions

our Lord means the scribes and Pharisees, whom he calls serpents and a brood of vipers, Matthew 23:33, because, through the subtlety and venom of the old serpent, the devil, they opposed him and his doctrine; and, by trampling on these, it is likely that he means, they should get a complete victory over such: as it was an ancient custom to trample on the kings and generals who had been taken in battle, to signify the complete conquest which had been gained over them.[5]

Again, Jesus stated:

> But I say to you that everyone who looks at a woman with lustful intent has already committed adultery with her in his heart. If your right eye causes you to sin [becomes a stumbling-block], tear it out and throw it away. For it is better that you lose one of your members than that your whole body be thrown into hell. And if your right hand causes you to sin, cut it off and throw it away. For it is better that you lose one of your members than that your whole body go into hell. (Matt. 5:28–30)

Some commentators have interpreted this teaching literally, with sometimes tragic consequences:

> The command is here laid down (v. 27), *Thou shalt not commit adultery*; which includes a prohibition of all other acts of uncleanness, and the desire of them . . . We are here taught, that there is such a thing as *heart-adultery*, adulterous thoughts and dispositions, which never proceed to the act of adultery or fornication . . .
> That such looks and such dalliances are so very dangerous and destructive to the soul, that it is better to lose the eye and the hand that thus offend then to give way to the sin, and perish eternally in it. This lesson is here taught us, v. 29, 30. Corrupt nature would soon object against the prohibition of heart-adultery, that it is impossible to governed by it; '*It is a hard saying, who can bear it?* Flesh and blood cannot but look with pleasure upon a beautiful woman; and it is impossible to forbear lusting after and dallying with such an object.' Such pretences as these will scarcely be overcome by reason, and therefore must be argued against with *the terrors of the Lord*, and so they are here argued against.

It is a severe operation that is here prescribed for the preventing of these fleshly lusts. *If thy right eye offend thee*, or *cause thee to offend*, by wanton glances, or wanton gazings, upon forbidden objects; *if thy right hand off end thee*, or *cause thee to offend*, by wanton dalliances; and if it were indeed impossible, as is pretended, to govern the eye and the hand, and they have been so accustomed to these wicked practices, that they will not be withheld from them; if there be no other way to restrain them (which, blessed be God, through his grace, there is), it were better for us to *pluck out the eye*, and *cut off the hand*, though the *right eye*, and *right hand*, the more honourable and useful, than to indulge them in sin to the ruin of the soul . . .

It is a startling argument that is made use of to enforce this prescription (v. 29), and it is repeated in the same words (v. 30), because we are loath to hear such rough things . . . *It is profitable for thee that one of thy members should perish, though it be an eye or a hand, which can be worse spared, and not that thy whole body should be cast into hell.*[6]

Others have sat on the fence:

> . . . there have been fanatical ascetics who have both advocated and practiced this, showing a very low apprehension of spiritual things . . . At the same time, just by cutting off a hand, or plucking out an eye, the power of acting and of seeing would be destroyed . . . our Lord certainly means that we are to strike at the root of such unholy dispositions, as well as to cut off the occasions which tend to stimulate them.[7]

However, most commentators agree that the severity of the directives preclude their literal interpretation and implementation. Christ also taught that God desired that in the hour that is coming, true worshippers approach Him 'in spirit and truth', that is, not in purely materialistic ways (John 4:23–24).

The metaphorical nature of many of the Gospel teachings is vividly illustrated at times in the language used by Christ:

> To another he said, 'Follow me.' But he said, 'Lord, let me first go and bury my father.' And Jesus said to him, 'Leave the dead to bury

their own dead. But as for you, go and proclaim the kingdom of God.' (Luke 9:59–60; also, Matt. 8:22)

When we examine this statement we note that there are four possible computations:

a) let the physically dead bury their physically dead
b) let the physically dead bury their spiritually dead
c) let the spiritually alive and physically alive bury the spiritually dead
d) let the spiritually dead but physically alive bury the physically dead

As explained by the evangelist Billy Graham, only the last option is reasonable:

> What did He mean by this? Jesus wasn't saying that people who were physically dead should bury other dead people; as you say, that wouldn't make sense. Instead He was speaking of those who were spiritually dead – those who were alive physically but dead toward God in their souls. We may be very strong and healthy physically, and yet be spiritually dead – which is far more serious.[8]

Christ was not being unsympathetic to the man's bereavement, but He wished it to be known that He had a very limited time to preach the Gospel – in contrast, the spiritually dead had ample opportunity to perform the burial rites of the physically dead. His disciples had to remain focused on the task at hand, namely, to preach the good news of the coming of the Kingdom.

Again, were the stars, each of which is many times larger than the earth, to fall literally to earth, and the sun to be darkened, (Matt. 24:29), humanity would not survive to witness the return of Christ at the Second Coming.

4. Belief in the exclusivity and finality of Christianity

As with the Synagogue, which asserts the supremacy of the Torah and celebrates God's special favours bestowed on Moses, the Church trumpets the superiority, exclusivity and finality of Christ and His revelation, thus hampering the ability of Christian institutions to respond befittingly to the anticipated revelation. We examine here the New Testament verses that are commonly quoted in support of the exclusivity and finality of Christianity.

Assertion: Unlike other intermediaries, Jesus is the exclusive path to God, the heavenly Father:

> Thomas said to him, 'Lord. We do not know where you are going. How can we know the way?' Jesus said to him, 'I am the way, and the truth, and the life. No one comes to the Father except through me . . . (John 14:5–6)

Understandably, this is interpreted as attesting that truth and salvation are only attainable through Jesus – and presumably not through any other religion or Christian denomination. However, we cannot ignore the fact that 'the way' is not identical with the destination, namely the Kingdom of God revealed at the Second Coming.

If the Prophet following Christ cannot establish a new covenant, how could Jesus contravene the injunctions of the Book of Deuteronomy and bring a 'new testament'? An examination of John 14:6 reveals additional profound explanations that are more inclusive than the traditional and narrow interpretation.

The phrase 'I am' at the beginning of the verse is reminiscent of the title of Yahweh 'I am who I am' in Exodus. In other words, the name of God 'I am' speaking through Jesus shows the way in the dispensation of Christ:

> Then Moses said to God, 'If I come to the people of Israel and say to them, "The God of your fathers has sent me to you", and they ask me, "What is his name?" what shall I say to them?' God said to Moses, "I am who I am." And he said, "Say this to the people of Israel: 'I AM has sent me to you.'" (Ex. 3:13–14)

Matthew Henry's commentary explains this name of God:

> A name that denotes what he is in himself, I AM THAT I AM. This explains his name Jehovah, and signifies, 1. That he is self-existent:

he has his being of himself. 2. That he is eternal and unchangeable, and always the same, yesterday, to-day, and for ever. 3. That he is incomprehensible; we cannot by searching find him out: this name checks all bold and curious inquiries concerning God. 4. That he is faithful and true to all his promises, unchangeable in his word as well as in his nature; let Israel know this, I AM hath sent me unto you. I am, and there is none else besides me. All else have their being from God, and are wholly dependent upon him.[9]

In every dispensation God's intermediary is 'the way', as He is entirely subject to the will of God. For example, for the duration of the dispensation of Moses, Jehovah showed 'the way' to the Children of Israel:

Thus saith the Lord, thy Redeemer, the Holy One of Israel; I am the Lord thy God which teacheth thee to profit, which leadeth thee by the way that thou shouldest go. (Is. 48:17)

I [the Lord] will instruct you and teach you in the way you should go; I will counsel you with my eye upon you. Be not like a horse or a mule, without understanding… (Ps. 32:8–9)

The Hebrew Bible describes that the Lord Yahweh has guided humanity in multiple 'ways' and 'paths':

Make me to know your ways, O Lord; teach me your paths. Lead me in your truth and teach me, for you are the God of my salvation; for you I wait all the day long . . . Good and upright is the Lord; therefore he instructs sinners in the way. He leads the humble in what is right, and teaches the humble his way. All the paths of the Lord are steadfast love and faithfulness, for those who keep his covenant and his testimonies. (Ps. 25:4–5, 8–10)

Notably, John the Baptist came to prepare and to straighten the way for the Messiah:

And this is the testimony of John, when the Jews sent priests and Levites from Jerusalem to ask him, 'Who are you?' He confessed, and did not deny, but confessed, 'I am not the Christ.' And they asked him, 'What then? Are you Elijah?' He said, 'I am not.' 'Are you the Prophet?' And he answered, 'No.' So they said to him, 'Who are you? We need to give an answer to those who sent us. What do you say about yourself?' He said, 'I am the voice of one crying out in the wilderness, "Make straight the way of the Lord," as the prophet Isaiah said.' (John 1:19–23)

Christ taught His followers to treat generously those of other belief systems, but who advocated the same ends.

> John said to him, 'Teacher, we saw someone casting out demons in your name,[10] and we tried to stop him, because he was not following us.' But Jesus said, 'Do not stop him, for no one who does a mighty work in my name will be able soon afterward to speak evil of me. For the one who is not against us is for us.' (Mark 9:38–41)

Rev. Albert Barnes has written:

> Christians should rejoice in good done by their brethren of any denomination. There are men calling themselves Christians who seem to look with doubt and suspicion on all that is done by those who do not walk with them. They undervalue their labors, and attempt to lessen the evidences of their success and to diminish their influence. True likeness to the Saviour would lead us to rejoice in all the good accomplished, by whomsoever it may be done – to rejoice that the kingdom of Christ is advanced, whether by a Presbyterian, an Episcopalian, a Baptist, or a Methodist.[11]

The commentary of Charles John Ellicott similarly states:

> The words are wide-reaching in their range. The true disciples of Christ are to hinder no one who is really doing His work. The very fact that they do it will bring with it reverence and sympathy. They will not quickly be found among those who speak evil of the Son of Man . . .[12]

Assertion: Christ's revelation is perfect and complete

At the end of the New Testament Christians are cautioned not to add to or subtract from the scripture:

> I warn everyone who hears the words of the prophecy of this book: if anyone adds to them, God will add to him the plagues described in this book, and if anyone takes away from the words of the book of this prophecy, God will take away his share in the tree of life and in the holy city, which are described in this book. (Rev. 22:18–19)

The individuals who are in a position to add to, or subtract from, the scriptures are primarily the religious leaders and theologians. The above warning is thus intended first and foremost for them – clearly, it was not meant to restrict the ability of God, for Whom 'all things are possible' (Matt. 19:26), to bring new truths at the time of the next dispensation (see John 16:12).

Assertion: Jesus was God incarnate

This doctrine, that Jesus was God made flesh, is not based on any direct statement of Jesus but was derived indirectly centuries later from testimonies such as:

> Behold, the virgin shall conceive and bear a son, and they shall call his name Immanuel (which means, God with us). (Matt. 1:23)

> In the beginning was the Word, and the Word was with God, and the Word was God. He was in the beginning with God . . . And the Word became flesh and dwelt among us, and we have seen his glory, glory as of the only Son from the Father, full of grace and truth. (John 1:1–2, 14)

The letter of Jude, one of the books with disputed authorship and authenticity, states ambiguously:

> . . . to the only God, our Savior, through Jesus Christ our Lord, be

glory, majesty, dominion, and authority, before all time and now and forever. Amen. (Jude 1:25)

Bahá'ís believe that all that Christ taught and did was directed by God and in accordance with the divine will. Hence they fully accept the statement of Christ that 'I and the Father are One' (John 10:30). However they do not accept that God incarnated His nature at the First Coming or today:

> The divinity attributed to so great a Being and the complete incarnation of the names and attributes of God in so exalted a Person should, under no circumstances, be misconceived or misinterpreted. The human temple that has been made the vehicle of so overpowering a Revelation must, if we be faithful to the tenets of our Faith, ever remain entirely distinguished from that 'innermost Spirit of Spirits' and 'eternal Essence of Essences' – that invisible yet rational God Who, however much we extol the divinity of His Manifestations on earth, can in no wise incarnate His infinite, His unknowable, His incorruptible and all-embracing Reality in the concrete and limited frame of a mortal being. Indeed, the God Who could so incarnate His own reality would, in the light of the teachings of Bahá'u'lláh, cease immediately to be God.[13]

Assertion: Jesus is the only Saviour

Rev. Joseph Benson writes:

> From the appellation here used, our Saviour, it is argued by some that this doxology is addressed to the Lord Jesus, whose proper title is our Saviour, and who is called God in other passages of Scripture, particularly Romans 9:5, where he is styled, God blessed for ever. Nevertheless, as in some passages of Scripture, particularly Luke 1:47; I Timothy 1:1; Titus 1:3, the Father is styled our Saviour, this argument is doubtful. They who contend that the doxology in this passage belongs to the Father, observe that the same doxology is unambiguously addressed to God the Father, Romans 16:27... [also, Is. 12:2 and 45:21][14]

Salvation is often regarded as uniquely applicable to Jesus and only attainable through Him. However, being freed from sin is not an exclusively Christian concept but, as noted previously, is also a teaching of the Tanakh. In reality, every religion provides the salvation of its peoples.

There are additionally the following statements of the Apostle Paul which appear to add credence to the claim of exclusivity, superiority, and finality of Christ and His message:

> And there is salvation in no one else, for there is no other name under heaven given among men by which we must be saved. (Acts 4:12)

> And he commanded us to preach to the people and to testify that he is the one appointed by God to be judge of the living and the dead. To him all the prophets bear witness that everyone who believes in him receives forgiveness of sins through his name. (Acts 10:42–43)

However, while these are true statements in the context of the Christian dispensation, they cannot be taken to imply that the All-Merciful God will not also provide for the salvation for the followers of other religions and for the rest of humanity. Furthermore, Hebrews asserts that God's Purpose as revealed through Jesus Christ was continuous with the past, and the future: 'Jesus Christ is the same yesterday, and today, and for ever' (Heb. 13:8). Again, God, having spoken at 'many times and in many ways' in the past through the Prophets, had 'in these last days spoken to us by his Son' (Heb 1:1–2).

Moreover, the concept of the finality and supremacy of Jesus must be judged with reference to descriptions such as 'the Alpha and Omega', 'the Beginning and the End', 'the first and the last' (Rev. 1:17; 21:6; 22:13), and 'Who is and who was and who is to come, the Almighty' (Rev. 1:4, 8; and 4:8). These imply that it is God's Light that is eternal. They testify that there is but one God, the revealer of all dispensations, and His Faith and Purpose are One. Clearly, Christ had a central role in this unfolding divine agenda.

One may also note that the view that Christ is the only Saviour that humanity has experienced or will experience inevitably leads to intolerance of other religions and the conviction that non-Christians are all condemned to hell-fire.

Assertion: Jesus is the 'only begotten Son' of the Father

The terms 'Son', 'only Son' (John 1:18), 'Son of God' (I John 5:20), and 'only begotten Son' (I John 4:9) are used to refer to Jesus in the New Testament. However, they are also part of the phraseology of the Hebrew Bible, but there they are not used in any form that would suggest a physical begetting by God. Indeed, a literal interpretation of 'Son' and 'begotten' would have been deemed utterly blasphemous by all Jews and many early Christians.

The Hebrew Bible and the New Testament refer to many other sons of God. Therefore, 'only Son' may be interpreted as referring to the special relationship of Christ to God, rather than in the sense of a 'solitary' or 'lone' Son.

One also notes that God tells Abraham to sacrifice His 'only' son Isaac (Gen. 22:2), when clearly Abraham had another son called Ishmael who was fourteen years older than Isaac.[15] This anomaly has been explained by the fact that Ishmael had been sent away, but this fact did not make Ishmael any less the son of Abraham, particularly in view of his glorious divinely ordained destiny (Gen. 17:20).

Some examples where the terms are understood figuratively are:

'Son(s) of God' denoting general humanity[16] or a Prophet

> When man began to multiply on the face of the land and daughters were born to them, the sons of God saw that the daughters of man were attractive. And they took as their wives any they chose. (Gen. 6:1–2)

> The Lord addressing His Anointed Davidic King, says: 'You are My Son; today I have begotten you . . . (Ps. 2:7).

'My son' and 'My first-born' (first-begotten), referring to the people of Israel

> Then you [Moses] shall say to Pharaoh, 'Thus says the Lord, Israel is my firstborn son, and I say to you, "Let my son go that he may serve me." If you refuse to let him go, behold, I will kill your firstborn son.' (Ex. 4:22–23)

When Israel was a child, I loved him, and out of Egypt I called my son. (Hos. 11:1)

'Son of God'

It was not uncommon for those who were the highest authority to be regarded as the son of God.[17] Christ acknowledged that the Jews, as recipients of the Word of God, had been referred to as gods.

> Jesus answered them, Is it not written in your law, I said, Ye are gods? If he called them gods, unto whom the word of God came, and the scripture cannot be broken. (John 10:34–35)

God is love: thus anyone who loves others is born of God:

> Ye are from God, little children . . . Beloved, let us love one another, for love is from God, and whoever loves has been born of God and knows God. Anyone who does not love does not know God, because God is love. (I John 4:4, 7–8)

Anyone who accepted God's light was to be regarded as a begotten son of God (John 1:12–13). Again,

> Everyone who believes that Jesus is the Christ has been born of God . . . (I John 5:1)

The phrase 'begotten son' is synonymous with being derived from the Spirit of God, denoting an intimate knowledge and purpose of God. It does not imply a physical relationship with God. The word 'only' used in association with 'begotten son' describes a special or specific relationship that the Author of a revelation has with God.

> No man hath seen God at any time; the only begotten[18] Son, which is in the bosom of the Father, he hath declared him. (King James Version: John 1:18)

Christ dismissed the notion of an exclusive inherited relationship to God – man must demonstrate his faith by the fruits of his labours and not by mere association:

> And do not presume to say to yourselves, 'We have Abraham as our father,' for I tell you, God is able from these stones to raise up children for Abraham. (Matt. 3:9)

Exclusivity leading to denial of other faiths

An exclusivist approach also contradicts Christ's statements of other sheep (non-Jews) that belong to other legitimate flocks (religions or dispensations) – presumably they also attained salvation through the same Creator (John 10:16). Thus, through misunderstanding of the teachings of Christ, exclusivity and intolerance unfortunately became a feature of Christianity, resulting in one denomination becoming estranged from another, and at times condemning it to eternal damnation.

According to the Gospel of Luke, Christ prohibited His followers from abusing or anathematizing others; this would include anyone who does not share their beliefs:

> . . . bless those who curse you, pray for those who abuse you. (Luke 6:28)

We note however, that the Apostle Paul invoked God's wrath against those who did not love Jesus and who preached any other gospel:

> If any man love not the Lord Jesus Christ, let him be Anathema Maranatha. [King James Version: I Cor. 16:22)

The biblical scholar Rev. Albert Barnes provides the following explanation:

> Anathema signifies a thing devoted to destruction, and it seems to have been customary with the Jews of that age, when they had pronounced any man anathema, to add the Syriac expression, Maranatha, that is, the Lord cometh; namely, to execute vengeance upon him . . . We may add further here, 'Anathema Maranatha' were the words with

which the Jews began their greatest excommunications, whereby they not only excluded sinners from their society, but delivered them to the divine Cherem, or Anathema; that is, to eternal perdition.[19]

And Paul reiterated his view in the Epistle to the Galatians:

> As we said before, so say I now again, If any man preach any other gospel unto you than that ye have received, let him be accursed [Greek: ἀνάθεμα ἔστω, *anathema estō*].[20] (King James Version: Gal. 1:9)

In time anathema became an instrument of intolerance, an ecclesiastical curse used to execrate and excommunicate individuals or communities that did not share the opinion of the church, consigning them to damnation or destruction. Infamously, an anathema was issued by the Catholic Church in 1054 CE against the Eastern Patriarch, who then issued an anathema against the prelate who delivered the message. Only as recently as 1965, after more than nine hundred years of interdenominational animosities and overt hostilities, did the Pope and the Ecumenical Patriarch of Constantinople nullify the anathemas. This nullification was essentially a goodwill gesture and did not constitute any sort of reconciliation or unification.

Nurturing a sense of religious superiority and exclusivity and confident in the knowledge of who is a believer and who is a disbeliever

As noted earlier, the message of Christ attempted to break through the overpowering orthodox Jewish inflexibility, exclusivity and insularity, and to encourage a more inclusive and loving relationship. The Apostle Paul condemned the hypocrisy and false sense of spiritual superiority exhibited by some Jews:

> But if you call yourself a Jew and rely on the law and boast in God and know his will and approve what is excellent, because you are instructed from the law; and if you are sure that you yourself are a guide to the blind, a light to those who are in darkness, an instructor of the foolish, a teacher of children, having in the law the embodiment of knowledge and truth – you then who teach others, do you

not teach yourself? While you preach against stealing, do you steal? You who say that one must not commit adultery, do you commit adultery? You who abhor idols, do you rob temples? You who boast in the law dishonor God by breaking the law. For, as it is written, 'The name of God is blasphemed among the Gentiles because of you.' (Rom. 2:17–24)

However, soon after Jesus's crucifixion, some of His followers became preoccupied with defining who was a true believer and who was not.

In his second letter to the troubled church in Corinth (c. 55 CE), Paul discouraged fellowship (particularly intermarriage) with non-Christians:

> Do not be unequally yoked [Greek: ἑτεροζυγοῦντες, heterozygountes][21] with unbelievers. For what partnership has righteousness with lawlessness? Or what fellowship has light with darkness? What accord has Christ with Belial? Or what portion does a believer share with an unbeliever? What agreement has the temple of God with idols? For we are the temple of the living God; as God said, 'I will make my dwelling among them and walk among them, and I will be their God, and they shall be my people. Therefore go out from their midst, and be separate from them, says the Lord, and touch no unclean thing; then I will welcome you, and I will be a father to you, and you shall be sons and daughters to me, says the Lord Almighty.' (II Cor. 6:14–18)

In his commentary, Joseph Benson states:

> **'Do not be unequally yoked with unbelievers'** – Christians with Jews or heathen, godly persons with the ungodly, spiritual with such as are carnal. The Apostle particularly speaks of marriage; but the reasons equally hold against any needless intimacy or society with them.[22]

And Ellicott writes:

> *Be ye not unequally yoked together with unbelievers.* – We seem at first to enter, by an abrupt transition, upon a new line of exhortation. The under-current of thought is, however, not difficult to

trace. There was a false latitude as well as a true. The baser party at Corinth might think it a matter of indifference whether they married a heathen or a Christian, whether they chose their intimate friends among the worshippers of Aphrodite or of Christ. Against that 'enlargement' the Apostle feels bound to protest . . . Cattle were unequally yoked together when ox and ass were drawing the same plough (Deut. 22:10). Men and women are so when they have no common bond of faith in God.[23]

However, it is difficult to reconcile these sentiments, which discriminate sharply between believers and non-believers, with Christ's parable of the Samaritan (Luke 10:25–37), His willingness to befriend a Roman centurion (Matt. 8:5–13), and His association with people deemed to be sinful and undesirable (Mark 2:16–17).

Intolerance of other religions

The belief that the doctrines and rituals of a particular church are, as ordained by God, the only way of attaining salvation has been the cause of many acts of interdenominational and interreligious intolerance over the past centuries. This interfaith hostility is particularly tragic, as most Christians have been and remain unaware of the truths and the scriptures of other belief systems, and cannot acknowledge the magnitude of their colossal spiritual and social achievements.

Sadly, exclusivism became part of the teaching of the Church early on. A Church father, Augustine of Hippo (354–430 CE), famously said:

> Whoever is without the Church will not be reckoned among the sons, and whoever does not want to have the Church as mother will not have God as father.[24]

This point has been driven home by several popes and church councils. Thus, Pope Pelagius II (578–590 CE) wrote that if individuals were not in the bosom of the Church, even martyrdom would be insufficient to ensure their salvation:

> Consider the fact that whoever has not been in the peace and unity of the Church cannot have the Lord . . . Although given over to

flames and fires, they burn, or, thrown to wild beasts, they lay down their lives, there will not be (for them) that crown of faith but the punishment of faithlessness . . . Such a one can be slain, he cannot be crowned . . . [If] slain outside the Church, he cannot attain the rewards of the Church.[25]

Pope Gregory the Great (490–604 CE) declared:

Now the holy Church universal proclaims that God cannot be truly worshipped saving within herself, asserting that all they that are without her shall never be saved.[26]

In 1215 the Fourth Lateran Council officially reaffirmed: 'There is but one universal Church of the faithful, outside which no one at all is saved' – *Extra Ecclesiam Nulla Salus* ('no salvation outside of the Christian *church*'), and established the Inquisition to root out all forms of heresy. These declarations of the Council, rather than strengthening faith, resulted in a pushback by those who felt that the Church had drifted too far from the original teachings of Christ and the Apostles. The fallout, and subsequent Council pronouncements and papal declarations eventually led to the Reformation. Nevertheless, Pope Boniface stated in his Bull *Unam Sanctum* in 1302:

We are compelled in virtue of our faith to believe and maintain that there is only one holy Catholic Church, and that one is apostolic. This we firmly believe and profess without qualification. Outside this Church there is no salvation and no remission of sins . . . We declare, say, define, and pronounce that it is absolutely necessary for the salvation of every human creature to be subject to the Roman Pontiff.[27]

The Council of Florence (1438–45) confirmed this uncompromising viewpoint:

The most Holy Roman Church firmly believes, professes and preaches that none of those existing outside the Catholic Church, not only pagans, but also Jews and heretics and schismatics, can have a share in life eternal; but that they will go into the 'eternal fire which was prepared for the devil and his angels' (Matthew 25:41), unless before death they are joined with Her; and that so important is the unity of this ecclesiastical body that only those remaining within this unity can profit by the sacraments of the Church unto salvation, and they alone can receive an eternal recompense for their fasts, their almsgivings, their other works of Christian piety and the duties of a Christian soldier. No one, let his almsgiving be as great as it may, no one, even if he pour out his blood for the Name of Christ, can be saved, unless he remain within the bosom and the unity of the Catholic Church.[28]

Pope Leo XII reiterated the supremacy of the church in 1824:

It is impossible for the most true God, who is Truth itself, the best, the wisest Provider, and the Rewarder of good men, to approve all sects who profess false teachings which are often inconsistent with one another and contradictory, and to confer eternal rewards on their members . . . by divine faith we hold one Lord, one faith, one baptism, and that no other name under heaven is given to men except the name of Jesus Christ of Nazareth in which we must be saved. This is why we profess that there is no salvation outside the Church.[29]

Promoting the concept that the Catholic Church deserved to be the official state religion, Pope Leo XIII (1810–1903) pronounced:

Justice therefore forbids, and reason itself forbids, the State to be godless; or to adopt a line of action which would end in godlessness – namely, to treat the various religions (as they call them) alike, and to bestow upon them promiscuously equal rights and privileges. Since, then, the profession of one religion is necessary in the State, that religion must be professed which alone is true, and which can be recognized without difficulty, especially in Catholic States, because the marks of truth are, as it were, engravers upon it. This religion, therefore, the rulers of the State must preserve and protect, if they would provide – as they should do – with prudence and usefulness for the good of the community.[30]

In an encyclical Pope Pius IX[31] wrote in 1863:

> And here, beloved Sons and Venerable Brothers, We should mention again and censure a very grave error in which some Catholics are unhappily engaged, who believe that men living in error, and separated from the true faith and from Catholic unity, can attain eternal life. Indeed, this is certainly quite contrary to Catholic teaching. It is known to Us and to you that they who labor in invincible ignorance of our most holy religion and who, zealously keeping the natural law and its precepts engraved in the hearts of all by God, and being ready to obey God, live an honest and upright life, can, by the operating power of divine light and grace, attain eternal life, since God who clearly beholds, searches, and knows the minds, souls, thoughts, and habits of all men, because of His great goodness and mercy, will by no means suffer anyone to be punished with eternal torment who has not the guilt of deliberate sin. But, the Catholic dogma that no one can be saved outside the Catholic Church is well-known; and also that those who are obstinate toward the authority and definitions of the same Church, and who persistently separate themselves from the unity of the Church, and from the Roman Pontiff, the successor of Peter cannot obtain eternal salvation . . .[32]

As recently as 1953 Pope Pius XII declared:

> By divine mandate the interpreter and guardian of the Scriptures, and the depository of Sacred Tradition living within her, the Church alone is the entrance to salvation: She alone, by herself, and under the protection and guidance of the Holy Spirit, is the source of truth.[33]

Attempts to counteract the enervating rigid exclusivism

The Second Vatican Council (1962–1965) introduced sweeping reforms that sought to create a more modern and open church. In an attempt to be more inclusive of other faiths without conceding that they each had their own path of salvation to God, a controversial formulation referred to as 'Anonymous Christianity' was articulated by the Jesuit theologian Karl Rahner (1904–1984), namely, that members of other religions who have never heard the Christian Gospel may not be deprived of salvation:

> 'Anonymous Christianity' means that a person lives in the grace of God and attains salvation outside explicitly constituted Christianity. A Protestant Christian is, of course, no 'anonymous Christian'; that is perfectly clear. But let us say, a Buddhist monk (or anyone else I might suppose) who, because he follows his conscience, attains salvation and lives in the grace of God, of him I must say that he is an anonymous Christian; if not, I would have to presuppose that there is a genuine path to salvation that really attains that goal, but that simply has nothing to do with Jesus Christ. But I cannot do that. And so if I hold that everyone depends upon Jesus Christ for salvation, and if at the same time I hold that many live in the world who have not expressly recognized Jesus Christ, there remains in my opinion nothing else but to make up the postulate of an anonymous Christianity.[34]

He concluded:

> Hinduism, Buddhism, and Islam cannot be considered simply as human inventions that have gone bad or as a deterioration of human religiosity that has to be judged negatively. But how they are to be more exactly interpreted, what can be learned from them, what differences and what common characteristics there may be already existing – all that has to be investigated much better so that there really can be a dialogue of Christianity with the other world religions.[35]

Subsequently, the concept of Anonymous Christianity received papal blessing:

> Nevertheless, God, who desires to call all peoples to himself in Christ and to communicate to them the fullness of his revelation and love, 'does not fail to make himself present in many ways, not only to individuals, but also to entire peoples through their spiritual riches, of which their religions are the main and essential expression even when they contain "gaps, insufficiencies and errors"'. Therefore, the sacred books of other religions, which in actual fact direct and

nourish the existence of their followers, receive from the mystery of Christ the elements of goodness and grace which they contain.[36]

Nevertheless, this revised viewpoint did not lead to a wholehearted acceptance of the legitimacy of the other major religions of mankind – that they too derived their inspiration from the same God through teachers other than Christ, and were in effect different facets of the same divine faith:

> According to the concept of Anonymous Christianity, the 'Mystery of Christ' is contained in varying degrees in non-Christian religions. Therefore, salvation is also available in those other religions.
> This teaching ostensibly affirms Jesus as the only way of salvation. However, it also locates Jesus (albeit imperfectly) in other religions outside Christianity. These religions variously deny Jesus (Judaism), call him a mere prophet (Islam), an ascended master (Buddhism), or know nothing of him (spiritism, animism, etc.). These other concepts of Jesus are not merely imperfect revelations of Jesus, but are, in fact, various forms of denying Jesus as Holy Scripture reveals Him.
> This teaching also ostensibly denies that there is salvation outside of Christianity. However, it does so by including as 'anonymous' Christians individual members of virtually every religion.
> In other words, the teaching denies what it claims to affirm – the teaching of salvation in Christ Alone, and affirms what it claims to deny – salvation outside the Christian faith.[37]

Furthermore, even this modest rapprochement has been criticized and met with hostility:

> Conservative Christians generally believe that the notion of Anonymous Christian explicitly contradicts the teachings of Peter, Paul and other Apostles. For example, Acts 4:12, 'there is salvation in no one else; for there is no other name under heaven that has been given among men, by which we must be saved.' This group of Christians believes in 'Christian exclusivism – the view that biblical Christianity is true, and that other religious systems are false'.[38]

Although several popes endorsed the ecumenism of Vatican II,[39] it has been denounced as false, heretical and an apostasy.[40] Traditional Catholics have criticized the decisions of the Council as contrary to the sacred traditions of the Catholic Church, citing many earlier anti-ecumenical statements by the church such as the ex-cathedra Papal Bull[41] of Pope Eugene IV which reiterated that not even a Christian martyr who has not been fully within the body of the Catholic Church can hope for salvation:

> It [the Roman Church] firmly believes, professes and preaches that none of those existing outside the Catholic Church, not only pagans, but also Jews, and heretics, and schismatics, can ever be partakers of eternal life, but that they are to go into the eternal fire 'which was prepared for the devil, and his angels,' (Matt. 25:41) unless before death they are joined with Her; and that so important is the unity of this Ecclesiastical Body, that only those remaining within this unity can profit from the sacraments of the Church unto salvation, and that they alone can receive an eternal recompense for their fasts, alms deeds, and other works of Christian piety and duties of a Christian soldier. No one, let his almsgiving be as great as it may, no one, even if he pour out his blood for the Name of Christ, can be saved unless they abide within the bosom and unity of the Catholic Church.[42]

Some fundamentalist Catholics have felt sufficiently aggrieved by the theological and disciplinary reforms of Vatican II and the Church's embrace of non-traditional modernism and pluralism principles and practices, as to support Sedevacantism (from the Latin *sede vacante*, 'vacant see'), the notion that the Holy See has not been occupied by a legitimate pope but has remained vacant since Pope Pius XII (d. 1958).[43] In parallel, the Eastern Orthodox Church regards itself as the 'one, holy, catholic church' as defined at the Council of Nicaea.[44] And continuing the exclusivist theological bent, Martin Luther said:

> For where Christ is not preached, there is no Holy Spirit to create, call and gather the Christian Church, and outside it no one can come to the Lord Christ.[45]

For their part, several Protestant churches, including the Lutheran, Baptist, Anabaptist, Methodist and Seventh-Day Adventist churches, also insist zealously that their particular denomination and reading of the scriptures is the only path to salvation and heaven.

Whatever the reasons for this divisive belief, it is certainly not a teaching that can any longer be justified, as it is destructive of faith, love and fellowship. In this connection, it has been insightfully observed that the conviction that the followers of a particular religion possess a monopoly on God's truth invariably fosters violence against those who are considered to be outsiders.[46]

For His part, Christ taught Christians to love the Creator and Father of all mankind (Mark 12:30), to love their fellow Christians (John 13:34–35) and to love their neighbours despite differences, as well as those they had considered to be their enemies (Matt. 5:43–47; see Chapter 2 above). Quite clearly, in this day all humanity has become our neighbours.

5. Heedlessness and ignoring the Divine Summons – slumbering through the Second Coming and being in need of reawakening

The followers of Christ might do well to ponder what has been the end result of all the animosity, bloodshed and division at the altar of dogma and tradition. Would they and humanity not have fared better if the institutions had confined their efforts to preaching the original message and the glad-tidings of the coming of the Kingdom and endeavored to live up to the standards of the spiritual teachings of Christ? Would Christ on His return be proud of their actions, or would He remind them of His warning: 'And then will I declare to them, "I never knew you; depart from me, you workers of lawlessness"'[47] (Matt. 7:23)?

First and foremost, God has summoned the children of Israel and the children of the Kingdom to reawaken spiritually. Christ in the Gospel of John had warned that at both the First Coming and the Second Coming, only those who hearkened to God's voice would live:

> Truly, truly, I say to you, an hour is coming, and is now here, when the dead will hear the voice of the Son of God, and those who hear will live. (John 5:25)

STUMBLING BLOCKS AT THE SECOND COMING

According to Ellicott's commentary on this verse:

> ***The hour is coming.*** *– . . .* The reference here, as in the whole of this paragraph (John 5:21–27), is to the spiritually dead. This is shown by the 'now is', which cannot be applied to the physical resurrection (comp. John 5:28), and cannot be explained by the instances of physical restoration to life during the earthly ministry of our Lord; and also by the last clause, where 'live' must mean the higher spiritual life, as it does in the whole context. It is shown too by the parallelism of the clauses with those of the previous verse: –
>
> ***'He that heareth'** . . . **'the dead shall hear'** . . . **'the voice of the Son of God'**, **'they that hear shall live'***. The world is as a vast moral graveyard where men lie dead in sin, – sense-bound hand and foot, with spirits buried in bodies which should be holy temples, but have become as unclean tombs; but the voice of the Son of God speaks, and spirit, love, life, passes through the chambers of death, quickening souls whose death is as yet but a sleep, and those who hear and obey come forth into new life.[48]

The Bible alerts us to the paralysis of faith that insidiously affects individuals. The Israelites were at various stages afflicted by this spiritual torpor and somnolence in spite of the signs that they witnessed:

> And Moses summoned all Israel and said to them: 'You have seen all that the Lord did before your eyes in the land of Egypt, to Pharaoh and to all his servants and to all his land, the great trials that your eyes saw, the signs, and those great wonders. But to this day the Lord has not given you a heart to understand or eyes to see or ears to hear.' (Deut. 29:2–4)

> For the Lord has poured out upon you a spirit of deep sleep, and has closed your eyes (the prophets), and covered your heads (the seers). (Is. 29:10)

The Prophet Isaiah (51:17 and 52:1–2) demanded that Israel wake up, particularly following all the dire tribulations that it had experienced.

The Apostle Paul bemoaned the tragic stupor that had become prevalent at the First Coming:

> What then? Israel failed to obtain what it was seeking. The elect obtained it, but the rest were hardened, as it is written, 'God gave them a spirit of stupor, eyes that would not see and ears that would not hear, down to this very day.' (Rom. 11:7–8)

Christ and the Apostles also repeatedly warned that at the Second Coming many would become aware that the Lord had come only after the event had taken place. They therefore called on Christians to remain awake and to be vigilant:

> . . . the hour has come for you to wake from sleep. For salvation is nearer to us now than when we first believed. The night is far gone; the day is at hand. So then let us cast off the works of darkness and put on the armour of light. (Rom. 13:11–12)

> . . . try to discern what is pleasing to the Lord. Therefore it says [Is. 60:1–2], 'Awake, O sleeper, and arise from the dead, and Christ will shine on you.' (Eph. 5:10, 14)

The same death-like spiritual slumber is responsible today for many Jews and Christians not recognizing the principal event for which they have waited and prayed for so long.

6. Professing to love Jesus but ignoring His admonitions concerning His advent in the Glory of the Father

For some time now the church has paid only lip service to the good news of the Gospels. Instead, it has continued to be preoccupied with earthly concerns and mundane interests – the actual expectation of the return of Christ and of the Second Coming has gradually receded into the background, diminishing in importance and coming to come to be regarded as one of its peripheral, and not central, teachings. Christ had warned them about this possible tragic development:

> . . . the master of that servant will come on a day when he does not expect him and at an hour he does not know . . . And that servant who knew his master's will but did not get ready or act according to his will, will receive a severe beating. But the one who did not know,

and did what deserved a beating, will receive a light beating. (Luke 12:46–48)

Every Sunday for the past two thousand years, Christians have flocked into the many churches of the various denominations and have there been reminded of the promise enshrined in the Lord's Prayer of the coming of the Kingdom of the Father. However, some learned theologians have decried the fact that the Second Coming, which is at the very heart and centre of New Testament teaching, has today been largely ignored by Christians and the church. For example, towards the end of the 19th century John Stuart Blackie (1809–1895) described that a basis of Christianity was 'a firm belief and a loving expectation of the Second Coming of a Saviour', adding that this factor now 'exists more as a vague belief than as an operative force. The few who live upon this idea now, do so as a matter of personal connection and private consolation; as a living power in the modern Christian church there is no such belief.'[49] More recently, Rev. William Barclay (1907–1978) wrote in his commentary on the Apostles' Creed that for many Christians 'it is a belief which has simply vanished from the forefront of their minds, taking its place on the circumference, and even among the eccentricities of Christian doctrine. They seldom preach on it, and simply lay it aside.'[50]

7. Novelty of the revelation, and lack of familiarity with its teachings and outward form

The Apostle Peter explained that it is to be expected that unbelievers will stumble, as they are inclined to object to God's chosen new revelation:

> So the honour is for you who believe, but for those who do not believe, 'The stone that the builders rejected has become the cornerstone,' And 'A stone of stumbling, and a rock of offense [the cornerstone which projects from the building causes them to dash themselves against it and fall].' They stumble because they disobey the word, as they were destined to do [they are disposed to reject the Gospel]. (I Peter 2:7–8; see Is. 8:13–15)

There is a genuine fear that by investigating a new divine message one is being unfaithful to one's previous faith. There is guilt in leaving familiar surroundings and like-minded fellow religionists. The unknown outward form of the new dispensation, its new name, its emergence from an unexpected place, and different social principles, are often major stumbling blocks that prevent its ready acceptance. As observed earlier, both the Hebrew Bible and the New Testament anticipate this major predicament by alerting both the Children of Israel and the Christians that God intends to do a new thing and reveal new heavens and a new earth and, in the process, once again to offer the water of life to the thirsty. In contrast, He does not intend to simply ratify the accumulated dogma, human explanations, rituals and traditions to which they have grown accustomed. Indeed, they should be aware that the new revelation will signal the passing of the old heaven and earth and 'former things' (Rev. 21:1, 4).

Fear of the new leads to institutional alarm and opposition

To the religious leaders, the unfamiliar teachings, background, and features of the new faith appear to be dangerous innovations which are not sanctioned by ancient tradition, and which challenge sacrosanct customs and practices on which the sacerdotal order largely depends for its revenues. The fear of the new name and the new revelation causes it to be regarded as a threat to faith – a deviation, a blasphemy, and a heresy.

The Jewish leaders expected their Messiah to re-establish and uphold the laws of the Torah, but not to change them or bring innovations. Christian clergy, in turn, would be distressed if Christ on His return did not approve of their particular church, or ascribe to their version of Christianity.

For these reasons, members of the religious hierarchy have been foremost in rejecting, and in the forefront of the persecution of, every new revelation.

8. Blindness and deafness caused by excessive love for the earlier Divine Messenger, and unquestioning devotion to time-expired dispensations and man-made institutions

As noted earlier, the Jews feel such a strong attachment to Moses that they fail to see the power and glory of Christ, and many Christians express a similar strong attachment to Jesus. This causes them to become apprehensive when presented with a divine revelation by another name. In consideration of this anxiety and fear, Jesus declared that the primary objective of His followers must be to look for the kingdom of the Father (Luke 12:29–32). Importantly, He also reassured His own disciples that a time would come when it would be expedient for them that He should go away, otherwise they would not be able to receive the next and 'another' Revealer of truth (John 14:16–17). Again,

> Nevertheless, I tell you the truth: it is to your advantage that I go away,[51] for if I do not go away, the Helper will not come to you. But if I go, I will send him to you. And when he comes, he will convict the world concerning sin and righteousness and judgment . . . (John 16:7–8)

One commentary explains:

> ***It is expedient for you that I go away.*** – 'There is no cause', He would say, 'for the deep sorrow which has filled your hearts. It is for your advantage that I, as distinct from the Paraclete, who is to come, should go away' (John 14:16). Yes; for those who had left all to follow Him; for those who had none to go to but Himself (John 6:68); for those whose hopes were all centred in Him, it was – hard and incomprehensible as the saying must have seemed – an advantage that He should go away.[52]

If one insists that the above passage refers to the third Person of the Trinity, one may wonder why the presence of the Holy Spirit was more valuable to the disciples than Jesus, presumably the second Person of the Trinity. It would only be to their advantage if through the aid of the Holy Spirit Christians were able to embrace the Second Coming.

9. Being blinded by dazzling titles, rituals, and charismatic personalities,[53] and placing undue reliance on the words of religious leaders

The Hebrew Bible chastises religious leaders for causing disunity and divisions, and for dispersing the flock:

> Woe to the shepherds who destroy and scatter the sheep of my pasture! declares the Lord. Therefore thus says the Lord, the God of Israel, concerning the shepherds who care for my people: 'You have scattered my flock and have driven them away, and you have not attended to them. Behold, I will attend to you for your evil deeds, declares the Lord. Then I will gather the remnant of my flock out of all the countries where I have driven them, and I will bring them back to their fold, and they shall be fruitful and multiply. I will set shepherds over them who will care for them, and they shall fear no more, nor be dismayed, neither shall any be missing, declares the Lord. (Jer. 23:1–4)

The Prophet Ezekiel warned of a day when false shepherds, acting out of self-interest, would prey on the scattered sheep. God would admonish the guilty shepherds. He would search for His sheep and seek them out, and He would rescue His flock:

> Son of man, prophesy against the shepherds of Israel; prophesy, and say to them, even to the shepherds, Thus says the Lord God: Ah, shepherds of Israel who have been feeding yourselves! Should not shepherds feed the sheep? You eat the fat, you clothe yourselves with the wool, you slaughter the fat ones, but you do not feed the sheep. The weak you have not strengthened, the sick you have not healed, the injured you have not bound up, the strayed you have not brought back, the lost you have not sought, and with force and harshness you have ruled them . . . my sheep have become a prey, and my sheep have become food for all the wild beasts, since there was no shepherd, and because my shepherds have not searched for my sheep, but the shepherds have fed themselves, and have not fed my sheep, therefore, you shepherds, hear the word of the Lord: Thus says the Lord God, Behold, I am against the shepherds, and I will require my sheep at their hand and put a stop to their feeding the sheep. No longer shall the shepherds feed themselves. I will rescue my sheep from their mouths, that they may not be food for them. (Ezek. 34:2–4, 8–10)

John the Baptist criticized the religious leaders of his time and warned them of the need to change their attitudes:

But when he saw many of the Pharisees and Sadducees coming to his baptism, he said to them, 'You brood of vipers! Who warned you to flee from the wrath to come? Bear fruit in keeping with repentance.' (Matt. 3:7–8)

Christ also reserved His strongest language for the religious leaders of His time who misguided their followers. He denounced their blindness and pride:

Let them alone; they are blind guides. And if the blind lead the blind, both will fall into a pit. (Matt. 15:14)

He denounced the hypocrisy of the Scribes and Pharisees for neither believing themselves nor allowing others to investigate and be transformed:

For they preach, but do not practise. They tie up heavy burdens, hard to bear, and lay them on people's shoulders, but they themselves are not willing to move them with their finger. They do all their deeds to be seen by others . . . But woe to you, scribes and Pharisees, hypocrites! For you shut the kingdom of heaven in people's faces. For you neither enter yourselves nor allow those who would enter to go in. Woe to you, scribes and Pharisees, hypocrites! For you travel across sea and land to make a single proselyte, and when he becomes a proselyte, you make him twice as much a child of hell as yourselves. (Matt. 23:3–5; 13–15)

He further accused them of being of the same ilk as those who had earlier rejected God's revelation and persecuted the Prophets, implying that not only had the light returned but so also had the darkness, objections, oppression, persecution, and false reverence:

Woe to you, scribes and Pharisees, hypocrites! For you build the tombs of the prophets and decorate the monuments of the righteous, saying, 'If we had lived in the days of our fathers, we would not have taken part with them in shedding the blood of the prophets.' Thus you witness against yourselves that you are sons of those who murdered the prophets. Fill up, then, the measure of your fathers. You serpents, you brood of vipers, how are you to escape being sentenced to hell? Therefore I send you prophets and wise men and scribes, some of whom you will kill and crucify, and some you will flog in your synagogues and persecute from town to town, so that on you may come all the righteous blood shed on earth, from the blood of righteous Abel to the blood of Zechariah the son of Barachiah,[54] whom you murdered between the sanctuary and the altar. (Matt. 23:29–35)

Jude, a brother of James, also severely chastises the Jews, describing their actions as being reminiscent of those of Cain, Balaam and Core (Korah).[55]

It must have been quite disconcerting to the Jewish leaders when Jesus asserted that they did not know their own Scriptures and were unaware that everything was within the power of the Omnipotent Lord (Matt. 22:29). At another time, He admonished them for neither loving God nor believing in Moses, for had they been in tune with Moses and the Scriptures, they would have recognized Him (Jesus) instead of being more concerned with preserving their status and privilege:

> But I know that you do not have the love of God within you. I have come in my Father's name, and you do not receive me. If another comes in his own name, you will receive him. How can you believe, when you receive glory from one another and do not seek the glory that comes from the only God? Do not think that I will accuse you to the Father. There is one who accuses you: Moses, on whom you have set your hope. For if you believed Moses, you would believe me; for he wrote of me. But if you do not believe his writings, how will you believe my words? (John 5:42–47)

In the same vein, the First Epistle of John states that seekers who believe in God will respond to His revelation:

> Little children, you are from God and have overcome them [false prophets], for he who is in you is greater than he who is in the world. They are from the world; therefore they speak from the world, and the world listens to them. We are from God. Whoever knows God listens to us; whoever is not from God does not listen to us. By this we know the Spirit of truth and the spirit of error. (I John 4:4–6)

Christ warned His followers not to distinguish themselves through titles

> But you are not to be called rabbi (teacher), for you have one Teacher and you are all brothers. And do not call anyone (in the church) on earth father, for you have one Father, Who is in heaven. And you must not be called masters (leaders), for you have one Master (Leader), the Christ. He who is greatest among you shall be your servant. Whoever exalts himself (with haughtiness and empty pride) shall be humbled (brought low), and whoever humbles himself (whoever has a modest opinion of himself and behaves accordingly) shall be raised to honour. (Amplified Bible, Classic Edition: Matt. 23:8–12)

Rev. Albert Barnes elaborates:

> Jesus forbade his disciples to seek such titles of distinction. The reason which he gave was that he was himself their Master and Teacher. They were on a level; they were to be equal in authority; they were brethren; and they should neither covet nor receive a title which implied either an elevation of one above another, or which appeared to infringe on the absolute right of the Saviour to be their only Teacher and Master. The direction here is an express command to his disciples not to receive such a title of distinction. They were not to covet it; they were not to seek it; they were not to do anything that implied a wish or a willingness that it should be appended to their names. Everything which would tend to make a distinction among them or destroy their parity – everything which would lead the world to suppose that there were ranks and grades among them as ministers, they were to avoid.[56]

And Ellicott comments:

> **Call no man your father.** – This also, under its Hebrew form of Abba, was one of the titles in which the scribes delighted. In its true use it embodied the thought that the relation of scholars and teachers was filial on the one side, paternal on the other; but precisely because it expressed so noble an idea was its merely conventional use full of

danger. The history of the ecclesiastical titles of Christendom offers in this respect a singular parallel to that of the titles of Judaism.[57]

When Cornelius, a Roman centurion, fell down at the feet of the Apostle Peter, he was ordered to stand up and not to pay homage, as the Apostle was a mere human being (Acts 10:25–26).

There is no specific mention in the Gospels of a need for Christians to act as leaders, and none existed in the first Christian century. The Apostle Peter mentions elders and considered himself to be one of several elders or presbyters – however, there was to be 'no domineering' (I Pet. 5:3), no 'lording it over those entrusted to them' (Berean Literal Bible), and no acting as 'lords of the flock over the flock' (Aramaic Bible in Plain English version). Rather the elders were to act with humility, a commission that they are given only until the coming of 'chief Shepherd':

> And when the chief Shepherd appears, you will receive the unfading crown of glory. Likewise, you who are younger, be subject to the elders. Clothe yourselves, all of you, with humility toward one another, for 'God opposes the proud but gives grace to the humble'. Humble yourselves, therefore, under the mighty hand of God so that at the proper time he may exalt you . . . (I Pet. 5:4–6)

There is a limited role for institutions and religious leadership in the New Testament

An early mis-step was perhaps the surprising readiness of Christians to assume the mantle of earthly authority when, after about three hundred years of sporadic persecution, their fortunes changed with the conversion of Emperor Constantine. Since then, the church's primary concern appears to have been to establish an earthly kingdom rather than to prepare the flock for the promised heavenly Kingdom of the Father. Christ stated unequivocally, 'My kingdom is not of this world. If my kingdom were of this world, my servants would have been fighting, that I might not be delivered over to the Jews. But my kingdom is not from the world' (John 18:36). This Message concerned chiefly the salvation of the individual, rather than being addressed at a societal level:

The Revelation associated with the Faith of Jesus Christ focused attention primarily on the redemption of the individual and the molding of his conduct, and stressed, as its central theme, the necessity of inculcating a high standard of morality and discipline into man, as the fundamental unit in human society. Nowhere in the Gospels do we find any reference to the unity of nations or the unification of mankind as a whole. When Jesus spoke to those around Him, He addressed them primarily as individuals rather than as component parts of one universal, indivisible entity.[58]

The Apostle Paul mentions 'bishop', 'presbyter', 'elder' or 'elders of the church' and 'pastor' but the terms are largely interchangeable. For example, there was no understanding that a bishop was exalted over presbyters. He admonishes them to 'pay careful attention to yourselves and to all the flock, in which the Holy Spirit has made you overseers, to care for the church of God' (Acts 20:28). He also admonished that no one should overstep the bounds of what had been prescribed, that is, he warned against theological speculations:

> I have applied all these things to myself and Apollos for your benefit, brothers . . . that you may learn by us not to go beyond what is written, that none of you may be puffed up in favour of one against another. For who sees anything different in you? What do you have that you did not receive? (I Cor. 4:6–7)

It was during the second century and later that Christianity began to adopt a clerical hierarchy and there arose a separation between the 'laity' (a word not found in the New Testament), or general Christian people, and the clergy. As noted earlier, the ecclesiastical institutions were further elaborated without authority whatsoever from the Gospels when Christianity came to power and assumed temporal responsibilities following the conversion of Emperor Constantine.

9

FURTHER IMPEDIMENTS

This chapter continues to examine obstacles that may prevent Christians from recognizing God's promised revelation, in particular those for which the institutions of the church bear a heavy responsibility.

'Churchianity'

According to most independent scholars, Jesus neither instituted sacraments nor founded a church.[1] Many Christians have been concerned for some time that the institutions of their faith have deviated far from the pristine purity of the Gospel teachings and early discipline. Prominent scholars have lamented that the love, unity and charity that characterized the early Christian community have been irretrievably lost:

> There was in the Church a true sympathy in which each felt for and with all the others. When the Jerusalem Christians were in need the Christians of Antioch were quick to send help (Acts 2:27–30).
>   The best example of all of this is Paul's scheme to help the Church in Jerusalem. The Jerusalem Church was a poor Church and Paul organized a collection from the younger Churches for the Church in Jerusalem (II Cor. 8:1–5; 9:1; Rom. 15:25–28). This was Paul's way of clearly and practically demonstrating the communion of saints, the fellowship of caring and sharing which should be the mark of the Church. A Church which has forgotten, not the obligation but the privilege of sharing has lost the mark of a Christian Church . . . So in this article of the creed [I believe in the Communion of Saints] we are again face to face with the tragedy of the Church . . . It is a tragedy of the Church that it has been marked by division and disunity rather than by this supreme unity which ought to be the closest of all unities. We should surely regard it as an astonishing

thing to go on repeating a creed which in action we deny, and go on affirming a belief which our practice bluntly and flatly contradicts.[2]

The term 'Churchianity' was coined to contrast the practices and preoccupations of the church with Christ's message and conduct in the apostolic age. In this context, the term has been defined as 'a usually excessive or narrowly sectarian attachment to the practices and interests of a particular church',[3] and 'any practices of Christianity that are viewed as placing a larger emphasis on the habits of church life or the institutional traditions of the church than on theology and spiritual teachings of Jesus; the quality of being too church-focused'.[4] In a famous article written in 1883 entitled 'Christianity vs. Churchianity', A. A. Phelps observed, 'there is religion enough, and Churchianity enough, but a great famine for real Christianity'. He added:

> Vast multitudes cling to some Church establishment as a drowning man would cling to a life-boat. They bow obsequiously to her priestly and official mandates, and imagine that the blind servility which they tender to the Church will be accounted acceptable service offered to Christ. The simplicity of the Gospel is lost in the imposing forms and glittering accompaniments of modern churchism. Splendid church edifices attract the eye. Splendid music charms the ear. Splendid prayers are addressed to the CONGREGATION. Splendid sermons please the fancy, and leave deluded sinners to slumber on. Church rivalry has achieved a glorious success, if success thundering organs, ostentatious dressing, theatrical singing, pointless praying, rhetorical preaching, careless hearing, and unscriptural practicing!
>
> Much of the current worship is done by proxy. Lazy religionists surrender their sacred rights to others. They take it for granted that the preacher is on the right track, and readily swallow whatever may be doled out from the pulpit, without using their own brains in searching for the hidden treasures of truth. Thus religious ideas are transmitted from generation to generation, until tradition exerts a more powerful influence than the Bible in molding the sentiments of men. There comes to be a fashionable faith, as well as a fashionable dress. To embrace a certain stereotyped circle of doctrinal views entitles a man to the claim of 'orthodoxy'; but let him not venture

one step out of the beaten track, if he would not be denounced as a deluded heretic! But few have the moral courage to question the decisions of the Church, much less to discard what she has labeled as 'orthodox'. The verdict of a few leading denominations has thus grown up into a threatening tyranny; and the multitude cannot think of stemming the mighty tide. So they bow down in their narrow enslavement and worship this curiously- fashioned but pious-looking idol – the Church! Since all idolatry is an abomination to God, we have no more right to worship a church than we have to worship a golden calf! We rob the Lord of His rightful honor, and ourselves of the highest bliss of Christianity, by looking to the Church too much, and 'looking unto Jesus' too little. What can be done to deal a staggering blow to this cruel church-worship of the day, and at the same time give us more exalted and ravishing views of Jesus Christ? There is a grand failure to carry out the ultimate design, when the appliances of the Gospel result only in the production of Churchianity. Our perception, our prayers, our faith and our adoration must overleap the narrow precincts of the outward Church, and rise up to the eternal throne! 'Worship God!'[5]

The dominance and lure of the pulpit

It often proves too difficult a test for the clergy to abandon the trappings of their faith and embrace an uncertain future by recognizing a new revelation. Christians originally met in caves and homes – there were no churches and no pulpits in the time of Jesus. At most, synagogues had a platform (bema) as a podium for speakers. The reader in the synagogue stood up out of reverence. Once the reader had finished he would sit down and participate in the discussion that followed. Christ rarely preached sermons without there being an opportunity for questions and discussion. He warned that no one should exalt himself or herself above others, indicating that there would be a future spiritual reversal: 'And behold, some are last who will be first, and some are first who will be last' (Luke 13:30). When at one time the disciples requested 'Grant us to sit, one at your right hand and one at your left, in your glory,' He replied, '. . . to sit at my right hand or at my left is not mine to grant, but it is for those for whom it has been prepared' (Mark 10:37, 40).

However, as the number of Christians grew it became necessary to erect a raised platform (Latin: pulpitum) so that the preacher could be seen and heard.

Paying homage to mere humans

It is a common practice in some denominations, such as the Catholic and Orthodox churches, for the laity to stoop and kiss the hand, ring, or feet of an individual who represents church authority, such as the Pope, cardinal and bishop, as an act of submission, respect, gratitude, supplication, neediness, and humility. There is no direct scriptural justification for it and, like the use of the pulpit, it denotes superiority of status among God's subjects.

Papal infallibility

The infallibility of the Pope has no basis in the actual statements of Jesus. It is a relatively recent doctrine of the Catholic Church, defined by the First Vatican Council in 1870. It states that by virtue of the promise made to Peter by Jesus, the Popes are preserved from the possibility of error when they make *ex cathedra* pronouncements.[6]

'Upon this rock' – a promise of Jesus to Peter?

> He said to them, 'But who do you say that I am?' Simon Peter replied, 'You are the Christ, the Son of the living God.'[7] And Jesus answered him, 'Blessed are you, Simon Bar-Jonah![8] For flesh and blood has not revealed this to you, but my Father who is in heaven. And I tell you, you are Peter, and on this rock I will build my church, and the gates of hell shall not prevail against it. I will give you the keys of the kingdom of heaven, and whatever you bind on earth shall be bound in heaven, and whatever you loose on earth shall be loosed in heaven.' Then he strictly charged the disciples to tell no one that he was the Christ. (Matt. 16:15–20)

The Bahá'í Faith accepts Peter's primacy among the Apostles. However, it is noted that the above account in Matthew is absent from the parallel Gospel accounts, and the phraseology indicates that it may have been a later addition – it is doubtful that Jesus would have used the word 'church' since the institution did not yet exist during that time; the word 'church' appears in the New Testament only one other time, in Matt. 18:17, to refer to the whole assembly of believers. Additionally, the phrase 'gates of hell' appears nowhere else in the New Testament.

The Catholic Church maintains that the passages clearly demonstrate that Peter was made the foundation of the church, and gave him a special place or primacy amongst the Apostles.[9] It also maintains his infallibility and hence, by inference, the primacy and infallibility of all of the Popes who have ever since claimed his mantle. In particular, the Pope is preserved from the possibility of error 'when, in the exercise of his office as shepherd and teacher of all Christians, in virtue of his supreme apostolic authority, he defines a doctrine concerning faith or morals to be held by the whole Church'.[10]

Pope Boniface VIII issued one *ex cathedra* bull in 1302, but it was during the pontificate of Pope Pius IX that the doctrine of papal infallibility became dogmatically defined by the First Vatican Council (1869–1870). It is considered one of the channels of the infallibility of the church.

In contrast, Protestant scholars dispute these conclusions. Some commentators, such as Rev. Albert Barnes, have concluded that the 'rock' was the confession of Peter as to the station of Christ and not meant to refer to the person of the Apostle. Certainly, they do not believe that the reference justifies papacy in perpetuity:

> Some have supposed that the word 'rock' refers to Peter's confession, and that Jesus meant to say, upon this rock, this truth that thou hast confessed, that I am the Messiah and upon confessions of this from all believers, I will build my church. Confessions like this shall be the test of piety, and in such confessions shall my church stand amid the flames of persecution, the fury of the gates of hell. Others have thought that Jesus referred to himself. Christ is called a rock (Is. 28:16; I Pet. 2:8). And it has been thought that he turned from Peter to himself, and said, 'Upon this rock, this truth that I am the Messiah – upon myself as the Messiah, I will build my church.' Both these interpretations, though plausible, seem forced upon the passage to avoid the main difficulty in it. Another interpretation is, that the word 'rock' refers to Peter himself.
>
> This is the obvious meaning of the passage; and had it not been

that the Church of Rome has abused it, and applied it to what was never intended, no other interpretation would have been sought for. 'Thou art a rock. Thou hast shown thyself firm, and suitable for the work of laying the foundation of the church. Upon thee will I build it. Thou shalt be highly honored; thou shalt be first in making known the gospel to both Jews and Gentiles.' . . . But Christ did not mean, as the Roman Catholics say he did, to exalt Peter to supreme authority above all the other apostles, or to say that he was the only one upon whom he would rear his church . . . More than all, it is not said here, or anywhere else in the Bible, that Peter would have infallible successors who would be the vicegerents of Christ and the head of the church. The whole meaning of the passage is this: 'I will make you the honored instrument of making known my gospel first to Jews and Gentiles, and I will make you a firm and distinguished preacher in building my church.'[11]

Notably, in this context only five verses further on Jesus rebukes Peter, calling him Satan and a stumbling block – again, it may be that the censure applies to what Peter had said rather than directed to him personally:

From that time Jesus began to show his disciples that he must go to Jerusalem and suffer many things from the elders and chief priests and scribes, and be killed, and on the third day be raised. And Peter took him aside and began to rebuke him, saying, 'Far be it from you, Lord! This shall never happen to you.' But he turned and said to Peter, 'Get behind me, Satan! You are a hindrance to me. For you are not setting your mind on the things of God, but on the things of man.' (Matt. 16:21–23)

Adulation of religious leaders is akin to idolatry

An idol is whatever takes away from the worship of God. Hence, it may take one of several forms – worship of a shrine, traditions and rituals. Excessive deferential attitude towards religious leaders can also be akin to idolatry.

The Bible promises that God will destroy the idols, for only He and His Faith will be exalted 'in that Day':

> Their land also is full of idols; they worship the work of their own hands, that which their own fingers have made: Enter into the rock, and hide thee in the dust, for fear of the Lord, and for the glory of his majesty. The lofty looks of man shall be humbled, and the haughtiness of men shall be bowed down, and the Lord alone shall be exalted in that day. For the day of the Lord of hosts shall be upon every one that is proud and lofty, and upon every one that is lifted up; and he shall be brought low: And the loftiness of man shall be bowed down, and the haughtiness of men shall be made low: and the Lord alone shall be exalted in that day. And the idols he shall utterly abolish. (Is. 2:8, 10–12, 17–18)

> I will sprinkle clean water on you, and you shall be clean from all your uncleannesses, and from all your idols I will cleanse you. (Ezek. 36:25)

Nevertheless, there is a vast array of paid church leaders who prevent Christians from investigating the truth and instead busy themselves with propagating effete dogmas and rituals.

The establishment of rules, regulations, and elaborate ceremonies that were not based on any direct teaching of Christ, such as the creation of monastic orders, promoting asceticism and celibacy

Ostentatious display of wealth side-by-side with ascetic practices

The inordinate opulence of the church, the lavish ceremonies and the immoderate lifestyles of some of its officials are in sharp contrast with the asceticism demanded of the members of some monastic orders, and contrast poorly with the example set by Christ. His instructions were:

> Whoever has two tunics is to share with him who has none, and whoever has food is to do likewise. (Luke 3:11)

> Sell your possessions, and give to the needy. Provide yourselves with moneybags that do not grow old, with a treasure in the heavens that

does not fail, where no thief approaches and no moth destroys. For where your treasure is, there will your heart be also. (Luke 12:33–34)

To a rich man who sought 'eternal life' Jesus said:

Sell all that you have and distribute to the poor, and you will have treasure in heaven; and come, follow me. (Luke 18:22)

The Jewish sects of the Essenes and the Therapeutae practised asceticism. However, the belief in asceticism which is practised by many monastic orders is in contrast to several biblical verses which encourage individuals to enjoy the bounties that God has provided:

Behold, what I have seen to be good and fitting is to eat and drink and find enjoyment in all the toil with which one toils under the sun the few days of his life that God has given him, for this is his lot. Everyone also to whom God has given wealth and possessions and power to enjoy them, and to accept his lot and rejoice in his toil – this is the gift of God. (Eccles. 5:18–19)

For early Christians, monasticism derived its inspiration from examples of holiness, such as the Prophet Elijah who fasted for forty days on his journey to Mount Horeb (I Kings 19:8), and John the Baptist who lived an ascetic life (Matt. 3:4) and 'was in the wilderness until the day of his public appearance to Israel' (Luke 1:80). It was also derived from Jesus's call to his disciples to follow Him (Matt. 10:38) and to emulate His life of sacrifice and service. There are several monastic and mendicant orders, and also orders of nuns, living under vows of poverty, chastity, and obedience.[12] Each order has its own particular mission and is recognizable by its religious clothing or habit. For example, the Franciscan orders focus on poverty and identifying with the poor and the destitute as well as concern for all creation. They wear simple brown habits with a corded rope with three knots tied around their waists, representing also poverty, chastity and obedience.

The Orthodox Church also values asceticism and monastic life. Mount Athos, a peninsula in northeastern Greece, is home to several of their monasteries that date back to the eighth century. To this day, only men and male animals are permitted to visit or stay there. Notably, the

Apostle Paul condemns excessive asceticism and describes those 'who forbid marriage and require abstinence from foods that God created to be received with thanksgiving by those who believe and know the truth' as insincere and liars (I Tim. 4:2–3).

The celibacy of Jesus and the celibacy of priests and nuns

Christ lived in meagre circumstances, not in palaces. The fact is that during His relatively brief and turbulent ministry He did not have a secure abode to establish a domestic life (Luke 9:57–58). His nomadic existence, fraught with danger and uncertainty, was imposed on him by authorities that were intent on taking His life. The New Testament discourages excessive materialism, but monasticism was not part of Jesus's teachings. He was never a mendicant and his lack of asceticism annoyed the strict Pharisees (Matt. 11:18–19).

If celibacy had been an important issue, Christ would have chosen His disciples from the strict religious sect of the Essenes who tended to be celibate. Some of the twelve disciples, including the Apostle Peter, were married. Christ and His disciples chose not to live ascetic lives but rather to live life fully, and in close association with people. Furthermore, Mary, the pregnant mother of Jesus, married Joseph before the birth of Jesus (Matt. 1:24–25), and according to the Gospels of Matthew and Mark, Jesus had several brothers and sisters:

> Is not this the carpenter's son? Is not his mother called Mary? And are not his brothers James and Joseph and Simon and Judas? And are not all his sisters with us? Where then did this man get all these things? (Matt. 13:55–56 and Mark 6:3)

> **His brethren, James** . . . – The fair interpretation of this passage is, that these were the sons and daughters of Joseph and Mary. The people in the neighborhood thought so, and spoke of them as such.[13]

The historian Edward Gibbon records that although celibacy became popular in the primitive church it was not without its problems:

> The chaste severity of the fathers in whatever related to the commerce of the two sexes flowed from the same principle – their

abhorrence of every enjoyment which may gratify the sensual and degrade the spiritual nature of man. It was their favourite opinion, that if Adam had preserved his obedience to the Creator, he would have lived for ever in a state of virgin purity, and that some harmless mode of vegetation might have peopled paradise with a race of innocent and immortal beings. The use of marriage was permitted only to his fallen posterity, as a necessary expedient to continue the human species, and as a restraint, however imperfect, on the natural licentiousness of desire . . . The sensual connection was refined into a resemblance of the mystic union of Christ with his church, and was pronounced to be indissoluble either by divorce or by death . . . Since desire was imputed as a crime, and marriage was tolerated as a defect, it was consistent with the same principles to consider a state of celibacy as the nearest approach to the Divine perfection . . . the primitive church was filled with a great number of persons of either sex, who had devoted themselves to the profession of perpetual chastity. A few of these, among whom we may reckon the learned Origen, judged it the most prudent to disarm the tempter. Before the fame of Origen had excited envy and persecution, this extraordinary action was rather admired than censured. . . Some were insensible and some were invincible against the assaults of the flesh. Disdaining an ignominious flight, the virgins of the warm climate of Africa encountered the enemy in the closest engagement; they permitted priests and deacons to share their bed, and gloried amidst the flames in their unsullied purity. But insulted Nature sometimes vindicated her rights, and this new species of martyrdom served only to introduce a new scandal into the church.[14]

In contrast, there has been a recent decline in the number of Catholic priests, and a corresponding increase in the ratio of lay persons to priests,[15] which has been attributed to recurrent scandals concerning the priesthood, and the requirements for celibacy, poverty and obedience.

Excessive reliance on accounts of physical miracles, which do not constitute a valid criterion for determining the truth

All religions ascribe miracles to their founders. Clearly, it is reasonable to assume that the Prophets, in their capacity as the agents of the

Ruler and Fashioner of the universe, can suspend the laws of nature and perform the miraculous.

A follower of Moses, for example, may point out the miracle of Balaam's unusually perceptive and talkative donkey (Num. 22:22–34),[16] or Moses changing His staff into a serpent before Pharaoh, partitioning the sea, providing manna from heaven and making water gush out from a rock in the desert. There was also the miracle of the High Priest Samuel being brought back to life by a female medium (I Sam. 28:6–19).

However, as proof of faith, miracles have their limitations. They are often observed only by a limited number of eyewitnesses during a snapshot in humanity's history. Many come to label them several centuries later as mere fables. Even the onlookers can dismiss them as a trick of the senses. The children of Israel who presumably witnessed the miracles of Moses – including the plagues that God visited on the Egyptians (Ex. 10 and 11), and the parting of the Red Sea (Ex. 13:17–14:29) – reverted to idolatry and the worship of the golden calf when Moses delayed to come down from the mountain (Ex. 32:1):

> They have turned aside quickly out of the way that I commanded them. They have made for themselves a golden calf and have worshiped it and sacrificed to it and said, 'These are your gods, O Israel, who brought you up out of the land of Egypt!' (Ex. 32:8)

A Christian may also rely on the many miracles in the New Testament attributed to Christ or His disciples. He may not consider that most of these, if not all, may be allegories for more profound spiritual truths. For example, when the disciples of John the Baptist asked Jesus (Matt. 11:3): 'Art thou he that should come, or do we look for another?' He replied by enumerating the miracles that He had performed. These may also be taken to refer to the manifold transformative effects of His teachings:

> And Jesus answered them, 'Go and tell John what you hear and see: the blind receive their sight and the lame walk, lepers are cleansed and the deaf hear, and the dead are raised up, and the poor have good news preached to them. And blessed is the one who is not offended by me.' (Matt. 11:4–6)

There would not have been any room for doubt if the above miracles had been witnessed literally. If, as in the case of Lazarus, bringing the physically dead back to life was critical to belief, Christ would not have dismissively stated earlier: 'leave the dead to bury their own dead' (Matt. 8:22).

The evidence for a spiritual explanation of curing 'blindness' is provided by Jesus's statement that He had also come to cause blindness (John 9:39).

Christ categorically declined to perform miracles during His lifetime

The advent of the Messiah was to be accompanied by many signs. But when Jesus was asked by the religious leaders to perform a miracle to prove to them that He was the Messiah, He stated that the only miracle that He would perform would be similar to that of the Prophet Jonas:

> Then some of the scribes and Pharisees answered him, saying, 'Teacher, we wish to see a sign [miracle] from you.' But he answered them, 'An evil and adulterous generation seeks for a sign, but no sign will be given to it except the sign of the prophet Jonah. For just as Jonah was three days and three nights in the belly of the great fish, so will the Son of Man be three days and three nights in the heart of the earth.'(Matt. 12:38–40)

Rev. Albert Barnes explains:

> ***There shall no sign be given to it* . . .** – They sought some direct miracle 'from heavens'. Jesus replied that no 'such' miracle should be given. He did not mean to say that he would work no more miracles, or give no more evidence that he was the Christ, but he would give 'no such miracle' as they required. He would give one that ought to be as satisfactory evidence to them that he was from God, as the miraculous preservation of Jonah was to the Ninevites that he was divinely commissioned. As Jonah was preserved three days by miracle and then restored alive, so he would be raised from the dead after three days.[17]

Matthew Henry has several explanations for this refusal. First, it was an insolent demand. Second, Christ had already given them other signs. Third, He took 'this occasion to represent the sad characters and condition of that generation in which he lived, a generation that would not be reformed, and therefore could not but be ruined . . .'[18] One notes that Jesus later performed several 'miracles': He fed 5,000 people with five loaves and two fishes (Matt. 14:16–21), walked on water (Matt. 14:25), and healed the sick (Matt. 14:35–36). And He did not perform, at least literally, the miracle of Jonah.

A plausible explanation is that the Jews wished for a physical miracle but Christ performed spiritual miracles – He thus fed people with the heavenly and life-giving bread of His teachings, healed spiritual blindness and deafness, resuscitated the spiritually dead, and cured them of their many spiritual diseases.

If the miracles recorded in the New Testament were all in fact literally true, they failed to have a lasting effect – most of the Jews to this day deny that Jesus was their Messiah. For example, as described in the Gospel of John, on the Sabbath day Jesus restored the sight of a man born blind (John 9:1–34). The Pharisees in their spiritual blindness reviled Him, declaring that He was a sinner and He could not be of God because the performance of such work during Sabbath was forbidden.

The inner significance of miracles

The inner meaning of miracles is, according to the Bahá'í Writings, more important than whether they actually occurred. Miracles do not constitute a proof of the validity of a divine revelation:

> . . . most of the miracles attributed to the Prophets have an inner meaning . . . Our purpose is not to deny, but merely to say that these accounts do not constitute a decisive proof, and that they have an inner meaning – nothing more.[19]

> For example, if a blind man is made to see, in the end he will again lose his sight, for he will die and be deprived of all his senses and faculties. Thus, causing the blind to see is of no lasting importance, since the faculty of sight is bound to be lost again in the end. And

if a dead body be revived, what is gained thereby, since it must die again? What is important is to bestow true insight and everlasting life, that is, a spiritual and divine life; for this material life will not endure and its existence is tantamount to non-existence.[20]

We entreat Our loved ones not . . . to allow references to what they have regarded as miracles and prodigies to debase Our rank and station, or to mar the purity and sanctity of Our name.[21]

The profound miracle of Christ is acknowledged:

He was a single, unique and lowly individual Who appeared at a time when the Israelitish nation had fallen from the heights of its glory to the lowest condition of bondage and contempt, subject to the tyranny of the Roman Empire, living under a yoke of humiliation, ignorant and negligent of God. The historical records of the Holy Books confirm these statements. Christ – this single and unique Personage – appeared amongst these despised and degraded people, reflecting a divine power and the potency of the Holy Spirit. He unified the various peoples and nations of the world, brought them together in fellowship and agreement and gathered them beneath the overshadowing protection of one Word. His prestige and mention were not confined to the children of Israel alone, who were at that time a limited race and people, but His spiritual power had also permeated and united great influential nations who had been warlike and hostile, such as the Romans, Greeks, Egyptians, Chaldeans, Syrians and Assyrians. He dispelled their hostility, healed their hatred, made them a united people, and by His Word created the utmost love amongst them so that they advanced immeasurably in the degrees of education and human perfection, thereby attaining a never-ending glory.

The Jews had become dispersed and widely scattered. This single and unique Personage overcame all the then known world, founding an everlasting sovereignty, a mighty nation indeed. Such a result proved Him to be a great man, the first Educator of His time, the first Teacher of His period. What proofs could be greater than these? What would be more convincing than this evidence that a single individual resuscitated so many nations and peoples, unified so many tribes and sects, removed so much warfare and hatred? Undoubtedly, such accomplishment could be wrought only through the power of God and not by mere human effort, which is altogether incapable of producing these mighty results.[22]

Ignoring the injunction not to 'add' or 'take away' from the scriptures: Dogma, tradition and rituals

A major difficulty preventing recognition of the Second Coming is the accumulated teachings of the church that have little to do with the original teachings of Jesus. Christ had to contend with a similar issue. Indeed, Jesus used the word 'adulterous' (Matt. 12:39) to describe the corruption and dilution of the revelation of Moses by unwarranted additions, interpretations and explanations. The Apostle Paul warns against those 'which corrupt the word of God' (II Cor. 2:17).

A prime example of unwarranted additions to the Torah is ritual cleanliness. Moses had taught the importance of washing oneself under certain circumstances – for example, quite reasonably, if there was a physical contact with a man with a bodily discharge that was likely to be infectious (Lev. 15:1–13). However, under rabbinic law, the practice became quite elaborate later. A common custom is to pour water from a vessel twice (Hasidic Jews: three times) on the right hand followed by twice on the left hand (*vice versa* for those who are left-handed). The ritual then requires recitation of a blessing. This practice continues to this day and 'is unrelated to personal hygiene, and an individual is required to perform the ritual even if the hands are quite clean. It is also customary not to speak following the recitation of this blessing until reciting the blessing for bread and partaking of some of it'.[23]

Thus the Jewish leaders objected that Jesus's disciples ignored the oral law of the Talmud concerning ritual hand washing (*Netilat Yadyim*) before a meal that included bread. Christ's reaction to the objections of the Jewish religious leaders was to express His disdain for the commandments of men:

> And the Pharisees and the scribes asked him, 'Why do your disciples not walk according to the tradition of the elders, but eat with defiled hands?' And he said to them, 'Well did Isaiah prophesy of

you hypocrites, as it is written, "This people honors me with their lips, but their heart is far from me; in vain do they worship me, teaching as doctrines the commandments of men." You leave the commandment of God and hold to the tradition of men.' (Mark 7:5–8)

He was referring to the complaint of the Prophet Isaiah, about 800 years earlier:

And the Lord said: 'Because this people draw near with their mouth and honour me with their lips, while their hearts are far from me, and their fear of me is a commandment taught by men . . . the wisdom of their wise men shall perish, and the discernment of their discerning men shall be hidden.' (Is. 29:13–14)

Despite these accounts, from early on some Christians were eager to make their own contributions to God's revelation, as evident from this appeal of the Apostle Paul:

As I urged you when I was going to Macedonia, remain at Ephesus so that you may charge certain persons not to teach any different doctrine, nor to devote themselves to myths and endless genealogies, which promote speculations rather than the stewardship from God that is by faith. The aim of our charge is love that issues from a pure heart and a good conscience and a sincere faith. Certain persons, by swerving from these, have wandered away into vain discussion. (I Tim. 1:3–6)

Perversion of the truth

Interpretations by teachers who pander to the wishes of their followers

For the time is coming when people will not endure sound teaching, but having itching ears they will accumulate for themselves teachers to suit their own passions, and will turn away from listening to the truth and wander off into myths.[24] (II Tim. 4:3–4)

According to the Apostle Peter, interpretation of the scriptures or statements by the Prophets belongs to God alone. He will reveal their truth when 'the Day' dawns. No Christian is licensed to interpret the prophetic statements of the Bible:

> And we have the prophetic word more fully confirmed, to which you will do well to pay attention as to a lamp shining in a dark place, until the day dawns and the morning star rises in your hearts, knowing this first of all, that no prophecy of Scripture comes from someone's own interpretation. For no prophecy was ever produced by the will of man, but men spoke from God as they were carried along by the Holy Spirit. (II Pet. 1:19–21)

Rev. Albert Barnes comments:

> ... the apostle teaches that the truths which the prophets communicated were not originated by themselves; were not of their own suggestion or invention; were not their own opinions, but were of higher origin, and were imparted by God ... it says nothing about 'the church' as empowered to give a public or authorized interpretation of the prophecies. There is not a hint, or an intimation of any kind, that the church is entrusted with any such power whatever. There never was any greater perversion of a passage of Scripture than to suppose that this teaches that any class of people is not to have free access to the Bible. The effect of the passage, properly interpreted, should be to lead us to study the Bible with profound reverence, as having a higher than any human origin, not to turn away from it as if it were unintelligible, nor to lead us to suppose that it can be interpreted only by one class of men. The fact that it discloses truths which the human mind could not of itself have originated, is a good reason for studying it with diligence and with prayer – not for supposing that it is unlawful for us to attempt to understand it; a good reason for reverence and veneration for it – not for sanctified neglect.[25]

Interpretative translations and errors in transcription

Christ as God incarnate. In the original King James Version of the Bible written in 1611, the letter of the Apostle Paul to Timothy states:

> And without controversie, great is the mysterie of godlinesse: God was manifest in the flesh, justified in the Spirit, seene of Angels, preached unto the Gentiles, beleeved on in the world, received up into glory. (I Tim. 3:16)

In 1715 CE John James Wettstein, a Swiss theologian, whilst studying the fifth-century manuscript of the Greek Bible Codex Alexandrinus in London, noted an important error in the transcription of I Tim. 3:16 passage in the New Testament – a scribe had changed the Omicron (O) to theta Θ, replacing the phrase 'He who' [Ὅς] by the word 'God' [Θεὸς]:

> The manuscript originally had O without a transverse stroke and without a bar above, such as would mark the contraction ς. The bar above is written by a later hand, while the – has got in the middle of the O from the bar of the first ε of εὐσέβειαν (ch, vi. 3) on the other side of the page showing through the vellum in the middle of O. [26]

The manuscript thus no longer read: 'He who appeared ['was manifested' or 'revealed'] in the flesh' but now read: 'God was manifest in the flesh.'

The discovery of this unfortunate substitution questioned the dogma that Christ was literally and physically God. The mistake was corrected in translations such as the New International Version; New Living Translation; English Standard Version; Berean Study Bible; Christian Standard Bible; Contemporary English Version; Good News Translation; and American Standard Version, but was replicated in a number of other translations that have been published more than a century after Wettstein's discovery, such as Webster's Bible (1833); Young's Literal Translation (1862); American Standard Bible (1901); New King James Version (1982); American King James Version (1999); and the Jubilee Bible 2000. The error is present in the widely disseminated Holy Bible by the Gideons (1978).

For his efforts, Wettstein's enemies brought 'against him the outrageous charge of tampering with the sacred text in the interests of Socinianism (a view that rejected orthodox Christian theology on the doctrine of the Trinity and the divinity of Christ) and depriving Christians of a clear proof of the Divinity of Christ'.[27]

Not only did some of the churches misinterpret and misrepresent the New Testament passages, but Jewish scholars also misunderstood Christ's identity with God, and they therefore considered them blasphemous (John 10:29–38).

The New Testament refers to Moses, Christ and the Prophets as mediators of God's revelation and the Manifestations of His attributes. They represent His 'express image' and their message and actions mirror and are 'imprints' of the Divine Purpose – this represents an identity of purpose and not of personalities (Heb. 1:3). 'To each is given the manifestation of the Spirit for the common good' (I Cor. 12:7).

'A son' versus 'his Son'. Though traditionally credited to the Apostle Paul, the authorship of the Epistle to the Hebrews is uncertain.[28] Verses 1:1–4 explain that Christ's revelation came after God had spoken to man through many Prophets in different ways. He had latterly spoken to us through 'a son' in several English translations of the Bible[29] and in others, through 'his Son'.[30] The word 'his' is italicized in some translations,[31] to indicate that it is not a verbatim English translation but an interpretation of the Greek word υἱῷ (huiō). The variations in translation have arisen in part due to difficulty in translating 'a' and 'the' from Greek to English. However, we have the following explanation from The Discovery Bible:[32]

> HELPS Word Studies 5207: *hyiós* – properly, a son (by birth or adoption); (figuratively) anyone sharing the same nature as their Father. For the believer, becoming a son of God begins with being reborn (adopted) by the Heavenly Father ... In the NT, 5207 / *hyiós* ('son') equally refers to female believers (Gal. 3:28).

Appearance of the Holy Spirit or Holy Ghost after the crucifixion versus the advent of 'he' or 'the Spirit of Truth' who will guide humanity to 'all Truth' at the Second Coming. As mentioned earlier, some Christians maintain that the Holy Spirit referred to in John 16:13

appeared to the disciples at Pentecost following the crucifixion of Jesus, and hence, Christians do not need to be concerned about its re-manifestation in a future dispensation. Evidently the post-crucifixion spiritual experiences were limited, for had the Holy Spirit revealed 'all truth' at Pentecost, the church would not have become so deeply divided over dogma during the subsequent centuries.

Inconsistencies and altered meaning in different translations of the Bible, presumably due to dissimilar source texts

Significant textual discrepancies (shown in italics) are demonstrated when the King James Version and other translations such as the Greek, the New International Version, the Revised Standard Version and the English Standard Version are compared. Two examples are provided here.

'Take up the cross'

King James Version:

> Then Jesus beholding him loved him, and said unto him, One thing thou lackest: go thy way, sell whatsoever thou hast, and give to the poor, and thou shalt have treasure in heaven: and come, *take up the cross*, and follow me. (Mark 10:21)

Several other translations omit entirely the reference to the cross, for example:

English Standard Version:

> And Jesus, looking at him, loved him, and said to him, 'You lack one thing: go, sell all that you have and give to the poor, and you will have treasure in heaven; and come, follow me.'

It is also unlikely that the phrase 'take up the cross' was a familiar term before Jesus's crucifixion.

Did Jesus rise from the dead on the third day or after the third day?

English Standard Version:

And when he is killed, after three days he will rise (Mark 9:31)

King James Version:

and after that he is killed, *he shall rise the third day.*

New International Version:

They will kill him, and *after three days he will rise.*

This discrepancy also affects Mark 10:34:

King James Version:

they shall mock him, and shall scourge him, and shall spit upon him, and shall kill him: and *the third day he shall rise again.*

New International Version:

who will mock him and spit on him, flog him and kill him. *Three days later he will rise.*

English Standard Version:

And they will mock him and spit on him, and flog him and kill him. *And after three days he will rise.*

Jonah 'was in the belly of the fish three days and three nights' (Jonah 1:17), Notably, if Jesus died on Friday evening and rose literally on early Sunday morning, the duration in the tomb would not amount to a complete three days and certainly not three nights. Rev. Barnes observes: 'It will be seen in the account of the resurrection of Christ that he was in the grave but two nights and a part of three days'.[33]

Attempts to define the unknowable and to codify divine revelation

Church theology and the commentaries of Christian scholars are often examples of fallible, unwarranted and contradictory interpretations. Only the next Revealer of God's Truth has the authority to explain the intent of earlier Scripture. Therefore, a Christian should resist being unduly influenced by human scriptural analyses that are intended to buttress church dogma. He should be aware that the statements of one scholar are often contradicted by others, and that the resulting disputes have in the past divided the church again and again, and been responsible for many bloody wars between fellow Christians. He should also note that it was the interpretation of clerics that in Judaism led to the rejection of Christ and caused His sufferings.

In the absence of an undisputed successor to Christ and interpreter of His teachings, many arguments broke out in early Christianity creating an array of schisms too numerous to mention here. The purpose of dogma was to create consistency of belief, buttress faith and maintain the unity and integrity of the church. The subjects that were pronounced on were often by their very nature beyond human understanding, such as the nature of God, Christ, and the Holy Spirit. Nevertheless, the discussions surrounding the creation of the dogmas were invested with intense feelings, and dogmas that were intended to settle issues instead generated additional controversies and schisms.

It is noteworthy that when Joseph was asked to interpret a dream of Pharaoh Apopis (2000–1600 BCE), his reaction was to rhetorically ask 'do not interpretations belong to God?' (Gen. 40:8). Furthermore, the Prophet Daniel, who had several dreams and visions about the coming of the Messiah and the end time, was himself not privy to their interpretation. When he enquired as to the meaning of his visions he was tersely informed that the explanation would only be manifest at a future day and time. Even then, 'only the wise will understand' (Dan. 12:4, 8–10).

The Apostle Paul also advised Christians not to explain what they could not discern adequately, and not to judge matters prematurely:

> Therefore do not pronounce judgment before the time, before the Lord comes, who will bring to light the things now hidden in darkness and will disclose the purposes of the heart (I Cor. 4:5).

Only the Author of the new revelation, the One whose advent represents the Second Coming, has the power to interpret the Scriptures, and to explain the mysteries and prophecies of the books of earlier religions.

Compelling individuals to submit and adhere to a particular church viewpoint

The church has from its early stages coerced Christians to conform to orthodox norms. The Apostle Paul describes attempts by early Jewish Christians to compel the Gentile Christians to become circumcised (Gal. 2:14). The difficulties facing the apostolic age of the church grew so dire during the late first century that some Christian leaders openly refused to receive believers from other communities, and were engaged in excommunicating their fellow Christians from the church (III John 1:9–10). Concerning this troubling initial period, the historian Edward Gibbon wrote: 'the scanty and suspicious materials of ecclesiastical history seldom enable us to dispel the dark cloud that hangs over the first age of the Church'.[34] He ascribed the rapid growth of the early Christian church in part to 'the inflexible, and if we may use the impression, the intolerant zeal of the Christians.'[35]

Although Emperor Constantine, in collaboration with Emperor Licinius, issued the Edict of Milan in 313 CE which granted freedom of worship to all citizens of Rome, during his reign those who opposed Christianity became labelled as enemies of true religion and were punished severely – all so-called pagan religions were persecuted and their temples were destroyed. Gibbon writes thus of this change in the role of Christianity, namely, from being persecuted to persecuting others:

> The edict of Milan, the great charter of toleration, had confirmed to each individual of the Roman world the privilege of choosing and professing his own religion. But this inestimable privilege was soon violated: with the knowledge of truth the emperor imbibed the maxims of persecution; and the sects which dissented from the Catholic Church were afflicted and oppressed by the triumph of Christianity. Constantine easily believed that the heretics, who presumed to dispute *his* opinions or to oppose *his* commands, were guilty of the most absurd and criminal obstinacy; and that a seasonable application of moderate severities might save those unhappy

men from the danger of an everlasting condemnation. Not a moment was lost in excluding the ministers and teachers of the separated congregations from any share of the rewards and immunities which the emperor had so liberally bestowed on the orthodox clergy . . .

The design of extirpating the name, or at least of restraining the progress, of these odious heretics, was prosecuted with vigour and effect. Some of the penal regulations were copied from the edicts of Diocletian [ruled as Emperor 284–285 CE; he tried ruthlessly to exterminate Christians] and this method of conversion was applauded by the same bishops who had felt the hand of oppression, and had pleaded for the rights of humanity.[36]

Examples of intolerance of other theological opinions and traditions

Emperor Constantine attempted to unify the Christians and resolve their differences concerning the Trinity, but ended up exposing greater divisions without resolving the issue. This created additional reason for Christians to persecute each other.

Arius, a Christian priest in Alexandria, Egypt, began to preach in 318 CE that Jesus was begotten by God at a certain point in time and was therefore distinct from and subordinate to the Father. 'It is told of Thomas Carlyle by his biographer that at one time he thought the early controversy as to Christ, whether He were Divine or a created demigod, was of trifling importance, "a matter a diphthong" (*Homoosios* "of the same substance" or *Homosiousios*, "of like substance with God").'[37] Trivial as the difference in the beliefs of Trinitarians and Arianism may sound, the controversy generated intense passions on both sides of the argument. Arianism was declared a heresy by the Council of Nicaea (325 CE) but Arius was exonerated by the Synod of Tyre in 335 CE and the Arians used their favoured position with the Emperor Constantinus, the son and successor of Constantine, to persuade him to persecute the Trinitarians:

> The celebrated Athanasius, and other bishops, were banished, and their sees filled with Arians. In Egypt and Lybia, thirty bishops were martyred, and many other Christians cruelly tormented; and, A.D. 386, George, the Arian bishop of Alexandria, under the authority

of the emperor, began a persecution in that city and its environs, and carried it on with the most infernal severity. He was assisted in his diabolical malice by Catophonius, governor of Egypt; Sebastian, general of the Egyptian forces; Faustinus, the treasurer; and Heraclius, a Roman officer.

The persecutions now raged in such a manner that the clergy were driven from Alexandria, their churches were shut, and the severities practiced by the Arian heretics were as great as those that had been practiced by the pagan idolaters. If a man, accused of being a Christian, made his escape, then his whole family were massacred, and his effects confiscated.[38]

The historian William James Durant (1885–1981) writes: 'Probably more Christians were slaughtered by Christians in these two years (342–343 CE) than by all the persecutions of Christians by pagans in the history of Rome'.[39] After the death of Arius, an anathema was issued against him, he was proclaimed to be a heretic, and the doctrine of the Trinity triumphed.

A church father, Augustine (354–430 CE), was involved in resisting another schism. The Donatists insisted that clergy performing baptism and other sacraments must be free of faults, including not having surrendered copies of the Scriptures to the civil authorities during Emperor Diocletian's great persecution. To combat schisms such as the Donatists, Augustine argued that the Christian Roman Emperors had 'an unquestioned right of *cohercitio* [coercion/correction], in the strict legal sense, to punish, to restrain and repress, those impious cults over which God's providence had given them dominion'.[40] In his letter outlining the reasons why it was legitimate to intimidate Donatist Christians to join the Catholic Church Augustine wrote:

> Not every one who is indulgent is a friend; nor is every one an enemy who smites. Better are the wounds of a friend than the proffered kisses of an enemy. (Prov. 27:6) It is better with severity to love, than with gentleness to deceive. More good is done by taking away food from one who is hungry, if, through freedom from care as to his food, he is forgetful of righteousness, than by providing bread for one who is hungry, in order that, being thereby bribed, he may consent to unrighteousness. He who binds the man who is

in a phrenzy, and he who stirs up the man who is in a lethargy, are alike vexatious to both, and are in both cases alike prompted by love for the patient. Who can love us more than God does? And yet He not only give us sweet instruction, but also quickens us by salutary fear, and this unceasingly. Often adding to the soothing remedies by which He comforts men the sharp medicine of tribulation, He afflicts with famine even the pious and devout patriarchs, disquiets a rebellious people by more severe chastisements, and refuses, though thrice besought, to take away the thorn in the flesh of the apostle, that He may make His strength perfect in weakness. (II Cor. Let us by all means <u>love</u> even our enemies, for this is right, and God commands us so to do, in order that we may be the children of our Father who is in heaven, who makes His sun to rise on the <u>evil</u> and on the good, and sends rain on the just and on the unjust. (Matt. 5:45) But as we praise these His gifts, let us in like manner ponder His correction of those whom He loves.

You are of opinion that no one should be compelled to follow righteousness; and yet you read that the householder said to his servants, Whomsoever you shall find, compel them to come in. (Luke 14: 23)[41]

Protestant commentators have expressed dismay at Augustine's interpretation of the Lukan parable: 'And the lord said unto the servant, Go out into the highways and hedges, and compel them to come in, that my house may be filled' (Luke 14:23), which changes an instruction to encourage Christians to respond to the divine call into a justification for compelling them to the Catholic viewpoint. Ellicott writes:

> **Compel them to come in.** [That my house may be filled.] It would have seemed all but incredible, had it not been too painfully and conspicuously true, that men could have seen in these words a sanction to the employment of force and pains and penalties as means of converting men to the faith of Christ. To us it seems almost a truism to say that such means may produce proselytes and hypocrites, but cannot possibly produce converts.[42]

The longstanding feud between the Catholic and the Orthodox churches, evident even today to tourists visiting the Church of the

Holy Sepulcher in Jerusalem, is another prominent example of denominational rivalry and antagonism.[43] The main theological difference between them is that the Catholics believe that the Holy Spirit proceeds from both the Father and the Son, but the Orthodox maintain, as did the original Nicene Creed, that the third person of the Trinity proceeds from the Father only. The theological and political difference caused an East–West break, also known as the Great Schism, and resulted in mutual excommunications by the Patriarch of Constantinople and the Pope in 1054 CE.[44]

The Fourth Crusade, sanctioned by Pope Innocent III, resulted in the sacking in 1203/1204 CE of Constantinople (Istanbul), the capital of the Eastern Orthodox Church, and the largest and richest European city, known as the Queen of Cities. The Catholic Crusaders never made it to the Holy Land. Fighting ostensibly under the banner of a holy war, but motivated mostly by greed, they decided that before conquering Muslim-controlled Jerusalem, their immediate spiritual duty was to restore the Eastern Christian Empire to Rome by crushing the heretical Greek Orthodox Church. The crusaders spared no one: thousands were raped and massacred, churches (including the Hagia Sophia) were plundered, and the city was torched.[45] The clergy played an ignoble role in urging the crusader army to fight on, describing the Greeks as dogs, 'worse than the Jews', by invoking the authority of God and the Pope, and by actively participating in the accompanying pillage.[46]

The Thirty Years War between the Protestants and Catholics (1618–1648) devastated Europe and killed a third of the German population.

Preoccupation with reforming the church from within instead of looking forward to a divinely ordained 'new heaven and a new earth'

The four Gospels clearly indicate that the mission of Christians was to proclaim the good news that the Messiah had come and Christ would return. Instead of repeated attempts to reform and update itself, the Church could have stressed the need for increased spiritual awareness and preparedness to facilitate recognition of the promised heavenly kingdom.

By the sixteenth century it became increasingly clear to several Christian scholars that a number of church dogmas and practices could not be justified from the explicit text of the Gospels. Individuals such as Calvin wrote that there was a dire need to reform the church because of the patent 'diseases both numerous and grievous'.⁴⁷

Christ did not merely reform Judaism but instead inaugurated a new dispensation

The reality of every religion is resurrected in the form of the next dispensation, referred to as a new Covenant (Jer. 31:31–34). The new Covenant is described as better (Heb. 7:18–19; 8:7), but this does not indicate a superior revelation, otherwise one would have to confess that God had previously provided humanity with a deficient revelation. A more accurate rendering would be that each dispensation is appropriate to the age in which it appears. The question is whether it is legitimate for human beings to reform God's faith, or should they instead rely on God to make the necessary changes through a new revelation. Human efforts to reform the church may be likened to a profoundly sick patient self-prescribing remedies that often aggravate his condition.

Notably, Jesus did not merely reform and reinvent Judaism but brought a new revelation, a new covenant and a new testament. In this manner, He was able to unite members of different Jewish sects, Greeks and Romans in a common faith. He reconciled their differences and renewed their outlook. This divinely-generated unity and amity would have not been possible through the mere introduction of innovations into the practice and teachings of one or all of the many Jewish sects. The necessary transformation required the creative power of the Divine Word and was independent of the erudition and scholarly endeavours of the Jewish leaders.

The Church cannot by itself effectively reform Christianity – it is God's domain to regenerate His Faith

The Apostle Peter taught that humanity should prepare for the divinely ordained 'time for restoring all the things about which God spoke by the mouth of his holy Prophets long ago', by repenting and turning back that its 'sins may be blotted out', and that times of refreshing may come from the presence of the Lord (Acts 3:19–21).

The selfless love that defined a Christian (John 13:35) and the elimination of prejudices that alienated the Jews and Gentiles (Matt.

5:43–45) did not arise out of church dogma but were inspired by the Holy Spirit and generated through the creative power of the divine Word.

Previously, human attempts to reform the church have resulted in persecution and violence

As might be anticipated, due to entrenched opinions and beliefs imposed by the temporal powers and military force, whenever voices of opposition were raised they were repressed with unchristian-like brutality. The following serve as a few examples.

John Wycliffe, a seminary professor at Oxford, translated the Gospels from Latin into English. He could not see any scriptural justification for the privileged status of the clergy, their pomp and lavish ceremonies, the concept of purgatory as a third or alternative state to heaven and hell, clerical celibacy, pilgrimages, the selling of indulgences and praying to saints. He defined 'the religion of Christ' as 'simply that which Christ expressly instituted, without any later admixture of human ceremony'.[48] He argued that the pure Christian religion was more perfect than 'private religions' which add rites and ceremonies and 'cut themselves off from the commonality and lay claim to superiority over them on the basis of a purely human assessment of what is required to please God'.[49] Ironically and tragically, his valiant efforts to reform the Church from within resulted in his movement being labelled 'a private religion'.[50]

Following his lead, his followers known as the Lollards argued against the veneration of saints, the sacraments, transubstantiation, monasticism, and existence of the papacy. In the years before his death in 1384 he increasingly argued for the unique authority of the Bible over the belief and life of the Christian, that the claims of the papacy were unhistorical, that monasticism was irredeemably corrupt, and that the moral unworthiness of priests invalidated their offices and their sacraments. He and his followers faced stiff opposition from the ecclesiastical establishment. Following his death, the persecution of Wycliffe's remaining followers was written into the Anti-Wycliffite Statute of 1401. In order to support the church's authority in all ecclesiastical matters, the 'Constitutions of Oxford' of 1408 banned his writings, effectively both excommunicating him retroactively and making him an early forerunner of Protestantism. Wycliffe's works were to be burned and his remains were to be removed from consecrated ground. This order, confirmed by Pope Martin V, was carried out in 1428. Wycliffe's corpse was exhumed, his bones burned and the ashes cast into a river.[51]

John Hus, a Czech priest and philosopher influenced by Wycliffe's ideas, became one of the earliest reformers, and a key predecessor to Protestantism. He was burned at the stake in 1415 for heresy against the doctrines of the Roman Catholic Church. This led to a revolt by his followers, the Hussites, who fought against the Catholic Church in five consecutive papal crusades (1420–1431).[52]

Martin Luther, a devout German Augustinian friar and university lecturer, launched an attack in 1517 on some of the Catholic Church's practices, including the granting of indulgences for monetary gain – the indulgencies were said to reduce the time spent in purgatory for those who had already died. Luther also challenged the Catholic Church's absolute authority and claim that it alone held the keys to salvation. His teachings, together with those of Calvin, Zwingli, Knox and others, were the foundation of the Protestant Reformation.

Huldrych Zwingli sparked a similar controversy in Switzerland in 1519 by preaching that salvation belonged only to God.

John Calvin (1509–1564) suffered bitter opposition and had to flee from France to Switzerland following publication of his book *Institutes of the Christian Religion*, expressing Protestant Reformation views that salvation belonged absolutely to God.

John Knox (1513–1572) led the Protestant Reformation in Scotland, and at one time was captured and confined in French galleys.

The radical ideas coalesced into many sects and rebellions throughout the Holy Roman Empire, plunging Europe into a series of devastating wars between the reformists and the counter-reformists. Early on, a widespread popular Protestant revolt, the German Peasants War, was suppressed by the Catholic aristocracy with the slaughter of between 100,000 and 300,000 poorly armed peasants and farmers. When Mary, the Catholic daughter of Henry VIII, came to the throne in 1553, about 300 Protestants were burned alive at the stake in Smithfield. She came to be denounced as 'Bloody Mary' by the Protestants.

Considering the past: Recognition of God's new message allows enlightened individuals to also refer to the teachings of previous dispensations

The Gospels teach that a religious scholar is able to refer to earlier teachings and supplement them with the new teachings only when, by embracing the new dispensation, he 'is instructed unto the kingdom of heaven':

> And he said to them, 'Therefore every scribe who has been trained for the kingdom of heaven is like a master of a house, who brings out of his treasure what is new and what is old.'[53] (Matt. 13:52)

Charles J. Ellicott provides the following commentary:

> ***Things new and old.*** – Our Lord's own teaching was, of course, the highest example of this union. There were the old eternal laws of righteousness, the proclamation of the true meaning of all that every true teacher had included in the idea of duty and religion, but there were also new truths, such as His own mission as the Head of the divine kingdom and the future Judge of all men, and the work of the Spirit as regenerating and sanctifying.[54]

Name-calling and vilification

Accusing a new revelation of being a heresy or a cult

The word 'heresy' comes from the Greek (*haireomai*, to choose) and implies a personal *choice* of belief or opinion contrary to orthodox religious doctrine, that is, one based on investigation and not imitation. To the Jewish leaders, Jesus posed a threat that was capable of dividing Judaism – He did not conform to their expectations of the Messiah but at the same time some Jews accepted him as such. They therefore accused His followers of being troublemakers and belonging to an unpopular sect, heresy or cult.

It is worth noting that in the early days Christians such the Apostle Paul were also accused of being part of a sect, heresy or cult:

For we have found this man a plague, one who stirs up riots among all the Jews throughout the world and is a ringleader of the sect of the Nazarenes (Greek: τῆς τῶν Ναζωραίων αἱρέσεως, tēs tōn Nazōraiōn haireseōs). (Acts 24:5)

But we desire to hear from you what your views are, for with regard to this sect (Greek: τῶν Ναζωραίων αἱρέσεως, tēs haireseōs) we know that everywhere it is spoken against. (Acts 28:22)

In his defence, the Apostle denied stirring up trouble but, importantly, embraced the accusation, using the occasion to explain that the new faith or 'way' that he had personally chosen was compatible with belief in God, following the Law and accepting the Jewish Prophets:

> ... and they did not find me disputing with anyone or stirring up a crowd, either in the temple or in the synagogues or in the city. Neither can they prove to you what they now bring up against me. But this I confess to you, that according to the Way, which they call a sect, I worship the God of our fathers, believing everything laid down by the Law and written in the Prophets ... (Acts 24:12–14)

He had previously admitted before the Sanhedrin[55] that he was 'a Pharisee and the son of Pharisees' (Acts 23:1–3, 6) and was also a Roman by birth (Acts 22:27). His choice to follow Jesus and his missionary zeal to teach both Jews and Romans[56] ultimately led to his arrest, flogging, and imprisonment and ultimately martyrdom. The reason for the seizure of Paul and Silas is given as follows:

> And when they had brought them to the magistrates, they said, 'These men are Jews, and they are disturbing our city. They advocate customs[57] that are not lawful for us as Romans to accept or practice.[58]

Ignoring this instructive precedent, some Christians denounce the followers of other religions, such as the Bahá'í Faith, as also being members of a heretical cult.[59]

Having an issue with certain aspects of the earthly life of the Divine Messengers

The earthly lives and actions of none of the Divine Prophets have lived up to the expectations of the followers of an earlier dispensation. They conform neither to traditional norms nor to all the social rules that they themselves teach. They were therefore ridiculed by the religious leaders of their time.

To walk in the footsteps of Jesus implies following the essential spiritual teachings of His Faith. As noted earlier, the Jews, following their written law and oral traditions, failed to understand this, and objected to Christ on multiple grounds of their own making. Thus, because of their limited perspective they failed to appreciate true godliness, and denied One Who was the Source of the spiritual life of humanity and the embodiment of God's grace and truth.

PART IV

CHURCH DOGMA AND REALIZED ESCATOLOGY

10

REVIEW OF SOME CHRISTIAN THEMES

We examine here certain Christian topics, in the context of the teachings of the Bible and in the light of the Bahá'í Writings.

The challenge of human interpretation

Scholars often give the impression that, due to their learning and erudition, they know the mind of God and have answers to all scriptural questions, and yet they are invariably at the forefront of those who deny God's latest revelation. Their prodigious writings and ample judgements, often relying on other authorities, have adulterated God's Faith (James 4:4) and irreparably shattered its unity. They profess piety and humility and yet obstinately fail to admit that it is the Creator and not man Who reveals the truth and judges between right and wrong, good and evil, and light and darkness. It is God Who, at the dawn of every revelation, informs humanity of the Divine Will for the new age; reminds the followers of the diverse religions about the true import of their scriptures; and guides individuals back to the straight path.

In the parable of the Sower, Christ warned about 'thorns' that would snuff out the spirit of faith and investigation – 'weeds' which He predicted would be 'pulled up and burnt in the fire . . . at the end of the age' (Matt. 13:36–43). The term thorns may apply to the elaborate institutional explanations, dogmas, and traditions that choke many a tender plant of faith (Mark 4:7) and hinder sincere seekers from recognizing the truth. One is reminded of the following graphic description in the Hebrew Bible:

> I passed by the field of a sluggard, by the vineyard of a man lacking sense, and behold, it was all overgrown with thorns; the ground was

covered with nettles, and its stone wall was broken down. (Prov. 24:30–31)

Therefore, it is an imperative that we investigate our beliefs diligently and objectively, and not counteract automatically every new teaching with traditional explanations. We should consult all relevant biblical passages and, importantly, remind ourselves that Jesus had promised that it will be the Spirit of Truth Who will bring what His early followers were not able to bear at that time. It will be He, Who speaking with God's authority, will guide them to 'all truth'; and it will be He, the Spirit of Truth, Who will take what Christ had mentioned and disclose it to them (John 16:12–15), that 'no good tree bears bad fruit, nor again does a bad tree bear good fruit, for each tree is known by its own fruit. For figs are not gathered from thornbushes, nor are grapes picked from a bramble bush . . .' (Luke 6:43–44)

The Apostle Paul urged his fellow Christians not to waste time formulating premature opinions that might cause dissension but instead wait for the Second Coming when all that is concealed will be revealed:

> Therefore do not pronounce judgement before the time, before the Lord comes, who will bring to light the things now hidden in darkness and will disclose the purposes[1] of the heart. Then each one will receive his commendation from God. I have applied all these things to myself and Apollos for your benefit, brothers, that you may learn by us not to go beyond what is written, that none of you may be puffed up in favour of one against another. (I Cor. 4:5–6)

> For nothing is hidden that will not be made manifest, nor is anything secret that will not be known and come to light. (Luke 8:17)

'Creation' – a reference to the birth of man's spiritual consciousness

The Book of Genesis begins with what is considered an account of the creation of the cosmos, the planet earth, and man. Thus, based on the Hebrew Bible, the Jewish historian Josephus and the fathers of the early church – Cyprian, Irenaeus, Clement of Alexandria, Julius Africanus, Origen, Lactantius, Chrysostom, Jerome and Augustine – estimated that the earth was less than 6,000 years old. We now know from irrefutable scientific evidence that the universe is at least 13.8 billion years old, the earth is about 4.5 billion years old, and man has evolved for the past several million years. The fact that the Genesis narrative mentions three days when the sun had not yet been created demonstrates that the statements have significances other than literal. Hence, the story in Genesis is symbolic, that is, not an account of the creation of man or the physical universe, but instead the beginnings of man's consciousness of his creator, and the awakening of his spirit through divine knowledge – 'and God said, "Let there be light," and there was light' (Gen. 1:3).

'Bread' and 'water'– a reference to spiritual sustenance and heavenly teachings

The Hebrew Bible equates famine with a dearth of spiritual receptivity to the Divine Word:

> 'Behold, the days are coming', declares the Lord God, 'when I will send a famine on the land – not a famine of bread, nor a thirst for water, but of hearing the words of the Lord. They shall wander from sea to sea, and from north to east; they shall run to and fro, to seek the word of the Lord, but they shall not find it.' (Amos 8:11–12)

Christ inculcated the paramount importance of seeking and working for spiritual nourishment rather than material well-being. For example, He eulogized those who had a keen hunger and thirst for righteousness (Matt. 5:6), and said:

> 'Do not work for the food that perishes, but for the food that endures to eternal life, which the Son of Man will give to you. For on him God the Father has set his seal'. . . Jesus said to them, 'I am the bread of life; whoever comes to me shall not hunger, and whoever believes in me shall never thirst . . . I am the bread of life. Your fathers ate the manna in the wilderness, and they died. This is the bread that comes down from heaven, so that one may eat of it and not die. I am the living bread that came down from heaven. If anyone eats of this bread, he will live forever . . .' (John 6:27, 35, 48–51)

The Bahá'í Writings explain the symbolic meaning of the 'bread' of revelation:

> He (Jesus) said, 'I am the living bread which came down from heaven; if any man eat of this bread, he shall live for ever.' When the Jews heard this, they took it literally and failed to understand the significance of His meaning and teaching. The spiritual truth which Christ wished to convey to them was that the reality of Divinity within Him was like a blessing which had come down from heaven and that he who partook of this blessing should never die. That is to say, bread was the symbol of the perfections which had descended upon Him from God, and he who ate of this bread, or endowed himself with the perfections of Christ, would undoubtedly attain to everlasting life. The Jews did not understand Him, and taking the words literally, said, 'How can this man give us his flesh to eat?' Had they understood the real meaning of the Holy Book, they would have become believers in Christ.
>
> All the texts and teachings of the holy Testaments have intrinsic spiritual meanings. They are not to be taken literally.[2]

While some scholars, such as John Calvin, have interpreted the bread principally as physical nourishment,[3] the 'daily bread', 'the living bread', 'the bread of life', and 'the bread that came down from heaven', mentioned in the New Testament refer to God's revelation and His teachings that descend from the heaven of His Will and Power in every dispensation. It is this spiritual 'bread' for which Christians supplicate in the Lord's Prayer. One notes that Christ had said earlier:

> Man shall not live by bread alone, but by every word that comes from the mouth of God. (Matt. 4:4)

The anticipated new divine teachings are also referred to as a concealed or hitherto unknown manna (Rev. 2:17).

Additionally, there are references to 'the water of life', 'living water', and 'life-giving water', which be offered to every sincere seeker:

> Jesus said to her,[4] 'Everyone who drinks of this water will be thirsty again, but whoever drinks of the water that I will give him will never

be thirsty again. The water that I will give them will become in him a spring of water welling up to eternal life.' (John 4:13–14)

Notably, in the Book of Revelation, God warns that only those who thirst will receive the water of life at the Second Coming:

> To the thirsty I will give from the spring of the water of life without payment.[5] (Rev. 21:6)

> And let the one who is thirsty come; let the one who desires take the water of life without price. (Rev. 22:17)

'Blindness', 'deafness' and 'hardness of heart'– references to heedlessness and lack of spiritual receptivity

Eyes that are closed and thus do not perceive the divine light, as in physical sleep and death, are often scriptural metaphors for sin and spiritual death, describing lack of spiritual insight and receptivity.

Prayers that 'God may open the eyes'

When Elisha and his servant were besieged by the army of the king of Syria, the Prophet prayed, not for victory, but for the eyes of his companion to be opened. Only then did his servant perceive that they were being protected by the hosts of heaven:

> When the servant of the man of God rose early in the morning and went out, behold, an army with horses and chariots was all around the city. And the servant said, 'Alas, my master! What shall we do?' He said, 'Do not be afraid, for those who are with us are more than those who are with them.' Then Elisha prayed and said, 'O Lord, please open his eyes that he may see.' So the Lord opened the eyes of the young man, 'and he saw, and behold, the mountain was full of horses and chariots of fire all around Elisha . . .' (II Kings 6:15–17)

King David also prayed that God might 'open his eyes':

> I will delight in your statutes; I will not forget your word. Deal

bountifully with your servant, that I may live and keep your word. Open my eyes, that I may behold wondrous things out of your law. (Ps. 119:16–18)

He praised God for endowing him with 'an open ear', that is, a receptive soul (Ps. 40:6). Isaiah couches the glad tiding of the coming of the Lord in similar allegorical language:

> Strengthen the weak hands, and make firm the feeble knees. Say to those who have an anxious heart, 'Be strong; fear not! Behold, your God will come with vengeance, with the recompense of God. He will come and save you.' Then the eyes of the blind shall be opened, and the ears of the deaf unstopped; then shall the lame man leap like a deer, and the tongue of the mute sing for joy. (Is. 3–6)

The Prophet instructs:

> Hear, you deaf, and look, you blind, that you may see! (Is. 42:18)

He equates blindness with lack of knowledge and understanding and observes with sadness:

> His watchmen[6] are blind; they are all without knowledge; they are all silent dogs; they cannot bark, dreaming, lying down, loving to slumber. The dogs have a mighty appetite; they never have enough. But they are shepherds who have no understanding; they have all turned to their own way, each to his own gain, one and all. (Is. 56:10–11)

The spiritual blindness and lack of receptivity continued to be an issue at the First Coming, obliging Christ to state:

> Then the disciples came and said to him, 'Why do you speak to them in parables?' And he answered them, 'To you it has been given to know the secrets of the kingdom of heaven, but to them it has not been given. For to the one who has, more will be given, and he will have an abundance, but from the one who has not, even what he has will be taken away. This is why I speak to them in parables,

because seeing they do not see, and hearing they do not hear, nor do they understand. Indeed, in their case the prophecy of Isaiah is fulfilled that says: "You will indeed hear but never understand, and you will indeed see but never perceive." For this people's heart has grown dull, and with their ears they can barely hear, and their eyes they have closed, lest they should see with their eyes and hear with their ears and understand with their heart and turn, and I would heal them.' But blessed are your eyes, for they see, and your ears, for they hear. For truly, I say to you, many prophets and righteous people longed to see what you see, and did not see it, and to hear what you hear, and did not hear it. (Matt. 13:10–17; see also John 12:40)

We must pray that the same paucity of spiritual capacity, resulting in heedlessness, does not characterize Christians at the Second Coming.

'Light' versus 'darkness' – references to divine guidance and mercy versus being deprived of insight, and God's grace and bounty

The light that emanates from God is the cause of man's spiritual guidance and life. Its source is God alone, man's Saviour. The Psalmist equates the Lord's light with spiritual deliverance: 'The Lord is my light and my salvation; whom shall I fear?'(Ps. 27:1). The Prophet Isaiah had a vision about the appearance of the divine light that would illuminate the spiritually dead living in darkness:

> The people who walked in darkness have seen a great light; those who dwelt in a land of deep darkness, on them has light shone (Is. 9:2)

At the First Coming, this Light of divine guidance which gives life to humanity was transmitted through Christ:

> In him was life, and the life was the light of men. (John 1:4)

> Again Jesus spoke to them, saying, 'I am the light of the world. Whoever follows me will not walk in darkness, but will have the light of life.' (John 8:12)

> While I am in the world, I am the light of the world. (John 9:5)

> I have come into the world as light, so that whoever believes in me may not remain in darkness. (John 12:46)

His disciples in turn transmitted His light and illuminated all humankind:

> You are the light of the world ... (Matt. 5:14)

> For you are all children of light, children of the day. We are not of the night or of the darkness ... (I Thess. 5:5)

Some individuals eagerly seek the light, but others prefer the dark. Although darkness represents the absence of light, it nonetheless has serious consequences – spiritual darkness promotes evil, divisions, blind opposition to the truth, and death. The divine light causes the darkness of imitation, prejudice, discord, disunity and enmity to recede.

Others react adversely and attempt to frustrate God's purpose. However, in every age, God's light is able to overcome darkness:

> In him was life, and the life was the light of men. The light shines in the darkness, and the darkness has not overcome it.[7] (John 1:4–5)

> And this is the judgement: the light has come into the world, and people loved the darkness rather than the light because their works were evil. For everyone who does wicked things hates the light and does not come to the light, lest his works should be exposed. But whoever does what is true comes to the light, so that it may be clearly seen that his works have been carried out in God. (John 3:19–21)

The 'sun' and the 'moon' – references to the spiritual and social laws of a dispensation

The sun often represents divine glory in the Bible: the Prophet Malachi describes the Messiah as the 'Sun of righteousness' who shall arise with healing in His wings (Mal. 4:2). Christ explains that this sun rises 'on the evil and on the good' (Matt. 5:45).

REVIEW OF SOME CHRISTIAN THEMES

The moon has no light of its own but reflects the light of the sun. Similarly, the social laws of a religion, represented by the moon, owe their light to the core ethical and moral teachings of a religion.

The spiritual sun is predicted to shine 'seven times' more brightly at the end time

The Prophet Isaiah predicts that the sun of the anticipated revelation will be 'transcendently more bright and glorious that ever it was before':[8]

> Moreover, the light of the moon will be as the light of the sun, and the light of the sun will be sevenfold, as the light of seven days, in the day when the Lord binds up the brokenness of his people, and heals the wounds inflicted by his blow. (Is. 30:26)

In his commentary Rev. Albert Barnes explains:

> *Moreover.* In addition to all the blessings . . .
> *The light of the moon.* Light is in the Scriptures an emblem of purity, intelligence, happiness, prosperity; as darkness is an emblem of ignorance, calamity, and sin . . .
> The sense of this passage is, that in those future days the light would shine intensely, and without obscurity; that though they had been walking in the light of the true religion, yet that their light would be greatly augmented, and that they would have much clearer views of the divine character and government. That this refers to the times of the Messiah there can be little or no room to doubt. It is language such as Isaiah commonly employs to describe those times; and there is a fullness and splendor about it which can suit no other period . . . There is nothing in the connection, moreover, which forbids such an interpretation of the passage.
> *Shall be as the light of the sun.* Shall be clear, bright, intense. The sense is, there shall be a great increase of light, as if the light of the moon were suddenly increased to the brightness of the meridian sun.
> *Shall be seven-fold.* Seven times as intense and clear as usual, as if the light of seven days were concentrated into one. The word 'seven' in the Scriptures often denotes a complete or perfect number; and

indicates 'completeness' or 'perfections' . . . The sense of the prophet is, that subsequent to the great calamities which were to befall them, there would be a time of glorious prosperity, and the design of this was to comfort them with the assurance that their nation would not be wholly destroyed.[9]

An imperishable and everlasting light:

> The sun shall be no more your light by day, nor for brightness shall the moon give you light; but the Lord will be your everlasting light, and your God will be your glory. Your sun shall no more go down, nor your moon withdraw itself; for the Lord will be your everlasting light, and your days of mourning shall be ended. (Is. 60:19–20)

Christ promised that His servants will also be a source of illumination:

> Then the righteous will shine like the sun in the kingdom of their Father. He who has ears, let him hear. (Matt. 13:43; also Dan. 12:3)

Furthermore, on the occasion of the Second Coming, the expected 'City of God', the 'new Jerusalem' or the new revelation will not rely on earlier illuminations but will be self-sufficient in this respect – 'the glory of God' will be its light, and 'by its light will all nations walk' – 'there will be no night there' (Rev. 21:23–26).

> And night will be no more. They will need no light of lamp or sun, for the Lord God will be their light . . . (Rev. 22:5)

These prophecies clearly refer to a future divine revelation, as the lights of the various dispensations have for a long time become dimmed and obscured.

The darkening of the sun – a reference to gloomy spiritual horizons, and the inability of earlier religions to shed light on humanity

The Prophet Isaiah correlates the darkening of the sun and moon with a rise in unrighteousness (Is. 13:10; 24:23; see also Joel 2:2, 30–31; 3:15).

Consistent with these prophecies, by the reckoning of the Apostles the spiritual sun had 'turned to darkness' (Acts 2:20). Christ predicted that the same phenomenon would affect the Second Coming (Matt. 24:29).

That the heavenly portents are to be understood allegorically and spiritually is demonstrated by the fact that the Apostle Peter stated that what he and the other eleven disciples were witnessing was exactly what the Prophet Joel had prophesied. Clearly, none of the heavenly signs and portents occurred visibly, indicating that the disciples understood them metaphorically. Indeed, the literal fulfilment of these prophecies, such as the moon turning to blood, would be absurd. Had the physical sun actually darkened, life on earth would have shortly thereafter ceased to exist.

The conversion of the moon into blood – a reference to old social laws of a religion causing hostility and bloodshed

As noted earlier, the Apostle Peter claimed that this prediction of the Prophet Joel had indeed been fulfilled:

> But this is what was uttered through the prophet Joel: And I will show wonders in the heavens above and signs on the earth below, blood, and fire, and vapor of smoke; the sun shall be turned to darkness and the moon to blood, before the day of the Lord comes, the great and magnificent day. (Acts 2:16, 19–20)

Clearly, the events had not occurred literally at the time of Peter's address. The Apostle must have understood that the prophecy had other explanations.

In his commentary on the Acts, Rev. Albert Barnes explains that the events referred to a time beyond the Pentecost:[10]

> Much of the difficulty of interpreting these verses consists in affixing the proper meaning to the expression 'that great and notable day of the Lord'. If it be limited to the day of Pentecost, it is certain that no such events occurred at that time. But there is, it is believed, no propriety in confining it to that time. The description here pertains to 'the last days' (Acts 2:17) . . . The day of the Lord is the day when God will manifest himself in a special manner; a day when he will

so strikingly be seen in his wonders and his judgments that it may be called his day. Thus, it is applied to the day of judgment . . .[11]

The traditional view has been that the prophecy refers to a change in the colour of the moon, as in the God's Word translation: 'the moon will become as red as blood'. Another explanation is that at the Second Coming the social principles (the moon) of the earlier dispensations provide reason for warfare and bloodshed.

The 'darkening' and 'fall of the stars' – references to the relatively lesser or diminished spiritual light emanating from religious leaders, and to their fall from grace

> Bahá'u'lláh explains that these prophecies about the sun, moon and stars, the heavens and the earth, are symbolical and are not to be understood merely in the literal sense. The Prophets were primarily concerned with spiritual, not material, things; with spiritual, not with physical, light. When They mention the sun, in connection with the Day of Judgement, They refer to the Sun of Righteousness. The sun is the supreme source of light, so Moses was a sun for the Hebrews, Christ for the Christians, and Muḥammad for the Muslims. When the Prophets speak of the sun being darkened, what is meant is that the pure teachings of these spiritual Suns have become obscured by misrepresentation, misunderstanding and prejudice, so that the people are in spiritual darkness. The moon and stars are the lesser sources of illumination, the religious leaders and teachers, who should guide and inspire the people. When it is said that the moon shall not give her light or shall be turned into blood, and the stars shall fall from heaven, it is indicated that the leaders of the churches shall become debased, engaging in strife and contention, and the priests shall become worldly minded, concerned about earthly instead of heavenly things.[12]

Again,

> In another sense, by these terms is intended the divines of the former Dispensation, who live in the days of the subsequent Revelations, and who hold the reins of religion in their grasp. If these divines be

illumined by the light of the latter Revelation they will be acceptable unto God, and will shine with a light everlasting. Otherwise, they will be declared as darkened, even though to outward seeming they be leaders of men, inasmuch as belief and unbelief, guidance and error, felicity and misery, light and darkness, are all dependent upon the sanction of Him Who is the Day-star of Truth.[13]

Bahá'u'lláh adds:

> In another sense, by the terms 'sun', 'moon', and 'stars' are meant such laws and teachings as have been established and proclaimed in every Dispensation, such as the laws of prayer and fasting . . .[14]

> It is unquestionable that in every succeeding Revelation the 'sun' and 'moon' of the teachings, laws, commandments, and prohibitions which have been established in the preceding Dispensation, and which have overshadowed the people of that age, become darkened, that is, are exhausted, and cease to exert their influence.[15]

In the deserts of the East the caravans relied on the stars for guidance. Hence, stars metaphorically refer to religious leaders who direct the spiritual welfare of others:

> And those who are wise shall shine like the brightness of the sky above; and those who turn many to righteousness, like the stars forever and ever. (Dan. 12:3)

Notably, in one of his dreams, Joseph sees his brothers (later the heads of the tribes of Israel) as eleven stars (Gen. 37:9–10).

The Hebrew Bible also implies that the stars will not only darken and withdraw their light, but will also be eclipsed by the greater brilliance of the future revelation:

> And the stars withdraw their shining. (Joel 2:10; also 3:15)

> For the stars of the heavens and their constellations will not give their light . . . (Is. 13:10)

The New Testament predicts that the stars will fall with the return of the Son of Man (Matt. 24:29; Mark 13:25; Rev. 6:13). When the religious leaders and scholars, the 'stars' of heavenly understanding, mislead their followers they are considered to have plummeted from their lofty positions, and as stars they have ceased to shine. This concept is consistent with descriptions of fallen angels in the New Testament (Luke 10:18; Rev. 12:9), and in the Hebrew Bible:

> How you are fallen from heaven, O Day Star, son of Dawn! How you are cut down to the ground, you who laid the nations low! (Is. 14:12)

The event cannot refer to the innumerable stars, all of which are many times larger than our planet, falling on earth since no one would be left on earth to receive the new revelation!

Bahá'u'lláh lovingly thus exhorts his followers:

> O friends! Be not careless of the virtues with which ye have been endowed, neither be neglectful of your high destiny. Suffer not your labours to be wasted through the vain imaginations, which certain hearts have devised. Ye are the stars of the heaven of understanding, the breeze that stirreth at the break of day, the soft-flowing waters upon which must depend the very life of all men, the letters inscribed upon His sacred scroll.[16]

He addresses the learned of His dispensation in the same language:

> Happy are ye, O ye the learned ones in Bahá [Glory]. By the Lord! Ye are the billows of the Most Mighty Ocean, the stars of the firmament of Glory, the standards of triumph waving betwixt earth and heaven. Ye are the manifestations of steadfastness amidst men and the daysprings of Divine Utterance to all that dwell on earth.[17]

'Heaven' refers to the spiritual realm which is the origin of divine revelation, and 'earth' signifies 'human understanding and knowledge'[18]

The Hebrew word for heavens ('heights' or 'high places') is *shomayim* or šá·má·yim (from *samu*, lofty, and *mayim*, meaning water, i.e. the high places that provide water of life). This word is used about seventy times in the Tanakh to denote almost exclusively a celestial heaven, as in:

> But Abram said to the king of Sodom, 'I have lifted my hand to the Lord, God Most High, Possessor of heaven and earth . . . (Gen. 14:22)

The Israelites were provided with 'manna', literally 'bread of heaven', as they wandered through the desert, perhaps a metaphor for spiritual nourishment, as discussed earlier.

Heaven is also the source of the 'bread', or the divine teachings provided by Christ (John 6:48–51)

It is clear that Christ did not literally come down from the sky, nor did any loaves of bread descend on the disciples. His allusions to bread, and sometimes to Himself, as coming down from heaven referred to the divine teachings that were essential for the spiritual advancement of His followers. His physical being came from Galilee but His spiritual reality and teachings emanated from a non-material realm:

> He said to them, 'You are from below; I am from above. You are of this world; I am not of this world . . .' (John 8:23)

We also note that Christ is expected to descend again from heaven (Matt. 24:30). Some Christians have mistakenly interpreted these statements, which are clearly allegorical, as referring to the appearance of Jesus coming down from the sky.

The discourse of Jesus with Nicodemus, a member of the Jewish council (John 3:1–2) also sheds light on the spiritual nature of heaven. In their conversation Jesus makes a number of allegorical statements which Nicodemus understands literally. Christ explained that He was already 'in heaven' whilst still alive and on earth – in this context, heaven alluded to His spiritual state and not to a physical place in the sky:

> Jesus answered him, 'Truly, truly, I say to you, unless one is born again he cannot see the kingdom of God.' Nicodemus said to him, 'How can a man be born when he is old? Can he enter a second

time into his mother's womb and be born?' Jesus answered, 'Truly, truly, I say to you, unless one is born of water and the Spirit, he cannot enter the kingdom of God. That which is born of the flesh is flesh, and that which is born of the Spirit is spirit . . . No one has ascended into heaven except he who descended from heaven, the Son of Man.[19] (John 3:3–6, 13)

If taken literally, no one will ever go to heaven because no one has come down physically from heaven. Interpretation of heaven as a spiritual reality solves this dilemma – Christ was in perfect harmony with God's Will and Purpose, and His teachings had descended from the heaven of revelation. He was therefore in heaven whilst sitting a few yards from Nicodemus. However, due to difficulty with this statement of Christ, the last four words of the verse are omitted from several translations such as the New International Version, English Standard Version, and Berean Study Bible. Rev. Ellicott explains:

> **Which is in heaven** – These words are omitted in some MSS, including the Sinaitic and the Vatican. The judgment of most modern editors (not including Westcott and Hort) retains them. It is an instance where it is hard to account for the insertion by a copyist, but where the omission is not unlikely, owing to their seeming difficulty. And yet the difficulty is one which vanishes before the true idea of heaven. If heaven is thought of as a place infinitely distant beyond clouds and sky, or as a time in the far future when this world's life shall end, then it is indeed hard to understand what is here meant by 'the Son of Man which is in heaven'; and a copyist may well have found in omission the easiest solution of the difficulty. But if heaven is something wholly different from this coldness of distance in space or time; if it is a state, a life, in which we are, which is in us – now in part, hereafter in its fulness – then may we understand and with glad hearts hold to the vital truth that the Son of Man, who came down from heaven, was ever in heaven . . .[20]

And according to Rev. Albert Barnes:

> **Which is in Heaven** – This is a very remarkable expression. Jesus, the Son of man, was then bodily on earth conversing with Nicodemus;

yet he declares that he is 'at the same time' in heaven. This can be understood only as referring to the fact that he had two natures: that his 'divine nature' was in heaven, and his 'human nature' on earth. Our Saviour is frequently spoken of in this manner . . . Since Jesus was 'in' heaven – as his proper abode was there – he was fitted to speak of heavenly things, and to declare the will of God to man . . .[21]

God does not reside physically in buildings. His abode (heaven) is in the hearts and souls of men, not a physical place in the sky

Stephen, the first Christian martyr, was charged at his arraignment with speaking against the temple. He responded by declaring that God's dwelling was not limited to any place – His throne is heaven:

> So it was until the days of David, who found favor in the sight of God and asked to find a dwelling place for the God of Jacob. But it was Solomon who built a house for him. Yet the Most High does not dwell in houses made by hands . . . (Acts 7:45–48)

The Lord's Prayer calls on the 'Father which art in Heaven' to bring His Kingdom on earth, when the world would evolve spiritually and become 'as it is in heaven' (Matt. 6:10). This spiritual transformation will be an inner experience and, again, not a physical change (Luke 17:20–21).

> Do you not know that you are God's temple and that God's Spirit dwells in you? If anyone destroys God's temple, God will destroy him. For God's temple is holy, and you are that temple. (I Cor. 3:16–17)

'Heaven' contrasted with 'hell'

The traditional explanation has been that hell is a place where sinners burn forever and heaven is a pleasant place reserved for believers. As discussed earlier, the concept of a heaven as a physical place is not in keeping with biblical statements. Similarly, the concept of hell as a physical place is not as straightforward as may be believed.

Those who regard the existence of a physical hell as an essential part of Christian belief may well consider the discrepancies concerning the word 'hell' in the various translations of the Bible. These have arisen because there is no single word in the Hebrew or Greek Bible that means hell. Notably, in the fourth century, Jerome in his Latin Bible translation, the Vulgate (400 CE), mistranslated four different words to mean hell. Hence, the vulgate Bible mentions 'hell' a total of 110 times, and the King James Version (1611 CE) mentions 'hell' 31 times in the Old Testament and 23 times in the New Testament, in contrast to Young's Literal Translation (1891 CE) which does not mention hell at all.

The word *Sheol* appears sixty-five times in the Hebrew manuscripts, where it refers to the grave or the pit, the place of the dead. The word *Hades* appears eleven times and is the equivalent of *Sheol* in the Greek translation of the New Testament; thus it also means the grave, the place of the dead, or the pit. *Tartarus* appears only once in the Greek manuscripts of the New Testament and refers to certain angels that had sinned and had been cast down and chained in darkness (II Pet. 2:4). The word *Gehenna* appears twelve times and is closest to the traditional understanding of hell. *Gehenna* is mentioned once in the Kethuvim part of the Tanakh or Old Testament, as a place where King Ahaz sacrificed his children to the Canaanite god Moloch in the fire (II Chron. 28:1–3). *Gehenna* is used eleven times by Jesus. In His time it referred literally to a place outside ancient Jerusalem which was used as the city dump. A fire was constantly kept alight to burn up the unwanted refuse.

It should be obvious that a literal hell, as a physical place of eternal damnation, torment and burning in an everlasting fire, is surely not in accordance with a loving and compassionate God whose mercies encompass the good and the evil (Matt. 5:45).

In the Bahá'í Writings, heaven and hell are described as spiritual states of this earthly world and the next – descriptions not of physical places, but of the condition of the soul of man; heaven is nearness to God and hell describes the torments of a soul which is not in harmony with the Divine Will. If an individual is in tune with the Spirit of God and His revelation, then his soul experiences heaven and is in heaven. Conversely: 'A soul that abhors the light of the lamp is, as it were, blind and cannot perceive the light, and this blindness is the cause of eternal deprivation.'[22] Also,

If the heart turns away from the blessings God offers how can it hope for happiness? If it does not put its hope and trust in God's Mercy, where can it find rest? Oh, trust in God! for His Bounty is everlasting, and in His Blessings, for they are superb. Oh! put your faith in the Almighty, for He faileth not and His goodness endureth for ever! His Sun giveth Light continually, and the Clouds of His Mercy are full of the Waters of Compassion with which He waters the hearts of all who trust in Him. His refreshing Breeze ever carries healing in its wings to the parched souls of men! Is it wise to turn away from such a loving Father, Who showers His blessings upon us, and to choose rather to be slaves of matter?[23]

Heaven is the state of perfection, and Hell that of imperfection; Heaven is harmony with God's will and with our fellows, and Hell is the want of such harmony; Heaven is the condition of spiritual life, and Hell that of spiritual death. A man may be either in Heaven or in Hell while still in the body. The joys of Heaven are spiritual joys; and the pains of Hell consist in the deprivation of these joys.[24]

True death is realized when a person dieth to himself at the time of His Revelation in such wise that he seeketh naught except Him.

True resurrection from the sepulchres means to be quickened in conformity with His Will, through the power of His utterance.

Paradise is attainment of His good-pleasure and everlasting hellfire His judgment through justice.

The Day He revealeth Himself is Resurrection Day which shall last as long as He ordaineth.[25]

When they [men] are delivered through the light of faith from the darkness of these vices, and become illuminated with the radiance of the sun of reality, and ennobled with all the virtues, they esteem this the greatest reward, and they know it to be the true paradise . . . Spiritual punishment . . . is to be subjected to the world of nature, to be veiled from God, to be brutal and ignorant, to fall into carnal lusts, to be absorbed in animal frailties, to be characterized with dark qualities . . . these are the greatest punishments and tortures.[26]

They say: 'Where is Paradise, and where is Hell?' Say: 'The one is reunion with Me; the other thine own self . . .'[27]

'Life' and 'death' refer, respectively, to spiritual life and its extinction; 'Resurrection' refers to spiritual reawakening and restoration of righteous (virtuous) living

Scriptural references to life, death and resurrection are allegorical and meant to be understood spiritually. For example, the Hebrew Bible predicts that there will be an abundance of dead people in that day:

> The songs of the temple shall become wailings[28] in that day declares the Lord God: '. . . So many dead bodies!' (Amos 8:3)

It also teaches that the soul of a man who sins and who lives a worldly and unspiritual existence is dead:

> Behold, all souls are mine; the soul of the father as well as the soul of the son is mine: the soul who sins shall die. (Ezek. 18:4)

This theme continues in the New Testament:

> For the wages of sin is death . . . (Rom. 6:23)

> For those who live according to the flesh set their minds on the things of the flesh, but those who live according to the Spirit set their minds on the things of the Spirit. For to set the mind on the flesh is death, but to set the mind on the Spirit is life and peace. For the mind that is set on the flesh is hostile to God, for it does not submit to God's law; indeed, it cannot. Those who are in the flesh cannot please God . . . For if you live according to the flesh you will die, but if by the Spirit you put to death the deeds of the body, you will live. For all who are led by the Spirit of God are sons of God. (Rom. 8:5–8, 13–14)

> And you were dead in the trespasses and sins in which you once walked, following the course of this world . . . because of the great love which he loved us . . . made us alive together with Christ. (Eph. 2:1, 4–5, also Col. 2:13)

As noted earlier, Christ's injunction 'follow me, and leave the dead to bury their own dead' (Matt. 8:22) illustrates powerfully that death in the New Testament often refers to spiritual demise. It is again evident that it was in a spiritual context that Jesus declared that those who accepted His revelation and believed in God would live forever:

> Truly, truly, I say to you, whoever hears my word and believes him who sent me has eternal life. He does not come into judgement, but has passed from death to life. (John 5:24)

It is also anticipated that there will be a spiritual resurrection at both the First Coming and the Second Coming:

> Truly, truly, I say to you, an hour is coming, and is now here, when the dead will hear the voice of the Son of God, and those who hear will live. For as the Father has life in himself, so he has granted the Son also to have life in himself. Do not marvel at this, for an hour is coming when all who are in the tombs will hear his voice and come out, those who have done good to the resurrection of life, and those who have done evil to the resurrection of judgment. (John 5:25–26, 28–29)

Referring to the resurrection and escape of His followers from this spiritual death, Christ also stated, 'I give unto them eternal life; and they shall never perish' (John 10:28). It was the Jewish leaders who interpreted what He said literally:

> Truly, truly, I say to you, if anyone keeps my word, he will never see death.' The Jews said to him, 'Now we know that you have a demon! Abraham died, as did the prophets, yet you say, "If anyone keeps my word, he will never taste death." Are you greater than our father Abraham, who died? And the prophets died! Who do you make yourself out to be?' (John 8:51–53)

Christ claimed that 'Whoever believes in the Son has eternal life; whoever does not obey the Son shall not see life,' that is, he will not experience the life of the spirit (John 3:36).

Also, in the parable of the prodigal son, the spiritual transformation of the wayward son is referred to as his resurrection:

For this my son was dead, and is alive again; he was lost, and is found. And they began to celebrate. (Luke 15:24)

Rev. Albert Barnes explained that the prodigal son 'was dead to virtue . . . Hence, to be restored to "virtue" is to be restored again to life.'[29] Similarly, Rev. Joseph Benson wrote:

> **For this my son was dead** – Was considered by me as dead; **and is alive again** – It is by a very common and beautiful emblem, that vicious persons are represented as dead, both by sacred and profane authors; and the natural death of their children would be less grievous to pious parents than to see them abandoned to such a course as this young sinner took.
> **He was lost and is found** – We looked upon him as utterly lost, but lo! he is come back again, beyond all expectation, in safety. Two things here are worthy of observation: 1st, That the conversion of a soul from sin to God is the raising of that soul from death to life, and the finding of that which seemed to be lost. It is a great, wonderful, and happy change: it is like that which passes upon the face of the earth when the spring returns.[30]

The Apostle Paul explained the essential nature of this inner transformation without which the individual would die (Eph. 2:1–6). Again, John the Evangelist declared that the love that Christ generated in their hearts was what distinguished them as having been resurrected from death:

> We know that we have passed out of death into life, because we love the brothers. Whoever does not love abides in death. (I John 3:14)

The Bahá'í Writings explain that 'By the terms "life" and "death", spoken of in the scriptures, is intended the life of faith and the death of unbelief.'[31]

> The world of humanity cannot advance through mere physical powers and intellectual attainments; nay, rather, the Holy Spirit is essential. The divine Father must assist the human world to attain maturity. The body of man is in need of physical and mental energy,

but his spirit requires the life and fortification of the Holy Spirit. Without its protection and quickening the human world would be extinguished ... Jesus Christ ... said, 'That which is born of the flesh is flesh; and that which is born of the Spirit is spirit' [John 3:6]. It is evident, therefore, according to Christ that the human spirit which is not fortified by the presence of the Holy Spirit is dead and in need of resurrection by that divine power; otherwise, though materially advanced to high degrees, man cannot attain full and complete progress.[32]

... whosoever in every dispensation is born of the Spirit and is quickened by the breath of the Manifestation of Holiness, he verily is of those that have attained unto 'life' and 'resurrection' and have entered into the 'paradise' of the love of God. And whosoever is not of them, is condemned to 'death' and 'deprivation', to the 'fire' of unbelief, and to the 'wrath' of God ... For the life of the flesh is common to both men and animals, whereas the life of the spirit is possessed only by the pure in heart who have quaffed from the ocean of faith and partaken of the fruit of certitude. This life knoweth no death, and this existence is crowned by immortality.[33]

'Judgement Day' or 'Resurrection Day' refer to the end of one dispensation and the birth of a new dispensation when the fate of all earlier concepts will be decided

Jews and Christians alike await the coming of the Judge and the Day of Judgement, an event synonymous with the Day of Resurrection, when the dead are expected to arise:

> And many of those who sleep in the dust of the earth shall awake, some to everlasting life, and some to shame and everlasting contempt. (Dan. 12:2)

Jesus stated in Luke 9:60: 'Leave the dead to bury their dead'. His concern had to do with the resuscitation of belief and faith and a reawakening of humanity's spirituality. Christ had come not only for those who were well and did not need a physician, but also to cure individuals who were spiritually moribund (Luke 5:31). He denied that He had personally passed sentence on any man – any apparent judgement was not His but that of the Father:

> You judge according to the flesh; I judge no one. Yet even if I do judge, my judgement is true, for it is not I alone who judge, but I and the Father who sent me ... (John 8:15–16)

The Gospel of John reminded Christians:

> For God did not send his Son into the world to condemn the world, but in order that the world might be saved through him ... (John 3:17)

Charles J. Ellicott's commentary gives the following explanation:

> Part of the current belief about the Messiah's advent was, that he would destroy the Gentile world. The authorised expositions of many texts of the Old Testament asserted this, and Nicodemus must oft times have heard it and taught it. God's love for, and gift to, the world has just been declared. This truth runs counter to their belief, and is now stated as an express denial of it. The purpose of the Messiah's mission is not to judge, but to save. The latter clause of the verse changes the order of the thought. It would naturally be 'but that He might save the world'.[34]

When the people of a Samaritan village did not extend hospitality to Jesus, His disciples wondered whether the inhabitants did not deserve God's wrath:

> And he sent messengers ahead of him, who went and entered a village of the Samaritans, to make preparations for him. But the people did not receive him, because his face was set toward Jerusalem. And when his disciples James and John saw it, they said, 'Lord, do you want us to tell fire to come down from heaven and consume them?' But he turned and rebuked them.[35] And they went on to another village. (Luke 9:52–56)

Christ taught that those who desire to honour God must not wish ill on any of His creation, a lesson that should perhaps be heeded by those who ascend pulpits and invoke fire and brimstone on presumed sinners.

Christ's revelation represented the Day of Judgement of the Dispensation of Moses – a time when the blind will be distinguished from those who comprehend

It is the nature of divine revelation that it restores insight and comprehension to some individuals but causes others to rebel against the truth:

> Jesus said, 'For judgement I came into this world, that those who do not see may see, and those who see may become blind.' Some of the Pharisees near him heard these things, and said to him, 'Are we also blind?' Jesus said to them, 'If you were blind, you would have no guilt; but now that you say, "We see," your guilt remains.' (John 9:39–41)

Rev. Joseph Benson has provided the following commentary:

> *For judgment*, as well as mercy, *I am come into this world that they which see not might see* – That the ignorant, who are willing and desirous to be instructed, might have divine knowledge and true wisdom imparted to them; *and that they which see* –Who are confident that they see, who are conceited of, or trust in, their supposed knowledge and wisdom; *might be made blind* – Might be confirmed in their ignorance and folly, and be abandoned to a greater degree thereof.[36]

In their commentary, Matthew Henry and Thomas Scott similarly wrote:

> *That those who see not might see, and that those who see might be made blind.* Such a difference of Christ's coming is often spoken of; to some his gospel is a saviour of life unto life, to others of death unto death. (1.) This is applicable to nations and people, that the Gentiles, who had long been destitute of the light of divine revelation, might see it; and the Jews, who had long enjoyed it, might have the things of their peace hid from their eyes, Hos. 1:10; 2:23. The Gentiles see a great light, while blindness is happened unto Israel, and their eyes

> are darkened. (2.) . . . Christ came into the world, [1.] Intentionally and designedly to give sight to those that were spiritually blind; by his word to reveal the object, and by his Spirit to heal the organ, that many precious souls might be turned from darkness to light. He came for judgment, that is, to set those at liberty from their dark prison that were willing to be released, Isa. 61:1 . . . Eventually, and in the issue, that those who see might be made blind; that those who have a high conceit of their own wisdom, and set up that in contradiction to divine revelation, might be sealed up in ignorance and infidelity.[37]

Clearly, Christ did not physically blind anyone. Hence, we may deduce that He was referring to the fact that the new teachings and the brilliant light of His revelation blinded the vision of some of those who had become accustomed to spiritual darkness. His rebuke of His disciples is consistent with this understanding:

> Do you not yet perceive or understand? Are your hearts hardened? Having eyes do you not see, and having ears do you not hear? And do you not remember? (Mark 8:17–18)

The Apostle Peter equated blindness with a lack of virtues:

> . . . make every effort to supplement your faith with virtue, and virtue with knowledge, and knowledge with self-control, and self-control with steadfastness, and steadfastness with godliness, and godliness with brotherly affection, and brotherly affection with love. For if these qualities are yours and are increasing, they keep you from being ineffective or unfruitful in the knowledge of our Lord Jesus Christ. For whoever lacks these qualities is so nearsighted that he is blind, having forgotten that he was cleansed from his former sins. (II Peter 5–9)

The Apostle Paul lamented that the people of his age were veiled and their minds blinded from seeing the beauty of the light of the Gospel (II Cor. 4:3–4). He prayed:

> . . . that the God of our Lord Jesus Christ, the Father of glory, may give you the Spirit of wisdom and of revelation in the knowledge of him, having the eyes of your hearts enlightened . . . (Ephes. 1:17–18)

11

RESURRECTION

At the First Coming

The resurrection of Christ after His death on the cross and a general resurrection at the Second Coming are considered essential Christian beliefs. However, the key to understanding these concepts is that the Hebrew Bible also speaks of a resurrection that will accompany the coming of the Messiah, when individuals will be granted everlasting life:

> Trust in the Lord forever, for the Lord God is an everlasting rock. Your dead shall live; their bodies shall rise. You who dwell in the dust, awake and sing for joy! For your dew is a dew of light, and the earth will give birth to the dead. (Is. 26:4,19)

> But I am the Lord your God from the land of Egypt; you know no God but me, and besides me there is no saviour. It was I who knew you in the wilderness, in the land of drought . . . I shall ransom them from the power of Sheol;[1] I shall redeem them from Death. O Death, where are your plagues? O Sheol, where is your sting? . . . (Hos. 13:4–5, 14)

> Therefore my heart is glad, and my whole being rejoices . . . For you will not abandon my soul to Sheol . . . You make known to me the path of life . . . (Ps. 16:9–11)

Maimonides' thirteen principles of faith are included in every Jewish prayer book. Notably, the thirteenth principle asserts Jewish belief in the resurrection of the dead: 'I believe with perfect faith, that there will be a revival of the dead at the time when it shall please the Creator, blessed be his Name, and exalted be his fame for ever and ever'.[2]

Expected resurrection at the Second Coming

The resurrection of the dead at the Second Coming has often been interpreted as a physical phenomenon, with those who have passed on rising from their graves literally. Once again, assertions about resurrection, for example by the Apostle Paul, would be consistent with the actual statements of Christ if the rising of the dead is understood in spiritual rather than in stark literal terms:

> But we do not want you to be uninformed, brothers, about those who are asleep, that you may not grieve as others do who have no hope. For since we believe that Jesus died and rose again, even so, through Jesus, God will bring with him those who have fallen asleep. For this we declare to you by a word from the Lord, that we who are alive, who are left until the coming of the Lord, will not precede those who have fallen asleep. For the Lord himself will descend from heaven with a cry of command, with the voice of an archangel, and with the sound of the trumpet of God. And the dead in Christ will rise first. Then we who are alive, who are left, will be caught up together with them in the clouds to meet the Lord in the air, and so we will always be with the Lord. Therefore encourage one another with these words. (I Thess. 4:13–18)

The Apostle Paul had also warned:

> I tell you this, brothers: flesh and blood[3] cannot inherit the kingdom of God, nor does the perishable inherit the imperishable. Behold! I tell you a mystery. We shall not all sleep, but we shall all be changed, in a moment, in the twinkling of an eye, at the last trumpet. For the trumpet will sound, and the dead will be raised imperishable, and we shall be changed. For this perishable body must put on the imperishable, and this mortal body must put on immortality. (I Cor. 15:50–53)

Jesus also anticipated a resurrection at the Second Coming, akin to the spiritual vitalization that accompanied the First Coming:

> Truly, truly, I say to you, an hour is coming, and is now here, when

the dead will hear the voice of the Son of God, and those who hear will live. (John 5:25)

The Book of Revelation states that at the Second Coming the spiritually dead will be judged for not having heeded the precepts, admonitions and promises recorded in their own scriptures. There will, however, be an additional book (revelation) that will confer life:

And I saw the dead, great and small,[4] standing before the throne, and books were opened. Then another book was opened [an additional new revelation], which is the book of life. And the dead were judged by what was written in the books [scriptures of the various dispensations], according to what they had done. (Rev. 20:12)

The traditional explanation of Rev. 20:12 is provided by Rev. Albert Barnes:

And the books were opened – That is, the books containing the record of human deeds. The representation is, that all that people have done is recorded, and that it will be exhibited on the final trial, and will constitute the basis of the last judgement.[5]

While it is reasonable to assume that individuals will be judged according to their deeds, as noted earlier, one must acknowledge that the Book of Revelation also prepares Christians for the fact that God will provide new understandings in the Day of the Father (Rev. 2:17) just as they were 'renewed in knowledge' at the First Coming (Col. 3:10). In this context, one may accept that the 'Books' refer to the scriptures and humanity will be judged as to how well they obeyed the divine ordinances. These scriptures prepare their followers for the Day of God.

The post-crucifixion resurrection

The Gospel of Matthew describes the events as follows:

And behold, the curtain of the temple was torn in two, from top to bottom. And the earth shook, and the rocks were split. The tombs also were opened. And many bodies of the saints who had fallen asleep were raised, and coming out of the tombs after his resurrection they went into the holy city and appeared to many. (Matt. 27:51–53)

Some Christian commentators such as Rev. Barnes[6] and Rev. Benson[7] have interpreted literally the opening of the graves, the earthquake and the emergence of the saints from their tombs. Other scholars do allow for the signs to be discerned allegorically – as poetic renderings worthy of the significance of Christ's mission and death. For example, in a commentary on the Gospel of Matthew, W. D. Davies, Emeritus Professor of Christian Origins, Duke University, and Dale C. Allison, Jr, Research Fellow, Friends University, Wichita, write:

> While verses 32–50 are seemingly devoid of supernatural activity, verses 51–4 offer an explosion of the supernatural. One cannot but recall the habit of world mythology and literature to encircle the ends of great figures with extraordinary events. Trees bloomed out of season and powder fell from the sky when Buddha slipped away. The heavens shook when Moses was taken to God (2 Bar. 59.3). As Francis of Assisi left the body, larks, otherwise only heralds of the dawn, sang at night. And when Milarepa, the Tibetan yogi, died, comets flashed, flowers floated to earth, and strange sounds were heard.[8]

A literal interpretation of these events has no historical or scientific merit. If these momentous events had occurred physically, it would be astonishing that the three other Gospels failed to mention them. Also, close examination of other New Testament scripture points to the validity of a spiritual understanding of these verses.

Rending or splitting of the rocks – softening the 'stubborn hearts', 'hard foreheads' and 'hard faces' with increased spiritual receptivity

> But the house of Israel will not be willing to listen to you, for they are not willing to listen to me: because all the house of Israel have a hard forehead and a stubborn heart. Behold, I have made your face as hard as their faces, and your forehead as hard as their foreheads. Like emery[9] harder than flint . . . (Ezek. 3:3:7–9; also, Dan. 5:20; Mark 6:52; John 12:40; Heb. 3:13)

Again,

> But they refused to pay attention and turned a stubborn shoulder and stopped their ears that they might not hear. They made their hearts diamond-hard lest they should hear the law and the words that the Lord of hosts had sent by his Spirit through the former prophets. (Zech. 7:11–12)

Conversely, the Hebrew Bible promises:

> And I will give them one heart, and a new spirit I will put within them. I will remove the heart of stone from their flesh and give them a heart of flesh, that they may walk in my statutes and keep my rules and obey them. And they shall be my people, and I will be their God. (Ezek. 11:19–20)

These verses remind one that, beyond the obvious, there may have been other meanings to the following account in the Torah of water gushing out of a stone:

> And Moses lifted up his hand and struck the rock with his staff twice, and water came out abundantly, and the congregation drank, and their livestock. (Num. 20:11)

In one sense, the quaking of the earth, the splitting of the rocks and the resurrection of the saints (Matt. 27:51–2) may refer to the fact that through the sacrifice of Christ, some hard hearts were softened and some blind eyes were opened to His reality. In addition, 'earthquake' would also be an apt reference to the social turmoil and upheaval that disturbed the foundations of Jewish thought and tradition.

Resurrection of the dead

It is likely that following Christ's crucifixion the faith of some was restored and resurrected. Jesus Himself predicted this: it would be after His death that some individuals would believe:

> So Jesus said to them, 'When you have lifted up the Son of Man,

then you will know that I am he, and that I do nothing on my own authority, but speak just as the Father taught me.' (John 8:28)

The Bahá'í Writings describe the transformation and changes brought about by Christ's crucifixion:

> Know thou that when the Son of Man yielded up His breath to God, the whole creation wept with a great weeping. By sacrificing Himself, however, a fresh capacity was infused into all created things. Its evidences, as witnessed in all the peoples of the earth, are now manifest before thee. The deepest wisdom which the sages have uttered, the profoundest learning which any mind hath unfolded, the arts which the ablest hands have produced, the influence exerted by the most potent of rulers, are but manifestations of the quickening power released by His transcendent, His all-pervasive, and resplendent Spirit.[10]

Bahá'u'lláh's followers are urged today to emulate the sacrificial efforts of Christ's disciples:

> The disciples of Christ forgot themselves and all earthly things, forsook all their cares and belongings, purged themselves of self and passion, and with absolute detachment scattered far and wide and engaged in calling the peoples of the world to the divine guidance; till at last they made the world another world, illumined the surface of the earth, and even to their last hour proved self-sacrificing in the pathway of that beloved One of God. Finally in various lands they suffered glorious martyrdom. Let them that are men of action follow in their footsteps![11]

However, the Bahá'í Writings explain that the signs accompanying the crucifixion were symbolic:

> ... it is recorded in the Gospel that upon the martyrdom of Christ darkness fell, the earth shook, the veil of the Temple was rent in twain, and the dead arose from their graves. If this had outwardly come to pass, it would have been a stupendous thing. Such an event would have undoubtedly been recorded in the chronicles of the

time and would have seized with dismay the hearts of men. At the very least the soldiers would have removed Christ from the cross or would have fled. But as these events have not been recorded in any history, it is evident that they are not to be understood literally but according to their inner meaning.[12]

The Bahá'í Writings also explain that by the resurrection of the dead, expected by both Jews and Christians, is meant the divinely ordained return of individuals to a holy life dedicated to the eternal virtues – hence, a reference to spiritual resuscitation rather than to bodily reanimation. John Esslemont comments:

> Resurrection has nothing to do with the gross physical body. That body, once dead, is done with. It becomes decomposed and its atoms will never be recomposed into the same body.
>
> Resurrection is the birth of the individual to spiritual life, through the gift of the Holy Spirit bestowed through the Manifestation of God. The grave from which he arises is the grave of ignorance and negligence of God. The sleep from which he awakens is the dormant spiritual condition in which many await the dawn of the Day of God. This dawn illumines all who have lived on the face of the earth, whether they are in the body or out of the body, but those who are spiritually blind cannot perceive it . . .[13]

In one sense, every new revelation represents the Day of Judgement and the Day of Resurrection of the earlier dispensations. Thus, the Day of Resurrection of Judaism began when Christ was baptized by John the Baptist and the Holy Spirit descended on Him:

> . . . from the inception of the mission of Jesus . . . till the day of His ascension was the Resurrection of Moses. For during that period the Revelation of God shone forth through the appearance of that divine Reality, Who rewarded by His Word everyone who believed in Moses, and punished by His Word everyone who did not believe; inasmuch as God's Testimony for that Day was that which He had solemnly affirmed in the Gospel.[14]

Today, the revelation of Bahá'u'lláh signifies the Day of Resurrection and Judgement of previous dispensations, including Judaism and Christianity. It is the Day when the spiritually dead are destined to be quickened. It is also the Day when those who deny God's revelation will have to explain the reasons for their failure to recognize the truth:

> Concerning the meaning of 'Resurrection'... this term is often used by Bahá'u'lláh in His Writings... its meaning is figurative. The tomb mentioned is also allegorical, i.e. the tomb of unbelief. The Day of Resurrection, according to Bahá'í interpretation, is the Judgement Day, the Day when unbelievers will be called upon to give account of their actions, and whether the world has prevented them from acknowledging the new Revelation.[15]

> By the Resurrection is meant... the appearance of a new Manifestation of the Sun of Truth. The raising of the dead means the spiritual awakening of those who are asleep in the graves of ignorance, heedlessness and lust. The Day of Judgement is the Day of the new Manifestation, by acceptance or rejection of Whose Revelation the sheep are separated from the goats, for the sheep know the voice of the Good Shepherd and follow Him.[16]

Bahá'u'lláh has brought all the truth that Jesus stated He had not revealed because His disciples could not 'bear them' (John 16:12). He has divulged the meaning of the truths of the Bible and proclaimed: 'Every hidden thing hath been brought to light by virtue of the Will of the Supreme Ordainer...'[17] He has discriminated between the social principles that must govern a global society and those beliefs and practices that are inimical to its well-being, peace and tranquility. It may well be asked: who other than the Author of 'the time of the end', anticipated by the Prophet Daniel, can elucidate the divine mysteries of the Scriptures, divulge 'the words that are shut up [closed up]', and 'unseal the book' (Dan. 12:8–9)?

The reappearance of Christ in the clouds of heaven

The clouds mentioned in the Bible do not necessarily refer literally to drops of water or ice crystals suspended in the atmosphere. The Hebrew Bible describes clouds darkening or obscuring the light of the sun (Is. 5:30). Therefore, another explanation of 'clouds' is that they refer to the many adverse conditions that would prevail at the Second Coming and which would prevent recognition of God's revelation (see also Chapter 6).

In this context, the Bahá'í Writings make reference to 'the thick clouds of waywardness',[18] and 'the dark and gloomy clouds of blind imitation and dogmatic variance'.[19] They further instruct:

> If we abandon these time-worn blind imitations and investigate reality all of us will be unified. No discord will remain; antagonism will disappear. All will associate in fellowship. All will enjoy the cordial bonds of friendship. The world of creation will then attain composure. The dark and gloomy clouds of blind imitations and dogmatic variances will be scattered and dispelled; the Sun of Reality will shine most gloriously . . .[20]

> By the term 'clouds' is meant those things that are contrary to the ways and desires of men . . . These 'clouds' signify, in one sense, the annulment of laws, the abrogation of former Dispensations, the repeal of rituals and customs current amongst men, the exalting of the illiterate faithful above the learned opposers of the Faith. In another sense, they mean the appearance of that immortal Beauty in the image of mortal man, with such human limitations as eating and drinking, poverty and riches, glory and abasement, sleeping and waking, and such other things as cast doubt in the minds of men, and cause them to turn away. All such veils are symbolically referred to as 'clouds' . . . Even as the clouds prevent the eyes of men from beholding the sun, so do these things hinder the souls of men from recognizing the light of the divine Luminary.[21]

Life after death, and the spiritual meaning of Christ's resurrection

The Bahá'í Writings teach that the soul of man is immortal:

> Know thou of a truth that the soul, after its separation from the body, will continue to progress until it attaineth the presence of God, in a state and condition which neither the revolution of ages

and centuries, nor the changes and chances of this world, can alter. It will endure as long as the Kingdom of God, His sovereignty, His dominion and power will endure. It will manifest the signs of God and His attributes, and will reveal His loving kindness and bounty ... The purpose underlying their (Prophets and Messengers) revelation hath been to educate all men, that they may, at the hour of death, ascend, in the utmost purity and sanctity and with absolute detachment, to the throne of the Most High. The light which these souls radiate is responsible for the progress of the world and the advancement of its peoples. They are like unto leaven which leaveneth the world of being, and constitute the animating force through which the arts and wonders of the world are made manifest. Through them the clouds rain their bounty upon men, and the earth bringeth forth its fruits... These souls and symbols of detachment have provided, and will continue to provide, the supreme moving impulse in the world of being. The world beyond is as different from this world as this world is different from that of the child while still in the womb of its mother. When the soul attaineth the Presence of God, it will assume the form that best befitteth its immortality and is worthy of its celestial habitation.[22]

The resurrection of Christ was not the reanimation of His crucified dead body but the restoration of His Faith and His teachings – the disciples came to realize that though physically dead, His spirit was always present with them, as He had promised:

'And behold I am with you always, to the end of the age.' (Matt. 28:20)

Unfortunately, the physical resurrection of Christ eventually became part of the Apostles' Creed. It is now not uncommon to hear that Christianity stands or falls by the dogma of the physical resurrection of Christ, a creed that separates Christianity from other religions, as Mohler writes:

The resurrection of Jesus Christ from the dead separates Christianity from all mere religion – whatever its form. Christianity without the literal, physical resurrection of Jesus Christ from the dead is merely one religion among many. 'And if Christ is not risen,' said the Apostle Paul, 'then our preaching is empty and your faith is in vain' (I Cor. 15:14.). Furthermore, 'You are still in your sins!' (I Cor. 15:17). Paul could not have chosen stronger language. 'If in this life only we have hope in Christ, we are of all men the most pitiable' (I Cor. 15:19).

Yet, the resurrection of Jesus Christ has been under persistent attacks since the Apostolic age. Why? Because it is the central confirmation of Jesus' identity as the incarnate Son of God, and the ultimate sign of Christ's completed work of atonement, redemption, reconciliation, and salvation. Those who oppose Christ, whether first century religious leaders or twentieth century secularists, recognize the Resurrection as the vindication of Christ against His enemies.

Those who would attack the Church and reject its gospel must direct their arrows at the most crucial truth claim of the New Testament and the disciples: That Jesus Christ, having suffered death on a cross, though sinless, having borne the sins of those He came to save, having been buried in a sealed and guarded grave, was raised by the power of God on the third day.

As Paul well understood, Christianity stands or falls with the empty grave. If Christ is not raised, we are to be pitied, for our faith is in vain. Those who would preach a resurrectionless Christianity have substituted the truth of the gospel for a lie. But, asserted Paul, Christ is risen from the dead. Our faith is not in vain, but is in the risen Lord. He willingly faced death on a cross and defeated death from the grave. The Resurrection is the ultimate sign of God's vindication of His Son.[23]

Some scholars, however, have argued that a non-literal interpretation of the events associated with Easter does not invalidate the profound spiritual truth of the resurrection of Christ. Prof. Marcus Joel Borg, an American New Testament theologian at Oregon State University, has stated, for example:

> I do believe in the resurrection of Jesus. I am just skeptical that it involved anything happening to his corpse . . . The truth of Easter really has nothing to do with whether the tomb was empty on a

particular morning 2,000 years ago or whether anything happened to the corpse of Jesus. I see the truth of Easter as grounded in the Christian experience of Jesus as a living spiritual reality of the present.[24]

Post-crucifixion accounts

A literal understanding of the stories of the empty tomb and Jesus walking the earth after His crucifixion presents a great many difficulties. To begin with, the accounts differ: in Matthew, Jesus appeared to His followers in Galilee, and in Luke, in Jerusalem. In one account Jesus walked through a door and materialized in the middle of a meeting His disciples were having. However, the anecdotes make two points that can be accepted without belief in a physical resurrection: Jesus did die, and He was seen afterwards.

The formulation of the dogma of physical resurrection relies primarily on a few fragmentary statements (I Cor. 15:12–20; Acts 3:15). There are several points that we must bear in mind. First, the Apostle Paul describes the resurrection of Christ, not as a physical fact but as a belief (Rom. 10:9–10). Second, all the biblical statements about the resurrection of the dead and the resurrection of Christ are more susceptible to spiritual than literal interpretation. Third, the use of the Apostle Paul's arguments by Christians to explain the resurrection of Christ literally is in many respects similar to the Jews using the writings of the great Rabbi Maimonides to refute the New Testament teachings.

It may be observed that had the physical resurrection of Jesus been a proven fact and universally accepted it would not have been necessary to formulate it as a dogma.

In addition, spiritual explanations of the resurrection of Christ are not only persuasive and compatible with His own statements on death, life and reawakening, but also infuse the subject with deeper and more transformative meanings. Christ's statement that He was the source of the spiritual life and resurrection of those who accepted His teachings – the body may die but the soul lives on – illustrates this:

> Jesus said to her, 'I am the resurrection and the life. Whoever believes in me, though he die, yet shall he live, and everyone who lives and believes in me shall never die . . .' (John 11:25–26)

> For Christ . . . being put to death in the flesh but made alive in the spirit . . . (I Peter 3:18)

An important Bahá'í understanding is that faith should accord with reason and science. Although there is not always a completely satisfactory logical explanation of every spiritual truth,[25] it is not necessary to insist on a physical interpretation of resurrection, as there are spiritual explanations. There are a number of passages in the Bible, the Qur'án and the Bahá'í Writings that indicate the spiritual nature of life, death and resurrection in the three scriptures. In addition, one encounters difficulties trying to reconcile the different accounts of the resurrection of Christ,[26] some of which will be examined here.

Jesus would be buried for three days and three nights before His resurrection

The events described do not appear to fulfil literally the promise recorded in the Gospel of Matthew that Jesus would be buried three days and three nights before His resurrection, whereas a figurative explanation does appear reasonable.

Origin of the three days and three nights

When pressed by the Jewish leaders to give them a sign to validate His claims of being the Messiah, Jesus said that the only miracle He would perform was the sign of Jonah:

> Then some of the scribes and Pharisees answered him, saying, 'Teacher, we wish to see a sign from you.' But he answered them, 'An evil and adulterous generation seeks for a sign, but no sign will be given to it except the sign of the prophet Jonah. For just as Jonah was three days and three nights in the belly of the great fish, so will the Son of Man be three days and three nights in the heart of the earth.' (Matt. 12:38–40)

The Prophet Jonah (or Jonas, c. 780–730 BCE) was sent by God to warn the town of Nineveh, the capital of Assyria, of its impending destruction. Realizing that his message was not going to be popular with the people of Nineveh, Jonah tried to escape the divine command by taking a boat away from the area. They were engulfed by a storm that threatened to sink the boat. Jonah, realizing that he was the cause of the danger that they faced, asked the sailors to throw him overboard. He was swallowed by a great fish or whale, and 'Jonah was in the belly of the fish three days and three nights' (Jonah 1:17).

Christian scholars have struggled with the statement of Matt. 12:40, as the length of time Jesus is reported to have been in His grave before rising does not amount to three days and three nights. Christ died on the cross late Friday afternoon. A disciple of Christ, Joseph of Arimathea, placed the wrapped body of Jesus in a tomb which he had cut out of stone, and rolled a great stone across the entrance to the tomb, whilst Mary Magdalene and 'the other Mary' were sitting opposite the tomb (Matt. 27:57–61). Two or more women (the exact number differs), including Mary Magdalene and Mary, the mother of James and John, found the tomb to be empty early Sunday morning. Based on the Bible (Gen. 1:5) a Jewish day starts with nightfall and continues to the next nightfall. If taken as a 'historical' account, the duration of time that Jesus spent in the tomb included Friday evening, Friday night, Saturday, and possibly a few hours of early Sunday morning – hardly three days and certainly only two nights. According to one commentary, 'not a few critics accordingly inferred . . . that the explanation given by Matthew was an addition to the words actually spoken by our Lord'. The commentary argues 'That the very difficulty presented by the prediction of "three days and three nights" as compared with the six-and-thirty hours (two nights and one day) of the actual history of the Resurrection, is against the probability of the verse having been inserted as a prophecy after the event.'[27]

One explanation that is often advanced is that any fraction of a day is considered by Jews to be equivalent to a whole day. This, however, fails to clarify the absence of three nights. Furthermore, in a parable related by Christ, a physical rising from the dead would be futile as it would not convince His detractors:

> He said to him, 'If they do not hear Moses and the Prophets, neither will they be convinced if someone should rise from the dead.' (Luke 16:31)

The three days and three nights likely refers to the period immediately following the crucifixion when the discouraged disciples left the scene and the light of Christ became eclipsed. In reality, Christianity died before His disciples realized that His spirit was alive and present with them. All the subsequent embellishments of the story are not based on any direct teaching of Christ, but are derived from certain statements of the Apostles Paul and Peter.

Bahá'ís accept the resurrection of Christ, but their faith in Jesus does not require the belief that He was physically raised back to life – after all, Christ was 'the way and the truth, and the life' before His crucifixion. They also consider the greater reality that although the Christian Faith underwent a brief demise, it was resurrected when the disciples realized that the spirit of Christ had not been destroyed on the cross, that He was still with them, and that they had a duty to perform:

> Go therefore and make disciples of all nations, baptizing them in the name of the Father and of the Son and of the Holy Spirit, teaching them to observe all that I have commanded you. And behold, I am with you always, to the end of the age. (Matt. 28:19–20)

It is with this perspective that one appreciates how a literal interpretation of the resurrection kills the spirit but a spiritual explanation gives life (II Cor. 3:6).

The ascent of Christ to heaven immediately following His death on the cross

In the following Gospel account, Jesus clearly states that He accompanied by the 'good thief', would ascend to paradise (heaven) on the same day as His crucifixion – that is, even before their bodies were laid in the grave:

> One of the criminals who were hanged railed at him, saying, 'Are you not the Christ? Save yourself and us!' But the other rebuked him, saying, 'Do you not fear God, since you are under the same sentence of condemnation? And we indeed justly, for we are receiving the due reward of our deeds; but this man has done nothing wrong.' And he said, 'Jesus, remember me when you come into your kingdom.' And he said to him, 'Truly, I say to you, today you will

be with me in paradise.'[28] Then Jesus, calling out with a loud voice, said, 'Father, into your hands I commit my spirit!' And having said this he breathed his last. (Luke 23:39–43, 46)

Rev. Albert Barnes comments:

> ***Today* . . .** – It is not probable that the dying thief expected that his prayer would be so soon answered. It is rather to be supposed that he looked to some 'future' period when the Messiah would rise or would return; but Jesus told him that his prayer would be answered that very day, implying, evidently, that it would be 'immediately' at death. This is the more remarkable, as those who were crucified commonly lingered for several days on the cross before they died; but Jesus foresaw that measures would be taken to 'hasten' their death, and assured him that 'that' day he should receive an answer to his prayer and be with him in his kingdom.
> ***Paradise*** – . . . from the narrative we may learn: . . . That the soul will exist separately from the body; for, while the thief and the Saviour would be in Paradise, their 'bodies' would be on the cross or in the grave.[29]

Jesus's ascent to heaven may be understood in the same context as His descent from heaven

Confusing the physical sky with heaven, the realm of the spirit, the Jews protested when Jesus claimed to have come down from heaven. Clearly, He was referring to His teachings and not His body:

> So the Jews grumbled about him, because he said, 'I am the bread that came down from heaven.' They said, 'Is not this Jesus, the son of Joseph, whose father and mother we know? How does he now say, "I have come down from heaven"?' (John 6:41–42)

Notably, the Book of Revelation mentions that John similarly went to heaven 'in the Spirit' (Rev. 4:1–2) and was carried 'in the Spirit' to be shown 'the Holy City, Jerusalem' (Rev. 21:10).

Christ was expected to descend from heaven a second time, at the Second Coming:

And while they were gazing into heaven[30] as he went; behold, two men stood by them in white robes. 'Men of Galilee, why do you stand looking into heaven?[31] This Jesus, who was taken up from you into heaven, will come in the same way as you saw him go into heaven.' (Acts 1:10–11)

Difficulty of reconciling church dogma with the Gospel accounts and science

Jonah describes himself as being in hell (Sheol) while he was in the belly of the whale:

> Then Jonah prayed to the Lord his God from the belly of the fish, saying, 'I called out to the Lord, out of my distress, and he answered me; out of the belly of Sheol I cried, and you heard my voice' (Jonah 2:1–2).

This may explain an early church understanding that Jesus descended on Saturday whilst in His tomb to Abraham's side of Hades, or Sheol, to preach to those who were imprisoned there (I Pet. 3:18–19), and to release them from their bondage. This account was neither part of the Nicene Creed (325 CE) nor its revised version, the Nicene–Constantinopolitan Creed (381 CE) but was inserted into the Apostles' Creed in 570 CE.

It defies belief that the All-Merciful God would allow individuals such as the Patriarch Abraham, who received His intimations directly from God, to remain in hell (Sheol) for centuries until being rescued by Jesus.[32] Also, bodily resurrection does not accord with reason – a major principle of the Bahá'í Faith is that religion and science must not disagree but be in harmony:

> Every religion which is not in accordance with established science is superstition. Religion must be reasonable. If it does not square with reason, it is superstition and without foundation. It is like a mirage, which deceives man by leading him to think it is a body of water. God has endowed man with reason that he may perceive what is true. If we insist that such and such a subject is not to be reasoned out and tested according to the established logical modes

of the intellect, what is the use of the reason which God has given man?[33]

Spiritual significance of the death, resurrection and ascension of Christ

To summarize, although the Bahá'í Writings do not support a literal understanding of the resurrection of Christ, they do acknowledge the spiritual forces and transformative power that were released through the sacrifice of Christ on the cross. They elevate the discourse and render it more compatible with the spiritual truths of the Bible. Bahá'u'lláh glorifies Christ – as anticipated in the Gospel of John (John 16:14) – and emphasizes His sacrifice for the salvation of humanity. He confirms that Jesus died for our sins of materialism, heedlessness and lack of righteousness, and that we might realize our full spiritual potential. In this context, the Bahá'í Writings pay the following tributes to Christ:

> Christ sacrificed Himself so that mankind might be freed from the imperfections of the material nature and endowed with the virtues of the spiritual nature . . . He sacrificed Himself that He might bestow the spirit of life, and perished in body that He might quicken others in spirit . . . Christ was like a seed, and this seed sacrificed its form so that the tree might grow and develop. Although the form of the seed was destroyed, its reality manifested itself, in perfect majesty and beauty, in the outward form of the tree . . .The form of the seed was sacrificed for the tree, but its perfections were revealed and manifested by virtue of this sacrifice: For the tree, its branches, its leaves, and its blossoms were latent and hidden within the seed, but when the form of the seed was sacrificed, its perfections were fully manifested in the leaves, blossoms, and fruit.[34]

> The exaltation of the Word, the revelation of the power of God, the conversion of God-fearing souls, the bestowal of everlasting life – it was following the Messiah's martyrdom that all these were increased and intensified.[35]

It is important to emphasize that the spiritual explanations of resurrection in the Bahá'í Writings do not in any way detract from the significance of the event and Christ's sacrifice. Instead, such an understanding elevates the biblical themes and glorifies Christ. According to the Baháʼí Writings, Christ sacrificed Himself for the unity and amity of mankind:

> The divine Prophets came to establish the unity of the Kingdom in human hearts. All of them proclaimed the glad tidings of the divine bestowals to the world of mankind. All brought the same message of divine love to the world. Jesus Christ gave His life upon the cross for the unity of mankind. Those who believed in Him likewise sacrificed life, honor, possessions, family, everything, that this human world might be released from the hell of discord, enmity and strife. His foundation was the oneness of humanity. Only a few were attracted to Him. They were not the kings andrulers of His time. They were not rich and important people. Some of them were catchers of fish . . . His essential teaching was the unity of mankind and the attainment of supreme human virtues through love. He came to establish the Kingdom of peace and everlasting life.[36]

Again,

> What an infinite degree of love is reflected by the divine Manifestations toward mankind! For the sake of guiding the people They have willingly forfeited Their lives to resuscitate human hearts. They have accepted the cross. To enable human souls to attain the supreme degree of advancement, They have suffered during Their limited years extreme ordeals and difficulties. If Jesus Christ had not possessed love for the world of humanity, surely He would not have welcomed the cross. He was crucified for the love of mankind. Consider the infinite degree of that love. Without love for humanity John the Baptist would not have offered his life. It has been likewise with all the Prophets and Holy Souls. If the Báb [the forerunner of Baháʼuʼlláh] had not manifested love for mankind, surely He would not have offered His breast for a thousand bullets. If Baháʼuʼlláh had not been aflame with love for humanity, He would not have willingly accepted forty years' imprisonment.[37]

The Baháʼí Writings explain that the Jewish prophecies about the Messiah were similarly fulfilled by Jesus spiritually and not literally:

... they (the Jews at the time Jesus) said, 'We have heard from our fathers and have read in the Old Testament that Christ must come from an unknown place; now we find that this one has come from Nazareth.' Steeped in the literal interpretation and imitating the beliefs of fathers and ancestors, they failed to understand the fact that although the body of Jesus came from Nazareth, the reality of the Christ came from the unknown place of the divine Kingdom. They also said that the scepter of Christ would be of iron – that is to say, He should wield a sword. When Christ appeared, He did possess a sword; but it was the sword of His tongue with which He separated the false from the true. But the Jews were blind to the spiritual significance and symbolism of the prophetic words. They also expected that the Messiah would sit upon the throne of David, whereas Christ had neither throne nor semblance of sovereignty; nay, rather, He was a poor man, apparently abject and vanquished; therefore, how could He be the veritable Christ? This was one of their most insistent objections based upon ancestral interpretation and teaching. In reality, Christ was glorified with an eternal sovereignty and everlasting dominion – spiritual and not temporal. His throne and Kingdom were established in human hearts, where He reigns with power and authority without end. . .[38]

All the words of the prophets were fulfilled, but because the Jews held tenaciously to hereditary [traditional] interpretations, they did not understand the inner meanings of the Holy Bible; therefore, they denied Jesus Christ, the Messiah. The purpose of the prophetic words was not the outward or literal meaning, but the inner symbolical significance. For example, it was announced that the Messiah was to come from an unknown place. This did not refer to the birthplace of the physical body of Jesus. It has reference to the reality of the Christ – that is to say, the Christ reality was to appear from the invisible realm – for the divine reality of Christ is holy and sanctified above place.

His sword was to be a sword of iron. This signified His tongue which should separate the true from the false and by which great sword of attack He would conquer the kingdoms of hearts. He did not conquer by the physical power of an iron rod; He conquered the East and the West by the sword of His utterance.

He was seated upon the throne of David, but His sovereignty was neither a Napoleonic sovereignty nor the vanishing dominion of a Pharaoh. The Christ Kingdom was everlasting, eternal in the heaven of the divine Will.

By His promulgating the laws of the Bible the reality of the Law of Moses was meant. The Sinaitic law (Law of Moses revealed from Mount Sinai) is the foundation of the reality of Christianity. Christ promulgated it and gave it higher, spiritual expression.

In His day, according to prophecy, the wolf and the lamb were to drink from the same fountain. This was realized in Christ. The fountain referred to was the Gospel, from which the water of life gushes forth. The wolf and lamb are opposed and divergent races symbolized by these animals. Their meeting and association were impossible, but having become believers in Jesus Christ those who were formerly as wolves and lambs became united through the words of the Gospel.

The purport is that all the meanings of the prophecies were fulfilled, but because the Jews were captives of ancestral imitations and did not perceive the reality of the meanings of these words, they denied Christ; nay, they even went so far as to crucify Him. Consider how harmful is imitation. These were interpretations handed down from fathers and ancestors, and because the Jews held fast to them, they were deprived.[39]

And again,

> According to the Jews, Jesus the Christ fulfilled none of these conditions, for their eyes were holden[40] and they could not see.
>
> He came from Nazareth, no unknown place. He carried no sword in His hand, nor even a stick. He did not sit upon the Throne of David, He was a poor man. He reformed the Law of Moses, and broke the Sabbath Day. He did not conquer the East and the West, but was Himself subject to the Roman Law. He did not exalt the Jews, but taught equality and brotherhood, and rebuked the Scribes and Pharisees. He brought in no reign of peace, for during His lifetime injustice and cruelty reached such a height that even He Himself fell a victim to it, and died a shameful death upon the cross.
>
> Thus the Jews thought and spoke, for they did not understand

the Scriptures nor the glorious truths that were contained in them. The letter they knew by heart, but of the life-giving spirit they understood not a word.[41]

Sin and sinners

A traditional dogma is that sin is the handiwork of the devil, and that Jesus died on the cross as a sacrificial lamb for our sins. Christians who confessed their transgressions and acknowledged their belief in Him would be saved. It reinforces the belief system that salvation comes exclusively through Christ and, by extension, the church. It also implies, for Catholics, that the priestly rituals are essential for absolution of sins and for salvation.

Another view is that Christ's sacrifice was necessary to remove the sins of blindness and heedlessness so that man, by accepting the new divine covenant and testament, would be reborn and attain eternal life. This is perhaps the true meaning of Jesus's giving Himself up as 'a ransom for all' (I Tim. 2:6). It is for precisely the same reason that so many other Prophets and their followers have suffered martyrdom.

Sin: a rectifiable error or an aberration

The word for sin is *hamartian* in Greek, a derivation of the word *hamartia* which translates as 'error', 'defect', or 'to miss the mark'. As illustration, a hamartoma is a growth in the body that has elements of normal tissue but by comparison to what is expected is different and flawed. By the above definition, sin is a relative term – any individual may appear sinful when compared to a righteous person endowed with greater virtues. Such a person may, through prayer and sincere efforts, discard the robe of sinfulness and achieve his or her destiny.

Sin: misjudging and opposing a new revelation

Earlier beliefs and social imperatives necessarily fall short in the Day that God chooses to modify or replace them, and under the new circumstances, perhaps nothing is more sinful than for individuals to insist on the old teachings and to use their understanding of them to cavil against God and His Messenger and refute the latest divine revelation. This understanding of sin enjoins great humility, for we all fall short of what God expects of us:

> For there is no distinction . . . for all have sinned and fall short of the glory of God . . . (Rom. 3:23–24)

In His exchanges with the Jewish religious leaders, Christ explained that their sin was in their belief that they perceived the truth whereas in actuality they were spiritually blind (John 9:39–41).

Sin: an opportunity for spiritual transformation

The author of Proverbs, most likely King Solomon, the son of King David, states that acknowledgement of one's sins attracts divine mercy:

> Whoever conceals his transgressions will not prosper, but he who confesses and forsakes them will obtain mercy. Blessed is the one who fears the Lord always, but whoever hardens his heart will fall into calamity (Prov. 28:13–14)

In numerous prayers the followers of Bahá'u'lláh also confess their sinfulness and supplicate for forgiveness from the kind Father 'Who overlookest the shortcomings of all mankind':[42]

> I am a sinner, O my Lord, and Thou art the Ever-Forgiving. As soon as I recognized Thee, I hastened to attain the exalted court of Thy loving-kindness. Forgive me, O my Lord, my sins which have hindered me from walking in the ways of Thy good-pleasure, and from attaining the shores of the ocean of Thy oneness.
>
> There is no one, O my Lord, who can deal bountifully with me to whom I can turn my face, and none who can have compassion on me that I may crave his mercy. Cast me not out, I implore Thee, of the presence of Thy grace, neither do Thou withhold from me the outpourings of Thy generosity and bounty. Ordain for me, O my Lord, what Thou hast ordained for them that love Thee, and write down for me what Thou hast written down for Thy chosen ones. My gaze hath, at all times, been fixed on the horizon of Thy gracious providence, and mine eyes bent upon the court of Thy tender mercies. Do

with me as beseemeth Thee. No God is there but Thee, the God of power, the God of glory, Whose help is implored by all men.[43]

God's response to man's sin is a way by which the divine attributes of forgiveness, mercy and compassion are demonstrated, and the transformative power of His Word is revealed.[44]

Associating with sinners

The Hebrew Bible warns against being biased and prejudiced:

> To show partiality is not good,[45] but for a piece a man will do wrong. (Prov. 28:21)

There is often a reluctance to engage with members of other faiths, and to show them love and respect. In contrast, Christ spoke against religious arrogance, and consorted with individuals from many walks of life, especially those who most needed His understanding, compassion, and gift of spiritual healing:

> And as he reclined at table in his house, many tax collectors and sinners were reclining with Jesus and his disciples, for there were many who followed him. And the scribes of the Pharisees, when they saw that he was eating with sinners and tax collectors, said to his disciples, 'Why does he eat with tax collectors and sinners?' And when Jesus heard it, he said to them, 'Those who are well have no need of a physician, but those who are sick. I came not to call the righteous, but sinners.'(Mark 2:15–17)

To those 'who trusted in themselves' and believed 'that they were righteous. And treated others with contempt', Jesus recounted the following parable:

> Two men went up into the temple to pray, one a Pharisee and the other a tax collector. The Pharisee, standing by himself, prayed thus: 'God, I thank you that I am not like other men, extortioners, unjust, adulterers, or even like this tax collector. I fast twice a week; I give tithes of all that I get.' But the tax collector, standing far off,

would not even lift up his eyes to heaven, but beat his breast, saying, 'God, be merciful to me, a sinner!' I tell you, this man went down to his house justified, rather than the other. For everyone who exalts himself will be humbled, but the one who humbles himself will be exalted. (Luke 18:9–14)

Not associating with sinners

In contrast, the Apostle Paul taught that Christians should shun fellow believers who did not follow the teachings of Christ:

> I wrote unto you in an epistle not to company with fornicators:[46] Yet not altogether with the fornicators of this world, or with the covetous, or extortioners, or with idolaters; for then must ye needs go out of the world. But now I have written unto you not to keep company, if any man that is called a brother be a fornicator, or covetous, or an idolater, or a railer, or a drunkard, or an extortioner; with such an one no not to eat. (King James Version: I Cor. 5:9–12)

As noted earlier, in his next letter to the Corinthians the Apostle Paul added that intercourse with unbelievers was to be avoided as well:

> Wherefore come out from among them, and be ye separate, saith the Lord, and touch not the unclean thing; and I will receive you, And will be a Father unto you, and ye shall be my sons and daughters, saith the Lord Almighty. (II Cor. 6:17–18).

Confessing one's sins to a priest and seeking absolution

Confession, also known as reconciliation or penance, refers to acknowledgment of one's sins, in public or in private, regarded as necessary to obtain divine forgiveness. The need for confession is stressed in the Bible. The mission of the Hebrew Prophets was to awaken an awareness of the divine, and a sense of sinfulness so that people might readily acknowledge their personal and collective guilt and trespasses.

> Before the destruction of the Temple of Jerusalem [70 CE], the sin offerings on the Day of Atonement [Yom Kippur] were prefaced

by a collective expression of sinfulness [Lev. 16:21] and, since the destruction of the Temple, the Day of Atonement has continued to be commemorated in Judaism as a day of prayer, fasting, and confession.[47]

In the Lord's Prayer, Christ taught His disciples to supplicate the Father privately for forgiveness of their trespasses, as they also forgave the trespasses of others.

The Bible encourages the individual to recognize his or her sinfulness and to show remorse (Job 42:5–6; Matt. 3:8; 6:12; 11:20; Rom. 2:4; Rev. 2:5). However, confession of sins, penance and absolution by a priest are not based on any explicit teaching of Christ, Instead they are deduced indirectly from interpretations of a few vague passages that are not accepted by all Christian denominations.

Confession to a priest appeared early in the Catholic Church's history and is now regarded as a sacrament. The practice has also been adopted by the Eastern Orthodox churches, but most Protestants believe that only God can forgive sins.

One such justification is based on the parable of the prodigal son who was remorseful for having disappointed his father. The Apostle James introduces a new concept which is used to support the Roman Catholic doctrine of confessing one's sins to a priest.

> Is any sick among you? let him call for the elders of the church; and let them pray over him, anointing him with oil in the name of the Lord: And the prayer of faith shall save the sick, and the Lord shall raise him up; and if he have committed sins, they shall be forgiven him. Confess *your* faults one to another,[48] and pray one for another, that ye may be healed. The effectual fervent prayer of a righteous man availeth much. (King James Version: James 5:14–16)

The word 'your' in the above verse is in italics because the possessive pronoun is absent from the original Greek translation. The verse simply stated that Christians should recall how they could fall short of what Christ expected of them, and that they should pray for the spiritual well-being of each other, with the reminder that God hears the supplications of the righteous.

However, it is argued that the passage supports the doctrine of ministerial priesthood, and confession of one's sins to a priest. For example, one Catholic apologist offers two arguments for why this passage must refer to the priesthood.[49] He writes:

> James had just told us to go to the *presbyter* in verse 14 for healing and the forgiveness of sins. Then, verse 16 begins with the word *therefore* – a conjunction connecting verse 16 back to verses 14 and 15. The context seems to point to the 'elder' as the one to whom we confess our sins.

While the expression 'to one another' is used, the context specifies that this only refers to elders. He further adds:

> Ephesians 5:21 employed this same phrase, 'to one another,' in the context of teaching about the sacrament of holy matrimony: 'Be subject to one another out of reverence for Christ.' Even though the text says 'to one another,' the context limits the scope of the meaning of 'to one another' specifically to a man and wife – not just anyone. Similarly, the context of James 5 bears out that the confession 'to one another' refers to the relationship between 'anyone' and specifically an 'elder' or 'priest' (Gk. Πρεσβυτέρους, *presbuteros*).[50]

Protestants do not share this understanding:

> **Confess your faults one to another.** – The meaning attributed to the words of this verse by many devout Catholics cannot be established either from the opinion of antiquity, or a critical examination of the Greek text according to modern schools.[51]

Rev. Albert Barnes provides the following detailed indictment:

> This passage is one on which Roman Catholics rely to demonstrate the propriety of 'auricular confession', or confession made to a priest with a view to an absolution of sin. The doctrine which is held on that point is, that it is a duty to confess to a priest, at certain seasons, all our sins, secret and open, of which we have been guilty; all our improper thoughts, desires, words, and actions; and that the priest has power to declare on such confession that the sins are forgiven.

But never was any text less pertinent to prove a doctrine than this passage to demonstrate that. Because:

(1) The confession here enjoined is not to be made by a person in health, that he may obtain salvation, but by a sick person, that he may be healed.

(2) as mutual confession is here enjoined, a priest would be as much bound to confess to the people as the people to a priest.

(3) no mention is made of a priest at all, or even of a minister of religion, as the one to whom the confession is to be made.

(4) the confession referred to is for 'faults' with reference to 'one another', that is, where one has injured another; and nothing is said of confessing faults to those whom we have not injured at all.

(5) there is no mention here of absolution, either by a priest or any other person.

(6) if anything is meant by absolution that is Scriptural, it may as well be pronounced by one person as another; by a layman as a clergyman. All that it can mean is, that God promises pardon to those who are truly penitent, and this fact may as well be stated by one person as another. No priest, no man whatever, is empowered to say to another either that he is truly penitent, or to forgive sin. 'Who can forgive sins but God only?' None but he whose law has been violated, or who has been wronged, can pardon an offence. No third person can forgive a sin which a man has committed against a neighbor; no one but a parent can pardon the offences of which his own children have been guilty towards him; and who can put himself in the place of God, and presume to pardon the sins which his creatures have committed against him?

(7) the practice of 'auricular confession' is 'evil, and only evil, and that continually'. Nothing gives so much power to a priesthood as the supposition that they have the power of absolution. Nothing serves so much to pollute the soul as to keep impure thoughts before the mind long enough to make the confession, and to state them in words. Nothing gives a man so much power over a female as to have it supposed that it is required by religion, and appertains to the sacred office, that all that passes in the mind should be disclosed to him...[52]

Penance

Penance is a voluntary self-punishment, a particular task often assigned by the priest to the person who has confessed his or her sins. It may consist of fasting, prayer and almsgiving, but individuals may also practise self-flagellation,[53] or the wearing of a hair shirt.[54] The act is meant to be accompanied by a transformation of the heart and spiritual conversion, referred to as *metanoia*.[55]

It was as late as 1215 CE that the Fourth Council of the Lateran's Canon 21 required that every Christian who had reached the age of discretion must confess all their sins at least once a year to their own priest. Notably, it was the same Council that defined the doctrine of transubstantiation, describing the method by which the bread and wine offered in the sacrament of the Eucharist becomes the actual blood and body of Christ. The Council also forbade Jews from holding public office, infamously required them (and Muslims) to wear distinctive clothing, and called for a crusade to recover the Holy Land from the Muslims.[56]

Penance became an established teaching of the Catholic Church at the Council of Trent in 1551 CE:

> As a means of regaining grace and justice, penance was at all times necessary for those who had defiled their souls with a mortal sin ... Before the coming of Christ, penance was not a sacrament, nor is it since His coming a sacrament for those who are not baptized. But the Lord then principally instituted the sacrament of Penance, when being raised from the dead, he breathed upon His disciples saying: 'Receive the Holy Ghost. Whose sins you shall forgive, they are forgiven them; and who sins you shall retain, they are retained' [John 20:22–23]. By which action so signal and words so clear the consent of all the Fathers has ever understood that the power of forgiving and retaining sins was communicated to the Apostles and to their lawful successors, for the reconciling of the faithful who have fallen after Baptisms.[57]

Penance is a sacrament of the Catholic, Orthodox and Lutheran churches. Anglican and Methodist churches regard confession of sins and penance as rites and not sacraments.

Original or ancestral sin

This church dogma is based on a literal understanding of the creation story narrated in the Book of Genesis. Adam and Eve disobeyed God and ate of the forbidden tree of knowledge. Consequently, they became aware of their nakedness and were expelled from the Garden of Eden (paradise).

> The formalized Church doctrine was first developed in the 2nd century by Irenaeus, Bishop of Lyon. Irenaeus believed that Adam's sin was the source of human sinfulness, mortality and enslavement to sin, and that all human beings participate in his sin and share his guilt.[58]

The Bahá'í Writings state that, if taken literally, this concept is unjust and therefore not attributable to divinity:

> . . . the majority of the Christians believe that Adam sinned and transgressed by eating from the forbidden tree, that the dire and disastrous consequences of this transgression were inherited for all time by His descendants, and that Adam has thus become the cause of the death of man. This explanation is irrational and clearly mistaken, for it implies that all men, even the Prophets and Messengers of God, through no fault or sin of their own, and for no other reason than their descent from Adam, became guilty sinners and suffered the torments of hell until the day of Christ's sacrifice. This would be far from the justice of God. If Adam was a sinner, what was the sin of Abraham? What was the fault of Isaac and of Joseph? What was the transgression of Moses?[59]

> Could we conceive of the Divinity, Who is Justice itself, inflicting punishment upon the posterity of Adam for Adam's own sin and disobedience? Even if we should see a governor, an earthly ruler punishing a son for the wrongdoing of his father, we would look upon that ruler as an unjust man. Granted the father committed a wrong, what was the wrong committed by the son? There is no connection between the two. Adam's sin was not the sin of His posterity . . . If the father of a thousand generations committed a sin, is it just to demand that the present generation should suffer the consequences thereof?[60]

The Bahá'í Faith explains the serpent in the story of creation as a metaphor for excessive attachment to the world. This attachment fetters man's spirit and is a sin. Therefore the sin inherited by the descendants of Adam is the attachment of their souls and spirits to the material world.[61]

Evil and the devil

Satan features prominently in Christian theology, but not so much in Judaism. Most mentions of Satan (*śāṭān* or 'the adversary') in the Hebrew Bible are generic and do not refer to a specific figure. In the Second Temple period (516 BCE–70 CE) Judaism was influenced by Zoroastrianism, the national religion of the Achaemenid Empire. A tradition of this faith is that a destructive being, *Ahriman* or *Angra Mainyu*, was the main adversary of Ahura Mazda (Ormuzd). This dualist tradition has been challenged and it has been proposed that Zoroastrianism was originally a monotheistic faith.[62]

The dualism of Zoroastrianism is countered by the following statement in the Hebrew Bible that there is no other divinity other than God. In other words, it is God Who is responsible for everything:

> That they may know from the rising of the sun, and from the west, that there is none beside me. I am the Lord, and there is none else. I form the light, and create darkness: I make peace, and create evil: I the Lord do all these things. (King James Version: Is. 45:6–7)

It is quite reasonable to suppose that Isaiah would be acquainted with the belief of the Persians and Medes, who had come in contact with the Assyrians as early as B.C. 830; and a warning against the chief error of their religion would be quite in place when he was holding up Cyrus to his countrymen as entitled to their respect and veneration. The nexus of the words, 'I am the Lord, and there is none else. I form the light, and create darkness,' is such as naturally to suggest an intended antagonism to the Zoroastrian system. Under that, Ormuzd created 'light' and 'peace', Ahriman 'darkness' and 'evil'. The two were eternal adversaries, engaged in an inter-ruinable contest. Ormuzd, it is true, claimed the undivided allegiance of mankind, since he was their maker; but Ahriman was a great power, terribly formidable – perhaps a god (diva) – certainly the chief of the devas.[63]

As darkness is the absence of light, evil is simply the absence of good. Therefore, by God defining what is good and righteous, 'light' and 'peace', and what conduces to spiritual life, He also identifies (creates) the converse, namely, evil, darkness, and spiritual death.

Nonetheless, there are passages in the New Testament that are interpreted literally by some Christians, such as the temptation of Christ by the devil (διάβολος, diabolos) (Matt. 4:1–11); the sowing of the tares by the devil (Matt. 13:39) and the need for sinners to escape the devil's trap:

> Then they will come to their senses and escape from the devil's trap. For they have been held captive by him to do whatever he wants. (II Timothy 2:26)

A commentator has written:

> They have been held captive by him to do whatever he wants . . . it signifieth the miserable state of sinners, who are captives at the devil's command and will, that if he saith to them, Go, they go; if he saith, Come, they come; if he saith, Do this, they do it.[64]

However, an allegorical understanding of the passages is supported by the following statement of Christ:

> If I had not come and spoken to them, they would not have been guilty of sin, but now they have no excuse for their sin . . . If I had not done among them the works that no one else did, they would not be guilty of sin . . . (John 15:22, 24)

View of the Bahá'í Faith on evil and the Devil

Similar to the biblical verses, the Bahá'í Faith teaches that evil is real but that it represents the absence of good and divine light:

> . . . the greatest evil is (man's) going astray and being veiled from Truth. Error is lack of guidance; darkness is absence of light; ignorance is lack of knowledge; falsehood is lack of truthfulness; blindness is lack of sight; and deafness is lack of hearing. Therefore,

error, blindness, deafness and ignorance are non-existent things . . . The darkness spoken of in the Bible as being created by God, signifieth that, verily, God hath not caused light to shine; inasmuch as where there is no light, there will be darkness; when there is no sight, there will be blindness; when there is no life, there will be death; when there is no riches, there will be poverty; and when there is no knowledge, there will be ignorance.[65]

The Baháʼí Writings also emphasize that the all-encompassing power of divine revelation is vouchsafed to all, and with the certitude that we are one, we must use that divine power to transform humanity:

> . . . the mercy of God encircles all mankind; that not a single individual is deprived of the mercy of God; and no soul is denied the resplendent bestowals of God. The whole human race is submerged in the sea of the mercy of the Lord and we are all the sheep of the one divine shepherd. Whatever shortcomings exist among us must be remedied. For example those who are ignorant must be educated so that they may become wise; the sick must be treated until they recover; those who are immature must be trained in order to reach maturity; those asleep must be awakened. All this must be accomplished through love and not through hatred and hostility.[66]

Hence, the Baháʼí Faith denies the existence of a personified devil who is the source of all evil and who is in competition with God. It regards the frequent references to Satan in the Bible as a means of indicating the power of the dark side, in the absence of divine influence and intervention, to create evil and mayhem.

12

THE TRINITY

The Trinity: Father, Son, and the Holy Spirit

Trinity as a church dogma

Trinity, or the triune God, the construct that God the Father, God the Son, and God the Holy Spirit (or Holy Ghost) are coexistent, coeternal and consubstantial Persons, is the central doctrine of most Christian denominations. It was formally adopted by the Council of Nicaea in 325 CE, representing a doomed attempt to explain the unknowable nature of Christ and His relationship to the Holy Spirit and to God. The dogma was based on Jesus's frequent mention of God as the Heavenly Father, His claim to therefore be the Eternal Son of God, and the promise, as His ministry was drawing to a close, that the Father would send the Holy Spirit in His place.

The concept was debated vociferously in the first centuries of Christianity. Both then and now it has been impossible to resolve the issues to the satisfaction of all parties. Some have maintained that it is a divine mystery and that believers should simply accept it and believe it. Others find helpful the analogy of the three states of water – ice, liquid and steam. However, clearly the flaw of this comparison is that the three states do not coexist simultaneously.

New Testament references that form the basis of church teaching

References to Christ as 'God' and 'the Son' have been discussed earlier in this book. Two other statements in the New Testament are consistent with a Trinitarian formulation. The first is to be found in the final verses of the Gospel of Matthew. Some of the eleven disciples had spiritual experiences of a post-crucifixion Christ when Jesus instructed them to baptize all nations in the name of the Trinity:

THE TRINITY

> And when they [disciples] saw him [Jesus] they worshipped him, but some doubted . . . And Jesus came and said to them. '. . . Go therefore and make disciples of all nations, baptizing them in the name of the Father and of the Son and of the Holy Spirit. teaching them to observe all that I have commanded you. And behold, I am with you always, to the end of the age.' (Matt. 28:17, 19–20)

Notably, Eusebius (263–339 CE), the Bishop of Caesarea and one of the early fathers of the church, mentioned baptizing in only the name of Jesus in his several citations of this verse, indicating that the formulation was a later addition.[1] Several instructions by the disciples also teach the believers to baptize in the name of Jesus only:

> And Peter said to them, 'Repent and be baptised every one of you in the name of Jesus Christ for the forgiveness of your sins, and you will receive the gift of the Holy Spirit . . .' (Acts 2:38; also 8:16; 10:48; 19:5; 22:16; Rom. 6:3; Gal. 3:27)

The second instance of a Gospel verse often cited in support of the Trinity is:

> For there are three that bear record in heaven, the Father, the Word, and the Holy Ghost: and these three are one. And there are three that bear witness in earth, the spirit, and the water, and the blood: and these three agree in one. (1 John 5:7–8; King James Version)

However, it has long been recognized that I John 5:7–8 has significant textual problems: the evidence – both external and internal – is decidedly against its authenticity.[2]

> Of all the Greek manuscripts, only two contain it. These two manuscripts are of very late dates, one from the fourteenth or fifteenth century and the other from the sixteenth century. Two other manuscripts have this verse written in the margin. All four manuscripts show that this verse was apparently translated from a late form of the Latin Vulgate.[3]

A footnote in the New International Version explains that the formulation 'was not found in any Greek manuscript before the fourteenth century'. The New Living Translation also adds in its footnote: 'A few very late manuscripts add *in heaven – the Father, the Word, and the Holy Spirit, and these three are one. And we have three witnesses on earth.*' Other translations, such as the Amplified Bible, simply exclude the above italicized portion of the verses.

Later developments: The Creed of Nicaea, the Nicene–Constantinopolitan Creed, and the Apostles' Creed

When Constantine became Emperor of Rome in 312 CE he elevated Christianity to a favoured status, in part to unify his empire. However, he discovered that it was a fractured religion with many contrary beliefs having developed during the period of time that it had been a secret and persecuted faith. To deal with this he convened a large body of prominent clerics and scholars in Nicaea to resolve their differences and arrive at a uniform set of beliefs. Initially, the main questions related to the relationship between the Father, the Son and the Holy Spirit.

The First Council of Nicaea (325 CE) formulated the following as core Christian belief:

> We believe in one God, the Father Almighty, Maker of all things visible and invisible. And in one Lord Jesus Christ, the Son of God, begotten of the Father [the only-begotten; that is, of the essence of the Father, God of God], Light of Light, very God of very God, begotten, not made, being of one substance with the Father; By whom all things were made [both in heaven and on earth]; Who for us men, and for our salvation, came down and was incarnate and was made man; He suffered, and the third day he rose again, ascended into heaven; From thence he shall come to judge the quick and the dead. And in the Holy Ghost.

The Nicene–Constantinopolitan Creed was formulated at the First and Second Ecumenical Councils (381 CE). The initial and orthodox version read:

> We believe in one God, the Father Almighty, Maker of heaven and

earth, and of all things visible and invisible. And in one Lord Jesus Christ, the only-begotten Son of God, begotten of the Father before all worlds (*æons*), Light of Light, very God of very God, begotten, not made, being of one substance with the Father; by whom all things were made; who for us men, and for our salvation, came down from heaven, and was incarnate by the Holy Ghost and of the Virgin Mary, and was made man; he was crucified for us under Pontius Pilate, and suffered, and was buried, and the third day he rose again, according to the Scriptures, and ascended into heaven, and sitteth on the right hand of the Father; from thence he shall come again, with glory, to judge the quick and the dead; whose kingdom shall have no end. And in the Holy Ghost, the Lord and Giver of life, who proceedeth from the Father, who with the Father and the Son together is worshipped and glorified, who spake by the prophets. In one holy catholic and apostolic Church; we acknowledge one baptism for the remission of sins; we look for the resurrection of the dead, and the life of the world to come. Amen.

The Apostles' Creed appears in a letter dated 390 CE. It is related to the Nicene Creed but contains certain additions (shown in italics) that were inserted in 570 CE:

I believe in God
    the Father Almighty,
    Maker of heaven and earth.
And in Jesus Christ
    His only Son our Lord;
    Who was conceived by the Holy Ghost,
    Born of the Virgin Mary,
    Suffered under Pontius Pilate,
    Was crucified, dead, and buried;
    He descended into hell;
    The third day he rose again from the dead;
    He ascended into heaven,
    And sitteth on the right hand of God the Father Almighty; from thence he shall come to judge the quick and the dead.
I believe in
    The Holy Ghost;

The Holy Catholic Church;
The communion of Saints;
The forgiveness of sins;
The resurrection of the body;
And the life everlasting.[4]

The *Filioque* clause 'and [from] the Son' was added to the original Nicene Creed in 589 CE, referring to whether the Holy Spirit emanates from the Father alone or from both the Father and the Son. The reference to the Holy Spirit now reads:

I believe in the Holy Spirit, the Lord, the giver of life,
who proceeds from the Father and the Son,
who with the Father and the Son is adored and glorified,
who has spoken through the prophets.

The dogma of Trinity was not adopted universally by Christians. This insertion was a major cause of the Great Schism between the Orthodox and the Catholic churches. Despite the weak and indirect scriptural evidence, as noted, the Trinity became part of both the Nicene Creed and the Apostles' Creed, and served as a baptismal rite for new Christian converts. Framed in the literal language of the creeds, the Trinity became less susceptible to a spiritual rendition.

Many early Christians such as the Arians and Unitarians objected to the Trinity and were persecuted for their beliefs. Members of the Unitarian Church believe that Christ was a Saviour and that His teachings were inspired by God. They do not perceive Him as a deity, and reject the doctrines of original sin, predestination and the infallibility of the Bible. Primarily, Unitarians maintain that the dogma of the Trinity is inconsistent with biblical teachings and statements of the oneness of God.

A literal understanding that God, Jesus, and the Holy Spirit are 'co-equal', 'co-eternal', and of the same substance as parts of a triune divinity are not in keeping with several New Testament teachings. Christ never claimed to be God or a god: Jesus did not at any time desire His followers to worship Him, either as God or as the Son of God, in the sense that the church now advocates. Some references from the New Testament are given below:

THE TRINITY

Declarations that God is One (I Cor. 8:4, 6; I Tim. 1:17).

Only God was to be worshipped at the First and Second Coming (John 4:23).

Only the Will of God is supreme (Mark 14:36; also, 26:39; John 6:38).

Supreme authority belongs to God alone (Matt. 20:23; also Mark 10:40).

Only God is the All-Knowing (Mark 13:32; Matt. 24:36).

All glory belongs to God alone (John 8:50, 54).

All good and righteousness emanates from God (Matt. 19:16).

The ultimate source of all spiritual life is God alone (I Tim. 6:13).

The gift of recognizing the truth is bestowed solely by God (John 6:65).

The relationship of Christ to the Holy Spirit and the Father

God is not material or visible – Christ declared Him (made Him known). (John 1:18).

Jesus's words were God's Word and not His own (John 12:49–50; 14:10, 24).

Christ revealed the divine attributes and teachings to the extent that the people of His time could appreciate it, and in that sense He identified Himself with God – a unity of Divine Purpose rather than an identity of the Person of Jesus with the Almighty (John 10:30 and 14:9).

The absolute dependence of Christ on God but not vice versa

> I can do nothing on my own. As I hear, I judge, and my judgement is just, because I seek not my own will but the will of him who sent

me. If I alone bear witness about myself, my testimony is not true . . . (John 5:30–31; see also John 8:28–29)

Christ also differentiates between Himself and the Holy Spirit by saying that all sins were forgivable, including slandering Him, but not the sin of blasphemy against the Holy Spirit:

> Therefore I tell you, every sin and blasphemy will be forgiven people, but the blasphemy against the Spirit will not be forgiven. And whoever speaks a word against the Son of Man will be forgiven, but whoever speaks against the Holy Spirit will not be forgiven, either in this age or in the age to come. (Matt. 12:31–32)

According to the Bahá'í Writings, the meaning is that people may not be conscious of the reality of Jesus and that it is forgivable since they may yet become aware. However, if they oppose the divine perfections that God manifested in Jesus, that would not be forgivable for it shows 'hatred of the light', which makes it impossible for such souls to draw near to God.[5]

Belief in Christ did not necessarily signify belief in Jesus but an acknowledgement of the God Who had sent Him

Hence, He protested loudly to the disbelieving Jews who misunderstood His intent:

> And Jesus cried out and said, 'Whoever believes in me, believes not in me but in him who sent me. And whoever sees me sees him who sent me.' (John 12:44–45)

Some translations of this verse add the words 'only' or 'alone' which are absent from the original Greek version, examples:

> Then Jesus cried out, 'Whoever believes in me does not believe in me only, but in the one who sent me'. (New International Version)

> Then Jesus cried out, 'Whoever believes in Me does not believe in Me alone, but in the One who sent Me'. (Berean Study Bible)

Also:

> Whoever receives you receives me, and whoever receives me receives him who sent me. (Matt. 10:40)

There is little support for the dogma of Trinity in the Hebrew Bible. Judaism, the prior faith of many early Christians, uncompromisingly inculcates monotheism (Is. 40:28; 44:6; 45:5–6; 18:21–22; 46:9). For His part, Christ described the *Shema*, a declaration of the oneness of God (Deut. 6:4–9), as the most important commandment of the Torah. He included the instruction to love thy neighbour as thyself as being one of the greatest commandments (Mark 12:28–31). It would therefore have been unthinkable to the early Christian converts from the Jewish Faith, who included Jesus's own mother and brethren and members of the early Jerusalem sect of the Ebionims, to believe that the person of Jesus was God or a god.

The 'Sonship' of Christ

The 'Sonship' of Jesus is accepted in the Bahá'í Writings but is explained in spiritual and not physical terms.

> It is true that Jesus referred to Himself as the Son of God, but this, as explained by Bahá'u'lláh in the *Íqán*, does not indicate any physical relationship whatever. Its meaning is entirely spiritual and points to the close relationship existing between Him and the Almighty God.[6]

> . . . since Christ had come into being through the Divine Spirit, He called Himself the Son of God.[7]

> As to the position of Christianity, let it be stated without any hesitation or equivocation that its divine origin is unconditionally acknowledged, that the Sonship and Divinity of Jesus Christ are fearlessly asserted, that the divine inspiration of the Gospel is fully recognized, that the reality of the mystery of the Immaculacy of the Virgin Mary is confessed, and the primacy of Peter, the Prince of the Apostles, is upheld and defended. The Founder of the Christian Faith is designated by Bahá'u'lláh as the 'Spirit of God', is proclaimed

as the One Who 'appeared out of the breath of the Holy Ghost', and is even extolled as the 'Essence of the Spirit'. His mother is described as 'that veiled and immortal, that most beauteous, countenance', and the station of her Son eulogized as a 'station which hath been exalted above the imaginings of all that dwell on earth' . . .[8]

The immaculacy of Mary

That Mary was sinless is not an overstatement. The problem lies in the church's explanations as to how this was the case. There are two ways in which the 'immaculacy' of Mary, the mother of Jesus, is understood. The first is the belief that she was chaste and a virgin when she conceived Christ, and as such was free of sin. As noted earlier, the belief in the virgin birth as a miracle is shared by Islam and the Bahá'í Faith:

> [Bahá'ís] believe [the virgin birth] to have been a miracle and a sign of His Prophethood. In this matter we are in entire agreement with the most orthodox church views.[9]

The second has to do with Mary not having inherited original sin at her own conception. Although Jesus did not have a physical father, He did have a mother whose ancestry the Gospel of Matthew traced to Adam. The dogma of sin inherited from parents therefore required that Mary be free of original sin if Jesus were also to be free from this ancestral sin.

It was the church that found the remedy to this predicament. Pope Pius IX in 1854 declared the dogma of the Immaculacy of Mary. Thus, on earth and after more than 1,800 years, the church, without any scriptural justification, arrogated to itself the need to pronounce its conclusions concerning a blessed soul who had long since ascended to heaven:

> We declare, pronounce and define that the doctrine which holds that the Blessed Virgin Mary, at the first instant of her conception, by a singular privilege and grace of the Omnipotent God, in virtue of the merits of Jesus Christ, the Saviour of mankind, was preserved immaculate from all stain of original sin, has been revealed by God, and therefore should firmly and constantly be believed by all the faithful.

Hence, if anyone shall dare – which God forbid! – to think otherwise than as has been defined by us, let him know and understand that he is condemned by his own judgment; that he has suffered shipwreck in the faith; that he has separated from the unity of the Church; and that, furthermore, by his own action he incurs the penalties established by law if he should are to express in words or writing or by any other outward means the errors he think in his heart.[10]

The Bahá'í Writings declare:

> . . . religion must conform to reason and be in accord with the conclusions of science. For religion, reason and science are realities; therefore, these three, being realities, must conform and be reconciled. A question or principle which is religious in its nature must be sanctioned by science. Science must declare it to be valid, and reason must confirm it in order that it may inspire confidence. If religious teaching, however, be at variance with science and reason, it is unquestionably superstition.[11]

The truth is that there is no scientific basis for believing that the sin committed by the allegorical original parents of humanity (Adam and Eve) could be literally transmitted to their progeny.

The Trinity in the Bahá'í Writings

The Bahá'í Writings recognize the difficulties with the Trinity as formulated by the early church fathers:

> The question of the Trinity, since the time of His Holiness Christ until now, is the belief of the Christians, and to the present time all the learned among them are perplexed and confounded. All have confessed that the question is beyond the grasp of reason, for three cannot become one, nor one three. To unite these is impossible; it is either one or three . . .
>
> But there are, in the Gospels, clear expressions indicative of Trinity; among them: 'The Father is in the Son and the Son is in the Father.' As Christians did not understand the meaning of this expression, their thoughts were scattered.

> The reality of this question is as follows ... The sun is one sun but manifesteth itself in different mirrors ... The sun ... hath not taken up its abode in this mirror, but hath manifested itself therein.[12]

In the Bible and the Bahá'í Writings God is represented metaphorically as the sun. Christ is also represented as a reflection of God, as in a polished mirror:

> God, who at sundry times and in divers manners spake in time past unto the fathers by the prophets, Hath in these last days spoken unto us by *his* Son,[13] whom he hath appointed heir of all things, by whom also he made the worlds; Who being the brightness of his glory, and the express image ...[14] (King James Version: Heb. 1:1–3)

In this analogy, the Holy Spirit is represented as the rays of the sun which are reflected in the mirror of Christ, bringing the light of the divine teachings to man. Hence, the Bahá'í Writings explain that Jesus Christ was the complete incarnation not of the essence of God but of His names and attributes.

> Know thou of a certainty that the Unseen can in no wise incarnate His Essence and reveal it unto men. He is, and hath ever been, immensely exalted beyond all that can either be recounted or perceived. From His retreat of glory His voice is ever proclaiming: 'Verily, I am God; there is none other God besides Me, the All-Knowing, the All-Wise. I have manifested Myself unto men, and have sent down Him Who is the Day Spring of the signs of My Revelation. Through Him I have caused all creation to testify that there is none other God except Him, the Incomparable, the All-Informed, the All-Wise.' He Who is everlastingly hidden from the eyes of men can never be known except through His Manifestation, and His Manifestation can adduce no greater proof of the truth of His Mission than the proof of His own Person.[15]

> ... all the Prophets of God, His well-favoured, His holy, and chosen Messengers, are, without exception, the bearers of His names, and the embodiments of His attributes.[16]

These Tabernacles of Holiness, these primal Mirrors which reflect the light of unfading glory, are but expressions of Him Who is the Invisible of the Invisibles.[17]

The human temple that has been made the vehicle of so overpowering a Revelation must . . . ever remain entirely distinguished from that 'innermost Spirit of Spirits' and 'eternal Essence of Essences' – that invisible yet rational God Who, however much we extol the divinity of His Manifestation on earth, can in no wise incarnate His infinite, His unknowable, His incorruptible and all-embracing Reality in the concrete and limited frame of a mortal being. Indeed, the God Who could so incarnate His own reality would, in the light of the teachings of Bahá'u'lláh, cease immediately to be God.[18]

The relationship of the Prophets[19] to God – an identity with divine will and purpose and not of persons

The essence of belief in Divine unity consisteth in regarding Him Who is the Manifestation of God and Him Who is the invisible, the inaccessible, the unknowable Essence as one and the same. By this is meant that whatever pertaineth to the former, all His acts and doings, whatever He ordaineth or forbiddeth, should be considered, in all their aspects, and under all circumstances, and without any reservation, as identical with the Will of God Himself.[20]

Biblical titles of Jesus

As noted earlier, the terms, 'son', 'his son' and 'the 'son' or 'sons 'of God' have a broader meaning in the Bible than a physical relationship to God. For example, in the Hebrew Bible, God's male creations are called 'sons of God' (Gen. 6:2). God also refers to Israel as 'My first-born son' (Ex. 4:22). He explains His special relationship to King Solomon by stating: 'I will be to him a father, and he shall be to Me a son' (II Sam. 7:14). The anointed king, David, is described as the Lord's begotten son (Ps. 2:7).

Notably, Jesus was never said to apply the title 'Son of God' to Himself in the Synoptic Gospels (Matthew, Mark and Luke). He called John and James 'Boanerges' or 'Sons of Thunder', which underlines the allegorical nature of the term 'sons' (Mark 3:17).

The Apostle Paul stated: 'For all who are led by the Spirit of God are sons of God' (Rom. 8:14). He declared that 'the creation waits with eager longing for the revealing of the sons of God' (Rom. 8:19), that is, individuals who were transformed by the creative power of the Word. He additionally referred to Timothy, one of his converts, as 'my [Paul's] beloved son' (King James Version, I Cor. 4:17), lending emphasis to the spiritual nature of sonship.

The Book of Revelation bestows the title of 'my son' on anyone who overcomes the spiritual hurdles at the Second Coming and recognizes 'the truth' – clearly again not in the sense of being the physical progeny of God, but being derived from His Spirit:

> The one who conquers [overcometh] will have this heritage, and I will be his God and he will be my son. (Rev. 21:7)

13

SACRAMENTS AND ORDINANCES

Sacraments are church rituals intended to impart divine grace and to consecrate Christians.

One notes, however, the following statement in the Epistle to Titus which downplays the necessity of rituals:

> To the pure, all things are pure, but to the defiled and unbelieving, nothing is pure; but both their minds and their consciences are defiled. (Titus 1:15)

Rev. Albert Barnes, a Presbyterian, explained this verse as follows:

> The principle of the declaration is, that a pure mind – a truly pious mind – will not regard the distinctions of food and drink; of festivals, rites, ceremonies, and days, as necessary to be observed in order to promote its purity. The conscience is not to be burdened and enslaved by these things, but is to be controlled only by the moral laws which God has ordained. But there may be a somewhat higher application of the words – that every ordinance of religion, every command of God, every event that occurs in divine Providence, tends to promote the holiness of one who is of pure heart. He can see a sanctifying tendency in everything, and can derive from all that is commanded, and all that occurs, the means of making the heart more holy. While a depraved mind will turn every such thing to a pernicious use, and make it the means of augmenting its malignity and corruption, to the pure mind it will be the means of increasing its confidence in God, and of making itself more holy. To such a mind everything may become a means of grace.
>
> But unto them that are defiled and unbelieving is nothing pure – Everything is made the means of increasing their depravity.[1]

Nevertheless, rituals play a central role in the lives of many Christian denominations, and are important to some churches as a means of binding the flock to the institutions. The latter insist that the ceremonies themselves are not merely symbolic of a determination to commit to a spiritual life but of vital importance as they *per se* confer spiritual benefits on the believer. The church attendee thereby becomes naturally more invested in the minutiae of the rituals rather than learning to investigate the reality and purpose of faith.

The Catholic Church considers that seven rites or sacraments – baptism, confirmation, the Eucharist, penance, anointing of the sick, marriage, and holy orders – convey God's grace in an inward, spiritual sense, rather than directly and literally to properly disposed or prepared individuals. It maintains that they derive their power from the work of Christ (*ex opere operato Christi*) rather than through human endeavour. The priest officiating at these rites is believed to be acting in place of the person of Christ.

Protestants and Evangelicals see most of these practices as ordinances, merely demonstrating the participants' faith. Rather than necessary for salvation, they believe that the rites serve as visual aids to help Christians appreciate what Christ accomplished in His redemptive work. Ordinances are considered sacraments by some churches, if they were instituted by Christ, taught by the Apostles, and practised by the early church – to most Protestants, baptism and communion (Eucharist or The Lord's Supper) are the only rites that qualify as sacraments, having unequivocally these three elements.

Baptism

As noted, baptism is one of the sacraments of the Catholic Church, but many Protestants in general do not believe that it is necessary for salvation and consider it an ordinance. The rite involves sprinkling of or immersion in water to ritually cleanse the body of sin. One method is immersion in natural flowing water or 'living water'[2] – a reminder that John the Baptist had baptized Jesus in the flowing waters of the river Jordan, and of the need for regeneration by the Holy Spirit. If the water is insufficient for immersion, it may be poured three times on the head.[3] According to several churches (including Catholic, Anglican, Eastern

Orthodox and Oriental Orthodox), the water used for the ritual must be 'holy water'; that is, water that has been sanctified by a priest and thereby given the ability to repel evil.

Baptism by John the Baptist

Individuals undergoing baptism by John the Baptist in the River Jordan symbolically cleansed their bodies of impurities and prepared themselves for the advent of the Messiah by repenting of their transgressions. According to the historian Flavius Josephus (c. 37–100 CE), as recorded in his book *Jewish Antiquities*, baptism was not sacramental; that is, it was not intended to wash the Jews of their sins. Rather, it was an exhortation to lead spiritual and righteous lives:

> . . . for Herod slew him (John the Baptist) who was a good man, and commanded the Jews to exercise virtue, both as to righteousness towards one another, and piety towards God, and so to come to baptism; for that the washing (with water) would be acceptable to him, if they made use of it, not in order to the putting away (or the remission) of some sins (only), but for the purification of the body; supposing still that the soul was thoroughly purified beforehand by righteousness.[4]

In this connection, John the Baptist stated that the Messiah would not baptize His followers with water but 'with [the] Holy Spirit and with fire'[5] (Matt. 3:11). Baptism by fire refers to the love of God which would, though not mentioned, include and be strengthened by the tribulations and persecution that are suffered because of one's faith, and which refine faith.

Baptism of Jesus by John the Baptist

The following explanation is found in the Bahá'í Writings:

> It is not that Christ was in need of baptism, but He submitted to it because at that time this action was praiseworthy and acceptable before God and presaged the glad-tidings of the Kingdom. However, He later said that true baptism was not with material water but with

spirit and with water, and, elsewhere, with spirit and with fire. What is meant here by 'water' is not material water, for elsewhere it is explicitly stated that baptism must be with spirit and with fire, and the latter makes it clear that the intention is not material fire and water, since baptism with fire is impossible.

Therefore, by 'spirit' is meant divine grace; by 'water', knowledge and life; and by 'fire', the love of God. For material water cleanses not the heart of man but his body. Rather, the heavenly water and spirit, which are knowledge and life, cleanse and purify the heart of man. In other words, the heart that partakes of the outpouring grace of the Holy Spirit and becomes sanctified is made goodly and pure. The purpose is that the reality of man be purified and sanctified from the defilements of the world of nature, which are vile attributes such as anger, lust, worldliness, pride, dishonesty, hypocrisy, deceit, self-love, and so on.

Man cannot free himself from the onslaught of vain and selfish desires save through the confirming grace of the Holy Spirit. That is why it is said that baptism must be with the spirit, with water, and with fire – that is, with the spirit of divine grace, the water of knowledge and life, and the fire of the love of God. It is with this spirit, this water, and this fire that man must be baptised, that he may partake of everlasting grace. For otherwise, of what avail is it to be baptised with material water? No, this baptism with water was a symbol of repentance and of seeking remission of sins.

But in the Dispensation of Bahá'u'lláh this symbol is no longer required, for its reality, which is to be baptised with the spirit and the love of God, has been established and realized.[6]

Jesus did not baptize anyone Himself

Over the passage of time, baptism in Christianity replaced circumcision (in Judaism) as a rite of initiation into the new religion, and as a means of attaining salvation.

The only Gospel describing baptism by Jesus is that of John, written probably between 90 and 120 CE. In three verses, 3:22, 3:26 and 4:1, it states that Jesus baptized, but in a parenthentical explanation, the Gospel itself states: 'Jesus himself did not baptise, but only his disciples' (John 4:2). Nevertheless, the ritual of baptism has continued, in part due to post-resurrection instructions by Christ to baptize all nations (Matt. 28:16–20).

Ernest W. Barnes makes the following comment with respect to the above passage in Matthew:

> But the use of this formula of baptism 'in the name the Trinity', instead of the earlier formula of baptism 'in the name of Lord Jesus, (Acts, 19:19:1–7)' shows that this passage represents not an early tradition, but late Christian opinion as to what the risen Christ should have said. It must have been formulated many years after the crucifixion of Jesus. Clearly the early tradition preserved no record either that Jesus himself baptised or that he instructed his disciples so to act.[7]

The Apostle Paul was quite reluctant to baptize his Christian converts:

> I thank God that I baptised none of you except Crispus and Gaius, so that no one may say that you were baptised in my name. (I did baptise also the household of Stephanas. Beyond that, I do not know whether I baptised anyone else.) For Christ did not send me to baptise but to preach the gospel, and not with words of eloquent wisdom, lest the cross of Christ be emptied of its power. (I Cor. 1:14–17)

This assertion of Paul does not comply with the following teaching attributed to the Apostle Peter:

> And Peter said to them, 'Repent and be baptised every one of you in the name of Jesus Christ for the forgiveness of your sins, and you will receive the gift of the Holy Spirit.' (Acts 2:38)

In another post-resurrection account Jesus apparently recommends baptism and exorcism of demons and handling of poisonous snakes (Mark 16:18). Again, it is generally accepted that this and other such accounts were later additions – some have questioned whether Mark 16:9–20 should even be included in the Bible.[8]

Infant baptism

Most Christian denominations baptize infants or young children. These include Catholics, Orthodox, Anglicans, Lutherans, Presbyterians and other reformed churches, Methodists, and the Moravian Church. The case for infant baptism is that (1) Jesus's Great Commission to the disciples that they should teach and baptize (Matt. 28:16–20) did not set an age limit for the ritual; (2) it is a sign of renewal and rebirth, marking the infant as belonging to a new covenant; (3) whole households were baptized in the New Testament; and (4) it frees the child from the bondage of original sin inherited from Adam and Eve.[9]

The Gospels do not directly condone infant baptism. Indeed, the children that Jesus said were destined for the Kingdom of God (Matt. 19:14) had not been baptized. As more infants were born into Christian families, infant baptism became the common pattern by the fifth century. Canon II of the Synod of Carthage (418 CE) confirmed officially that infants are to be baptized for the remission of sins.

The true meaning of baptism

> . . . John would first admonish the people, lead them to repent of sin, and exhort them to anticipate the advent of Christ.[10]

John the Baptist taught that the Messiah would not continue the ritual of baptism with water. His baptism would be spiritual and involve sacrifice:

> I baptise you with water for repentance, but he who is coming after me is mightier than I, whose sandals I am not worthy to carry. He will baptise you with the Holy Spirit and fire. (Matt. 3:11; see also Mark 1:8; Luke 3:3)

Baptism is used in a spiritual and transformative context in the Bahá'í Writings:

> To be pure and holy in all things is an attribute of the consecrated soul and a necessary characteristic of the unenslaved mind. The best of perfections is immaculacy and the freeing of oneself from every

defect. Once the individual is, in every respect, cleansed and purified, then will he become a focal centre reflecting the Manifest Light.

First in a human being's way of life must be purity, then freshness, cleanliness, and independence of spirit. First must the stream bed be cleansed, then may the sweet river waters be led into it. Chaste eyes enjoy the beatific vision of the Lord and know what this encounter meaneth; a pure sense inhaleth the fragrances that blow from the rose gardens of His grace; a burnished heart will mirror forth the comely face of truth.[11]

In the Gospel according to St John, Christ has said: 'Except a man be born of water and the Spirit, he cannot enter into the Kingdom of Heaven.' The priests have interpreted this into meaning that baptism is necessary for salvation. In another Gospel it is said: 'He shall baptise you with the Holy Ghost and with fire.'

Thus the water of baptism and the fire are one! It cannot mean that the 'water' spoken of is *physical* water, for it is the direct opposite of 'fire', and one destroys the other. When in the Gospels, Christ speaks of 'water', He means *that which causes life*, for without water no worldly creature can live . . .

Water is the cause of life, and when Christ speaks of water, He is symbolizing that which is the cause of *Everlasting Life*.

This life-giving water of which He speaks is like unto fire, for it is none other than the Love of God, and this love means life to our souls.

By the fire of the Love of God the veil is burnt which separates us from the Heavenly Realities, and with clear vision we are enabled to struggle onward and upward, ever progressing in the paths of virtue and holiness, and becoming the means of light to the world.

There is nothing greater or more blessed than the Love of God! It gives healing to the sick, balm to the wounded, joy and consolation to the whole world, and through it alone can man attain Life Everlasting. The *essence* of all religions is the Love of God, and it is the foundation of all the sacred teachings.

It was the Love of God that led Abraham, Isaac, and Jacob, that strengthened Joseph in Egypt and gave to Moses courage and patience . . .

Finally, it was the Love of God that gave to the East Bahá'u'lláh, and is now sending the light of His teaching far into the West, and from Pole to Pole.

Thus I exhort each of you, realizing its power and beauty, to sacrifice all your thoughts, words and actions to bring the knowledge of the Love of God into every heart.[12]

The Eucharist and Communion

The symbolism of the bread and the wine

The Gospel of Matthew describes thus the Last Supper of Christ:

> Now as they were eating, Jesus took bread, and after blessing it broke it and gave it to the disciples, and said, 'Take, eat; this is my body.' And he took a cup, and when he had given thanks he gave it to them, saying, 'Drink of it, all of you, for this is my blood of the covenant, which is poured out for many for the forgiveness of sins. I tell you I will not drink again of this fruit of the vine until that day when I drink it new with you in my Father's kingdom.' (Matt. 26:26–29)

Christ had earlier described His teachings as the true bread of life that came from God (John 6:32). The red wine symbolized the blood that He and His followers were to sacrifice to resuscitate the spiritually dead. Unfortunately, the simple spiritual message was interpreted literally in time: the bread and wine offered by the priest to re-enact the Last Supper became physically the flesh and blood of Jesus Christ (doctrine of transubstantiation). As it is believed that Jesus is literally present even in the smallest particle of the communion bread, known as the Host, care is taken to avoid even the smallest crumb falling to the ground. The rite of the Last Supper, the Eucharist or Holy Communion gradually became a bedrock of the church. It was stated dogmatically quite late at the Council of Trent (1545–1563 CE), prompted by the Protestant Reformation and described as the embodiment of the Counterreformation. This ecumenical council stated that Christ is present in every part of the sacrament.

> The Holy Eucharist is a sacrament and a sacrifice. In the Holy Eucharist, under the appearances of bread and wine, the Lord Christ is contained, offered, and received.

(a) The whole Christ is really, truly, and substantially present in the Holy Eucharist. We use the words 'really, truly, and substantially' to describe Christ's presence in the Holy Eucharist in order to distinguish Our Lord's teaching from that of mere men who falsely teach that the Holy Eucharist is only a sign or figure of Christ, or that He is present only by His power.[13]

The Eucharist also rises to the level of a sacrament in some Protestant churches because Jesus presided over the Last Supper and broke bread with His disciples, but for them the ritual is not necessary for conveying grace and for salvation. Protestants, who believe that grace is free, regard the rite as a church ordinance and interpret it symbolically:

This 'breaking' of the bread represented the sufferings of Jesus about to take place – his body 'broken' or wounded for sin. Hence, Paul (I Cor. 11:24) adds, 'This is my body which is broken for you;' that is, which is about to be broken for you by death, or wounded, pierced, bruised, to make atonement for your sins.
This is my body – This represents my body. This broken bread shows the manner in which my body will be broken; or this will serve to recall my dying sufferings to your remembrance. It is not meant that his body would be literally 'broken' as the bread was, but that the bread would be a significant emblem or symbol to recall to their recollection his sufferings. It is not improbable that our Lord pointed to the broken bread, or laid his hands on it, as if he had said, 'Lo, my body!' or, 'Behold my body! – that which "represents" my broken body to you.' This 'could not' be intended to mean that that bread was literally his body. It was not. His body was then before them 'living'. And there is no greater absurdity than to imagine his 'living body' there changed at once to a 'dead body', and then the bread to be changed into that dead body, and that all the while the 'living' body of Jesus was before them.
Yet this is the absurd and impossible doctrine of the Roman Catholics, holding that the 'bread' and 'wine' were literally changed into the 'body and blood' of our Lord. The language employed by the Saviour was in accordance with a common mode of speaking among the Jews, and exactly similar to that used by Moses at the institution of the Passover (Ex. 12:11).[14]

The Ebionites, the earliest Jewish converts to Christianity, believed that drinking the wine at Passover to remember the work of Jesus was symbolic – one was not uniting with God by drinking it. The Greek bishop Irenaeus, who saw it as his duty to stamp out heresy, wrote *circa* 180 CE:

> Vain also are the Ebionites, who do not receive by faith into their soul the union of God and man, but who remain in the old leaven of [the natural] birth, and who do not choose to understand that the Holy Ghost came upon Mary, and the power of the Most High did overshadow her: wherefore also what was generated is a holy thing, and the Son of the Most High God the Father of all, who effected the incarnation of this being, and showed forth a new [kind of] generation; that as by the former generation we inherited death, so by this new generation we might inherit life. Therefore do these men reject the commixture of the heavenly wine.[15]

The non-Christian origins of church dogma and ritual

The early Christian converts imported many ideas and practices of the pre-Christian Greek, Roman, and Egyptian religions into their newly adopted faith, in particular the ancient rites and terminology of several secret religious cults or mystery religions which co-existed in the Roman Empire for the first three centuries of the Christian era.

Eucharist

Several Greco-Roman secret ('mystery') religions 'shared a communal meal in which they symbolically ate the flesh and drank the blood of their god'.[16] For example, initiates of Mithraism, the religion of Mithras, an Indo-Iranian deity and mediator between Ahura Mazda and men, celebrated a communion involving bread and wine in memory of the last meal that the sun god Helios and Mithras, his son, shared together on earth before Mithras ascended to heaven.[17] The bread and wine were believed to be the flesh and blood of a great bull that was slain by Mithras.

The likenesses between Mithraism and Christianity were many. Each faith borrowed from the other, 'and the borrowings of Christianity were perhaps the more extensive'.[18] In a scholarly study, Dr Martin Luther King Jr. provided the following assessment:

> That Christianity did copy and borrow from Mithraism cannot be denied, but it was generally a natural and unconscious process rather than a deliberate plan of action. It was subject to the same influences from the environment as were the other cults, and it sometimes produced the same reaction. The people were conditioned by the contact with the older religions and the background and general trend of the time.
>
> Many of the views, while passing out of Paganism into Christianity were given a more profound and spiritual meaning by Christians, yet we must be indebted to the source. To discuss Christianity without mentioning other religions would be like discussing the greatness of the Atlantic Ocean without the slightest mention of the many tributaries that keep it flowing.[19]

Trinity

Variations of a Trinity exist in several other religions. For example, the concept of *trimurti* (Sanskrit: 'three forms') in Hinduism embraces a triad of gods (Brahma, Vishnu and Shiva): 'The *trimurti* collapses the three gods into a single form with three faces. Each god is in charge of one aspect of creation, with Brahma as creator, Vishnu as preserver, and Shiva as destroyer.'[20] Mithraism, as a religion popular amongst the Roman military, may also have contributed significantly to Trinity.

Baptism

Baptism was widely practised before the advent of Christianity. The followers of Mithras underwent a form of baptism using sprinkling of holy water or total immersion, designed to wash away sins. Baptism was performed on adults in the Mithraic mysteries during initiation. Similar to the Christian rite, the priest made a sign upon the forehead of the person being baptised.

In the cult of Cybele, the rite of Taurobolium involved baptism in the blood of a sacrificed bull.

The ritual of baptism was also practised by the Essenes, a sect of

Judaism that flourished in Syria and Palestine from 200 BCE to 100 CE, and is a feature of Judaism up to the present time. Washing, symbolically representing one's intention to purify oneself from evil, may be understood from the Book of Isaiah (1:16–17). Baths (*mikvoths*) were constructed for the purpose of ritual immersion and purification required by the Torah, as, for example, after childbirth or menstruation; a bride before her wedding; temple priests before certain religious services; preparing a dead person for burial; and for purification of individuals with an infectious disease (Num. 19:7–8, 11–20). Later, ritual washing (*tevilah*) was performed seven days after circumcision as part of a ceremony for receiving a Gentile as a proselyte.[21] The Essenes can repeat the ritual of baptism during their lifetime, as opposed to Christian baptism which is normally performed only once.

Resurrection

The physical resurrection of gods was a common belief in the mystery religions of the Roman Empire. For example, in one such religion/cult, the god Attis was born of the Virgin Nana on 25 December. He was a shepherd, who was miraculously brought back to life three days after his death.[22] The Bishop of Birmingham, Ernest William Barnes, wrote:

> Above all, men craved the immortality that the mysteries of the Great Mother [of gods] professed to give. Attis died and rose again: those mystically joined to him would likewise after death rise to newness of life.[23]

In Mithraism the god Mithras, whose birthday was also celebrated on 25 December, rose from the dead and ascended to heaven.

Reactions against Mithraism by the church

The early church Fathers tried to blame the similarities between Mithraism and the beliefs of the church on Satan copying the teachings from Judeo-Christianity. They explained that Mithras had been conceived by Satan as a pre-emptive strike against the Gospel centuries before Christ was born: 'The devil got there first to sow confusion';[24] 'a diabolical mimicry' ('a plagiarism by anticipation').[25] The disconcerting similarity of a last supper rite in Mithraism to Communion for example, caused Justin Martyr, a second-century Christian writer, and other Christian writers, to accuse Mithraism of imitating the Christian rite despite the fact that Mithraism predated Christianity:

> . . . the wicked devils have imitated in the mysteries of Mithras, commanding the same thing to be done. For, that bread and a cup of water are placed with certain incantations in the mystic rites of one who is being initiated, you either know or can learn.[26]

Tertullian declared that the Devil must have engineered the coincidence for his wicked ends:

> Who interprets the meaning of these passages which make for heresies? The Devil, we cannot doubt; for it is his character to overturn the Truth who emulously rivals the very realities of the Divine sacraments in the idol-mysteries. For he too baptises certain persons – his own believers and faithful ones; he promises a putting away of sins by means of the laver [a large basin containing water]; and if my memory still serves me, Mithras seals there on the foreheads his own soldiers. He celebrates, too, an oblation of bread, and introduces a representation of the resurrection.[27]

The fact that some elements of the Christian rituals and practices such as baptism, the Trinity, Christmas, the Last Supper, and the Crucifixion and Resurrection of Christ were clearly adopted from other religions does not, however, detract from the profound and spiritual aspects of the traditions if they are explained figuratively and not literally or dogmatically.

The Bahá'í Writings do not deny the church dogmas, but emphasize the importance of spiritual and allegorical explanations rather than literal understandings and ritual observances.

14

BIBLICAL CRITERIA TO VALIDATE TRUTH

Those of us who identify ourselves as followers of Christ must avoid repeating the mishaps associated with the First Coming, when although some of the followers of Moses heeded the biblical warnings and came to recognize Jesus as their Messiah, others objected to His every word and action. They remain as adamant today that He was a false Messiah or Christ as they did two thousand years ago.

Was the reason perhaps that the testimonies of the Hebrew Prophets were insufficient or deficient? If so, it would hardly have been fair for a just God to withhold His grace and truth from them, and punish them for their heedlessness. Or was it, as suggested by some church leaders, that they were simply too obstinate to receive the Divine Word or Logos?[1] A more plausible explanation may be that few Jews investigated the Cause of Jesus for themselves and instead were preoccupied with the rules and reasoning of others to guide them to the truth. They were warned in the Hebrew Bible:

> Trust in the Lord with all your heart, and do not lean on your own understanding. In all your ways acknowledge him, and he will make straight your paths. Be not wise in your own eyes; fear the Lord, and turn away from evil. (Prov. 3:5–7)

Christians have been admonished similarly:

> If any of you lacks wisdom, let him ask God, who gives generously to all without reproach, and it will be given him. (James 1:5)

It therefore behooves us to reflect prayerfully on what constitutes valid scriptural criteria of truth.

1. True faith invites investigation

Christ encouraged His followers to ask for the bread of divine teachings and to knock at the gates of heaven:

> Ask, and it will be given to you; seek, and you will find; knock, and it will be opened to you. For everyone who asks receives, and the one who seeks finds, and to the one who knocks it will be opened. Or which one of you, if his son asks him for bread, will give him a stone? Or if he asks for a fish, will give him a serpent? If you then, who are evil, know how to give good gifts to your children, how much more will your Father who is in heaven give good things to those who ask him! (Matt. 7:7–11)

Hence, there must be a genuine desire for truth – a longing for the divine Word that is as earnest as that of a baby crying for milk:

> Like newborn infants, long for the pure spiritual milk, that by it you may grow up into salvation – if indeed you have tasted that the Lord is good. (I Pet. 2:2–3)

As noted earlier, the Scriptures invite the thirsty to partake of the water of life, wine and milk offered freely by the merciful God:

> Come, everyone who thirsts, come to the waters; and he who has no money, come, buy and eat! Come, buy wine and milk without money and without price. (Is. 55:1)

> To the thirsty I will give from the spring of the water of life without payment. (Rev. 21:6)

Christ blessed those who 'hunger and thirst after righteousness' for only then 'will they be filled' (Matt. 5:6) – the divine response was contingent on following the commandments: 'ask', 'seek' and 'knock'. (Matt. 7:7)

2. True faith accords with reason

In the Hebrew Bible, God invites us to use both our hearts and our rational faculties (Jer. 17:10). The Prophet Isaiah taught that the Lord is a reasonable God (1:18). The Bahá'í Writings explain that the shining spark of truth is often revealed only after the clash of differing but sincerely held and reasoned opinions.[2]

The Apostle Peter admonished his fellow Christians to be long-suffering in their interactions with those who do not share their opinions:

> ... always being prepared to make a defence to anyone who asks you for a reason for the hope that is in you; yet do it with gentleness and respect, having a good conscience, so that, when you are slandered, those who revile your good behavior in Christ may be put to shame. For it is better to suffer for doing good, if that should be God's will, than for doing evil. (I Pet. 3:15–17)

We also note that the Apostle Paul's method of teaching non-Christians was not to threaten his audience with brimstone and hell-fire, but to engage them in meaningful conversations:

> So he reasoned in the synagogue with the Jews and the devout persons, and in the marketplace every day with those who happened to be there. (Acts 17:17; also, Acts 18:4)

He recommended that Christians heed what is said in the name of God (prophecies), and also 'test everything' and do what is right:

> Now concerning the times and the seasons, brothers, you have no need to have anything written to you. For you yourselves are fully aware that the day of the Lord will come like a thief in the night. Do not quench the Spirit. Do not despise prophecies, but test everything; hold fast what is good. (I Thess. 5:1–2, 19–21)

The seeker must be humble, pay attention to the new message and not be quick to judge, for in every age, God alone is the ultimate Judge and Arbiter of the truth

Those engaged in this high spiritual endeavour cannot be arrogant, as we note that it was pride that prevented many of the religious leaders from recognizing Christ at the First Coming. The Hebrew Bible warns:

> When pride comes, then comes disgrace, but with the humble is wisdom. (Prov. 11:2)

> ... if my people ... humble themselves, and pray and seek my face and turn from their wicked ways, then I will hear from heaven and will forgive their sin ... (II Chron. 7:14)

The seeker should realize that spiritual conversations are only productive if the participants are sincere and receptive

A 'hearing ear' and a 'seeing eye' are essential for appreciation of the Divine Word, and attainment of a spiritual life:

> Listen diligently to me (the Lord) ... Incline your ear, and come to me; hear, that your soul may live ... Seek the Lord while he may be found; call upon him while he is near ... (Is. 55:2–3, 6)

Jesus praised His disciples for having perceived and embraced the newly revealed truth:

> Then turning to the disciples he said privately, 'Blessed are the eyes that see what you see! For I tell you that many prophets and kings desired to see what you see, and did not see it, and to hear what you hear, and did not hear it.' (Luke 10:23–24)

The seeker should appreciate that every dispensation brings novel spiritual insights that are accepted by pure, simple and humble souls but hidden from the haughty and worldly-wise

> At that time Jesus declared, 'I thank you, Father, Lord of heaven and earth, that you have hidden these things from the wise and understanding and revealed them to little children; yes, Father, for such was your gracious will.' (Matt. 11:25–26)

The Apostle Paul explained that revealed truth was not acquired but had been revealed to them by God. It must be understood spiritually and not literally or through theological wisdom. This is as true today as it was at the First Coming:

> Howbeit we speak wisdom among them that are perfect: yet not the wisdom of this world, nor of the princes of this world, that come to nought: But we speak the wisdom of God in a mystery, even the hidden wisdom, which God ordained before the world unto our glory: Which none of the princes of this world knew: for had they known it, they would not have crucified the Lord of glory. But as it is written, Eye hath not seen, nor ear heard, neither have entered into the heart of man, the things which God hath prepared for them that love him . . . Now we have received, not the spirit of the world, but the spirit which is of God; that we might know the things that are freely given to us of God. Which things also we speak, not in the words which man's wisdom teacheth, but which the Holy Ghost teacheth; comparing spiritual things with spiritual. But the natural man receiveth not the things of the Spirit of God: for they are foolishness unto him: neither can he know them, because they are spiritually discerned. (King James Version: I Cor. 2:6–9, 12–14)

3. The 'fruits' of a new revelation should be manifestly 'good' and beneficial to individuals as well as to society

True faith is born of the Holy Spirit – it educates the character of individuals, and edifies society through the transformative power of the Divine Word

A distinguishing feature of God's revelation, and its greatest proof, is the creative power of the Divine Word – its ability to open the eyes of the blind and the ears of the deaf; to soften 'hardened' hearts; to change hatred and hostility into love; to replace division and estrangement with unity and fellowship; and to renew faith and resuscitate the spiritually dead. By transforming the individual, the whole fabric of society is changed and the evolution of human civilization advances.

The Hebrew Bible compares this creative power of the Divine Word to rain and snow that bring life to the earth and make it productive:

> For as the rain and the snow come down from heaven and do not return there but water the earth, making it bring forth and sprout, giving seed to the sower and bread to the eater, so shall my word be that goes out from my mouth; it shall not return to me empty, but it shall accomplish that which I purpose, and shall succeed in the thing for which I sent it. (Is. 55:10–11)

It promises a future transformation and purification of the Jews (Ezek. 36:23).

The Apostle Paul defined the fruits of the Spirit (Gal. 5:22–23), and thanked God for His mercies of rebirth and renewal:

> For we ourselves were once foolish, disobedient, led astray, slaves to various passions and pleasures, passing our days in malice and envy, hated by others and hating one another. But when the goodness and loving kindness of God our Saviour [a reference to God the Father] appeared, he saved us, not because of works done by us in righteousness, but according to his own mercy, by the washing of regeneration and renewal of the Holy Spirit. (Titus 3:3–5)

The 'blind' religious leaders dismissed the spiritual changes as the work of the devil:

> And all the people were amazed, and said, 'Can this be the Son of David?' But when the Pharisees heard it, they said, 'It is only by Beelzebul, the prince of demons, that this man casts out demons.' (Matt. 12:24)

Jesus, however, reasoned with them that His revelation created 'good' and thus could not emanate from an evil source:

> Knowing their thoughts, he said to them, 'Every kingdom divided against itself is laid waste, and no city or house divided against itself will stand. And if Satan casts out Satan, he is divided against himself. How then will his kingdom stand?' (Matt. 12:25–6)

> Either make the tree good and its fruit good, or make the tree bad and its fruit bad, for the tree is known by its fruit . . . (Matt. 12: 33)

True faith transcends the limitations of the environment into which it is born, and proclaims an agenda that involves a greater section of humanity.

Revelation, if divine, is transformative

The alteration in the character and lives of the believers in the apostolic age of Christianity is well known – the conversion of Saul to Paul and Simon to Peter serve as examples. The Bahá'í Writings state that God has always revealed His Message amongst the most difficult and unpromising lands and peoples to remind humanity of the creative power of His Word. Today, the very same transformation is evident through Bahá'u'lláh, exemplified by the 'impact on the lives and standards of those who have chosen to enlist under His banner'. 'The calling into being of a new race of men' is regarded as 'the supreme and distinguishing function' of His revelation:[3]

> How often have the Prophets of God, not excepting Bahá'u'lláh Himself, chosen to appear, and deliver their Message in countries

and amidst peoples and races, at a time when they were either fast declining, or had already touched the lowest depths of moral and spiritual degradation. The appalling misery and wretchedness to which the Israelites had sunk, under the debasing and tyrannical rule of the Pharaohs, in the days preceding their exodus from Egypt under the leadership of Moses;[4] the decline that had set in in the religious, the spiritual, the cultural, and the moral life of the Jewish people, at the time of the appearance of Jesus Christ; the barbarous cruelty, the gross idolatry and immorality, which had for so long been the most distressing features of the tribes of Arabia and brought such shame upon them when Muḥammad arose to proclaim His Message in their midst; the indescribable state of decadence, with its attendant corruption, confusion, intolerance, and oppression, in both the civil and religious life of Persia, so graphically portrayed by the pen of a considerable number of scholars, diplomats, and travellers, at the hour of the Revelation of Bahá'u'lláh – all demonstrate this basic and inescapable fact.

... not by reason of any racial superiority, political capacity, or spiritual virtue which a race or nation might possess, but rather as a direct consequence of its crying needs, its lamentable degeneracy, and irremediable perversity, has the Prophet of God chosen to appear in its midst, and with it as a lever has lifted the entire human race to a higher and nobler plane of life and conduct. For it is precisely under such circumstances, and by such means that the Prophets have, from time immemorial, chosen and were able to demonstrate their redemptive power to raise from the depths of abasement and of misery, the people of their own race and nation, empowering them to transmit in turn to other races and nations the saving grace and the energizing influence of their Revelation.[5]

Christians are urged to prepare themselves for another spiritual transformation and regeneration associated with the Second Coming of Christ

Repent ye therefore, and be converted, that your sins may be blotted out, when the times of refreshing shall come from the presence of the Lord; And he shall send Jesus Christ, which before was preached unto you: Whom the heaven must receive until the times of restitution of all things, which God hath spoken by the mouth of all his holy prophets since the world began. (Acts 3:19–21)

Once again, God promises to 'make all things new' because 'the former things are passed away' (Rev. 21:4–5). Those who remain attached to the old and refuse to become transformed will be part of the 'second death' (Rev. 21:8). As with the First Coming, the greatest danger to the sheep lies within the flock:

> Beware of false prophets, who come to you in sheep's clothing but inwardly are ravenous wolves. You will recognize them by their fruits. Are grapes gathered from thornbushes, or figs from thistles? So, every healthy tree bears good fruit, but the diseased tree bears bad fruit. A healthy tree cannot bear bad fruit, nor can a diseased tree bear good fruit. Every tree that does not bear good fruit is cut down and thrown into the fire. Thus you will recognize them by their fruits. (Matt. 7:15–20)

Rev. Albert Barnes wrote:

> ***False prophets.*** As prophets, however, were commonly regarded as public instructors on the subject of religion, the word came to denote all who were religious teachers. In this sense it is probably used here . . . 'Who come in sheep's clothing' – The sheep is an emblem of innocence, sincerity, and harmlessness. To come in sheep's clothing is to assume the appearance of sanctity and innocence, when the heart is evil.
> ***Ravening wolves*** – Rapacious; voraciously devouring; hungry even to rage. Applied to the false teachers, it means that they assumed the appearance of holiness in order that they might the more readily get the property of the people. They were full of extortion and excess.
> ***Ye shall know them by their fruits*** – He gives the proper test of their character. Men do not judge a tree by its leaves, or bark, or flowers. The flowers may be handsome and fragrant; the foliage, thick and green; but these are merely ornamental. It is the fruit that is of chief service to man; and he forms his opinion of the nature of the tree by that fruit. So of the pretensions to religion. The profession may

be fair; but the conduct – the fruit in the eye of the world – is to determine the nature of the principles.[6]

And Matthew Henry also wrote:

> We have need to be very cautious, because their pretences are very fair and plausible, and such as will deceive us, if we be not upon our guard. They come in sheep's clothing, in the habit of prophets We must take heed of being imposed upon by men's dress and garb, as by that of the scribes, who desire to walk in long robes, Lu. 20:46. Or it may be taken figuratively; they pretend to be sheep, and outwardly appear so innocent, harmless, meek, useful, and all that is good, as to be excelled by none; they feign themselves to be just men, and for the sake of their clothing are admitted among the sheep, which gives them an opportunity of doing them a mischief ere they are aware. They and their errors are gilded with the specious pretences of sanctity and devotion.[7]

It is quite clear that early Christian theologians such as Tertullian, c. 155/160–c. 220 CE, understood that the ravening wolves referred to false preachers who would appear amongst the flock and teach in the name of Christ:

> The Lord taught that many ravening wolves would come in sheep's clothing. And what is sheep's clothing but the outward profession of the Christian name? What are the ravening wolves but crafty intentions and dispositions lurking within to molest the flock of Christ? Who are the false prophets but false preachers? Who are false Apostles but spurious evangelizers?[8]

St Augustine cautioned:

> '. . . how many sheep are outside, how many wolves within! And how many sheep are inside, how many wolves without! . . .'[9]

The Hebrew Bible states that God assesses the fruit of man's deeds:

> I the Lord search the heart and test the mind, to give every man according to his ways, according to the fruit of his deeds. (Jer. 17:10)

A true seeker, one who possesses a heart and mind that are sanctified from bias, will readily realize that the divine tree of the revelation of Bahá'u'lláh has borne good fruits – justice, love, unity, harmony and peace. It has promoted interfaith dialogue, and reawakened the spirit of self-sacrifice and service to humanity. These are the same fruits of the heavenly 'good tree' to which Christ referred.

4. A true Prophet's words come true

The Torah teaches that if a prediction fails, the Prophet is not from God:

> And if you say in your heart, 'How may we know the word that the Lord has not spoken?'– when a prophet speaks in the name of the Lord, if the word does not come to pass or come true, that is a word that the Lord has not spoken; the prophet has spoken it presumptuously. You need not be afraid of him. (Deut. 18:21–22)[10]

The Prophet Jeremiah reiterates this point:

> As for the prophet who prophesies peace, when the word of that prophet comes to pass, then it will be known that the Lord has truly sent the prophet. (Jer. 28:9)[11]

Veracity of Jesus Christ and of the Prophets of the Hebrew Bible

The predictions in the Tanakh of the dispersion of the Jews and their re-gathering have been realized, confirming our faith in the Bible, the Patriarchs, Moses and the Prophets of Israel. The primary prediction of the Gospels, the 'good news' of the advent of the Day when the Will of the Father will 'be done in earth, as it is in heaven' (Matt. 6:10) remained merely a promise until the advent of the Second Coming. If, despite all the evidence, Christians maintain that the prophecies of the New Testament have not yet come to pass, they would in effect be undermining the veracity of Christ's teachings.

False narratives

Joseph Smith (1805–1844 CE), the founder-prophet of the Church of Jesus Christ of Latter Day Saints (LDS), and the LDS Church have made a number of predictions that have failed to materialize.[12] As an example, in 1842 Joseph Smith published the Book of Abraham, which was based on his translation of the hieroglyphics from some Egyptian papyri that he had purchased, and that had been found in the coffins of four Egyptian mummies. This work was canonized by the LDS Church in 1880, and thus became part of its doctrine. As expounded by Joseph Smith, the preface to the book explains that it is 'the writings of Abraham while he was in Egypt . . . written by his own hand, upon papyrus'.[13] The discovery of the Rosetta Stone which contains Greek and Ancient Egyptian versions of the same text finally allowed an accurate translation of the hieroglyphic script. In 1861 the Egyptologist Théodule Devéria examined the papyri, and declared that Joseph Smith's translation was entirely mistaken.[14] Other scholars have since confirmed that Joseph Smith's prediction that the papyri were written by Abraham was not true – the papyri were common Egyptian funerary documents like the Book of the Dead.[15]

Predictions of Bahá'u'lláh fulfilled: A brief account

Bahá'u'lláh wrote to several of the civil and ecclesiastical rulers of His time warning them of their hypocrisy, heedlessness, neglect of their subjects, and hunger for earthly glory.

In a second epistle to Napoleon III, He warned the French Emperor that he would suffer a humiliating defeat, that his kingdom would be 'thrown into confusion'; his empire would pass from his hands; and that his people would experience great 'commotions'.[16] This indictment of Napoleon III was widely published, and soon after he was defeated and captured at the Battle of Sedan in 1870. He was subsequently deposed, and died a sick man as an exile in Kent, England.

Bahá'u'lláh also predicted the demise of Kaiser Wilhelm I, the conqueror of Napoleon III. 'Do thou remember,' Bahá'u'lláh thus addressed him, 'the one [Napoleon] whose power transcended thy power, and whose station excelled thy station . . . Think deeply, O king, concerning him, and concerning them who, like unto thee, have conquered cities and ruled over men.'[17] And again: 'O banks of the Rhine! We have seen you covered with gore, inasmuch as the swords of retribution were drawn against you; and you shall have another turn. And We hear the lamentations of Berlin, though she be today in conspicuous glory.'[18]

> [Wilhelm I] sustained two attempts on his life, and was succeeded by a son who died of a mortal disease, three months after his accession to the throne, bequeathing the throne to the arrogant, the headstrong and short-sighted William II. The pride of the new monarch precipitated his downfall. Revolution, swiftly and suddenly, broke out in his capital, communism reared its head in a number of cities . . . and he himself, fleeing ignominiously to Holland, was compelled to relinquish his right to the throne . . . the terms of an oppressively severe treaty provoked 'the lamentations' which, half a century before, had been ominously prophesied.[19]

Bahá'u'lláh also predicted the ignominious fall from power and the deaths of the powerful Sultan 'Abdu'l-'Azíz, the Caliph of the Ottoman Empire, and his two ministers, who had decreed His exile to 'Akká.[20]

5. A true Prophet glorifies God and not Himself – He is subservient to the Divine Will

Moses showed a greater humility before God than any of His followers (Num. 12:3). He did not desire the homage of the Israelites but instead prayed that God might reveal to Him His glory (Ex. 3:18). Neither did Christ seek praise or honour, or to exalt or vindicate Himself:

> I do not receive glory from people.[21] (John 5:41)

> The one who speaks on his own authority seeks his own glory; but the one who seeks the glory of him who sent him is true, and in him there is no falsehood. (John 7:18)

> Yet I do not seek my own glory; there is One who seeks it, and he is the judge . . . If I glorify myself, my glory is nothing. It is my Father who glorifies me, of whom you say, 'He is our God.' (John 8:50, 54)

And Jesus cried out and said, 'Whoever believes in me, believes not in me but in him who sent me.' (John 12:44)

He maintained that the one expected to come after Him would glorify Him:

He will glorify me, for he will take what is mine [teachings] and declare it to you... he will take what is mine and declare it.[22] (John 16:14–15)

6. A true Prophet confirms earlier revelations and His Message is consistent and harmonious with the spiritual themes of earlier scriptures

In view of humanity's spiritual steps and development being guided by God, it stands to reason that the teachings of Moses would follow naturally those of Noah and the patriarchs. Christ stated that His teachings were in accord with the teachings of Moses and the promises of the Hebrew Bible, but that the Jewish leaders did not truly believe in Moses or fully understand their own Scriptures, otherwise they would also have believed in Him (John 5:45–46). He pointed out that 'the scripture cannot be broken' (John 10:35).

The revelation following the Dispensation of Christ confirms categorically the truth of the Hebrew Bible and the Gospels, and describes them as part of the same *deen* or religion as itself.[23]

7. A true Prophet's knowledge is innate – His revelation is not acquired and is not dependent on human learning

Moses's revelation of the Torah

In the book of Deuteronomy Moses describes Himself as a Prophet Who had spoken only what God had told Him to reveal – He had not spoken of His own volition. Stephen, the first Christian martyr, states that 'Moses was educated in all the wisdom of the Egyptians and was powerful in speech and action' (Acts 7:22). However, His teachings delivered from Mount Sinai had nothing in common with the understanding of the Children of Israel or the learning of their masters in

Egypt. His eloquence and actions emanated from God alone. The same would hold true for a future prophet (Deut. 18:18–19).

Jesus's teachings were not His own and were not founded on rabbinical training

The Jews therefore marvelled, saying, 'How is it that this man has learning, when he has never studied?' So Jesus answered them, 'My teaching is not mine, but his who sent me.' (John 7:15–16)

So Jesus said to them, 'When you have lifted up the Son of Man, then you will know that I am he, and that I do nothing on my own authority, but speak just as the Father taught me. And he who sent me is with me. He has not left me alone, for I always do the things that are pleasing to him.' (John 8:28–29)

Whoever does not love me does not keep my words. And the word that you hear is not mine but the Father's who sent me. (John 14:24)

Bahá'u'lláh, the Author of a vast revelation, had no formal scriptural or scholarly training – His knowledge, like that of Moses and Christ, was divine

This Wronged One hath frequented no school, neither hath He attended the controversies of the learned. By My life! Not of Mine own volition have I revealed Myself, but God, of His own choosing, hath manifested Me.[24]

O King! I was but a man like others, asleep upon My couch, when lo, the breezes of the All-Glorious were wafted over Me, and taught Me the knowledge of all that hath been. This thing is not from Me, but from One Who is Almighty and All-Knowing. And He bade Me lift up My voice between earth and heaven, and for this there befell Me what hath caused the tears of every man of understanding to flow. The learning current amongst men I studied not; their schools I entered not.[25]

8. A true Prophet guides humanity back to the right path

God's Messengers warn of heedlessness and the consequences of turning away from God:

> Whoever heeds instruction is on the path to life, but he who rejects reproof leads others astray. (Prov. 10:17)

> A man who wanders from the way of understanding will rest in the assembly of the dead. (Prov. 21:16)

> And the word of the Lord came to me: 'Son of man, when a land sins against me by acting faithlessly, and I stretch out my hand against it and break its supply of bread and send famine upon it...' (Ezek. 14:12)

The Hebrew Bible speaks of the children of Israel being misled:

> All we like sheep have gone astray; we have turned – every one – to his own way (Is. 53:6).

> In those days and in that time, declares the Lord, the people of Israel and the people of Judah shall come together, weeping as they come, and they shall seek the Lord their God. They shall ask the way to Zion, with faces turned toward it, saying, 'Come, let us join ourselves to the Lord in an everlasting covenant that will never be forgotten.' My people have been lost sheep. Their shepherds have led them astray, turning them away on the mountains. From mountain to hill they have gone. They have forgotten their fold. (Jer. 50:4–6).

> Woe to them, for they have strayed from me! Destruction to them, for they have rebelled against me! I would redeem them, but they speak lies against me. They do not cry to me from the heart... (Hos 7:13–14)

Consequently:

> . . . in that day, that the Lord shall punish the host of the high ones that are on high, and the kings of the earth upon the earth . . . Then the moon shall be confounded, and the sun ashamed, when the Lord of hosts shall reign in mount Zion, and in Jerusalem, and before his ancients gloriously. (Is. 24:21, 23)

The New Testament warns the Jews to be alert and not to go astray as they did at the time of Moses:

> Therefore, as the Holy Spirit says, 'Today, if you hear his voice, do not harden your hearts as in the rebellion, on the day of testing in the wilderness, where your fathers put me to the test and saw my works for forty years.' Therefore I was provoked with that generation, and said, 'They always go astray in their heart; they have not known my ways.' As I swore in my wrath, 'They shall not enter my rest.' (Heb. 3:7–11)

Bahá'u'lláh entreats God to assist humanity to repent and to turn to Him:

> Assist them, O my Lord, to return unto Thee, and to repent before the door of Thy grace. Powerful art Thou to do what Thou willest, and in Thy grasp are the reins of all that is in the heavens and all that is on earth. Praise be unto God, the Lord of the worlds.[26]

> We entreat God – exalted and glorified be He – to aid all men to be just and fair-minded, and to graciously assist them to repent and return unto Him. He, verily, heareth, and is ready to answer.[27]

9. A true Prophet eliminates misunderstandings and provides the spiritual explanations of previous scriptures

Chapter 5 of Matthew consists almost entirely of new teachings from Jesus. Throughout His ministry, the truths that He brought, and the corrections that He made to Jewish belief, were often deliberately conveyed in parables, and expressed in allegorical terms. This demanded that His listeners search for the underlying spiritual explanations of His statements, an essential requirement at both the First Coming and the Second Coming (John 4:23–24; I Cor. 2:12–14). The Apostle Paul wrote:

> So we do not lose heart. Though our outer self is wasting away, our inner self is being renewed day by day . . . as we look not to the things that are seen but to the things that are unseen. For the things that are seen are transient, but the things that are unseen are eternal. (II Cor. 4:16, 18)

10. A true Prophet's life and those of his early followers exemplify self-sacrifice – in spite of inevitable persecutions by the civil and ecclesiastical authorities, God's Word endures

The divine Word eventually triumphs over adversities:

> The Light shines in the darkness, and the darkness has not overcome it. (John 1:1)

> . . . since you have been born again, not of perishable seed but of imperishable, through the living and abiding word of God; for 'All flesh is like grass and all its glory like the flower of grass. The grass withers, and the flower falls, but the word of the Lord remains forever'.[28] And this word is the good news that was preached to you. (I Pet. 1:23–25)

Christ reminded His followers that every true faith has been maligned and its followers persecuted:

> Blessed are you when others revile you and persecute you and utter all kinds of evil against you falsely on my account. Rejoice and be glad, for your reward is great in heaven, for so they persecuted the prophets who were before you. (Matt. 5:11–12)

> If the world hates you, know that it has hated me before it hated you. If you were of the world, the world would love you as its own; but because you are not of the world, but I chose you out of the world, therefore the world hates you. (John 15:18–19)

At his arraignment, St Stephen, the first Christian martyr, made a similar point:

> You stiff-necked people, uncircumcised in heart and ears, you always resist the Holy Spirit. As your fathers did, so do you. Which of the prophets did your fathers not persecute? And they killed those who announced beforehand the coming of the Righteous One, whom you have now betrayed and murdered . . . (Acts 7:51–53)

The Epistle of James explains that the Prophets have always endured their hardships with steadfastness:

> As an example of suffering and patience, brothers, take the prophets who spoke in the name of the Lord. (James 5:10)

Approval by the majority does not ensure that one is on the right path:

> Woe to you, when all people speak well of you, for so their fathers did to the false prophets. (Luke 6:26)

Christ taught that those who are prepared to sacrifice themselves for the divine teachings will gain spiritual life, but this will not happen to those who are attached to this world:

> And he said to all, 'If anyone would come after me, let him deny himself and take up his cross daily and follow me. For whoever would save his life will lose it, but whoever loses his life for my sake will save it. For what does it profit a man if he gains the whole world and loses or forfeits himself? . . .'(Luke 9:23–25)

He encouraged commitment and the spirit of self-sacrifice (Luke 18:22). When the Apostle Peter declared that the disciples had sacrificed everything for Him, Jesus replied that whatever they had lost they would gain many times over:

> And Peter said, 'See, we have left our homes and followed you.' And he said to them, 'Truly, I say to you, there is no one who has left house or wife or brothers or parents or children, for the sake of

the kingdom of God, who will not receive many times more in this time, and in the age to come eternal life.' (Luke 18:28–30)

In the same way, in a general Tablet to the kings of Christendom, Bahá'u'lláh expresses confidence concerning the eventual victory of His much maligned and persecuted Faith:

> Warn and acquaint the people, O Servant, with the things We have sent down unto Thee, and let the fear of no one dismay Thee, and be Thou not of them that waver. The day is approaching when God will have exalted His Cause and magnified His testimony in the eyes of all who are in the heavens and all who are on the earth. Place, in all circumstances, Thy whole trust in Thy Lord, and fix Thy gaze upon Him, and turn away from all them that repudiate His truth. Let God, Thy Lord, be Thy sufficing succorer and helper. We have pledged Ourselves to secure Thy triumph upon earth and to exalt Our Cause above all men . . .[29]

15

BIBLICAL PROMISES FULFILLED

As noted earlier, both the Hebrew Bible and the New Testament have many promises about the advent of a world-encompassing revelation. This chapter describes the fulfilment of the biblical expectations of a universal Redeemer and the Second Coming of Christ in the Glory of the Father, in relation to the Faith of Bahá'u'lláh.

The place and the time

Persia, a country in close proximity to, and directly to the east, of Israel, was the birthplace of the revelations of the Báb and Bahá'u'lláh in the 19th century. It was also the birthplace of Zoroastrianism, one of the oldest monotheistic religions. The Magi ('Wise Men' or 'Kings') (Matt. 2:1–12) who came from the East and paid homage to the newly born Christ were from a priestly caste of Zoroastrianism. Cyrus the Great (600–530 BCE) was the founder of the Achaemenid Empire, the first Persian Empire, and respected the customs and religions of the lands under his rule. He is praised in the Bible which states that he was anointed by God. (Is. 45:1)

In the creation account in Genesis, God planted a garden in the east called Eden (Gen. 2:8), home to the Tree of Life and the Tree of Knowledge of good and evil, and described in the Bible as 'the garden of God' (Ezek. 28:13). Eden has also been translated as 'paradise', related to an ancient Persian word *paridayda*, a walled enclosure of harmony. The Aramaic root word means 'fruitful, well-watered', that is, blessed by divine bounties.[1] Some Christians believe that the Genesis account is literally true. Because of the biblical reference: 'A river flowed out of Eden to water the garden, and there it divided and became four rivers' (Gen. 2:10), they have suggested that the location of Eden is at the head of the Persian Gulf where there are four rivers, Tigris, Euphrates, Pishon and Gihon.[2]

The Prophet Ezekiel was transported in a vision from God to the land of Israel and to a very high mountain. From this vantage point he had visions of the coming of the glory of the God of Israel from the east:

> 'Son of man, look with your eyes, and hear with your ears, and set your heart upon all that I shall show you, for you were brought here in order that I might show it to you. Declare all that you see to the house of Israel.' . . . Then he went into the gateway facing east . . . (Ezek. 40:4, 6)

> Then he led me to the gate, the gate facing east. And behold, the glory of the God of Israel was coming from the east. And the sound of his coming was like the sound of many waters, and the earth shone with his glory . . . And I fell on my face. As the glory of the Lord entered the temple by the gate facing east . . . and behold, the glory of the Lord filled the temple. (Ezek. 43:1–2, 4–5)

Adam Clarke (1762–1832), a Methodist theologian and Bible scholar, wrote insightfully in his *Commentary*:

> And this glory, coming from the east, is going to enter into the eastern gate of the temple, and thence to shine out upon the whole earth. Is there not a mystery here? All knowledge, all religion, and all arts and sciences, have traveled, according to the course of the sun, From East To West! From that quarter the Divine glory at first came; and thence the rays of Divine light continue to diffuse themselves over the face of the earth. From thence came the Bible, and through that the new covenant. From thence came the prophets, the apostles, and the first missionaries, that brought the knowledge of God to Europe, to the isles of the sea, and to the west first, and afterwards to these northern regions.[3]

It may be noted that there would have been no need for the Prophet to be taken to the apex of a very high mountain to see the temple, so a literal interpretation of 'high mountain' may not be assumed. Traditionally, 'the gate facing east', has been interpreted as referring to the eastward-looking gate of the court of priests. However, another plausible explanation is that the 'Glory of God', Bahá'u'lláh in Arabic, would come to Israel from the east.

The Prophet Jeremiah stated that God would establish His throne in Elam, a western province of Persia and east of the Holy Land, which includes a small part of modern Iraq:

> I will set my throne in Elam . . . declares the Lord. But in the latter days I will restore the fortunes of Elam, declares the Lord. (Jer. 49:38–39)

Persia is also the region where the Prophet Daniel was taken into captivity by Nebuchadnezzar (Dan. 1:1–6).[4] It is in this region, described as a 'holy place' by Christ (Matt. 24:15) that he had dreams alluding to 1844 (Dan. 8:2; 12:11), the year when the Báb, the Forerunner of Bahá'u'lláh, declared in the city of Shiraz at 25 years of age, that the world would soon witness the appearance of 'Him Whom God shall make manifest'. Notably, the modern-day city of Shiraz lies south-east of the province of Llám, from the name Elam, referred in the above quotation from Jeremiah.

Prophecies in the Book of Daniel and the Book of Revelation

The date 1260 appears seven times in the Bible; twice in Daniel and five times in the Book of Revelation. Sir Isaac Newton (1643–1727) commented:

> [It is] therefore a part of this Prophecy, that it should not be understood before the last age of the world; and therefore it makes for the credit of the Prophecy, that it is not yet understood. But if the last age, the age of opening these things, be now approaching, as by the great successes of late Interpreters it seems to be, we have more encouragement than ever to look into these things. If the general preaching of the Gospel be approaching, it is to us and our posterity that those words mainly belong: In the time of the end the wise shall understand, but none of the wicked shall understand (Dan. 12:4, 10).[5]

The date is expressed in several ways: (a) 'a thousand two hundred and three score' (1,260) days:

BIBLICAL PROMISES FULFILLED

And I will grant authority to my two witnesses, and they will prophesy for 1,260 days, clothed in sackcloth. (Rev. 11:3)

She gave birth to a male child, one who is to rule all the nations with a rod of iron, but her child was caught up to God and to his throne, and the woman fled into the wilderness, where she has a place prepared by God, in which she is to be nourished for 1,260 days. (Rev. 12:5–6)

(b) 'a time and times' and 'the dividing of a time' (or half a time): that is, one year or 360 days, plus two years or 720 days plus half a year or 180 days – a total of 1,260 days.

And someone said to the man clothed in linen, who was above the waters of the stream, 'How long shall it be till the end of these wonders?' And I heard the man clothed in linen, who was above the waters of the stream; he raised his right hand and his left hand toward heaven and swore by him who lives forever that it would be for a time, times, and half a time . . . (Dan. 12:6–7; see also 7:25, and Rev. 12:13–14)

(c) 'Forty-two months' or 42 x 30 days = 1,260 days (Rev. 11:2 and 13:5).

Coincidence of the year 1260 AH in the Muslim calendar with 1844 CE

As Islam was the primary actor in the events leading to the cleansing of the sanctuary (from non-Jewish foreign elements), the year 1260 should be reckoned according to the Muslim calendar which was in operation in that part of the world. The Muslim calendar is reckoned in lunar months from the migration of Muhammad, or *hegira*, from Mecca to Medina. The observation was not lost on Christians in the 1840s that the Muslims of their period were using a calendar that documented 1844 CE as 1260 AH (after *hegira*). For example, Rev. Edward Bickersteth, the evangelical Bishop of Exeter, wrote the following in the intolerant language of his coreligionists in 1845 concerning the prophecy of 'one thousand two hundred and three score days' or 1,260 years in Revelation 11:3:

Besides the mystical application of this to Rome; it is also a more visible and manifest fulfilment in the duration of the Mahomedan imposture and dominion. The Mahomedan Anti-Christ reckons by the lunar year, and has fixed his own era, that of Hegira, A. D. 622. Through his dominions, and through the civilized world, this is known as the 1,260th year of the Mohamodan religion. It terminates in January 1845. Forty months, according to the eastern reckoning of months, contains 1260 days; the date being expressed in months, gives it a correspondence with the Mahomedan reckoning of lunar years, and for that period the Mahomedan is the prevailing power in the East. The Gentiles have literally trodden down the city of Jerusalem for a large part of that period. The city was given to idolatry under a Christian name, and was taken by the Caliph Omar, in 636, and with the exception of 88 years in the time of the crusaders, who were also full of superstition and idolatry, has been in the possession of Mahomedans ever since. This again furnishes another sign of the times in which we live, and marks farther the passing of the second woe.[6]

And in the words of the Irish evangelist and author Henry Grattan Guinness (1835-1910):

The restoration of the sacrifice continued with slight exceptions to the destruction of Jerusalem by the Romans, since which Jerusalem has been trodden of the Gentiles, to the period of March 20, 1844; makes 2300 years; and on the first of Nisan, 1844, the power of the Mohammadans to persecute Christianity passed away, and liberty is given for Christian worship, the true cleansing of the sanctuary. THIS IS THE MORE REMARKABLE ALSO AS THIS IS THE 1260th YEAR OF HEJIRA (the date fixed by the Mohammadan AntiChrist as the rise of this branch of the Apostasy), and so the closing year in Mohammadanism of that remarkable prophetical period 1260 years. In a letter from Tangiers, dated June 20th, 1844, given in the public journals, speaking of the difficulties besetting the kingdom of Morocco, it is stated that the Moors have always had forebodings of this year. For a long time they have been exhorting each other to beware of 1260 (that is of the Hejira), which according to our reckoning is the present year.[7]

Protestant Adventists who were unaware that 1260 AH coincided with 1844 CE had another explanation for the 1260 date. They believed that it referred to the duration of the fearful power that would persecute and wage war against God's true church, and which they attributed to papal dominion. Thus the Millerites, in common with the Seventh-Day Adventists and the earlier biblical students of the Reformation and post-Reformation eras, understood the 1260 'days' to be the period that the Papacy ruled in Rome. Their explanation was that this period began in 538 CE when the Ostragoths were forced by General Belisarius to abandon their siege of Rome. This left the Bishop of Rome to exercise the prerogatives of Justinian's decree of 533 CE, and the power and the authority of the Papacy steadily increased. The period ended 1260 years later when in 1798 the French General Berthier, with Napoleon's army, marched into Rome and proclaimed the end of the political rule of the Papacy. The Pope was taken prisoner and was removed to France where he died in exile.

The fifth and sixth trumpets, and the end of 'the abomination that maketh desolate'

The Book of Revelation (9:1–11) speaks of dire calamities that would arise in the vicinity of the river Euphrates in the Middle East: an immense army like locusts would be unleashed from that region – 'the locusts looked like horses prepared for battle' (Rev. 9:7) and suggested an Arabian calvary.[8]

The reference to the 'fifth trumpet' and 'first woe' was increasingly interpreted by Christians of the late eighteenth and early nineteenth centuries, such as the historian Edward Gibbon and the biblical scholar Rev. Albert Barnes, as referring to the rise of Islam which had inflicted unprecedented pain, suffering and loss on Christian countries:

> With surprising unanimity, commentators have agreed in regarding this as referring to the empire of the Saracens, or to the rise and progress of the religion and the empire set up by Muhammed.[9]

The conviction of the Adventists that the events were related to Islam was strengthened as they noted the acceleration of the misfortunes of Ottomans in the 1840s and the weakening of their grip on the Holy

Land. They interpreted the extraordinary developments as being consistent with the 'sixth trumpet' of Revelation 9, the passing of the 'second woe', and removal at long last of the 'abomination that maketh desolate', signalling the fulfilment of the end of time (Rev. 9:13–15).[10] They noted that this event coincided with the fulfilment of other prophecies concerning the Second Coming, including the proclamation of the Gospel to all humanity and easing of conditions for the return of the Jews to their homeland.

Josiah Litch (1809–86), a New England Methodist Episcopal preacher, writing a commentary on Revelation 9, predicted in 1838 that the demise of the Ottoman Empire would occur in August 1840.[11] In 1838 Turkey had suppressed a rebellion by Egypt, but Egypt successfully attacked the following year, capturing the Turkish naval fleet and decimating its army. England, Russia, Austria and Prussia, four Christian nations with massive fleets, came to Turkey's assistance and established ultimatums against Egypt. They reduced the boundaries of Egyptian rule and forced the *pasha* of Egypt, Mehemet Ali, to return the fleet to the Turkish Sultan. This ultimatum was hand-delivered to the Egyptians by the Turkish envoy on 11 August 1840, thereby forcing the weakened Ottoman Empire to legally admit that its existence depended upon the support and guarantees of Christian nations. The humbled Sultan of the Ottoman Empire saved his reign and probably his life by accepting the protection of those Christian powers. He then watched the dismemberment of his weakened empire as his 'protectors' appropriated parts of his territories for their own use, piece by piece. Thus, an Adventist, with justification, observed that 'its [Caliphate of Islam] power to afflict Christendom had been removed'.[12]

The Ottoman edict of toleration[13] of 1844[14] and the Imperial Reform Edict of 1856 provided further evidence of the approaching end time, the elimination of the oppression by the Caliphate and of the 'abomination that maketh desolate'. The emerging limits of the ability of the Ottoman Caliphate to impose its wishes by applying Islamic laws on Jews and Christians became evident following certain notable events in 1843/144. These are described by an Adventist writing in 1845:

> It has long been known, and universally acknowledged that the Mahomedan empire has been for many years in the course of decay. This fact is one visible in the face of all men, and particularly since

the French revolution in 1793. This has been still more marked since the year 1822, since which time some of its largest and fairest provinces have been wrested from it by conquest or treaty. Its population and its inward resources have been continually wasting ...

When the Mahommedan rulers then, under the dictation of Christian powers, solemnly and officially relinquish the power of persecuting Christians, we may then fully and emphatically say the second woe is past.

Such an event appears to me to have taken place in 1844. Till this year Turkey retained in the face of Europe, as a principle of their religion, and a law of their Koran, the power of putting all Mahomedans who forsook their religion and embraced Christianity to death.[15] In accordance with this, an Armenian was put to death for forsaking Mohamedanism, and returning to the Armenian Church in 1843. The barbarity of the act shocked the European nations, and our ambassador obtained a general promise that the practice should cease. In violation of this general engagement, a Greek was, in Dec. 1843, executed for the same cause. This roused the Christian states of Europe, and the five European powers, England, France, Prussia, Austria, and Russia interposed with earnest remonstrances. The great impediment to complying with these remonstrances was this: Their supposed divine law, the Koran, in their view required this severe penalty, and hence there was in their judgment no possibility of a change. But the European powers would take no denial, and after much delay, and with infinite difficulty, they at length procured an official statement, abandoning all persecutions of Christianity. It was given in these words, 'The Sublime Porte engages to take effectual measures to prevent henceforth the execution and putting to death of the Christian who is an apostate. March 21, 1844.' The Sultan also declared to our ambassador, Sir Stratford Canning, 'Henceforth neither shall Christianity be insulted in my dominions, nor shall Christians be in any way persecuted for their religion. March 23, 1844.'[16]

The Imperial Reform Edict (*Islâhat Hatt-ı Hümâyûnu* or *Islâhat Fermânı*) issued in 1856 by Sultan Abdülmecid I improved further the situation of the Jews and Christians in the Ottoman Empire. The decree, the result of the influence of France and England due to their assistance to the Ottoman Empire against the Russians during the Crimean War

(1853–56), promised equality in education, government appointments, and administration of justice to all, regardless of creed. These Ottoman reforms, which facilitated life for Jews in the Holy Land, coupled with the holocaust in Europe a hundred years later, ensured continued migration and the return of the Jews to their traditional homeland.

Dispersion of the Jews and their return to the Holy Land

The scattering of the Jews, or the Diaspora

The Children of Israel were warned that if they did not faithfully follow God's Law and did not revere His glorious and exalted name they would be visited by many tribulations.

> If you are not careful to do all the words of this law that are written in this book, that you may fear this glorious and awesome name, the Lord your God, then the Lord will bring on you and your offspring extraordinary afflictions, afflictions severe and lasting, and sicknesses grievous and lasting . . . And the Lord will scatter you among all peoples, from one end of the earth to the other, and there you shall serve other gods of wood and stone, which neither you nor your fathers have known. And among these nations you shall find no respite, and there shall be no resting place for the sole of your foot, but the Lord will give you there a trembling heart and failing eyes and a languishing soul. Your life shall hang in doubt before you. Night and day you shall be in dread and have no assurance of your life. In the morning you shall say, 'If only it were evening!' and at evening you shall say, 'If only it were morning!' because of the dread that your heart shall feel, and the sights that your eyes shall see. (Deut. 28:58–59, 64–67)

Several of the later Prophets repeatedly warned them that their ungodliness would eventually have dire consequences, but their admonitions fell on deaf ears. Finally, after lasting about two centuries, the northern Kingdom of Israel was destroyed by the Assyrians in 722 BCE. It was the policy of the Assyrians to relocate to other parts of the Empire the inhabitants of the countries that they conquered, particularly their affluent classes. This was the beginning of the widespread dispersion (diaspora, or scattering) of the Jews. The southern kingdom of Judea was also conquered in turn by the Chaldeans, Egyptians and Babylonians. Following the conquest of the kingdom of Judah in 598/597 and 587/586 BCE[17] by Nebuchadnezzar, Jerusalem and the Temple were destroyed, and again thousands of prominent Jews were taken captive to Babylon. This forced detention of the Jews is known as the Babylonian Captivity, or Babylonian Exile.[18] The captivity formally ended in 538 BCE, when the Persian conqueror of Babylonia, Cyrus the Great, gave the Jews permission to return to Palestine; however, most elected to stay in Babylon. The author of the second Book of Chronicles saw the tragedy as an inevitable consequence of the evil that had been perpetrated despite repeated admonishments (II Chron. 36:12–16).

The third large dispersion occurred a century after Christ. Judea became a protectorate of Rome in 63 BCE and was reorganized as a Roman province in 6 CE. Roman rule was harsh; the Jews were heavily taxed and their chief religious official, the High Priest, became a political appointee. The Jews rebelled under Bar Kokhba against the Roman Emperor Hadrian, whose army defeated the Jewish armies in 135 CE and Jewish independence was lost, thereby as punishment for their rebellion, Hadrian exiled more Jews, sold them into slavery, turned Jerusalem into a pagan Roman city and forbade the Jews from living there. Judea and Samaria were renamed Syria Palestina as a means of erasing the land's Jewish identity. Since then, and until the re-establishment of Israel in 1948, most Jews have lived in the diaspora.

The gathering of the scattered Jews in the Holy Land – Aliyah

The second event predicted by the Patriarch Jacob in Genesis is the gathering of the Jews. This is also associated with Shiloh and the Messiah, and is presumably a reference to the Second Coming.

Christians, writing in the 1840s, underlined the close relationship between the restoration of the fortunes of Israel and the Second Coming:

> This appearing is again intimately connected with the Restoration of the Jewish nation. The general voice of prophecy is when the Lord shall build up Zion, then shall he appear in his glory, Ps. 102:16. There shall come out of Zion the Deliverer, and shall turn away ungodliness from Jacob, (Rom. 11:26, 27). And unequalled since the Apostolic age is the interest that has manifested for this people

in recent years and Christian nations in general. May it grow to that fulness of love which marked the Apostle of the Gentiles, (Rom. ix. x.) and our Saviour Christ Himself. (Isaiah lx, lxi. Matt. xxiii, 37. Luke xix. 41–44).[19]

The exiled Jews were persecuted in many localities throughout the world. This prompted the creation of Modern Zionism in the 1800s. In 1841, the first modern Jewish School was founded in Vilna, Lithuania; students of the Vilna Gaon moved to Palestine in the 1860s and were also part of the 'First Aliyah' (the first large wave of Jewish settlers to the Holy Land) in the 1880s. In 1897 the First Zionist Congress was held in Switzerland and influential Jews agreed on the imperative of a homeland for their people. In 1917 General Allenby took Jerusalem, ending 400 years of Ottoman rule.

The Balfour Declaration was a letter dated 2 November 1917 from the British Foreign Secretary Arthur James Balfour to Walter Rothschild, a leader of the British Jewish community, for transmission to the Zionist Federation of Great Britain and Ireland. It read:

November 2nd, 1917

Dear Lord Rothschild,
    I have much pleasure in conveying to you, on behalf of His Majesty's Government, the following declaration of sympathy with Jewish Zionist aspirations which has been submitted to, and approved by, the Cabinet.
    'His Majesty's Government view with favour the establishment in Palestine of a national home for the Jewish people, and will use their best endeavours to facilitate the achievement of this object, it being clearly understood that nothing shall be done which may prejudice the civil and religious rights of existing non-Jewish communities in Palestine, or the rights and political status enjoyed by Jews in any other country.'
    I should be grateful if you would bring this declaration to the knowledge of the Zionist Federation.
    Yours sincerely,
        Arthur James Balfour[20]

Continued persecution prompted waves of Jews to migrate from countries of Eastern Europe, such as Russia and Poland, to what was then called Palestine. The coming of Hitler to power in 1933 further accelerated the migration. In 1939 alone, 62,000 Jews settled in Palestine. Britain, which had been given a mandate by the League of Nations to govern Palestine, attempted to limit not only the Jewish immigration to Palestine, but also the purchase of land by Jews. However, the British were unable to maintain peace in the region, and in 1947 decided to withdraw their forces. In 1948 open fighting broke out between Jews and Arabs in Palestine. Israel was proclaimed an independent State by David Ben Gurion on 14 May 1948. From 1948 to 1952 hundreds of thousands of Jews migrated to Israel from European and Arab countries.

The Great Disappointment

William Miller, a Baptist preacher, predicted in 1838 that the Second Advent of Jesus Christ would occur in 1839.[21] He then predicted that the world would be destroyed by fire in 1843, but later changed the date to before 21 March 1844.[22] Miller provided the following description of the Second Advent:

> A small bright spot will first appear in the east, which will gradually expand as it approaches the earth. Bye and bye, a small cloud will appear before the luminous ball, and between it and the earth. On this cloud will be seen the Son of Man, standing erect, his figure plainly visible to the spectators on the earth. At the sound of a trumpet (or some other signal,) the bright spot having gradually illuminated the whole heavens, the righteous dead shall arise from their resting places—and the risen and living saints shall together be caught up and meet the Saviour in the air, when they will instantly be changed and clothed with mortality. The Saviour will then present them to the Father . . .[23]

In the approaching days, Miller wrote:

> I am now seated at my old desk in my east room. Having obtained help of God until the present time, I am still looking for the Dear

Savior... The time, as I have calculated it, is now filed up; and I expect every moment to see the Savior descend from heaven. I have now nothing to look for but this glorious hope...[24]

When this date passed, a new date was predicted: 18 April 1844.[25] When this revised date also passed, one of his followers, Samuel S. Snow, predicted the date of 22 October 1844.[26]

The followers of the Adventist movements were devastated when their expectations were not fulfilled literally and Christ did not materialize from the sky, a setback called the Millerite Great Disappointment.[27] A follower of Miller wrote in his journal:

> I waited all Tuesday [October 22] and dear Jesus did not come; – I waited all the forenoon of Wednesday, and was well in body as I ever was, but after 12 o'clock I began to feel faint, and before dark I needed someone to help me up to my chamber, as my natural strength was leaving me very fast, and I lay prostrate for 2 days without any pain – sick with disappointment.[28]

Until his death in 1849, Miller clung to the belief that the end of the world was near.

The Jehovah's Witnesses proposed the alternative dates of 1874 and 1914 for the Second Coming. When they were again disappointed, the explanation was given that Christ had indeed come but that the event had not been visible. It is noteworthy that Seventh-Day Adventists continue to have a literal interpretation of the biblical prophecies, and clearly, as long as they persist in this, they will continue to be disappointed:

> The Second Coming of Christ is the blessed hope of the church, the grand climax of the gospel. The Saviour's coming will be literal, personal, visible, and worldwide. When He returns, the righteous dead will be resurrected, and together with the righteous living will be glorified and taken to heaven, but the unrighteous will die. The almost complete fulfilment of most lines of prophecy, together with the present condition of the world, indicates that Christ's coming is imminent.[29]

The fate of the Millerites and the Adventists is a profound tragedy – Miller failed to realize the accuracy with which he had forecast the Second Coming. Notably, the Báb, the Forerunner of Bahá'u'lláh Whose advent the Bahá'ís believe represents the Second Coming of Christ in the Glory of the Father, declared His mission in the East on 23 May 1844. He did not descend literally from the sky in Boston where Miller and his followers lived, but His teachings, the bread of life, were revealed from the heaven of divine knowledge.

The Declaration of the Báb in 1844 CE and the fulfilment of the biblical prophecies

The Báb declared in 1844 that God would soon manifest the promise of all religions. He and His followers suffered extreme religious persecution at the hands of the Islamic civil and ecclesiastical authorities. The youthful Báb was suspended against a barrack square wall and was made the target of a hail of musket fire.[30] Many thousands of His followers also suffered martyrdom:

> A persecution, kindling a courage which . . . has been unsurpassed by that which the fires of Smithfield evoked, mowed down, with tragic swiftness, no less than twenty thousand of its heroic adherents, who refused to barter their newly born faith for the fleeting honours and security of a mortal life.[31]

Bahá'u'lláh's banishment to the Holy Land

Born into nobility and extreme wealth, Bahá'u'lláh, due to His support of the Báb, lost all His earthly possessions, was tortured by bastinado, suffered imprisonment in a dark and loathsome dungeon, the 'black pit' of Tehran, and was then banished under guard to Iraq, a province of the Ottoman Empire, where in 1863 He announced that He was the One foretold by the Báb and all earlier Messengers:

> He Who in such dramatic circumstances was made to sustain the overpowering weight of so glorious a Mission was none other than the One Whom posterity will acclaim, and Whom innumerable followers already recognize, as the Judge, the Lawgiver and Redeemer

of all mankind, as the Organizer of the entire planet, as the Unifier of the children of men, as the Inaugurator of the long-awaited millennium, as the Originator of a new 'Universal Cycle', as the Establisher of the Most Great Peace, as the Fountain of the Most Great Justice, as the Proclaimer of the coming of age of the entire human race, as the Creator of a new World Order, and as the Inspirer and Founder of a world civilization.

To Israel He was neither more nor less than the incarnation of the 'Everlasting Father', [Is. 9:6] the 'Lord of Hosts' come down 'with ten thousands of saints' [Deut. 33:2]; to Christendom Christ returned 'in the glory of the Father' [Matt. 16:27] . . .[32]

Many of His followers were also martyred. Bahá'u'lláh testifies to the suffering of all Prophets and the sacrifice of their followers:

> . . . consider the hardships and the bitterness of the lives of those Revealers of the divine Beauty. Reflect, how single-handed and alone they faced the world and all its peoples, and promulgated the Law of God! No matter how severe the persecutions inflicted upon those holy, those precious, and tender Souls, they still remained, in the plenitude of their power, patient, and, despite their ascendancy, they suffered and endured.[33]

He attests to the cruel treatment He and His followers experienced:

> Glorified art Thou, O Lord my God! Thou seest what hath befallen this Wronged One at the hands of them that have not associated with Me, and who have arisen to harm and abase Me, in a manner which no pen can describe, nor tongue recount . . . I beseech Thee, O my Lord . . . to protect Thy loved ones from the cruelty of such as have remained unaware of the mysteries of Thy Name, the Unconstrained. Assist them . . . and aid them to be patient and long-suffering . . .[34]

The Greek word 'martyr' signifies someone whose death is a testimony to his faith. Bahá'u'lláh underlines the discriminating value of the sacrifices borne in God's path:

> Glory to Thee, O my God! But for the tribulations which are sustained in Thy path, how could Thy true lovers be recognized; and were it not for the trials which are borne for love of Thee, how could the station of such as yearn for Thee be revealed? ... Let me quaff in Thy Cause, O my God and my Master, whatsoever Thou didst desire, and send down upon me in Thy love all Thou didst ordain. By Thy glory! I wish only what Thou wishest, and cherish what Thou cherishest. In Thee have I, at all times, placed My whole trust and confidence.[35]

As a prisoner of the Ottoman Empire, He was further banished from Iraq to Constantinople, Adrianople and finally to the penal colony of 'Akká.

'Akká and the valley of Achor

Bahá'u'lláh's banishment to 'Akká was tantamount to a death sentence because of its foul air and dire conditions:

> 'Akká, the ancient Ptolemais, the St. Jean d'Acre of the Crusaders, that had successfully defied the siege of Napoleon, had sunk, under the Turks, to the level of a penal colony to which murderers, highway robbers and political agitators were consigned from all parts of the Turkish empire. It was girt about by a double system of ramparts ... was devoid of any source of water within its gates; was flea-infested, damp and honey-combed with gloomy, filthy and tortuous lanes. [Bahá'u'lláh has stated] 'it is the most desolate of the cities of the world, the most unsightly of them in appearance, the most detestable in climate, and the foulest in water. It is as though it were the metropolis of the owl.' So putrid was its air that, according to a proverb, a bird when flying over it would drop dead.[36]

Bahá'u'lláh wrote of the fortified city of 'Akká situated in northern Israel:

> Lend an ear unto the song of David. He saith: 'Who will bring me into the Strong City?' The Strong City is 'Akká, which hath been named the Most Great Prison, and which possesseth a fortress and mighty ramparts.[37]

The Prophet Hosea spoke that the Lord through His Mercy would change the valley of Achor, which symbolized trouble, rebellion and treachery[38] to a 'door of hope':

> And there I will give her her vineyards and make the Valley of Achor a door of hope and expectation. (Hos. 2:15)

As it is likely that some may fail to see the association of the valley of Achor with the city of 'Akká, the following details are presented for consideration:

(i) The five references to the valley of Achor (Josh. 7:26; 15:7; Is. 65:10; and Hos. 2:15) do not specify unequivocally the exact location of the valley. Notably, in his commentary, Rev. Albert Barnes states, 'its exact site is uncertain'. Indeed, there is uncertainty about many places named in the Bible 2,500 years ago.

Some presume that the valley of Achor is literally in the vicinity of Jericho, about 30 miles from Jerusalem. Others have written that the valley refers to a ravine to the south of Jericho. 'Akká is a city to the north. Notably, of the 12 minor prophets mentioned in the Bible, only Hosea belonged to the Northern Kingdom of Israel (Samaria). Thus, he has been described as 'a northerner, and he spoke to his own people of the north'.[39] This indicates strongly that Hosea's mention of the valley of Achor referred to a place and conditions in the north and not to a geographical area in the south in the Kingdom of Judah.

(ii) The term 'valley' is often used figuratively in the Bible as a symbol of life and civilization or to describe a state of trouble, spiritual depression and loss of hope, for example Ps. 84:5–6. Thus the advent of John the Baptist was associated with uplifting or raising up of 'every valley'. The valley of Achor means 'the valley of trouble, a place for herds to lie down (Is. 65:10), the valley of trouble for a door of hope (Hos. 2:15), as a way of describing the redemption promised by God'.[40]

(iii) In the Bahá'í Writings, the valley of Achor is associated with the city of 'Akká, not because of the similarity of the names Achor and

'Akká but because of the symbolism associated with the advent of Bahá'u'lláh. Certainly, 'Akká fitted the description of a valley of trouble and affliction, a place where Christians and Muslims fought each other for many years. With the arrival of Bahá'u'lláh it has become a door of hope to many nations (herds).

(iv) The New Testament states that 'no prophecy of the scripture is of any private interpretation'. The right to interpret the abstruse passages of earlier scripture belongs to God's new revelation – the passages of the Hebrew Bible interpreted in the New Testament as referring to Jesus and the First Coming attest to this. For Bahá'ís, 'Abdu'l-Bahá, who was imprisoned and resided in Akká for several years, is the authorized Interpreter of the Bahá'í Faith and the scriptures. This is His interpretation:

> It is recorded in the Torah:[41] And I will give you the valley of Achor for a door of hope. This valley of Achor is the city of 'Akká, and whoso hath interpreted this otherwise is of those who know not.[42]

We also have:

> 'Akká, itself, flanked by the 'glory of Lebanon' and lying in full view of the 'splendor of Carmel', at the foot of the hills which enclose the home of Jesus Christ Himself, had been described by David as 'the Strong City', designated by Hosea as 'a door of hope', and alluded to by Ezekiel as 'the gate that looketh towards the East', whereunto 'the glory of the God of Israel came from the way of the East', His voice 'like a noise of many waters'.[43]

'This Day' of the First Coming has transitioned into 'that Day' of the Second Coming

The Bible refers to the anticipated Redeemer in the Bible as the 'Ancient of Days' (Dan. 7:9, 13, 22). God has expressed His Will through many dispensations.[44] In this connection, the New Testament refers to earlier dispensations as 'long ago', 'past occasions', 'time past', and 'yesterday'

(Heb. 1:2; 13:8); to the Dispensation of Christ and to the First Coming as 'today', 'this day' or 'this hour'(Matt. 6:11; 13:8; John 12:27); and the future revelation of the Lord or Father as 'that day' and 'that hour' (Zeph. 1:15; Amos 5:18; Mark 13:32). The Apostle Paul gave the following warning at the First Coming, an admonishment which is equally relevant today: 'Today, if you hear his voice, do not harden your hearts' (Heb. 4:7 quoting Ps. 95:8).

Bahá'u'lláh thus praises today, the Day that has witnessed the advent of His revelation:

> For this day is the Lord of all days, and whatsoever hath been revealed therein by the Source of divine Revelation is the truth and the essence of all principles. This day may be likened to a sea and all other days to gulfs and channels that have branched therefrom. That which is uttered and revealed in this day is the foundation, and is accounted as the Mother Book and the Source of all utterance. Although every day is associated with God, magnified be His glory, yet these days have been singled out and adorned with the ornament of intimate association with Him, for they have been extolled in the books of the Chosen Ones of God . . . as the 'Day of God'.[45]

> All glory be to this Day, the Day in which the fragrances of mercy have been wafted over all created things, a Day so blest that past ages and centuries can never hope to rival it, a Day in which the countenance of the Ancient of Days hath turned towards His holy seat.[46]

> This is the King of Days . . . the Day that hath seen the coming of the Best-Beloved, Him Who, through all eternity, hath been acclaimed the Desire of the World . . . The Scriptures of past Dispensations celebrate the great jubilee that must needs greet this most great Day of God. Well is it with him that hath lived to see this Day and hath recognized its station.[47]

> Say: O men! This is a matchless Day. Matchless must, likewise, be the tongue that celebrateth the praise of the Desire of all nations, and matchless the deed that aspireth to be acceptable in His sight. The whole human race hath longed for this Day, that perchance it

may fulfil that which well beseemeth its station, and is worthy of its destiny. Blessed is the man whom the affairs of the world have failed to deter from recognizing Him Who is the Lord of all things.[48]

He Who is the King of Kings hath appeared, arrayed in His most wondrous glory, and is summoning you unto Himself, the Help in Peril, the Self-Subsisting. Take heed lest pride deter you from recognizing the Source of Revelation; lest the things of this world shut you out as by a veil from Him Who is the Creator of heaven. Arise, and serve Him Who is the Desire of all nations...[49]

Great indeed is this Day! The allusions made to it in all the sacred Scriptures as the Day of God attest its greatness. The soul of every Prophet of God, of every Divine Messenger, hath thirsted for this wondrous Day. All the divers kindreds of the earth have, likewise, yearned to attain it...[50]

The Kingdom of the Father (the New Jerusalem) has descended from heaven

One viewpoint is that Christ represented the advent of the 'Son' and of a new covenant for the Jews. Jesus taught His followers to pray that the Heavenly Father might hasten His Kingdom, a time when His Purpose would be done 'on earth as it is in heaven' (Matt. 6:10).

To His followers, the Dispensation of Bahá'u'lláh signifies the advent of the Day of the Father. Its import is thus far greater than a literal reappearance of Jesus and a repetition of the day of the Son, as it represents a faith that is the promise of all religions, and addresses the concerns all humanity. Indeed, Jesus portrayed the Second Coming so vividly that His disciples wished to know more about it, even though He was still with them (Matt. 24:3; also Mark 13:4; Luke 21:7). Jesus warned Christians that if they wished to be part of the new divine plan they could not afford to yearn for the past (Luke 9:62). The Apostle Paul rejoiced that they were 'forgetting what lies behind and straining forward to what lies ahead' (Philip. 3:13). The Book of Revelation warns Christians that they will not be harmed by 'the second death' and will suffer spiritual demise if at the Second Coming they do not let go of 'the former things'.

The 'Great Shepherd' has come to feed and unite the flocks

Christ belonged to the lineage of King David, who as a shepherd had tended to the flock of his father. As noted earlier, David refers to the Lord as his shepherd (Ps. 23:1–3). The Prophet Isaiah promised that the Lord Himself will tend His flock (Is. 40:9–11).

Christ referred to Himself figuratively as the good shepherd who cares for the sheep and protects the flock.

The Apostle Peter also refers to the coming of the Chief or Great Shepherd at the Second Coming when they 'will receive the unfading glory' (I Pet. 5:4). Irrespective of the background of their faith, 'everyone who calls upon the name of the Lord shall be saved' (Acts 2:21). Christ also promised that God will establish one fold out of the many flocks:

> I am the good shepherd. The good shepherd lays down his life for the sheep . . . And other sheep I have, which are not of this fold: them also I must bring, and they shall hear my voice; and there shall be one fold, and one shepherd. (John 10:11, 16)

The 'other sheep' in the above passage is likely a reference to the Gentiles. Bahá'u'lláh has facilitated and accelerated that process by announcing that although there are many religions, faith is one: and that faith is now addressing all humanity, declaring its oneness.

The Lord of the vineyard has come to expel the evil husbandmen

In a parable recorded in the Gospel of Matthew, the Dispensation of Moses is depicted as a vineyard planted by God, the Father. He sends His servants (the Prophets) to gather the fruits of divine labour, but they are one by one persecuted or killed. He ultimately sends Jesus, His Son, who is also killed. The parable then warns that when the Father, the Lord of the vineyard, comes He will evict the evil-doers and give the vineyard to more deserving tenants.

> Hear another parable. There was a master of a house who planted a vineyard and put a fence around it and dug a winepress in it and

built a tower and leased it to tenants, and went into another country. When the season for fruit drew near, he sent his servants to the tenants to get his fruit. And the tenants took his servants and beat one, killed another, and stoned another. Again he sent other servants, more than the first. And they did the same to them. Finally he sent his son to them, saying, 'They will respect my son.' But when the tenants saw the son, they said to themselves, 'This is the heir. Come, let us kill him and have his inheritance.' And they took him and threw him out of the vineyard and killed him. When therefore the owner of the vineyard comes, what will he do to those tenants? They said to him, 'He will put those wretches to a miserable death and let out the vineyard to other tenants who will give him the fruits in their seasons.' (Matt. 21:33–41)

It is important to note that, despite all man's trespasses and evil, the Father does not destroy the earth but arranges for it to realize its full potential. The parable has its roots in the Tanakh. The word 'Carmel' means 'the vineyard of God' in Hebrew (Orthodox Jewish Bible: Is. 16:10). Today Mount Carmel, the biblical mountain of the Lord, is the site of the administrative centre of the Bahá'í Faith.

After citing the prophecies of Psalms, Isaiah and Amos concerning 'Akká, Jerusalem, Palestine and Zion, Bahá'u'lláh states:

> Carmel, in the Book of God, hath been designated as the Hill of God, and His Vineyard. It is here that, by the grace of the Lord of Revelation, the Tabernacle of Glory hath been raised. Happy are they that attain thereunto; happy they that set their faces towards it . . .[51]

Notably, after His martyrdom in 1850 in Persia, the remains of the Báb were brought to the Holy Land and have been placed in a shrine on Mount Carmel. Bahá'u'lláh visited Mount Carmel several times while still a prisoner of the Ottoman Empire. At the same time, a German evangelical Protestant sect, the Templers (no relationship to the Templar Crusaders), a splinter group from the Lutheran Church that was persecuted in its homeland, settled in the Holy Land at the urging of its leaders, Christoff Hoffman and David Hardegg, in anticipation of the Second Coming of Christ. The front of one of their buildings in Haifa, at the foot of Mount Carmel, is engraved with a verse in German from

Is. 60:1: 'Arise, shine, for your light has come, and the glory of the Lord has risen upon you.' Another inscription quotes Ps. 87:2: 'The Lord loves the gates of Zion more than all the dwellings of Jacob.' Yet another inscription on a building dated 1871 reads *'Der Herr ist nahe'* or 'The Lord is nigh,' a common refrain in the Bible (Ps. 145:18; Is. 13:6; Zeph. 1:7, 14; Ezek. 30:3; Obad. 1:15, Joel 1:15, 3:14; Philip 4:5; James 5:8).

Many shall run to and fro, and knowledge shall be increased (Daniel 12:4)

This prophecy concerning the 'end of time'[52] is interpreted by some Christian scholars as the great evangelical efforts to proclaim the 'Gospel of the kingdom', 'throughout the world as a testimony to all nations', before the coming of the end (Matt. 24:14):

> **Many shall run to and fro** – Many shall diligently search into these prophecies, and make use of all the means in their power to arrive at a true knowledge of them; shall improve all opportunities of getting their mistakes rectified, their doubts resolved, and their acquaintance with divine things in general, and with these and the other prophecies of God's word in particular, improved and perfected. **And knowledge shall be increased** – By these means great light shall be thrown on every part of divine revelation, and especially on the parts that are prophetic: the more the predictions are accomplished, the better will they be understood; and future ages will receive more instruction and edification from them than we do. The words have an especial reference to gospel days; and the expression of running to and fro, doubtless points to the journeys, voyages, and labours of gospel ministers, whether apostles, evangelists, pastors, or teachers, who should traverse sea and land, and travel from place to place, from country to country, to spread the knowledge of divine truth, and testify the gospel of the grace of God.[53]

Another explanation is that the means of travel and transport, the acquisition of knowledge and the pace of discovery will be vastly accelerated.[54]

He will come like a thief in the night – suddenly and unexpectedly

Perhaps the best indication of the magnitude of the stumbling blocks that Christians will encounter is the frequency of the warnings that most will miss the event for which they have prayed for two thousand years, only learning about it after it has occurred. In this context, the Second Coming is referred to as a 'thief in the night':

> ... you should remember the predictions of the holy prophets and the commandment of the Lord and Savior through your apostles, knowing this first of all, that scoffers will come in the last days with scoffing, following their own sinful desires. They will say, 'Where is the promise of his coming? For ever since the fathers fell asleep, all things are continuing as they were from the beginning of creation.' ...The Lord is not slow to fulfil his promise as some count slowness, but is patient toward you, not wishing that any should perish, but that all should reach repentance. But the day of the Lord will come like a thief, and then the heavens will pass away with a roar, and the heavenly bodies will be burned up and dissolved, and the earth and the works that are done on it will be exposed. (II Pet. 3:2–4, 9–10)

Bahá'u'lláh has come indeed like a thief in the night, with most Christians as yet unaware of His advent and teachings.

The Creative Word of God expressed through His appointed Servant and Divine Physician is again healing the maladies of humanity

A name of God in the Bible is Rapha or 'the Lord Who Heals' (Ex. 15:26; also II Chron. 32:24; Prov. 28:25; Is. 38:16; 57:19; 61:1; Jer. 3:22; 17:14). It is He who 'gives sight to the blind' (Ps. 146:8); and restores faith (Jer. 3:22); and spiritual health (38:16). A 'dewdrop' of His teachings is sufficient to heal humanity spiritually and enlighten them.[55] Such healing is described in association with forgiveness of sins or iniquities (Ps. 103:3); and saving souls from hell (Ps. 30:2–3; Jer. 17:14). Whilst in the process of giving the good news of the coming of the kingdom, Christ cured his listeners of 'every disease and sickness'

(Matt. 9:35). Few would dispute that humanity today requires again the healing power of the Divine Word. Sadly, humanity has so far been slow to accept the Divine prescription for its ills:

> The All-Knowing Physician hath His finger on the pulse of mankind. He perceiveth the disease, and prescribeth, in His unerring wisdom, the remedy. Every age hath its own problem, and every soul its particular aspiration. The remedy the world needeth in its present-day afflictions can never be the same as that which a subsequent age may require. Be anxiously concerned with the needs of the age ye live in, and centre your deliberations on its exigencies and requirements.
>
> We can well perceive how the whole human race is encompassed with great, with incalculable afflictions. We see it languishing on its bed of sickness, sore-tried and disillusioned. They that are intoxicated by self-conceit have interposed themselves between it and the Divine and infallible Physician. Witness how they have entangled all men, themselves included, in the mesh of their devices. They can neither discover the cause of the disease, nor have they any knowledge of the remedy. They have conceived the straight to be crooked, and have imagined their friend an enemy.[56]

Also, a prayer revealed by Bahá'u'lláh reads:

> Thy name is my healing, O my God, and remembrance of Thee is my remedy. Nearness to Thee is my hope, and love for Thee is my companion. Thy mercy to me is my healing and my succour in both this world and the world to come. Thou, verily, art the All-Bountiful, the All-Knowing, the All-Wise.[57]

The creation of unity in diversity – the destiny of mankind

The Prophet Haggai promised the advent of 'the Desire of all nations'[58] when God's house will be filled with glory (King James Version: Hag. 2:7). The Book of Isaiah promises that 'in the latter days' 'all the nations shall flow' to 'the mountain of the house of the Lord' (Is. 2:2–4), and 'all the ends of the earth shall see the salvation of our God' (Is. 52:10). The Lord shall teach his ways to many nations (Micah 4:1–3). All humanity shall come to worship before the Lord (Is. 66:23). A similar prophecy is voiced by the Prophet Zechariah:

> And the Lord will be king over all the earth. On that day the Lord will be one and his name one. (Zech. 14:9)

Christ stated that 'many shall come from the east and the west, and shall sit down with Abraham, and Isaac, and Jacob, in the kingdom of heaven' (Matt. 8:11). He also promised a day when there would 'one fold and one shepherd' (John 10:16). The Book of Revelation predicts that 'every eye shall see him' [perceive Christ on His return] (Rev. 1:7).

True to these promises, the followers of Bahá'u'lláh come from all walks of life, and represent the diverse nationalities and ethnic groups of humanity. As followers of Moses, Christ, and the many other religions of mankind, each and every one of them have come to recognize their new faith as a natural extension of their former religion:

> The Faith of Bahá'u'lláh has assimilated, by virtue of its creative, its regulative and ennobling energies, the varied races, nationalities, creeds and classes that have sought its shadow, and have pledged unswerving fealty to its cause. It has changed the hearts of its adherents, burned away their prejudices, stilled their passions, exalted their conceptions, ennobled their motives, coordinated their efforts, and transformed their outlook. While preserving their patriotism and safeguarding their lesser loyalties, it has made them lovers of mankind, and the determined upholders of its best and truest interests. While maintaining intact their belief in the Divine origin of their respective religions, it has enabled them to visualize the underlying purpose of these religions, to discover their merits, to recognize their sequence, their interdependence, their wholeness and unity, and to acknowledge the bond that vitally links them to itself. This universal, this transcending love which the followers of the Bahá'í Faith feel for their fellow-men, of whatever race, creed, class or nation, is neither mysterious nor can it be said to have been artificially stimulated. It is both spontaneous and genuine. They whose hearts are warmed by the energizing influence of God's creative love cherish His creatures for His sake, and recognize in every human face a sign of His reflected glory.[59]

PART V
RENEWAL AND RESURRECTION

16

BAHÁ'U'LLÁH'S PROCLAMATION

Following more than three thousand years of prayerful expectation in Judaism, two thousand years in Christianity, and fourteen hundred years in Islam, Bahá'u'lláh has announced that the sacred pledges have finally been fulfilled. God has once again 'breathed a new life into every human frame, and instilled into every word a fresh potency'.[1] He has restored and revitalized the spiritual foundations of faith and prescribed a world order based on spiritual principles.

Bahá'u'lláh's general announcement to humankind

With great clarity and forthrightness, Bahá'u'lláh declares in many of His Writings that through Him God has once again revealed His purpose to all humanity:

> The Eternal Truth is now come. He hath lifted up the Ensign of Power, and is now shedding upon the world the unclouded splendor of His Revelation.[2]

> Verily I say, this is the Day in which mankind can behold the Face, and hear the Voice, of the Promised One. The Call of God hath been raised, and the light of His countenance hath been lifted up upon men. It behoveth every man to blot out the trace of every idle word from the tablet of his heart, and to gaze, with an open and unbiased mind, on the signs of His Revelation, the proofs of His Mission, and the tokens of His glory.[3]

Bahá'u'lláh writes that His revelation is the promise of all ages and religions:

> Verily I say, in this most mighty Revelation, all the Dispensations of the past have attained their highest, their final consummation.[4]

> The Revelation which, from time immemorial, hath been acclaimed as the Purpose and Promise of all the Prophets of God, and the most cherished Desire of His Messengers, hath now, by virtue of the pervasive Will of the Almighty and at His irresistible bidding, been revealed unto men. The advent of such a Revelation hath been heralded in all the sacred Scriptures . . .[5]

Individuals are challenged to respond to the divine summons, undeterred by any obstacle that friend or foe may place in their path, fortified with the certitude that the rejection of God's revelation today would be a repudiation of all earlier Prophets and dispensations:

> Verily this is that Most Great Beauty, foretold in the Books of the Messengers, through Whom truth shall be distinguished from error and the wisdom of every command shall be tested. Verily He is the Tree of Life that bringeth forth the fruits of God . . . the people are wandering in the paths of delusion, bereft of discernment to see God with their own eyes, or hear His Melody with their own ears . . . Thus have their superstitions become veils between them and their own hearts and kept them from the path of God . . . Be thou assured in thyself that verily, he who turns away from this Beauty hath also turned away from the Messengers of the past and showeth pride towards God from all eternity to all eternity.[6]

He pleads with humanity:

> How long is chaos and confusion to reign amongst men? How long will discord agitate the face of society? . . . The winds of despair are, alas, blowing from every direction, and the strife that divideth and afflicteth the human race is daily increasing. The signs of impending convulsions and chaos can now be discerned, inasmuch as the prevailing order appeareth to be lamentably defective.[7]

Bahá'u'lláh's call

The prophecies have been fulfilled

Bahá'u'lláh writes:

> Call out to Zion, O Carmel, and announce the joyful tidings: He that was hidden from mortal eyes is come! His all-conquering sovereignty is manifest; His all-encompassing splendour is revealed. Beware lest thou hesitate or halt. Hasten forth and circumambulate the City of God that hath descended from heaven, the celestial Kaaba round which have circled in adoration the favoured of God, the pure in heart, and the company of the most exalted angels. Oh, how I long to announce unto every spot on the surface of the earth, and to carry to each one of its cities, the glad-tidings of this Revelation . . .[8]

> . . . from the heights of the Kingdom the voice of the Son of God is heard proclaiming: 'Bestir yourselves, ye proud ones of the earth, and hasten ye towards Him.' Carmel hath in this day hastened in longing adoration to attain His court, whilst from the heart of Zion there cometh the cry: 'The promise of all ages is now fulfilled. That which had been announced in the holy writ of God, the Beloved, the Most High, is made manifest'. . .By the one true God, Elijah hath hastened unto My court and hath circumambulated in the day-time and in the night-season My throne of glory.'[9]

The invitation could not have been more direct or urgent: the Father is come, open your hearts and minds to Him:

> 'Followers of the Gospel,' Bahá'u'lláh addressing the whole of Christendom exclaims, 'behold the gates of heaven are flung open. He that had ascended unto it is now come. Give ear to His voice calling aloud over land and sea, announcing to all mankind the advent of this Revelation . . . The Father hath come. That which ye were promised in the Kingdom of God is fulfilled. This is the Word which the Son veiled when He said to those around Him that at that time they could not bear it . . . Verily the Spirit of Truth is come to guide you

unto all truth . . . He is the One Who glorified the Son and exalted His Cause . . .' 'The Comforter Whose advent all the scriptures have promised is now come that He may reveal unto you all knowledge and wisdom. Seek Him over the entire surface of the earth, haply ye may find Him.'[10]

> We, verily, have come for your sakes, and have borne the misfortunes of the world for your salvation. Flee ye the One Who hath sacrificed His life that ye may be quickened? Fear God, O followers of the Spirit [Jesus], and walk not in the footsteps of every divine that hath gone far astray . . . He, verily, hath again come down from heaven, even as He came down from it the first time. Beware lest ye dispute that which He proclaimeth, even as the people before you disputed His utterances . . .[11]

Christians are warned not to repeat the apathy, heedlessness and errors of the First Coming. Bahá'u'lláh thus urged the Pope and the entire body of Christians:

> O concourse of Christians! We have, on a previous occasion, revealed Ourself unto you, and ye recognized Me not. This is yet another occasion vouchsafed unto you. This is the Day of God; turn ye unto Him . . . The Beloved One loveth not that ye be consumed with the fire of your desires. Were ye to be shut out as by a veil from Him, this would be for no other reason than your own waywardness and ignorance. Ye make mention of Me, and know Me not. Ye call upon Me, and are heedless of My Revelation . . .[12]

Alluding to the Gospel assertion that whereas many non-Christians will accept the divine revelation, most Christians, the ones for whom the Kingdom of Heaven was primarily intended, will hesitate (Matt. 7:21–23; 8:11–12), He adds:

> O people of the Gospel! They who were not in the Kingdom have now entered it, whilst We behold you, in this day, tarrying at the gate. Rend the veils asunder by the power of your Lord, the Almighty, the All-Bounteous, and enter, then, in My name My Kingdom. Thus biddeth you He Who desireth for you everlasting life . . .

We behold you, O children of the Kingdom, in darkness. This, verily, beseemeth you not. Are ye, in the face of the Light, fearful because of your deeds? Direct yourselves towards Him . . . Verily, He [Jesus] said: 'Come ye after Me, and I will make you to become fishers of men' [Matt. 4:19]. In this day, however, We say: 'Come ye after Me, that We may make you to become the quickeners of mankind.'[13]

Addresses to the ecclesiastical orders of Christendom

Announce thou unto the priests: Lo! He Who is the Ruler is come. Step out from behind the veil in the name of thy Lord, He Who layeth low the necks of all men. Proclaim then unto all mankind the glad-tidings of this mighty, this glorious Revelation. Verily, He Who is the Spirit of Truth is come to guide you unto all truth. He speaketh not as prompted by His own self, but as bidden by Him Who is the All-Knowing, the All-Wise.

Say, this is the One Who hath glorified the Son and hath exalted His Cause. Cast away, O peoples of the earth, that which ye have and take fast hold of that which ye are bidden by the All-Powerful, He Who is the Bearer of the Trust of God. Purge ye your ears and set your hearts towards Him that ye may hearken to the most wondrous Call which hath been raised from Sinai, the habitation of your Lord, the Most Glorious. It will, in truth, draw you nigh unto the Spot wherein ye will perceive the splendour of the light of His countenance which shineth above this luminous Horizon.

O concourse of priests! Leave the bells, and come forth, then, from your churches. It behoveth you, in this day, to proclaim aloud the Most Great Name among the nations. Prefer ye to be silent, whilst every stone and every tree shouteth aloud: 'The Lord is come in His great glory!' Well is it with the man who hasteneth unto Him. Verily, he is numbered among them whose names will be eternally recorded and who will be mentioned by the Concourse on High. Thus hath it been decreed by the Spirit in this wondrous Tablet. He that summoneth men in My name is, verily, of Me, and he will show forth that which is beyond the power of all that are on earth. Follow ye the Way of the Lord and walk not in the footsteps of them that are sunk in heedlessness. Well is it with the slumberer who is stirred by the Breeze of God and ariseth from amongst the dead, directing his steps towards the Way of the Lord. Verily, such a man is regarded, in the sight of God, the True One, as a jewel amongst men and is reckoned with the blissful . . .

O concourse of bishops! Ye are the stars of the heaven of My knowledge. My mercy desireth not that ye should fall upon the earth. My justice, however, declareth: 'This is that which the Son hath decreed.' And whatsoever hath proceeded out of His blameless, His truth-speaking, trustworthy mouth, can never be altered. The bells, verily, peal out My Name, and lament over Me, but My spirit rejoiceth with evident gladness . . .

O concourse of monks! If ye choose to follow Me, I will make you heirs of My Kingdom; and if ye transgress against Me, I will, in My long-suffering, endure it patiently, and I, verily, am the Ever-Forgiving, the All-Merciful . . .

Bethlehem is astir with the Breeze of God. We hear her voice saying: 'O most generous Lord! . . . The sweet savours of Thy presence have quickened me . . . Praised be Thou in that Thou hast raised the veils, and come with power in evident glory.', . . 'O Bethlehem! This Light hath risen in the orient, and traveled towards the occident, until it reached thee in the evening of its life. Tell Me then: Do the sons recognize the Father, and acknowledge Him, or do they deny Him, even as the people aforetime denied Him (Jesus)?'[14]

O concourse of patriarchs! He Whom ye were promised in the Tablets is come. Fear God, and follow not the vain imaginings of the superstitious. Lay aside the things ye possess, and take fast hold of the Tablet of God by His sovereign power. Better is this for you than all your possessions. Unto this testifieth every understanding heart, and every man of insight. Pride ye yourselves on My Name, and yet shut yourselves out as by a veil from Me? This indeed is a strange thing!

Say: O concourse of archbishops! He Who is the Lord of all men hath appeared . . . He calleth mankind, whilst ye are numbered with the dead! Great is the blessedness of him who is stirred by the Breeze of God, and hath arisen from amongst the dead in this perspicuous Name.

Say: O concourse of bishops! . . . He Who is the Everlasting Father calleth aloud between earth and heaven. Blessed the ear that hath heard, and the eye that hath seen, and the heart that hath turned unto Him Who is the Point of Adoration of all who are in the heavens and all who are on earth.[15]

He warned the Christian clergymen not to follow in the footsteps of the Jewish leaders and not to be deterred by the new name of the Promised One:

> Say, O followers of the Son! Have ye shut out yourselves from Me by reason of My Name? Wherefore ponder ye not in your hearts? Day and night ye have been calling upon your Lord, the Omnipotent, but when He came from the heaven of eternity in His great glory, ye turned aside from Him and remained sunk in heedlessness.
> ... How numerous the Pharisees who had secluded themselves in synagogues in His name, lamenting over their separation from Him, and yet when the portals of reunion were flung open and the divine Luminary shone resplendent from the Dayspring of Beauty, they disbelieved in God, the Exalted, the Mighty ... No one from among them turned his face towards the Dayspring of divine bounty except such as were destitute of any power amongst men. And yet, today, every man endowed with power and invested with sovereignty prideth himself on His Name. Moreover, call thou to mind the one who sentenced Jesus to death. He was the most learned of his age in his own country, whilst he who was only a fisherman believed in Him. Take good heed and be of them that observe the warning.
> Consider likewise, how numerous at this time are the monks who have secluded themselves in their churches, calling upon the Spirit, but when He appeared through the power of Truth, they failed to draw nigh unto Him and are numbered with those that have gone far astray. Happy are they that have abandoned them and set their faces towards Him Who is the Desire of all that are in the heavens and all that are on the earth.
> They read the Evangel and yet refuse to acknowledge the All-Glorious Lord, notwithstanding that He hath come through the potency of His exalted, His mighty and gracious dominion. We, verily, have come for your sakes, and have borne the misfortunes of the world for your salvation. Flee ye the One Who hath sacrificed

His life that ye may be quickened? Fear God, O followers of the Spirit, and walk not in the footsteps of every divine that hath gone far astray. Do ye imagine that He seeketh His own interests, when He hath, at all times, been threatened by the swords of the enemies; or that He seeketh the vanities of the world, after He hath been imprisoned in the most desolate of cities? Be fair in your judgement and follow not the footsteps of the unjust.[16]

Summons to Pope Pius IX

Pope Pius IX had the longest pontificate in history, from 1846 until his death in 1878. His reign was marked by increasing conservatism in the face of almost universal European demand for papal reform. He is notable for the declaration of the dogma of the Immaculate Conception in 1854, the publication of the *Syllabus of Errors* in 1864, and sessions of the First Vatican Council which took place from 1869 to 1870, during which the doctrine of papal infallibility was authoritatively defined. In 1870 the forces of King Emmanuel captured Rome and made it the capital of Italy, thereby ending more than a thousand years of temporal domination of the Popes over central Italy. Pope Pius IX came to be known as the 'prisoner of the Vatican',[17] ruling over only 109 acres of land, a small fraction of his previous large domain.

Bahá'u'lláh, whilst a prisoner of the Ottoman Sultan 'Abdu'l-'Azíz, the Caliph of the Sunni Muslim world, wrote an epistle to Pope Pius IX in 1867, and described thus His mission and station:

> O Pope! Rend the veils[18] asunder. He Who is the Lord of Lords is come overshadowed with clouds,[19] and the decree hath been fulfilled by God, the Almighty, the Unrestrained . . . He, verily, hath again come down from Heaven even as He came down from it the first time.[20] Beware that thou dispute not with Him even as the Pharisees disputed with Him [Jesus] without a clear token or proof. On His right hand flow the living waters of grace,[21] and on His left the choice Wine[22] of justice, whilst before Him march the angels of Paradise, bearing the banners of His signs. Beware lest any name[23] debar thee from God, the Creator of earth and heaven. Leave thou the world behind thee, and turn towards thy Lord, through Whom the whole earth hath been illumined [Rev. 21:23–24]

... Dwellest thou in palaces whilst He Who is the King of Revelation liveth in the most desolate of abodes? Leave them unto such as desire them, and set thy face with joy and delight towards the Kingdom.

... Arise in the name of thy Lord, the God of Mercy, amidst the peoples of the earth, and seize thou the Cup of Life with the hands of confidence, and first drink thou therefrom, and proffer it then to such as turn towards it amongst the peoples of all faiths ...

Tear asunder the veils of human learning lest they hinder thee from Him Who is My name, the Self-Subsisting. Call thou to remembrance Him Who was the Spirit [Jesus], Who, when He came, the most learned of His age pronounced judgement against Him in His own country, whilst he who was only a fisherman[24] believed in Him. Take heed, then, ye men of understanding heart! Thou, in truth, art one of the suns of the heaven of His names. Guard thyself, lest darkness spread its veils over thee,[25] and fold thee away from His light ...

Consider those who opposed the Son [Jesus], when He came unto them with sovereignty and power. How many the Pharisees who were waiting to behold Him, and were lamenting over their separation from Him! And yet, when the fragrance of His coming was wafted over them, and His beauty was unveiled, they turned aside from Him and disputed with Him ... None save a very few, who were destitute of any power amongst men, turned towards His face. And yet today every man endowed with power and invested with sovereignty prideth himself on His Name! In like manner, consider how numerous, in these days, are the monks who, in My Name, have secluded themselves in their churches, and who, when the appointed time was fulfilled, and We unveiled Our beauty, knew Us not, though they call upon Me at eventide and at dawn. We behold them clinging to My name, yet veiled from My Self. This, verily, is a strange thing.

... The Word which the Son concealed is made manifest.[26] It hath been sent down in the form of the human temple in this day. Blessed be the Lord Who is the Father! He, verily, is come unto the nations in His most great majesty. Turn your faces towards Him, O concourse of the righteous!

... This is the day whereon the Rock [Peter] crieth out and

shouteth, and celebrateth the praise of its Lord, the All-Possessing, the Most High, saying: 'Lo! The Father is come, and that which ye were promised in the Kingdom is fulfilled!'

... My body hath borne imprisonment that your souls may be released from bondage, and We have consented to be abased that ye may be exalted ... My body longeth for the cross, and Mine head waiteth the thrust of the spear, in the path of the All-Merciful, that the world may be purged from its transgressions ...

O Supreme Pontiff![27] Incline thine ear unto that which the Fashioner of mouldering bones counselleth thee, as voiced by Him Who is His Most Great Name. Sell all the embellished ornaments thou dost possess, and expend them in the path of God, Who causeth the night to return upon the day, and the day to return upon the night. Abandon thy kingdom unto the kings, and emerge from thy habitation, with thy face set towards the Kingdom, and, detached from the world, then speak forth the praises of thy Lord betwixt earth and heaven ... Exhort thou the kings and say: 'Deal equitably with men. Beware lest ye transgress the bounds fixed in the Book.' This indeed becometh thee. Beware lest thou appropriate unto thyself the things of the world and the riches thereof. Leave them unto such as desire them, and cleave unto that which hath been enjoined upon thee by Him Who is the Lord of creation. Should anyone offer thee all the treasures of the earth, refuse to even glance upon them. Be as thy Lord hath been.

... Should the inebriation of the wine of My verses seize thee, and thou determinest to present thyself before the throne of thy Lord, the Creator of earth and heaven, make My love thy vesture, and thy shield remembrance of Me, and thy provision reliance upon God, the Revealer of all power ... .[28]

Bahá'u'lláh's announcement to Christian secular rulers

Napoleon III (1808–1873) and the prediction of the defeat of France

Napoleon III, Emperor of France (Louis-Napoléon Bonaparte) was the nephew of Napoleon I. In 1867, during His banishment in Adrianople, Bahá'u'lláh wrote to this powerful and arrogant Emperor:

> O King of Paris! Tell the priest to ring the bells no longer. By God, the True One! The Most Mighty Bell hath appeared in the form of Him Who is the Most Great Name, and the fingers of the will of thy Lord, the Most Exalted, the Most High, toll it out in the heaven of Immortality, in His Name, the All-Glorious . . .
>
> Give ear, O King, unto the Voice that calleth from the Fire which burneth in this Verdant Tree, upon this Sinai which hath been raised above the hallowed and snow-white Spot, beyond the Everlasting City . . . Arise thou to serve God and help His Cause. He, verily, will assist thee with the hosts of the seen and unseen . . .[29]

The pealing of the bell every Sunday alerts Christians to gather and, amongst other acts of worship, to pray for the Father to send down His Kingdom. Bahá'u'lláh here personifies himself as the 'Bell' which today summons the faithful to enter the Kingdom of God. Furthermore, He asserts here that the same divine voice that addressed Moses and the Jewish people from the 'burning bush' on Mount Sinai is today addressing the Christians and humanity through Him. Furthermore, he writes:

> O King! The stars of the heaven of knowledge have fallen, they who seek to establish the truth of My Cause through the things they possess, and who make mention of God in My Name. And yet, when I came unto them in My glory, they turned aside. They, indeed, are of the fallen. This is, truly, that which the Spirit of God [Jesus] hath announced, when He came with truth unto you, He with Whom the Jewish doctors disputed, till at last they perpetrated what hath made the Holy Spirit to lament, and the tears of them that have near access to God to flow.[30]

Since the Emperor failed to respond, Bahá'u'lláh sent him a second epistle in 1869 from 'Akká warning him of impending catastrophe that would befall his empire. A year later, Napoleon III was defeated and captured by Germany during the Battle of Sedan. Two days after this battle, he was deposed by the French who subsequently declared the Third Republic of France in 1870. He died in exile in England in 1873.

Wilhelm I, King of Prussia (1797–1888) and the prediction of the defeat of Germany

To the Lutheran German Emperor who had defeated Napoleon III, Bahá'u'lláh wrote this warning in 1873:

> O King of Berlin! . . . Do thou remember the one whose power transcended thy power [Napoleon III] and whose station excelled thy station. Where is he? Whither are gone the things he possessed? Take warning, and be not of them that are fast asleep. He it was who cast the Tablet of God behind him, when We made known unto him what the hosts of tyranny had caused Us to suffer. Wherefore, disgrace assailed him from all sides, and he went down to dust in great loss. Think deeply, O King, concerning him, and concerning them who, like unto thee, have conquered cities and ruled over men. The All-Merciful brought them down from their palaces to their graves. Be warned, be of them who reflect.[31]

And in a fateful prediction:

> O banks of the Rhine! We have seen you covered with gore, inasmuch as the swords of retribution were drawn against you; and you shall have another turn. And We hear the lamentations of Berlin, though she be today in conspicuous glory.[32]

Esslemont provides the following insight:

> During the period of German successes in the Great War of 1914–1918, and especially during the last great German offensive in the spring of 1918, this well-known prophecy was extensively quoted by the opponents of the Bahá'í Faith in Persia, in order to discredit Bahá'u'lláh; but when the forward sweep of the victorious Germans was suddenly transformed into crushing, overwhelming disaster, the efforts of these enemies of the Bahá'í Cause recoiled on themselves, and the notoriety which they had given to the prophecy became a powerful means of enhancing the reputation of Bahá'u'lláh.[33]

Francis Joseph (1830–1916), Emperor of Austria–Hungary

Bahá'u'lláh reprimanded the Emperor for not taking the opportunity to investigate His Faith when he had visited 'Akká:

> O Emperor of Austria! He who is the Dayspring of God's Light dwelt in the prison of 'Akká, at the time when thou didst set forth to visit the Aqṣá Mosque [in Jerusalem]. Thou passed Him by, and inquired not about Him, by Whom every house is exalted, and every lofty gate unlocked. We, verily, made it a place whereunto the world should turn, that they might remember Me, and yet thou hast rejected Him Who is the Object of this remembrance, when He appeared with the Kingdom of God, thy Lord and the Lord of the worlds. We have been with thee at all times, and found thee clinging unto the Branch and heedless of the Root. Thy Lord, verily, is a witness unto what I say. We grieved to see thee circle round Our Name, whilst unaware of Us, though We were before thy face. Open thine eyes, that thou mayest behold this glorious Vision, and recognize Him Whom thou invokest in the daytime and in the night season, and gaze on the Light that shineth above this luminous Horizon.[34]

Czar Alexander II (1818–1881)

When Bahá'u'lláh was arrested, the representative in Tehran of the Russian government, Prince Dolgorouki, had attempted to assist him.[35] Addressing the Czar, Bahá'u'lláh acknowledged this and at the same time admonished the Russian potentate thus:

> O Czar of Russia! Incline thine ear unto the voice of God, the King, the Holy . . . Beware lest thy desire deter thee from turning towards the face of thy Lord, the Compassionate, the Most Merciful . . . Whilst I lay chained and fettered in the prison, one of thy ministers extended me his aid. Wherefore hath God ordained for thee a station which the knowledge of none can comprehend except His knowledge. Beware lest thou barter away this sublime station . . .
>
> Beware lest thy sovereignty withhold thee from Him Who is the Supreme Sovereign. He, verily, is come with His Kingdom, and all

the atoms cry aloud: 'Lo! The Lord is come in His great majesty!' He Who is the Father is come, and the Son [Jesus], in the holy vale, crieth out: 'Here am I, here am I, O Lord, My God!', whilst Sinai circleth round the House, and the Burning Bush calleth aloud: 'The All-Bounteous is come mounted upon the clouds! Blessed is he that draweth nigh unto Him, and woe betide them that are far away.'[36]

Queen Victoria (1819–1901), Queen of Great Britain and Empress of India

Bahá'u'lláh rebuked all but one of the monarchs for their unjust practices, their greed, and burdensome excessive military expenditures. He praised Queen Victoria and the British Empire for abolishing the slave trade, saying it had also been forbidden in His revelation:

> We have been informed that thou hast forbidden trading in slaves, both men and women. This, verily, is what God hath enjoined in this wondrous Revelation.[37]

He also commended her for having 'entrusted the reins of counsel' [parliamentary governance] 'into the hands of the people':

> We have also heard that thou hast entrusted the reins of counsel into the hands of the representatives of the people. Thou, indeed, hast done well, for thereby the foundations of the edifice of thine affairs will be strengthened, and the hearts of all that are beneath thy shadow, whether high or low, will be tranquillized. It behoveth them, however, to be trustworthy among his servants, and to regard themselves as the representatives of all that dwell on earth.[38]

Bahá'u'lláh concluded this address with a prayerful invitation – that she open her heart to the Bahá'í revelation. She reportedly responded, 'If this is of God it will endure; if not, it can do no harm.' Victoria's neutral response to the Bahá'í teachings gradually became more emphatically positive over time, from both her country and her progeny. In 1926, one of her granddaughters, the dowager Queen Marie of Romania, accepted Bahá'u'lláh's teachings and became the first monarch to accept the Bahá'í Faith. Queen Marie's declarations of faith reached millions of people when she decided to send letters about the beauty and power of the Bahá'í teachings to hundreds of newspapers.[39]

Immediately after writing His letter to Queen Victoria, Bahá'u'lláh addressed the 'elected representatives of the people in every land', explaining that His mission was to bring the prescriptions for the ills of today that will renew and unify humanity:

> That which the Lord hath ordained as the sovereign remedy and mightiest instrument for the healing of all the world is the union of all its peoples in one universal Cause, one common Faith. This can in no wise be achieved except through the power of a skilled, an all-powerful and inspired Physician. This, verily, is the truth, and all else naught but error . . .
>
> Consider these days in which He Who is the Ancient Beauty hath come in the Most Great Name, that He may quicken the world and unite its peoples.[40]

17

CONTINUITY OF DIVINE PURPOSE: MULTIPLE RELIGIONS BUT ONE COMMON FAITH

E pluribus unum: 'Out of many, one'

Several world religions compete for the attention and allegiance of humanity, each with its own historical narrative, scripture, rituals and traditions. Their rivalries periodically boil over and disturb the peace of mankind. According to one source, religious conflicts now account for most global conflagrations.[1]

A convenient starting point for the study of Judaism and Christianity and the diversity of religious beliefs is their shared conviction that God is the one and single source of their inspiration and teachings.

God is One: He is called by many names and possesses many attributes but has one reality

Judaism

The Hebrew Bible refers to God by several names, including Yahweh (Lord, Jehovah); Adonai (my Lord, my Master); Elohim (God, Mighty Creator); El Shaddai (Lord God Almighty); El-Elyon (The Most High God); El Olam (The Everlasting God); El Roi (the God Who Sees Me); Yahweh-Rapha (the Lord our Healer); and Yahweh Tsebaoth (The Lord of Hosts).

Nevertheless, the Jewish Bible unequivocally states that 'the Lord is God; there is no other besides him' (Deut. 4:35, also, 4:39; 6:4; II Sam. 7:22; I Kings 8:60; Is. 43:10–11; 44:6; 45:14). It further explains that God is infinite but man is finite, and that divine nature and understanding are beyond human comprehension (Job 5:8–9; 11:7–9; 36:26;

Is. 40:28; 55:8–11). It states that what has hitherto been seen of God, and what He has made known 'are but the outskirts of his ways',[2] and merely a 'whisper' (Job 26:14) compared with His full and glorious reality.

God loves His creation (Ps. 86:5) and wishes to give man hope and peace, and assist him to prosper (Jer. 29:11; 31:3). Hence, the divine teachings revealed by His Prophets, embody this love and God's tender mercies (Ps. 147:5, 8). One therefore concludes that the divine beneficence is unlimited, and man's duty to know God and to worship Him is not limited to any one dispensation. He is the source of spirituality and of all good:

> The Lord is my light and my salvation; whom shall I fear? The Lord is the stronghold of my life; of whom shall I be afraid? (Ps. 27:1; also Is. 60:3)

By focusing on the spiritual light in every religion, God simultaneously defines what constitutes spiritual darkness and evil:

> I am the Lord, and there is no other. I form light and create darkness; I make well-being and create calamity; I am the Lord, who does all these things. (Is. 45:6–7)

Christianity

Certainly, it would have been inconceivable for the Jewish Christians to believe that God the Father mentioned in the New Testament was a different Being from Yahweh who had revealed the Torah and sent the earlier Prophets. In addition to the Hebrew names of God which would have been familiar to Jesus and His disciples, such as Eloi or Eli – my God (the words of Jesus on the cross, Mark 15:34); Hashem or the Name (II Cor. 9:7–8) and the Lord Jehovah (Acts 3:24: Aramaic Bible in Plain English), the New Testament also refers to God by several Greek names and attributes: Theos; Kyrios (the Lord or owner); Patēr (πατήρ), the Father of glory (Eph. 1:17) and the Father of spirits (Heb. 12:9: Πατρὶ τῶν πνευμάτων – Patri tōn pneumatōn); the Father of lights (James 1:17: Πατρὶ τῶν φώτων – Patros tōn phōtōn).

Nevertheless, as noted earlier, Jesus identified the *Shema*, a teaching of Moses which unconditionally states that the Lord God is one (Deut. 6:4), as also being the most important principle of His dispensation (Mark 12:28-31).

Christ did not seek to be worshipped by His followers. His purpose was to make 'known'[3] 'the only God' (John 1:18). It would have been contrary to the *Shema* had He simultaneously taught that there was another god besides the Lord. Hence, the Book of Revelation describes Christians as 'priests', not to a dual or triune god, but 'to his [Christ's] God and Father' (Rev. 1:6). The Apostle Paul added that righteousness comes from God but that it had been conveyed through faith in Christ (Rom. 3:22; 10:11-13).

Reasons for the diversity of religious experience

Several explanations may be advanced as to why, if there is one Creator, there are so many religions.

One reason may be that regional religions came to exist because sections of humanity, with dissimilar backgrounds, were separated by vast distances. Clearly, in a contracting world and an increasingly interdependent global society, there is less reason today for having a multiplicity of religious beliefs. Indeed, unity of values and faith would lessen the confusion, misunderstanding and escalating religious hostilities.

Progressive revelation

Perhaps the most important explanation for the multiplicity of religions is that divine truth has been revealed to man not in absolute but in relative terms – not spasmodically, only once, and to only a particular people – but in an evolutionary way. God's teachings have been revealed progressively in steps and according to the needs of a people and the exigencies of time and environment.[4] Thus, the various religions may be regarded as different expressions of the same faith, which is renewed from one dispensation to another.

> [The Bahá'í] teachings revolve around the fundamental principle that religious truth is not absolute but relative, that Divine Revelation is progressive, not final. Unequivocally and without the least reservation it proclaims all established religions to be divine in origin,

identical in their aims, complementary in their functions, continuous in their purpose, indispensable in their value to mankind.[5]

Bahá'u'lláh explains that God prescribes remedies at the appropriate time and for specific spiritual ailments:

> The All-Knowing Physician hath His finger on the pulse of mankind. He perceiveth the disease, and prescribeth, in His unerring wisdom, the remedy. Every age hath its own problem, and every soul its particular aspiration. The remedy the world needeth in its present-day afflictions can never be the same as that which a subsequent age may require. Be anxiously concerned with the needs of the age ye live in, and centre your deliberations on its exigencies and requirements.[6]

The concept of progressive revelation, that is, God has revealed His Will for humanity in increments and through the agency of many mediators, is amplified in the Bahá'í Writings, since the aim of Bahá'u'lláh's teachings is to establish the oneness of mankind; the promotion of the oneness of faith is essential to that effort. However, it is also an important teaching of several religions, including Judaism and Christianity. The Bible is an account of several successive Prophets – each mediator proclaiming the same faith but also foretelling of One to come. Here is a brief summary of some of the Prophets and their predictions. Please note that the chronology is only approximate

Jacob (2200 BCE)	The coming of Shiloh (Gen. 49:10)
Moses (1500 BCE)	Advent of a 'prophet like Moses' (Deut. 18:15–19)
Joel (790–760 BCE)	Advent of the Day of the Lord (Joel 2:1–2, 11)
Hosea (785–725 BCE)	The latter days; Valley of Akka will become a door of hope (Hos. 3:4; 2:15)

Micah (745–725 BCE)	The coming of a Redeemer, the Lord of hosts'; 'the Holy One of Israel' (Micah 7:7,9)
Isaiah (740 BCE)	The coming of the Messiah the king; new Jerusalem; the Judge, the Redeemer, the Mighty God, the Everlasting Father, Prince of Peace; new heavens and a new earth (Is. 2:4; 47:4; 54:5; 59:20)
Jeremiah (628–588 BCE)	The 'righteous Branch' of King David; a new covenant (Jer. 23:5–6; 31:31–33)
Ezekiel (596–574 BCE)	The coming of the Lord God; 'the Glory of the God of Israel'; 'the One Shepherd' (Ezek. 34:23; 37:26–28; 43:4)
Daniel (606–534 BCE)	Death of the Messiah; ' a son of man'; the latter days and the Ancient of Days (Dan. 7:9, 13–14, 22)
Zephaniah (630–620 BCE)	The coming of the great day of the Lord (Zeph. 1:14)
Haggai (520–518 BCE)	The Desire of all nations (Hag. 2:7)
Zechariah (520–510 BCE)	The coming of the King and the Lord (Zech. 9:9–10; 14:9)
Malachi (420–397 BCE)	The return of Elijah; The Sun of Righteousness (Mal 4:2)
Jesus (30–33 CE)	The re-return of Elijah; the return of Christ in the glory of the Father; the advent of the Spirit of truth, the Advocate; the Lord of the vineyard, the Son of man, (Luke 20:9–16; John 14:16–17, 16:12–15)

Every dispensation adds to the spiritual life of humanity

The Book of Isaiah states:

> To whom will he teach knowledge, and to whom will he explain the message? Those who are weaned from the milk, those taken from the breast? For it is precept upon precept, precept upon precept, line upon line, line upon line, here a little, there a little. (Is. 28:9–10)

Christ did not claim to be the exclusive source of divine guidance for all time – instead He said that had come to endow the people with a greater measure of spiritual life (John 10:10). Christians were to wait to attain 'all truth', which would happen at the Second Coming (John 16:12–13). The Apostle Paul reminded his fellow Christians:

> Love never ends. As for prophecies, they will pass away; as for tongues, they will cease; as for knowledge, it will pass away. For we know in part and we prophesy in part, but when the perfect comes, the partial will pass away. When I was a child, I spoke like a child, I thought like a child, I reasoned like a child. When I became a man, I gave up childish ways. For now we see in a mirror dimly, but then face to face. Now I know in part; then I shall know fully, even as I have been fully known. (I Cor. 13:8–12).

He explained that the 'one God' is the 'Father of all' (Eph. 4:6). Ecclesiastes states that there is an appropriate time for everything – every dispensation is prescribed for a certain length of time:

> For everything there is a season, and a time for every matter under heaven: a time to be born, and a time to die; a time to plant, and a time to pluck up what is planted . . . a time to keep, and a time to cast away; a time to tear, and a time to sew; a time to keep silence, and a time to speak . . . (Eccl. 3:1–2, 6–7)

The reality of God's Messengers transcends time – Christ: 'before Abraham was I am'

The Prophets have had a single purpose, which has been to faithfully deliver the divine message. The spiritual component of that message is eternal and one. This is illustrated by the dialogue between Jesus and the Pharisees recorded in the Gospel of John. During the exchange, to the annoyance of the Jewish leaders, who had a literal view of the world and time and space, Christ claimed that His reality existed at the time of Abraham, and indeed pre-existed the ancestral father of the Jews (John 8:56–58). The statement in Hebrews conveys a similar understanding:

> Jesus Christ the same yesterday and today and for ever.[7] (Heb. 13:8)

These verses imply that the divine teachings have been revealed progressively. Throughout, the Christ-like reality has remained the same: the Divine has nourished humanity's spiritual well-being in former times by means of Noah, Abraham, Moses and the other Prophets; through Jesus at the First Coming, and will be re-manifested in future dispensations.

Spiritual and social evolution portrayed allegorically as advances in building materials

> The bricks have fallen, but we will build with dressed stones;[8] the sycamores have been cut down, but we will put cedars in their place. (Is. 9:10)

The explanation given by Rev. Albert Barnes is:

> Bricks, in oriental countries, were made of clay and straw, and were rarely turned. Hence, exposed to suns and rains, they soon dissolved. Walls and houses constructed of such materials would not be very permanent, and to build with them is strongly contrasted with building in a permanent and elegant manner with hewn stone.
>
> The sycamores – These trees grew abundantly on the low lands of Judea, and were very little esteemed . . . They are contrasted with

cedars here – (1) Because the cedar was a much more rare and precious wood. (2) Because it was a much more smooth and elegant article of building. (3) Because it was more permanent. The grain and texture of the sycamore is remarkably coarse and spongy, and could, therefore, stand in no competition with the cedar for beauty and ornament . . .[9]

And, in Isaiah:

> For you shall go out in joy and be led forth in peace; the mountains and the hills before you shall break forth into singing, and all the trees of the field shall clap their hands. Instead of the thorn shall come up the cypress; instead of the brier shall come up the myrtle; and it shall make a name for the Lord, an everlasting sign that shall not be cut off. (Is. 55:12–13)

A time for 'milk' and a time for 'solid food'; and a period of infancy followed by adulthood

I Corinthians explains the progressive nature of revelation allegorically in terms of milk and the type of food consumed by adults. Both foods contain almost identical nutrients, but the former is suitable for the digestive system of a nursing infant, whereas the latter provides more solid nourishment that satisfies an adult:

> However, brothers and sisters, I could not talk to you as to spiritual people, but [only] as to worldly people, mere infants in Christ! I fed you with milk, not solid food; for you were not yet able to receive it. Even now you are still not ready. (Amplified Bible: I Cor. 3:1–2)

Explaining the need for renewal and increased spiritual capacity the Apostle Paul wrote:

> Concerning this we have much to say, and it is hard to explain, since you have become dull and sluggish in (your spiritual) hearing and disinclined to listen. For though by this time you ought to be teachers (because of the time you have had to learn these truths), you actually need someone to teach you again the elementary principles

of God's word (from the beginning), and you have come to be continually in need of milk, not solid food. For everyone who lives on milk is (doctrinally inexperienced and) unskilled in the word of righteousness, since he is a spiritual infant. But solid food is for the (spiritually) mature, whose senses are trained by practice to distinguish between what is morally good and what is evil. (Amplified Bible: Heb. 5:11–14)

Divine teachings are referred to as variable amounts of the water of life

God provides this life-giving water from the heaven of His mercy according to man's needs: thus, is described as 'dew' (Gen. 27:28; Deut. 32:2; Prov. 3:20; Hosea 14:5; Hag. 1:10); 'rain' (Deut. 32:2; Job. 36:27–28; Ecc. 11:3); 'spring,' 'wells,' or 'fountain' (Prov. 14:27; Is. 12:3; 58:11; John 4:14; Rev. 21:6); 'streams' (Is. 35:6; 43:3); 'river' (John 7:38; Rev. 22:1); 'sea' (Amos 8:12; Rev. 21:1); or an 'ocean' (Ps. 36:6).

Revelation as 'Light'

This Divine Light is at the heart of creation. The Hebrew Bible begins with the following command:

> And God said, 'Let there be light,' and there was light . . . And God separated the light from the darkness. (Gen. 1:3–4)

Again, light is light and is measured in the units called photons. However, it is of variable intensity, consisting of a variety of colours of varying wavelengths. Its power may be that of a candle or a lamp (Ps. 18:28) or the sun. From time to time, man rejects the light and descends into spiritual darkness. The Bible is an account of successive Prophets who were sent by God to invite man back to the Light. Christ, the creative Divine Word, is described as the Source of that light: 'in Him was life; and the life was the light of men' (John 1:4). The Gospel of John also declares that the Light that shone through Christ's revelation was the same 'true Light, which lighteth every man that cometh into the world'. (King James Version: John 1:9).

The Bahá'í Writings explain that the Light originates from the same spiritual sun but that its intensity is adapted to the varying needs of mankind

All the Prophets have acted as mediators between God and His creation, and reflected or transmitted His eternal light:

> Likewise, the divine religions . . . are in reality one, though in name and nomenclature they differ. Man must be a lover of the light, no matter from what dayspring it may appear. He must be a lover of the rose, no matter in what soil it may be growing. He must be a seeker of the truth, no matter from what source it come. Attachment to the lantern is not loving the light. Attachment to the earth is not befitting, but enjoyment of the rose which develops from the soil is worthy... The word of truth, no matter which tongue utters it, must be sanctioned . . .[10]

> The Sun of Reality is one Sun, but it has different dawning-places, just as the phenomenal sun is one although it appears at various points of the horizon . . . These daysprings or dawning points differ widely, but the sun is ever the same sun – whether it be the phenomenal or spiritual luminary. Souls who focus their vision upon the Sun of Reality will be the recipients of light no matter from what point it rises, but those who are fettered by adoration of the dawning point are deprived when it appears in a different station upon the spiritual horizon.[11]

The light of the sun of Bahá'u'lláh's revelation is thus the same as that manifested by Moses and Christ, but of greater intensity as it needs to unite all humanity and religions:

> . . . all the Prophets are the Temples of the Cause of God, Who have appeared clothed in divers attire. If thou wilt observe with discriminating eyes, thou wilt behold them all abiding in the same tabernacle, soaring in the same heaven, seated upon the same throne, uttering the same speech, and proclaiming the same Faith. Such is the unity of those Essences of being, those Luminaries of infinite and immeasurable splendor.[12]

> They [Prophets of God] only differ in the intensity of their revelation, and the comparative potency of their light . . .[13]

> It is clear and evident, therefore, that any apparent variation in the intensity of their light is not inherent in the light itself, but should rather be attributed to the varying receptivity of an ever-changing world.[14]

This divinely ordained gradual unfolding of divine light and spiritual truth is in the best interests of man:

> . . . in every Dispensation the light of Divine Revelation hath been vouchsafed unto men in direct proportion to their spiritual capacity. Consider the sun. How feeble its rays the moment it appeareth above the horizon. How gradually its warmth and potency increase as it approacheth its zenith, enabling meanwhile all created things to adapt themselves to the growing intensity of its light. How steadily it declineth until it reacheth its setting point. Were it, all of a sudden, to manifest the energies latent within it, it would, no doubt, cause injury to all created things . . . In like manner, if the Sun of Truth were suddenly to reveal, at the earliest stages of its manifestation, the full measure of the potencies which the providence of the Almighty hath bestowed upon it, the earth of human understanding would waste away and be consumed; for men's hearts would neither sustain the intensity of its revelation, nor be able to mirror forth the radiance of its light.[15]

> At a time when darkness had encompassed the world, the ocean of divine favour surged and His Light was made manifest . . . This, verily, is that Light which hath been foretold in the heavenly scriptures. Should the Almighty so please, the hearts of all men will be purged and purified through His goodly utterance, and the light of unity will shed its radiance upon every soul and revive the whole earth.[16]

> The Day Star of Truth that shineth in its meridian splendour beareth Us witness! . . . Every discerning eye can, in this Day, perceive the dawning light of God's Revelation, and every attentive ear can

recognize the Voice that was heard from the Burning Bush . . . The portals of grace are wide open before the face of all men.[17]

The light of the sun of revelation in the Day of Bahá'u'lláh is predicted to be especially intense, an indication of the spiritual needs of today:

> Moreover, the light of the moon will be as the light of the sun, and the light of the sun will be sevenfold, as the light of seven days, in the day when the Lord binds up the brokenness of his people, and heals the wounds . . . (Is. 30:26)

The scope of the anticipated revelation is to include followers of all religions – a Promised Day when God's Name and Faith will be One. The Bible predicts a Day when all humanity will recognize their one Lord, and His Faith and worship will be one:

> The Lord has bared his holy arm before the eyes of all the nations, and all the ends of the earth shall see the salvation of our God. (Is. 52:10)

> From new moon to new moon, and from Sabbath to Sabbath, all flesh shall come to worship before me, declares the Lord. (Is. 66:23)

> And the Lord will be king over all the earth. On that day the Lord will be one and his name one. (Zech. 14:9)

The concepts of 'return', image' or 'reflection' or 'likeness', and 'revival' are further indications of a sequence of divine revelations

Return

It is clear that by 'return' is not meant the reappearance of the physical form, but the re-manifestation of spiritual attributes:

> . . . a return is indeed referred to in the Holy Scriptures, but by this is meant the return of the qualities, conditions, effects, perfections, and inner realities of the lights which recur in every dispensation.

The reference is not to specific, individual souls and identities.

It may be said, for instance, that this lamplight is last night's come back again, or that last year's rose hath returned to the garden this year. Here the reference is not to the individual reality, the fixed identity, the specialized being of that other rose, rather doth it mean that the qualities, the distinctive characteristics of that other light, that other flower, are present now, in these. Those perfections, that is, those graces and gifts of a former springtime are back again this year. We say, for example, that this fruit is the same as last year's; but we are thinking only of the delicacy, bloom and freshness, and the sweet taste of it; for it is obvious that that impregnable centre of reality, that specific identity, can never return.[18]

John the Baptist: the return of Elijah

Two Prophets are often viewed, unlike Jesus, as having gone to heaven without dying beforehand– Enoch[19] and Elijah (c. 800 BCE: Elias in Greek, a name meaning 'my God is *JAH* or Jehovah', or 'Jehovah is my strength'). Concerning Enoch, Rev. Joseph Benson wrote:

> *Enoch was translated* — μετετέθη, was removed, namely, in a miraculous manner, from among men, God taking him out of this sinful and miserable world to himself. See notes on Genesis 5:22–24. That he should not see death.[20]

Similarly John Albert Bengel's *Gnomen* has the following:

> He was therefore translated from mortality without death to immortality. –(πρὸ, *before*) Construed with εὐηρεστηκέναι, *to have pleased* [He had the testimony that he pleased God before his translation].[21]

While talking to his disciple and successor, Elisha, Elijah was suddenly transported to heaven on a chariot of fire (II Kings 2:11). In the closing verses of the Hebrew Bible the Prophet Malachi promises that Elijah, 'the messenger of the covenant', will return, presumably from heaven, before the coming of the Messiah (Mal. 3:1–2; 4:5–6). Centuries later, when the disciples asked Jesus why Elijah had not physically appeared from heaven, they were told that Elijah would come again in the future, but that the power and spirit of Elijah had also become manifest in John the Baptist (Luke 1:17).

One notes that Christ's prediction 'Elias [Elijah] truly shall first come. And restore all things' (Matt. 17:11) took place after the beheading of John the Baptist, and hence is a reference to yet another Prophet with attributes of Elijah. An explanation is given in *The Pulpit Commentary*:

> Elias truly shall first come (ἔρχεται, cometh). Many of the best manuscripts and editions omit 'first'. The Vulgate has merely, **Elias quidem venturus est.** It is probably inserted in our text from the parallel passage in Mark, where it is certainly genuine. Christ is here alluding to his own second coming, which shall be preceded by the appearance of Elijah in person. This seems to be the plain meaning of the prophecy in Malachi, and of Christ's announcement, and is confirmed by St. John's statement concerning the two witnesses (Revelation 11:3, 6).[22]

Similarly, Ellicott comments:

> ***Elias truly shall first come.*** – Better, *cometh*, Our Lord's words are obviously enigmatic in their form . . . they seem to say that Elijah shall come in person before the yet future day of the Lord, the great second Advent of the Christ.[23]

The similarity between Elijah and John the Baptist was that they were both divine messengers who warned the people and the rulers (King Ahab and King Herod, respectively) of their time.

The return of the sovereignty of King David

As noted earlier, the Hebrew Bible promises the advent of the Messiah, a descendant of King David:

> But they shall serve the Lord their God and David their king, whom I will raise up for them. (Jer. 30:9)

> And I will set up over them one shepherd, my servant David, and

he shall feed them: he shall feed them and be their shepherd. (Ezek. 34:23)

For the children of Israel shall dwell many days without king or prince, without sacrifice or pillar, without ephod or household gods. Afterward the children of Israel shall return and seek the Lord their God, and David their king, and they shall come in fear to the Lord and to his goodness in the latter days. (Hos. 3:4–5)

Clearly, the New Testament teaches that Jesus fulfilled that promise:

The book of the genealogy of Jesus Christ, the son of David, the son of Abraham. (Matt. 1:1)

And behold, you will conceive in your womb and bear a son, and you shall call his name Jesus. He will be great and will be called the Son of the Most High. And the Lord God will give to him the throne of his father David, and he will reign over the house of Jacob forever, and of his kingdom there will be no end. (Luke 1:31–33)

Despite the efforts of the Gospels to link Jesus with King David physically and literally, including through two different depictions of Jesus's genealogy, the two persons could not have been more different – King David had temporal dominion but, in contrast, Jesus did not even have somewhere to lay His head. The return of King David as Christ can therefore be best understood as referring to the return of the spiritual attributes of David, not to the return of his physical being.

Bahá'u'lláh: The return of Christ in the Glory of the Father

Christians have prayed for God the Father to reveal His heavenly Kingdom (Matt. 6:9–10), and they await the return of Jesus Christ in the glory of His Father:

For the Son of Man is going to come with his angels in the glory of his Father, and then he will repay each person according to what he has done. (Matt. 16:27; see also Luke 9:26)

Bahá'u'lláh, referring to Himself, declared to Pope Pius IX: 'He, verily, hath again come down from Heaven even as He came down from it the first time.'[24] Most Christians are, however, unfamiliar with the name of Bahá'u'lláh, and fail to see how He could be a return of Christ. Their initial reaction is to consider that to follow Bahá'u'lláh would be a betrayal of Christ. Jesus, they know, was from Nazareth in Galilee, had spear wounds in His side and nail wounds in His hands and feet, confirmed by the observations of doubting Thomas (John 20:24–29), and was lifted to heaven about 30–33 CE. In contrast, Bahá'u'lláh came from Persia and passed away in 'Akká in 1892 CE. What, they may ask, is the resemblance between the two? In what sense is Bahá'u'lláh the 'return' of Christ?

The return of previous spiritual life and transformation: the reopening of the eyes and ears

The Prophet Isaiah, speaking of receptive souls, stated:

> Bring out the people who are blind, yet have eyes, who are deaf, yet have ears! (Is. 43:8)

Jesus also explained that the light of a new revelation gives sight to some but blinds others:

> Jesus said, 'For judgement I came into this world, that those who do not see may see, and those who see may become blind.' (John 9:39)

Re-manifestation not only of heavenly power, but also of the spiritual darkness, lack of receptivity and opposition and hostility towards God's faith

False expectations can blind individuals to the truth. The Prophet Isaiah predicted that this would be a prominent feature of the First Coming:

> And I heard the voice of the Lord saying, 'Whom shall I send, and who will go for us?' Then I said, 'Here I am! Send me.' And he said, 'Go, and say to this people: "Keep on hearing, but do not understand; keep on seeing, but do not perceive." Make the heart of this people dull, and their ears heavy, and blind their eyes; lest they see

with their eyes, and hear with their ears, and understand with their hearts, and turn and be healed.' (Is. 6:8–10)

Christ stated that this prophecy of Isaiah had been fulfilled in His time (Matt. 13:14–15). A similar lack of faith and receptivity is expected to characterize the Second Coming (Luke 18:8; II Thess. 2:3; II Tim. 4:3–4).

The 'return' of the Divine Spirit in other religions of mankind

There is so much that could be written about the expectations of other religions. Here is a brief synopsis:

Hinduism teaches the re-manifestation of Lord Krishna when evil predominates, and there is a need for righteousness to prosper:

> When Righteousness [Dharma] declines, O Bharata! when Wickedness [adharma] Is strong, I rise, from age to age, and take visible shape, and move a man with men, succouring the good, thrusting the evil back, and setting Virtue on her seat again.[25]

Buddhism teaches the expectation of other Buddhas, and of a Holy One, a Supremely Enlightened One, who will also proclaim righteousness and eternal truths. To His disciple Ananda, Buddha uttered, on His death bed, the following reassuring words:

> Suppressing his tears, Ananda asked Buddha, 'Who shall teach us when You are gone?' 'I am not the first Buddha to come upon earth; nor shall I be the last. In due time, another Buddha will arise in this world, a Holy One, a Supremely Enlightened One, endowed with wisdom . . . He will reveal to you the same Eternal Truths which I have taught you. He will proclaim a religious life, wholly perfect and pure; such as I now proclaim.' 'How shall we know him?' asked Ananda. The Buddha replied, 'He will be known as Maitreya which means kindness or friendliness.'[26]

In *Islam*, every *ummah* (such as *ummat al-Islám*, the Islamic community) has a preordained end but there is no finality to faith:

> ... when their appointed term is completed they cannot delay it an hour, nor can they advance it. O children of Adam! Verily, there will come to you apostles from amongst you, narrating unto you my signs; then whoever fears God and does what is right, there is no fear for them, nor shall they grieve. (Qur'án 7:34–35, trans. Edward Henry Palmer)

> If all the trees on the earth were pens, and the sea replenished with seven more seas [were ink], the words of God would not be spent. Indeed God is All-Mighty, All-Wise. (Qur'án 31:27)

> None of Our revelations do We abrogate or cause to be forgotten, but We substitute something better or similar: Knowest thou not that God Hath power over all things? (Qur'án 2:106)

Image, reflection or likeness

The creation of men and women in the image or likeness of God

> Then God said, 'Let us make man in our image, after our likeness...'
> So God created man in his own image, in the image of God he created him; male and female he created them. (Gen. 1:26–27)

If taken literally, this statement does not make sense, as God's image cannot mirror both genders and the diverse forms of humanity. Further, God is invisible and the Bible mostly conveys Him through metaphors.

However, Michelangelo, intent on portraying physical forms, was not deterred by these constraints when he painted the creation of Adam on the ceiling of the Sistine Chapel at the Vatican. He painted God as a man in a gown with white hair and a long beard, indicating ancient age, surrounded by a bevy of angelic forms – a great artistic achievement but depictions that some would regard as blasphemous and clear violations of the second commandment:

> You shall not make for yourself a carved image, or any likeness of anything that is in heaven above, or that is in the earth beneath, or that is in the water under the earth. (Ex. 20:4)

According to Bahá'í understanding, this 'likeness' indicates the potential of every man and woman to reflect the divine attributes such as love, unity, forbearance, compassion, mercy and truthfulness:

> According to the words of the Old Testament God has said, 'Let us make man in our image, after our likeness.' This indicates that man is of the image and likeness of God – that is to say, the perfections of God, the divine virtues, are reflected or revealed in the human reality. Just as the light and effulgence of the sun when cast upon a polished mirror are reflected fully, gloriously, so, likewise, the qualities and attributes of Divinity are radiated from the depths of a pure human heart.[27]

> ... in [man] are potentially revealed all the attributes and names of God...[28]

> They whose hearts are warmed by the energizing influence of God's creative love cherish His creatures for His sake, and recognize in every human face a sign of His [God's] reflected glory.[29]

Another likeness mentioned in the Bible is a return to conditions that prevailed in the day of Noah:

> For as were the days of Noah, so will be the coming of the Son of Man. For as in those days before the flood they were eating and drinking, marrying and giving in marriage, until the day when Noah entered the ark, and they were unaware until the flood came and swept them all away, so will be the coming of the Son of Man. (Matt. 24:37–39)

Expectation of a Prophet like Moses

Towards the end of His life Moses informed His followers that they would not have to consult diviners (soothsayers) in the future as God would provide them with a Prophet Who would guide them with spiritually:

> The Lord your God will raise up for you a prophet like me from among you, from your brothers – it is to him you shall listen – just

as you desired of the Lord your God at Horeb on the day of the assembly, when you said, 'Let me not hear again the voice of the Lord my God or see this great fire any more, lest I die.' And the Lord said to me, 'They are right in what they have spoken. I will raise up for them a prophet like you from among their brothers. And I will put my words in his mouth, and he shall speak to them all that I command him. And whoever will not listen to my words that he shall speak in my name, I myself will require it of him. But the prophet who presumes to speak a word in my name that I have not commanded him to speak, or who speaks in the name of other gods, that same prophet shall die.' And if you say in your heart, 'How may we know the word that the Lord has not spoken?'– when a prophet speaks in the name of the Lord, if the word does not come to pass or come true, that is a word that the Lord has not spoken; the prophet has spoken it presumptuously. You need not be afraid of him. (Deut. 18:15–22)

The above passage is understood in one of two ways: (1) God will raise up not an individual but a succession of Prophets for the instruction of His people; and (2) the text speaks of one Prophet and not of many. Second, the Messiah, and none other, was the same stature (like unto) as Moses (Deut. 34:10; Num. 12:6–8).[30] Some therefore understand that the prophecy refers to Christ[31] and the other Prophets of succeeding dispensations.

Christ as the image of God, reflected in the divine mirror

Hebrews states that God had again disclosed His purpose through Jesus, Who was a 'reflection of God's glory], and 'the exact likeness of God's own being'.[32] Colossians (1:15) also portrays Jesus as 'the image of the invisible God' – clearly an oxymoron if interpreted literally. But the statements do make sense if they are understood as referring to Christ's mission to reveal the attributes and perfections of God, and to express His Will and Purpose.

'That Day' and 'that Hour' of the Second Coming destined to mirror 'this Day' and 'this Hour' of the First Coming

'That day' in the Hebrew Bible (Is. 2:11 and 17: 24:21; 26:1–2; 52:6; Zech. 9:16) may refer to the day of the Messiah (Christ). However, we find that the New Testament continues to use the phrases 'that Day' and 'that Hour' to refer to a future time:

> But the hour is coming, and is now here, when the true worshippers will worship the Father in spirit and truth, for the Father is seeking such people to worship him. God is Spirit: and those that worship him must worship in spirit and truth. (John 4:23–24)

> Behold, the hour is coming, indeed it has come,[33] when you will be scattered, each to his own home, and will leave me alone. (John 16:32; also, Matt. 24:36; John 16:23).

Thus, one reasonable explanation is that the First and Second Coming of Christ mirror one another.

Christ also used the phrase 'shall come and is come already' to indicate similarities between the advent of the original Elijah, the return of Elijah as John the Baptist, and a re-return of Elijah in the future (Matt. 17:11–12).

Revival

As noted earlier, 'life' denotes spiritual life bestowed through the revelation of divine teachings and conversely, 'death' is the extinction of spiritual life. Restoration of faith and spiritual life by a new revelation, referred to as reanimation, resuscitation, resurrection, rebirth, quickening or to be made alive again, healing, and return to righteousness, is an important theme of the Scripture.

In Judaism, the Psalmist prayed: 'Create in me a clean heart, O God; and renew a right spirit within me' (Ps. 51:10). He appealed:

> . . . give us life, and we will call upon your name! Restore us, O Lord God of hosts! Let your face shine, that we may be saved! (Ps. 80:18–19)

He supplicated God to grant His salvation and revive the Jewish people so that they could rejoice again (Ps. 85:6–7). The Prophet Habakkuk pleaded with God that, in His righteous wrath, He should remember His mercy and revive His works (Hab. 3:2).

This revival occurred at the First Coming. The Apostle Paul described the early Christians as having been dead in (spiritual) transgressions, but being revived by 'God, who is rich in mercy', because of 'his great love' for them (Eph. 2:4).

The Gospels certainly anticipate a further darkening of the spiritual horizons; the spiritually dead cannot resuscitate anyone (Matt. 8:22) and the blind make others similarly affected to go in the wrong direction (Matt. 15:14). Only through the power of the creative Word of God can the dead rise again from their tombs of heedlessness and the blind see the Divine light. Thus, the Apostle Peter entreated individuals to 'repent', to 'turn back' and to return to God, so that 'the times of refreshing may come from the presence of the Lord' (Acts 3:19–20).

Rebirth of religions

> These divinely-revealed religions . . . are doomed not to die, but to be reborn . . . Does not the child succumb in the youth and the youth in the man; yet neither child nor youth perishes?[34]

In this connection Bahá'u'lláh has written:

> We can well perceive how the whole human race is encompassed with great, with incalculable afflictions. We see it languishing on its bed of sickness, sore-tried and disillusioned. They that are intoxicated by self-conceit have interposed themselves between it and the Divine and infallible Physician. Witness how they have entangled all men, themselves included, in the mesh of their devices. They can neither discover the cause of the disease, nor have they any knowledge of the remedy. They have conceived the straight to be crooked, and have imagined their friend an enemy.
>
> Incline your ears to the sweet melody of this Prisoner. Arise, and lift up your voices, that haply they that are fast asleep may be awakened. Say: O ye who are as dead! The Hand of Divine bounty proffereth unto you the Water of Life. Hasten and drink your

fill. Whoso hath been reborn in this Day, shall never die; whoso remaineth dead, shall never live.[35]

Progressive revelation: Different Prophets or Messengers proclaiming the same Faith

Hebrews reminded the Jews that the divine message had been revealed 'at sundry times' and 'in diverse manners' (Heb. 1:1). The sequence of Prophets in the Bible, including Christ, illustrates undeniably that God has revealed His purpose and educated mankind progressively. As a follow-up, Christ stated that there were more truths yet to be revealed, but that it was not timely to do so, and that there would be further revelations through the 'Spirit of truth' and the 'Comforter' (John 16:12–14). He therefore gave instruction to His followers to pray for the Day when the Father would establish His Heavenly Kingdom on earth where His Will shall be done (Matt. 6:10). He spoke of His teachings as the spiritual 'bread' that comes down from the Heaven of Divine Will (John 6:51). Humanity is preoccupied in obtaining physical bread. Christ taught His followers to pray for the daily bread (Matt. 6:11) – that is in addition to physical sustenance, the spiritual nourishment that is offered to mankind in every Day of God or divine dispensation:

> The Spirit breathing through the Holy Scriptures is food for all who hunger. God Who has given the revelation to His Prophets will surely give of His abundance daily bread to all those who ask Him faithfully.[36]

Jesus explained that there is room for everyone in the Kingdom of the Father – presumably, this includes the followers of all faiths:

> In my Father's house are many rooms.[37] If it were not so, would I have told you that I go to prepare a place for you? (John 14:2)

Multiple flocks of sheep destined to be united and fed by one Chief Shepherd

The Hebrew Bible describes the Lord as a Shepherd (Ps. 23:1), and His creation as the sheep of His pasture (Ezek. 34:31). He shall in due time feed His flock (Is. 40:11). In Christ's time the flock consisted primarily of the Jews. Hence, He explained that His disciples should preach primarily to the Jews who were wandering like sheep without a shepherd:

> These twelve Jesus sent out, instructing them, 'Go nowhere among the Gentiles and enter no town of the Samaritans, but go rather to the lost sheep of the house of Israel.' (Πορεύεσθε δὲ μᾶλλον πρὸς τὰ πρόβατα τὰ ἀπολωλότα οἴκου Ἰσραήλ) (Matt. 10:5–6)

Again,

> He answered [the Canaanite woman], 'I was sent only to the lost sheep of the house of Israel.' (Matt. 15:24]

Rev. Albert Barnes explains:

> The 'lost sheep of the house of Israel' were the Jews. He came first to them. He came as their expected Messiah. He came to preach the gospel himself to the Jews only. Afterward it was preached to the Gentiles, but the ministry of Jesus was confined almost entirely to the Jews.[38]

Christ elaborates in the Gospel of John that there were other sheep that belonged to other flocks, and were cared for by other shepherds. He anticipated that a day would come when all of these flocks would receive their guidance from one shepherd (John 10:16).

I Peter (5:4) reminds Christians that when the Chief (Great) Shepherd (Greek: Ἀρχιποίμενος, Archioimenos – an overseer of the shepherds when the flocks became too large to be handled by single shepherds) they will receive an unfading crown of glory.[39] This Chief Shepherd would represent the return of Christ, Jesus having after His ascension been described as 'the great shepherd of the sheep' (Heb. 13:20).

As we have seen, the Bahá'í explanation is that God's Faith is a living religion that evolves and grows.[40] By way of analogy, it sees the teachings of Moses as the 'bud', those of Christ as the 'flower', and those of Bahá'u'lláh as the 'fruit'.[41] The flower may be regarded as the fulfilment of the purpose of the bud, and the fruit as the fulfilment of the purpose of both the bud and the flower. The bud's scales must fall in order that the flower may bloom, and the petals must fall in order that the fruit may grow and ripen. It is not because the bud's scales and the petals were 'wrong' or did not serve their purpose that they had to be discarded, for without the bud there would be no flower and without the bud and the flower there would be no fruit. The flower is thus the transformation of the bud, not its annihilation, and the fruit does not signify the destruction of the bud and the flower, but their natural evolution. Similarly, the external features of God's religion may change from age to age, but each revelation represents the fulfilment of its predecessors and not their destruction – they are not separate or incongruous, but different stages in the life history of One Faith, which has in turn been revealed as a seed, as a bud and as a flower, and enters the stage of fruition:

> There are certainly wide differences among the world's major religious traditions with respect to social ordinances and forms of worship. Given the thousands of years during which successive revelations of the Divine have addressed the changing needs of a constantly evolving civilization, it could hardly be otherwise. Indeed, an inherent feature of the scriptures of most of the major faiths would appear to be the expression, in some form or other, of the principle of religion's evolutionary nature . . .
>
> It may be objected that, if all the great religions are to be recognized as equally Divine in origin, the effect will be to encourage, or at least to facilitate, the conversion of numbers of people from one religion to another. Whether or not this is true, it is surely of peripheral importance when set against the opportunity that history has at last opened to those who are conscious of a world that transcends this terrestrial one – and against the responsibility that this awareness imposes.[42]

Each successive dispensation accepts its predecessor, and affirms their common moral and ethical truths, but endows God's nascent Faith with a new spiritual vigour and life. Each modifies or abrogates earlier social principles and laws in accordance with the changing times and conditions, but enjoins that its own precepts be kept sacrosanct during its particular period. Hence the phrases used in the Bible, such as 'forever' and 'throughout your generations' are to be understood as enjoining observance of the law for the duration of a particular age.[43]

CONTINUITY OF DIVINE PURPOSE: MULTIPLE RELIGIONS BUT ONE COMMON FAITH

Indeed, an important reason for the polarization of both the Jewish and Christian communities into conservative (fundamentalist, orthodox) and liberal factions is the conservative group's insistence that the social rules and regulations must continue to be followed, even after their expiration date. Conversely, the liberal factions, concerned that many of the laws are no longer applicable today, alter them according to their whim. However, if changes are necessary they are more appropriately prescribed by God alone.

> Religion is the outer expression of the divine reality. Therefore it must be living, vitalized, moving and progressive. If it be without motion and non-progressive it is without the divine life; it is dead. The divine institutes are continuously active and evolutionary; therefore, the revelation of them must be progressive and continuous. All things are subject to reformation. This is a century of life and renewal. Sciences and arts, industry and invention have been reformed. Law and ethics have been reconstituted, reorganized. The world of thought has been regenerated. Sciences of former ages and philosophies of the past are useless today. Present exigencies demand new methods of solution; world problems are without precedent. Old ideas and modes of thought are fast becoming obsolete. Ancient laws and archaic ethical systems will not meet the requirements of modern conditions, for this is clearly the century of a new life . . .
>
> From the seed of reality, religion has grown into a tree which has put forth leaves and branches, blossoms and fruit. After a time this tree has fallen into a condition of decay. The leaves and blossoms have withered and perished; the tree has become stricken and fruitless. It is not reasonable that man should hold to the old tree, claiming that its life forces are undiminished, its fruit unequalled, its existence eternal. The seed of reality must be sown again in human hearts in order that a new tree may grow therefrom and new divine fruits refresh the world. By this means the nations and peoples now divergent in religion will be brought into unity, imitations will be forsaken and a universal brotherhood in the reality itself will be established.[44]

Hence, the Bahá'í Faith cannot accept that any particular religion or Prophet is superior to others, nor does it accept that any of the dispensations is the final Word of God: 'The Bahá'í Faith upholds the unity of God, recognizes the unity of His Prophets, and inculcates the principle of the oneness and wholeness of the entire human race.'[45] It acknowledges that the station of the Prophets of God is beyond human experience and understanding, and sanctified above all comparisons. To speculate on their nature is futile, as they manifest the attributes of an infinite and unknowable One God. Their revelations are not for personal profit or self-aggrandizement. They are all obedient to the Will of Him Who sent Them.

The Gospel of Matthew and the progressive nature of divine revelation

The first four chapters of Matthew deal mainly with the genealogy of Christ and His early life. Chapter 5 of the Gospel of Matthew is devoted almost entirely to Jesus's teachings and how they relate to the Law of Moses:

1. Christians must be ready to investigate the truth which in part entails an admission of their spiritual poverty:

> Blessed are the poor in spirit . . . Blessed are those who hunger and thirst for righteousness . . . Blessed are the pure in heart . . . (Matt. 5:3, 6 and 8).

2. There has to be a spiritual preparedness – His followers were to be true to the moral laws that had been revealed earlier:

> Therefore whoever relaxes one of the least of these commandments and teaches others to do the same will be called least in the kingdom of heaven, but whoever does them and teaches them will be called great in the kingdom of heaven. For I tell you, unless your righteousness exceeds that of the scribes and Pharisees, you will never enter the kingdom of heaven. (Matt. 5:19–20)

Christ did not wish to add to the Laws of the Torah, but instead, He discouraged the Jews from following the letter of the Law blindly, emphasizing the spiritual aspects of the teachings. He thus fulfilled the intent of the Law, training at the same time His disciples to become more perfect and more righteous than the teachers of the Law. The Jewish leaders, in contrast, were inattentive to the spiritual transformation that was necessary if their followers were to receive the Word of God through Jesus Christ. Instead, they were preoccupied with examining and discussing the minutiae of the Law, an effort that provided them with their stature in the community and paid for their upkeep. Over the past centuries the church has also distorted the original message of Christ and introduced many innovations into Christian belief.

3. Christ's teaching was to renew and elaborate on the virtues of the Faith of Moses. Beyond what the Law had dictated, He encouraged individuals to correct their own shortcomings and to improve their spirituality.

> . . . if you greet only your brothers, what more are you doing than others? Do not even the Gentiles do the same? You therefore must be perfect, as your heavenly Father is perfect. . . (Matt. 5:47–48).

He did however, modify some aspects of the Law. In certain cases He made it even more binding; for example, the Torah's Seventh Commandment 'Thou shalt not commit adultery' (Ex. 20:14) was made more stringent by Christ's teaching that one commits adultery if he looks at a woman lustfully (Matt. 5:27–28), rendering discussion of other sexual offences superfluous. He annulled divorce except on the grounds of sexual immorality (Greek: πορνείας, porneias) (Matt. 5:31–32),[46] asked His followers not to retaliate against evil (Matt. 5:39) and to settle disputes quickly rather than litigate (Matt. 5:25).

4. Christ often prefaced His amplifications or modifications to the Law by stating, 'You have heard that it was said by them of old time,' clearly indicating that His power to make the changes to the Law was identical to that of Moses (Matt. 5: 21, 27, 31, 33 and 38).

5. One may also reflect on who was responsible for the initial teachings which Christ referred to as being 'of old time'. Clearly, they originated with God and not with Moses, for it is stated plainly that God 'put [His] words' in the mouth of Moses and Moses spoke 'all that God commanded Him' (Deut. 18:18).

Again, one may ask who is the 'I' in 'But I say unto you . . .'? Once again the answer is not Jesus but God, because Christ also declared that 'the word which ye hear is not mine, but the Father's which sent me' (John 14:24). As the Father spoken of by Jesus was one and the same as the Yahweh referred to by Moses, it was God Who was responsible for the original teachings, deemed to be eternal, and the changes to His own Law in the new dispensation.

It may then be asked why the new truths revealed by Jesus were omitted from God's original message. It would be unlikely that God's practice and knowledge had improved in the interim millennium and that consequently He was now capable of revealing greater truths and a superior covenant. The only reasonable conclusion is that the Dispensation of Moses allowed the Jews to grow spiritually so that they could receive the new revelation to humanity that was now conducive to their further spiritual and material advancement, and more in keeping with the enhanced social, intellectual and spiritual capacity of a larger and more learned community of mankind.

6. It may be argued that the Western Christian democracies have not adhered to several of the social teachings of Christ. A couple of examples may suffice to make this point.

The predilection to sue and to engage in adversarial legal practices are contrary to Christ's teaching of forbearance (Matt. 5:25):

> Not in regard to acts of violence only, but also in dealing with the petty litigation that disturbs so many men's peace, it is better to yield than to insist on rights. St. Paul gives the same counsel to the believers at Corinth: 'Why do ye not rather suffer yourselves to be defrauded?' (1 Cor. 6:7)[47]

Matt. 5:42: 'Give to the one who begs from you, and do not refuse the one who would borrow from you' has been debated:

> **Give to him that asketh thee:** This verse has been often adduced by unbelievers to prove the incompatibility of our Lord's utterances with the conditions of modern society. Wrongly. Because our Lord is inculcating the proper spirit of Christian life, not giving rules to be literally carried out irrespective of circumstances.[48]

Conversely, others have stated that modern banking practices of borrowing and lending are not in keeping with these teachings:

> **From him that would borrow.** – The force of the precept depends on its connection with the Jewish Law, which forbade not only what we call usury, i.e., excessive interest, but all interest on loans where debtor and creditor alike were Israelites (Exodus 22:25; Leviticus 25:37; Deuteronomy 23:19–20). From our modern point of view that law cannot be regarded as in harmony with the present order of society, nor consistent with our modern views of financial justice.[49]

7. Every dispensation introduces a new covenant. An understanding that is implicit in this early chapter of the Gospel of Matthew is that the old covenant, described in Hebrews as consisting largely of 'regulations for worship and an earthly place of holiness' (Heb. 9:1) and representing 'regulations for the body imposed until the time of reformation' (Heb. 9:10) should give way to the new covenant:

> In speaking of a new covenant, he makes the first one obsolete. And what is becoming obsolete and growing old is ready to vanish away. (Heb. 8:13)

As noted by the church father Augustine, Bishop of Hippo, this is akin to an alteration in the condition of a patient which demands a change in the prescription:

> The eminent physician of our own times, Vindicianus, being consulted by an invalid, prescribed for his disease what seemed to him a suitable remedy at that time; health was restored by its use. Some years afterwards, finding himself troubled again with the same disorder, the patient supposed that the same remedy should be applied; but its application made his illness worse. In astonishment, he again returns to the physician, and tells him what had happened; whereupon he, being a man of very quick penetration, answered: The reason of your having been harmed by this application is, that I did not order it . . . When he was afterwards questioned by some who were amazed at his words, he explained what they had not understood, namely, that he would not have prescribed the same

remedy to the patient at the age which he had now attained. While, therefore, the principle and methods of art remain unchanged, the change which, in accordance with them, may be made necessary by the difference of times is very great.[50]

Surely, these pragmatic considerations also apply to many of the church traditions today.

8. The interval between the time that God spoke through Moses ('old time') and when Christ spoke ('but now I say unto you') was allegedly about 1,500 years. Thus one may ask whether, after a lapse of a further 2,000 years, the time has not finally come for the God Who revealed the two earlier dispensations to update His purpose and renew His covenant, thus eliminating the need for religious leaders to make their own changes. If it were possible for the Faith of God to be reformed by human beings, there would surely have been no need for the revelation of Christ.

This step by step unfolding of the divine purpose, referred to as progressive revelation in the Bahá'í Writings, is a harmonizing principle of faith

By acknowledging the contribution of all major religions to the advancement of the spiritual evolution of mankind, the root cause of religious intolerance is eliminated. It thus promotes reconciliation, unity and amity. Bahá'ís 'view all the Prophets and Messengers of God as one soul and one body, as one light and one spirit':[51]

> It is clear and evident . . . that all the Prophets are the Temples of the Cause of God, Who have appeared clothed in divers attire. If thou wilt observe with discriminating eyes, thou wilt behold them all abiding in the same tabernacle, soaring in the same heaven, seated upon the same throne, uttering the same speech, and proclaiming the same Faith.[52]

> These Countenances [Divine Manifestations] are the recipients of the Divine Command, and the day-springs of His Revelation. This Revelation is exalted above the veils of plurality and the exigencies of number.[53]

> The foundations of all the divine Prophets and Holy Books are one. The difference among them is one of terminology only. Each springtime is identical with the former springtime. The distinction between them is only one of the calendar – 1911, 1912 and so on. The difference between a Christian and a Bahá'í, therefore, is this: There was a former springtime, and there is a springtime now. No other difference exists because the foundations are the same. Whoever acts completely in accordance with the teachings of Christ is a Bahá'í. The purpose is the essential meaning of Christian, not the mere word. The purpose is the sun itself and not the dawning points. For though the sun is one sun, its dawning points are many. We must not adore the dawning points but worship the sun. We must adore the reality of religion and not blindly cling to the appellation Christianity . . . Be seekers of light, no matter from which lantern it shines forth. Be not lovers of the lantern . . .[54]

The aim of religion is to assist humanity in its struggle to reverse the disintegration that has set in, and to continue its progress towards the Light:

> To contend that any particular religion is final, that 'all Revelation is ended, that the portals of Divine mercy are closed, that from the daysprings of eternal holiness no sun shall rise again, that the ocean of everlasting bounty is forever stilled, and that out of the Tabernacle of ancient glory the Messengers of God have ceased to be made manifest' would indeed be nothing less than sheer blasphemy.[55]

The Bahá'í Writings explain that the elimination of the estrangement afflicting the various sections of humanity is an important function of the Bahá'í Faith today:

> And among the teachings of Bahá'u'lláh is the oneness of the world of humanity; that all human beings are the sheep of God and He is the kind Shepherd. This Shepherd is kind to all the sheep, because He created them all, trained them, provided for them and protected them. There is no doubt that the Shepherd is kind to all the sheep, and should there be among these sheep ignorant ones, they must be educated; if there be children, they must be trained until they

reach maturity; if there be sick ones, they must be cured. There must be no hatred and enmity . . . religion must be the cause of fellowship and love. If it becomes the cause of estrangement then it is not needed, for religion is like a remedy; if it aggravates the disease then it becomes unnecessary.[56]

A stated goal of the revelation of Bahá'u'lláh, indeed its primary purpose, is therefore to enable Jews and Christians to become better acquainted with the purpose of Judaism and Christianity. Focusing on scripture and the fundamentals of faith, we realize the unity of the religions. It follows that by accepting the Faith of Bahá'u'lláh, Bahá'ís in no way reject their former religions, but come to recognize that the new revelation represents the fulfilment and latest expression of their earlier affiliation. If anything, their faith in their previous religion becomes confirmed, because they see the Bahá'í Faith as the latest stage in the evolution of an eternal faith – a faith that today is 'at once the essence, the promise, the reconciler, and the unifier of all earlier religions'.[57]

> . . . the Revelation identified with Bahá'u'lláh abrogates unconditionally all the Dispensations gone before it, upholds uncompromisingly the eternal verities they enshrine, recognizes firmly and absolutely the Divine origin of their Authors, preserves inviolate the sanctity of their authentic Scriptures, disclaims any intention of lowering the status of their Founders or of abating the spiritual ideals they inculcate, clarifies and correlates their functions, reaffirms their common, their unchangeable and fundamental purpose, reconciles their seemingly divergent claims and doctrines, readily and gratefully recognizes their respective contributions to the gradual unfoldment of one Divine Revelation, unhesitatingly acknowledges itself to be but one link in the chain of continually progressive Revelations, supplements their teachings with such laws and ordinances as conform to the imperative needs, and are dictated by the growing receptivity, of a fast evolving and constantly changing society, and proclaims its readiness and ability to fuse and incorporate the contending sects and factions into which they have fallen into a universal Fellowship, functioning within the framework, and in accordance with the precepts, of a divinely conceived, a world-unifying, a world-redeeming Order.[58]

Indeed one cannot espouse the Bahá'í Faith and deny the validity of any of the major religions of humanity. Coming from contending religions, the followers of Bahá'u'lláh find themselves organically united in one common Faith, a coming together of diverse peoples attracted to the same revelation, and, as noted earlier, an event promised in the Bible.

It naturally follows that the Bahá'í Faith seeks to help followers of the various religions to have a better understanding of their own Faith, for to comprehend a part is to appreciate the whole. Individuals have the ability to distinguish truth from error, and should be encouraged to exercise their scriptural right to do so.

In the absence of paid priesthood, Bahá'ís have a duty to share their beliefs with others and, should any feel within their heart the spark of faith, they are welcome, and indeed, are invited to become an active participant in the Bahá'í community, contributing to the unification of all humanity. Bahá'ís are forbidden to proselytize, and when they share their beliefs, no attempt is made to coerce anyone, or otherwise to forcefully prove a particular point. Rather, they engage in meaningful conversations and endeavour to remove misconceptions:

> The aim of Bahá'u'lláh, . . . He whose advent fulfils the prophecies of the Old and New Testaments . . . is not to destroy but to fulfil the Revelations of the past, to reconcile rather than accentuate the divergences of the conflicting creeds which disrupt present-day society.[59]

> . . . refusing to be labelled as a mere philosophy of life, or as an eclectic code of ethical conduct, or even as a new religion . . . Far from wishing to add to the number of the religious systems, whose conflicting loyalties have for so many generations disturbed the peace of mankind, this Faith is instilling into each of its adherents a new love for, and a genuine appreciation of the unity underlying, the various religions represented within its pale.[60]

18

REAFFIRMATION OF EARLIER MORAL AND ETHICAL TEACHINGS

Bahá'u'lláh, the Prophet-Founder of the Bahá'í Faith, appeared at a time when humanity had once again drifted far away from its Lord and Creator and from righteousness. In the words of Timothy, it instead now heeds 'seducing spirits, and doctrines of devils',[1] alien to the original teachings of their faith. Like Christ, Bahá'u'lláh has come so that humanity may once again have spiritual 'life and have it more abundantly' (John 10:10).

One cannot dismiss the Bahá'í Faith as a sect and its teachings as being a mere philosophy of life or an eclectic code of ethical conduct. The Faith of Bahá'u'lláh provides ample evidence of the redemptive power of the Holy Spirit transforming the individual and societies. It is a vision of an 'organic and spiritual unity of the whole body of nations'[2] that comprise this planet:

> Theirs is the duty to hold, aloft and undimmed, the torch of Divine guidance, as the shades of night descend upon, and ultimately envelop the entire human race. Theirs is the function, amidst its tumults, perils and agonies, to witness to the vision, and proclaim the approach, of that re-created society, that Christ-promised Kingdom, that World Order whose generative impulse is the spirit of none other than Bahá'u'lláh Himself, whose dominion is the entire planet, whose watchword is unity, whose animating power is the force of Justice, whose directive purpose is the reign of righteousness and truth, and whose supreme glory is the complete, the undisturbed and everlasting felicity of the whole of human kind.[3]

Within a relatively brief period of time, and despite merciless persecution in the land of its origin, the Bahá'í Faith has demonstrated its ability to assimilate the diversified elements of humanity, and to cleanse them of all forms of prejudice – clear evidence of the efficacy of the new teachings, and its transformative power born of the Holy Spirit 'which a disillusioned and sadly shaken society can ill afford to ignore'.[4]

Bahá'u'lláh has reaffirmed the spiritual truths of Judaism and Christianity, endowing their virtues and ethical principles with new vigour and direction, and framing them in terms that relate to, and are to the benefit of the present global society.

Investigation of religious truth, freed from preconceived notions and the restraints of tradition

The Bahá'í Writings emphasize that the individual has a sacrosanct scriptural responsibility to investigate reality and ascertain the truth of his or her faith. Christians must free themselves from the shackles of dogma, obsolete tradition and sectarianism and search earnestly for the fulfilment of the 'good news' of the Gospels:

> The first teaching of Bahá'u'lláh is the investigation of reality. Man must seek reality himself, forsaking imitations and adherence to mere hereditary forms. As the nations of the world are following imitations in lieu of truth and as imitations are many and various, differences of belief have been productive of strife and warfare. So long as these imitations remain, the oneness of the world of humanity is impossible. Therefore, we must investigate reality in order that by its light the clouds and darkness may be dispelled. Reality is one reality; it does not admit multiplicity or division. If the nations of the world investigate reality, they will agree and become united.[5]

Excessive love for the trappings of a religious institution can cause one to err, as can irrational prejudice against a new faith:

> He [the seeker] must so cleanse his heart that no remnant of either love or hate may linger therein, lest that love blindly incline him to error, or that hate repel him away from the truth. Even as thou dost witness in this Day how most of the people, because of such love and hate, are bereft of the immortal Face, have strayed far from the Embodiments of the Divine mysteries, and, shepherdless, are roaming through the wilderness of oblivion and error.[6]

Christians must be receptive and not act as the unresponsive people described by Christ:

> For this people's heart has grown dull, and with their ears they can barely hear, and their eyes they have closed, lest they should see with their eyes and hear with their ears and understand with their heart and turn, and I would heal them. (Matt. 13:15)

They will then readily appreciate that the spiritual message and moral teachings of Christianity and of the Bahá'í Writings are one and the same. The latter is simply a continuation of the former, but with a Message that has been expanded to include the followers of the other great faiths of mankind. Indeed, it is a central conviction of the Bahá'í Faith that all religions are expressions of the Divine Will – a theme that promotes greater inter-faith understanding and encourages the establishment of the unity of mankind. This is only feasible if man lets go of ancestral beliefs and prejudices:

> Reality or truth is one, yet there are many religious beliefs, denominations, creeds and differing opinions in the world today. Why should these differences exist? Because they do not investigate and examine the fundamental unity, which is one and unchangeable. If they seek reality itself, they will agree and be united; for reality is indivisible and not multiple. It is evident, therefore, that there is nothing of greater importance to mankind than the investigation of truth.[7]

> Likewise . . . if all the existing religious systems will turn away from ancestral imitations and investigate reality, seeking the real meanings of the Holy Books, they will unite and agree upon the same foundation, reality itself. As long as they follow counterfeit doctrines or imitations instead of reality, animosity and discord will exist and increase.[8]

It is the fruits of faith that matter – markers that identify one's religion or denomination are less important:

> The difference between a Christian and a Bahá'í, therefore, is this.

There was a former springtime, and there is a springtime now. No other difference exists because the foundations are the same. Whoever acts completely in accordance with the teachings of Christ is a Bahá'í. The purpose is the essential meaning of Christian, not the mere word.[9]

Seekers after truth are counselled to put their trust in God:

> Say: God sufficeth all things above all things, and nothing in the heavens or in the earth or in whatever lieth between them but God, thy Lord, sufficeth. Verily, He is in Himself the Knower, the Sustainer, the Omnipotent.[10]

> Say: God sufficeth unto me; He is the One Who holdeth in His grasp the kingdom of all things. Through the power of His hosts of heaven and earth and whatever lieth between them, He protecteth whomsoever among His servants He willeth. God, in truth, keepeth watch over all things.[11]

Divine guidance, love and assistance are contingent on the seeker making a sincere effort, which will then be rewarded and attract divine confirmations. An individual with sincere intentions is assured of God's assistance:

> O Son of Being! Love Me, that I may love thee. If thou lovest Me not, My love can in no wise reach thee. Know this, O servant.[12]

> He verily, will aid everyone that aideth Him, and will remember everyone that remembereth Him.[13]

The seeker has the potential to independently ascertain the truth – there is no need to imitate others:

> . . . every man hath been, and will continue to be, able of himself to appreciate the Beauty of God, the Glorified. Had he not been endowed with such a capacity, how could he be called to account for his failure? . . . the faith of no man can be conditioned by anyone except himself.[14]

... no man should blindly follow his ancestors and forefathers ... each must see with his own eyes, hear with his own ears and investigate the truth himself in order that he may follow the truth instead of blind acquiescence and imitation of ancestral beliefs.[15]

Consider the people and nations of the earth today and observe this same tenacious allegiance to ancestral belief. He whose father was a Zoroastrian is a Zoroastrian. He whose father was a Buddhist remains a Buddhist. The son of a Muslim continues a Muslim, and so on throughout. Why is this? Because they are slaves and captives of mere imitation. They have not investigated the reality of religion and arrived at its fundamentals and conclusions. The Jew, for instance, has not proved the validity of Moses by investigating reality. He is a Jew because his father was a Jew. He imitates the forms and belief of his fathers and ancestors. There is no thought or mention of reality. And so it is with the other peoples of religion.[16]

Imitation destroys the foundation of religion, extinguishes the spirituality of the human world, transforms heavenly illumination into darkness and deprives man of the knowledge of God. It is the cause of the victory of materialism and infidelity over religion; it is the denial of Divinity and the law of revelation; it refuses Prophethood and rejects the Kingdom of God. When materialists subject imitation to the intellectual analysis of reason, they find them to be mere superstitions; therefore, they deny religion. For instance, the Jews have ideas as to the purity and impurity of religion, but when you subject these ideas to scientific scrutiny, they are found to be without foundation.[17]

It is evident that prejudices arising from adherence to religious forms and imitation of ancestral beliefs have hindered the progress of humanity thousands of years. How many wars and battles have been fought, how much division, discord and hatred have been caused by this form of prejudice![18]

... if the nations of the world forsake imitations and investigate the reality underlying the revealed Word of God, they will agree and become reconciled. For reality is one and not multiple.[19]

Truth by any name is truth:

> No one truth can contradict another truth. Light is good in whatsoever lamp it is burning! A rose is beautiful in whatsoever garden it may bloom! A star has the same radiance if it shines from the East or from the West. Be free from prejudice, so will you love the Sun of Truth from whatever point in the horizon it may arise! You will realize that if the Divine Light of Truth shone in Jesus Christ, it also shone in Moses and Buddha. This is what is meant by the 'Search after Truth'.[20]

A grape by any other name is still a grape:

> A certain person bestowed a coin upon five beggars. They resolved to spend it for food. The Englishman said, 'Buy grapes.' The Turk wanted *uzum*, the Arab *anáb*, the Greek *stafi'li*, the Persian *angúr*. Not understanding each other's language, they quarrelled and fought. A stranger came along. He was familiar with all five languages. He said, 'Give me the coin; I will buy what you wish.' When he brought them grapes, they were all satisfied. They wanted the same thing but differed in the term only. Briefly, when reality dawns in the midst of the religions, all will be unified and reconciled.[21]

Religion should be of proven value to mankind

Religion should be conducive to the oneness of humanity, inculcate morality, purify the hearts, impel men to achieve praiseworthy deeds, unify and strengthen the bonds of friendship and amity, and be constructive:

> The essential purpose of the religion of God is to establish unity among mankind. The divine Manifestations were Founders of the means of fellowship and love. They did not come to create discord, strife and hatred in the world. The religion of God is the cause of love, but if it is made to be the source of enmity and bloodshed, surely its absence is preferable to its existence; for then it becomes satanic, detrimental and an obstacle to the human world.[22]

Religion should unite all hearts and cause wars and disputes to vanish from the face of the earth, give birth to spirituality, and bring life and light to each heart. If religion becomes a cause of dislike, hatred and division, it were better to be without it, and to withdraw from such a religion would be a truly religious act. For it is clear that the purpose of a remedy is to cure; but if the remedy should only aggravate the complaint it had better be left alone. Any religion which is not a cause of love and unity is no religion.[23]

The function and purpose of a shepherd is to gather and not disperse his flock. The prophets of God have been divine shepherds of humanity. They have established a bond of love and unity among mankind, made scattered peoples one nation and wandering tribes a mighty kingdom. They have laid the foundation of the oneness of God and summoned all to universal peace.[24]

The [divine Prophets] did not reveal themselves for the purpose of founding a nation, sect or faction. They did not appear in order that a certain number might acknowledge their prophethood. They did not declare their heavenly mission and message in order to lay the foundation for a religious belief. Even Christ did not become manifest that we should merely believe in him as the Christ, follow him and adore his mention. . . Nay, rather . . . Christ appeared in order to illumine the world of humanity, to render the earthly world celestial, to make the human kingdom a realm of angels, to unite the hearts, to enkindle the light of love in human souls, so that such souls might become independent, attaining complete unity and fellowship, turning to God, entering into the divine Kingdom, receiving the bounties and bestowals of God and partaking of the manna from heaven. Through Christ they were intended to be baptised by the Holy Spirit, attain a new spirit and realize the life everlasting . . .[25]

The Baháʼí Faith wishes to be judged mainly by its fruit and scrutinized by legitimate criteria:

Nowhere but in the purity of its precepts, the sublimity of its standards, the integrity of its laws, the reasonableness of its claims, the comprehensiveness of its scope, the universality of its programme, the flexibility of its institutions, the lives of its founders, the heroism of its martyrs, and the transforming power of its influence, should the unprejudiced observer seek to obtain the true criterion that can enable him to fathom its mysteries or to estimate its virtue.[26]

Transformation of human character and of society

Each new religion aims to spiritualize humanity through a fresh outpouring of the creative Divine Word. Bahá'u'lláh states that religion is futile without this necessary transformation:

> ... is not the object of every Revelation to effect a transformation in the whole character of mankind, a transformation that shall manifest itself, both outwardly and inwardly, that shall affect both its inner life and external conditions? For if the character of mankind be not changed, the futility of God's universal Manifestations would be apparent.[27]

> ... the purpose of the Manifestation of God and the dawning of the limitless lights of the Invisible is to educate the souls of men, and refine the character of every living man.[28]

This prescribed transmutation of character, this ordained spiritual resurrection and rebirth of individuals, will in due time renew the life and outlook of the global society.

> Every word that proceedeth out of the mouth of God is endowed with such potency as can instill new life into every human frame ... every created thing will, according to its capacity and limitations, be invested with the power to unfold the knowledge of the most marvellous sciences, and will be empowered to manifest them in the course of time at the bidding of Him Who is the Almighty, the All-Knowing.[29]

Bahá'u'lláh envisages further emanations and unfolding of this transformative spirit:

> All the wondrous achievements ye now witness are the direct consequences of the Revelation of this Name. In the days to come, ye will, verily, behold things of which ye have never heard before.[30]

The creative power of the Divine Word is today healing the seemingly intractable divisions in religion and human society:

> Today nothing but the power of the Word of God which encompasses the realities of things can bring the thoughts, minds, hearts and spirits under the shade of one Tree. He is the potent in all things, the vivifier of souls, the preserver and the controller of the world of mankind . . . in this day the light of the Word of God has shone forth upon all regions; and from all sects, communities, nations, tribes, peoples, religions and denominations, souls have gathered together under the shadow of the Word of Oneness, and have in the utmost fellowship united and harmonized![31]

This transformation, bringing forth spiritual fruit, is conclusive evidence of the validity and relevance of the Faith of Bahá'u'lláh. The achievements attained in a relatively short period of time prompted Shoghi Effendi[32] to pen the following:

> The Faith of Bahá'u'lláh . . . has changed the hearts of its adherents, burned away their prejudices, stilled their passions, exalted their conceptions, ennobled their motives, coordinated their efforts, and transformed their outlook. While preserving their patriotism and safeguarding their lesser loyalties, it has made them lovers of mankind, and the determined upholders of its best and truest interests. While maintaining intact their belief in the Divine origin of their respective religions, it has enabled them to visualize the underlying purpose of these religions, to discover their merits, to recognize their sequence, their interdependence, their wholeness and unity, and to acknowledge the bond that vitally links them . . .
> Of such men and women it may be truly said that to them 'every foreign land is a fatherland, and every fatherland a foreign land'. For their citizenship . . . is in the Kingdom of Bahá'u'lláh. Though willing to share to the utmost the temporal benefits and the fleeting joys which this earthly life can confer, though eager to participate

in whatever activity that conduces to the richness, the happiness and peace of that life, they can, at no time, forget that it constitutes no more than a transient, a very brief stage of their existence, that they who live it are but pilgrims and wayfarers whose goal is the Celestial City, and whose home the Country of never-failing joy and brightness.[33]

Bahá'ís appreciate that once they have ascertained the truth of Bahá'u'lláh's revelation they must heed its admonitions and act in accordance with its teachings. Bahá'u'lláh writes:

The first duty prescribed by God for His servants is the recognition of Him Who is the Dayspring of His Revelation and the Fountain of His laws, Who representeth the Godhead in both the Kingdom of His Cause and the world of creation. Whoso achieveth this duty hath attained unto all good; and whoso is deprived thereof hath gone astray, though he be the author of every righteous deed. It behoveth every one who reacheth this most sublime station, this summit of transcendent glory, to observe every ordinance of Him Who is the Desire of the world. These twin duties are inseparable. Neither is acceptable without the other. Thus hath it been decreed by Him Who is the Source of Divine inspiration.[34]

O ye peoples of the world! Know assuredly that My commandments are the lamps of My loving providence among My servants, and the keys of My mercy for My creatures . . . Think not that We have revealed unto you a mere code of laws. Nay, rather, We have unsealed the choice Wine with the fingers of might and power.[35]

O Son of Being! Walk in My statutes for love of Me and deny thyself that which thou desirest if thou seekest My pleasure.[36]

Expressions of belief alone, however, are not sufficient for building a better world – faith must be validated and reinforced through action. Bahá'u'lláh writes:

Beware, O people of Bahá, lest ye walk in the ways of them whose words differ from their deeds. Strive that ye may be enabled to manifest to the peoples of the earth the signs of God, and to mirror forth His commandments. Let your acts be a guide unto all mankind, for the professions of most men, be they high or low, differ from their conduct. It is through your deeds that ye can distinguish yourselves from others. Through them the brightness of your light can be shed upon the whole earth.[37]

It is incumbent upon every man of insight and understanding to strive to translate that which hath been written into reality and action.[38]

O people! Words must be supported by deeds, for deeds are the true test of words. Without the former, the latter can never quench the thirst of the yearning soul, nor unlock the portals of vision before the eyes of the blind.[39]

Testifying to the Divine Word: A spiritual requirement

At the beginning of His dispensation, all followers of Christ were required to proclaim the Gospel. The Apostle Paul equates belief with proclaiming the truth of one's convictions:

> Since we have the same spirit of faith according to what has been written, 'I believed, and so I spoke,' we also believe, and so we also speak . . . (II Cor. 4:13)

It is also the duty of every Bahá'í, who, after diligent investigation, has come to accept the Faith of Bahá'u'lláh, to arise and teach its message:

> This is the day in which to speak. It is incumbent upon the people of Bahá to strive, with the utmost patience and forbearance, to guide the peoples of the world to the Most Great Horizon. Every body calleth aloud for a soul. Heavenly souls must needs quicken, with the breath of the Word of God, the dead bodies with a fresh spirit. Within every word a new spirit is hidden. Happy is the man that attaineth thereunto, and hath arisen to teach the Cause of Him Who is the King of Eternity.[40]

REAFFIRMATION OF EARLIER MORAL AND ETHICAL TEACHINGS

Say: To assist Me is to teach My Cause. This is a theme with which whole Tablets are laden. This is the changeless commandment of God, eternal in the past, eternal in the future.[41]

In a prayer revealed by Bahá'u'lláh, His followers ask for assistance in this spiritual enterprise:

Do Thou destine for me, O my God, what becometh the greatness of Thy majesty, and assist me, by Thy strengthening grace, so to teach Thy Cause that the dead may speed out of their sepulchers, and rush forth towards Thee, trusting wholly in Thee, and fixing their gaze upon the orient of Thy Cause, and the dawning-place of Thy Revelation.[42]

They are urged, as were the Christians, to act as farmers and to plant the seed:

. . . revive the hearts by the fragrances of God and plant the seed of guidance in the field of the souls, by a help from thy Lord, the Merciful, the Clement.[43]

For unless the seed is sown, the bounty and blessing will not be attained; until the tree be planted, the fresh fruit will not be produced; unless the candle contact with fire, it will not ignite; and until a light dawn, the darkness will not vanish. Therefore, the beloved of God must sow the seeds and plant the fresh plants in that garden. They must ignite the extinguished candles so that the purpose may be attained and the beloved intent unveil its face.[44]

Now you must become heavenly farmers and scatter pure seeds in the prepared soil. The harvest of every other seed is limited, but the bounty and the blessing of the seed of the divine teachings is unlimited. Throughout the coming centuries and cycles many harvests will be gathered. Consider the work of former generations. During the lifetime of Jesus Christ the believing, firm souls were few and numbered, but the heavenly blessings descended so plentifully that in a number of years countless souls entered beneath the shadow of the Gospel . . . we must not consider our ability and capacity, nay, rather, we must fix our gaze upon the favours and bounties of God, in these days, Who has made of the drop a sea, and of the atom a sun.'[45]

However, the final outcomes belong to God and should be left entirely to Him. Religious followers ought not to be unduly concerned as to who is, and who is not, one of them, as such concerns perpetuate disunity. Instead, Bahá'u'lláh states 'Be anxiously concerned with the needs of the age ye live in and centre your deliberations on its exigencies and requirements.'[46]

Transforming one's own character

The process of bearing witness to one's faith and presenting its truths is prescriptive *per se*, as it demands that the individual first transform his own character:

> God hath prescribed unto every one the duty of teaching His Cause. Whoever ariseth to discharge this duty, must needs, ere he proclaimeth His Message, adorn himself with the ornament of an upright and praiseworthy character, so that his words may attract the hearts of such as are receptive to his call. Without it, he can never hope to influence his hearers.[47]

> Whoso ariseth to teach Our Cause must needs detach himself from all earthly things . . .[48]

In their attempts to carry out this injunction, Bahá'ís are reminded that their individual and collective lives must attest to the 'good fruits' of the tree of Bahá'u'lláh's revelation. In order to be effective in teaching, their conduct should be unblemished and they should prove themselves to be of value to mankind:

> The triumph of this Cause hath depended, and will continue to depend, upon the appearance of holy souls, upon the showing forth of goodly deeds, and the revelation of words of consummate wisdom.[49]

REAFFIRMATION OF EARLIER MORAL AND ETHICAL TEACHINGS

Not by the force of numbers, not by the mere exposition of a set of new and noble principles, not by an organized campaign of teaching – no matter how worldwide and elaborate in its character – not even by the staunchness of our faith or the exaltation of our enthusiasm, can we ultimately hope to vindicate in the eyes of a critical and sceptical age the supreme claim of the [Bahá'í] Revelation. One thing and only one thing will unfailingly and alone secure the undoubted triumph of this sacred Cause, namely, the extent to which our own inner life and private character mirror forth in their manifold aspects the splendor of those eternal principles proclaimed by Bahá'u'lláh.[50]

The most vital duty, in this day . . . is to purify your characters, to correct your manners, and improve your conduct. The beloved of the Merciful must show forth such character and conduct among His creatures, that the fragrance of their holiness may be shed upon the whole world, and may quicken the dead . . .[51]

Those engaged in this vital spiritual endeavour come to realize early on that they too must be occupied with matters that advance their spiritual growth and fulfil the real purpose of their existence – they cannot be too preoccupied with the mundane:

O Son of Spirit! The bird seeketh its nest; the nightingale the charm of the rose; whilst those birds, the hearts of men, content with transient dust, have strayed far from their eternal nest, and with eyes turned towards the slough of heedlessness are bereft of the glory of the divine presence. Alas! How strange and pitiful; for a mere cupful, they have turned away from the billowing seas of the Most High, and remained far from the most effulgent horizon.[52]

In their presentations of the Faith of Bahá'u'lláh they are to refrain from being 'arrogant in the affirmation of its claims',[53] and are instead to show kindness and friendliness:

Consort with all men, O people of Bahá, in a spirit of friendliness and fellowship. If ye be aware of a certain truth, if ye possess a jewel, of which others are deprived, share it with them in a language of utmost kindliness and goodwill. If it be accepted, if it fulfil its purpose, your object is attained. If anyone should refuse it, leave him unto himself, and beseech God to guide him. Beware lest ye deal unkindly with him. A kindly tongue is the lodestone of the hearts of men. It is the bread of the spirit, it clotheth the words with meaning, it is the fountain of the light of wisdom and understanding . . .[54]

Beware lest ye contend with any one, nay, strive to make him aware of the truth with kindly manner and most convincing exhortation. If your hearer respond, he will have responded to his own behoof, and if not, turn ye away from him, and set your faces towards God's sacred Court, the seat of resplendent holiness.

Dispute not with any one concerning the things of this world and its affairs, for God hath abandoned them to such as have set their affection upon them. Out of the whole world He hath chosen for Himself the hearts of men—hearts which the hosts of revelation and of utterance can subdue.[55]

Characteristics of a re-sanctified life

A pure heart, a tranquil conscience, and selfless motives

In a prayer revealed by Bahá'u'lláh His followers supplicate:

> Create in me a pure heart, O my God, and renew a tranquil conscience within me, O my Hope! Through the spirit of power confirm Thou me in Thy Cause, O my Best-Beloved, and by the light of Thy glory reveal unto me Thy path, O Thou the Goal of my desire! Through the power of Thy transcendent might lift me up unto the heaven of Thy holiness, O Source of my being, and by the breezes of Thine eternity gladden me, O Thou Who art my God! Let Thine everlasting melodies breathe tranquillity on me, O my Companion, and let the riches of Thine ancient countenance deliver me from all except Thee, O my Master, and let the tidings of the revelation of Thine incorruptible Essence bring me joy, O Thou Who art the most manifest of the manifest and the most hidden of the hidden![56]

And Bahá'u'lláh enjoins on them:

O Son of Spirit! My first counsel is this: Possess a pure, kindly and radiant heart, that thine may be a sovereignty ancient, imperishable and everlasting.[57]

To be effective in presenting their Faith the followers of Bahá'u'lláh must cultivate righteous living, and hearts and souls cleansed of all impurities:

The sword of a virtuous character and upright conduct is sharper than blades of steel.[58]

It is easy to read the Holy Scriptures, but it is only with a clean heart and a pure mind that one may understand their true meaning.[59]

The most important thing is to polish the mirrors of hearts in order that they may become illumined and receptive of the divine light.[60]

Know that thy true adornment consisteth in the love of God and in thy detachment from all save Him, and not in the luxuries thou dost possess.[61]

An outlook that is purified from all inordinate desires and attachments

And when the sanctified souls rend asunder the veils of all earthly attachments and worldly conditions, and hasten to the stage of gazing on the beauty of the Divine Presence and are honoured by recognizing the Manifestation and are able to witness the splendour of God's Most Great Sign in their hearts, then will the purpose of creation, which is the knowledge of Him Who is the Eternal Truth, become manifest.[62]

O Son of Spirit! There is no peace for thee save by renouncing thyself and turning unto Me; for it behooveth thee to glory in My name, not in thine own; to put thy trust in Me and not in thyself, since I desire to be loved alone and above all that is.[63]

O Son of Man! If thou lovest Me, turn away from thyself; and if thou seekest My pleasure, regard not thine own; that thou mayest die in Me and I may eternally live in thee.[64]

Avoid purely materialistic pursuits and existence

He is not to be numbered with the people of Bahá who followeth his mundane desires, or fixeth his heart on things of the earth. He is My true follower who, if he come to a valley of pure gold will pass straight through it aloof as a cloud, and will neither turn back, nor pause. Such a man is assuredly of Me. From his garment the Concourse on high can inhale the fragrance of sanctity . . .[65]

O Son of Being! Busy not thyself with this world, for with fire We test the gold and with gold We test Our servants.[66]

Promote love, unity and amity

It is Our wish and desire that every one of you may become a source of all goodness unto men, and an example of uprightness to mankind. Beware lest ye prefer yourselves above your neighbours. Fix your gaze upon Him Who is the Temple of God amongst men. He, in truth, hath offered up His life as a ransom for the redemption of the world . . . We love to see you at all times consorting in amity and concord within the paradise of My good-pleasure, and to inhale from your acts the fragrance of friendliness and unity, of loving-kindness and fellowship . . . We shall always be with you; if We inhale the perfume of your fellowship, Our heart will assuredly rejoice, for naught else can satisfy Us.[67]

Become a 'living sacrifice'

. . . the spiritual descendants of the dawn-breakers of an heroic Age, who by their death proclaimed the birth of that Faith – must, in turn, usher in, not by their death but through living sacrifice, that promised World Order, the shell ordained to enshrine that priceless jewel the world civilization, of which the Faith itself is the sole begetter.[68]

Let your conduct be ethical and virtuous

Moral rectitude is one of the 'spiritual prerequisites' of success and forms 'the bedrock' of all Bahá'í activities:

> A rectitude of conduct, an abiding sense of undeviating justice, unobscured by the demoralizing influences which a corruption-ridden political life so strikingly manifests; a chaste, pure, and holy life, unsullied and unclouded by the indecencies, the vices, the false standards, which an inherently deficient moral code tolerates, perpetuates, and fosters; a fraternity freed from that cancerous growth of racial prejudice, which is eating into the vitals of an already debilitated society – these are the ideals which the . . . believers must . . . individually and through concerted action, strive to promote, in both their private and public lives . . .
>
> This rectitude of conduct, with its implications of justice, equity, truthfulness, honesty, fair-mindedness, reliability, and trustworthiness, must distinguish every phase of the life of the Bahá'í community. 'The companions of God,' Bahá'u'lláh Himself has declared, 'are, in this day, the lump that must leaven the peoples of the world. They must show forth such trustworthiness, such truthfulness and perseverance, such deeds and character that all mankind may profit by their example.'[69]

Be faithful to God's Cause

> That which is of the greatest importance is to have firmness, steadfastness and constancy.[70]

Forget not My bounties while I am absent. Remember My days during thy days, and My distress and banishment in this remote prison. And be thou so steadfast in My love that thy heart shall not waver, even if the swords of the enemies rain blows upon thee and all the heavens and the earth arise against thee.[71]

O ye beloved of the Lord! Beware, beware lest ye hesitate and waver. Let not fear fall upon you, neither be troubled nor dismayed. Take ye good heed lest this calamitous day slacken the flames of your ardour, and quench your tender hopes. Today is the day for steadfastness and constancy. Blessed are they that stand firm and immovable as the rock and brave the storm and stress of this tempestuous hour. They, verily, shall be the recipients of God's grace; they, verily, shall receive His divine assistance, and shall be truly victorious. They shall shine amidst mankind with a radiance which the dwellers of the Pavilion of Glory laud and magnify.[72]

Fear God

Awareness of the 'presence of God' or the 'fear of God' must educate and regulate the daily activities of Bahá'ís:

> We have admonished Our loved ones to fear God, a fear which is the fountain-head of all goodly deeds and virtues.[73]

> Their hearts [followers of Bahá'u'lláh] are illumined with the light of the fear of God, and adorned with the adornment of His love.[74]

Be chaste

> . . . let each one of you be as a lamp shining forth with the light of the virtues of the world of humanity. Be trustworthy, sincere, affectionate and replete with chastity. Be illumined, be spiritual, be divine, be glorious, be quickened of God, be a Bahá'í.[75]

Such a chaste and holy life, with its implications of modesty, purity, temperance, decency, and clean-mindedness, involves no less than the exercise of moderation in all that pertains to dress, language, amusements, and all artistic and literary avocations. It demands daily vigilance in the control of one's carnal desires and corrupt inclinations. It calls for the abandonment of a frivolous conduct, with its excessive attachment to trivial and often misdirected pleasures. It requires total abstinence from all alcoholic drinks, from opium, and from similar habit-forming drugs. It condemns the prostitution of art and of literature, the practices of nudism and of companionate marriage, infidelity in marital relationships, and all manner of promiscuity, of easy familiarity, and of sexual vices. It can tolerate no compromise with the theories, the standards, the habits, and the excesses of a decadent age. Nay rather it seeks to demonstrate, through the dynamic force of its example, the pernicious character of such theories, the falsity of such standards, the hollowness of such claims, the perversity of such habits, and the sacrilegious character of such excesses.[76]

Show love indiscriminately – do not prefer or exalt yourself above others

O Children of Men! Know ye not why We created you all from the same dust? That no one should exalt himself over the other.[77]

You must manifest complete love and affection toward all mankind. Do not exalt yourselves above others, but consider all as your equals, recognizing them as the servants of one God. Know that God is compassionate toward all; therefore, love all from the depths of your hearts . . . be filled with love for every race, and be kind toward the people of all nationalities.[78]

He must never seek to exalt himself above any one, must wash away from the tablet of his heart every trace of pride and vainglory, must cling unto patience and resignation, observe silence, and refrain from idle talk . . .[79]

Be charitable, hospitable, and trustworthy – demonstrate humility and integrity

And among the teachings of Bahá'u'lláh is voluntary sharing of one's property with others among mankind. This voluntary sharing is greater than equality, and consists in this, that man should not prefer himself to others, but rather should sacrifice his life and property for others. But this should not be introduced by coercion so that it becomes a law and man is compelled to follow it. Nay, rather should man voluntarily and of his own choice sacrifice his property and life for others, and spend willingly for the poor . . .[80]

Be generous in prosperity, and thankful in adversity. Be worthy of the trust of thy neighbour, and look upon him with a bright and friendly face. Be a treasure to the poor, an admonisher to the rich, an answerer to the cry of the needy, a preserver of the sanctity of thy pledge. Be fair in thy judgment, and guarded in thy speech. Be unjust to no man, and show all meekness to all men. Be as a lamp unto them that walk in darkness, a joy to the sorrowful, a sea for the thirsty, a haven for the distressed, an upholder and defender of the victim of oppression. Let integrity and uprightness distinguish all thine acts. Be a home for the stranger, a balm to the suffering, a tower of strength for the fugitive. Be eyes to the blind, and a guiding light unto the feet of the erring. Be an ornament to the countenance of truth, a crown to the brow of fidelity, a pillar of the temple of righteousness, a breath of life to the body of mankind, an ensign of the hosts of justice, a luminary above the horizon of virtue, a dew to the soil of the human heart, an ark on the ocean of knowledge, a sun in the heaven of bounty, a gem on the diadem of wisdom, a shining light in the firmament of thy generation, a fruit upon the tree of humility.[81]

Do not abase yourself

O Son of Spirit! I created thee rich, why dost thou bring thyself down to poverty? Noble I made thee, wherewith dost thou abase thyself? Out of the essence of knowledge I gave thee being, why seekest thou enlightenment from anyone beside Me? Out of the clay of love I molded thee, how dost thou busy thyself with another? Turn thy sight unto thyself, that thou mayest find Me standing within thee, mighty, powerful and self-subsisting.[82]

O Son of Spirit! Noble have I created thee, yet thou hast abased thyself. Rise then unto that for which thou wast created.[83]

Be just and equitable in your dealings

O Son of Spirit! The best beloved of all things in My sight is Justice; turn not away therefrom if thou desirest Me, and neglect it not that I may confide in thee. By its aid thou shalt see with thine own eyes and not through the eyes of others, and shalt know of thine own knowledge and not through the knowledge of thy neighbor. Ponder this in thy heart; how it behooveth thee to be. Verily justice is My gift to thee and the sign of My loving-kindness. Set it then before thine eyes.[84]

No light can compare with the light of justice. The establishment of order in the world and the tranquillity of the nations depend upon it.[85]

Be fair to yourselves and to others that the evidences of justice may be revealed through your deeds among Our faithful servants . . . Equity . . . is the most fundamental among human virtues. The evaluation of all things must needs depend upon it.[86]

Note that, like Christ, Bahá'u'lláh endured many injustices and deprivations so as to bring about justice:

Glorified be the All-Merciful, the Revealer of so inestimable a bounty. Say: Because He bore injustice, justice hath appeared on earth, and because He accepted abasement, the majesty of God hath shone forth amidst mankind.[87]

Avoid being judgmental and preoccupied with the faults of others – do not backbite or slander anyone

O Son of Being! How couldst thou forget thine own faults and busy thyself with the faults of others? . . .[88]

O Son of Man! Breathe not the sins of others so long as thou art thyself a sinner.[89]

. . . backbiting quencheth the light of the heart, and extinguisheth the life of the soul . . .[90]

Never speak disparagingly of others, but praise without distinction. Pollute not your tongues by speaking evil of another. Recognize your enemies as friends, and consider those who wish you evil as the wishers of good . . . Act in such a way that your heart may be free from hatred. Let not your heart be offended with anyone. If some one commits an error and wrong toward you, you must instantly forgive him. Do not complain of others. Refrain from reprimanding them, and if you wish to give admonition or advice, let it be offered in such a way that it will not burden the bearer. Turn all your thoughts toward bringing joy to hearts. Beware! Beware! lest ye offend any heart ... Be the source of consolation to every sad one, assist every weak one, be helpful to every indigent one, care for every sick one, be the cause of glorification to every lowly one, and shelter those who are overshadowed by fear.[91]

Be dissatisfied with oneself – a sign of spiritual progress

The soul who is satisfied with himself is the manifestation of Satan, and the one who is not contented with himself is the manifestation of the Merciful. If a person has a thousand good qualities he must not look at them; nay, rather he must strive to find out his own defects and imperfections ... However much a man may progress, yet he is imperfect, because there is always a point ahead of him. No sooner does he look up towards that point than he become dissatisfied with his own condition, and aspires to attain to that. Praising one's own self is the sign of selfishness.[92]

Be truthful

God is the source of all truth; hence, the followers of Bahá'u'lláh must be true to themselves and honest with their fellow men.

> Truthfulness ... is the foundation of all human virtues. Without truthfulness progress and success, in all the worlds of God, are impossible for any soul ...[93]

> Beautify your tongues, O people ... with truthfulness, and adorn your souls with the ornament of honesty. Beware, O people, that ye deal not treacherously with anyone. Be ye the trustees of God amongst His creatures, and the emblems of His generosity amidst His people ... Let your eye be chaste, ... your hand faithful, your tongue truthful, and your heart enlightened ... Be an ornament to the countenance of truth ... a crown to the brow of fidelity, a

> pillar of the temple of righteousness, a breath of life to the body of mankind, an ensign of the hosts of justice, a luminary above the horizon of virtue . . . Let truthfulness and courtesy be your adorning . . .[94]

> Truthfulness and good-will have, at all times, marked their relations with all men. Their outward conduct is but a reflection of their inward life, and their inward life a mirror of their outward conduct.[95]

Writing to an immensely rich and powerful Muslim clergyman who had been responsible for the persecution and death of many Bahá'ís, Bahá'u'lláh wrote:

> We beseech God to aid thee to be just and fair-minded . . . We ask thee to reflect upon that which hath been revealed, and to be fair and just in thy speech, that perchance the splendours of the daystar of truthfulness and sincerity may shine forth, and may deliver thee from the darkness of ignorance, and illumine the world with the light of knowledge.[96]

Be sincere and imbued with piety, trustworthiness, resignation, kindliness, uprightness, wisdom, fidelity and courtesy

> The purpose of the one true God in manifesting Himself is to summon all mankind to truthfulness and sincerity, to piety and trustworthiness, to resignation and submissiveness to the Will of God, to forbearance and kindliness, to uprightness and wisdom. His object is to array every man with the mantle of a saintly character, and to adorn him with the ornament of holy and goodly deeds.[97]

> Adorn your heads with the garlands of trustworthiness and fidelity, your hearts with the attire of the fear of God, your tongues with absolute truthfulness, your bodies with the vesture of courtesy.[98]

Be courteous

O people of God! I admonish you to observe courtesy. For above all else it is the prince of virtues. Well is it with him who is illumined with the light of courtesy and is attired with the vesture of uprightness. Whoso is endued with courtesy hath indeed attained a sublime station.[99]

Exercise moderation

Overstep not the bounds of moderation, and deal justly with them that serve thee.[100]

It is incumbent upon them who are in authority to exercise moderation in all things. Whatsoever passeth beyond the limits of moderation will cease to exert a beneficial influence.[101]

Pray and consume every evil thought; be considerate of the destitute – evince a compassion and kindness that extends even to animals

He should be content with little, and be freed from all inordinate desire. He should treasure the companionship of those that have renounced the world, and regard avoidance of boastful and worldly people a precious benefit. At the dawn of every day he should commune with God, and with all his soul persevere in the quest of his Beloved. He should consume every wayward thought with the flame of His loving mention, and, with the swiftness of lightning, pass by all else save Him. He should succour the dispossessed, and never withhold his favour from the destitute. He should show kindness to animals, how much more unto his fellow-man, to him who is endowed with the power of utterance.[102]

Do not desire for others that which you do not wish for yourself – pray for the remission of their sins

He should not wish for others that which he doth not wish for himself, nor promise that which he doth not fulfil. With all his heart he should avoid fellowship with evil-doers, and pray for the remission of their sins. He should forgive the sinful, and never despise his low estate, for none knoweth what his own end shall be. How often hath a sinner attained, at the hour of death, to the essence of faith, and, quaffing the immortal draught, hath taken his flight unto the Concourse on high! And how often hath a devout believer, at the hour of his soul's ascension, been so changed as to fall into the nethermost fire![103]

Do not revile or execrate anyone

Defile not your tongues with the cursing and reviling of any soul, and guard your eyes against that which is not seemly. Set forth that which ye possess. If it be favourably received, your end is attained; if not, to protest is vain. Leave that soul to himself and turn unto the Lord, the Protector, the Self-Subsisting. Be not the cause of grief, much less of discord and strife . . . Ye are all the leaves of one tree and the drops of one ocean.[104]

When the light of Bahá'u'lláh dawned . . . anathema and execration were utterly abrogated. He said, 'It is not becoming in man to curse another; it is not befitting that man should attribute darkness to another; it is not meet that one human being should consider another human being as bad; nay, rather, all mankind are the servants of one God; God is the Father of all; there is not a single exception to that law. There are no people of Satan; all belong to the Merciful. There is no darkness; all is light. All are the servants of God, and man must love humanity from his heart. He must, verily, behold humanity as submerged in the divine mercy.'[105]

Be clean

And although bodily cleanliness is a physical thing, it hath, nevertheless, a powerful influence on the life of the spirit. It is even as a voice wondrously sweet, or a melody played: although sounds are but vibrations in the air which affect the ear's auditory nerve, and these vibrations are but chance phenomena carried along through the air, even so, see how they move the heart. A wondrous melody is wings for the spirit, and maketh the soul to tremble for joy. The purport is that physical cleanliness doth also exert its effect upon the human soul.[106]

Honour your parents

> The fruits that best befit the tree of human life are trustworthiness and godliness, truthfulness and sincerity; but greater than all, after recognition of the unity of God, praised and glorified be He, is regard for the rights that are due to one's parents. [107]

Bahá'ís pray for forgiveness for their parents and for the progress of their souls in all the realms of God:

> It is seemly that the servant should, after each prayer, supplicate God to bestow mercy and forgiveness upon his parents . . . Blessed is he who remembereth his parents when communing with God. There is, verily, no God but Him, the Mighty, the Well-Beloved.[108]

They also must seek parental approval concerning their choice of spouse.

• • • • •

Finally, here are some of the 'beatitudes' of Bahá'u'lláh mentioned in a Tablet addressed to a believer of Christian background:

> Say: Blessed the slumberer who is awakened by My Breeze.

> Blessed the lifeless one who is quickened through My reviving breaths.

> Blessed the wayfarer who directeth his steps towards the Tabernacle of My glory and majesty.

> Blessed the sore athirst who hasteneth to the soft-flowing waters of My loving-kindness.

> Blessed the insatiate soul who casteth away his selfish desires for love

of Me and taketh his place at the banquet table which I have sent down from the heaven of divine bounty for My chosen ones.

Blessed the abased one who layeth fast hold on the cord of My glory; and the needy one who entereth beneath the shadow of the Tabernacle of My wealth.

Blessed the ignorant one who seeketh the fountain of My knowledge; and the heedless one who cleaveth to the cord of My remembrance.

Blessed the soul that hath been raised to life through My quickening breath and hath gained admittance into My heavenly Kingdom.

Blessed the ear that hath heard and the tongue that hath borne witness and the eye that hath seen and recognized the Lord Himself, in His great glory and majesty, invested with grandeur and dominion.

Blessed is he who hath heard of My grief and hath arisen to aid Me among My people.

Blessed is he who hath laid down his life in My path and hath borne manifold hardships for the sake of My Name.

Blessed the man who, assured of My Word, hath arisen from among the dead to celebrate My praise.

Blessed is he who hath remained faithful to My Covenant, and whom the things of the world have not kept back from attaining My Court of holiness.[109]

One may well ask: Do these words and virtues not evoke the spirit of the Gospels? – do they not embody the reality and purpose of Christ's teachings in this day, while simultaneously inviting Christians to heed the fulfilment of the promises of their scriptures?

19

NEW SOCIAL PARADIGMS FOR A GLOBAL SOCIETY

In addition to reanimating the spiritual truths of earlier dispensations, Bahá'u'lláh has abrogated their obsolete social laws, replacing them with new ordinances that advance a global human society and ensure its peace, unity, and tranquillity.

Elimination of all prejudices

The oneness of mankind

The oneness of all mankind is 'the pivot round which all the teachings of Bahá'u'lláh revolve'.[1] It is primarily a universal human rights issue and hence independent of religious affiliation or any other considerations. Today, mankind is invited to reconcile its differences and promote this unity:

> ... the peoples of the world, of whatever race or religion, derive their inspiration from one heavenly Source, and are the subjects of one God.[2]

> In every Dispensation the light of Divine Guidance has been focused upon one central theme ... In this wondrous Revelation, this glorious century, the foundation of the Faith of God, and the distinguishing feature of His Law, is the consciousness of the oneness of mankind.[3]

> O ye children of men! The fundamental purpose animating the Faith of God and His Religion is to safeguard the interests and promote the unity of the human race, and to foster the spirit of

love and fellowship amongst men. Suffer it not to become a source of dissension and discord, of hate and enmity. This is the straight Path, the fixed and immovable foundation. Whatsoever is raised on this foundation, the changes and chances of the world can never impair its strength, nor will the revolution of countless centuries undermine its structure . . .[4]

The unity of the human race, as envisaged by Bahá'u'lláh, implies the establishment of a world commonwealth in which all nations, races, creeds and classes are closely and permanently united, and in which the autonomy of its state members and the personal freedom and initiative of the individuals that compose them are definitely and completely safeguarded.[5]

The oneness of mankind is an extension of Christ's commandment that Christians should become the embodiment of love (Matt. 5:45–46). In this way the Bahá'í Faith has expanded the perception of 'brotherhood' to include all humanity, unconditionally and without exception.

In cycles gone by, though harmony was established, yet, owing to the absence of means, the unity of all mankind could not have been achieved. Continents remained widely divided, nay even among the peoples of one and the same continent association and interchange of thought were well nigh impossible. Consequently intercourse, understanding and unity amongst all the peoples and kindreds of the earth were unattainable. In this day, however, means of communication have multiplied, and the five continents of the earth have virtually merged into one . . . In like manner all the members of the human family, whether peoples or governments, cities or villages, have become increasingly interdependent. For none is self-sufficiency any longer possible, inasmuch as political ties unite all peoples and nations, and the bonds of trade and industry, of agriculture and education, are being strengthened every day. Hence the unity of all mankind can in this day be achieved.[6]

This principle of the oneness of mankind is highly developed in the Bahá'í Faith:

[It] is no mere outburst of ignorant emotionalism or an expression of vague and pious hope. Its appeal is not to be merely identified with a reawakening of the spirit of brotherhood and good-will among men, nor does it aim solely at the fostering of harmonious cooperation among individual peoples and nations. Its implications are deeper, its claims greater than any which the Prophets of old were allowed to advance. Its message is applicable not only to the individual, but concerns itself primarily with the nature of those essential relationships that must bind all the states and nations as members of one human family. It does not constitute merely the enunciation of an ideal, but stands inseparably associated with an institution adequate to embody its truth, demonstrate its validity, and perpetuate its influence. It implies an organic change in the structure of present-day society, a change such as the world has not yet experienced. It constitutes a challenge, at once bold and universal, to outworn shibboleths of national creeds – creeds that have had their day and which must, in the ordinary course of events as shaped and controlled by Providence, give way to a new gospel, fundamentally different from, and infinitely superior to, what the world has already conceived. It calls for no less that the reconstruction and the demilitarization of the whole civilized world – a world organically unified in all the essential aspects of its life, its political machinery, its spiritual aspiration, its trade and finance, its script and language, and yet infinite in the diversity of the national characteristics of its federated units.

It represents the consummation of human evolution – an evolution that has had its earliest beginnings in the birth of family life, its subsequent development in the achievement of tribal solidarity, leading in turn to the constitution of the city-state, and expanding later into the institution of independent and sovereign nations.

The principle of the Oneness of Mankind, as proclaimed by Bahá'u'lláh, carries with it no more and no less than a solemn assertion that attainment to this final stage in this stupendous evolution is not only necessary but inevitable, that its realization is fast approaching, and that nothing short of a power that is born of God can succeed in establishing it.[7]

The many seemingly irreconcilable religions with their numerous denominations are guilty of alienating other members of the human family. Bahá'u'lláh writes:

> The well-being of mankind, its peace and security, are unattainable unless and until its unity is firmly established.[8]

The achievement of this unity is Bahá'u'lláh's declared mission and the aim of all Bahá'í activities.

There are many underlying causes for the divisions that exist between human beings: differences of race, skin colour, tribe, nationality, and educational, economic and social standing. The Bahá'í Faith declares that these distinctions, which have unleashed so much hostility, no longer have any validity, are not part of the Divine Will today, and must be eliminated. Only then will humanity's full potential be realized.

> Whatsoever hath led the children of men to shun one another, and hath caused dissensions and divisions amongst them, hath, through the revelation of these words, been nullified and abolished.[9]
>
> All prejudices, whether of religion, race, politics or nation, must be renounced, for these prejudices have caused the world's sickness. It is a grave malady which, unless arrested, is capable of causing the destruction of the whole human race. Every ruinous war, with its terrible bloodshed and misery, has been caused by one or other of these prejudices.[10]
>
> A new religious principle is that prejudice and fanaticism – whether sectarian, denominational, patriotic or political – are destructive to the foundation of human solidarity; therefore man should release himself from such bonds in order that the oneness of the world of humanity may become manifest.[11]

Racism and racial harmony

The belief that race is a significant determinant of human capacities, that racial differences justify belief in an inherent superiority of a particular section of humanity, and that this should form the basis of our human values, has little scientific merit. The Human Genome Project, completed in 2003, showed that we share the same number of identical genes and thus demonstrated for the first time that scientifically humanity is one species.[12] Where we differ is variations (known as alleles) of the same genes. We are genetically far more nuanced and variable than is reflected in just skin coloration (surrogate for race). Hence we are all 'coloured' to varying degrees by having inherited a set of three genes that affects the production of melanin.

Nevertheless, the concept of race, with its attendant prejudices, is likely to persist. Hence, apart from scientific considerations the power of faith is necessary to combat racial bigotry.

Racism is the antithesis of Bahá'í belief:

> For a Bahá'í racial prejudice, in all its forms, is simply a negation of faith, an attitude wholly incompatible with the very spirit and actual teachings of the Cause.[13]

> Racism, one of the most baneful and persistent evils, is a major barrier to peace. Its practice perpetrates too outrageous a violation of the dignity of human beings to be countenanced under any pretext. Racism retards the unfoldment of the boundless potentialities of its victims, corrupts its perpetrators, and blights human progress. Recognition of the oneness of mankind, implemented by appropriate legal measures, must be universally upheld if this problem is to be overcome...[14]

In an interview in 1890 with the orientalist Professor E. G. Browne of the University of Cambridge, Bahá'u'lláh stressed the importance of the oneness of humanity in His revelation:

> We desire but the good of the world and the happiness of the nations; yet they deem us a stirrer up of strife and sedition worthy of bondage and banishment... That all nations should become one in faith and all men as brothers; that the bonds of affection and unity between the sons of men should be strengthened; that diversity of religion should cease, and differences of race be annulled – what harm is there in this? ... this bloodshed and discord must cease, and all men be as one kindred and one family... Let not a man glory in this, that he loves his country; let him rather glory in this, that he loves his kind...[15]

'Abdu'l-Bahá, the son of Bahá'u'lláh and His successor, frequently spoke of the need to bring about harmony between the blacks and whites. As early as 1912, during his journey to North America, He warned of the possible consequences of failing to address this issue:

> This opposition, enmity, and prejudice among the white race and the colored cannot be effaced except through faith, assurance, and the teachings of [Bahá'u'lláh] . . . This question of the union of the white and the black is very important . . . for if it is not realized, erelong great difficulties will arise, and harmful results will follow . . . If this matter remaineth without change . . . enmity will be increased day by day, and the final result will be hardship and may end in bloodshed. [16]

Since then there has indeed been considerable bloodshed, and racial prejudice has moved to the forefront of the issues facing and dividing not only the United States[17] but many other countries.

The belief that a particular race is pure, and that its purity and superiority must be safeguarded by forbidding interracial marriage, is false – we all share a rich genetic legacy.

> . . . that the principle of the oneness of mankind prevents any true Bahá'í from regarding race itself as a bar to union is in complete accord with the Teachings of the Faith on this point. For both Bahá'u'lláh and 'Abdu'l-Bahá never disapproved of the idea of interracial marriage, nor discouraged it. The Bahá'í Teachings, indeed, by their very nature transcend all limitations imposed by race, and as such can and should never be identified with any particular school of racial philosophy.[18]

Diversity should be embraced as it adds to the beauty of humanity:

> God maketh no distinction between the white and the black. If the hearts are pure both are acceptable unto Him. God is no respecter of persons on account of either colour or race. All colours are acceptable unto Him . . . Inasmuch as all were created in the image of God, we must bring ourselves to realize that all embody divine possibilities . . . In the estimation of God, all men are equal. There is

no distinction or preference for any soul, in the realm of His justice and equity . . . .there is no distinction of colour; all are one in the colour and beauty of servitude to Him. Colour is not important; the heart is all-important . . . God doth not behold differences of hue and complexion. He looketh at the hearts. He whose morals and virtues are praiseworthy is preferred in the presence of God; he who is devoted to the Kingdom is most beloved. In the realm of genesis and creation the question of colour is of least importance.[19]

One of the important questions . . . which affect the unity and the solidarity of mankind is the fellowship and equality of the white and coloured races . . . The diversity in the human family . . . should be the cause of love and harmony, as it is in music where many different notes blend together in the making of a perfect chord . . . If you meet . . . those of a different race and colour from yourself, do not mistrust them, and withdraw yourself into your shell of conventionality, but rather be glad and show them kindness . . . In the world of being . . -the meeting is blessed when the white and coloured races meet together with infinite spiritual love and heavenly harmony. . . Strive earnestly . . . and put forth your greatest endeavour toward the accomplishment of this fellowship and the cementing of this bond of brotherhood between you. Such an attainment is not possible without will and effort on the part of each; from one, expressions of gratitude and appreciation; from the other, kindliness and recognition of equality. Each one should endeavour to develop and assist the other toward mutual advancement . . . Love and unity will be fostered between you, thereby bringing about the oneness of mankind. For the accomplishment of unity between the coloured and white will be an assurance of the world's peace . . .[20]

Given the above admonishments, the Bahá'ís have special responsibilities with regard to race and the protection of the rights of minorities:

To discriminate against any tribes because they are in a minority is a violation of the spirit that animates the Faith of Bahá'u'lláh. As followers of God's Holy Faith it is our obligation to protect the just interests of any minority element within the Bahá'í Community. In fact in the administration of our Bahá'í affairs, representatives of minority groups are not only enabled to enjoy equal rights and privileges, but they are even favoured and accorded priority. Bahá'ís should be careful never to deviate from this noble standard.²¹

If we allow prejudice of any kind to manifest itself in us, we shall be guilty before God of causing a setback to the progress and real growth of the Faith of Bahá'u'lláh. It is incumbent upon every believer to endeavour with a fierce determination to eliminate this defect from his thoughts and acts.

The fundamental purpose of the Faith of Bahá'u'lláh is the realization of the organic unity of the entire human race . . .²²

. . . a fraternity freed from that cancerous growth of racial prejudice, which is eating into the vitals of an already debilitated society . . .²³

. . . verily the faces of these are as the pupil of the eye; although the pupil is created black, yet it is the source of light. I hope God will make these black ones the glory of the white ones and as the depositing of the lights of love of God. And I ask God to assist them in all circumstances, that they may be encompassed with the favours of their Loving Lord throughout centuries and ages.²⁴

I hope that ye may cause that downtrodden race to become glorious, and to be joined with the white race, to serve the world of man with the utmost sincerity, faithfulness, love, and purity. This opposition, enmity, and prejudice among the white race and the coloured cannot be effaced except through faith, assurance, and the teachings of the Blessed Beauty . . . This question of the union of the white and the black is very important, for if it is not realized, erelong great difficulties will arise, and harmful results will follow.²⁵

Let the white make a supreme effort in their resolve to contribute their share to the solution of this problem, to abandon once for all their usually inherent and at times subconscious sense of superiority, to correct their tendency towards revealing a patronizing attitude towards the members of the other race, to persuade them through their intimate, spontaneous and informal association with them of the genuineness of their friendship and the sincerity of their intentions, and to master their impatience of any lack of responsiveness on the part of a people who have received, for so long a period, such grievous and slow-healing wounds.[26]

If any discrimination is at all to be tolerated, it should be a discrimination not against, but rather in favour of the minority, be it racial or otherwise . . . every organized community, enlisted under the banner of Bahá'u'lláh should feel it to be its first and inescapable obligation to nurture, encourage, and safeguard every minority belonging to any faith, race, class, or nation within it.[27]

Prejudices based on partisan politics

As with ecclesiastical institutions, every follower of the Faith of Bahá'u'lláh can, no doubt, subscribe to some of the principles and ideals animating political parties. However, by their very nature political parties are divisive, and a Bahá'í cannot therefore identify himself with institutions that promote partisan politics, 'nor can he unreservedly endorse the creeds, the principles and programs on which they are based'.[28] They are significant barriers to unity.

> Shun (partisan) politics like the plague, and be obedient to the Government in power in the place where we reside . . . We must obey in all cases except where a spiritual principle is involved, such as denying our Faith. For these spiritual principles we must be willing to die. What we Bahá'ís must face is the fact that society is disintegrating so rapidly that moral issues which were clear a half century ago are now hopelessly confused and what is more, thoroughly mixed up with battling political interests . . . If they become involved in the issues the Governments of the world are struggling over, they will be lost. But if they build up the Bahá'í pattern they can offer it as a remedy when all else has failed.[29]

Gender equality

Among the fundamental teachings of the Bahá'í Faith is that both sexes must be given the same opportunities, respect, and treatment:

The world of humanity has two wings – one is women and the other men. Not until both wings are equally developed can the bird fly. Should one wing remain weak, flight is impossible. Not until the world of women becomes equal to the world of men in the acquisition of virtues and perfections, can success and prosperity be attained as they ought to be.[30]

In the world of humanity . . . the female sex is treated as though inferior, and is not allowed equal rights and privileges. This condition is due not to nature, but to education. In the Divine Creation there is no such distinction. Neither sex is superior to the other in the sight of God. Why then should one sex assert the inferiority of the other, withholding just rights and privileges as though God had given His authority for such a course of action? If women received the same educational advantages as those of men, the result would demonstrate the equality of capacity of both for scholarship.

In some respects woman is superior to man. She is more tenderhearted, more receptive, her intuition is more intense. [31]

. . . woman has not been afforded the same educational facilities as man. For if she had received the same opportunities for training and development as man has enjoyed, undoubtedly she would have attained the same station and level. In the estimate of God no distinction exists; both are as one and possess equal degrees of capacity. Therefore, through opportunity and development woman will merit and attain the same prerogatives.[32]

Men and women are taught to live by spiritual principles, but God's Faith today does not discriminate against women, nor does it dictate their choices or how they should lead their lives. No male dominance or subjugation is to be tolerated. Rather than being deprived of education, girls must be given preferential training, and the feminine counsel on human affairs is to be taken fully into account – world peace and prosperity are dependent on achieving this goal.

The emancipation of women, the achievement of full equality between the sexes, is one of the most important, though less acknowledged prerequisites of peace. The denial of such equality perpetrates an injustice against one half of the world's population and promotes in men harmful attitudes and habits that are carried from the family to the workplace, to political life, and ultimately to international relations. There are no grounds, moral, practical, or biological, upon which such denial can be justified. Only as women are welcomed into full partnership in all fields of human endeavor will the moral and psychological climate be created in which international peace can emerge.[33]

... there must be an equality of rights between men and women. Women shall receive an equal privilege of education. This will enable them to qualify and progress in all degrees of occupation and accomplishment.[34]

The world in the past has been ruled by force, and man has dominated over woman by reason of his more forceful and aggressive qualities both of body and mind. But the balance is already shifting; force is losing its dominance, and mental alertness, intuition, and the spiritual qualities of love and service, in which woman is strong, are gaining ascendancy. Hence the new age will be an age less masculine and more permeated with the feminine ideals, or, to speak more exactly, will be an age in which the masculine and feminine elements of civilization will be more evenly balanced.[35]

Religious prejudice

... religious, racial, political, economic and patriotic prejudices destroy the edifice of humanity. As long as these prejudices prevail, the world of humanity will not have rest.[36]

Wherefore, O my loving friends! Consort with all the peoples, kindreds and religions of the world with the utmost truthfulness, uprightness, faithfulness, kindliness, good-will and friendliness, that all the world of being may be filled with the holy ecstasy of the grace of Bahá, that ignorance, enmity, hate and rancor may vanish from the world and the darkness of estrangement amidst the peoples and kindreds of the world may give way to the Light of Unity. Should other peoples and nations be unfaithful to you show your fidelity unto them, should they be unjust toward you show justice towards them, should they keep aloof from you attract them to yourselves, should they show their enmity be friendly towards them, should they poison your lives, sweeten their souls, should they inflict a wound upon you, be a salve to their sores. Such are the attributes of the sincere! Such are the attributes of the truthful.[37]

The fellowship and unity that are evident amongst Baháʼís, many of whom were formerly members of one of the various denominations of Christianity or of other faiths, stem from the realization that their former religious affiliation shares the same core spiritual principles as the Baháʼí Faith, but that God has once again provided humanity with new social laws that are compatible with the needs of today.

It is equally evident that, in turn, the unity of mankind is impossible unless there is organic unity of religion. This oneness of faith is far more than a slogan, a pious hope or even a plea that the religions tolerate each other and live in peace. This aim requires Baháʼís to associate freely with members of all faiths, an injunction inculcated by Baháʼu'lláh:

> That the divers communions of the earth, and the manifold systems of religious belief, should never be allowed to foster the feelings of animosity among men, is, in this Day, of the essence of the Faith of God and His Religion . . .
>
> Gird up the loins of your endeavour, O people of Bahá, that haply the tumult of religious dissension and strife that agitateth the peoples of the earth may be stilled, that every trace of it may be completely obliterated. . .
>
> The utterance of God is a lamp, whose light is these words: Ye are the fruits of one tree, and the leaves of one branch. Deal ye one with another with the utmost love and harmony, with friendliness and fellowship. . . So powerful is the light of unity that it can illuminate the whole earth.[38]

Baháʼu'lláh thus explains the unity of God's Prophets:

> They Who are the Luminaries of Truth and the Mirrors reflecting the light of Divine Unity . . . in whatever age and cycle they are sent down from their invisible habitations of ancient glory unto this world to educate the souls of men and endue with grace all created things, are

invariably endowed with an all-compelling power and invested with invincible sovereignty . . . These sanctified Mirrors, these Day-Springs of ancient glory are one and all the exponents on earth of Him Who is the central Orb of the universe, its essence and ultimate purpose. From Him proceed their knowledge and power; from Him is derived their sovereignty. The beauty of their countenance is but a reflection of His image, and their revelation a sign of His deathless glory . . . Through them is transmitted a grace that is infinite, and by them is revealed the light that can never fade . . . they therefore are regarded as one soul and the same person . . . They all abide in the same tabernacle, soar in the same heaven, are seated upon the same throne, utter the same speech, and proclaim the same Faith.[39]

Bahá'u'lláh has announced that the foundation of all the religions of God is one, that oneness is truth and truth is oneness which does not admit of plurality. This teaching is new and specialized to this Manifestation.[40]

Scientific truth and endeavour should complement religion

Science and religion are both based on truth and therefore must not be in conflict. Rather, they should complement one another. The Bahá'í Faith enjoins the acquisition of knowledge and the study of the arts and sciences. It upholds the standard that scientific freedom and truth must not be restricted by preconceived religious notions. It teaches that 'religion must be in conformity with science and reason, so that it may influence the hearts of men. The foundation must be solid and must not consist of imitations.'[41]

Whatever the intelligence of man cannot understand, religion ought not to accept. . . any religion contrary to science is not the truth.[42]

Religion must stand the analysis of reason. It must agree with scientific act and proof so that science will sanction religion and religion fortify science. Both are indissolubly welded and joined in reality. If statements and teachings of religion are found to be unreasonable and contrary to science, they are outcomes of superstition and imagination.[43]

Religion and science are the two wings upon which man's intelligence can soar into the heights, with which the human soul can progress. It is not possible to fly with one wing alone! Should a man try to fly with the wing of religion alone he would quickly fall into the quagmire of superstition, whilst on the other hand, with the wing of science alone he would also make no progress, but fall into the despairing slough of materialism.[44]

Learning a profession or skill

Bahá'u'lláh counsels His followers to study such sciences and arts as are 'useful' and would further 'the progress and advancement' of society. He cautions against sciences which 'begin with words and end with words', the pursuit of which leads to 'idle disputation', 'fruitless excursions into metaphysical hair-splitting', and 'those theological treatises and commentaries that encumber the human mind rather than help it to attain the truth'.[45]

Consider work as worship

> It is enjoined upon every one of you to engage in some form of occupation, such as crafts, trades and the like. We have graciously exalted your engagement in such work to the rank of worship unto God, the True One . . . Waste not your time in idleness and sloth. Occupy yourselves with that which profiteth yourselves and others.[46]

Universal education and the spiritual training of children

Bahá'u'lláh declares that all human beings should attain knowledge and acquire an education. This is a new and a necessary principle of religious belief.

> The education of children is therefore compulsory in the Bahá'í Faith. They are required to receive 'systematic training' from earliest childhood, with explanations of the sciences through play and verbal interactive sessions, and not merely through reading books.[47]

Educators are encouraged to be particularly sensitive to the inclination, desire, and talents of a particular youth when considering long-term choices about contributing to society and earning a living.[48]

Education of girls is of paramount importance

... most important of all is the education of girl children, for these girls will one day be mothers, and the mother is the first teacher of the child. In whatever way she reareth the child, so will the child become, and the results of that first training will remain with the individual throughout his entire life, and it would be most difficult to alter them. And how can a mother, herself ignorant and untrained, educate her child? It is therefore clear that the education of girls is of far greater consequence than that of boys ... .[49]

Evolving towards a united global society

The Bahá'í Writings observe:

Today, humanity faces the limits of a social order inadequate to meet the compelling challenges of a world that has virtually shrunk to the level of a neighborhood. On this small planet, sovereign nations find themselves caught between cooperation and competition. The well-being of humanity and of the environment are too often compromised for national self-interest. Propelled by competing ideologies, divided by various constructs of us versus them, the people of the world are plunged into one crisis after another – brought on by war, terrorism, prejudice, oppression, economic disparity, and environmental upheaval, among other causes.[50]

Just as the organic evolution of mankind has been slow and gradual, and involved successively the unification of the family, the tribe, the city-state, and the nation, so has the light vouchsafed by the Revelation of God, at various stages in the evolution of religion, and reflected in the successive Dispensations of the past, been slow and progressive. Indeed the measure of Divine Revelation, in every age, has been adapted to, and commensurate with, the degree of social progress achieved in that age by a constantly evolving humanity.[51]

A new vision for humanity – spiritual solutions to global issues

> For Bahá'u'lláh, we should readily recognize, has not only imbued mankind with a new and regenerating Spirit. He has not merely enunciated certain universal principles, or propounded a particular philosophy, however potent, sound and universal these may be. In addition to these He, as well as 'Abdu'l-Bahá after Him, has, unlike the Dispensations of the past, clearly and specifically laid down a set of Laws, established definite institutions, and provided for the essentials of a Divine Economy. These are destined to be a pattern for future society, a supreme instrument for the establishment of the Most Great Peace, and the one agency for the unification of the world, and the proclamation of the reign of righteousness and justice upon the earth.[52]

Bahá'u'lláh envisages a social order that is fundamentally different from what exists today – one that considers the welfare of all mankind:

> It is incumbent upon all the peoples of the world to reconcile their differences, and, with perfect unity and peace, abide beneath the shadow of the Tree of His care and loving-kindness. It behoveth them to cleave to whatsoever will, in this Day, be conducive to the exaltation of their stations, and to the promotion of their best interests.[53]

He solemnly asserts:

> Soon will the present day order be rolled up, and a new one spread out in its stead.[54]

He has brought the blueprint for global transformation and the creation of a spiritual world civilization:

> The most glorious fruit of the tree of knowledge is this exalted word: Of one tree are ye all the fruit, and of one bough the leaves. Let not man glory in this that he loveth his country, let him rather glory in this that he loveth his kind.[55]

Shoghi Effendi further explains:

> This New World Order, whose promise is enshrined in the Revelation of Bahá'u'lláh . . . involves no less than the complete unification of the entire human race. This unification should conform to such principles as would directly harmonize with the spirit that animates, and the laws that govern the operation of, the institutions that already constitute the structural basis of the Administrative Order of His Faith.[56]

As noted earlier, creating a just and harmonious global society is intimately dependent on the realization that the whole world is essentially one country and all mankind are its citizens.

> The distinguishing feature of humanity's coming of age is that, for the first time in its history, the entire human race is consciously involved, however dimly, in the awareness of its own oneness and of the earth as a single homeland. This awakening opens the way to a new relationship between God and humankind. As the peoples of the world embrace the spiritual authority inherent in the guidance of the Revelation of God for this age, Bahá'u'lláh said, they will find in themselves a moral empowerment which human effort alone has proven incapable of generating. 'A new race of men' will emerge as the result of this relationship, and the work of building a global civilization will begin.[57]

Humanity is ready for a change and the adoption of new ways of managing its affairs: 'Every system, short of the unification of the human race, has been tried, repeatedly tried, and been found wanting.'[58]

> No doubt after so many years of deep suffering and bitter disillusion there are many souls eager for the truth, and more awakened to the need of a spiritual solution for the world's problems.[59]

Bahá'u'lláh recommends that we develop a new set of priorities by cultivating a desire for the betterment of the world instead of promoting our selfish longings:

O people of God! Do not busy yourselves in your own concerns; let your thoughts be fixed upon that which will rehabilitate the fortunes of mankind and sanctify the hearts and souls of men. This can best be achieved through pure and holy deeds, through a virtuous life and a goodly behavior. Valiant acts will ensure the triumph of this Cause, and a saintly character will reinforce its power . . . Let your vision be world-embracing, rather than confined to your own self. [60]

Their purpose is to obliterate differences, and quench the flame of hatred and enmity, so that the whole earth may come to be viewed as one country.[61]

Promotion of global peace, unity and amity

Therefore, it is our duty to put forth our greatest efforts and summon all our energies in order that the bonds of unity and accord may be established among mankind. For thousands of years we have had bloodshed and strife. It is enough; it is sufficient. Now is the time to associate together in love and harmony. For thousands of years we have tried the sword and warfare; let mankind for a time at least live in peace. Review history and consider how much savagery, how much bloodshed and battle the world has witnessed. It has been either religious warfare, political warfare or some other clash of human interests. The world of humanity has never enjoyed the blessing of universal peace. Year by year the implements of warfare have been increased and perfected.[62]

Elimination of world hunger and poverty

The inordinate disparity between rich and poor, a source of acute suffering, keeps the world in a state of instability, virtually on the brink of war. Few societies have dealt effectively with this situation. The solution calls for the combined application of spiritual, moral and practical approaches. A fresh look at the problem is required, entailing consultation with experts from a wide spectrum of disciplines, devoid of economic and ideological polemics, and involving the people directly affected in the decisions that must urgently be made. It is an issue that is bound up not only with the necessity for eliminating extremes of wealth and poverty but also with those spiritual verities the understanding of which can produce a new universal attitude. Fostering such an attitude is itself a major part of the solution.[63]

Consultation as an instrument for promoting the well-being of the community

Bahá'u'lláh has established consultation – described by 'Abdu'l-Bahá as 'spiritual conference and not the mere voicing of personal views'[64]– as one of the fundamental principles of His Faith, to be practised at all levels of administration of its affairs:

> . . . consultation must have for its object the investigation of truth. He who expresses an opinion should not voice it as correct and right but set it forth as a contribution to the consensus of opinion, for the light of reality becomes apparent when two opinions coincide. A spark is produced when flint and steel come together. Man should weigh his opinions with the utmost serenity, calmness and composure. Before expressing his own views he should carefully consider the views already advanced by others. If he finds that a previously expressed opinion is more true and worthy, he should accept it immediately and not wilfully hold to an opinion of his own. By this excellent method he endeavours to arrive at unity and truth. Opposition and division are deplorable.[65]

> . . . at the very root of the Cause lies the principle of the undoubted right of the individual to self-expression, his freedom to declare his conscience and set forth his views . . . Let us also bear in mind that the keynote of the Cause of God is not dictatorial authority but humble fellowship, not arbitrary power, but the spirit of frank and loving consultation. Nothing short of the spirit of a true Bahá'í can hope to reconcile the principles of mercy and justice, freedom and submission, of the sanctity of the right of the individual and of self-surrender, of vigilance, discretion and prudence on the one hand, and fellowship, candor, and courage on the other.[66]

Adoption of a universal auxiliary language

Bahá'u'lláh has proclaimed the adoption of a universal language. A language shall be agreed upon by which unity will be established in the world. Each person will require training in two languages: his native tongue and the universal auxiliary form of speech. This will facilitate intercommunication and dispel the misunderstandings which the barriers of language have occasioned in the world. All people worship the same God and are alike His servants. When they are able to communicate freely, they will associate in friendship and concord, entertain the greatest love and fellowship for each other, and in reality the Orient and Occident will embrace in unity and agreement.[67]

A world commonwealth fortified by the principle of collective security

Sane patriotism and love and respect for the diverse cultures

Far from aiming at the subversion of the existing foundations of society, it [the Law of Bahá'u'lláh] seeks to broaden its basis, to remold its institutions in a manner consonant with the needs of an ever-changing world. It can conflict with no legitimate allegiances, nor can it undermine essential loyalties. Its purpose is neither to stifle the flame of a sane and intelligent patriotism in men's hearts, nor to abolish the system of national autonomy so essential if the evils of excessive centralization are to be avoided. It does not ignore, nor does it attempt to suppress, the diversity of ethnical origins, of climate, of history, of language and tradition, of thought and habit, that differentiate the peoples and nations of the world. It calls for a wider loyalty, for a larger aspiration than any that has animated the human race. It insists upon the subordination of national impulses and interests to the imperative claims of a unified world. It repudiates excessive centralization on one hand, and disclaims all attempts at uniformity on the other. Its watchword is unity in diversity . . .[68]

Unbridled nationalism, as distinguished from a sane and legitimate patriotism, must give way to a wider loyalty, to the love of humanity as a whole . . . The concept of world citizenship is a direct result of the contraction of the world into a single neighbourhood through scientific advances and of the indisputable interdependence of nations. Love of all the world's peoples does not exclude love of one's country. The advantage of the part in a world society is best served by promoting the advantage of the whole. Current international activities in various fields which nurture mutual affection and a sense of solidarity among peoples need greatly to be increased.[69]

Though loyal to their respective governments, though profoundly interested in anything that affects their security and welfare, though anxious to share in whatever promotes their best interests, the Faith with which the followers of Bahá'u'lláh stand identified is one which they firmly believe God has raised high above the storms, the divisions, and controversies of the political arena. Their Faith they conceive to be essentially non-political, supra-national in character, rigidly non-partisan, and entirely dissociated from nationalistic ambitions, pursuits, and purposes. Such a Faith knows no division of class or of party. It subordinates, without hesitation or equivocation, every particularistic interest, be it personal, regional, or national, to the paramount interests of humanity, firmly convinced that in a world of inter-dependent peoples and nations the advantage of the part is best to be reached by the advantage of the whole, and that no abiding benefit can be conferred upon the component parts if the general interests of the entity itself are ignored or neglected.[70]

Changes to earlier social laws

Today, in addition to renewing and revitalizing the moral and ethical prescriptions that must dictate human conduct, Bahá'u'lláh has abrogated a number of the social principles of Judaism, Christianity and Islam, largely accrued, that in a global society promote division and perpetuate prejudices. Some of these social laws had become distorted over time and have been replaced by laws that create harmony in the family of mankind.

> O ye that dwell on earth! The distinguishing feature that marketh the preeminent character of this Supreme Revelation consisteth in

that We have, on the one hand, blotted out from the pages of God's book whatsoever hath been the cause of strife, of malice and mischief amongst the children of men, and have, on the other, laid down the essential prerequisites of concord, of understanding, of complete and enduring unity. Well is it with them that keep My statutes.[71]

Abolition of 'holy' or religious war

The Bahá'í Faith does not condone war with people who have different beliefs, but instead it protects their rights and uses the power of reason, logic and example to demonstrate its own validity and vision for mankind. Thus, holy war[72] by individuals to advance the interests of a religion has been eliminated from God's Faith. Bahá'u'lláh declares:

> O people of the earth! The first Glad-Tidings which the Mother Book hath, in this Most Great Revelation, imparted unto all the peoples of the world is that the law of holy war hath been blotted out from the Book. Glorified be the All-Merciful, the Lord of grace abounding, through Whom the door of heavenly bounty hath been flung open in the face of all that are in heaven and on earth.[73]

> Beware lest ye shed the blood of anyone. Unsheathe the sword of your tongue from the scabbard of utterance, for therewith ye can conquer the citadels of men's hearts. We have abolished the law to wage holy war against each other. God's mercy, hath, verily, encompassed all created things, if ye do but understand. Aid ye your Lord, the God of Mercy, with the sword of understanding. Keener indeed is it, and more finely tempered, than the sword of utterance, were ye but to reflect upon the words of your Lord.[74]

However, it is important to note the following clarification:

> Bahá'ís recognize the right and duty of governments to use force for the maintenance of law and order and to protect their people. Thus, for a Bahá'í, the shedding of blood for such a purpose is not necessarily wrong. The Bahá'í Faith draws a very definite distinction between the duty of the an individual to forgive and 'to be killed

rather than kill' and the duty of society to uphold justice . . . In the present condition of the world Bahá'ís try to keep themselves out of the internecine conflicts that are raging among their fellow men and to avoid shedding in struggles, but this does not mean that we are absolute pacifists . . .[75]

With reference to the absolute pacifists, or conscientious objectors to war; their attitude, judged from the Bahá'í standpoint is quite anti-social and due to its exaltation of the individual conscience leads inevitably to disorder and chaos in society. Extreme pacifists are thus very close to the anarchists, in the sense that both of these groups lay an undue emphasis on the rights and merits of the individual. The Bahá'í conception of social life is essentially based on the subordination of the individual will to that of society. It neither suppresses the individual nor does it exalt him to the point of making him an anti-social creature, a menace to society. As in everything, it follows the 'golden mean'. The only way that society can function is for the minority to follow the will of the majority.

The other main objection to the conscientious objectors is that their method of establishing peace is too negative. Non-cooperation is too passive a philosophy to become an effective way for social reconstruction. Their refusal to bear arms can never establish peace. There should first be a spiritual revitalization which nothing, except the Cause of God, can effectively bring to every man's heart.[76]

Priestly confession

Although Bahá'ís must recognize and sincerely repent of their sins, Bahá'u'lláh prohibits constitutional confession:

> When the sinner findeth himself wholly detached and freed from all save God, he should beg forgiveness and pardon from Him. Confession of sins and transgressions before human beings is not permissible, as it hath never been nor will ever be conducive to divine forgiveness. Moreover such confession before people results in one's humiliation and abasement, and God – exalted be His glory – wisheth not the humiliation of His servants. Verily He is the

Compassionate, the Merciful. The sinner should, between himself and God, implore mercy from the Ocean of mercy, beg forgiveness from the heaven of generosity.[77]

Bahá'u'lláh's prohibition concerning the confession of sins (to a priest) does not prevent an individual from admitting transgressions in the course of consultations held under the aegis of Bahá'í institutions. Likewise, it does not preclude the possibility of seeking advice from a close friend or of a professional counsellor regarding such matters.[78]

The daily life of Bahá'ís, in the framework of the Administrative Order of Bahá'u'lláh

Individual daily prayer and private reflection are confirmed and prescribed in the Bahá'í Faith, whose Central Figures have revealed many prayers and meditations. Bahá'ís recite one of three obligatory prayers daily, and fast from sunrise to sunset for 19 days each year. They meditate on the Bahá'í Sacred Writings as well as the scriptures of all religions. In addition, they observe commemorate Holy Days such as the Declarations of the Báb and Bahá'u'lláh.

The Bahá'í Faith has no paid clergy. At a local level, the affairs of the Bahá'í community are administered by the Local Spiritual Assembly. Again, once a year delegates from various communities elect a National Spiritual Assembly. Once every five years members of National Spiritual Assemblies elect the nine members[79] of the Universal House of Justice, the supreme governing council of the Faith, which has its seat in Haifa, Israel.

Every Bahá'í month, which comprises nineteen days, Bahá'ís participate in a meeting that forms the bedrock of Bahá'í community life. It includes a devotional portion, an administrative portion where members of the community consult with one another and make recommendations for the Local Spiritual Assembly to consider, and a social portion during which refreshments are served and members of the community can converse.

Summary

As anticipated by the major religions of mankind, God has once again revealed His purpose, in preparation for the establishment of His kingdom on earth. The following quotation describes the attitude of the Bahá'í Faith to its sister religions:

> The Revelation, of which Bahá'u'lláh is the source and centre, abrogates none of the religions that have preceded it, nor does it attempt, in the slightest degree, to distort their features or to belittle their value. It disclaims any intention of dwarfing any of the Prophets of the past, or of whittling down the eternal verity of their teachings. It can, in no wise, conflict with the spirit that animates their claims, nor does it seek to undermine the basis of any man's allegiance to their cause. Its declared, its primary purpose is to enable every adherent of these Faiths to obtain a fuller understanding of the religion with which he stands identified, and to acquire a clearer apprehension of its purpose. It is neither eclectic in the presentation of its truths, nor arrogant in the affirmation of its claims. Its teachings revolve around the fundamental principle that religious truth is not absolute but relative, that Divine Revelation is progressive, not final. Unequivocally and without the least reservation it proclaims all established religions to be divine in origin, identical in their aims, complementary in their functions, continuous in their purpose, indispensable in their value to mankind.[80]

BIBLIOGRAPHY

'Abdu'l-Bahá. *'Abdu'l-Bahá in London* (1912, 1921). London: Bahá'í Publishing Trust, 1982.
— *Japan Will Turn Ablaze!* Tokyo: Bahá'í Publishing Trust of Japan, rev. ed. 1992.
— *Paris Talks: Addresses given by 'Abdu'l-Bahá in 1911* (1912). London: Bahá'í Publishing Trust, 12th ed. 1995.
— *The Promulgation of Universal Peace: Talks Delivered by 'Abdu'l-Baha During His Visit to the United States and Canada in 1912* (1922, 1925). Comp. H. MacNutt. Wilmette, IL: Bahá'í Publishing Trust, 2nd ed. 1982.
— *The Secret of Divine Civilization.* Trans. M. Gail. Wilmette, IL: Bahá'í Publishing Trust, 1957.
— *Selections from the Writings of 'Abdu'l-Bahá.* Comp. Research Department of the Universal House of Justice. Haifa: Bahá'í World Centre, 1978.
— *Some Answered Questions* (1908). Comp. and trans. Laura Clifford Barney. Haifa: Bahá'í World Centre, rev. ed. 2014.
— *Tablets of 'Abdu'l-Bahá* (etext in the Ocean search engine; originally published as *Tablets of Abdul-Baha Abbas*. 3 vols. Chicago: Bahá'í Publishing Society, 1909–1916). Wilmette, IL: National Spiritual Assembly of the Bahá'ís of the United States, 1980.
— *Tablets of the Divine Plan.* Wilmette, IL: Bahá'í Publishing Trust, rev. ed. 1977.
— *Will and Testament of 'Abdu'l-Bahá.* Wilmette, IL: National Spiritual Assembly of the Bahá'ís of the United States, 1944.

AlJazeera. 'Pope apologises for church's role in Rwanda genocide', 20 March 2017.

Angier, Natalie. 'Do races differ? Not really, genes show', in *The New York Times*, 22 August 2000.

'Antisemitism, Christianity and Anti-semitism, Jewish deicide', online article, February 2018, at https://www.antisem.eu/jewish-deicide/.

Anti-Slavery International. 'What is modern slavery?', online article at: https://www.antislavery.org.

Augustine, Saint (Augustine of Hippo). *Contra Faustum Manichaeum.* https://www.newadvent.org/fathers/140622.htm.
— *De Symbolo ad Catechumenos* (On the Creed: A Sermon to Catechumens). www.ewtn.com.

— *The Letters of St. Augustine.* North Charleston, SC: Createspace, 1972.
— *The Works of Saint Augustine: A Translation for the 21st Century.* New City Press, 2005.

The Báb. *Selections from the Writings of the Báb.* Comp. Research Department of the Universal House of Justice. Haifa: Bahá'í World Centre, 1976.

Bahá'í Education: A Compilation. Research Department of the Universal House of Justice. Wilmette, IL: Bahá'í Publishing Trust, 1977.

Bahá'í International Community, Office of Public Information. *Bahá'u'lláh.* Haifa; Bahá'í World Centre, 1992.

Bahá'í Prayers: A Selection of Prayers Revealed by Bahá'u'lláh, the Báb, and 'Abdu'l-Bahá. Wilmette, IL: Bahá'í Publishing Trust, 1991.

The Bahá'í World online, at: https://bahaiworld.bahai.org.

Bahá'í World Faith: Selected Writings of Bahá'u'lláh and 'Abdu'l-Bahá. Wilmette, IL: Bahá'í Publishing Trust, 1976.

Bahá'u'lláh. *Epistle to the Son of the Wolf.* Trans. Shoghi Effendi. Wilmette, IL: Bahá'í Publishing Trust, rev. ed. 1976.
— *Gems of Divine Mysteries: Javáhiru'l-Asrár.* Haifa: Bahá'í World Centre, 2002.
— *Gleanings from the Writings of Bahá'u'lláh.* Trans. Shoghi Effendi. Wilmette, IL: Bahá'í Publishing Trust, 2nd ed. 1976.
— *The Hidden Words of Bahá'u'lláh.* Trans. Shoghi Effendi. Wilmette, IL: Bahá'í Publishing Trust, 1970; New Delhi: Bahá'í Publishing Trust, 1987.
— *The Kitáb-i-Aqdas: The Most Holy Book.* Haifa: Bahá'í World Centre, 1992.
— *Kitáb-i-Íqán: The Book of Certitude.* Trans. Shoghi Effendi. Wilmette, IL: Bahá'í Publishing Trust, 2nd ed. 1950, 1981.
— *Prayers and Meditations by Bahá'u'lláh.* Trans. Shoghi Effendi. Wilmette, IL: Bahá'í Publishing Trust, 1938, 1987.
— *The Summons of the Lord of Hosts: Tablets of Bahá'u'lláh.* Haifa: Bahá'í World Centre, 2002.
— *The Tabernacle of Unity.* Haifa: Bahá'í World Centre, 2006.
— *Tablets of Bahá'u'lláh Revealed after the Kitáb-i-Aqdas.* Comp. Research Department of the Universal House of Justice. Haifa: Bahá'í World Centre, 1978.

Barclay, William. *The Plain Man Looks at the Apostles Creed.* London: Collins, 1977, 1990.
— *The Plain Man Looks at the Lord's Prayer.* Glasgow: Collins, 1965.

Baltimore Catechism. Rev. ed. 1941. https://www.catholicity.com/baltimore-catechism/.

Barna Group, 2018. 'Atheism doubles among generation Z' (2018). https://www.barna.com/research/atheism-doubles-among-generation-z/

Barnes, Albert. *Albert Barnes' Notes on the Whole Bible*, at StudyLight.org/Bible Commentaries.

— *Notes, Explanatory and Practical, on the Book of the Prophet Isaiah*. New York: Leavitt & Allen, 1853. www.sacred-texts.com/bib/cmt/barnes/index.htm.
— *Notes on the New Testament, Explanatory and Practical*. Ed. Robert Frew. London: Baker Book House, 1956.
— *Notes, Explanatory and Practical on the Gospels*. 2 vols. London: George Routledge, 1846, 1857.
— *Barnes' Notes, Explanatory and Practical, on the Gospels*, New York: Harper & Brothers, 1855.
— *Notes, Explanatory and Practical, on The Gospels: Designed for Sunday School and Bible Classes*. New York: Harper & Brothers, 1847.
— *Notes, Explanatory and Practical, on the Book of Revelation*. London: Knight and Son, 1853.
— *Notes, Explanatory and Practical, on the Acts of the Apostles: Designed for Sunday-School Teachers and Bible Classes*. New York: Harper & Brothers, rev. ed. 1870.
— *Notes, Explanatory and Practical, on the First Epistle of Paul to the Corinthians*. London: Knight and Son, 1852.
— *Notes, Explanatory and Practical, on the Second Epistle to the Corinthians and the Epistle to the Galatians*. New York: Harper & Brothers, 1846, 1847.
— *Barnes' Notes, Explanatory and Practical, on the Second Epistle to Corinthians and the Epistle to Galatians*. Ed. Rev. Ingram Cobbin. London: Knight and Son, 1852.
— *Notes, Explanatory and Practical on the Epistles of Paul to the Thessalonians, to Timothy, to Titus, and to Philemon*. New York: Harper & Brothers, 1846; London: Knight and Son, 1852.
— *Notes, Explanatory and Practical, on the General Epistles of James, Peter, John, & Jude*. London: Knight and Son, 1854. New York: Harper & Brothers, 1857.

Barnes, Ernest William. *The Rise of Christianity*. Longmans, Green and Co., 1947.

Bates, Stephen. 'Synod approves church remarriage for divorcees', in *The Guardian*, 14 November 2002.

Baumann, Jonas; Finnbogason, Daniel; Svensson, Isak. 'Rethinking mediation: Resolving religious conflicts', Center for Security Studies (CSS), 2 February 2018. www.css.ethz.ch/gess/cis/services/digital-library/articles/article.html.

BBC News. 'Child abuse: 7% of Australian Catholic priests alleged to be involved', 6 February 2017. www.bbc.com/newettsteinws/world-australia-38877158.

Bendavid, Naftali. 'Europe's empty churches go on sale', in *The Wall Street Journal*, 2 January 2015.

Bengel, John Albert (Albrecht). *John Albert Bengel's Gnomen of the New Testament, Pointing Out from the Natural Force of the Words, the Simplicity, Depth, Harmony and Saving Power of the Divine Thoughts*. Trans. Charlton T. Lewis and Marvin R. Vincent. Philadelphia: Perkinpine and Higgens; New York: Sheldon & Co., 1862.

Benson, Joseph. *The Holy Bible, Containing the Old and New Testaments according to the Present, Authorized Version with Critical, Explanatory, and Practical Notes*. New York: G. Lane & C. B. Tippett, for the Methodist Episcopal Church, 1846.

— *The New Testament of Our Lord and Saviour Jesus Christ, with Critical, Explanatory, and Practical Notes.* New York: Lane & Tippett, 1846; Carlton & Phillips, 1854.

Bhagavad Gita. Trans. Sir Edwin Arnold. Dover Thrift Editions, 1993.

Bible. The translations used in this book, unless otherwise indicated in the quotations, are from the English Standard Version, available online at Biblehub.com/Online Bible Study Suite. Other versions cited in the quotations are mainly at the same online source; if not, the publishers are indicated in the list below:

American Standard Version (first published 1901, rev. ed. 2010) also known as the Revised Version, Standard American Edition of the Bible.

Amplified Bible, Classic Edition (AMPC). Republished as Amplified Bible: The Comparative Study Bible, A Parallel Bible. Grand Rapids, MI: Zondervan Bible Publishers, 1965.

Aramaic Bible in Plain English (published in 2010 by Lulu.com).

Berean Literal Bible, and Berean Study Bible (2016).

Darby Bible. Trans. 1867, with revised editions in 1872 and 1884.

The Discovery Bible. https://thediscoverybible.com.

The Expositor's Greek Testament. Ed. Rev. W. Robertson Nicoll. New York: George H. Doran & Co., 1897.

Gideon Bible. The Holy Bible containing the Old and New Testaments, commonly known as the Authorized (King James) Version.

God's Word Translation (GW). Trans. God's Word to the Nations Bible Mission Society. Iowa Falls, Iowa: World Publishing, 1995.

Good News Translation (GNT). Trans. The American Bible Society. First published as the New Testament under the name *Good News for Modern Man* in 1966.

Jubilee Bible (2000). BibleGateway.com.

King James Version (Authorized Version, 1611); also New King James Version (1982 revision); and the American King James Version, 6th revision, 2018, at www.kneelingmedia.org.

Net Bible (2005). A completely new translation.

New American Standard Bible (1995). Translation first published by the Lockman Foundation in 1971.

New Heart English Bible (NHEB) (2008). A modern English translation of the New Testament based on the American Standard Version first published in 1901.

New International Version (NIV), International Bible Society. Grand Rapids, MI: Zondervan Bible Publishers, 1984.

The New Layman's Parallel Bible. Grand Rapids, MI: Zondervan Bible Publishers, 1987.

New Living Translation (1996).

Orthodox Jewish Bible. Trans. Philip E. Goble. New York: AFI International, 4th ed. 2011.

Revised Standard Version. Authorized revision of the American Standard Version of 1901.

Webster's Bible Translation (1833). A revision of the King James Version.

World English Bible (also known as the WEB) (2000). An updated revision of the American Standard Version (1901).

Young's Literal Translation (1862).

Bickersteth, Edward. *The Signs of the Times in the East; A Warning to the West. Being a A Practical View of Our Duties in the Light of the Prophecies which Illustrate the Present and Future State of the Church and of the World.* London: Seeley, Burnside and Seeley, 1845. (Kessinger Legacy Reprints).

Billy Graham Evangelistic Association. 'What did Jesus mean when He said to let the dead bury the dead?', online article, 5 October 2004, at: https://billygraham.org.

Blackie, John Stuart. *The Day-book of John Stuart Blackie*, Selected and Transcribed from the Manuscript by his Nephew, Archibald Stodard-Walker. London: Grant Richards, 1901 (Harvard College Library).

Booth, Robert. 'Christians could be minority by 2018', in *The Guardian*, 11 December 2012.

Borg, Marcus Joel. 'The Resurrection of Jesus', in *Religion & Ethics Newsweekly*, 26 March 1999.

Bourne, George. *A Condensed Anti-Slavery Bible Argument.* New York: S. W. Benedict, 1845.

Boyd Carpenter, W. *The New Testament Commentary: The Revelation of St. John the Divine.* Ed. Charles John Ellicott. London, Paris & New York: Cassell, Peter, Galpin & Co., 1879.

Brown, Peter. 'Augustine's attitude to religious coercion', in *Journal of Roman Studies*, vol. 54 (1964).

Butler, Declan. 'Vatican toughens stance on embryo research', in *Nature*, December 2008.

Cairns, David S. *The Reasonableness of the Christian Faith.* London, New York, Toronto: Hodder and Stoughton, 3rd ed. 1920.

Calvin, John. *Institutes of the Christian Religion.* Trans. Henry Beveridge, ed. Anthony Uyl. Ingersoll, Ontario: Devoted Publishing, 2014.
— *The Necessity of Reforming the Church* (1544). Trans. Henry Beveridge. E-book, First Rate Publishers, 2014.

The Cambridge Bible for Schools and Colleges. Cambridge: Cambridge University Press, 1893.

Carter, Jimmy. *A Call to Action: Women, Religion, Violence, and Power.* New York: Simon and Schuster, 2014.

Carter, Joe. 'Are all Christian denominations in decline?' in *The Gospel Coalition*, 17 March 2015.

Carus, Paul. *The Gospel of Buddha According to Old Records* (1894). Chicago: Open Court Publishing, 11th ed.

Catechism of the Catholic Church. Online at: www.vatican.va/archive/.

Catholic Answers. 'What the early Church believed: Peter's primacy'. https://www.catholic.com/tract/peters-primacy.

The Catholic Encyclopedia: An International Work of Reference on the Constitution, Doctrine, Discipline, and History of the Catholic Church. 15 vols. New York: The Encyclopedia Press, 1911.

Catholicism.org. 'The Popes on *Extra Ecclesiam Nulla Salus*'. 31 January 2005.
— 'The Council of Florence (1438-1445) from *Cantate Domino*: Papal Bull of Pope Eugene IV', 16 March 2005.

Chabad, org. Website of the Chabad-Lubavitch Hasidic movement.

Chou, Vivian. 'How science and genetics are shaping the race debate of the 21st century', Harvard University Blog Opinion, 17 April 2017.

Church of Jesus Christ of Latter-Day Saints. 'The Book of Abraham', with papyri facsimiles, in *Holy Bible, Book of Mormon, Doctrine and Covenants, Pearl of Great Price* (compilation). Salt Lake City, Utah, 1979.

Clarke, Adam. *Adam Clarke's Commentary on the Whole Bible* (1810–1826). Online at: https://www.studylight.org/commentaries/acc.html.

Claster, Jill N. *Sacred Violence: The European Crusades to the Middle East, 1095–1396.* Toronto: University of Toronto Press, 2009.

Cline, Austin. 'Jesus: Contradictions in resurrection and ascension', 25 June 2019, online at: https://www.learnreligions.com.

Clinton, Stephen M. *Peter, Paul and the Anonymous Christian: A Response to The Mission Theology of Rahner and Vatican II.* The Orlando Institute, Leadership Forum, November 1998, Evangelical Theological Society.

Coffey, John. *Persecution and Toleration in Protestant England 1588-1689.* Harlow: Longman Pearson Education, 2000.

Cohen, Chaim. 'Eden', in Adele Berlin and Maxine Grossman: *The Oxford Dictionary of the Jewish People.* Oxford: Oxford University Press, 2011.

Cohn, Nate. 'Big drop in share of Americans calling themselves Christian', in *The New York Times*, 12 May 2015.

Collinge, William J. *Historical Dictionary of Catholicism*. Lanham, MD: Scarecrow Press, 2nd ed. 2002.

Congregation for the Doctrine of the Faith. *Declaration 'Dominus Iesus' on the Unicity and Salvific Universality of Jesus Christ and the Church*, 2000. Online at: www.vatican.va/roman.../rc_con_cfaith_doc_20000806_dominus-iesus_en.html.

Cowles, Henry. *The Holy Bible with a Commentary Explanatory and Practical and Introductions to the Several Books, by Clergymen of the Church of England*. Oxford, Cambridge, and London: J. Parker & Co., 1879.

Cross, F. L. (ed). 'Great Schism (1)', in *The Oxford Dictionary of the Christian Church*. New York: Oxford University Press, 2005.

Crossan, John Dominic; Watts, Richard G. *Who is Jesus? Answers to Your Questions About the Historical Jesus*. Louisville, Kentucky: Westminster John Knox Press, 1996.

Daniel, E. Randolph; Murphy, Thomas Patrick. 'The Holy War (review)', in *Speculum*, vol. 53 (1978), no. 3, pp. 602–3.

Davidson, James D. 'Fewer and fewer', in *America Magazine*, vol. 189 (2003), no. 18.

Davies, W. D.; Allison, Dale C. Jr. *A Critical and Exegetical Commentary on The Gospel According to Saint Matthew*. London and New York: T&T Clark International, 2004.

The Dawn-Breakers: Nabíl's Narrative of the Early Days of the Bahá'í Revelation. Trans. Shoghi Effendi. Wilmette, IL: Bahá'í Publishing Trust, 1932, 1999.

Deringil, Selim. *Conversion and Apostasy in the Late Ottoman Empire*. Cambridge: Cambridge University Press, 2012.

Dorgan, Michael. 'Irish priests disappointed at Pope's reluctance to ordain female deacons', in *IrishCentral*, 15 May 2019.

Drews, Wolfram. *The Unknown Neighbour: The Jew in the Thought of Isidore of Seville*. Leiden: Brill Academic, 2006.

Durant, Will. *The Story of Civilization: The Age of Faith*. New York: Simon and Schuster, 1950.

Earle, Alice Morse. *The Sabbath in Puritan New England*. New York: Charles Scribner's Sons, 1891.

Easton, M. G. *Illustrated Bible Dictionary*. London: Thomas Nelson, 1897.

The Economist. 'The Bible v the Koran: The battle of the books', 19 December 2007.

Edmundson, George. *The Church in Rome in the First Century*. Reprint from the collection of the University of California Libraries. London, New York, Bombay and Calcutta: Longmans, Green & Co., 1913.

Egbert, Elaine. *Till Morning Breaks: A Story of the Millerite Movement and the Great Disappointment*. Adventist Heritage Library. Nampa, Idaho: Pacific Press, 1993.

Ellicott, Charles John. *Ellicott's Commentary on the Whole Bible* (originally published by Cassell as *A Bible Commentary for English Readers*, 1897). Eugene, OR: Wipf & Stock, 2015. https://biblehub.com and https://www.studylight.org.

— *An Old Testament Commentary for English Readers*. London, Paris, & New York: Cassell, 1884.

— *The New Testament Commentary for English Readers*. London, Paris & New York: Cassell, 1884. www.DelmarvaPublications.com.

— (ed.). *A New Testament Commentary for English Readers by Various Writers*. London, Paris & Melbourne: Cassell, 1897.

— *The New Testament Commentary for Schools*. London, Paris & New York: Cassell & Galpin, 1879.

— *The Epistles to the Colossians, Thessalonians, and Timothy*: Cassell, 1879.

Elliott, Neil. *Liberating Paul: The Justice of God and the Politics of the Apostle*. Minneapolis: Fortress Press, 2006.

Encyclopaedia Britannica. Online at www.britannica.com.

The Epistle to Diognetus. Early Church Classics (1908), republished online by Forgotten Books, 2012.

Esslemont, J. E. *Bahá'u'lláh and the New Era*. Wilmette IL: Bahá'í Publishing Trust, 1980.

European-American Evangelistic Crusades. 'Cult 007A Bahá'í World Faith', online article at: http://www.eaec.org/cults/bahai.htm.

Evans, G. R. *John Wyclif*. Oxford, UK: Lions Books, 2007.

Fahlbusch, Erwin; Bromiley, William (eds). *The Encyclopedia of Christianity*. Eerdmans, 2003.

Fairchild, Mary. 'Catholic beliefs about Mary that lack Biblical support', at *Learn Religions*, 17 April 2019. https://www.learnreligions.com/misconceptions-about-mary-700365.

Ferrar, W. J. *The Proof of the Gospel Being the Demonstratio Evangelica of Eusebius of Cæsarea*. Translations of Christian Literature, Series I, Greek Texts. London and New York: SPCK, 1920.

Frazer, James G. *The Golden Bough: A Study in Magic and Religion* (1890). Many editions, e.g. ed. Robert Fraser. Oxford: Oxford University Press, 1994.

Fuller, Robert C. *Spiritual, but Not Religious: Understanding Unchurched America*. New York: Oxford University Press.

Gall, Carlotta. 'Ukrainian Orthodox Christians formally break from Russia', in *The New York Times*, 6 January 2019.

Giangravè, Claire. 'Catholic women divided over Pope's remarks on female deacons', in *Angelus News*, 15 May 2019.

Gibbon, Edward. *The Decline and Fall of the Roman Empire*. New York, London and Toronto: Knopf, 1999.

Gill, John. *Exposition on the Whole Bible* (1748–63). https://www.studylight.org/commentaries/geb.html.

— *Exposition of the Old and New Testament* (1748–63). https://www.sacred-texts.com/bib/cmt/gill/index.htm.

Gilman, Sander L.; Katz, Steven T. *Anti-Semitism in Times of Crisis*. New York: NYU Press, 1993.

Gottheil, Richard; König, Eduard. 'The Tomb of Daniel', in *The Jewish Encyclopedia* (1906). JewishEncyclopedia.com.

Grant, R. M. 'Five apologists and Marcus Aurelius', in *Vigiliae Christianae*, vol. 42 (1988), pp. 1–17.

Grant, Tobin. 'The Great Decline: 60 years of religion in one graph', at *Religion News Service*, 27 January 2014. https://religionnews.com/2014/01/27/great-decline-religion-united-states-one-graph/.

'The Great Apostasy of Vatican II'. romancatholicfaith.weebly.com.

Guinness, Henry Grattan. *The Approaching End of the Age: Viewed in the Light of History, Prophecy, and Science*. London: Hodder and Stoughton, 8th ed. 1882.

Hein, Avi. 'Women in Judaism: A history of women's ordination as rabbis', online article, no date, at jewishvirtuallibrary.org.

Harris, Stephen L. *Understanding the Bible*. New York: McGraw-Hill, 2011.

Hayes, Justin S. *Jupiter's Legacy: The Symbol of the Eagle and Thunderbolt in Antiquity and Their Appropriation by Revolutionary America and Nazi Germany: The General Symbolism of the Eagle*. Siddhartha Hayes GRST 360–04 Senior Thesis, 2014. http://digitalwindow.vassar.edu/senior_capstone.

Henn, Alexander. *Hindu-Catholic Encounters in Goa: Religion, Colonialism, and Modernity*. Bloomington, Indiana: Indiana University Press, 2014.

Henry, Matthew. *Commentary on the Whole Bible*. Edited by Ernie Stefanik. Grand Rapids, MI: Christian Classics Ethereal Library, 2000.

— *Matthew Henry's Concise Commentary*. https://biblehub.com/commentaries/matthew.

—; Scott, Thomas. *A Commentary upon the Holy Bible: Matthew to Acts*. London: The Religious Tract Society, 1835.

Herbermann, Charles, ed. (1913). 'Ancient Diocese of Mâcon', in *The Catholic Encyclopedia*. New York: Robert Appleton Company, 1913.

Hillerbrand, Hans J. *The Reformation: A Narrative History Related by Contemporary Observers and Participants*. London and New York: SCM Press and Harper & Row, 1964.

Hodal, Kate. 'One in 200 people is a slave. Why?', in *The Guardian*, 25 February 2019.

Horowitz, Jason. 'Pope issues first rules for Catholic Church worldwide to report sex abuse', in *The New York Times*, 9 May 2019.

Hulbert-Powell, C. L. *John James Wettstein (1693–1754): An Account of His Life, Work and Some of His Contemporaries*. Church Historical Society. London: SPCK, 1937.

Hunt, James. *The Negro's Position in Nature*, paper read before the London Anthropological Society.

Anti-abolish tracts No. 4. New York: Van Evrie, Horton and Company,1864. (Harvard College Library).

Iamblichus. *Life of Pythagoras,* Trans. Thomas Taylor. London: J. M. Watkins, 1818.

Ibsen, Henrick. *Emperor and Galilean: A World Historic Drama*. Ed. William Archer. New York: Scribner & Welford, 1890.

Ice, Thomas D. 'Running to and fro'. Liberty University, 2009: Article Archives 31. https://digitalcommons.liberty.edu/pretrib_arch/31.

Imhof, Paul; Biallowons, Hubert. *Karl Rhaner in Dialogue: Conversations and Interviews 1965-1982*. New York: The Crossroad Publishing Company, 1986.

Institute for Religious Research. 'Failed prophecies of Joseph Smith', online article, 16 August 2011, at: mit.irr.org/failed-prophecies-of-joseph-smith.

International Standard Bible Encyclopedia. Online at: https://www.biblestudytools.com.

Irenaeus of Lyons (c. 180). 'Against the heresies', in Alexander Roberts and James Donaldson (eds): *The Ante-Nicene Fathers: The Writings of the Fathers down to A.D. 325*. Buffalo: The Christian Literature Publishing Company, 1885. Christian Classics Ethereal Library, http://www.ccel.org/fathers2/ANF-01/TOC.htm.

Jackson, John R. Jr.; Weidman, Nadine M. *Race, Racism, and Science: Social Impact and Interaction*. New Brunswick: Rutgers University Press, 2006.

Jackson, Wayne. 'The Baha'i Movement', online article, 2020, at: ChristianCourier.com.

Jamieson, Robert; Fausset, A. R.; Brown, David. *Commentary, Critical and Explanatory on the Old and New Testament*. Glasgow, Edinburgh and London, 1863. Republished by Delmarva Publications, 2013.

Jobes, Karen. 'I Peter', in *Baker Exegetical Commentary on the New Testament*. Grand Rapids, MI: Baker Academic, 2005.

BIBLIOGRAPHY

St. John of Damascus. *Writings, The Fount of Knowledge: The Philosophical Chapters, On Heresies, & On the Orthodox Faith.* The Fathers of the Church, vol. XXXVII. Fontibus, 2015.

Johnson, Gaines R. 'The lost rivers of the Garden of Eden – found', online article, n.d., at: https://www.kjvbible.org/rivers_of_the_garden_of_eden.html.

Johnson, Todd M.; Grim, Brian J. 'Global religious populations, 1910–2010', in *The World's Religions in Figures: An Introduction to International Religious Demography.* London: Wiley, 2013.

Jones, Jeffrey M. 'U.S. church membership down sharply in past two decades', in *Gallup: Politics,* 18 April 2019.

Josephus, Flavius. *The Works of Flavius Josephus: The Learned and Authentic Jewish Historian, and Celebrated Warrior, to which are added, Three Dissertations, concerning Jesus Christ, John the Baptist, James the Just, God's Command to Abraham.* Trans. William Whiston. London: William Milner, 1849. penelope.uchicago.edu/josephus/ant-18.html.

Justin Martyr. *Dialogue with Trypho.* www.earlychristianwritings.com/Church Fathers/Justin Martyr.
— *First Apology.* saintfactory.com/old_site/Justin_Martyr.html.

Kelly, Brian. 'The saints on Mohammadinism', online article, 21 December 2016, at Catholicism.org.

Kelly, J. N. D. *Early Christian Doctrines.* San Francisco: Harper Collins, 1978.
— (ed). *Oxford Dictionary of the Popes.* New York: Oxford University Press, 1986.

Kertzer, David I. *Prisoner of the Vatican.* New York: Houghton Mifflin, 2004.

King, L. W. (trans). *The Code of Hammurabi.* Yale Law School, Lillian Goldman Law Library, The Avalon Project, 2008. avalon.law.yale.edu/ancient/hamframe.asp.

King, Martin Luther, Jr., 'The influence of the mystery religions on Christianity', essay published in C. Carson, R. Luker and P.A. Russell (eds): *The Papers of Martin Luther King, Jr: Called to Serve,* Stanford, The Martin Luther King, Jr. Research and Education Institute. Berkeley and Los Angeles: University of California Press, 1992.

King, Peter J. (ed). *Christianity and Violence,* Middleton, DE: CreateSpace, 2016.

Klein, Rabbi Isaac. *A Guide to Jewish Religious Practice.* The Jewish Theological Seminary of America. New York and Jerusalem: KTAV, 1979, 1992.

Knight, George R. *Millennial Fever and the End of the World: A Study of Millerite Adventism.* Boise, Idaho: Pacific Press, 1993.

Kosmin, Barry A.; Keysar, Alriela. *The American Religious Identification Survey (ARIS) of 2008.* Summary Report. Trinity College, Hartford, Connecticut, March 2009. https://commons.trincoll.edu.

Krejcir, Richard J. 'Statistics and reasons for Church decline', online article, 2007, at ChurchLeadership.org.

Levesque, Douglas. 'Iran, the Persia of the Bible'. https://biblenation.org/ Global.

Library of Congress, National Endowment for the Humanities. *Chronicling America: Historic American Newspapers.*

Lightfoot, J. B. (trans. and ed). *The Didache or Teaching of the Apostles*, (1885), in *The Whole Works of the Late Rev. John Lightfoot*. 13 vols. London: Hatchard, 1825.

Lightfoot, Neil R. *How We Got the Bible.* Grand Rapids, MI: Baker Books, 1963, 1988, 2003.

Lights of Guidance: A Bahá'í Reference File. Comp. H. Hornby. New Delhi: Bahá'í Publishing Trust, 5th ed. 1997.

Litch, Josiah. *The Probability of the Second Coming of Christ about CE 1843: Shown by a Comparison of Prophecy with History, up to the Present Time, and an Explanation of those Prophecies which are Yet to be Fulfilled.* New York: David H. Ela, 1938.

Longman, Timothy. *Christianity and Genocide in Rwanda.* New York: Cambridge University Press, 2010.

Louth, Andrew (ed). *Early Christian Writings: The Apostolic Fathers.* London: Penguin Classics, 1987.

Lupton, J. H. 'On the Mahometan controversy', in Lupton: *St. John of Damascus.* London: SPCK, 1882. Reproduced by First Rate Publishers.

Luther, Martin. 'On the Jews and their Lies', Wittenberg, 1543.

Lützow, Count. *The Hussite Wars.* New York: E. P. Dutton, 1914. Reproduced by Forgotten Books, 2015.

Maimonides, Rabbi Moshe ben. *Melachim uMilchamot* (The Laws of the Kings and Their Wars). Trans. E. Touger. www.chabod.org.
— 'The Thirteen Principles of Faith', in *The Authorized Daily Prayer Book.* Trans. Joseph N. Hertz. New York: Bloch & Co, 1948. www.hebrew-streams.org/judaism/13-principles.
— *The Thirteen Principles of the Faith.* Trans. David R. Blumenthal. js.emory.edu/Blumenthal.

Marler, Penny Long; Hadaway, C. Kirk. '"Being religious" or "being spiritual" in America: A zero sum proposition?', in *Journal for the Scientific Study of Religion*, June 2002, p. 41.

Martin, Walter. *Kingdom of the Cults.* Minneapolis, MN: Bethany House, 1997.

Marty, Martin E.; Appleby, R. Scott, *Fundamentalism Observed.* American Academy of Arts and Sciences. Chicago and London: The University of Chicago Press, 1994.

Marx, Dalia. 'The morning ritual in the Talmud: The reconstitution of one's body and personal identity through the Blessings', in *Hebrew Union College Annual*, vol. 77 (2006), pp. 103–29.

Masci, David. 'Split between Ukrainian, Russian churches show political importance of Orthodox Christianity', Pew Research Center, 14 January 2019.

McLaren, Brian D. *The Great Spiritual Migration: How the World's Largest Religion Is Seeking a Better Way to Be Christian.* New York and London: Convergent Books, 2016.

McSwain, Steve. 'Why nobody wants to go to church anymore', in *HuffPost*, 14 October 2014.

Meotti, Giulio. 'Gatestone Institute: 500 closed churches in London', online article, April 2017, at WorldNetDaily.com.

Meyer, Heinrich August Wilhelm. *Critical and Exegetical Commentary on the New Testament.* Edinburgh: Murray and Gibb, 1874.

Millman, Peter A. 'The falling of the stars', in *The Telescope*, vol. 7 (May–June 1940) no. 57.

Mi Yodeya. 'How many of the 613 Mitzvos can we do only in Israel?' https://judaism.stackexchange.com/questions/11044/how-many-of-the-613-mitzvos-can-we-do-only-in-Israel.

Mohler, Albert. 'Christianity stands or falls on the Resurrection?'. Jesus.org.

Montefiore, Simon Sebag. *Jerusalem: The Biography.* London: Weidenfeld and Nicolson, 2011.

Montgomery Watt, W. 'Islamic conceptions of the Holy War', in Murphy, *The Holy War.* Ohio State University Press, Center for Medieval and Renaissance Studies, 1976.

Muggah, Robert; Velshi, Ali. 'Religious violence is on the rise. What can faith-based communities do about it?' *World Economic Forum*, 25 February 2019.

Murdock, D. M. (Acharya S). 'Early Church Fathers on Mithraism: The devil got there first'. http://www.truthbeknown.com/mithraism.html.

Murphy, Thomas Patrick (ed). *The Holy War.* Ohio State University Press, Center for Medieval and Renaissance Studies, 1976.

Nabarz, Payam. *The Mysteries of Mithras: The Pagan Belief that Shaped the Christian World.* Rochester, VT: Inner Traditions, 2005.

Nailor, Daimon. 'Why is Christianity declining in the West?', in *Quora*, 11 April 2017.

Neturei Karta International. 'Why Orthodox Jews are opposed to a Zionist state'. www.nkusa.org/aboutus/zionism/opposition.cfm.

Newton, Isaac. *Observations upon the Prophecies of Daniel and the Apocalypse of St. John*. London: Darby and Browne, 1733.

New World Encyclopedia. https://www.newworldencyclopedia.org.

Niewwhof, Carey. '5 reasons people have stopped attending your church (especially millennials)', online article, 29 April 2015, at https://careynieuwhof.com.

O'Brien, Conor Cruise. *States of Ireland*. New York: Pantheon, 1972.

Onnekink, David. *War and Religion after Westphalia, 1648–1713*. London: Ashgate, 2013.

Padovano, A. 'Joseph's son', in *National Catholic Reporter*, 12 April 1996.

Pardon, Bob. 'A closer look at Bahá'í'. Online article at http://www.neirr.org/bahai1.htm.

Peter Chrysologus. *St Peter Chrysologus: Selected Sermons*. Vol. 6. Trans. W. B. Palardy, Fathers of the Church Series. Catholic University of America, 2004.

Peters, Edward N. (trans). *The 1917 Pio-Benedictine Code of Canon Law*. Ignatius Press, 2001.

Pew Research Center. 'America's changing religious landscape', in Pew Research Center, Religion and Public Life, 12 May 2015. http://www.pewforum.org/2015/05/12/americas-changing-religious-landscape/.

— 'Perception of conflict between science and religion', in Pew Research Center, Religion and Science, 22 October 2015. www.pewresearch.org/science/.../perception-of-conflict-between-science-and-religion/.

Phelps, A. A: 'Christianity vs. Churchianity' (1883), in *Zion's Watch Tower and Herald of Christ's Presence*. Periodical ed. C. T. Russell, Pittsburgh, PA.

Phillips, Jonathan. *The Fourth Crusade and the Sack of Constantinople*. New York: Viking, 2004.

Pinedo, Moisés. 'Infant baptism', online article, 17 February 2017, at https://compositebiblereflections.blogspot.com/2017/02/infant-baptism-by-moises-pinedo.html.

Pivarunas, Mark A. 'The Last Days and false ecumenism', Advent letter, 1995. www.cmri.org/95prog9-3.htm.

Plumptree, E. H. *The Gospel According to St. Matthew, with Commentary*. London, Paris & New York: Cassell, Petter, Galpin & Co., 1879.

Poole, Matthew. *English Annotations on the Holy Bible* (1696). Many online editions.

Pope Eugene IV. *Cantate Domino*. Papal Bull, 4 February 1442. https://catholicism.org/cantate-domino.html.

Pope Leo XII, *Ubi Primum*, Encyclical on His Assuming the Pontificate, 1824. Papal Encyclicals Online, www.papalencyclicals.net.

Pope Leo XIII, *Liberatas,* Encyclical on the Nature of Human Liberty, 20 June 1988. www.vatican.va/leo-xiii/documents.

Pope Pius IX. *Quanto conficiamur moerore,* On the Promotion of False Doctrines, 19 August 1863. Papal Encyclicals Online, www.papalencyclicals.net.

— *Ineffablis Deus,* 8 December 1854. Papal Encyclicals Online, www.papalencyclicals.net.

Pricket, Stephen. *Origins of Narrative: The Romantic Appropriation of the Bible.* New York: Cambridge University Press, 1996.

Priolkar, Anant Kakba. *The Goa Inquisition: Being a Quatercentenary Commemoration Study of the Inquisition in India.* New Delhi: Voice of India 1998.

Pulvermacher, Lucian. 'Vatican II Council accepts freedom of religion, teaches heresy and Apostasies', in *Caritas Newsletter,* 19 August 1989.

Ranke-Heinemann. *Eunuchs for the Kingdom of Heaven.* New York: Doubleday, 1990.

Reichberg, Gregory M. *Thomas Aquinas on War and Peace.* Cambridge, UK: Cambridge University Press, 2017.

Remy, Jules; Brenchley, Julius. *A Journey to Great-Salt-Lake City, with a Sketch of the History, Religion, and Customs of the Mormons.* London, W. Jeffs, 1861. Reissued Miami, FL: Hard Press, 2017.

Revelation Revolution. 'The abomination that causes desolation explained'. Fort Worth, TX. https://revelationrevolution.org/the-abomination-that-causes-desolation-explained/.

Roberts, B. H. *A Comprehensive History of the Church.* Orem, Utah: Sonos, 1991.

Rood, Rick. *The Christian Attitude towards Non-Christian Religions,* Probe Ministries International, 1999. www.leaderu.com/orgs/probe/docs/non-xrel.html.

Schaff, Philip. *The Creeds of Christendom.* 3 vols. Grand Rapids, MI: Baker Books, 1977.

Schoenherr, Richard A.; Young, Lawrence A.; Cheng, Tsan-Yuang. *Full Pews and Empty Altars: Demographics of the Priest Shortage in United States Catholic Dioceses.* Madison, WI: University of Wisconsin Press.

Schwartz, Regina M., *The Curse of Cain: The Violent Legacy of Monotheism.* Chicago: University of Chicago Press, 1997.

Sefaria: A Living Library of Jewish Texts. Online library, at sefaria.org.

Shattuck, Kelly. '7 startling facts: An upclose look at church attendance in America', online article, 29 December 2015, at ChurchLeaders.com.

Sherwood, Harriet. 'People of no religion outnumber Christians in England and Wales', in *The Guardian,* 23 May 2016 (modified 28 November 2017).

— 'Christianity as default is gone: The rise of a non-Christian Europe', in *The Guardian,* 21 March 2018.

Shoghi Effendi. *The Advent of Divine Justice* (1939). Wilmette, IL: Bahá'í Publishing Trust, 1984.
— *Bahá'í Administration: Selected Messages 1922–1932*. Wilmette: Bahá'í Publishing Trust, 1980.
— *Dawn of a New Day: Messages to India 1923–1957*. New Delhi: Bahá'í Publishing Trust, n.d.
— *Directives from the Guardian*. Comp. Gertrude Garrida. New Delhi: Bahá'í Publishing Trust, 1973.
— *God Passes By* (1944). Wilmette, IL: Bahá'í Publishing Trust, rev. ed. 1974.
— *High Endeavours: Messages to Alaska*. Anchorage: National Spiritual Assembly of the Bahá'ís of Alaska, 1976.
— *The Light of Divine Guidance: The Messages from the Guardian of the Bahá'í Faith to the Bahá'ís of Germany and Austria*. 2 vols. Hofheim-Langenhain: Bahá'í-Verlag, 1982, 1985.
— *Messages to America 1932–1946*. Wilmette, IL: Bahá'í Publishing Trust, 1947. Published online by the Project Gutenberg.
— *The Promised Day Is Come* (1941). Wilmette, IL: Bahá'í Publishing Trust, rev. ed. 1980.
— *A Summary of the Origin, Teachings and Institutions of the Bahá'í Faith*, prepared in 1947 for the United Nations Special Committee on Palestine by Shoghi Effendi in his capacity as Head of the Bahá'í Faith. Wilmette, IL: Bahá'í Publishing Trust, 1947.
— *This Decisive Hour*. Wilmette, IL: Bahá'í Publishing Trust, 1992.
— *Unfolding Destiny: The Messages from the Guardian of the Bahá'í Faith to the Bahá'í Community of the British Isles*. London: Bahá'í Publishing Trust, 1981.
— *The World Order of Bahá'u'lláh: Selected Letters by Shoghi Effendi* (1938). Wilmette, IL: Bahá'í Publishing Trust, 2nd rev. ed. 1974.

Smietana, Bob. 'Americans are fond of the Bible, don't actually read it', in *LifeWay Research*, 25 April 2017.

Snapp, Allen. 'Christianity stands or falls on the Resurrection', Series: Letter to a Really Messed up Church, 16 August 2005. https://www.gracecorning.org/sermons/.

Snow, Samuel S. 'The Exeter Campmeeting', in *The Advent Herald*, 21 August 1844. In Stone, Jon R.; Farer, Tom: *Transnational Crime in Americas: An Inter-American Dialogue*. New York: Routledge, 2000.

Spalding, F. S. *Joseph Smith Jr. as a Translator*. Arrow Press, 1912. Reissued in Classic Reprint Series, www.ForgottenBooks.com.

Spence, H. D. M.; Exell, Joseph S. *The Pulpit Commentary*. London: Kegan Paul, Trench, Trübner & Co., 1894.

Spurgeon, Charles Haddon. 'Churchianity versus Christianity' (1868). https://archive.spurgeon.org/s_and_t/c_v_c.php.

Stanford, Miles J. *Fox's Book of Martyrs or A History of the Lives, Sufferings, and Triumphant Deaths of the Primitive Protestant Martyrs, from the Introduction of*

Christianity to the Latest Periods of Pagan, Popish, and Infidel Persecutions. New York: Worthington, 1887.

Staples, Tim. 'The priesthood is both universal and ministerial', in *This Rock*, vol. 21 (2010), no. 2.

Star of the West: The Bahai Magazine. Periodical, 25 vols. 1910–1935. Vols. 1–14 RP Oxford: George Ronald, 1978. Complete CD-ROM version: Talisman Educational Software/Special Ideas, 2001.

Stenhouse, T. B. H. *The Rocky Mountain Saints: A Full and Complete History of the Mormons from the First Vision of Joseph Smith to the Last Courtship of Brigham Young.* New York: D Appleton and Company, 1873.

Strange, Daniel. 'Exclusivisms: "Indeed their rock is not like our rock"', in Paul Hedges and Alan Race (eds): *Christian Approaches to Other Faiths*. London: SCM, 2008.

Strochilic, Nina. 'Christian monks square off at one of Jerusalem's holiest sites: A multi-century-long battle has been raging between six Christian sects at the Church of the Holy Sepulchre', in *Daily Beast*, 4 July 2013.

Suran, Melissa. 'The separation of church and science', in *EMBO Reports*, vol. 11 (2010), no. 8, pp. 586–9.

Svensson, Isak; Nilsson, Desirée. 'Disputes over the divine: Introducing the Religion and Armed Conflict (RELAC) Data', *Journal of Conflict Resolution*, 30 October 2017.

Talmud. *The William Davidson Talmud.* https://www.sefaria.org/ william-davidson-talmud.

The Telegraph. 'Child abuse scandals faced by Roman Catholic Church', 12 March 2010.

Tertullian. *De Praescriptione Haereticorum: On the Testimony of the Soul and the 'Prescription' of Heretic* (1914). Trans. T. Herbert Bindley, Reproduced by Forgotten Books.

Thomas à Kempis (c. 1418-1427). *The Imitation of Christ.* Ed. Paul Negri and Susan L. Rattner. New York: Dover, 2003.

Thompson, Damian. '2067: The end of British Christianity. Projections aren't predictions. But there's no denying that churches are in deep trouble', in *The Spectator*, 13 June 2015.

Titelman, Gregory Y. *Random House Dictionary of Popular Proverbs and Sayings.* New York: Random House, 1996.

Toner, P. J. 'Infallibility', in *The Catholic Encyclopedia* (1911).

Tosefta Berakot. Trans. Eliyahu Gurevich. Las Vegas, NV: Eliyahu Gurevich. www.toseftaonline.org.

Trumbower, Jeffrey A. *Rescue for the Dead: The Posthumous Salvation of Non-Christians in Early Christianity*. Oxford Studies in Historical Theology. Oxford: Oxford University Press, 2001.

Tucker, Garland. 'Quo vadis? The philosophical, spiritual floundering of Europe in 2017', in *National Review*, 21 October 2017.

Turtledove, Harry (trans and ed). *The Chronicle of Theophanes: An English translation of Anni mundi 6095–6305 (A.D. 602–813)*. Philadelphia, PA: University of Pennsylvania Press, 1982.

United Methodist Church. 'History of hymns': Onward, Christian Soldiers'. www.umcdiscipleship.org.

The United Methodist Hymnal. https://www.hymnsite.com.

The Universal House of Justice. *Message to the World's Religious Leaders*. Haifa: Bahá'í World Centre, April 2002.
— *Messages from the Universal House of Justice 1963–1986: The Third Epoch of the Formative Age*. Comp. Geoffry W. Marks. Wilmette, IL: Bahá'í Publishing Trust, 1996.
— *One Common Faith*. Wilmette, IL: Bahá'í Publishing Trust, 2005.
— *The Promise of World Peace*. Haifa: Bahá'í World Centre, 1995.

Vatican II: Its Heresies, Errors and Rites. Website. http://www.truecarpentry.org/tc-cwww/cathwww/v2heresies.htm.

Vidmar, John. *The Catholic Church Through the Ages: A History*. New York: Paulist Press, 2014.

Vincent, Marvin R. *Vincent's Word Studies in the New Testament*. Peabody, MA: Hendrickson, 1886.

Vischer, Robert K. 'Racial segregation in American churches and its implications for school vouchers', in *Florida Law Review*, 2001.

The Washington Post. 'Rwanda: Catholic bishops apologize for role in genocide', 20 November 2016.

Weaver, J. Denny. 'Violence in Christian theology', in *Cross Currents*, vol. 51 (2001), issue 2.

Weaver, Mary Jo, R. Scott Appleby. *Being Right: Conservative Catholics in America*. Indiana University Press, 1995.

de Wette, Wilhelm Martin Leberecht. *A Critical and Historical Introduction to the Canonical Scriptures of the Old Testament*. Trans. Theodore Parker. University of Michigan Library, 2006.

Wheeler, Carolynne. 'Monks brawl at Jerusalem's Church of the Holy Sepulchre, site of Jesus's Crucifixion', in *The Telegraph*, 9 November 2008.

White, James Emery. *The Rise of the Nones: Understanding and Reaching the Religiously Unaffiliated*. Grand Rapids, MI: Baker Books, 2014.

Whitworth, Lou. 'The religion of Baha'i: What does a Baha'i believe'. Online article, 22 May 1997, at probe.org.

Wilken, Todd. 'What is the Catholic teaching of "Anonymous Christianity"'? Online article at www.issuesetcarchive.org/issues_site/resource/archives/anonchrs.htm.

Winters, Michael Sean. 'Hostility to Vatican II runs deep with Pope Francis' critics', in *National Catholic Reporter*, 8 January 2018.

Yale Law School, Lillian Goldman Law Library, *The Avalon Project*.

Zaimov, Stoyan. '500 UK churches closed while 423 mosques were built on "sad ruins of English Christianity"', in *The Christian Post*, 3 April 2017.

Zion's Watch Tower and Herald of Christ's Presence. Periodical, 1873 et seq. Ed. C. T. Russell, Pittsburgh, PA.

NOTES AND REFERENCES

Foreword

1. See for example: Booth, 'Christians could be minority by 2018'; Joe Carter, 'Are all Christian denominations in decline?'; Fuller, *Spiritual, but Not Religious*, p. 11; Krejcir; 'Statistics and reasons for Church decline'; McSwain, 'Why nobody wants to go to church anymore'; Meotti, 'Gatestone Institute: 500 closed churches in London'; Pew Research Center, 'America's changing religious landscape'; Shattuck, '7 startling facts: An upclose look at church attendance in America'; Zaimov, '500 UK churches closed while 423 mosques were built on "sad ruins of English Christianity"'.
2. McSwain, 'Why nobody wants to go to church anymore'.
3. Pew Research Center, 'America's changing religious landscape'.
4. ibid.
5. White, *The Rise of the Nones: Understanding and Reaching the Religiously Unaffiliated*, p. 21.
6. McSwain, 'Why nobody wants to go to church anymore'.
7. Joe Carter, 'Are all Christian denominations in decline?'; Cohn, 'Big drop in share of Americans calling themselves Christian'; Fuller, *Spiritual, but Not Religious*; Marler and Hadaway, '"Being religious" or "being spiritual" in America: A zero sum proposition?'
8. The Universal House of Justice, *One Common Faith*, p. 23.
9. ibid.
10. 'Abdu'l-Bahá, *Tablets of the Divine Plan*, 14.9 (also see Shoghi Effendi, *God Passes By*, p. 100); Bahá'u'lláh, *Gleanings from the Writings of Bahá'u'lláh*, CIX.
11. 'Abdu'l-Bahá, *Tablets of the Divine Plan*, 14.11.
12. Bahá'u'lláh, *Gleanings from the Writings of Bahá'u'lláh*, LXX, p. 136.
13. Shoghi Effendi, *God Passes By*, p. 100.
14. McLaren, *The Great Spiritual Migration*, pp. 2–3.
15. Jimmy Carter, *A Call to Action: Women, Religion, Violence, and Power*, p. 23.
16. 'Abdu'l-Bahá, *Tablets of the Divine Plan*, 14.9.

Introduction

1. Bahá'u'lláh, *Gleanings from the Writings of Bahá'u'lláh*, XLIII, p. 94.
2. Shoghi Effendi, *The Advent of Divine Justice*, pp. 74–5.
3. Bahá'u'lláh, *Epistle to the Son of the Wolf*, p. 14.
4. Spurgeon, 'Churchianity versus Christianity'.
5. 'Abdu'l-Bahá, *The Promulgation of Universal Peace*, p. 5.

6. Shoghi Effendi, *The World Order of Bahá'u'lláh*, p. 114.
7. Paraphrased from Shoghi Effendi, *The Promised Day Is Come*, para. 265, p. 108.
8. 'Abdu'l-Bahá, *The Promulgation of Universal Peace*, p. 361.
9. ibid. p. 363.
10. Bahá'u'lláh, *Gleanings from the Writings of Bahá'u'lláh*, XCIX, p. 200.
11. Shoghi Effendi, *The World Order of Bahá'u'lláh*, pp. 186–7.
12. Bahá'u'lláh, *The Tabernacle of Unity*, p. 6.
13. Shoghi Effendi, *The World Order of Bahá'u'lláh*, p. 185.
14. ibid. p. 191.
15. The authoritative Writings and guidance of the Báb, Bahá'u'lláh and 'Abdu'l-Bahá.

1. Taking stock: The darkening spiritual horizons

1. Amplified Bible: 'that is, grafted in, joined to Him by faith in Him as Savior'.
2. ibid: 'he is a new creature' [reborn and renewed by the Holy Spirit].
3. ibid: 'because spiritual awakening brings a new life'.
4. Barclay, *The Plain Man Looks at the Apostles' Creed*, pp. 10–11.
5. ibid. p. 297.
6. *The Epistle to Diognetus*, pp. 61–6, 67. Paraphrased in part by Shoghi Effendi in *The World Order of Bahá'u'lláh*, p. 198, to describe the followers of Bahá'u'lláh today.
7. T. Grant, 'The Great Decline: 60 years of religion in one graph' (2014).
8. Thompson, '2067: The end of British Christianity' (2015); Sherwood, 'People of no religion outnumber Christians in England and Wales' (2017).
9. Tucker, 'Quo vadis? The philosophical, spiritual floundering of Europe in 2017'.
10. Bendavid, 'Europe's empty churches go on sale' (2015).
11. ibid.
12. Tucker, 'Quo vadis? The philosophical, spiritual floundering of Europe in 2017'.
13. Kosmin and Keysar, *The American Religious Identification Survey (ARIS) of 2008*.
14. Pew Research Center, 'America's changing religious landscape' (2015).
15. Bendavid, 'Europe's empty churches go on sale' (2015); Sherwood, 'Christianity as default is gone: The rise of a non-Christian Europe' (2018).
16. Barna Group, 'Atheism doubles among generation Z' (2018).
17. Smietana, 'Americans are fond of the Bible, don't actually read it' (2017).
18. *The Economist*, 'The Bible v the Koran: The battle of the books' (2007).
19. *Catechism of the Catholic Church*, part I, ch. 3, para. 143.
20. ibid. para. 159.
21. Suran, 'The separation of church and science' (2010).
22. Butler, 'Vatican toughens stance on embryo research' (2008).
23. Pew Research Center, 'Perception of conflict between science and religion' (2015).
24. Niewwhof, '5 reasons people have stopped attending your church (especially millennials)' (2015).

25. *The Telegraph*, 'Child abuse scandals faced by Roman Catholic Church' (2010); BBC News, 'Child abuse: 7% of Australian Catholic priests alleged to be involved' (2017).
26. A. Barnes, *Notes, Explanatory and Practical, on the First Epistle of Paul to the Corinthians*, p. 331.
27. Jones, 'U.S. church membership down sharply in past two decades' (2019).
28. Vischer, 'Racial segregation in American churches and its implications for school vouchers' (2001), pp. 193, 196–7, 204–5.
29. Fairchild, 'Catholic beliefs about Mary that lack biblical support' (2019).
30. The Center for the Study of Global Christianity at Gordon-Conwell Theological Seminary estimates that there were 1,600 denominations or churches in 1900 CE. This mushroomed to 34,000 in 2000 CE and to 43,000 in 2012 CE.
31. Longman, *Christianity and Genocide in Rwanda*; AlJazeera, 'Pope apologises for church's role in Rwanda genocide' (2017); *The Washington Post*, 'Rwanda: Catholic bishops apologize for role in genocide' (2016).
32. Gall, 'Ukrainian Orthodox Christians formally break from Russia' (2019); Masci, 'Split between Ukrainian, Russian churches show political importance of Orthodox Christianity' (2019).
33. 'Abdu'l-Bahá, *The Promulgation of Universal Peace*, pp. 5–6.
34. Benson, *The Holy Bible, Containing the Old and New Testament according to the Present, Authorized Version with Critical, Explanatory, and Practical Notes*, vol. 1. ch. VII, p. 81.
35. A. Barnes, *Notes on the New Testament, Explanatory and Practical*, Matthew and Mark, p. 78.
36. Amplified Bible: 'spiritually wise', that is, those who are in tune with God's Purpose.
37. Nailor, 'Why is Christianity declining in the West?' (2017).
38. King James Version: 'iniquity'; New International Version: 'wickedness'.
39. King James Version: 'there come a falling away first'; New Living Translation: 'a great rebellion against God'; Berean Literal Bible: 'until the apostasy shall come first'.
40. Edmundson, *The Church in Rome in the First Century*, p. 151.
41. Meyer, *Critical and Exegetical Commentary on the New Testament*, part II: *The Gospel of John*, vol. 1, p. 265.
42. Professor of Divinity and Biblical Criticism at Glasgow University and Visiting Professor at the University of Strathclyde (d. January 1978).
43. Barclay, *The Plain Man Looks at the Apostles' Creed*, pp. 178, 197.
44. King James Version: 'He that overcometh shall inherit all things; and I will be his God, and he shall be my son.'

2. Revisiting Christian virtues and relearning to walk in Christ's footsteps

1. Spence and Exell, *The Pulpit Commentary:* Peter 4: 16.
2. New International Version: 'obey my teachings'.
3. Benson, *The New Testament of Our Lord and Saviour Jesus Christ*, vol. 1, p. 826.
4. Berean Study Bible: 'bond of perfect unity'.
5. Henry, *Commentary on the Whole Bible*, vol. 6 (Acts to Revelation), p. 1901 (I John 3:14–19).

6. Reference to the fourth Gospel by its common and traditional name without necessarily ascribing authorship.
7. Calvin, *Institutes of the Christian Religion*, vol. 2, p. 440.
8. Good News Translation: 'needy fellow Christians'.
9. Contemporary English Version: 'welcome strangers into your home'; International Standard Version: 'extend hospitality to strangers'.
10. King James Version: 'be converted'; New International Version: 'change'.
11. Benson, *The New Testament of Our Lord and Saviour Jesus Christ*, vol. 1, p. 154.
12. A. Barnes, *Notes on the New Testament, Explanatory and Practical*, p. 78.
13. Berean Study Bible: 'the essence'.
14. Apparently a common proverb amongst the Jews in Jesus's time.
15. King James Version: 'bishop' – *episkopos*: term first used for officials in government, and later for church leaders.
16. A. Barnes, *Notes, Explanatory and Practical on the Gospels*, vol. I, p. 422.
17. King James Version: 'prove all things'; New American Standard Bible: 'examine everything carefully'.
18. Several translations including New Living Translation: 'the Good News about the Kingdom', and Darby Bible Translation: 'glad tidings of the Kingdom'.
19. New Living Translation: 'the Good News to everyone'.
20. King James Version: 'Let your waist be girded'.

3. Discarding obsolete teachings, outworn shibboleths and injurious superstitions

1. Shoghi Effendi, *Messages to America*, p. 15.
2. Shoghi Effendi, *The World Order of Bahá'u'lláh*, p. 170.
3. The Universal House of Justice, *The Promise of World Peace*, p. 6.
4. Commentary by Cowles: 'The minor prophets; Zechariah', in *The Holy Bible with a Commentary Explanatory and Practical and Introductions to the Several Books, by Clergymen of the Church of England*, p. 560.
5. Gill, *Exposition on the Whole Bible*.
6. *Ellicott's Commentary on the Whole Bible*. vol. 6. p. 312.
7. A. Barnes, *Notes: Explanatory and Practical, on the Second Epistle to the Corinthians and the Epistle to the Galatians*, p. 374.
8. www.plymouthbrethren.com/references.htm.
9. Mi Yodeya, 'How many of the 613 Mitzvos can we do only in Israel?'
10. New Living Translation: 'man-made ideas'; New International Version: 'merely human rules'.
11. English Revised Version: 'Jewish fables'; Good News Translation: 'Jewish legends'.
12. Earle, *The Sabbath in Puritan New England*, ch. XVII: 'The observance of the day', pp. 245–7.
13. *The Washington Post*, 17 October 2013. See also: www.criticalcommons.org/.../clips/this-map-shows-where-the-world2019s-30-million; Anti-Slavery International, 'What is modern slavery?'; Hodal, 'One in 200 people is a slave. Why?'.
14. Jackson and Weidman, *Race, Racism, and Science: Social Impact and Interaction*, p. 4.

15. Good News Translation: 'a slave'.
16. Elliott, *Liberating Paul: The Justice of God and the Politics of the Apostle*, section 2: 'The canonical betrayal of the apostle', pp. 32–52.
17. ibid. section 2: 'Facing the facts of pseudepigraphy', p. 25. This is reminiscent of the Qur'án verses: 'A part of them do conceal the truth, though acquainted with it' (Qur'án 2:141) and 'They shift the words of Scripture from their places, and have forgotten part of what they were taught' (Qur'án 5:13).
18. Bourne, *A Condensed Anti-Slavery Bible Argument*.
19. Hunt, *The Negro's Position in Nature* (1864).
20. Ellicott, *The Epistles to the Colossians, Thessalonians, and Timothy*, p. 255.
21. Berean Study Bible: 'all humanity'.
22. *Tosefta Sanhedrin* 13:2; see https://www.mechon-mamre.org/ jewfaq/gentiles.
23. King James Version: 'children'.
24. 'Magi', in the *New World Encyclopedia*.
25. Ellicott, *A New Testament Commentary for English Readers*, vol. II, pp. 205–6.
26. Henry, *Commentary on the Whole Bible, vol. VI (Acts to Revelation), II Corinthians 6:11–18*, p. 1091.
27. A. Barnes, *Notes: Explanatory and Practical, on the Second Epistle to the Corinthians and the Epistle to the Galatians*, p. 152.
28. *Tosefta Berakot*, Tosefta 23, ch. 6, p. 404.
29. *The William Davidson (Babylonian) Talmud*, ch. 10, Pesachim 111a, in *Sefaria: A Living Library of Jewish Texts*.
30. *Midrash, Sifrei Devarim*, ch. 11. para. 46, ibid.
31. A. Barnes, *Notes: Explanatory and Practical, on the First Epistle of Paul to the Corinthians*, pp. 246–7.
32. See Hein, 'Women in Judaism: A history of women's ordination as rabbis'.
33. Aramaic Bible: 'assemblies'.
34. New American Standard Bible: 'improper; Berean Study Bible: 'dishonorable'; Contemporary English Version: 'must not be allowed to speak'.
35. Amplified Bible: 'But I do not allow a woman': Greek: γυναικὶ οὐκ ἐπιτρέπω οὐδὲ αὐθεντεῖν, gynaiki ouk epitrepō.
36. New International Version: 'became a sinner'.
37. A. Barnes, *Notes: Explanatory and Practical, on the First Epistle of Paul to the Corinthians*, pp. 332–3.
38. A village in Corinth, Greece.
39. Dorgan, 'Irish priests disappointed at Pope's reluctance to ordain female deacons'; Giangravè, 'Catholic women divided over pope's remarks on female deacons'.
40. Henry, *Commentary on the Whole Bible, vol. VI, I Timothy, 2: 9–15*, pp. 1430–31.
41. Peters, *The 1917 Pio-Benedictine Code of Canon Law*, no. 1262.
42. Hillerbrand, *The Reformation: A Narrative History Related by Contemporary Observers and Participants*. p. 377.
43. De Wette, *A Critical and Historical Introduction to the Canonical Scriptures of the Old Testament*, vol. 2, pp. 329–30.
44. See Hillerbrand, *The Reformation*.
45. Bates, 'Synod approves church remarriage for divorcees'.

46. Padovano, 'Joseph's Son'.
47. The Apostolic Constitutions (375–380) contain eight treatises on Christian discipline, worship and doctrine, intended to serve mainly as a manual of guidance for the clergy.
48. J. N. D. Kelly, *Oxford Dictionary of the Popes*.
49. Ranke-Heinemann. *Eunuchs for the Kingdom of Heaven*, p. 110.
50. Vidmar, *The Catholic Church Through the Ages: A History*, p. 69.
51. Sanhedrin 73a, in *Sefaria: A Living Library of Jewish Texts*.
52. King, *The Code of Hammurabi*, codes 195–200.
53. A. Barnes, *Notes, Explanatory and Practical on the Gospels*, vol. II, Luke and John, p. 171.
54. Coffey, *Persecution and Toleration in Protestant England 1588–1689*, p. 22.
55. Augustine, *Contra Faustum Manichaeum*, book 22, sections 69–76.
56. Reichberg, *Thomas Aquinas on War and Peace*, chs. 6 and 7, pp. 114–172.
57. Claster, *Sacred Violence: The European Crusades to the Middle East, 1095–1396*, pp. xvii–xviii.
58. Crocker, 'Early crusade songs', in Murphy, *The Holy War*, p. 96.
59. ibid. p. 4.
60. ibid. with reference to Montgomery Watt, 'Islamic conceptions of the Holy War', pp. 141-56.
61. Daniel and Murphy, 'The Holy War (review)'.
62. King, *Christianity and Violence*, pp. 1–4.
63. J. D. Weaver, 'Violence in Christian theology'.
64. United Methodist Church, 'History of Hymns: Onward, Christian Soldiers'.
65. Baring-Gould, in *The United Methodist Hymnal*, no. 575.
66. Onnekink, *War and Religion after Westphalia, 1648–1713*, pp. 1–8.
67. Bickersteth, *The Signs of the Times in the East; A Warning to the West*, p. 7.
68. Pricket, *Origins of Narrative: The Romantic Appropriation of the Bible*, p. 64.
69. O'Brien, *States of Ireland*, Epilogue, pp. 308–9,
70. Ferdinand Bauer (1792–1860); Adolf Hilgenfeld (1823–1907); and Albert Schwegler (1819–1857).
71. *The Epistle to Diognetus*, pp. 58–61.
72. Louth, *Early Christian Writings: The Apostolic Fathers*, p. 73.
73. Macon Council (581–583). 'Documenta Catholica Omnia', Cooperatorum Veritatis Societas; see also Herbermann, 'Ancient Diocese of Mâcon'.
74. Sebag Montefiore, *Jerusalem: The Biography*, p. 400.
75. 'Antisemitism, Christianity and Anti-semitism, Jewish deicide'.
76. R. M. Grant, 'Five apologists and Marcus Aurelius'.
77. Gilman and Katz, *Anti-Semitism in Times of Crisis*, p. 47.
78. Peter Chrysologus, 'Sermon CLXXII', in *Sermons of Peter Chrysologus*, vol. 6, p. 116; see also Drews, *The Unknown Neighbour: The Jew in the Thought of Isidore of Seville*, p. 187.
79. St John of Damascus, *Writings, The Fount of Knowledge: The Philosophical Chapters, On Heresies and On the Orthodox Faith*; see also Lupton, *St. John of Damascus*, ch. VIII: 'On the Mahometan controversy'.
80. Turtledove, *The Chronicle of Theophanes*, p. 34.
81. Brian Kelly, 'The saints on Mohammadinism'.

82. Priolkar, *The Goa Inquisition*, ch. VIII, 'Anti-Hindu laws in Goa', pp. 114–49; ch. IX, 'Use of torture by the Inquisition and the Palace of the Goa inquisition', pp. 150–62; see also Henn, *Hindu-Catholic Encounters in Goa: Religion, Colonialism, and Modernity*, pp. 1, 7, 46–7, 61.
83. King, *Christianity and Violence*, ch. 8, p. 74.
84. Ellicott, *A Bible Commentary for English Readers*.
85. *Cambridge Bible for Schools and Colleges*.
86. *Matthew Henry's Concise Commentary*.

4. The times of rebirth and renewal of faith

1. Ellicott, *An Old Testament Commentary for English Readers*. vol. IV, p. 531.
2. A. Barnes, *Notes, Explanatory and Practical, on the Book of the Prophet Isaiah*, vol. II, p. 108.
3. New Living Translation: 'He uncovers mysteries hidden in darkness; he brings light to the deepest gloom.'
4. A sign of respect as in Job 29:9–10.
5. New International Translation: 'turn to God'.
6. New International Version: 'For whatever is hidden is meant to be disclosed, and whatever is concealed is meant to be brought out into the open.'
7. A. Barnes, *Notes, Explanatory and Practical, on the Book of Revelation*, p. 109.
8. Jamieson, Fausset and Brown, *Commentary Critical and Explanatory on the Whole Bible*, vol. 4: *Philippians to Revelation*.

5. The advent of the world redeemer in the Hebrew Bible (Old Testament)

1. Compare: 'He [Jesus] answered, "Elijah does come, and he will restore all things . . ."' (Matt. 17:11); '. . . whom [Jesus] heaven must receive until the time for restoring all the things about which God spoke by the mouth of his holy prophets long ago'. (Acts 3:21)
2. King James Version: 'a rod out of the stem of Jesse'.
3. 'my holy mountain': Several mountains are considered holy, such as Sinai, the site of Moses's revelation. Mount Carmel was considered particularly holy from ancient times and is often cited in the Tanakh for its beauty and fertility. The sixth-century Greek mathematician Pythagoras is claimed to have visited Mount Carmel, which he described as 'more sacred than other mountains, and quite inaccessible to the vulgar. . .' (Iamblichus, *Life of Pythagoras*, pp. 7–8). Mount Carmel was where God destroyed idolatry and restored monotheism to Israel (I Kings). King Ahab had married the Phoenician princess Jezebel who turned his allegiance from Yahweh to her god Baal and had Yahweh's prophets slaughtered. Elijah called on Ahab to assemble the 450 priests of Baal on Mount Carmel. There he challenged the priests to call on fire from Baal to light a sacrifice. Baal failed to respond to the priests' cries. Then Elijah rebuilt the ruined altar of the Lord and offered a sacrifice. Immediately fire from heaven consumed the offering, even though it had been soaked in water.

   At the western edge of Mount Carmel is Stella Maris Monastery, the world headquarters of the Carmelites, a Catholic religious order. A small cave under the monastery is traditionally held to be a place where Elijah lived. Opposite the monastery, a footpath down towards the Mediterranean leads to another grotto called Elijah's Cave. Here the Prophet is said to have meditated before his encounter with the priests of Baal.

Both the Prophet Malachi in the Tanakh and Christ in the Gospels stated that the Prophet Elijah will return. It is noteworthy that Bahá'u'lláh pitched His tent on Mount Carmel and visited the cave of Elijah. The Shrine of the Báb, the Herald of the Bahá'í Faith, is also on Mount Carmel. The site is a sacred place for Bahá'ís around the world and home to their world administrative and spiritual centre.

4. The painting by Pietro Lorenzetti, 1320, depicts Jesus entering Jerusalem triumphantly riding the ass with the colt in tow.
5. 'Rod', in *International Standard Bible Encyclopedia*.
6. A. Barnes, *Notes, Explanatory and Practical, on the Book of Revelation*, p. 120.
7. King James Version: 'the crooked shall be made straight'.
8. See also Chapter 6.
9. Lord Shaftesbury's 'Memorandum to Protestant Monarchs of Europe for the restoration of the Jews to Palestine', published in the *Colonial Times* in 1841.
10. Neturei Karta International, 'Why Orthodox Jews are opposed to a Zionist state':
FIRST – . . . The only time that the People of Israel were permitted to have a state was two thousand years ago when the glory of the creator was upon us, and likewise in the future when the glory of the creator will once more be revealed, and the whole world will serve Him, then He Himself (without any human effort or force of arms) will grant us a kingdom founded on Divine Service. However, a worldly state, like those possessed by other peoples, is contradictory to the true essence of the People of Israel. . .
SECOND – Because of all of this and other reasons the Torah forbids us to end the exile and establish a state and army until the Holy One, blessed He, in His Glory and Essence will redeem us. This is forbidden even if the state is conducted according to the law of the Torah because arising from the exile itself is forbidden, and we are required to remain under the rule of the nations of the world . . . If we transgress this injunction, He will bring upon us (may we be spared) terrible punishment.
THIRD – Aside from arising from exile, all the deeds of the Zionists are diametrically opposed to the Faith and the Torah. Because the foundation of the Faith and Torah of Israel is that the Torah was revealed from heaven, and there is reward for those who obey it and punishment for those who transgress it. The entire People of Israel is required to obey the Torah, and whoever doesn't want to, ceases to be part of the congregation of Israel.
FOURTH – Aside from the fact that they themselves do not obey the Torah they do everything they can to prevent anyone they get under their power from fulfilling the commands of the Torah, the claims to freedom of religion are lies. They fight with all of their strength to destroy the Faith of Israel.
11. Attributed to R. Alexandri (Midrash on Psalms 22:2) in Marx, 'The morning ritual in the Talmud', p. 109.

6. The 'good news' of the Gospels and the signs of the times in the New Testament

1. A messianic title – Greek: ὁ ἐρχόμενος ἥξει, ho erchomenos hēxei.
2. This is attested to by Bahá'u'lláh: 'The Day of Return is inscrutable unto all men until after the divine Revelation hath been fulfilled' (*Tablets of Bahá'u'lláh Revealed after the Kitáb-i-Aqdas*, p. 186).
3. New Living Translation: 'home'; Amplified Bible: 'tabernacle'; International Standard Version: 'tent'.
4. Glory: 'Bahá' in Arabic.
5. In Arabic: 'Bahá'u'lláh'.
6. A prophecy fulfilled by Christ, but which applies also to subsequent Prophets.
7. English Standard Version: 'Author'.
8. Prince is also used for the devil as the ruler of demons (Matt. 9:34).
9. King James Version: 'the Comforter'; New International Version: 'the Advocate'.
10. Greek: *Paraklētos*.
11. Benson, *The New Testament of our Lord and Saviour Jesus Christ*, vol. I, p. 640.
12. A. Barnes, *Notes, Explanatory and Practical on the Gospels*, vol. II, p. 359.
13. Letter written on behalf of Shoghi Effendi to an individual, 21 April 1939, in *Lights of Guidance*, no. 1578.
14. Description of the *Kitáb-i-Íqán* (Book of Certitude) in Shoghi Effendi, *God Passes By*, p. 139.
15. Including the *Kitáb-i-Íqán* (Book of Certitude), the *Epistle to the Son of the Wolf*, *Gleanings from the Writings of Bahá'u'lláh*, the *Tablets of the Divine Plan*, and *Some Answered Questions* of 'Abdu'l-Bahá,
16. 'Abdu'l-Bahá, *The Promulgation of Universal Peace*, p. 5.
17. Bahá'u'lláh, *Gleanings from the Writings of Bahá'u'lláh*, XXXVI, pp. 85–6.
18. See for example thefuelproject.org/blog/list-of-people-who-claimed-to-be-jesus.
19. Henry, *Commentary on the Whole Bible*, vol. V, p. 555-7.
20. King James Version adds: 'and pestilences'.
21. Two examples may be cited: the extensive famine and cholera outbreak in Yemen caused by hostilities between S͟hí'ihs, (Houthis backed by Iran), and the Saudi Arabia-led Sunni coalition (2011–); and the civil war in Sudan (1955–) between Muslims and Christians which has resulted in more than two million dead to date from the war and from war-induced famine.
22. King James Version: 'And then shall many be offended'; 'New International Version: 'many will turn away from the faith'.
23. King James Version: 'iniquity shall abound'.
24. Henry, *Commentary on the Whole Bible*, vol. V, p. 561.
25. Benson, *The New Testament of our Lord and Saviour Jesus Christ*, vol. I, p. 194.
26. A. Barnes, *Notes, Explanatory and Practical on the Gospels*, vol. II, p. 145.
27. Jamieson, Fausset and Brown, *Commentary, Critical and Explanatory on the Old and New Testament*, vol. II.
28. A. Barnes, *Notes, Explanatory and Practical. on the Epistles of Paul to the Thessalonians, to Timothy, to Titus, and to Philemon*, p. 100.
29. ibid. p. 103.
30. 'Abdu'l-Bahá, *The Promulgation of Universal Peace*, p. 6.

31. Benson, *The New Testament of our Lord and Saviour Jesus Christ*, vol. I, p. 195.
32. A. Barnes, *Notes on the New Testament, Explanatory and Practical*, p. 254.
33. *Ellicott's Commentary on the Whole Bible*, vol. VI: The Four Gospels, p. 147.
34. Bickersteth, *The Signs of the Times in the East; A Warning to the West* (1845), p. 305.
35. Vatican City, 'Bible translated into 2,454 languages, almost 4,500 more to go', in *AsiaNews*, 14 October 2008. *Ethnologue*, an encyclopedic reference work, estimates that there are 7,105 world languages.
36. http://www.wycliffe.net/statistics.
37. Eldest son and successor of Bahá'u'lláh.
38. 'Abdu'l-Bahá, *Some Answered Questions*, no. 11, pp. 53–4 (talk given in 1904–1906).
39. Bahá'u'lláh, *Tablets of Bahá'u'lláh Revealed after the Kitáb-i-Aqdas*, p. 13.
40. Bethlehem, birthplace of Jesus and Christianity.
41. Bahá'u'lláh, quoted in Shoghi Effendi, *The Promised Day Is Come*, p. 103.
42. Ellicott, *The New Testament Commentary for Schools*, p. 346.
43. Translation of ἀετός in Matthew 24:28, in *Biblical Hermeneutics*: https://hermeneutics.stackexchange.com. Many eagles also eat carrion. However, this does not invalidate the intent of Matthew.
44. Bahá'u'lláh, *Kitáb-i-Íqán*, paras. 28–9, pp. 29–32.
45. ibid. para. 31, pp. 33–4.
46. A social agenda of conflict, bloodshed, and holy war.
47. Millman, 'The falling of the stars', p. 57.
48. Bahá'u'lláh, quoted in Shoghi Effendi, *The Promised Day Is Come*, p. 106.
49. Shoghi Effendi, ibid. p. 102.
50. Bahá'u'lláh, *Kitáb-i-Íqán*, para. 35, p. 37.
51. Lightfoot, *The Whole Works of the Late Rev. John Lightfoot*, vol. XI, p. 304.
52. Gill, *Exposition of the Old and New Testament*.
53. A. Barnes, *Notes on the New Testament, Explanatory and Practical*: Matthew and Mark, p. 59.
54. Spence and Exell, *The Pulpit Commentary*: St. Matthew, vol. II. p. 439.
55. Henry, *Commentary on the Whole Bible*, vol. V, p. 572.
56. ibid.
57. Bahá'u'lláh, *Kitáb-i-Íqán*, para. 74, pp. 66–7.
58. A. Barnes, *Notes on the New Testament, Explanatory and Practical*, Matthew and Mark, p. 260.
59. Bahá'u'lláh, *Kitáb-i-Íqán*, para. 25, p. 27.
60. 'Abdu'l-Bahá, *Some Answered Questions*, no. 13, pp. 76–7.
61. Bahá'u'lláh, *Kitáb-i-Íqán*, paras. 217–219, pp. 197–9; also in *Gleanings from the Writings of Bahá'u'lláh*, CXXV, pp. 268–70.
62. Weymouth New Testament: 'I am re-creating all things.'
63. Ellicott, *The New Testament Commentary for English Readers*, vol. III, p. 627.
64. Easton, *Illustrated Bible Dictionary* (1897).
65. Emblem of authority.
66. Hebrew: until Shiloh comes.
67. Ellicott, *The New Testament Commentary for English Readers*, vol. I, p. 84.
68. Benson, *The Holy Bible containing The Old and the New Testaments with Notes, Critical, Explanatory, and Practical*, vol. III.

69. **The abomination of desolation of Nebuchadnezzar:**
The description of this event associated with Nebuchadnezzar is preserved on a clay inscription by his chronicler: 'the Babylonian king marched to the land of Hatti (Syria), besieged the City of Judah (Jerusalem) and on the second day of the month of Adar (16 March 597) took the city and captured the king.' Nebuchadnezzar plundered the Temple and deported the king and 10,000 nobles, artisans and young men to Babylon. He placed the exiled king's uncle, Zedekiah, on the throne. The latter launched a rebellion that was utterly defeated by Nebuchadnezzar. Jerusalem was besieged for eighteen months and in August 586 Nebuchadnezzar broke into the city and set fire to it and once again took into captivity 20,000 inhabitants. A month later a further attempt was made to obliterate Jerusalem, The Temple was destroyed, it's gold and silver vessels plundered, and the Ark of the Covenant vanished forever.

In 539 BCE the Persian Kourosh (Cyrus the Great) conquered Babylon and ordered to the delight of the exiles that the Temple in Jerusalem be rebuilt, in 537 BCE. More than 42,000 Jews returned to Jerusalem.

Darius, who succeeded Cyrus, confirmed the edict of his predecessor for Jerusalem to be rebuilt, and between 520–515 BCE Zerubbabel, the grandson of the last king of Judah and the priest Jeshua, built the Second Temple. The walls of the City were in severe disrepair fifty years later. Nehemiah, the cupbearer and a friend of Artaxerxes I, the grandson of Darius, appealed apprehensively to the King. Artaxerxes was sympathetic, influenced in part in his decisions by his Jewish queen, Esther. He appointed Nehemiah as the governor and giving him the necessary resources.

The abomination that maketh desolate of Antiochus Epiphanes:
In 167 BCE attempting to eradicate the Jewish religion, the Greek ruler Antiochus Epiphanes captured Jerusalem, slaughtered thousands, destroyed her wall and built a new citadel, the Acra. The Temple was desecrated and consecrated to the Olympian god Zeus. Between 164 and 166 BCE, following a rebellion led by Judah (the Hammer), Jewish independence was restored. Jonathan, Judah's brother, regained Jerusalem, restored the walls, and re-sanctified the Temple.

Abomination of desolation of the Romans:
The Romans annexed Syria and took control of Jerusalem and placed Herod as a puppet king (66–40 BCE). Herod expanded and embellished the Temple. The Jews mounted a spirited war against the Romans (66–70 CE). The last of three major Jewish–Roman wars was fought in 132–136 CE. The Romans eventually put down the Jewish revolt with great ferocity. Hundreds of Jewish communities in Israel were destroyed. The Jews were scattered from the Promised Land for the second time. Thus this loss of sovereignty coincided with the advent of Jesus, or the First Coming, when the Jews became dispersed and lost their national identity.

The abomination that maketh desolate of the Muslim Caliphs:
In 638 CE Caliph Omar conquered Jerusalem. Under the banner of Islam some of the Jews were able to return to the city. However, in 1099 CE Jerusalem was captured by the Crusaders and the Jewish and the Muslim inhabitants were slaughtered. The Muslims reconquered Jerusalem under Saladin in 1187 CE and the city then remained under Muslim domination.

70. Hayes, *Jupiter's Legacy: The Symbol of the Eagle and Thunderbolt in Antiquity and Their Appropriation by Revolutionary America and Nazi Germany*, p. 2.
71. Revelation Revolution, 'The abomination that causes desolation explained'.

7. Objections to Jesus as the Messiah

1. It is worth noting that Bahá'ís consider Jesus as the Messiah and the Lord. The stumbling blocks referred to in this section are to alert us to the issues faced by the followers of Moses at the First Coming and to avoid having similar objections today.
2. King James Version: a stone of stumbling and for a rock of offence.
3. Orthodox Jewish Bible: many rabbim or religious scholars.
4. A. Barnes, *Critical, Explanatory, and Practical, on the Book of The Prophet Isaiah*, vol. 1, p. 195.
5. Maimonides, *Melachim uMilchamot*, Ch. 11.
6. Proverb by John Heywood (1546) according to Titelman, *Random House Dictionary of Popular Proverbs and Sayings*.
7. 'Abdu'l-Bahá, *The Promulgation of Universal Peace*, pp. 291–3.
8. Bahá'u'lláh, *Kitáb-i-Íqán*, para. 6, p. 6.
9. Strong soap used to remove grime and to bleach clothes.
10. Steinberg, 'Was Jesus born in a different Bethlehem?'
11. The Pharisees would surely have known that several Prophets, including Jonah, Nahum and Hosea, came from Galilee. Christians have assumed that the Pharisees were either ignorant or being derisive. However, to be fair, another possibility may be that it was the writer of the Gospel of John reporting the exchange who was unaware of this fact.
12. Examples: Ezra 2:36; Neh. 3:9; 7:7, 11, 43; 8:17; 12:1, 10.
13. Zech. 6:9–13 mentions a high priest Joshua, the son of Jehozadak who is credited with the building of the temple (Ezra 5:1–2). This passage is interpreted as foreshadowing the coming of Jesus, the Messiah, the (spiritual) king. The Apostle Paul refers to Christ as a High Priest in the order of Melchizedek (Heb. 5:6) but the rest of the New Testament, including the Gospels, is silent on this point. His kingdom was not of this world, He predicted the destruction of the temple and did not speak of its reconstruction.

    Bahá'ís do not have an issue with this interpretation as they believe that some prophecies have spiritual implications beyond their immediate historical explanations and relevance. Christians might give the same consideration to the biblical prophecies that are said to apply to Bahá'u'lláh when alternative explanations may be advanced that apply to an earlier age.
14. King James Version: 'a mover of sedition'; Berean Literal Bible: 'a pest'.
15. New Living Translation: 'cult'; Weymouth New Testament: 'heresy'.
16. Followers of Jesus Who came from Nazareth.
17. Also, *Baalsebub*, 'the Lord of the flies', a Philistine god, and a major devil – 'the prince or king of demons'.
18. A male name of Greek origin (Ζακχαῖος or Zakaios) related to the Hebrew form Zaccai (Exra 2:9, Neh. 7:14) which meant 'pure', clean or 'innocent'. Tax collectors were regarded as traitors as they worked for Rome, and were among the most unpopular people in Israel.

19. Or Elias (c. 800 BCE), the Greek name meaning 'my God is *JAH* or Jehovah', or 'Jehovah is my strength'.
20. With few exceptions, most Bibles: 'virgin', but JPS Tanakh Translation: 'a young woman shall conceive'; Good News Translation: 'a young woman who is pregnant will have a son'; NET Bible: 'young woman'.
21. Maimonides, *The Thirteen Principles of the Faith*.
22. Is. 6:1, and Dan. 7:1; 8:1–2.
23. Gen. 6:13; 8:15; 12:1, 4; 22:1–2.
24. Maimonides, *The Thirteen Principles of the Faith*.
25. Expressed as 'throughout' their 'generations', or 'throughout the generations to come' for example, Gen. 17:12; Ex. 12:7; 30:8, 31; Lev. 22:3; 23:41; Numbers 15:21.
26. In a similar language, the Qur'án (5:64) denies finality of divine revelation: 'the Jews say: God's hand is fettered. Their hands are fettered... Nay, but both His hands are spread out wide in bounty. He bestoweth as He will'.
27. New International Version: 'my feet from stumbling'; Aramaic Bible in Plain English: my feet from slipping'.
28. Two closely but independent events, as demonstrated by the phrases ἐλήλυθεν, elēlythen (is come) and ἔρχεται, erchetai (cometh, is coming). Examples:
First event: 'The Son of man is come' [Greek: ἐλήλυθεν elēlythen] (Luke 7:34)
Future event: Watch therefore: for ye know not what hour your Lord doth come [Greek: ἔρχεται, erchetai]. But know this, that if the goodman of the house had known in what watch the thief would come [Greek: ἔρχεται, erchetai], he would have watched, and would not have suffered his house to be broken up. Therefore be ye also ready: for in such an hour as ye think not the Son of man cometh [Greek: ἔρχεται, erchetai]. (Matt. 24:42–44)

The hour is coming [ἔρχεται, erchtai] when I will no longer speak to you in figures of speech but will tell you plainly about the Father. (John 16:25)
Immediate and future events:

He answered, 'Elijah does come [ἔρχεται, erchetai] and he will restore [ἀποκαταστήσει, apokatastēsei] all things. But I tell you that Elijah has already come [ἦλθεν, ēlthen: 'is come'], and they did not recognize him, but did to him whatever they pleased. So also the Son of Man will certainly suffer at their hands. (Matt. 17:11–12)

... the hour is coming [ἔρχεται, erchetai] when neither on this mountain nor in Jerusalem will you worship the Father . . . But the hour is coming, [ἔρχεται, erchetai] and is now here [νῦν ἐστιν, nyn estin] when the true worshipers will worship the Father in spirit and truth, for the Father is seeking such people to worship him. (John 4:21, 23)

Truly, truly, I say to you, an hour is coming [ἔρχεται, erchetai], and is now here [νῦν ἐστιν, nyn estin], when the dead will hear the voice of the Son of God, and those who hear will live . . . Do not marvel at this, for an hour is coming [ἔρχεται, erchetai] when all who are in the tombs will hear [ἀκούσουσιν, akousousin] his voice (John 5:25, 28)
29. King James Version: 'strait gate' that is, narrow and difficult.
30. Isaac Watts, English Christian minister (1674–1748).

31. A. Barnes, *Notes on the New Testament, Explanatory and Practical*, Matthew and Mark, p. 78.
32. King James Version: 'children of the kingdom'; Amplified Bible: 'the sons *and heirs of the kingdom*'.
33. Benson, *The New Testament of our Lord and Saviour Jesus Christ*, vol. I: Matthew to the Acts of the Apostles, p. 141.
34. 'Abdu'l-Bahá, *The Promulgation of Universal Peace*, p. 199.

8. Stumbling blocks at the Second Coming

1. King James Version: 'prove all things'.
2. New Living Translation: 'Now our knowledge is partial and incomplete, and even the gift of prophecy reveals only part of the whole picture!'
3. A. Barnes, *Notes, Explanatory and Practical, on the Second Epistle to Corinthians and the Epistle to Galatians*, p. 60.
4. Crossan and Watts, *Who is Jesus? Answers to Your Questions about the Historical Jesus*, p. 79.
5. Clarke, *Commentary on the Whole Bible*, Luke 10:19.
6. Henry, *Commentary on the Whole Bible*, vol. V, Matthew to John, pp. 105-7.
7. Jamieson, Fausset and Brown, *A Commentary: Critical, Practical and Explanatory, on the Old and New Testament*, vol. 1, p. 47.
8. Graham, 'What did Jesus mean when He said to let the dead bury the dead?'
9. Henry, *Commentary on the Whole Bible*: Exodus.
10. Some manuscripts add 'who do not follow us'.
11. A. Barnes, *Notes on the New Testament, Explanatory and Practical*, Matthew and Mark, p. 364.
12. Ellicott, 'The Gospel according to St. Mark', in Ellicott, *The New Testament Commentary for Schools*, p. 138.
13. Shoghi Effendi, *The World Order of Bahá'u'lláh*, p. 112.
14. Benson, *The New Testament of our Lord and Saviour Jesus Christ*, vol. II, p. 692.
15. According to Gen. 16:16 Abraham was 86 years old but Gen. 21:5 states that he was 100 years old when Isaac was born.
16. The genealogy of Jesus describes Adam as the 'son of God' (Luke 3:38).
17. For example, Julius Caesar was formally deified as 'the Divine Julius', and Caesar Augustus became *Dvi Filius* ('the Son of the Divine One').
18. The word 'begotten' is absent from several translations.
19. A. Barnes, *Notes, Explanatory and Practical, on the First Epistle of Paul to the Corinthians*.
20. Good News translation: 'may he be condemned to hell!'; Aramaic Bible in Plain English: 'he shall be damned'; God's Word translation: 'that person should be condemned to hell'; NET Bible: 'let him be condemned to hell'.
21. ἑτεροζυγοῦντες: bearing a different kind of yoke.
22. Benson, *The Holy Bible Containing the Old and New Testaments with Notes, Critical, Explanatory, and Practical*, vol. V, book 4, ch. 13.
23. Ellicott, *The New Testament Commentary for English Readers*.
24. Augustine, *De symbolo ad catechumenos* (On the Creed: A Sermon to Catechumens), book 4, ch. 13.
25. *Catholicism.org*, 'The Popes on *Extra Ecclesiam Nulla Salus*', 31 January 2005.

26. ibid.
27. 'Unam Sanctum', *Catholic Encyclopedia*.
28. Catholicism.org, 'The Council of Florence (1438–1445) from *Cantate Domino*: Papal Bull of Pope Eugene IV', 16 March 2005.
29. Pope Leo XII, *Ubi Primum*, Encyclical, para. 14.
30. Pope Leo XIII, *Liberatas,* Encyclical on the Nature of Human Liberty, para. 21, 20 June 1988.
31. The recipient of Bahá'u'lláh's Tablet.
32. Pope Pius IX, *Quanto conficiamur moerore*, 19 August 1863.
33. Allocution to the Gregorian University, 17 October 1953.
34. Imhof and Biallowons, *Karl Rhaner in Dialogue: Conversations and Interviews 1965–1982*, p. 207.
35. ibid. p. 325.
36. Congregation for the Doctrine of the Faith, *Dominus Iesus*, I, 8.
37. Wilken, 'What is the Catholic teaching of "Anonymous Christianity"?'
38. Clinton, *Peter, Paul and the Anonymous Christian: A Response to The Mission Theology of Rahner and Vatican II*.
39. John XXIII, Paul VI, John Paul I, John Paul II, Benedict XVI and Pope Francis.
40. See, for example, Pulvermacher, 'Vatican II Council: Accepts freedom of religion, teaches heresy and apostasies', *Caritas Newsletter*, 19 August 1989; Pivarunas, 'The Last Days and false ecumenism'; Rood, *The Christian Attitude towards Non-Christian Religions*; Anonymous, 'The Great Apostasy of Vatican II', online article; Winters, 'Hostility to Vatican II runs deep with Pope Francis' critics', *National Catholic Reporter*, 8 January 2018.
41. A papal declaration made 'from the chair' on issues of faith or morals that is considered infallible.
42. Catholicism.org, 'The Council of Florence (1438–1445) from *Cantate Domino*: Papal Bull of Pope Eugene IV'.
43. See Weaver and Appleby, *Being Right: Conservative Catholics in America*, pp. 25–27; Marty and Appleby, *Fundamentalism Observed*, p. 88; Collinge, *Historical Dictionary of Catholicism*, p. 399.
44. Fahlbusch and Bromiley, *The Encyclopedia of Christianity*, vol. 3, p. 867.
45. Strange, 'Exclusivisms: "Indeed their rock is not like our rock"', p. 41.
46. Schwartz, *The Curse of Cain: The Violent Legacy of Monotheism*, pp. 3–5.
47. King James Version: 'iniquity'.
48. Ellicott, *Ellicott's Commentary for English Readers*, John 5.
49. Blackie, *The Day-book of John Stuart Blackie*, p. 38.
50. Barclay, *The Plain Man Looks at The Apostles' Creed*, p. 178.
51. New International Version: 'it is for your good'.
52. Watkins, 'The Gospel According to St. John', 'in Ellicott, *A New Testament Commentary for English Readers by Various Writers*, vol. 1, p. 515.
53. Referred to in Bahá'í Writings as 'veils of glory'.
54. A Hebrew Prophet.
55. Jude 1:10–11, referring in part to Numbers 16: 2–3:
    Korah along with 250 other prominent leaders of the Jewish community incited a rebellion against Moses: They united against Moses and Aaron and said, 'You have gone too far! The whole community of Israel has been set apart

by the Lord, and he is with all of us. What right do you have to act as though you are greater than the rest of the Lord's people?'

Balaam was a Prophet who in the end misled the Jews: for a bribe he advised the Moabites on how to entice the Israelites with prostitutes and idolatry.

56. A. Barnes, *Notes on the New Testament, Explanatory and Practical*, Matthew and Mark, p. 242.
57. Ellicott, *Ellicott's Commentary on the Whole Bible*. vol. VI: The Four Gospels. Previously published as *A Bible Commentary for English Readers*, vol. I, p. 141.
58. Shoghi Effendi, *The Promised Day Is Come*, pp. 119-20.

9. Further impediments

1. E. W. Barnes, *The Rise of Christianity*, p. 267.
2. Barclay, *The Plain Man Looks at the Apostles' Creed*, pp. 294–5.
3. *Merriam-Webster Dictionary*.
4. 'Churchianity'. Wiktionary, at https://en.wiktionary.org/wiki/Churchianity.
5. *Zion's Watch Tower and Herald of Christ's Presence* (1879), vol. 1, no. 3.
6. The *cathedra* was the raised throne of a bishop in the early Christian basilica; hence, ex-cathedra: 'from the chair'. 'It was applied to decisions made by Popes from their thrones. According to Roman Catholic doctrine, a Pope speaking ex cathedra on issues of faith or morals is infallible. In general use, the phrase has come to be used with regard to statements made by people in positions of authority, and it is often used ironically to describe someone speaking with overbearing or unwarranted self-certainty' (*Merriam-Webster Dictionary*).
7. In contrast to inanimate idols.
8. Son of Jonah, the name of Peter's father.
9. *Catholic Answers*, 'What the early Church believed: Peter's primacy'.
10. Infallibility means more than exemption from actual error; it means exemption from the possibility of error; see Toner, 'Infallibility'; also, Pius IX, Vatican I, at Ewtn.com.
11. A. Barnes, *Notes on the New Testament, Explanatory and Practical*: Matthew and Mark, p. 170.
12. Mendicant orders, such as Franciscans and Dominicans, rely chiefly on charitable donations. In contrast to the monastic model of living they have renounced owning property and living in stable communities, instead embracing a life of poverty and travelling and ministering to the poor in urban areas.
13. A. Barnes, *Notes on the New Testament, Explanatory and Practical*: Matthew and Mark, p. 150.
14. Gibbon, *The Decline and Fall of the Roman Empire*, vol. I. ch. 15, pp. 528–30.
15. Davidson, 'Fewer and fewer'; see also Schoenherr, Young and Cheng, *Full Pews and Empty Altars: Demographics of the Priest Shortage in United States Catholic Dioceses*, p. 6.
16. The Prophet Balaam's donkey would not budge at the sight of an angel blocking the road. It protested when Balaam kept hitting it because he could not see the angel. Thus, it is not quite clear whether the miracle was attributable to the Prophet or to his extraordinarily perceptive and gifted donkey!
17. A. Barnes, *Notes on the New Testament, Explanatory and Practical*: Matthew and Mark, p. 134.

18. Henry, *Commentary on the Whole Bible*, vol. V, Matthew to John, pp. 284-5.
19. 'Abdu'l-Bahá, *Some Answered Questions*, no. 10, p. 44.
20. ibid. no. 22, pp. 114–15.
21. Bahá'u'lláh, *Epistle to the Son of the Wolf*, p. 33.
22. 'Abdu'l-Bahá, *The Promulgation of Universal Peace*, pp. 412–13.
23. https://www.myjewishlearning.com/article/hand-washing; see also Klein, *A Guide to Jewish Religious Practice*, ch. III, p. 49.
24. King James Version: 'fables'; Weymouth New Testament: 'but, wanting to have their ears tickled, they will find a multitude of teachers to satisfy their own fancies'.
25. A. Barnes, *Notes, Explanatory and Practical. On the General Epistles of James, Peter, John, & Jude*, p. 291.
26. Hulbert-Powell, *John James Wettstein (1693–1754): An Account of His Life, Work and Some of His Contemporaries*, ch. II. p. 23.
27. ibid.
28. *Encyclopaedia Britannica*: Letter to the Hebrews. Online at: https://www.britannica.com/topic/Letter-to-the-Hebrews.
29. For example, International Standard Version; NET Bible; New Heart English Bible; Weymouth New Testament; and Young's Literal Translation.
30. For example, New International Version; New Living Translation; English Standard Version; Berean Study Bible' King James Bible; New American Standard Bible; and English Revised Version.
31. For example: the King James Version and New American Standard Bible.
32. See https://thediscoverybible.com.
33. A. Barnes, *Notes, Explanatory, and Practical on the Gospels*, vol. I, p. 150.
34. Gibbon, *The Decline and Fall of the Roman Empire*, vol. I, ch. 15, pp. 487–9.
35. ibid.
36. ibid. vol. I, ch. 21, pp. 295–6.
37. Cairns, *The Reasonableness of the Christian Faith*, p. 176.
38. Stanford, *Fox's Book of Martyrs*, ch. III, p. 51.
39. Durant, *The Story of Civilization: The Age of Faith*, vol. IV, p. 5.
40. Brown, 'Augustine's attitude to religious coercion', p. 110; also Augustine, *Contra Epistulam Parmeniani*, 8:15.
41. Augustine, 'Letter 93 to Vincentius' (AD 408), in *The Letters of St. Augustine*, ch. II, pp. 178–180.
42. Ellicott, *Ellicott's Commentary for English Readers*, Luke 14:23.
43. Wheeler, 'Monks brawl at Jerusalem's Church of the Holy Sepulchre, site of Jesus's crucifixion'; Strochilic, 'Christian monks square off at one of Jerusalem's holiest sites: A multi-century-long battle has been raging between six Christian sects at the Church of the Holy Sepulchre'.
44. Cross, 'Great Schism (1)', in *The Oxford Dictionary of the Christian Church*.
45. Phillips, *The Fourth Crusade and the Sack of Constantinople*.
46. ibid. ch. 13, p. 245 and ch. 14, p. 266.
47. Calvin, *The Necessity of Reforming the Church*, Introduction: 'The evils which compelled us to seek remedies'.
48. Evans, *John Wyclif*, p. 224.
49. ibid. p. 224.

50. ibid. p. 251.
51. 'Sed postea per sententiam universalem Ecclesia fuit exhumatum et ossa sua fuerunt combusta.' Eulogium, III, p. 367. Quoted ibid. p. 210.
52. Lützow, *The Hussite Wars*.
53. New Living Translation: 'new gems of truth as well as old'.
54. Ellicott, *The New Testament Commentary for English Readers*, vol. I: *Genesis – Esther*, p. 84.
55. A rabbinical court.
56. 'It was contrary to strict Roman law for the Jews to propagate their opinions among the Romans, though they might make proselytes of other nations' (Vincent, *Vincent's Word Studies in the New Testament*, Acts 16:21).
57. *Expositor's Greek Testament*: ἔθη: religious customs here; the charge ostensibly put forward was really that of introducing a *religio illicita*, *licita* as it was for the Jews themselves.
58. Acts 16:21.
59. Examples: Jackson, 'The Baha'i Movement', in *ChristianCourier.com*, 2020; Martin, *Kingdom of the Cults*, ch. 10 (this book is discussed at Bahá'í Library Online).

10. Review of some Christian themes

1. Berean Study Bible: 'will expose the motives of men's hearts'.
2. 'Abdu'l-Bahá, *The Promulgation of Universal Peace*, pp. 459–60.
3. Calvin, *Institutes of the Christian Religion*, p. 398.
4. 'A woman from Samaria'.
5. King James Version: 'freely'.
6. Irresponsible leaders of the children of Israel.
7. New Living Translation: darkness can never extinguish it.
8. Benson, *The Holy Bible, Containing the Old and New Testaments*, vol. III, p. 180. Benson interprets the moon shining as brightly as the sun as metaphorically referring to 'that glorious and happy state of the church which should take in future times' – as a Methodist, he probably envisages this to apply to his own institution.
9. A. Barnes, *Notes, Critical Explanatory, and Practical on the Book of The Prophet Isaiah*, p. 485.
10. Pentecost: Fifteenth day from Easter Sunday, commemorating the descent of the Holy Spirit upon the Apostles and other followers of Jesus Christ while they were in Jerusalem.
11. A. Barnes, *Notes, Explanatory and Practical, on the Acts of the Apostles: Designed for Sunday-School Teachers and Bible Classes*, p. 43.
12. Esslemont, *Bahá'u'lláh and the New Era*, pp. 227–8.
13. Bahá'u'lláh, *Kitáb-i-Íqán*, para. 34, p. 36.
14. ibid. para. 38, p. 38.
15. ibid. para. 42, p. 41.
16. Bahá'u'lláh, *Gleanings from the Writings of Bahá'u'lláh*, XCVI, p. 196.
17. Bahá'u'lláh, *The Kitáb-i-Aqdas*, para. 173, p. 82.
18. Bahá'u'lláh, *Kitáb-i-Íqán*, para. 51, p. 48.

19. King James Version: 'even the Son of man which is in heaven'.
20. Ellicott, *The New Testament Commentary for Schools*: The Gospel According to St. John, p. 79.
21. A. Barnes, *Notes, Explanatory and Practical, on The Gospels*, vol. 2, p. 214.
22. 'Abdu'l-Bahá, *Some Answered Questions*, no. 31, p. 144.
23. 'Abdu'l-Bahá, *Paris Talks*, no. 34, pp. 108–9.
24. Esslemont, *Bahá'u'lláh and the New Era*, pp. 190–91.
25. The Báb, *Selections from the Writings of the Báb*, pp. 157–8.
26. 'Abdu'l-Bahá, quoted in Esslemont, *Bahá'u'lláh and the New Era*, p. 191.
27. Bahá'u'lláh, *Tablets of Bahá'u'lláh Revealed after the Kitáb-i-Aqdas*, p. 118.
28. King James Version: 'howlings'; Good News Translation: 'cries of mourning'.
29. A. Barnes, *Notes, Explanatory and Practical on the Gospels*, vol. II, p. 121.
30. Benson, *The Holy Bible, Containing the Old and New Testaments according to the Present, Authorized Version with Critical, Explanatory, and Practical Notes*, vol. I. ch. VII, p. 446.
31. Bahá'u'lláh, *Kitáb-i-Íqán*, para. 120, p. 114.
32. 'Abdu'l-Bahá, *The Promulgation of Universal Peace*, p. 182.
33. Bahá'u'lláh, *Kitáb-i-Íqán*, paras. 125, 128, pp. 118, 120.
34. Ellicott, *The New Testament Commentary for Schools*: The Gospel According to St. John, p. 81.
35. King James Version adds: 'For the Son of man is not come to destroy men's lives, but to save them.'
36. Benson, *The New Testament of our Lord and Saviour Jesus Christ with Critical, Explanatory and Practical Notes*; vol. I, p. 594.
37. Henry and Scott, *A Commentary upon the Holy Bible*: Matthew to Acts, p. 425.

11. Resurrection

1. King James Version: 'death'.
2. Maimonides, 'The Thirteen Principles of Faith', trans. Hertz.
3. New Living Translation: 'our physical bodies'.
4. 'of small and great consequence', as in Ps. 115:13.
5. A. Barnes, *Notes, Explanatory and Practical, on the Book of Revelation*, p. 574.
6. A. Barnes, *Notes on the New Testament, Explanatory and Practical* (ed. Robert Frew), Matthew and Mark, p. 314.
7. Benson, *The New Testament of Our Lord and Saviour Jesus Christ*, vol. I, Matthew to Acts of the Apostles, p. 239.
8. Davies and Allison, *A Critical and Exegetical Commentary on the Gospel According to Saint Matthew*, vol. III, p. 639.
9. New International Version: 'the hardest stone'.
10. Bahá'u'lláh, *Gleanings From the Writings of Bahá'u'lláh*, XXXVI, pp. 85–6.
11. 'Abdu'l-Bahá, *The Will And Testament of 'Abdu'l-Bahá*, pp. 10–11.
12. 'Abdu'l-Bahá, *Some Answered Questions*, no. 10, p. 44.
13. Esslemont, *Bahá'u'lláh and the New Era*, p. 222.
14. The Báb, *Selections from the Writings of the Báb*, p. 107.
15. Shoghi Effendi, *Dawn of a New Day*, p. 79.
16. Esslemont, quoting the Báb in *Bahá'u'lláh and the New Era*, p. 21.

17. Bahá'u'lláh, *The Kitáb-i-Aqdas*, para. 81, p. 49.
18. Bahá'u'lláh, *Epistle to the Son of Wolf*, p. 28.
19. 'Abdu'l-Bahá, *Japan Will Turn Ablaze!* p. 44.
20. ibid.
21. Bahá'u'lláh, *Kitáb-i-Íqán*, para. 79, pp. 71–2.
22. Bahá'u'lláh, *Gleanings from the Writings of Bahá'u'lláh*, LXXXI, pp. 155–7.
23. Mohler, 'Christianity stands or falls on the Resurrection?' See also Snapp, 'Christianity stands or falls on the Resurrection': 'The Christian faith is built on the resurrection. You can't deny the resurrection without denying the saving work of Christ . . .'
24. Borg, 'The Resurrection of Jesus'.
25. For example, the miracle of the virgin birth is accepted by both Islam and the Bahá'í Faith. However, the Qur'án states that God does not beget nor is He begotten (112:3).
26. Cline, 'Jesus: Contradictions in resurrection and ascension'.
27. Plumptree, *The Gospel According to St. Matthew, with Commentary* (in substance identical to Ellicott's *New Testament Commentary for English Readers*), p. 173.
28. Weymouth New Testament: 'this very day you shall be with me in Paradise'.
29. A. Barnes, *Notes, Explanatory and Practical on the Gospels*, vol. II, Luke and John, p. 181.
30. New International Version: 'looking intently into the sky'.
31. New International Version: 'sky?'
32. Trumbower, *Rescue for the Dead: The Posthumous Salvation of Non-Christians in Early Christianity*, p. 8.
33. 'Abdu'l-Bahá, *The Promulgation of Universal Peace*, p. 63 .
34. 'Abdu'l-Bahá, *Some Answered Questions*, no. 29, pp. 132–6.
35. 'Abdu'l-Bahá, *Selections from the Writings of 'Abdu'l-Bahá*, no. 31, p. 65.
36. 'Abdu'l-Bahá, *The Promulgation of Universal Peace*, p. 5.
37. ibid. pp. 256–7.
38. ibid. pp. 291–2.
39. ibid. p. 199.
40. 'holden': appears in Luke 24:16 and denotes that they did not know who He was.
41. 'Abdu'l-Bahá, *Paris Talks*, no. 16, pp. 47–8.
42. 'Abdu'l-Bahá, in many Bahá'í prayer books; also quoted in Esslemont, *Bahá'u'lláh and the New Era*, p. 90.
43. Bahá'u'lláh, *Prayers and Meditations by Bahá'u'lláh*, XXV, pp. 29–30.
44. See Bahá'u'lláh, *Gleanings from the Writings of Bahá'u'lláh*, CXLII, 311–12.
45. New Living Translation: 'showing partiality is never good...'
46. New International Version: 'sexually immoral people'.
47. *Encyclopaedia Britannica*: Confession, Religion.
48. Ἐξομολογεῖσθε (acknowledge, agree fully, confess, profess, promise) οὖν ἀλλήλοις (therefore to one another) τὰς ἁμαρτίας (the sins or mistakes).
49. Staples, 'The priesthood is both universal and ministerial'.
50. ibid.
51. Ellicott, *Commentary for English Readers*.

52. A. Barnes, *Notes, Explanatory and Practical, on the General Epistles of James, Peter, John, & Jude*, p. 110.
53. Enacting the flagellation of Jesus before his crucifixion was popular in the thirteenth century until it was condemned by the church in the fourteenth century. Pope John Paul II (d. 2005) allegedly whipped himself with a belt and sometimes lay prostrate all night on the floor. Mother Teresa wore a cilice, a strap secured around the thigh that inflicts pain with inward-pointing spikes. Self-flagellation is also practised by some Catholic organizations such as Opus Dei, and amongst some Catholic communities of Philippines, Mexico and Peru.
54. A garment of rough cloth made from animal hair and worn in the form of a shirt to induce discomfort or pain, as a girdle around the loins, by way of mortification and penance, similar to the garment of camels' hair worn by John the Baptist (Matt. 3:4). Elijah also had a girdle of leather around his loins (II Kings 1:8+). Albert Barnes explains:

    His costume was that of a thorough ascetic. Generally the Jews wore girdles of linen or cotton stuff, soft and comfortable. Under the girdle they wore one or two long linen gowns or shirts, and over these they had sometimes a large shawl. Elijah had only his leather girdle and his sheepskin cape or 'mantle'. (Barnes, *Notes on the Whole Bible*, II Kings 8)

55. *Catechism of the Catholic Church*, Part II, section 2, The Seven Sacraments of the Church, ch. 2: 'Interior Penance, 1430–1432'.
56. 'Fourth Lateran Council, 1215', in *Papal Encyclicals Online*.
57. 'Penance', in *The Catholic Encyclopedia*, vol. XI, p. 619.
58. J. N. D. Kelly, *Early Christian Doctrines*, p. 171.
59. 'Abdu'l-Bahá, *Some Answered Questions*, no. 29, pp. 134–5.
60. 'Abdu'l-Bahá, *The Promulgation of Universal Peace*, p. 49.
61. See 'Abdu'l-Bahá, *Some Answered Questions*, no. 30.
62. Haug, *Essays on the Sacred Language, Writings and Religion of the Parsis* (1884).
63. Spence and Exell, *The Pulpit Commentary*: Isaiah 45.
64. Poole, *English Annotations on the Holy Bible* (1696), at https://www.biblecomments.org / 2-timothy.
65. 'Abdu'l-Bahá *Tablets of Abdul-Baha Abbas*, pp. 609–10.
66. 'Abdu'l-Bahá, *The Promulgation of Universal Peace*, p. 444.

12. The Trinity

1. See for example Ferrar, *The Proof of the Gospel Being the Demonstratio Evangelica of Eusebius of Cæsarea*, book III, ch. 6, 132 (a), p. 152; ch. 7, 136 (a-d), p. 157.
2. 'The textual problem in 1 John 5:7-8', at https://bible.org/article/textual-problem-1-john-57-8.
3. Neil R. Lightfoot. *How We Got the Bible*, pp. 100–01.
4. Barclay, *The Plain Man Looks at the Apostles' Creed*, p. 9.
5. 'Abdu'l-Bahá, *Some Answered Questions*, no. 31, pp. 127–8.
6. Letter written on behalf of Shoghi Effendi to an individual, 29 November 1937, in *Lights of Guidance*, no. 1644.

7. 'Abdu'l-Bahá, *Some Answered Questions*, no. 12, p. 72.
8. Shoghi Effendi, *The Promised Day Is Come*, pp. 109–10.
9. Shoghi Effendi, *High Endeavours: Messages to Alaska*, p. 70.
10. Pope Pius IX, *Ineffablis Deus*, 8 December 1854.
11. 'Abdu'l-Bahá, *The Promulgation of Universal Peace*, p. 394.
12. 'Abdu'l-Bahá, *Tablets of Abdul-Baha Abbas*, pp. 513–14.
13. The correct translation uses the indefinite article 'a son' and not '*his* son' as appears in several translation such as the NET Bible, Weymouth New Testament, International Standard Version, New Heart English Bible, and Young's Literal Translation.
14. New International Version, Berean Study Bible and New American Standard: 'exact representation'; English Standard Version: 'exact imprint'; Good News Translation: 'exact likeness'; Aramaic Bible in Plain English: 'the image of His Being'.
15. Bahá'u'lláh, *Gleanings from the Writings of Bahá'u'lláh*, XX, p. 49.
16. Bahá'u'lláh, *Kitáb-i-Íqán*, para. 110, pp. 103–4.
17. ibid. para. 109, p. 103.
18. Shoghi Effendi, *The World Order of Bahá'u'lláh*, p. 112.
19. A Prophet, most commonly, *navi* or speaker in Hebrew (Deut. 18:15; Luke 24:19); προφήτης or an interpreter of God's will in Greek; and *nabi* in Arabic (Qur'án 7:157), is a divinely inspired and chosen Person who speaks for God. Also, one who is the bearer of God's Word or Message and Who transmits God's truth to others; hence, He is also referred to also as a Messenger in the Bible (Mal. 3:1). In the Qur'án a Prophet is sometimes referred to God's Messenger, *Rasúl*, or Apostle (7:35). Sometimes a Prophet is given by God a prophecy to convey. In the early church, elders were also referred to Apostles or Prophets (I Cor. 12:28; Ephes. 2:20; 3:5).
20. Bahá'u'lláh, *Gleanings from the Writings of Bahá'u'lláh*, LXXXIV, p. 167.

13. Sacraments and Ordinances

1. A. Barnes, *Notes, Explanatory and Practical on the Epistles of Paul to the Thessalonians, to Timothy, to Titus, and to Philemon*, p. 308.
2. J. B. Lightfoot (ed), *The Didache or Teaching of the Apostles* ((1885), vii. This is a brief early Christian treatise dated to late first or early second century.
3. ibid.
4. Josephus, *The Works of Flavius Josephus*, book XVIII, ch. 5, para. 2, p. 666.
5. Greek: πυρί, pyri.
6. 'Abdu'l-Bahá, *Some Answered Questions*, no. 19, pp. 103–4.
7. E. W. Barnes, *The Rise of Christianity*, p. 272.
8. The King James version of the Bible, as well as the New King James, contains vv. 9–20 because the King James version used medieval manuscripts as the basis of its translation. Since 1611, however, older and more accurate manuscripts have been discovered and they affirm that vv. 9–20 were not in the original Gospel of Mark. In addition, the fourth-century church fathers Eusebius and Jerome noted that almost all Greek manuscripts available to them lacked vv. 9–20. See http://www.gotquestions.org/Mark-16-9-20.html.
9. Pinedo, 'Infant baptism'.

10. 'Abdu'l-Bahá, *Some Answered Questions*, no. 20, p. 107.
11. 'Abdu'l-Bahá, *Selections from the Writings of 'Abdu'l-Bahá*, no. 129, p. 140.
12. 'Abdu'l-Bahá, *Paris Talks*, no. 27, pp. 79–81.
13. *Baltimore Catechism*, Lesson 26 – The Holy Eucharist, qq. 343–78.
14. A. Barnes, *Notes on the New Testament, Explanatory and Practical*, Matthew and Mark, p. 282.
15. Irenaeus, 'Against the heresies' (c. 180), book V, ch. 1, para. 3.
16. Harris, *Understanding the Bible*, p. 286.
17. Nabarz, *The Mysteries of Mithras: The Pagan Belief that Shaped the Christian World*, pp. 4–5, 19–27.
18. E. W. Barnes, *The Rise of Christianity*, p. 61.
19. Dr. Martin Luther King Jr., 'The influence of the mystery religions on Christianity'.
20. *Encyclopædia Britannica*: Trimurti, Hinduism.
21. Klein, *A Guide to Jewish Religious Practice*, ch. XXXI, pp. 442–5, 448.
22. Frazer, *The Golden Bough*, ch. 34: 'The myth and ritual of Attis'.
23. E. W. Barnes, *The Rise of Christianity*, p. 56.
24. Murdock, 'Early Church Fathers on Mithraism: The Devil got there first'.
25. Justin Martyr, *Dialogue with Trypho*, chs. LXIX and LXX.
26. Justin Martyr, *First Apology*, ch. LXVI, 'Of the Eucharist'.
27. Tertullian, *De Praescriptione Haereticorum*, ch. 40.

14. Biblical criteria to validate truth

1. For example, see the views of the Reformation leader Martin Luther expressed in 'On the Jews and their Lies', Wittenberg, 1543.
2. 'Abdu'l-Bahá, quoted in Shoghi Effendi, *Unfolding Destiny*, p. 7.
3. Shoghi Effendi, *The Advent of Divine Justice*, p. 16.
4. Further attestation to this divinely ordained transformation in the lives of the Jews is described by 'Abdu'l-Bahá, *The Secret of Divine Civilization*, pp. 75–7.
5. Shoghi Effendi, *The Advent of Divine Justice*, p. 17.
6. A. Barnes, *Notes, Explanatory and Practical, on The Gospels*, p. 105.
7. Henry, *Commentary on the Whole Bible*, vol. 6: Acts to Revelation.
8. Tertullian, *De Praescriptione Haereticorum*, ch. 3, p. 38.
9. St Augustine of Hippo, tractate 45 on the Gospel of John, in the *Catholic Encyclopedia*.
10. 'The test by which it was to be discovered which was the true prophet and which the false, was the fulfillment or non-fulfillment of his prediction' (Spence and Exell, *The Pulpit Commentary*: Jeremiah, Verses 21, 22).
11. The occasion for this statement by Jeremiah was that the Prophet Hananiah had predicted peace although all the Prophets of the Lord had prophesied of war and calamity. Ellicott's *Commentary for English Readers* states:

   The prophet which prophesieth of peace. –'Peace', with its Hebrew associations, includes all forms of national prosperity, and is therefore contrasted with famine and pestilence, not less than with war. The obvious reference to the test of a prophet's work, as described in Deuteronomy 18:22, shows, as other like references, the impression which that book had made on the prophet's mind.

12. Institute for Religious Research, 'Failed prophecies of Joseph Smith'.
13. Church of Jesus Christ of Latter-Day Saints, *'The Book of Abraham'*, pp. 29–42.
14. Account of the controversy given in Roberts, *A Comprehensive History of the Church*, vol II, pp. 136–9; Remy and Brenchley, *A Journey to Great-Salt-Lake City*, vol II, p. 539; Stenhouse, *The Rocky Mountain Saints*, ch. 3, pp. 21–8.
15. See Spalding, *Joseph Smith Jr. as a Translator* (1912).
16. Note 118 in Bahá'u'lláh, *The Kitáb-i-Aqdas*, pp. 216-17.
17. Bahá'u'lláh, *The Kitáb-i-Aqdas*, para. 86, p. 51.
18. ibid. para. 90, p. 53.
19. Shoghi Effendi, *God Passes By*, p. 226.
20. ibid. p. 225.
21. King James Version: 'honour from men'.
22. Greek: λαμβάνει καὶ ἀναγγελεῖ ὑμῖν, lambanei kai anangelei hymin – 'will disclose it to you'.
23. 'To thee We sent the Scripture in truth, confirming the scripture that came before it, and guarding it in safety: so judge between them by what God hath revealed, and follow not their vain desires, diverging from the Truth that hath come to thee . . .' (Qur'án 5:48)

    The same religion has He established for you as that which He enjoined on Noah – the which We have sent by inspiration to thee – and that which We enjoined on Abraham, Moses, and Jesus: Namely, that ye should remain steadfast in religion, and make no divisions therein . . .' (Qur'án 42:13)
24. Bahá'u'lláh, *Epistle to the Son of the Wolf*, p. 11.
25. Bahá'u'lláh, addressing the Shah of Persia, in Bahá'u'lláh, *The Summons of the Lord of Hosts*, p. 98.
26. Bahá'u'lláh, *Epistle to the Son of the Wolf*, p. 107.
27. ibid. p. 35.
28. Is. 40:7–8.
29. Bahá'u'lláh, *The Summons of the Lord of Hosts*, p. 195.

15. Biblical promises fulfilled

1. Cohen, 'Eden', in Berlin and Grossman, *The Oxford Dictionary of the Jewish People*.
2. Gaines R. Johnson, 'The lost rivers of the Garden of Eden – found'.
3. *Adam Clarke's Commentary on the Whole Bible*, Ezekiel 43.
4. Tradition has named Shushán (Susa), the capital of Elam, as a possible site where Daniel is buried (Gottheil and König, 'The Tomb of Daniel', 1906).
5. Newton, *Observations upon the Prophecies of Daniel and the Apocalypse of St. John*, p. 805.
6. Bickersteth, *The Signs of the Times in the East: A Warning to the West*, p. 28.
7. Guinness, *The Approaching End of the Age: Viewed in the Light of History, Prophecy, and Science*, p. 438.
8. See Benson, *The New Testament of Our Lord and Saviour Jesus Christ*.
9. A. Barnes, *Notes, Explanatory and Practical on the Book of Revelation*, p. 291.
10. Bickersteth, 'Testimonies of Christian divines for several centuries as to the application of the Sixth Trumpet to the Turks', in Bickersteth, *The Signs of the Times in the East: A Warning to the West*, pp. xvii–xxv.

NOTES AND REFERENCES

11. Litch, *The Probability of the Second Coming of Christ about CE 1843*.
12. Bickersteth, *The Signs of the Times in the East: A Warning to the West*, pp. 22–3.
13. An edict of toleration is a declaration, made by a ruling power, that members of a given religion will not be persecuted for engaging in their religious practices and traditions. It implies a tacit acceptance of the religion but not its endorsement. There have been several edicts of toleration. An early example is the one issued by the Roman Emperor Galerius in 311 CE, officially ending the dictates by Emperor Diocletian that had resulted in severe persecution of the Christians.
14. Deringil, *Conversion and Apostasy in the Late Ottoman Empire*, p. 73.
15. The Qur'án does not prescribe death for apostasy. The death penalty for apostasy comes from several hadiths and is practised under Shariah law.
16. Bickersteth, *The Signs of the Times in the East: A Warning to the West*, pp. 22–5. A full abstract of the Parliamentary paper on this subject was provided by Bickersteth in the Second Appendix to the seventh edition of his *Practical Guide to the Prophecies*, pp. 387–94. (quoted in full in Guinness, *The Approaching End of the Age: Viewed in the Light of History, Prophecy, and Science*, pp. 431–5):

    The papers entitled 'Correspondence Relating to Executions in Turkey for Apostasy from Islamism', were presented to Parliament, May 3, 1844, and having come before me through the kindness of Lord Ashley, I give the following abstract of them. The correspondence occupied a considerable part of a year – from Aug. 27, 1843, to April 19, 1844.

    The difficulties in the way were thus stated by the Grand Vizier, Aug. 24, 1843: 'The laws of the Koran compel no man to become a Mussulman; but they are inexorable, both as respects Mussulman who embraces another religion, and as respects a person, not a Mussulman, who, after having his own accord publicly embraced Islamism, is convicted of having renounced that faith. No consideration can produce a commutation of the capital punishment, to which the law condemns him without mercy. The only mode of escaping death is for the accused to declare that he has again become a Mussulman.' The same difficulties were pressed Dec. 1, 1843, when our Ambassador was assured, that although the Porte wished to avoid any recurrence of the atrocity, yet as such executions were obligatory under the law, considered by Mohammedans Divine, it would be embarrassing to give an official declaration. And again, Feb. 10, 1844, the Ottoman Minister for Foreign Affairs drew a strong line of distinction between custom and Divine law, intimating that a law prescribed by God Himself was not to be set aside by any human power; and that the Sultan in attempting it might be exposed to a heavy, perhaps even a dangerous, responsibility.

    The causes of this intervention of the European Powers are remarkable. In August, 1843, an Armenian youth, who after, under fear of punishment, becoming a Turk, had returned to his Christian faith, was put to death. This called for the interposition of our Government and its serious remonstrance, and produce in November, 1843, some promises of termination such affairs without capital punishment. In December, however, a young Greek, who had become a Mussulman, having returned to his own creed as a Greek Christian, at Biligik, adjoining to Brussa, was executed. This taking place in the midst of the correspondence, called forth Lord Aberdeen's decisive letter of Jan. 16. Thus we are indebted to the faithfulness of the Greek and Armenian martyrs for this remarkable change. The energy put forth to accomplish this change required the concurrent exertions of the five European Powers – Austria, Prussia, France, Russia, and England.

The able dispatch of Lord Aberdeen of Jan. 16, 1844, is peculiar, and very honorable to our country. It is as follows, – 'Despatch to Sir Stratford Canning, our Ambassador at the Porte, from the Earl of Aberdeen.' Foreign Office, January 16, 1844.

'Sir, – I have received your Excellency's despatch of the 17th of December, reporting that a Greek had been executed near Brussa as an apostate from Islamism, and enclosing a copy of the communication which you had directed Mr. Dragoman Frederick Pisani to make to the Porte in consequence of that transaction.

'I have to state to your Excellency that her Majesty's Government entirely approve the promptitude with which you acted on this occasion. But the repetition of the scene of this revolting kind so soon after that which had, in the course of last summer, excited the horror and indignation of Europe, evinces such total disregard, on the part of the Porte, for the feelings and remonstrances of the Christian Powers, that it is incumbent upon Her Majesty's Government, without loss of time, to convey their sentiments on the matter still more explicitly to the knowledge of the Porte. They take this course singly, and without waiting for the co-operation of the other Christian Powers, because they desire to announce to the Porte a determination which, though, it doubtless will be concurred in by all, Great Britain is prepared to act upon alone. Her majesty's Government fell, too, that they have an especial right to require to be listened to by the Porte on the a matter of this nature; for they can appeal to the justice ant to the favour with which the vast number of Mohammedans subject to British rule are treated in India, in support of their demand that all persons, subject of the Porte, and professing Christianity, shall be exempt from cruel and arbitrary persecution on account of their religion, and shall not be made the victims of a barbarous law, which it may be sought to enforce for their destruction. Whatever may have been tolerated in former times, by the weakness of indifference of Christian Powers, those Powers will now require from the Porte due consideration for their feelings as members of a religious community, and interested as such in the fate of all who, notwithstanding shades of difference, unite in a common belief in the essential doctrines of Christianity; and they will not endure that the Porte should insult and trample on their faith by treating as a criminal any person who embraces it. Her Majesty's Government require the Porte to abandon, once for all, so revolting a principle. They have no wish to humble the Porte by imposing upon it an unreasonable obligation; but as a Christian government, the protection of those who profess a common belief with themselves, form persecution or oppression, on that account alone, by their Mohammedan rulers, is a paramount duty with them, and one form which they cannot recede. Your Excellency will therefore press upon the Turkish Government, that if the Porte has any regard for the friendship of England – if it has any hope that, in the hour of peril or of adversity, that protection, which has more than once saved it from destruction, will be extended to it again, it must renounce absolutely, and without equivocation, the barbarous practice which has called forth: the remonstrance now addressed to it. Your Excellency will require an early answer; and you will let the Turkish Ministers understand that if that answer does not fully correspond with the expectations which Her Majesty's Government entertain, your Excellency is instructed to seek an audience of the Sultan and to explain to his Highness, in the most forcible terms, the feelings of the British Government, and the consequences, so injurious to Turkey, which a disregard for those feelings will involve. Her Majesty's Government are so anxious for the continuance of a good understanding with Turkey, and that the Porte should entitle itself to their good offices in the hour of need, that they wish to leave no expedient untried before they shall be compelled to admit the conviction that all their interest and friendship is misplaced, and that nothing remains for them but to look forward to, if not promote the arrival of, the day when the force of circumstances shall bring about a change which they will have vainly hoped to procure from the prudence and humanity of the Porte itself. 'Your Excellency will seek an interview with the Reis Effendi, and having read to him this despatch, leave a copy of it, with an accurate translation, in his hands.

'I am , etc., (Signed) ABERDEEN.'

Count Nesserode's despatch of February 27, 1844, on the part of the Russian Government, is instructive as opening out the weakness of the Ottoman Government. 'it is the Emperor's intention that you should declare to the Ottoman Porte, in the form of friendly counsel, that we positively expect no longer to witness executions which array against it the indignation of all Christendom. It is with a view to its own interest, that we address to it this demand. The Porte must not delude itself with regard to the elements now in state of fermentation in Turkey. Instead of alienation from itself the feelings of the Christina population, the Ottoman Government ought more than ever to labour to conciliate them to itself.'

The magnitude of the question is thus forcible stated, February 22, 1844, by the Turkish minister. 'No fresh step was requisite to make us sensible of the importance of this question, with which we are deeply impressed. We are dealing with it with all the seriousness and all the care which its gravity requires. Yes, what your respective chiefs say is true; this question has its political as also its religious side. It is requisite, in fact, that we should separate ourselves from the nation, or other wise from the Christian Powers; those are two great evils to be equally avoided. The Sultan has commanded that this question shall be discussed in the council of Oulemas (the learned), which will be opened on next Saturday, at the Sheik-ul-Islam's, to which the Gazi-Askes, and the other principal persons among the men of the law will be summoned; after which the council of ministers will again apply themselves to it. Do not suppose, however, that we have confined ourselves to direction their attention, purely and simply, to the question as it regard religion; we have likewise submitted to them the protocols of the conferences, the despatches of the two Governments, and even the extract of the newspapers which have discussed this question and we shall likewise communicate to them the instruction which you have just delivered to me, and which, although superfluous as far as the Porte is concerned, may still add to the impression produced by the other documents in their hands.

17. *Encyclopaedia Britannica*: Babylonian Captivity, Jewish history.
18. About 25% were deported but the remainder stayed behind.
19. Bickersteth, *The Signs of the Times in the East: A Warning to the West*, pp. 305–6.
20. Balfour Declaration 1917, available, among other sources, from Yale Law School, Lillian Goldman Law Library, *The Avalon Project*.
21. Library of Congress, National Endowment for the Humanities. *Chronicling America, Historic American Newspapers*. 'The Middlebury People's Press: From the Rev. Mr. Bronson's lectures on prophecy, April 26, 1843', p. 1.
22. Library of Congress, National Endowment for the Humanities, *Chronicling America, Historic American Newspapers*. 'Burlington Free Press, William Miller, February 17, 1843', p. 1.
23. ibid.
24. William Miller, quoted in Knight, *Millennial Fever and the End of the World: A Study of Millerite Adventism*, pp. 161–2.
25. ibid.
26. Snow, 'The Exeter Campmeeting', in *The Advent Herald*, 21 August 1844.
27. See Egbert, *Till Morning Breaks: A Story of the Millerite Movement and the Great Disappointment*.
28. Quoted in Knight, *Millennial Fever and the End of the World*, pp. 217–18.
29. Fundamental Belief No. 25 of the Seventh-day Adventist Church.
30. *The Dawn-Breakers: Nabíl's Narrative of the Early Days of the Bahá'í Revelation*, ch. 23, pp. 500–27.
31. Shoghi Effendi, *The Promised Day Is Come*, p. 7.
32. Shoghi Effendi, *God Passes By*, pp. 93–4.
33. Bahá'u'lláh, *Kitáb-i-Íqán*, para. 47, p. 45.
34. Bahá'u'lláh, *Epistle to the Son of the Wolf*, pp. 35–6.
35. ibid. p. 95.
36. Shoghi Effendi. *God Passes By*, p. 184.
37. Bahá'u'lláh, *Epistle to the Son of the Wolf*, p. 144.
38. See the story of Achan (Josh. 7:10–23).
39. Smith, 'Hosea', in *The Twentieth Century Bible Commentary*. p. 300.
40. https://en.wikipedia.org/wiki/Achor .
41. Reference not to the Pentateuch but to the Hebrew Bible in Islam and the Bahá'í Faith.
42. 'Abdu'l-Bahá, *Selections From the Writings of 'Abdu'l-Bahá*, p. 162.
43. Shoghi Effendi, *God Passes By*, p. 184.
44. Heb. 1:1: 'sundry times', Πολυμερῶς, polymerós; literally, many partedly; and in divers manners πολυτρόπως, polytropós]
45. Bahá'u'lláh, *The Tabernacle of Unity*, pp. 25–6.

46. Bahá'u'lláh, *Gleanings from the Writings of Bahá'u'lláh*, XI, p. 14.
47. Bahá'u'lláh, quoted in Shoghi Effendi, *The World Order of Bahá'u'lláh*, p. 106.
48. Bahá'u'lláh, *Gleanings from the Writings of Bahá'u'lláh*, XVI, p. 39.
49. Bahá'u'lláh, *The Kitáb-i-Aqdas*, par. 82, p. 49.
50. ibid. VII, p. 11.
51. Bahá'u'lláh, *Epistle to the Son of the Wolf*, p. 145.
52. The phrase 'end of time' occurs five times in the Hebrew Bible; all are found in the Book of Daniel.
53. Benson, *The Holy Bible containing The Old and the New Testaments with Notes, Critical, Explanatory, and Practical*, vol. III.
54. Ice, 'Running to and fro'.
55. Dew/dewdrop: a distillate of the water of life and a metaphor for divine teachings and mercy – healing herbs that resuscitate:
    Hebrew Bible:
    > May my teaching drop as the rain, my speech distill as the dew, like gentle rain upon the tender grass, and like showers upon the herb. (Deut. 32:2)
    > O Lord, we wait for you; your name and remembrance are the desire of our soul ... Your dead shall live; their bodies shall rise. You who dwell in the dust, awake and sing for joy! For your dew is a dew of light, and the earth will give birth to the dead. (Is. 26:8, 19)

    Bahá'í Writings:
    > O wayfarer in the path of God! Take thou thy portion of the ocean of His grace, and deprive not thyself of the things that lie hidden in its depths ... A dewdrop out of this ocean would, if shed upon all that are in the heavens and on earth, suffice to enrich them with the bounty of God, the Almighty, the All-Knowing, the All-Wise. With the hands of renunciation draw forth from its life-giving waters, and sprinkle therewith all created things, that they may be cleansed from all man-made limitations, and may approach the mighty seat of God, this hallowed and resplendent Spot. (Bahá'u'lláh quoted by Shoghi Effendi, in *The Advent of Divine Justice*, p. 61)
    > Praise be to the all-perceiving, the ever-abiding Lord Who, from a dewdrop out of the ocean of His grace, hath reared the firmament of existence, adorned it with the stars of knowledge, and admitted man into the lofty court of insight and understanding. This dewdrop, which is the Primal Word of God, is at times called the Water of Life, inasmuch as it quickeneth with the waters of knowledge them that have perished in the wilderness of ignorance. (Bahá'u'lláh, *The Tabernacle of Unity*, p. 3)
56. Bahá'u'lláh, *Gleanings from the Writings of Bahá'u'lláh*, CVI, p. 213.
57. *Bahá'í Prayers*, p. 87.
58. New International Version: 'what is desired by all nations'; GOD'S WORD Translation: 'the one whom all nations desire to come'.
59. Shoghi Effendi, *The World Order of Bahá'u'lláh*, pp. 197–8.

16. Bahá'u'lláh's proclamation

1. Bahá'u'lláh, quoted in Shoghi Effendi, *The World Order of Bahá'u'lláh*, p. 107.
2. Bahá'u'lláh, *Gleanings from the Writings of Bahá'u'lláh*, XXV, p. 60.
3. ibid. VII, pp. 10–11.
4. ibid. CLXI, p. 340.
5. ibid. III, p. 5.
6. Bahá'u'lláh, The Tablet of Aḥmad, in *Bahá'í Prayers*, pp. 210–12.
7. Bahá'u'lláh, *Gleanings from the Writings of Bahá'u'lláh*, CX, p. 216.
8. ibid. XI, p. 16.
9. Shoghi Effendi, *The World Order of Bahá'u'lláh*, p. 105.
10. ibid. pp. 104–5.
11. Bahá'u'lláh, Tablet to the Christians, *Tablets of Bahá'u'lláh Revealed after the Kitáb-i-Aqdas*, pp. 10–11.
12. Bahá'u'lláh, Súriy-i-Haykal, in Bahá'u'lláh, *The Summons of the Lord of Hosts*, pp. 65–6.
13. ibid. pp. 66–7.
14. Bahá'u'lláh, Tablet to the Christians, in *Tablets of Bahá'u'lláh Revealed after the Kitáb-i-Aqdas*, pp. 12–14.
15. Bahá'u'lláh, quoted in Shoghi Effendi, *The Promised Day Is Come*, p. 165.
16. Bahá'u'lláh, Tablet to the Christians, in *Tablets of Bahá'u'lláh Revealed after the Kitáb-i-Aqdas*, pp. 9–10.
17. See Kertzer, *Prisoner of the Vatican*.
18. Veils: All the numerous man-made obstacles that prevent people from seeing the truth, and their feet to slip – in this case, the dogmas, traditions, misunderstandings and misinterpretation, and rituals and tradition that veil or conceal the truth and prevent Christians from beholding the Glory of God.
19. Some explanations of 'clouds' by Bahá'u'lláh:

    > Consider again the sun when it is completely hidden behind the clouds. Though the earth is still illumined with its light, yet the measure of light which it receiveth is considerably reduced. Not until the clouds have dispersed, can the sun shine again in the plenitude of its glory. Neither the presence of the cloud nor its absence can, in any way, affect the inherent splendour of the sun (*Gleanings from the Writings of Bahá'u'lláh*, LXXX, p. 155).

    > Pay thou no heed to the humiliation to which the loved ones of God have in this Day been subjected . . . The day is approaching when the intervening clouds will have been completely dissipated, when the light of the words, 'All honour belongeth unto God and unto them that love Him,' will have appeared, as manifest as the sun, above the horizon of the Will of the Almighty (ibid, CXL, pp. 305–6).

20. Bahá'u'lláh, the 'return of Christ in the Glory of the Father'.
21. As in John 7:38 concerning Christians at the First Coming: 'He that believeth on me, as the scripture hath said, out of his belly shall flow rivers of living water.' And in Rev. 21:6 concerning believers at the Second Coming: 'I will give unto him that is athirst of the fountain of the water of life freely.'
22. Carefully chosen or well refined wine that will be offered by God, as in Is.

25:6: 'On this mountain the Lord Almighty will prepare a feast of rich food for all peoples, a banquet of aged wine – the best of meats and the finest of wines.'
23. New name, 'Bahá' or 'Glory' vs. the more familiar 'Christ' or 'the Anointed'.
24. Simon Peter, who with John, was an ordinary fisherman; they are traditionally known as having been illiterate.
25. As in Is. 25:7–8 referring to the spiritual death veil and shroud enveloping humanity, which the Bible promises to lift: 'On this mountain he will destroy the shroud that enfolds all peoples, the sheet that covers all nations; he will swallow up death forever.'
26. John 16:12–13; Luke 8:17: reference to Bahá'u'lláh bringing to light the many truths that Christ stated he had not disclosed because of limitations of the people of His time to understand.
27. The word 'pontiff' means 'bridge builder' and was used to describe individuals who symbolically bridged the gap between gods and men. It was initially the title of anyone who held high office in the church, and later more specifically to the Bishops of Rome. The Popes have assumed the title since the 1600s.
28. Bahá'u'lláh, Súriy-i-Haykal, in Bahá'u'lláh, *The Summons of the Lord of Hosts*, pp. 54–62. II Pet. 3:10–13 explains the evanescent nature of earthly life and concerns, and also, the impermanence of dispensations. He asks what type of Christian they must be, considering that everything will be dissolved.
29. ibid. pp. 67–9.
30. ibid. pp. 69–70.
31. Bahá'u'lláh, *The Kitáb-i-Aqdas*, para. 86, p. 51.
32. ibid. para. 90, p. 53.
33. Esslemont, *Bahá'u'lláh and the New Era*. p. 238.
34. Bahá'u'lláh, *The Kitáb-i-Aqdas*, para. 85, pp. 50–51.
35. See Shoghi Effendi, *God Passes By*, p. 71, for an account of this.
36. Bahá'u'lláh, Súriy-i-Haykal, in Bahá'u'lláh, *The Summons of the Lord of Hosts*, pp. 83–4.
37. ibid. p. 89.
38. ibid. p. 90.
39. See BahaiTeachings.org.
40. Bahá'u'lláh, Súriy-i-Haykal, in Bahá'u'lláh, *The Summons of the Lord of Hosts*, pp. 91–2.

17. Continuity of divine purpose: Multiple religions but one common faith

1. See Baumann, Finnbogason and Svensson. 'Rethinking mediation: Resolving religious conflicts'; Svensson and Nilsson, 'Disputes over the divine: Introducing the Religion and Armed Conflict (RELAC) Data'; Muggah and Velshi, 'Religious violence is on the rise: What can faith-based communities do about it?'
2. New Living Translation: 'the beginning of all he does'.
3. New Living Translation: 'reveal'.
4. Shoghi Effendi, *The World Order of Bahá'u'lláh*, p. 115.
5. ibid. p. 58.
6. Bahá'u'lláh, Tablet to Mánikchí Sáhib, in Bahá'u'lláh. *The Tabernacle of Unity*, p. 5.

7. Berean Literal Bible: 'to all ages'; Darby Bible Translation: 'the ages to come'.
8. King James Version: 'hewn stones'.
9. A. Barnes, *Notes, Explanatory and Practical, on the Book of the Prophet Isaiah*, vol. I, p. 212.
10. 'Abdu'l-Bahá, *The Promulgation of Universal Peace*, pp. 151–2.
11. ibid. p. 94.
12. Bahá'u'lláh, *Kitáb-i-Íqán*, para. 162, pp. 153–4.
13. ibid. para. 110, p. 104.
14. Bahá'u'lláh, *Gleanings from the Writings of Bahá'u'lláh*, XXXIV, p. 74.
15. ibid. XXXVIII, pp. 87–8.
16. Bahá'u'lláh, Tablet to Mánikchí Ṣáḥib, in Bahá'u'lláh. *The Tabernacle of Unity*, p. 8.
17. Bahá'u'lláh, *Gleanings from the Writings of Bahá'u'lláh*, CXXVI, pp. 271–2.
18. 'Abdu'l-Bahá, *Selections from the Writings of 'Abdu'l-Bahá*, no. 156, pp. 183–4.
19. 'By faith Enoch was taken up so that he should not see death, and he was not found, because God had taken him. Now before he was taken he was commended as having pleased God.' (Heb. 11:5)
20. See https://biblehub.com/commentaries/hebrews.
21. ibid.
22. Spence and Exell, *The Pulpit Commentary*.
23. Ellicott, *Ellicott's Commentary on the Whole Bible*, vol. 6. p. 105.
24. Bahá'u'lláh, *The Summons of the Lord of Hosts*, p. 55.
25. *Bhagavad Gítá*, 4:7–8.
26. Carus, *The Gospel of Buddha*, pp. 217–18.
27. 'Abdu'l-Bahá, *The Promulgation of Universal Peace*, p. 69.
28. Bahá'u'lláh, *Gleanings from the Writings of Bahá'u'lláh*, XC, p. 177.
29. Shoghi Effendi, *The World Order of Bahá'u'lláh*, pp. 197–8.
30. See commentary by Benson at https://biblehub.com and https://www.studylight.org.
31. See *Cambridge Bible for Schools and Colleges*: Deuteronomy 18, at: https://biblehub.com/commentaries/deuteronomy.
32. God's Word Translation: Heb. 1:1–3.
33. New International Version: 'A time is coming and in fact is come'.
34. Shoghi Effendi, *The World Order of Bahá'u'lláh*, pp. 197–8, quoting Ibsen, *Emperor and Galilean: A World Historic Drama*, p. 273.
35. Bahá'u'lláh, Tablet to Mánikchí Ṣáḥib, in Bahá'u'lláh, *The Tabernacle of Unity*, pp. 5–6.
36. 'Abdu'l-Bahá, *Paris Talks*, no. 16, p. 50. William Barclay wrote in *The Plain Man Looks at the Lord's Prayer*: 'The prayer may mean bread for our essential being. This then will be a prayer for the "suprasubstantial" bread, the bread that is real, essential, spiritual bread for our spiritual nourishment and growth . . .' (p. 91).
37. King James Version: 'mansions'.
38. *Albert Barnes' Notes on the Whole Bible*: Matthew 15:24.
39. Jobes, 'I Peter'.
40. Shoghi Effendi, *The World Order of Bahá'u'lláh*, p. 114.
41. Esslemont, *Bahá'u'lláh and the New Era*, p. 123.

42. The Universal House of Justice, *Message to the World's Religious Leaders*, April 2002.
43. It may be worth noting that the New Testament word 'forever' (John 6:51; 14:16), in the original αἰῶν, properly means 'for an age'.
44. 'Abdu'l-Bahá, *The Promulgation of Universal Peace*, pp. 140–42.
45. Shoghi Effendi, *The Promised Day Is Come*, p. v, quoting Shoghi Effendi, *A Summary of the Origin, Teachings and Institutions of the Bahá'í Faith*, prepared in 1947 for the United Nations Special Committee on Palestine.
46. An explanation by 'Abdu'l-Bahá:
    During the cycle of Christ, inasmuch as divorce was not in conformity with the time and conditions, Jesus Christ abrogated it. In the cycle of Moses plurality of wives was permissible. But during the time of Christ the exigency which had sanctioned it did not exist; therefore, it was forbidden. (*The Promulgation of Universal Peace*, p. 393)
47. Ellicott, *Commentary for English Readers*.
48. Spence and Exell, *The Pulpit Commentary*.
49. Ellicott, *Commentary for English Readers*.
50. St Augustine, Letter 138 (412 CE) to Marcellinus, in *The Works of Saint Augustine: A Translation for the 21st Century*, vol. II, p. 225.
51. Bahá'u'lláh, *Gems of Divine Mysteries (Javáhiru'l-Asrár)*, p. 33.
52. Bahá'u'lláh, *Kitáb-i-Íqán*, para. 162, pp. 153–4.
53. ibid. para. 161, p. 153.
54. 'Abdu'l-Bahá, *The Promulgation of Universal Peace*, pp. 247–8.
55. Shoghi Effendi, *The World Order of Bahá'u'lláh*, p. 58.
56. 'Abdu'l-Bahá, *Selections from the Writings of 'Abdu'l-Bahá*, no. 227, pp. 298–9.
57. Shoghi Effendi, *The Promised Day Is Come*, p. 112 (p. 184 in the 1996 pocket-size edition).
58. Shoghi Effendi, *God Passes By*, p. 100.
59. Shoghi Effendi, *A Summary of the Origin, Teachings and Institutions of the Bahá'í Faith*, prepared in 1947 for the United Nations Special Committee on Palestine by Shoghi Effendi in his capacity as Head of the Bahá'í Faith.
60. Shoghi Effendi, *The World Order of Bahá'u'lláh*, pp. 196–7.

18. Reaffirmation of earlier moral and ethical teachings

1. King James Version: I Timothy 4:1,
2. Shoghi Effendi, *The World Order of Bahá'u'lláh*, p. 163.
3. Shoghi Effendi, *Messages to America*, p. 28; also in Shoghi Effendi, *This Decisive Hour*, no. 58.
4. Shoghi Effendi, *The World Order of Bahá'u'lláh*, p. 155.
5. 'Abdu'l-Bahá, *The Promulgation of Universal Peace*, p. 180.
6. Bahá'u'lláh, *Gleanings from the Writings of Bahá'u'lláh*, CXXV, p. 264.
7. 'Abdu'l-Bahá, *The Promulgation of Universal Peace*, pp. 62–3.
8. ibid. p. 198.
9. ibid. pp. 247–8.
10. The Báb, *Selections from the Writings of the Báb*, p. 123.
11. ibid. p. 172.
12. Bahá'u'lláh, *Hidden Words*, Arabic no. 5.

13. Bahá'u'lláh, quoted in Shoghi Effendi, *The Advent of Divine Justice*, para. 109, p. 64.
14. Bahá'u'lláh, *Gleanings from the Writings of Bahá'u'lláh*, LXXV, p. 143.
15. 'Abdu'l-Bahá, *The Promulgation of Universal Peace*, p. 454.
16. ibid. pp. 273–4.
17. ibid. pp. 161–2.
18. ibid. p. 39.
19. ibid. p. 141.
20. 'Abdu'l-Bahá, *Paris Talks*, no. 41, p. 140.
21. 'Abdu'l-Bahá, *The Promulgation of Universal Peace*, p. 248.
22. ibid. p. 202.
23. 'Abdu'l-Bahá, *Paris Talks*, no. 40, p. 132.
24. 'Abdu'l-Bahá, *The Promulgation of Universal Peace*, p. 151.
25. ibid. pp. 442–3.
26. Shoghi Effendi, *The World Order of Bahá'u'lláh*, p. 54.
27. Bahá'u'lláh, *Kitáb-i-Íqán*, para. 270, pp. 240–41.
28. 'Abdu'l-Bahá, quoted in Shoghi Effendi, *The Advent of Divine Justice*, p. 22.
29. Bahá'u'lláh, *Gleanings from the Writings of Bahá'u'lláh*, LXXIV, pp. 141–2.
30. ibid. p. 142.
31. 'Abdu'l-Bahá, Tablet to the Hague, in *Bahá'í World Faith*, p. 296.
32. The great-grandson of Bahá'u'lláh, appointed Guardian and head of the Bahá'í Faith from 1921 until his death in 1957.
33. Shoghi Effendi, *The World Order of Bahá'u'lláh*, pp. 197–8.
34. Bahá'u'lláh, *The Kitáb i Aqdas*, para. 1, p. 19.
35. ibid. para. 3, p. 20.
36. Bahá'u'lláh, *Hidden Words*, Arabic no. 38.
37. Bahá'u'lláh, quoted in Shoghi Effendi, *The Advent of Divine Justice*, p. 21.
38. Bahá'u'lláh, *Tablets of Bahá'u'lláh Revealed after the Kitáb-i-Aqdas*, p. 166.
39. Bahá'u'lláh, Tablet to Mánikchí Ṣáḥib, in Bahá'u'lláh, *The Tabernacle of Unity*, p. 8.
40. Bahá'u'lláh, quoted in Shoghi Effendi, *The Advent of Divine Justice*, pp. 69–70.
41. Bahá'u'lláh, *Tablets of Bahá'u'lláh Revealed after the Kitáb-i-Aqdas*, p. 196.
42. Bahá'u'lláh, *Prayers and Meditations by Bahá'u'lláh*, XL, pp. 56–7.
43. 'Abdu'l-Bahá, *Tablets of Abdul-Baha Abbas*, p. 110.
44. ibid. pp. 632–3.
45. 'Abdu'l-Bahá, *Tablets of the Divine Plan*, no. 1, pp. 6–7.
46. Bahá'u'lláh, *The Tabernacle of Unity*, p. 21.
47. Bahá'u'lláh, *Gleanings from the Writings of Bahá'u'lláh*, CLVIII, p. 335.
48. ibid. CLVII, p. 334.
49. Bahá'u'lláh, quoted in Shoghi Effendi, *The Advent of Divine Justice*, p. 70.
50. Shoghi Effendi, *Bahá'í Administration*, p. 66.
51. 'Abdu'l-Bahá, quoted in Shoghi Effendi, *The Advent of Divine Justice*, pp. 21–2.
52. Bahá'u'lláh, *Hidden Words*, Persian no. 2.
53. Shoghi Effendi, *The World Order of Bahá'u'lláh*, p. 58.
54. Bahá'u'lláh, *Gleanings from the Writings of Bahá'u'lláh*, CXXXII, p. 289.
55. ibid. CXXVIII, p. 279.

56. Bahá'u'lláh, *Prayers and Meditations by Bahá'u'lláh*, CLV, p. 248.
57. Bahá'u'lláh, *Hidden Words*, Arabic no. 1.
58. Bahá'u'lláh, *Epistle to the Son of the Wolf*, p. 29.
59. 'Abdu'l-Bahá, *Paris Talks*, no. 16, p. 49.
60. 'Abdu'l-Bahá, *The Promulgation of Universal Peace*, p. 14.
61. Bahá'u'lláh, Tablet to Pope Pius IX, para. 119, in Bahá'u'lláh, *The Summons of the Lord of Hosts*, p. 62.
62. 'Abdu'l-Bahá, quoted in note 23, in Bahá'u'lláh, *The Kitáb-i-Aqdas*, p. 176.
63. Bahá'u'lláh, *Hidden Words*, Arabic no. 8.
64. ibid. no. 7.
65. Bahá'u'lláh, *Gleanings from the Writings of Bahá'u'lláh*, LX, p. 118.
66. Bahá'u'lláh, *Hidden Words*, Arabic no. 55.
67. Bahá'u'lláh, *Gleanings from the Writings of Bahá'u'lláh*, CXLVI, pp. 315-16.
68. Shoghi Effendi, *The Advent of Divine Justice*, p. 6, written to the Bahá'ís 'in the American continent'. Dawn-breakers of an heroic Age: reference to the many thousands of the followers of the Báb and Bahá'u'lláh whose martyrdom testified to their faith (see *The Dawn-Breakers: Nabíl's Narrative of the Early Days of the Bahá'í Revelation*).
69. ibid. p. 19.
70. 'Abdu'l-Bahá, *Tablets of Abdul-Baha Abbas*, p. 322.
71. *Bahá'í Prayers*, p. 211.
72. 'Abdu'l-Bahá, *Selections from the Writings of 'Abdu'l-Bahá*, no. 5, pp. 17–18.
73. Bahá'u'lláh, *Epistle to the Son of the Wolf*, p. 135.
74. ibid. p. 122.
75. 'Abdu'l-Bahá, *The Promulgation of Universal Peace*, p. 453.
76. Shoghi Effendi, *The Advent of Divine Justice*, p. 21.
77. Bahá'u'lláh, *Hidden Words*, Arabic no. 68.
78. 'Abdu'l-Bahá, *The Promulgation of Universal Peace*, p. 453.
79. Bahá'u'lláh, *Kitáb-i-Íqán*, para. 213, p. 193.
80. 'Abdu'l-Bahá, *Selections from the Writings of 'Abdu'l-Bahá*, no. 227, p. 302.
81. Bahá'u'lláh, *Epistle to the Son of the Wolf*, p. 95; also in *Gleanings from the Writings of Bahá'u'lláh*, CXXX, p. 285.
82. Bahá'u'lláh, *Hidden Words*, Arabic no. 13.
83. ibid. no. 22.
84. ibid. no. 2.
85. Bahá'u'lláh, *Epistle to the Son of the Wolf*, pp. 28–9.
86. Bahá'u'lláh, quoted in Shoghi Effendi, *The Advent of Divine Justice*, p. 20.
87. Bahá'u'lláh, *The Kitab-i-Aqdas*, para. 158, p. 76.
88. Bahá'u'lláh, *Hidden Words*, Arabic no. 26.
89. ibid. no. 27.
90. Bahá'u'lláh, *Kitáb-i-Íqán*, para. 214, p. 193.
91. 'Abdu'l-Bahá, *The Promulgation of Universal Peace*, p. 453.
92. Diary of Mírzá Aḥmad Sohrab (1914), quoted in Esslemont, *Bahá'u'lláh and the New Era*, p. 84.
93. 'Abdu'l-Bahá, *Tablets of Abdul-Baha Abbas*, p. 459.
94. Bahá'u'lláh, quoted in Shoghi Effendi, *The Advent of Divine Justice*, p. 21.
95. Bahá'u'lláh, *Gleanings from the Writings of Bahá'u'lláh*, CXXVI, p. 271.

96. Bahá'u'lláh, *Epistle to the Son of the Wolf*, pp. 10–11.
97. Bahá'u'lláh, *Gleanings from the Writings of Bahá'u'lláh*, CXXXVII, p. 299.
98. Bahá'u'lláh, *The Kitab-i-Aqdas*, para. 120, p. 62.
99. Bahá'u'lláh, *Tablets of Bahá'u'lláh Revealed after the Kitáb-i-Aqdas*, p. 88.
100. Bahá'u'lláh, addressing the Ottoman Sultan, in *The Summons of the Lord of Hosts*, p. 212.
101. Bahá'u'lláh, *Tablets of Bahá'u'lláh Revealed after the Kitáb-i-Aqdas*, p. 169.
102. Bahá'u'lláh, *Kitáb-i-Íqán*, para. 214, pp. 193–4.
103. ibid. pp. 194–5.
104. Bahá'u'lláh, *Tablets of Bahá'u'lláh Revealed after the Kitab-i-Aqdas*, p. 27.
105. 'Abdu'l-Bahá, *The Promulgation of Universal Peace*, p. 266.
106. 'Abdu'l-Bahá, *Selections from the Writings of 'Abdu'l-Bahá*, no. 129, p. 147.
107. 'Questions and Answers', no. 106, in Bahá'u'lláh, *The Kitab-i-Aqdas*, p. 139.
108. The Báb, Persian Bayán, VIII:16, in *Selections from the Writings of the Báb*, p. 94.
109. Bahá'u'lláh, Lawḥ-i-Aqdas (The Most Holy Tablet), sometimes referred to as Tablet to the Christians, in Bahá'u'lláh, *Tablets of Bahá'u'lláh Revealed after the Kitáb-i-Aqdas*, pp. 16–17.

19. New social paradigms for a global society

1. Shoghi Effendi, *The World Order of Bahá'u'lláh*, p. 42.
2. Bahá'u'lláh, *Gleanings from the Writings of Bahá'u'lláh*, CXI, p. 217.
3. Bahá'u'lláh, quoted in Shoghi Effendi, *The Promised Day Is Come*, p. 119.
4. Bahá'u'lláh, *Gleanings from the Writings of Bahá'u'lláh*, CX, p. 215.
5. Shoghi Effendi, *The World Order of Bahá'u'lláh*, p. 203.
6. 'Abdu'l-Bahá, *Selections from the Writings of 'Abdu'l-Bahá*, no. 15, pp. 31–2.
7. Shoghi Effendi, *The World Order of Bahá'u'lláh*, p. 42.
8. ibid. CXXXI, p. 286.
9. Bahá'u'lláh, *Tablets of Bahá'u'lláh Revealed after the Kitáb-i-Aqdas*, p. 87.
10. 'Abdu'l-Bahá, *Paris Talks*, no. 45, p. 151.
11. 'Abdu'l-Bahá, *The Promulgation of Universal Peace*, p. 455.
12. Chou, 'How science and genetics are shaping the race debate of the 21st century.' Also, in the year 2000:
    'Race is a social concept, not a scientific one,' said Dr. J. Craig Venter, head of the Celera Genomics Corp. in Rockville, Md. Venter and scientists at the National Institutes of Health recently announced that they had put together a draft of the entire sequence of the human genome, and the researchers unanimously declared that there is only one race – the human race.' (Angier, 'Do races differ? Not really, genes show', in *The New York Times*, 22 August 2000)
13. Letter written on behalf of Shoghi Effendi to an individual, 22 November 1936, in *Lights of Guidance*, no. 1812, p. 533.
14. The Universal House of Justice, *The Promise of World Peace*, p. 8.
15. Quoted in Esslemont, *Bahá'u'lláh and the New Era*, p. 39.
16. 'Abdu'l-Bahá, quoted in Shoghi Effendi, *The Advent of Divine Justice*, p. 33.
17. Jackson and Weidman, *Race, Racism, and Science*.
18. Shoghi Effendi, *Directives from the Guardian*, no. 117, pp. 43–4.
19. 'Abdu'l-Bahá, quoted in Shoghi Effendi, *The Advent of Divine Justice*, p. 31.

20. ibid. pp. 32–3.
21. The Universal House of Justice, letter to National Spiritual Assemblies in Africa, 8 February 1970, in *Messages from the Universal House of Justice, 1963–86*, no. 77, p. 166.
22. The Universal House of Justice, letter to all National Spiritual Assemblies, 13 July 1972, ibid. no. 117, p. 222.
23. Shoghi Effendi, *The Advent of Divine Justice*, p. 19.
24. 'Abdu'l-Bahá, *Tablets of Abdul-Baha Abbas*, vol. 2, p. 292.
25. 'Abdu'l-Bahá, quoted in Shoghi Effendi, *The Advent of Divine Justice*, p. 33.
26. Shoghi Effendi, ibid.
27. ibid, p. 29.
28. Shoghi Effendi, *The World Order of Bahá'u'lláh*, p. 199.
29. Shoghi Effendi, *Directives from the Guardian*, no. 153, p. 57.
30. 'Abdu'l-Bahá, *Selections from the Writings of 'Abdu'l-Bahá*, no. 227, p. 302.
31. 'Abdu'l-Bahá, *Paris Talks*, no. 30, pp. 169–70.
32. 'Abdu'l-Bahá, *The Promulgation of Universal Peace*, p. 395.
33. The Universal House of Justice, *The Promise of World Peace*.
34. 'Abdu'l-Bahá, *The Promulgation of Universal Peace*, p. 318.
35. 'Abdu'l-Bahá, remarks made on arrival in New York, in *Star of the West*, vol. 8, no. 3, p. 4.
36. 'Abdu'l-Bahá, *Selections from the Writings of 'Abdu'l-Bahá*, no. 227, p. 299.
37. 'Abdu'l-Bahá, *The Will and Testament of 'Abdu'l-Bahá*, pp. 13–14.
38. Bahá'u'lláh, *Epistle to the Son of the Wolf*, pp. 13–14.
39. Bahá'u'lláh, quoted in Shoghi Effendi, *The World Order of Bahá'u'lláh*, pp. 114–15.
40. 'Abdu'l-Bahá, *The Promulgation of Universal Peace*, p. 454.
41. 'Abdu'l-Bahá, *Selections from the Writings of 'Abdu'l-Bahá*, no. 227, p. 299.
42. 'Abdu'l-Bahá, *Paris Talks*, no. 40, p. 133.
43. 'Abdu'l-Bahá, *The Promulgation of Universal Peace*, p. 175.
44. 'Abdu'l-Bahá, *Paris Talks*, no. 44, p. 147.
45. Note 110 in Bahá'u'lláh, *The Kitáb-i-Aqdas*, p. 215.
46. Bahá'u'lláh, *Tablets of Bahá'u'lláh Revealed after the Kitáb-i-Aqdas*, p. 26.
47. 'Abdu'l-Bahá, in *Bahá'í Education*, p. 73.
48. ibid. p. 42.
49. 'Abdu'l-Bahá, ibid. p. 46; see also *'Abdu'l-Bahá in London*, p. 91.
50. 'Religion in an ever-advancing civilization', in *The Bahá'í World* online.
51. Shoghi Effendi, *The Promised Day Is Come*, p. 118.
52. Shoghi Effendi, *The World Order of Bahá'u'lláh*, p. 19.
53. Bahá'u'lláh, *Gleanings from the Writings of Bahá'u'lláh*, IV, p. 6.
54. ibid. p. 7.
55. Bahá'u'lláh, *Tablets of Bahá'u'lláh Revealed after the Kitab-i-Aqdas*, pp. 127–8.
56. Shoghi Effendi, *The World Order of Bahá'u'lláh*, p. 162.
57. Bahá'í International Community, *Bahá'u'lláh*, p. 27.
58. Shoghi Effendi, *The World Order of Bahá'u'lláh*, p. 190.
59. Letter written on behalf of Shoghi Effendi, 5 November 1945, in *The Light of Divine Guidance*, vol. 1, p. 99.
60. Bahá'u'lláh, *Gleanings from the Writings of Bahá'u'lláh*, XLIII, pp. 93–4.

61. Bahá'u'lláh, *Epistle to the Son of the Wolf*, p. 123.
62. 'Abdu'l-Bahá, *The Promulgation of Universal Peace*, p. 31.
63. The Universal House of Justice, *The Promise of World Peace*, p. 8.
64. 'Abdu'l-Bahá, *The Promulgation of Universal Peace*, p. 72.
65. ibid.
66. Shoghi Effendi, *Bahá'í Administration*, pp. 63–4.
67. 'Abdu'l-Bahá, *The Promulgation of Universal Peace*, p. 300.
68. Shoghi Effendi, *The World Order of Bahá'u'lláh*, pp. 41–2.
69. The Universal House of Justice, *The Promise of World Peace*, p. 8.
70. Shoghi Effendi, *The World Order of Bahá'u'lláh*, p. 198.
71. Bahá'u'lláh, *Gleanings from the Writings of Bahá'u'lláh*, XLIII, p. 97.
72. *Jihád* in Islam.
73. Bahá'u'lláh, *Tablets of Bahá'u'lláh Revealed after the Kitáb-i-Aqdas*, p. 21.
74. Bahá'u'lláh, *The Summons of the Lord of Hosts*, p. 23.
75. From a letter of the Universal House of Justice to the National Spiritual Assembly of the United States, 9 February 1967.
76. Shoghi Effendi, *Directives from the Guardian*, no. 144, pp. 53–4.
77. Bahá'u'lláh, *Tablets of Bahá'u'lláh Revealed after the Kitáb-i-Aqdas*, p. 24.
78. Note 58 in Bahá'u'lláh, *The Kitáb-i-Aqdas*, p. 194.
79. Although nine members is the present practice, this number may well increase in future.
80. Shoghi Effendi, *The World Order of Bahá'u'lláh*, pp. 57–8.

INDEX

Aaron 70, 122, 192, 549
Abdu'l-Bahá xii, 152, 176, 401, 495, 505, 508
abomination of desolation 151, 169-71, 545
Abraham 17, 60, 61, 66, 72, 79, 115, 136, 183, 186-7, 192, 193, 201, 202, 220, 222, 299, 321, 334, 357, 375, 409, 434, 442, 548, 558
absolution 326, 329-32
Abu Bakr 100
Achaemenid Empire 335, 384
Achor 399-401
adultery 43, 46, 86. 211. 223. 255. 328. 455
Advent
    of Antichrist 147
    of Christ 66, 176, 207, 356, 403
    of Day of the Father, Lord 135, 191, 234, 374, 403, 431
    of the Helper 139
    of Kingdom of God 24, 27, 121, 133
    of Messiah 24, 111, 128, 166, 175, 255, 302, 353, 441
    Second 395. 441
    of Second Coming 166, 203, 262-3, 266, 374, 395, 397, 441
    of Spirit of Truth, the Comforter 262-3, 416-17, 432
    of universal revelation 70, 113, 384, 402, 414-15
    of World Redeemer, Manifestation of God 116, 118
Africa, Africans 65-6, 253, 280
African-Americans 18
agnosticism 25
Ahaz, King 296
Ahura Mazda 335, 360
'Akká 376, 405, 423, 425, 431, 443
    and valley of Achor 399-401
Alexander II, Czar 425-6
Alexandria, Egypt 267-8
Aliyah 393-4

Allenby, General 394
Allison, Dale C. Jr 308
almsgiving 227, 231, 333
Alpha and Omega 135-6, 219
Ambrose of Milan, St 98
Ananda 444
anathema 222-3, 268, 487
Andrew, Apostle 11, 50-51
angel(s) 31, 36, 37, 56, 134, 137-8, 162-3, 188-9, 193, 207, 227, 231, 261, 306, 415, 420, 442, 468, 550
    fallen 292, 296
Anointed One 27, 100, 116, 122, 170-71, 220, 349, 384, 565
anointing of the sick (sacrament) 352
Anonymous Christianity 228-30
Antichrist 20, 147-8, 388
Antioch 27, 64, 97, 136, 244
anti-Semitism xi, 94, 96
Antiochus (Epiphanes) 168-9, 545
Aphrodite 225
Apollos 57, 243, 280
Apostle(s) *see separate entries*
Apostolic Constitutions 88, 540
Aquinas, Thomas 93
Arabia 150, 371, 389
Arabs, Arab countries 395, 467, 543
Argentina 87
Aristotle 169
Arius, Arians 267-8, 342
asceticism 87, 148, 212, 250-52, 555
    in monastic orders 250
Asia 65, 150
Assyria, Assyrians 127, 257, 317, 335, 392
Assumption 19
Artaxerxes 171, 545
Athanasius 267
atheism 25
Attis 362
Augustine, Saint, of Hippo 89, 93, 98, 225, 268-9, 280, 373, 457

authorities, civil, religious 93, 102-3, 181,
  184, 252, 268, 381, 397
awake, staying awake 22, 26, 53, 55, 134,
  163, 203, 207, 234

Báb, the 3, 152, 323, 384, 386, 397, 405,
  513, 542
Bahá'í Faith x-xii, 1-3, 462, 468, 491, 493
  Administrative Order of 506, 513
  history of 3, 424
  Writings on
    allegorical explanations of scripture
      365
    baptism 353-4
    'clouds' 313
    dispensations 61, 453-4
    education 502-3
    evil and the Devil 336-7
    faith and reason, and science 317,
      321, 347, 366, 502-3
    global society 504-11
    heaven and hell 296
    holy war, abrogation of 511
    immortality of the soul 313
    Jewish prophecies (Messiah) 323-4
    life and death, meaning of 300
    Jesus Christ 3-4, 142, 205, 218, 257,
      282, 310-12, 319, 322, 344-5,
      348, 353, 465
    investigation of truth 463-4
    man in image of God 446
    miracles 256-7
    moral life 471-89, 493, 496-501, 508
    original sin 334-5
    Peter (Apostle) 247
    racism 494-6
    religion, revelation x-xii, 4-7, 141,
      164, 317, 337, 370, 430, 437, 451,
      458-61, 282, 514
    resurrection 311-12, 319
    Trinity 347
    virgin birth 345
    see also oneness of humanity; progressive
      revelation
Bahá'ís 409, 461, 513
  standards of behaviour 471-89, 493, 496-
    501, 508
baptism 73, 227, 238, 268, 319, 333, 338-9,
  341-2, 352-7, 361-3, 468
  of Christ 311, 352-4
  of infants 356
Babylon 90, 95, 122, 169, 393, 545

Babylonian Captivity 393
Bahá'u'lláh
  imprisonment of 323, 397, 399, 405,
    420, 422, 425, 449, 479
  life of 3, 152-3, 323, 378, 397-9, 405
  Glory of God 164, 386
  predictions by 2, 375-6, 413-31 passim
  proclamation of 413-31
  return of Christ 443pp.
  World Order of 7, 398, 413, 462, 478,
    492, 506
  see also Bahá'í Faith, Writings on various
    subjects
Balaam 240, 254, 550
Balfour, Arthur James 394
Balfour Declaration 394
banking 102, 457
Barclay, William 12, 24, 235, 566
Barnes, Albert 18
  commentaries 18, 21, 61, 75, 80-81, 92,
    111, 124, 146, 150, 159, 162, 175,
    201, 209, 216, 222, 241, 248, 255,
    260, 264, 287, 289, 294, 300, 307-8,
    320, 331, 372, 389, 400, 434, 451, 555
Barnes, Ernest William 355, 362
baptism 73, 227, 268, 311, 319, 333, 338-9,
  341, 352-7, 361-3, 468
Beatitudes 39, 40, 52, 488-9
Beelzebel 185, 370
Belial 74-5, 224
Belisarius, General 389
Ben Gurion, David 395
Benson, Joseph 21, 552
  commentaries 31, 37-8, 146, 149, 168,
    205, 218, 224, 300, 303, 308, 440,
    552
Berlin 376, 424
Berthier, General 389
Bethlehem 72, 152-3, 181, 189, 418
  two towns 181
Bible
  translations 151, 154, 261-3, 296, 330,
    518, 556
  Vulgate 296, 339, 441
  see Gospels; also separate entries for Books
    of the Bible
Bickersteth, Edward 387, 559
birth pangs of new era 145
Blackie, John Stuart 235
Blacks 66, 69, 495, 497
blasphemy 4, 179, 182-3, 220, 224, 236,
  262, 344, 445, 459

blindness, spiritual 33, 51-3, 59, 63, 110-11, 142, 162, 176-9, 197, 199, 203, 223, 236-7, 239, 245, 254-6, 283-4, 296, 303-4, 309, 311, 324, 326-7, 336-7, 369-70, 407, 443, 449, 463, 466, 472, 482
    blind imitation 5, 176, 206, 313 *see also* imitation
Borg, Marcus Joel 315-16
bread,
    spiritual, of heaven 49-50, 256, 258, 281-2, 293, 320, 365, 379, 397, 450, 476, 566
    symbolism at Eucharist 333, 358-60, 363
Britain, British 14, 150, 394-5, 426, 560, 561
Browne, E. G. 494
Buddhism 61, 229, 230, 308, 444, 466-7
Byzantine Empire 94

Caesar 103, 121
    Augustus 548
    Julius 548
Caesarea 68, 339
Caiaphas, High Priest 51, 91
Cain 240
Caliphate 376, 388, 390, 420, 545
Calvin, John 34, 147, 271, 273, 282
Canaan, son of Ham 65-6
Canaanites 70, 73, 95 296, 451
Canning, Stratford 391, 560
Capernaum 72, 190
capital punishment 63, 94, 559
Carmel, Mount 128, 401, 405, 415, 541-2
Carlyle, Thomas 267
celibacy 87-9, 252-3, 272
character, human 16, 475, 476-85, 507
    transformation of 34, 115, 369-70, 469, 474
charity 34, 46, 83-4, 244, 481, 550
chastity 142, 251-3, 346, 357, 479, 480, 484
child, children 50, 207, 223, 300, 314, 332, 365, 382, 433, 449, 503-4
    baptism of 356
    Christian 13, 43, 64, 87, 94, 98, 221, 356
    counsel to become like 37-8, 49, 50-51, 368
    of God 34
    of the Kingdom 232, 417
    of light 12, 203, 286
    Jesus 182, 189-90
    sacrifice of 296
    slavery 65, 89

Children of Israel 49, 95-6, 107-9, 111, 161, 168, 178, 190, 192, 194, 215, 221-2, 232, 236, 254, 257, 377, 379, 392, 442
    In prophecies 120, 123, 191, 387
Chile 87
Christ, Jesus
    in Baháʼí Writings 3-4, 142, 205, 218, 257, 282, 310-12, 319, 322, 344-5, 348, 353, 465
    body of, in Eucharist 333, 359
    crucifixion 20, 23, 99, 128, 139, 141-2, 153, 171-2, 199, 262-3, 307, 309-10, 316, 319-20, 323, 325, 341, 355, 363, 368
    divinity of xi, 20, 218, 262, 282, 342, 345
    First Coming of 24, 35, 50, 55, 62, 113, 116, 120, 127, 135, 141, 143, 153, 160, 178-80, 203, 205, 207, 218, 232-3, 284-5, 299, 305-7, 364, 367-8, 380, 401-2, 416, 434, 443, 448-9, 545, 546, 564
    genealogies 188, 442, 454, 548
    names and titles
        Anointed 27, 100, 115, 349, 565
        Emmanuel 182, 189, 217
        Jesus 182
        Saviour 21, 116, 138, 201, 216, 218-19, 241, 295, 320, 342, 346, 359, 394, 395-6
        Son of God 7, 49, 125, 220-21, 232-3, 262, 299, 307, 315, 342, 345, 349, 415, 547, 548; only begotten 220, 340-41
        Son of Man 22, 26, 36, 56, 63, 120, 125, 137, 146, 152, 160, 163, 185-7, 207, 216, 255, 281, 292, 294, 309-10, 317, 344, 378, 395, 432, 442, 446, 547
    ransom 32, 326
    resurrection 96, 141, 255, 263-4, 305, 307-9, 314-25, 363, 554
    Second Coming of
        and Baháʼu'lláh 284, 397, 407
        challenge to Christians 24-5, 52-56, 61-2, 180, 199, 206-8, 213, 232, 234-5, 237, 238, 262, 285, 350, 371, 374
        in New Testament 25, 50, 55, 113-14, 124, 135, 140, 148, 151-2, 163, 232, 262, 280, 285, 288, 374, 381, 390, 396, 403-4, 433, 448
        and resurrection 305-7

signs of 127-8, 143, 145, 147, 151-2, 155-6, 159-60, 163, 166, 213, 289-90, 313, 320, 390, 393, 396-7, 441
Christianity
  Anonymous 228-30
  challenges of present day 3, 7, 13-22, 25, 58
  exclusivity, belief in 213-32, 314
  'good news' 24, 26, 40, 53-4, 56, 92, 128, 149-50, 199, 213, 234, 254, 270, 374, 381, 407, 463
  history x, 5, 92-8, 243, 265-70, 340
  and other religions 61, 96
    Bahá'í Faith 3-8, 345, 462, 464, 501
    Hinduism 100
    Islam 99-11, 388, 391
    Judaism 28, 61, 96-9, 103, 176, 179, 429
  physical resurrection of Christ 314-15, 318 *see also* resurrection
  Second Coming, belief in 235 *see also* Christ, Second Coming of
  teachings
    fundamental, spiritual 6, 29-57
    social subject to change 59, 61-103, 510-12
  see also Christians, Churches
Christians ix-xii, 15, 16, 18-19, 22, 24, 27, 34-5, 59, 75-6, 116, 133, 135, 145-6, 203, 225, 235, 244, 250, 262, 265, 270, 326, 330, 347, 371, 407, 463-4
  attachment to person of Jesus 236-7
  and Bahá'u'lláh 416, 423, 442-3
  challenge of Second Coming 206pp *see also* Christ, Second Coming of
  early 11-13, 27, 30-31, 41-3, 65, 85, 116, 133, 220, 242, 246-7, 251, 266-8, 274, 280, 342, 449
  injunctions
    of Christ 21, 26, 30-31, 62, 102, 134, 143, 232, 403, 454, 491
    of St Paul 11-13, 34-5, 37, 39, 55, 60, 86-8, 134, 178, 203, 224, 259, 265, 329, 366, 433
    to stay awake (and sober) 22, 26, 53, 55, 134, 163, 203, 207, 234
  love
    for enemies 102, 232
    for fellow Christians 30-31, 37, 91, 232
  see also Christianity; Churches
Christmas 363
Chronicles, Second Book of 393
Churchianity 3, 244-6
Churches, Christian
  Adventist 18, 151, 157, 171, 389-90, 396-7
  Anglican (Church of England) 13, 14, 19, 87, 95, 102, 338, 353, 356
  Anabaptist 13, 86, 232
  Armenian 391, 559
  Baptist 18, 59, 158, 216, 232, 395
  Catholic 13, 15-16, 18, 19, 82, 84, 87, 89, 94-6, 98-100, 147, 151, 223, 226-8, 231, 247, 248-9, 253, 266, 268-70, 273, 326, 330-31, 333, 341-2, 352, 356, 359, 550, 555
  Episcopalian 216
  Evangelical ix, 210, 213, 352, 387-8, 405-6
  Jehovah's Witnesses 396
  Jesus Christ of Latter Day Saints (LDS) 375
  Lutheran 18, 19 23, 232, 333, 356, 405
  Methodist 21, 216, 232, 333, 356, 385, 390, 552
  Moravian 356
  Orthodox 18, 19, 94, 147, 247, 251, 269-70, 333, 342, 356
    Eastern 13, 84, 89, 231, 270, 330, 352-3
    Greek 270
    Oriental 353
    Russian 19
    Ukrainian 19
  Presbyterian 18, 216, 356
  Protestant 13, 18, 19, 34, 82, 85, 94-6, 147-8, 151, 229, 232, 248, 269-70, 272-3, 330-31, 352, 358-9, 389, 405
  Restorationist 13
  Sabbatarian 64
  Seventh Day Adventist 64, 232, 389, 396
  Syrian 18
  Unitarian 342
City, Holy, of God (religion of God) 163-5, 217, 288, 415 *see also* Jerusalem
civil rights 66
Clarke, Adam 385
Claster, Jill 93
cleanliness
  physical 258, 357
  ritual, spiritual 72, 75, 87, 110, 136, 142, 185, 194, 198-9, 211, 224, 233, 250, 258, 304, 329, 357-8, 448, 480, 546, 563

Clement of Alexandria 280
clouds 117, 120, 130, 137, 158, 160-62, 312-13, 395, 420, 426, 564
Codex Alexandrinus 261
collective security 509
compassion 38, 44, 47, 66, 71, 73, 101, 110, 198, 296-7, 327-8, 446, 481, 486, 513
communion of saints 12, 244, 342
confession 327, 329-32, 333, 512-13
confirmation (sacrament)
Constantine, Emperor 63, 92, 242, 243, 266-7, 340
Constantinople (Istanbul) 94, 147, 223, 270, 399
consultation 507, 508-9, 513
contention 51, 83, 102, 290, 460-61, 476
Corinth 79, 224-5, 329, 456
Cornelius 72, 242
Council(s)
    Christian 225-6
    of Clermont 93
    of Nicaea, 231, 267, 338, 340
    First and Second Ecumenical 340
    of Florence 226
    Fourth Lateran 226, 333
    of Jerusalem 65
    of the Synod of Macon, second 98
    of Trent 333, 358
    Vatican I 247-8, 420
    Vatican II 228, 231
    Jewish 293
    of Oulemas 561
courtesy 36, 35, 485-6
covenant of God 59, 108-10, 164, 180, 187, 215, 358, 440, 489
    Ark of the 545
    everlasting 108-9, 379
    new 109, 209, 214, 271, 326, 356, 385, 403, 432, 456, 457-8
Covid-19 1
Cranmer, Thomas 147
creation accounts 84, 280-81, 334-5, 361, 384, 445
creationism 16
Creed, Christian 244-5, 340-42
    Apostles' 12, 235, 314, 321, 340-2
    Nicene 270, 321, 340-2
    Nicene-Constantinopolitan 321, 340-41
Crimean War 391
Crocker, Richard L. 93
Cross, the 3, 32, 94, 263, 305, 311, 318-26, 355, 421, 429

Crossan, John 209
Crusade(s), Crusaders 94, 98, 100, 270, 273, 333, 388, 399, 405, 545
    Fourth 270
Cybele, Cult of 361
Cyprian 280
Cyrus, King 122, 170, 335, 384, 393, 545

Daniel, Prophet 22, 112 130, 151, 157, 168-72, 193, 265, 312, 386, 406, 432, 558
darkness 8, 59-60, 72, 110, 116, 117, 126, 130-31, 136, 154-6, 159-60, 162, 180, 202, 296, 310, 443, 449, 482
    and light 11, 22, 33, 74-5, 111-2, 129, 190-91, 203, 223-4, 234, 239, 260, 265, 279-80, 285-91, 297, 304, 312-13, 335-7, 381, 417, 421, 429, 436, 438, 463, 466, 473, 485, 487, 500
Darius, King 171, 545
David, King 70, 109, 120, 121-2, 124, 168, 177, 179, 181, 188-9, 191, 220, 283, 295, 324, 325, 327, 349, 370, 399, 401, 404, 432, 441-2
Davies, W. D. 308
Day
    of Atonement 329-30
    of God 25-33
    of Judgement 147-9, 157, 164-5, 237, 290, 249, 301-4, 307, 311-12
    of Resurrection 301, 311-12
dead, the 7, 120, 156, 212, 232-4, 254-5, 296, 299, 379, 418, 472
    Book of 375
    and judgement 149, 165, 219, 301, 340-41
    resurrection of 132, 162, 199, 234, 255, 263, 301, 305-18, 333, 341, 362, 418, 449, 473, 475, 489, 547
deafness, spiritual 110, 152, 162, 199, 236, 254, 256, 283-4, 336-7, 369, 392, 443
death 20, 63, 90, 95, 98, 187, 199, 227, 231, 253, 283, 308, 314, 362, 398, 440, 478, 487, 559
    of Jesus 20, 125, 141-2, 305, 308, 315, 317, 319-20, 322, 325, 259, 419
    life after 313-14, 316
    spiritual 33, 40, 113, 118, 132, 153, 163-5, 191-2, 198, 201-2, 233-4, 283, 286, 297, 298-301, 305, 309, 317, 336-7, 372, 403, 448, 565

deicide 99
demons, evil spirits 22, 148, 185, 186, 192, 216, 299, 355, 370, 543, 546
   casting out 17, 185, 355, 370
denominationalism 5, 17-19
Deuteronomy 214, 377, 557
Devéria, Théodule 376
Devil 51, 56, 75, 144, 211, 227, 231, 326, 335-7, 362-3, 372, 462, 543, 546
Diocletian, Emperor 267-8, 559
Diognetus 12, 97
dispensation(s) x, 61-2, 117, 120, 154, 165, 178, 195, 219, 222, 236, 271, 274, 282, 286, 290-91, 301, 307, 368, 401, 429, 430, 433, 438, 450, 452-4, 457, 490, 565
   of Bahá'u'lláh 164, 203, 292, 354, 403
   of Christ 135, 199, 214-15, 219, 271, 377, 401, 456, 458, 472
      earlier, past 7, 135, 164, 276, 288, 290-91, 311-13, 401, 402, 414, 460, 490, 504, 505
      future 434
   of Moses 28, 49, 62, 74, 191, 194, 215, 303, 404, 430, 439, 456, 458
   of Noah 197
diversity 408, 428, 430, 492, 494-6, 509
divorce 85, 86-7, 177, 189, 253, 455, 567
dogma xii, 3, 5, 7, 18, 28, 61, 136, 161, 236, 258, 279, 313, 463, 564
   Christian 19, 99 158 179 228, 232, 248, 258, 261, 263, 270-02, 314, 316, 321, 326, 334, 338-48, 360-65, 420
   purpose of 265
Domenicans 550
Donatists 268
Dolgourouki, Prince 425
dreams 156, 188, 192-3, 265, 284, 291, 386
Durant, William James 268

eagle(s) 153-4, 169-70, 178
Earle, Alice 63
earth
   faith on, shall he find? 146
   God, Lord over 32, 51, 101, 119, 130, 196, 293, 341, 380, 409, 420, 439
   and heaven 117, 196, 207, 247, 378, 418-19, 422, 465, 479
      destruction of, signs 62, 113, 131, 134, 144-5, 156-60, 163-4, 236, 289-90, 310, 405, 407
      new 108-9, 113, 135, 145, 157, 163-4, 166, 236, 270, 432
   of human understanding 438
   judgement of 120, 210, 301, 305
   justice hath appeared on 483, 501
   Kingdom of God on 53, 121, 129-30, 135, 158, 295, 374, 403, 450, 514
   metaphorical meaning of 292
   one homeland 506-7
   peace on 91, 121, 123
   people of, all that dwell on 22, 32, 59, 95, 111-12, 118, 127, 129, 132, 133, 137, 149-51, 160, 164, 192, 292, 310-11, 346, 383, 392, 395, 403, 408, 415-17, 419, 241, 426, 439, 466, 472, 491, 501
   physical 13, 16, 41, 101, 108, 169, 213, 255, 280-81, 289, 292, 307-9, 369, 564
   shining with Glory of God 385
earthly
   authority, kingdom, powers 92, 103, 121, 134, 124, 136, 138, 158, 242, 334, 380, 426
   life, world, 42, 103, 183, 194, 276, 468, 470, 565
   possessions, concerns 40, 91, 234, 290, 310, 375, 397, 422, 437, 474, 477-8
earthquakes 117, 144-5, 308, 309
Easter 96, 98, 315-16
Ebionims, Ebionites 345, 360
edict(s) 171, 559
   of Cyrus 545
   of Diocletian 267, 559
   Imperial Reform (1856) 390-91
   of Milan 266
   Ottoman, of toleration (1844) 390-91, 559
Egypt, Egyptians 95, 108, 127, 181, 190, 192, 197, 221, 233, 254, 257, 267-8, 305, 357, 360, 371, 377-8, 390, 393
   and Joseph Smith 375
Elam 127, 386, 558
Elijah, Elias, Prophet, 117, 182, 187, 216, 251, 415, 432, 440-41, 448, 541-2, 547, 555
Elisha, Prophet 187, 283, 440
Ellicott, Charles John 60
   commentaries 60, 69, 74, 101, 108, 150, 166, 167, 216, 233, 241, 269, 274, 294, 302, 441
Emmanuel (Jesus) *see* Christ
Emmanuel, King of Italy 420
England 87, 390-91, 423, 560-61

enlightenment, spiritual 50, 130, 158, 194, 304, 407, 444, 482, 484
Enoch 440, 566
Ephesus 259
Ephraim the Syrian 98
epidemics, plagues 1, 75, 144, 217, 254
Epistles
   of Bahá'u'lláh
      to Napoleon III 375, 423
      to Pope Pius IX 420
   of Ignatius 97
   to Diognetus 12, 97
   in New Testament
      Colossians 60, 67, 447
      Corinthians 79, 329, 435
      Ephesians 67, 79, 331
      Galatians 223
      Hebrews 60, 219, 262, 434, 447, 450, 457
      James 42, 362
      John I 40
      Peter 68
      Romans 74, 82, 218
      Titus 351
equality 70, 325, 392, 481
   gender 498-500
   racial 496
Esslemont, John E. 311, 424
Essenes 87, 251, 252, 361-2
Esther, Queen 171, 545
Ethiopia 150, 192
Eucharist 333, 352, 358-60
Euphrates, river 384, 389
Europe, Europeans ix, 14, 17, 19, 65, 87, 94, 270, 273, 385, 391-2, 395, 420, 559-60
Eusebius 339, 556
Evans, Rachel Held ix
evil 6, 17, 29, 38, 39, 40, 45, 49, 51-2, 56, 74, 90, 101-3, 126, 147-8, 160, 161, 171, 198, 206, 216, 279, 286, 332, 335-7, 353, 364, 370, 372, 384, 393, 429, 436, 444, 455
   speaking, wishing 216, 381, 483, 486 *see also* Devil, reviling
   spirits 185
evildoers 13, 53, 71, 90, 103, 201, 206, 238, 255, 269, 296, 299, 317, 365-6, 404-5, 486
evolution 16
   spiritual, human and social 4, 61, 70, 369, 434, 452-3, 458, 460, 492, 504
ex-cathedra 231, 247-8, 550

excommunication 223, 266, 270, 272
Exodus 214
exorcism 355
Ezekiel 52, 109-10 198, 238, 385, 401

faith 5-7, 11, 52-3, 73, 107, 206, 404, 460, 464-5
   and action 222, 471-2, 474
   decline in 5, 14, 17, 19, 22, 24-5, 145-7, 148, 156, 160, 233, 245, 444
   faithfulness, firmness, steadfastness in 24, 28, 41, 44, 63, 109-10, 145, 160, 164, 179, 192, 215, 218, 226, 265, 297, 304, 392, 423, 434, 450, 475, 479, 484, 489, 497, 500
   faithlessness 86, 146, 226, 235, 379, 500
   justification by 141
   and love 31-2, 81, 84, 203, 232
   oneness of 129, 404, 427, 428, 430-31, 437, 439-61, 494, 501-2
   outward forms of 29, 58-9, 245-6, 352
   power of 5, 494-5
   purpose, function of 34, 145, 352, 369
   and reason, science 7, 15-16, 206, 317, 321, 347, 366, 502-3
   renewal of 2, 35, 59, 107, 113, 132, 271, 301, 309, 369, 407, 413, 448-9
   and spiritual life 297, 300-01
   tests of 41, 44, 48, 279, 347, 353, 398, 463
   true, sincere 6, 16, 21, 30, 68, 71-3, 78, 161, 182, 187, 259, 330, 365-6, 369-70
false prophets, false Christs 21, 22, 38, 99-100, 143-4, 240, 372-3, 382
famine 110, 144, 245, 269, 281, 379, 543, 557
farmers 56, 473
fasting 64, 97, 185, 291, 330, 333
Father, the 24, 28, 53, 62, 70, 92, 121, 134-5, 139, 153, 158, 199, 200, 205, 207, 214, 218, 234, 240, 307, 395, 397, 403-5, 418, 422, 423, 429
   Day of 403
   Kingdom of 203, 235, 237, 242, 374, 403, 450
   and the Son 121, 134, 135, 163, 182, 207, 217-18, 220-21, 267, 270, 299, 302, 310, 319, 338-43, 347, 360, 378, 384, 421-2, 426
fear 67, 159, 184, 235, 236-7, 284-5, 383, 417, 429, 479, 484

of God 6, 33-4, 109, 124, 168, 175, 194, 197, 250, 259, 269, 319, 322, 327, 364, 392, 416, 418, 420, 442, 445, 480, 485
flagellation 333, 555
food 13, 47, 50, 53, 60, 148, 185, 252, 268, 281, 351, 435, 467
  spiritual 114-15, 166, 435-6, 450, 565
forgiveness 39, 45, 47, 90-91, 94, 182, 187, 219, 327-33, 339, 342, 344, 355, 358, 367, 407, 484, 487, 488, 512-13
  and justice 90, 511
France, French 14, 273, 375, 389, 391, 422-3, 560
Francis of Assisi, St 308
Franciscans 100, 251, 550
Francis Joseph, Emperor 425
freedom
  through Christ 60-61
  of conscience 508
  from hatred 483
  from love of money 43
  and marriage 86-8
  personal 491
  from prejudice 50, 180, 467, 479, 497
  of religion, worship 266, 542
  from restrictions of the Law 60
  from sin 20, 60, 66, 110, 219, 268, 322, 346, 354, 356-7, 512
  and slavery 66-8, 69, 73
  spiritual 66
  from tradition 463
  and truth 48, 66, 502
  and women 81

Gaels 95-6
Galatia, Galatians 60, 223
Galilee 11, 54, 153, 181, 188, 190, 293, 316, 321, 443, 546
Galileo 15-16
Garden of Eden 334, 384
garments, old, new 29, 42, 59, 61, 131
gate(s) 35, 119, 136, 165, 406, 416, 425
  eastern 385, 401
  of heaven 365, 415
  of hell 247-8
  narrow, strait 144, 200-01
  title of the Báb 152
Gaul 150
Gehenna 296
Genesis, Book of 81, 90, 280-81, 334, 384, 393

Gentiles 46, 59, 60, 64-5, 70-71, 73-4, 76,, 82, 97, 129, 141, 150, 169, 172, 190, 224, 249, 261, 266, 271, 302-3, 362, 388, 394, 404, 451, 455
George, bishop of Alexandria 267
Germany, Germans 14, 17, 23, 85, 94, 270, 273, 405, 423-4
German Peasants War 273
Gibbon, Edward 252, 266, 389
Gill, John 59, 158
global society 1-2, 6, 28, 130, 312, 428, 463, 469, 490-01, 504-10
Glory of God 3, 119, 136, 164, 288, 386, 564
Goa, India 100
God
  image, likeness of 445-7, 495
  justice of 39, 126, 178, 297, 334, 418, 420, 496
  Kingdom of see Kingdom
  mercy of 17, 44, 46, 103, 219, 321, 329, 337, 365, 418, 422, 424, 425, 473, 483, 484, 511, 513
  names of 428-9, 446
  oneness of 28, 342, 345, 468
  vengeance of 154, 222, 284
  Word of xi, 4, 6, 98, 107, 140, 142, 148, 157, 159, 165, 191, 194, 221, 258, 381, 407, 449, 454, 455, 466, 470, 472, 563
  see also Father
golden calf 246, 254
golden rule 38
good works 39, 83, 103, 182-3
Gospels 24, 27-8, 42, 49, 59, 91, 101, 179, 206, 209, 212, 229, 242-6, 303-4, 321, 325, 377, 489
  in Bahá'í Writings 310-11, 345, 347, 415-16, 473, 489
  'good news' of 26, 40, 53, 133, 149-51, 234, 374, 463
  and Islam 377
  John 25, 33, 52, 79, 139, 145, 181, 232, 302, 322, 339, 354, 357, 434, 436, 451, 546
  Luke 17, 70, 188, 190, 222, 256, 319-20
  Mark 54, 252, 556
  Matthew 53, 59, 98, 143, 149, 151, 163, 181, 189-90, 202, 247, 252, 274, 307-8, 317, 338, 346, 358, 404, 449, 454, 457
  proclamation, preaching of 54, 73-4,

149-51, 213, 222-3, 249, 270, 355, 386, 390, 406, 451, 472-3
Synoptic 349
translations 140, 151, 153-4, 266, 261-2, 272, 294, 296, 326, 339-40, 344
Graham, Billy 213
Great Mother (of gods) 362
Great Schism 270, 342
Greece 150, 251, 539
Greeks xi, 12, 13, 65, 73-4, 257, 270, 271, 391, 545, 559-60
Guinness, Henry Gratton 388

Habakkuk, Prophet 449
Hades 296, 321
Hadrian, Emperor 393
Haggai, Prophet 119, 408, 432
Hagia Sophia, Istanbul 270
Ham, son of Noah 65-6
Hammurabi, Code of 90
hand washing 258
Hardegg, David 405
heaven(s), heavenly
    ascent to 314, 320, 360, 362, 396
        of Elijah 187, 440
        of Enoch 440
        of Jesus Christ 23, 113, 294, 311, 319-21, 340-41
        of Virgin Mary 19, 346
    of divine Will 282, 325, 350
    and earth *see* earth
    descent from 161-4, 187, 282, 293-4, 306, 321, 341, 395-6, 415, 416, 419-20, 443
    destruction of *see* earth
    Father 17, 45, 46, 49, 53, 66, 92, 121, 135, 214, 141, 247, 262, 269, 295, 338, 365, 368, 403, 455
    and hell 272, 295-7, 341
    hosts of 4, 283
    kingdom of 33, 35, 37, 40, 42-3, 50, 53, 62, 67, 71-3, 85, 103, 125, 135, 138, 158, 202, 209, 239, 242, 247, 270, 274, 284, 295, 357, 374, 403, 409, 416, 442, 450, 454, 489
    manna from 254, 468
    meaning of 161, 164, 292-7
    miracles, signs from demanded 204, 255
    new *see* earth
    power(s) of 6, 22, 154, 159-60, 443
    reward, treasure in 250-51, 263, 381
    signs in 289 *see also* clouds, earth, stars

souls 472
way, path to 201, 232
Hebrew Bible 77-8, 85, 91, 101, 107-12, 116-32, 155, 175, 180-02, 187, 190-91, 195, 197, 203, 207, 215, 220, 236-7, 279-81, 291-2, 298, 303, 309, 312, 328, 335, 345, 349, 364, 366-7, 369, 373-4, 377, 379, 384, 401, 428, 436, 440-41, 448, 450 *see also* separate entries for Prophets
Helios 360
hell 211-12, 219, 239-40, 272, 295-8, 321, 334, 407
    of discord, enmity 323
    gates of 247-8
    and heaven 272, 295-7, 341
    Jesus's descent into 341
Helper, the 139, 237
Henry, Matthew 33
    commentaries 74-5, 83, 102, 144-5, 160, 214, 236, 303, 373
heresy, heretics 94, 99, 159, 182, 226, 231, 236, 246, 266-8, 270, 273, 275, 360
Herod the Great 190, 545
Herod, King 99, 353, 441
Herodians 103
Heywood, John 176
Hinduism, Hindus 61, 100, 229, 361, 444
Hitler 395
Hoffmann, Christoff 405
Holy Land 194, 270, 333, 397, 405
    return of Jews to 127-8, 151, 179, 392-4
Holy Roman Empire 273
Holy Spirit 20, 24, 107, 139, 141, 208, 228, 231, 237, 243, 257, 260, 262-3, 265, 270, 272, 300-01, 311, 319, 338-44, 348, 352-5, 356, 369, 380, 382, 423, 462-3, 468, 552
holy war 91-4, 270
    abolition of 511
honour of parents 488
Hosea, Prophet 168, 198, 400-01, 431, 546
hospitality 37, 43, 302, 481
humility 16, 36-8, 46-7, 50, 81, 118, 123-4, 126-7, 160, 195, 215, 241-2, 247, 250, 279, 327, 329, 367-8, 376, 481-2, 508
Hus, John; Hussites 273
Hussites 273
hypocrisy 35, 44, 46, 103, 209, 223, 239, 259, 269, 354, 375

idols, idolatry 16, 40, 59, 70, 74-6, 89, 110,

118, 126, 169, 170, 198-9, 224, 246, 249-50, 254, 268, 329, 363, 371, 388, 541, 550
Immaculate Conception 19, 346, 420
imitation 5, 110, 176-7, 205, 206, 274, 286, 313, 325, 453, 463-4, 466, 502
immorality 371
    sexual 16, 40, 86-7, 455
incarnation 99, 179, 217-18, 261, 315, 340-41, 348-9, 360, 398
India 100, 150, 426, 560
infallibility 247-8, 420, 550
infidelity 76, 86, 304, 466, 480
infidels 76
Inquisition 16, 94, 226
interpretation of scripture
    Bahá'í, authorized 312, 401
    divine 117, 142, 207, 260, 266
    human 203, 218, 260, 279
    literal 26, 81, 117, 177-8, 180, 208-12, 220, 294, 299, 306, 308, 315-19, 324, 336, 358, 385, 396, 447
    by religious leaders and scholars
        Christian 12, 85, 93, 101, 140, 149, 153, 214, 248-9, 250, 260, 262, 265, 269, 287, 289, 293, 330, 357, 359, 363, 386, 389-90, 406, 546
        Jewish 159, 177, 197, 204-5, 262, 265, 299, 324-5
    in translation 261-2
    of oral tradition 63
intolerance 123, 222, 371, 458
    religious 219, 223, 225, 267
investigation of truth 15-17, 48, 52, 154, 158, 176, 200, 206, 229, 325, 239, 250, 274, 279, 280, 313, 352, 364, 365, 454, 463-4, 466, 508
Iraq 77, 386, 397, 399
Ireland 87, 95-6
Irenaeus of Lyons 280, 334, 360
Isaac 72, 201-2, 220, 334, 357, 409, 548
Isaiah, Prophet 107-12, 118-19, 122, 175, 189-91, 193-196-8, 204, 233, 258-9, 284-5, 287-8, 335, 362, 366, 404-5, 408, 432, 433, 435, 443-4
Ishmael 220
Islam vii, 5, 61, 99-100, 152, 179, 229-30, 346, 387, 389-90, 397, 413, 444, 510, 545, 554, 559-60
Israel 28, 49, 70-72, 77, 103, 108-9, 115, 127, 131, 167, 169, 171, 176, 190, 194-5, 198, 215, 220-21, 233-4, 238, 251, 254, 303, 349, 384-6, 393, 398, 399, 513, 545
    Children of 49, 95-6, 107-8, 111, 161, 168, 178, 190, 192, 194, 215, 232, 236, 254, 257, 377, 379, 392, 442
    God of 86, 97, 119, 238, 385, 401, 432
    Holy One of 118-19, 127, 215, 432
    house(s) of 73, 108, 121, 175-6, 198, 308, 385, 451
    kingdoms of 392, 400
    people of 127, 167, 192, 214, 220, 379, 542
    Prophets of 28, 137, 374 *see also* separate named entries
    State of 62, 128, 393, 395
Israelites 95, 122, 167, 233, 257, 291, 293, 371, 376, 457, 549
Italy 14, 87, 150, 420

Jacob 72, 78, 109, 118, 127, 167, 188, 191, 201-2, 295, 357, 393, 406, 409, 431, 442
James (Apostle) 37, 41, 42 50-51, 65, 96, 102, 115, 136, 302, 330, 331, 349, 382
James, brother of Jesus 183, 252
Japheth, son of Noah 65
Jeremiah, Prophet 25, 29, 48, 58, 108-10, 112, 125, 161, 178, 198, 374, 386, 432, 557
Jericho 71, 95, 186, 400
Jerome, St 98, 280, 296, 556
Jerusalem 71, 101, 124, 128, 150, 152, 155, 170, 172, 175, 181, 185, 190, 215, 249, 270, 296, 302, 316, 345, 380, 394, 400, 405, 425
    Church in 65, 96, 244
    Council of 65
    destruction of 149-50, 168-70, 329, 388, 393
    holy city 152, 170, 171, 308, 320
    new 113, 163-6, 288, 403, 432
    Temple 170, 190, 329
Jesse 122
Jesuits 100, 228
Job 44, 112
Joel, Prophet 111, 130, 155, 156, 289, 431
John the Baptist 54, 117, 189, 199, 205, 215, 238, 251, 254, 311, 323, 352-5, 356, 400, 440-01, 448, 555
John Chrysostom, St 98, 99, 280
John of Damascus 99
Jonah 255-6, 264, 317-18, 328, 546
Joseph of Arimathea 318

Joseph, brother of Jesus 183, 252
Joseph, husband of Mary 181-2, 188-90, 252, 320
Joseph, son of Jacob 90, 188, 197, 265, 291, 334, 357
Josephus, Flavius 168, 280, 353
Joshua 70, 95, 182, 546
Judaism 5, 23, 25, 38, 77, 79, 81-2, 87, 98, 103, 141, 143, 153, 176, 230, 242, 265, 271, 274, 311-12, 330, 335, 345, 354, 362, 413, 428-9, 431, 448, 460, 463, 510
   Babylonian Captivity 393
   circumcision 64-5, 97, 208, 266, 354, 362, 382
   Conservative 80, 453
   High Priests 51, 122, 254, 393, 546
   kings 103 *see also* David, Solomon
   Law, the 28-9, 32, 38, 59-65, 71, 72, 81, 86, 88, 89, 97-8, 103, 121, 125, 141, 168, 177, 184, 194-5, 208-9, 221, 223-4, 236, 275-6, 309, 392, 454-5, 457
      dietary 64-5
      of Moses 23, 32, 60, 62-4, 89, 141, 167, 177, 181, 195, 209, 325, 454-6
      of Noah 61-2, 70, 195
      oral 76, 258, 276
      ritual cleanliness 185, 258
   Mishna 76
   oral law 76, 258
   Orthodox 77, 80, 128, 223, 453
   Patriarchs 191, 269, 374, 377
   Pentateuch 161, 177, 194
   rabbis(s 62, 63, 76, 77, 80, 159, 197, 241
      rabbinic law 258
      teaching 378
      see also Maimonides
   Reconstructionist 80
   Reform 80
   Sanhedrin 51, 275
   Shema 28, 345, 429-30
   Talmud 23, 66, 70, 76-7, 86, 159, 167, 185, 197, 258
   Tanakh 197, 219, 293, 296, 374, 405, 541-2
   Tosefta 76
   see also antii-Semitism
Jude 217-18, 240
Judea 29, 149, 155, 169, 181, 183, 189-90, 392-3, 434
Judge, the 51, 120, 301, 397, 432

judgement
   by Bahá'u'lláh 397, 432
   by Christ 125, 148-9, 219, 274, 299, 302, 303, 340-41, 343, 443
   civil, religious, scholarly 101, 158, 279, 421
   day of, last 147-9, 157, 164-5, 237, 290, 249, 301-4, 307, 311-12
   by God 41, 51, 120, 135, 148-9, 165, 210, 279, 302, 307, 367, 376
   human 23, 39, 50, 60, 83, 88, 229, 253, 265, 279-80, 294, 326, 347, 372, 391, 420, 421, 468, 482, 558
   of others 35, 45, 51, 123, 178, 483
Julius Africanus 280
Jupiter 169-70
justice 6, 70, 121-2, 191, 227, 333, 374, 392, 457, 462, 479, 482-3, 485, 505
   courts of 102
   and forgiveness 90, 511
   of God 39, 126, 178, 297, 334, 418, 420, 496
   human 34, 90, 178, 325, 392, 499-500, 512
   and mercy 126, 508
   Most Great 398
Justin Martyr 97, 363

Katherina von Bora 85
kindness 18, 32-3, 37-8, 47, 51, 103, 475-8, 481, 485-6, 496
   of God, loving-kindness 156, 314, 327, 369, 444, 459, 483, 488, 505
King, Martin Luther, Jr. 361
King of Glory 119
Kingdom
   animal 178
   of Bahá'u'lláh 416-18, 470-71, 489
   of Christ 4, 16, 20, 27, 88, 142, 149, 177, 188, 191, 200, 216, 242, 319-20, 324-5, 406-7, 415
   divine 24, 36, 38, 56, 92, 120, 137, 141, 161, 167, 323-4, 353, 462, 468, 496
   of the Father 62, 92, 121, 135, 158, 203, 235, 237, 242, 288, 341, 357, 374, 403, 422-3, 442 450
   of God 16, 24, 43, 50, 54-5, 71-2, 102, 114, 121, 125, 133, 142, 162, 200-01, 208, 2113-14, 293-4, 306, 314, 356, 383, 415, 423, 425, 466
   on earth 53, 121, 295, 514
   of heaven 35, 37, 40, 42-3, 50, 62, 72-3,

85, 202, 209, 239, 247, 270, 274, 284, 357, 409, 416, 454
  of Satan 370
  temporal 18, 121, 141, 144, 159, 176, 242, 375, 392-3, 400, 422, 468
Korah (Core) 240, 549
Knox, John 147, 273
Krishna 444
Kutha, Iraq 77

Lactantius 280
language, universal auxiliary 509
Last Supper 358-9, 363
law(s)
  Baháʾí, of Baháʾuʾlláh 397, 460, 468, 471, 481, 487, 490, 501, 505, 506, 509-11
  Canon Law, 1983 Code 84
  of change 58
  of Christ 151, 177, 325
    of forgiveness 90
    of love 40
  and Christians 13, 20, 40, 59-60, 62-5, 71, 98, 185-6, 347, 453
  of God 164, 176, 194-5, 284, 298, 351, 392, 398, 456, 471, 490
  Jewish *see* Judaism
  Islamic 390-91
  natural, of nature 228, 254
  new 107-8, 128, 274, 456, 460
  moral, ethical 15, 29, 58, 274, 351, 453-4
  Roman 325
  social x, xi, 61, 286-7, 289, 490, 501, 510
lawlessness 22, 74, 145, 147, 224, 232
Lazarus 255
League of Nations 395
lending and borrowing with interest 102-3, 457
leprosy 75, 142
Levites 71, 215
Licinius, Emperor 266
life, significance of 298, 300-01
life after death 313-14, 316
light
  in the Baháʾí Writings 290-91, 296-7, 348-9, 357-8, 413, 417-18, 425, 436-40, 469-70, 477-90 passim, 501-2
  of Christ 33, 285-6, 304, 319, 340-41, 348, 436
  and darkness 11-12, 22, 33, 72, 74-5, 111-12, 118-19, 126, 131, 156, 160, 190-91, 223-4, 234, 239, 279-80, 285-6, 290-91, 304, 336-7, 381, 421,
    436, 473, 487
  divine, of God 33, 52, 72, 117, 130, 155, 161, 203, 219, 221, 228, 281, 283, 285, 288, 335, 337, 385, 406, 413, 417, 425, 429, 436-7, 449
  from the East 152-3, 385, 418
  of faith 297
  of Glory of God 156, 164
  hatred of 344
  of justice 483
  of love 469
  of Manifestations of God 156, 290-91, 313-14, 458-9, 467, 487, 501-2
  for the nations 59, 110, 129, 136
  of reality 463, 508
  of reason 15
  of religion, revelation 6, 7, 117, 158, 203, 287-8, 303-4, 406, 429, 436-9, 443, 459, 468, 504
  of the sun *see* sun
  of truth 162, 467
  of understanding 72, 476
  of unity 136, 500-01
  of the Word of God 470, 501
Lightfoot, John 158
Litch, Josiah 390
Lollards 272
Lord of Hosts 86, 119-21, 126, 129, 175, 180, 191, 250, 309, 380, 398, 428, 432
Lord's Prayer 135, 235, 282, 295, 330
love 6, 369, 446, 463, 478, 500
  of Baháʾís
    for Christ 3-4
    for mankind 409, 470, 481
  and the Best-Beloved 402, 415-16, 476
  Christian 11-13, 18, 20, 27-8, 30-32, 36-40, 47, 66, 71, 80, 91, 93, 96, 102, 103, 107, 137, 148, 203, 222, 232-3, 234, 237, 244, 257, 259, 263, 268-9, 271, 298, 300, 304, 310, 323, 345, 378, 394, 433, 468, 491
  of darkness 286
  for enemies 102, 269
  of God 29-30, 44, 135, 156, 165, 190, 196, 215, 221, 229, 232, 240, 269, 301, 302, 327, 353-4, 357-8, 368, 398-9, 408, 422, 429, 446, 449, 465, 471, 477, 479-80, 482, 488, 497
  growing cold 22, 145-6
  for humanity 32-3, 35, 66, 337, 409, 481, 487, 494, 496, 505, 507, 509-10
  in Judaism 86, 90, 236, 406

of Manifestations of God 323, 467-8
of money 43
religion as the cause of 460, 467-8, 490-91
self-love 354
universal 178, 328, 337, 374, 437, 461, 467, 481, 501, 505, 507
and the world 381
Luther, Martin 85, 147, 231, 273

Macedonia 259
Magi, the 72 152, 190, 384
Maimonides 62, 176, 179, 193, 195-7, 305, 316
Malachi 86, 187, 286, 432, 440, 441, 542
Malta 87
Manifestations, Messengers, of God, divine x, 3, 118-19, 156, 161, 179, 197, 218, 236, 262, 311-12, 323, 348-9, 403, 441, 458, 467, 469, 477
earthly life of 276
Marcus Antonius Felix 29
Marie of Romania, Queen 426-7
marriage 75. 79-80, 85-8, 148, 163, 189, 224, 252-3, 352, 446
companionate 480
forced 65
interfaith ix, 224
interracial 70, 495
polygamous 85, 177
of priests 88-9
a sacrament 352
martyrdom, martyrs 3, 11, 40, 225, 231, 253, 267, 275, 295, 310, 322, 326, 377, 382, 397-8, 405, 469, 560, 569
Mary Magdalene 318
Mary, mother of Christ *see* Virgin Mary
Mary, Queen (Bloody Mary) 273
materialism, material life 2, 42-3, 49-50, 101, 103, 193, 212, 252, 257, 281, 290, 301, 322, 335, 353-4, 456, 466, 478, 503
McSwain, Steve ix
Mehemet Ali, of Egypt 390
Melito of Sardis 99
mendicancy 251-2, 550
mercy 47, 71, 103, 186, 446, 508
of God 17, 44, 46, 103, 219, 321, 329, 337, 365, 418, 422, 424, 425, 473, 483, 484, 511, 513
Messiah 23-4, 51, 84, 98-100, 116, 120, 122-9, 138, 143, 145, 166-71, 175-89, 200, 209, 215, 236, 248, 255-6, 265, 270, 274, 286-7, 302, 317, 320, 322-4, 353, 364, 393, 432, 440, 441, 447-8, 451, 546
Meyer, Heinrich August Wilhelm 23-4
Micah, Prophet 119, 432
Michelangelo 445
Milarepa, Tibetan yogi 308
Miller, William 395-7
Millerites 389, 396-7
minority rights 496-8, 512
miracles 17, 21, 143-4, 180, 182, 253-7, 346, 362, 440, 550, 554
Miriam 70, 192
missionaries 92, 100, 385
Mithras, Mithraism 360-63
Moabites 70, 550
Mohler, Albert 314-15
Moloch 296
monasticism 76, 85, 229, 250-52, 272, 418-19, 421, 550
Montgomery Watt, W. 93
moon
  metaphor
    for Church 159, 552
    for government 158
    for spiritual knowledge 136, 160, 164, 286-8, 291, 439
  new 60, 97, 109, 439
  and sun, darkening of 22, 117, 126, 131, 136, 154, 156, 159-60, 180, 213, 288-91, 312-13
  turning to blood 156, 180, 289-90
morality, moral life 6, 15-17, 25, 29, 58, 86, 107, 156, 233, 243, 248, 287, 351, 371, 436, 452, 454, 462-89, 496, 498, 500, 507, 510, 549, 550
Moses
  in Bahá'í Writings 290, 311, 325, 334, 357, 371, 451, 466, 366
  belief in 24, 240, 311, 374, 377
  and Christ 23-4, 62, 177, 181, 240, 258, 318, 325, 359, 377, 430-31, 455
  dispensation, time of 61, 63, 119, 191, 194, 215, 303, 404, 456
  family of 70, 192
  followers of xi, 7, 17, 23-4, 28, 53, 61, 175, 184, 191, 208, 236, 254, 364, 409, 546
  humility, meekness of 192, 376
  Law of 23, 32, 60, 62-4, 89, 141, 167, 177, 181, 195, 209, 325, 454-6
  looked on, spoke with, God 100, 192-3, 214, 455, 458

Manifestation of God 156, 290, 434, 437
miracles performed by 182, 254, 309
in New Testament 262, 380
and Pharaoh 192, 220, 233, 254, 371
primacy of 193
and Prophet 'like unto' 138, 431, 446-7
In the Qur'án 558
revelation to 61, 62, 193, 195, 258, 311, 377, 423, 455, 541
Moses of Crete 143
Mount Athos 251
Muhammad, Prophet 99-100, 290, 371, 387
murder, murderers 33, 43, 89-90, 202, 239-40, 382, 399
Murphy, Thomas Patrick 93-4
Muslims 93, 100, 147, 270, 290, 333, 387, 401, 420, 466, 485, 543, 545
mystery religions 360, 362

Napoleon Bonaparte 325, 389, 399, 422
Napoleon III 375, 422-4
Nathaniel 131
nationalism 2, 19, 509-10
Nazareth 153, 177, 180-81, 183, 188-90, 227, 324-5, 443
Nebuchadnezzar, King 169, 386, 393, 545
Nehemiah, Prophet 171, 545
Nero, Emperor 147
new name 111, 114-15, 165-6, 236, 419, 565
New Testament *see* Gospels, *and separate entries for themes*
Newton, Isaac 386
Nicodemus 293-4, 302
Nineveh 317-18
Noah 61-2, 65-6, 70, 163, 193, 195, 197, 377, 434, 446, 558

oaths 101-2
obedience 15, 27-8, 30, 67, 79, 103, 107, 110, 148, 167, 194-5, 251, 253, 299, 307, 498, 542
disobedience 20, 235 334
O'Brien, Conor Cruise 95
Old Testament 85, 116, 177, 209, 296, 302, 324, 446 *see also* Hebrew Bible, Tanakh; *also individual entries for Prophets*
oneness of humanity, mankind 4, 7, 69, 323, 431, 467, 490-96
Onesimus 68
oppression 95, 100, 123, 154-5, 178-9, 191, 239, 267, 371, 390, 482, 504, 560

ordinances 35, 159, 307, 351-2, 359, 452, 460, 471, 490
Origen 253, 280
Ostragoths 389
Ottoman
 Caliphate 376, 390, 420
 Empire 376, 389-92, 394, 397, 399, 405, 559, 561
 edict of toleration 390-91, 559
 Sultans 390, 391, 559, 561
  'Abdu'l-Azíz 376, 420
  Abdülmecid 391

paganism, pagans 70, 76, 95, 97, 226, 231, 266, 268, 361, 393
Palestine 178, 362, 393-5, 405
papal infallibility 247-8, 420
Passover 98-9, 359-60
patriotism 2, 96, 409, 470, 493, 500, 509-10
Paul, St, Apostle
 life 29, 63, 64-5, 68, 70, 73-4, 87, 88, 96, 136, 147, 149-50, 183, 244, 266, 274-5, 366, 370
 writings: throughout, for themes *see separate entries*
peace
 and Bahá'u'lláh 374, 398
 and Christ 20, 39, 91, 121, 178, 323, 325, 456
 and Christians 93, 102, 134, 225
 and gender equality 499-500
 global, universal 123, 312, 468, 490, 493, 496, 499-500, 505, 507
 God of 17-18, 335-6, 429
 in Hebrew Bible 109, 119, 133, 210, 374, 429, 435
 and Messiah 122-3, 128, 138, 167
 Most Great 398, 505
 Prince of 120-21, 138, 191, 432
 racism a barrier to 494-5
 role of religion in 2, 6, 18, 298, 428, 461, 477, 501, 512
peacemakers 39, 91
penance 329-30, 333, 352, 555
Pentateuch 161, 177, 194
Pentecost 140, 263, 289, 552
Perpetual Virginity, doctrine of 19
persecution 353, 381-2, 398, 404
 of Abrahamic revelations 5
 of Báb and Bábís 397
 of Bahá'u'lláh and Bahá'is 383, 398, 462, 485

of Christians 11, 13, 32, 40, 44, 71, 92, 96, 114, 139, 147, 200, 242, 248, 253, 268, 340, 381, 388, 391
   by Christians 267-8, 272-3, 342, 389, 405
of Jews 98, 394-5
of Hindus 100
of 'pagain' religions 266
by religious authorities 92, 98, 100, 236, 239-40, 266-7, 381
Persian Gulf 384
Peter, St, Apostle 11, 23, 27, 34, 37, 41, 44-5, 48, 50, 55, 64-5, 68, 72, 79, 84, 88, 92, 96, 113, 136, 145, 155-6, 235, 242, 249, 252, 260, 271, 289, 304, 319, 339, 355, 366, 370, 382, 404, 449
   in Bahá'í Writings 345, 421
   and the papacy 147, 228, 247-9
   primacy of 247, 345
Peter Chrysologus 99
Pharaoh(s) 95, 192, 220, 233, 254, 325, 377
Pharaoh Apopis 265
Pharisees 23, 46, 53, 62-3, 76, 103, 181, 184-7, 204, 208, 211, 239, 252, 255-6, 258, 275, 303, 317, 325, 328, 370, 419-21, 434, 454, 546
Phelps, a. A. 245
Philemon 68
Philip of Hesse 85
Philippines 87, 555
Phoebe (Priscilla) 82
Physician, Divine 407-8, 427, 431, 449
Platina 147
Poland 395
politics ix, 270, 371, 389, 393-4, 479, 491-3, 500, 507, 510
   partisan 498
Pontius Pilate 92, 99, 341
Popes
   Boniface VIII 226, 228
   Gelasius 82
   Gregory the Great 226
   Gregory VII 93
   Eugene IV 231
   Innocent III 270
   Leo XII 227
   Leo XIII 227
   Martin V 273
   Pelagius 225
   Pius IX 19, 228, 248, 346, 420, 443
   Pius XII 19, 228, 231
   Urban II 89, 93-4

Portuguese, the 100
poverty 1, 47, 313, 337, 482, 507-8
prayer 22, 38, 45-6, 71, 118, 146, 148, 285, 291, 326-7, 333, 408, 473, 476, 486-8, 513
   in Bahá'í Faith 513
   by Christians 22, 24, 42, 45-6, 52, 82, 147, 222, 245-6, 403
      Lord's Prayer 135, 235, 282, 295, 330, 403
   in Judaism 28, 76, 82, 195, 198, 305, 330, 423, 442, 450
prejudice 1, 6, 26, 32, 50-51, 52, 70, 72, 141, 180, 206, 271, 290, 328, 409, 463-7, 470, 479, 490-500, 504, 510
Preterits 149
pride 51, 97, 118, 126, 207, 239, 241, 354, 367, 376, 403, 414, 418-19, 421, 481
priests 51, 71, 72, 87, 125, 152, 184, 189, 215, 249, 253, 254, 267, 272, 290, 326, 353, 357, 361-2, 384, 385, 393, 430, 541-2, 546
   anointed 122
   celibacy of 252-3
   confession to 329-33, 512-13
   marriage of 88-9
   and Christian sacraments 352-8
   summons of Bahá'u'lláh to 417
priesthood 82, 141, 253, 331-2, 461
Prince, the 138, 170-71 543, 546
   of Peace 120-21, 138, 191, 432
prison, prisoner(s) 36-7, 68, 89, 101, 275, 321, 389, 420
   'Abdu'l-Bahá 401
   Bahá'u'lláh 323, 397, 399, 405, 420, 422, 425, 449, 479
   of self 59-60, 110, 198, 304
prodigal son, parable of 299-300, 330
progressive revelation 4, 430-38, 450-61, 504, 514
prophecy (ies) 52, 203, 217, 366
   authority to interpret 207, 260, 266, 401
   concerning
      the Báb 152, 397
      Islam 152, 387
      return of Jews to Holy Land 127-8, 390, 393
      'that Day', last days, Messiah, Second Coming 124, 128-72, 180, 191, 288-9, 386-90, 444
   fulfilment of 117, 149-51, 155, 157, 172, 176-7, 290, 323-5, 396-405-9, 451,

424, 441, 444, 447
  disagreements concerning 98, 179-80, 189-90, 205, 374
  in Bahá'u'lláh 461
  role of 116-17
Proverbs, Book of 29, 327
Prussia 390-91, 424, 560
Psalms 49, 118, 198-9, 295, 405, 448
pulpits 245, 246-7, 303
purity of heart, mind 4, 16, 29, 50-52, 107, 259, 301, 314, 332, 351, 354, 356-7, 368, 415, 444, 446, 454, 476-7, 479-80, 495

quarrels 43, 45, 51, 467
Qur'án (Koran) 317, 391, 445, 547, 554, 556, 558, 559

racism xi, 1, 18, 69, 371, 493-8, 570
Rahab (Canaanite) 70
Rahner, Karl 228-9
reason, reasoning 3, 90, 155, 207, 211, 213, 227, 321-2, 347, 433, 453, 466, 502, 511
  and faith 15-16, 317, 321, 366
  and science 321-2, 347, 502
Redeemer 112, 116, 118-19, 125, 176, 195, 215, 401, 432
  Universal 54, 116, 122, 384, 397-8
redemption 107, 127, 196, 243, 305, 315, 379, 400, 460, 478
Red Sea 254
Reformation, the 85, 94, 147, 226, 273, 358, 389
  Counter-Reformation 94, 358
religious leaders 158, 162, 175, 236, 242, 249, 276, 290-92, 315, 458
  Christian 158, 217, 236
  Jewish 62, 178, 184, 197, 236-9, 255, 258, 327, 367, 370
  Muslim 3
repentance 47, 51, 54, 113, 198, 239, 271, 330-32, 339, 353-6, 371, 380, 407, 449, 512
resurrection
  of Christ 96, 141, 255, 263-4, 305, 307-9, 314-25, 363, 554
  day of 301, 311-12
  of the dead 132, 162, 199, 234, 255, 263, 301, 305-18, 333, 341, 362, 418, 449, 473, 475, 489, 547
  spiritual 33, 131, 148, 298-9, 469
return, concept of 439-45

revenge 39, 90
revelations(s)
  attempts to codify 256-6
  of Bahá'u'lláh 3-4, 6, 117, 152, 162, 311-12, 370-71, 374, 378, 384, 402-6, 413-21, 437-9, 442, 470-74, 490, 502, 506, 514
  of Christ 3-5, 51-2, 117, 134, 140, 191, 240, 243, 262, 271, 282, 294, 299, 303-4, 322, 370, 378, 436, 460-61
  claims to finality, superiority, exclusivity 191, 194-5, 213-14, 2117, 221, 229-30, 271, 454, 459
  continuity of vii, 62, 135, 161, 165, 262, 279, 282, 296, 303, 314, 348, 371, 377, 413-14, 428-45, 450-54, 502
  good fruits of 11, 369-70, 374, 470
  of Moses 61, 62, 193, 195, 258, 311, 377, 423, 455, 541
  new 24, 107, 113-14, 117, 135, 149, 158, 194, 200-03, 235-6, 246, 271, 274, 288-92, 307, 311-12, 326, 401, 448, 456
  name 111, 114-15, 165-6, 236-7, 419, 565
  teachings 25, 107, 112, 114, 274, 280, 304, 380, 463, 502, 510-11
  and 'oppression' 155
  progressive 4, 430-38, 450-61, 504, 514
  proof of 256, 470, 475
  purpose of x, 5, 314, 458, 469-70
  renewal, return 24, 107, 113-14, 239, 413, 439-45, 448, 458
  and social laws x, 65, 101, 107, 504, 510
  universal 70, 123, 129, 141, 384, 402, 404
Revelation, Book of (New Testament) 32, 95, 320, 430
  and Second Coming 124, 151-2, 163-4, 283, 307, 350, 386, 389, 403, 409
reviling 13, 41, 51, 67, 256, 366, 381, 487
revival, rebirth 448-50
riches see wealth
ritual(s) vi, 3, 7, 11, 15, 18-19, 61, 98, 127, 136, 158, 225, 236, 237, 249, 250, 313, 326, 351-6, 359, 360, 363, 428, 564
  cleanliness 158, 258, 352-3, 361-2 see also baptism
  Hindu 100
rock(s)
  metaphor
    for God's support 198, 305

for steadfastness 480
   for stumbling and offence 175-6, 235
 splitting of 254, 308-9
 and St Peter 247-9, 421
rod of iron 124-5, 387
Rome (city, empire) 11, 23, 51, 68, 74, 87, 93, 95, 98-9, 169-70, 266, 268, 340, 388-9, 393, 420, 546
   Romans 29, 32, 71-2, 87, 92, 149-50, 170, 178, 225, 242, 257, 268, 271, 275, 388, 393, 545, 552, 559
   see also Popes
Rothschild, Walter 394
Russia 390-91, 424, 560
Ruth (Moabite) 70
Rwanda 19

sacraments (of Christian Church) 227, 231, 244, 268, 272, 230-31, 331, 333, 351-3, 358-9, 363
sacrifice, self-, living s. 4, 20, 40-41, 96, 251, 310, 323, 358, 374, 381-2, 398, 478, 481
   Abraham 296
   Bahá'u'lláh 416, 419
   Christ 4, 11, 60, 96, 142, 309-10, 322-3, 326, 334, 356
   Eucharist 358
   human 296
   Jewish, Roman 141, 168, 170-71, 186, 254, 388, 422, 541
saints 12, 153, 171, 272, 307-9, 395, 398
Sabbatarians 64
Sabbath 60, 63-4, 97, 109, 141, 169, 177, 185-6, 256, 325, 439
Sadducees 204, 239
salvation
   and angels 162
   and Bahá'u'lláh 322, 416, 419
   in Christianity 48, 54-5, 63, 74, 95, 121, 187, 200, 203, 234, 315, 340-41, 352, 354, 357, 359, 365
      claim of exclusivity to 214, 219, 222, 225-32, 273, 326
      of individual 121, 242
   in Hebrew Bible 90, 118-19, 123, 128, 131, 196, 197-9, 215, 285, 408, 429, 439, 449
   not exclusive to any one religion 7
Samaritan(s) 73, 77, 302, 451
   Parable of Good Samaritan x, 32, 71, 225
Samuel, High Priest 254
Sanhedrin 51, 275

Saracens 100, 389
Sarah (wife of Abraham) 79
Satan, satanic 6, 20, 59, 249, 335, 337, 362, 370, 467, 484, 487
Saul, King 122
Saviour 24, 59, 68, 112, 182, 197, 235, 285, 303, 305, 369
   title of Christ 21, 79, 116, 138, 201, 216, 218-19, 241, 295, 320, 342, 346, 359, 394, 395-6
scholars, scholarship 274, 279, 371, 375, 499
   Christian 66, 96, 100, 147, 151-2, 170, 244, 248, 265, 270, 292, 308, 315, 318, 340, 406 *see also* Barnes, Benson, Calvin, Clarke, Ellicott, Gill, King, Meyer
   Jewish 132, 179, 181, 184, 189, 190, 193, 241, 262, 271, 274 *see also* Maimonides
science 2, 15-16, 26, 53, 281, 308, 385, 453, 466, 469, 493-4, 503, 510, 570
   and faith, reason, religion 7, 15-16, 206, 317, 321, 347, 502-3
Scott, Thomas 303
Scribes 23, 29, 62, 182, 185, 211, 239-41, 249, 255, 258, 317, 325, 328, 373, 454
sectarianism x, 5, 19, 38, 94-5, 144, 148, 245, 463, 493
sect(s) 460, 462, 468, 470
   Christian 18, 20, 227, 266, 273, 345, 405
   Jewish 87, 251-2, 258, 271, 361-2
   'of the Nazarene' 183, 274-5
Sedan, Battle of 375, 423
Sedevacantism 231
seed(s) 40, 56, 107, 137, 210, 322, 369, 381, 452, 453, 473
Sermon on the Mount x, 15, 52
Serpent(s), snakes 49, 77, 84, 210-11, 240, 254, 335, 355, 365
service
   by Christians 20, 21, 41 56, 67-9, 82, 153, 241, 245, 251, 288
   to God 33, 48, 51, 109, 111-12, 121, 124, 139, 156, 192-3, 403, 404-5, 407, 423, 441, 465, 471, 478, 481, 483, 487, 488, 486, 509, 512
   to humanity 374, 497
   to others 36, 39-40, 67-8, 251, 374, 497, 500
   spiritual quality of 500
Shem, son of Noah 65
Sheol 196, 199, 296, 305, 321

shepherd(s) 118, 121, 124, 204, 238, 248, 284, 312, 337, 379, 409, 432, 441-2, 459, 468
    Chief, Great 136, 242, 404, 450-51
Shiloh 167, 171, 393, 431
Shoghi Effendi 470, 506
Silas 275
Simon bar Kokhba 143
sin 25, 29, 34, 46, 59-60, 66, 68, 72, 90, 98, 102, 114, 119, 126, 147, 180, 188, 211-12, 223, 228, 233, 245, 283, 298, 300, 326-36, 379, 483
    association with sinners 186-7, 225, 328-30
    forgiveness of 45, 182, 187, 219, 327, 330, 332, 339, 342, 344, 355, 358, 367, 407, 487, 512-13
    and marriage 88
    original 334-5, 342, 346-7, 356
    remission of 94, 226, 341, 353-4, 356, 487
    repentance of 54, 113, 271, 339, 355-6, 371, 512
    salvation from 198, 219
    and Second Coming 138, 140, 170-71, 237, 407
    sinlessness
        of Christ 41, 315
        of Mary 20, 346
    and women 79, 84
    see also baptism, confession, Eucharist, hell
Sinai, Mount 23, 61, 325, 377, 417, 423, 426, 541
sincerity 30, 31, 46-8, 113, 206, 259, 279, 282, 326, 366, 367, 465, 485, 488, 497, 501
Sistine Chapel 445
slavery, slaves, bondsmen xi, 1, 60-61, 65-9, 73, 79, 89, 90, 94, 197, 393, 426
Snow, Samuel A. 396
Society of Friends 101-2
Socinianism 262
Solomon, King 70, 295, 327, 349
Spain 87, 150, 179
Spirit of truth 139-42, 240, 262, 280, 415, 417, 432, 450
Spiritual Assemblies 513
stars
    darkening of 126, 131, 158, 291-2
    falling of from heaven 22, 117, 126, 131, 154, 157-60, 180, 213, 290-92, 418, 423

metaphor
    for laws and teachings 291
    for religious leaders 158, 160-61, 290-92, 418, 423
Stephen, St 295, 377, 382
stumbling 33, 175-6, 178, 211, 235-6, 249, 407, 546; *see* Chs. 7 and 8
Sudan 543
suffering
    of the Báb, Bábís 397-8
    of Bahá'u'lláh 3, 397-8, 424
    of believers 353, 398
        Baha'ís 397-8
        Christians 12, 43, 95-6, 113, 273, 310, 366, 389
    of Christ 23, 41, 96, 142, 249, 265, 315, 326, 340-41, 359
    endurance of 41, 68, 102, 366, 382, 398, 418
    of humanity 506-7
    of individuals healed by Christ 72, 78
    of Messengers, Prophets 44, 51, 323, 326, 334, 382, 398
    of others, attitude towards 39, 482
sun
    metaphor
        for dispensation, revelation 136, 156, 158-9, 160, 161, 164, 281, 286-90, 297, 313, 348, 385, 436-9, 446, 459, 467, 564
    laws and teachings 291
    and moon, darkening of 22, 117, 126, 131, 136, 154, 156, 159-60, 180, 213, 288-91, 312-13
    physical 16, 71, 116-17, 118, 251, 269, 434
    of Reality 297, 313, 437
    of Righteousness 120, 290, 432
    of Truth 155-6, 158, 312, 438, 467
Switzerland, Swiss 261, 273, 394
Synods
    Carthage 356
    Macon 98
    Tyre 267

Talmud 23, 66, 70, 76-7, 86, 159, 167, 185, 197, 258
Tanakh 197, 219, 293, 296, 374, 405, 541-2
Tartarus 296
tax, tax collector(s) 46, 50-51, 71, 103, 121, 186, 189, 328, 393, 546
temple(s) 46, 74, 100, 165, 170, 179, 180,

190, 266, 275, 295, 307, 310, 328, 385
  destruction of 168-70, 266, 329, 393,
    545-6
  Second 335, 545
Templers, German 405-6
Ten Commandments 61, 63
terrorism 1, 91, 144, 504
Tertullian 363, 373
Theophanes the Confessor 100
Therapeutae 251
thief (in the night) 53, 134, 157, 163, 203,
    207
  'good thief' 319-20
time, biblical measures of 166-7
Thirty Years War 94, 270
Thomas (Apostle) 214, 443
Thomas á Kempis 17
Timothy 65, 261, 350, 462
Torah 23, 39, 52, 62-6, 70, 77, 86, 89-90,
    97, 176-9, 185, 191, 194-7, 213, 236,
    258, 309, 345, 362, 374, 377, 401, 429,
    454-5, 542
tradition(s) 58, 61, 161, 236, 249, 276,
    279-80, 428, 452, 463, 509
  Christian 16-19, 28, 61, 94, 136, 158,
    214, 232, 236, 245, 262, 267, 290,
    295, 307, 326, 355, 363, 385, 458,
    463
    Catholic 228, 231
  Jewish 52, 53, 79, 81, 84, 159, 185, 236,
    258-9, 296, 309, 324, 385
  oral 145
  Zoroastrian 335
transubstantiation 272, 333, 358
tribulation 22, 145, 154, 169, 233, 333,
    392, 399
Trinity, the 179, 237, 262-8, 270, 338-50,
    355, 361, 363
  in Bahá'í writings 347-9
trumpet(s) 162, 306, 309, 390, 385
truth
  acceptance, obedience to, recognition of
    50-51, 107, 116, 279, 312, 343, 350,
    367, 471, 476
  and Bahá'í Faith 437, 492, 514
  and Bahá'u'lláh 312, 322, 336, 402,
    413-14, 423, 427, 462-3, 471, 484
  of Christ's message 15, 33, 37, 42, 48, 66,
    117, 159, 214, 217, 237, 248, 282,
    294, 302, 319, 326, 380, 423, 448,
    456
    and Christian Church 227-8, 248

  and resurrection 315-17, 322
  denial of, opposition to, rejection of,
    rebellion against, turning away from
    63, 72, 144, 203, 259, 286, 303, 312,
    363, 383, 443, 463
  desire for, seeking 48-50, 155, 365, 437,
    465-7, 506
  of former religions 5, 7, 225, 377, 461,
    463, 467, 490, 514
  God, revealer, source of 227, 279, 291,
    368, 456, 484
  gradual unfolding of 438
  interpretation of 259-60, 265
  investigation of 52, 154, 158, 178, 206,
    245, 250, 365, 454, 463-7, 508
  Manifestation of God, Prophets, proof of
    348, 501
  path, way of 215, 319
  and miracles 253-4
  new 110, 141, 217, 274, 380, 456
  power of 419
  and reason, science 15, 317, 366, 502
  religious 180, 196, 206, 232, 502
    not absolute but relative 430, 514
  and religious leaders 162, 250, 327, 503
  scriptural criteria for 364-83
  Spirit of 139-42, 240, 262-3, 280, 312,
    415-17, 432, 450
  Sun of 155-6, 158, 438, 467
truthfulness 44, 336, 446, 479, 484-5, 488,
    500-01
Turkey 60, 390-91, 399, 561 *see also*
  Ottoman

unbelievers 74-6, 86-7, 224, 235, 312, 329,
    456
United Kingdom 14
United States 495
unity xi, 19, 136, 369, 430, 446, 498, 511
  and Bahá'í Faith 6, 374, 409, 446, 454,
    458, 460-62, 468, 478, 490-91, 493,
    497, 500-01, 505, 507
  and Christianity 20, 36, 38, 73, 91, 136,
    225, 227-8, 231, 244, 265, 271, 323,
    347
  and consultation 508
  in diversity 408, 509
  Divine (of God) 155, 161, 343, 349, 454,
    488, 501
  of mankind 4, 20, 32, 243, 323, 438,
    453, 462, 464, 467-8, 490-91, 493-4,
    497, 500-01, 505, 507

of Prophets, Manifestations of God 437, 454, 458, 501
racial 496
of religions 460-61, 468, 470, 474, 494, 501
and religious leaders and scholars 237, 279
and universal auxiliary language 509
Universal House of Justice 513

Van Evrie, J. H. 69
Van Leyden (Leiden), Jan (John) 86
Vatican (city) 87, 420, 446
vengeance of God 154, 222, 284
Vestal Virgins 87
Victoria, Queen 426-7
veils 84
  symbolic 118, 142, 193, 297, 304, 313, 336, 346, 357, 403, 414-18, 420-21, 458, 473, 477, 564, 565
Vilna, Lithuania 394
violence vi, 6, 69, 86, 89, 91-100, 272, 456
  religious, sectarian 2, 94-100, 232
  self-defence 89, 92
virgin birth 188-9, 346, 554
Virgin Mary 19, 84, 182, 183, 188-90, 252, 318, 341, 345-6, 360
  immaculacy of 345-6
virtue(s) 20, 24, 28, 31-57, 107, 226, 292, 297, 300, 304, 311, 322-3, 326, 353, 357, 371, 444, 446, 455, 463, 474-89, 496, 499
visions 156, 193, 265, 385 see also dreams
vultures 153-4

war 20, 69, 91-4, 100, 123, 144, 257-8, 265, 273, 290, 389, 463, 466, 468, 493, 504, 507, 512, 543, 545, 557
  Crimean 391
  German Peasants 273
  holy 93-5, 270
    abolition of 511
  just, justifiable 93-5
  Thirty Years 94, 270
  World Wars I and II 1, 19, 94, 144
washing of feet 35-6
water of life, living, life-giving 20, 29, 58, 77-8, 109, 110-13, 136, 161, 236, 282-3, 293, 325, 352, 357, 365, 420, 436, 449, 563, 564
  dew, dewdrop 161, 305, 407, 436, 482, 563

fountains 29, 58, 110-11, 113, 158, 161, 178, 325, 398, 436, 471, 476, 480, 489, 564
ocean 301, 436, 459, 563
rain 56, 71, 161, 314, 369, 436, 563
river 108, 357, 436, 564
sea 108, 123, 210, 402, 436, 475, 482
snow 369
springs 29, 78, 136, 178, 283, 365, 436
streams, streambed 59, 111, 156, 357, 436
wells 436
Watt, James 64
Watts, Isaac 201
Watts, Richard 209
way, the 102, 127, 155, 201, 214-16, 275, 319, 417-18
wealth, riches 424-3, 46, 165, 250-51, 397, 422, 482, 489
  and poverty 1, 47, 313, 337, 482, 507-8
Weaver, J. Denny 94
Wettstein, John James 261-2
Wilhelm I, Emperor 375-6, 424
Wilhelm II, Emperor 376
wine 44, 65, 71, 155, 166, 360, 564
  at Eucharist 333, 358, 360
  of justice 420
  spiritual 29, 50, 59, 110-11, 365, 422, 471
wineskins 29, 59, 61
wisdom 108, 155, 158, 183, 197, 202, 259, 303, 310, 355, 364, 367, 368, 377, 414, 476, 482, 485
  blinded by 51, 303-4
  divine 90, 112, 161, 304, 408, 416, 431, 444, 474
wolves 325, 372-3
women xi, 64, 70, 73, 76-89, 94, 169, 187, 189, 192, 211, 225, 318, 387, 426, 445-6, 455, 470, 499-500
work 44, 67, 68, 132, 281, 503
  on the Sabbath 63, 64, 256
world commonwealth 491, 509
World War I (Great War) 19, 94, 144, 424
World War II 1, 19, 144
worship
  Christian 14, 17, 45-6, 210, 212, 226, 245-6, 341-2, 388, 423, 540
  freedom of 266
  forms of 74-5, 452
  of God 17, 29, 109, 168-9, 246, 249, 275, 343, 409, 429, 439, 448, 509

of idols 89, 170, 246, 249-50, 254
of Jesus 339, 342, 430
and new covenant 457
public 81
spiritual 40-41, 209
work as 503
Wycliffe, John 272-3

Yahweh 95, 192, 198, 214-15, 428, 429, 456, 541
Yemen 543

Yom Kippur (Day of Atonement) 329-30
Yudghan 143

Zacchaeus 186-7
Zechariah of Nazareth 189
Zechariah, Prophet 60, 123, 240, 409, 432
Zephaniah, Prophet 161-2, 432
Zionism 394
Zoroastrianism 61, 72, 152, 335, 384, 466
Zwingli, Huldrych 273

ABOUT THE AUTHOR

Lameh Fananapazir was born in Iran and spent his youth in Gambia, Morocco and Kenya. He is a graduate of Edinburgh Medical School, specializing in Cardiovascular Diseases. He was elected as a Fellow of the Royal College of Physicians of Edinburgh, He specialized further in Electrophysiology at Duke Medical Center in North Carolina, following which he was recruited to investigate the mechanisms of sudden death in athletes and patients with genetic cardiac conditions at the National Institutes of Health where he became the chief of the Section of Inherited Heart Diseases. He was subsequently appointed the director of Health Services at the Bahá'í World Centre and Visiting Professor of Cardiology at Technion, Israel Institute of Technology. He retired from private practice in Cumberland, Maryland in 2016.

As religion continues to cause conflict, suffering and death in many parts of the world, apart from his scientific pursuits Dr Fananapazir has also been keenly interested in the Abrahamic religions, Judaism, Christianity and Islam. Following 9/11 he wrote *Islam at the Crossroads* which examined the issues that Islam faces and their potential solutions. He has also authored *A Companion to the Study of Epistle to the Son of the Wolf.*

www.ingramcontent.com/pod-product-compliance
Lightning Source LLC
Chambersburg PA
CBHW021713300426
44114CB00009B/123